Aligning Financial Reporting Standards With Global Trade Needs

Luan Vardari
University "Ukshin Hoti" Prizren, Kosovo

Isuf Qabrati
University "Ukshin Hoti" Prizren, Kosovo

IGI Global
Scientific Publishing
Publishing Tomorrow's Research Today

Vice President of Editorial | Melissa Wagner
Director of Acquisitions | Mikaela Felty
Director of Book Development | Jocelynn Hessler
Production Manager | Mike Brehm
Cover Design | Jose Rosado

Published in the United States of America by
IGI Global Scientific Publishing
701 East Chocolate Avenue
Hershey, PA, 17033, USA
Tel: 717-533-8845
Fax: 717-533-7115
Website: https://www.igi-global.com E-mail: cust@igi-global.com

Library of Congress Cataloging-in-Publication Data

Names: Vardari, Luan, 1985- editor. | Qabrati, Isuf, 1997- editor.
Title: Aligning financial reporting standards with global trade needs / edited by: Luan Vardari, Isuf Qabrati.
Description: Hershey, PA : IGI Global Scientific Publishing, [2025] | Includes bibliographical references and index. | Summary: "The book explores the evolving landscape of financial reporting in an increasingly interconnected global economy. The publication will address these challenges by examining emerging trends such as the digitization of trade, sustainability reporting, technological disruptions like AI and blockchain, and the growing importance of transparency and ethical considerations"-- Provided by publisher.
Identifiers: LCCN 2024059671 (print) | LCCN 2024059672 (ebook) | ISBN 9798337308876 (hardcover) | ISBN 9798337308883 (paperback) | ISBN 9798337308890 (ebook)
Subjects: LCSH: Financial statements. | Artificial intelligence--Financial applications. | Financial statements--Technological innovations--Moral and ethical aspects. | Blockchains (Databases)
Classification: LCC HG4028.B2 A45 2025 (print) | LCC HG4028.B2 (ebook) | DDC 657/.3--dc23/eng/20250326
LC record available at https://lccn.loc.gov/2024059671
LC ebook record available at https://lccn.loc.gov/2024059672
British Cataloguing in Publication Data
A Cataloguing in Publication record for this book is available from the British Library.

Table of Contents

Detailed Table of Contents

underscores the challenges of regulatory compliance, particularly in the context of ESG and AI-related frameworks.

With an emphasis on how they work together to improve compliance, transparency, and cross-border investment, this chapter explores the complex link between international trade regulations and International Financial Reporting Standards (IFRS). It looks at the benefits and drawbacks of their convergence, focusing on how IFRS and trade regulations should be harmonised to guarantee accuracy in financial reporting and compliance with trade regulations. The conversation focuses on how bringing these frameworks into alignment reduces financial risks in cross-border transactions and increases investor confidence and trust. The chapter emphasises the significance of unified policies by examining the regulatory obstacles encountered by multinational corporations. The ramifications of integrating IFRS principles with trade rules are shown via case studies, best practices, and practical techniques. The conclusion highlights how important it is for businesses, governments, and regulatory agencies to work together in order to maximise global economic integration.

In the dynamic realm of contemporary business, financial and non-financial audits are crucial for transparency, reliability, and sustainability. With rising concerns over Environmental, Social, and Governance (ESG) issues, stakeholders demand assurance on both financial and non-financial reporting. Accounting firms audit financial statements, both accounting and non-accounting firms provide non-financial reporting assurance. Given its novelty, regulators and investors focus on extended external reporting quality. Few nations mandate non-financial reporting and assurance, though global standards are emerging. Harmonizing audit practices remains challenging, yet necessary. Traditional audit reports had limited communicative value, leading to the introduction of Key Audit Matters (KAMs) reporting. This chapter shows application of KAMs reporting in Europe. Auditor competence and independence are crucial for financial and non-financial reporting, and audit quality. Future auditors are more likely to verify and report on both the financial and non-financial aspects of the firms.

Preface

INTRODUCTION

In an increasingly interconnected global economy, the need for transparent, harmonized, and forward-looking financial reporting standards has never been more pressing. As businesses expand across borders, and global trade becomes more reliant on technological innovation, environmental accountability, and regulatory compliance, the role of financial reporting transforms from a transactional necessity to a strategic imperative. *Aligning Financial Reporting Standards with Global Trade Needs* brings together a rich tapestry of scholarly insights and empirical research to explore how international financial standards—especially IFRS—can better serve the evolving demands of cross-border commerce, sustainability, digital innovation, and economic integration.

This edited volume is a product of interdisciplinary and cross-national collaboration, uniting academics and professionals from institutions across Asia, Africa, Europe, and Australia. Their contributions address the convergence of financial reporting with global trade policy, environmental governance, technological advancement, and risk management—critical issues for stakeholders ranging from regulators and investors to multinational corporations and policymakers.

The following chapter overview provides a roadmap to the themes and perspectives explored throughout the book:

CHAPTER OVERVIEW

Chapter 1: Bridging the Gap: Aligning ESG with Financial Disclosures for a Sustainable Global Trade System

This chapter analyzes the growing integration of ESG metrics into financial disclosures. Drawing on empirical data and case studies, the authors propose that standardizing ESG reporting is vital to achieving sustainable trade systems. The chapter offers actionable policy suggestions for governments, corporations, and trade bodies.

Chapter 2: Harmonizing Financial Reporting Standards: Driving Cross-Border Mergers and Acquisitions in a Globalized Economy

Exploring how unified reporting standards like IFRS simplify cross-border mergers and acquisitions, this chapter highlights the role of emerging technologies—such as blockchain and AI—in streamlining due diligence and compliance. The authors emphasize the growing investor demand for transparent and harmonized reporting in global M&A activity.

Chapter 3: Green Auditing: A Mechanism for Aligning with Climate Objectives via Emissions Reduction

Focusing on green auditing as a tool for aligning corporate practices with climate goals, the chapter uses quantitative methods to uncover the mediating effects of emissions reduction and the moderating influence of sector-specific variables. It concludes with a call for sectoral tailoring of audit practices and technical upskilling.

Chapter 4: Financial Reporting for E-commerce and Digital Trade Platforms

This chapter explores how digital trade demands new reporting frameworks that incorporate blockchain, AI, and big data. By examining multinational case studies, the authors argue for an overhaul of IFRS to account for real-time data flows, intangible asset valuation, and algorithm-driven financial decisions.

Chapter 5: Assessing the Challenges and Incentives for Companies to Incorporate Green Financing into Their CSR

Through a conceptual analysis, this chapter investigates the incentives for businesses to embrace green finance in CSR programs, while identifying obstacles such as funding scarcity and greenwashing risks. Strategic frameworks are recommended to align CSR with environmental sustainability more effectively.

Chapter 6: Aligning Financial Reporting Standards: A Catalyst for Global Mergers and Acquisitions

A companion to Chapter 2, this study reinforces the importance of IFRS in facilitating global M&As. It provides case-based evidence showing how standardized financial disclosures increase investor confidence and improve cross-border business synergies, especially in emerging markets.

Chapter 7: A Half-Century of International Accounting Standards: Assessing the Mandatory Adoption, Impact, and Morocco's Position in the Convergence Process

Providing a historical lens, this chapter charts the 50-year evolution of IAS/IFRS, assessing adoption rates, macroeconomic impacts, and Morocco's partial alignment with the standards. It emphasizes the ongoing need for capacity building and institutional reform in developing economies.

Chapter 8: Navigating Financial Risk: Hedging and Derivatives in International Reporting and Cross-Border Deals

The authors delve into the complexity of financial risk in global transactions, discussing how derivatives, predictive analytics, and AI can help firms manage currency volatility, geopolitical threats, and environmental uncertainty. The chapter also highlights compliance issues in a rapidly changing regulatory landscape.

Chapter 9: Navigating the Intersection of IFRS and Global Trade Regulations: Enhancing Compliance, Transparency, and Cross-Border Investment Flows

This chapter explores how harmonizing IFRS with international trade rules can reduce financial risk and increase investor trust. Through case studies, it illustrates how regulatory convergence supports accurate disclosures and compliant trade practices, and recommends collaborative action among regulators and firms.

Chapter 10: The Future of Auditing – Aligning International Audit Practices with Global Trade Needs

Auditing is undergoing a transformation driven by ESG concerns and digital expectations. This chapter highlights innovations such as Key Audit Matters (KAMs) and argues for global alignment of both financial and non-financial assurance practices. Auditor independence and competence are framed as cornerstones of future audit quality.

Chapter 11: The Role of Digital Currencies in Global Trade and Financial Reporting Standards

Focusing on digital currencies like CBDCs and cryptocurrencies, this chapter examines their implications for global trade efficiency and regulatory harmonization. With examples from China, El Salvador, and the EU, the authors discuss blockchain's potential to modernize both cross-border transactions and financial reporting.

CONCLUSION

Aligning Financial Reporting Standards with Global Trade Needs aims to be a timely contribution to the discourse at the intersection of finance, technology, sustainability, and policy. Whether addressing ESG integration, digital currencies, green finance, or global M&A, each chapter reflects a collective recognition: financial reporting is no longer a static discipline but a dynamic tool for shaping the future of global trade. We hope this book inspires further scholarship, policy innovation, and cross-sector collaboration.

Luan Vardari
University "Ukshin Hoti" Prizren, Kosovo

Isuf Qabrati
University "Ukshin Hoti" Prizren, Kosovo

Chapter 1

Bridging the Gap: Aligning ESG With Financial Disclosures for a Sustainable Global Trade System

Manish Gurung
NIET Business School, Greater Noida, India

Sanjay Taneja
https://orcid.org/0000-0002-3632-4053
Graphic Era University (Deemed), India

Gurinderpal Singh
Chandigarh University, India

Manpreet Kaur
Guru Nanak Dev University, India

Dixit Kalra
https://orcid.org/0000-0002-1744-6717
Chandigarh Group of Colleges Jhanjeri, Mohali, India

ABSTRACT

This study explores the integration of Environmental, Social, and Governance (ESG) criteria into financial disclosures within global trade systems, focusing on regulatory frameworks, technological innovations, and corporate practices. By examining the evolution of ESG adoption across diverse regions, the research highlights the challenges and opportunities in aligning ESG metrics with traditional financial reporting standards. Through a mixed-methods approach, the study synthesizes empirical data, case studies, and theoretical insights to explore the convergence of

DOI: 10.4018/979-8-3373-0887-6.ch001

ESG and financial disclosures, emphasizing the pivotal role of innovation, policy harmonization, and global collaboration. Key findings underscore the growing global trend toward standardized ESG reporting, particularly on sustainable trade practices. The study offers actionable policy recommendations for governments, trade organizations, and corporations to bridge the gap between ESG reporting and financial disclosures, facilitating a more sustainable global trade ecosystem.

1. ESG (ENVIRONMENTAL, SOCIAL, AND GOVERNANCE) AND FINANCIAL DISCLOSURES IN INTERNATIONAL TRADE

The emergence of Environmental, Social, and Governance (ESG) criteria has revolutionized international trade by redefining corporate performance metrics through a threefold framework that assesses ethical, environmental, and governance dimensions (Tang & Zhang, 2020). This framework is a benchmark for corporate responsibility and a key driver of sustainable trade systems grounded in sustainability approach, CSR, and governance studies (Rendtorff, 2023).

The theoretical bases of ESG in international trade are rooted in sustainability, values, and the "triple bottom line" theory, highlighting environmental, social, and financial accountability while aligning with social contract theory to support ethical business traditions that benefit all stakeholders above mere financial performance (Krahnen et al., 2023).

The ESG framework contains three interrelated dimensions: environmental sustainability, which concentrates on ecological effect and climate action; social responsibility, which manages diversity; fair labor and human rights; and governance integrity, which assures corporate accountability, transparency, and anti-corruption efforts (Kukreti et al., 2025). These measurements position firms as key drivers of sustainable, ethical, and trustworthy global trade systems (Sehajpal & Kaur, 2025).

The Contribution of Financial Disclosures Enabling Global Trade

Conventional financial disclosures, concentrated on economic performance through income reports, balance sheets, and cash flow reports, need to be more recognized for overlooking non-financial factors like social equity, environmental effect, and governance, limiting their relevance in addressing broader sustainability concerns in contemporary international trade dynamics (X. Liu, 2017).

Conventional financial disclosures, though necessary for evaluating direct business performance, lack standardized integration of ESG factors, limiting their capacity to address long-term risks from environmental, social, and governance collapses.

Thus, they highlight the urgent requirement for a complete reporting framework that contemplates the complexities of sustainability in a globalized business ecosystem (Filipovic et al., 2018).

Despite advancement through initiatives like TCFD and GRI, the fragmented nature of existing ESG reporting frameworks arises from a need for universal consensus on material ESG information. This results in inconsistent, supplementary disclosures that hinder investors, regulators, and customers from making fully reported, comparable determinations within core financial reporting systems (Abdullah et al., 2020).

Gap Recognition: Aligning ESG and Financial Disclosures

The gap between ESG reporting and financial disclosures originates from a conceptual and functional disconnect. Conventional financial reporting prioritizes short-term, quantifiable metrics. In contrast, ESG reporting highlights long-term value creation, posing challenges in aligning sustainability and governance concerns with historically limited financial frameworks (Zhang et al., 2022).

The absence of universally accepted standards strengthens the conceptual gap in ESG integration within financial reporting. Frameworks like GRI and TCFD's voluntary and fragmented nature divert global harmonization, compromising clarity and limiting stakeholders' capacity to assess risks and opportunities in international trade (Wang & Wen, 2022).

Aligning ESG with financial disclosures is critical for sustainable global trade. It delivers a comprehensive picture of corporate performance, stimulates informed decision-making, encourages sustainable practices, and reshapes business into a more ethical, equitable approach.

2. THE ADVANCEMENT AND EVOLUTION OF ESG AND FINANCIAL REPORTING

Developing Environmental, Social, and Governance (ESG) criteria within international trade has been a difficult, multi-faceted voyage marked by transformations in societal anticipations, regulatory frameworks, and corporate courses. Originally, the association between business performance and wider societal influences was tenuous, concentrating almost solely on financial returns and economic efficiency (Khanna et al., 2023). Over time, however, growing understanding of environmental degradation, social imbalances, and governance failures has emphasized the necessity for integrating ESG aspects into corporate strategies and the systems governing international trade. The chronological trajectory of ESG integration within business and financial reporting is a testament to the increasingly compulsory need for sustainable practices within the transnational economic framework (Upreti & Malhotra, 2024).

Chronological Route of ESG Integration in Trade

Trade accountability concerning environmental, social, and governance issues was underdeveloped until the late 20th century. Earlier trade methods concentrated primarily on economic outcome while overlooking environmental and social outcomes.

ESG began influencing trade practices in the late 20th century, with the environmental activity and troubles over human rights, labor criteria, and governance driving the emergence of corporate social responsibility (CSR) in the 1980s and 1990s.

The turn of the 21st century witnessed a significant shift in integrating ESG factors into trade and business policies, marked by international agreements like the MDGs, SDGs, Kyoto Protocol, and Paris Agreement, highlighting the link between economic development, environmental sustainability, and social well-being.

Progress of Financial Reporting Practices Corresponding to ESG Criterion Over a Period of Time

Initially, financial reporting concentrated on economic performance, delivering stakeholders with information on financial health and profitability, while ESG elements were deemed secondary or irrelevant to industry success. The growing recognition of ESG topics in the late 1990s and early 2000s led to the emergence of institutions like the GRI, which approved a new framework to systematize non-financial reporting on environmental effects, social equity, and governance patterns. In the 2010s, the landscape of ESG reporting moved significantly, driven by growing institutional investor demands and elevated awareness of climate change risks, with the structure of the Task Force on Climate-related Financial Disclosures (TCFD) in 2015, which played a key role in aligning climate risks with financial reporting by urging firms to disclose the financial importance of climate-related risks and possibilities, while the Sustainability Accounting Standards Board (SASB) developed industry-specific approaches to enable more granular ESG reporting that could better manage investor needs. As a result, financial reporting grew from focusing mainly on economic metrics to integrating ESG concerns with regulators, particularly in the EU, formalizing mandatory corporate disclosures through ambitions like the 2014 Non-Financial Reporting Directive (NFRD), which needed large corporations to disclose non-financial data on environmental effect, social responsibility, and governance (Neha et al., 2023).

Institutional Design and Regulatory Principles for ESG Reporting

Global standards and frameworks, such as the TCFD, GRI, and SASB, have shaped the institutionalization of ESG reporting, desiring to make ESG disclosures more wide and comparable across borders. Established in 1997, the GRI set the standard for international sustainability reporting, delivering a framework for companies to reveal their ESG effects (Bukhari et al., 2020). The TCFD connected climate-related disclosures to financial risk, and the SASB created industry-specific reporting standards to manage unique ESG challenges across sectors. While frameworks like the GRI, TCFD, and SASB have driven firms, the regulatory landscape deviates. The EU requires ESG disclosures through the NFRD and CSRD, whereas the U.S., traditionally volunteer, is moving toward standardized, mandatory reporting through SEC submissions.

Table 1. Regulatory frameworks for ESG disclosure in key economies (2023)

Country	Key ESG Regulatory Frameworks	ESG Reporting Mandates/ Requirements	Implementation Timeline
European Union (EU)	Corporate Sustainability Reporting Directive (CSRD)	Mandatory ESG disclosures for all large companies	2024 onwards
United States (US)	SEC ESG Disclosures Proposal, TCFD	SEC's mandatory disclosure on climate risks, diversity, and governance practices	2024 (proposed)
China	Green Finance Guidelines, China ESG Guidelines	ESG disclosures for listed companies and financial institutions	2023 ongoing
India	Business Responsibility and Sustainability Report (BRSR)	Mandatory sustainability reporting for top 1,000 listed companies	2023
Japan	Japan's Stewardship Code, GPIF ESG Investment Principles	Voluntary ESG disclosures, increasing push for governance transparency	2023
Australia	ASX Corporate Governance Council Guidelines	Voluntary disclosures, with a push towards standardization	2024 (recommendations)

Source: International Financial Reporting Standards (IFRS), 2023

The table 1 highlights the evolving regulatory landscape for ESG disclosures in key economies, with the United States and European Union introducing mandatory reporting frameworks, whereas nations like India, Japan, China and Australia continuc to refine their approaches, ranging from intended disclosures to rigorous mandates for listed firms, set to impacting in the near future.

Progress and Challenges in ESG Disclosure Practices

Integrating ESG standards into financial reporting faces challenges, such as the lack of standardization in ESG metrics, which leads to difficulties comparing performance across firms, industries, and regions. Deviations in reporting practices sabotage data comparability and reliability for regulators and investors (Kumar, Khannna Malholtra, et al., 2023). Corporate responsiveness to ESG disclosure provisions remains uneven. Some companies adopt transparency, whereas others lag due to imprecise regulatory motivations, view ESG as secondary, or face resource limitations in implementing robust reporting instruments, which can be incredibly challenging for smaller firms (Kaur et al., 2024).

Despite challenges, considerable progress has been made in ESG disclosure practices, pushed by increasing regulatory stress and recognizing ESG aspects as material to long-term performance (Malhotra et al., 2022). This has led to more significant transparency and a stronger integration of ESG into financial reporting for a more sustainable multinational trade system.

Table 2. ESG disclosure performance in global corporations (2022)

Company	ESG Disclosure Score (Out of 100)	Primary ESG Focus Areas	Reporting Framework Used
Apple	92	Climate Change, Responsible Supply Chain	TCFD, GRI
Microsoft	89	Carbon Neutrality, Social Responsibility	TCFD, SASB
Unilever	85	Waste Reduction, Fair Labor Practices	GRI, UN Global Compact
ExxonMobil	70	Carbon Emissions, Governance Practices	SASB, TCFD
Nestlé	80	Water Usage, Fair Trade	GRI, UN Global Compact
Amazon	75	Renewable Energy, Employee Welfare	GRI, TCFD

Source: Corporate Sustainability Disclosure Report, 2022

Table 2 emphasizes the ESG disclosure performance of leading international corporations, showcasing a degree of focus areas from climate change to social accountability. Institutions like Microsoft and Apple score most elevated, utilizing TCFD, GRI, and SASB frameworks. In contrast, others like Amazon and ExxonMobil show varying engagement classes in environmental practices and governance.

3. ESG'S ROLE IN SHAPING GLOBAL TRADE SYSTEMS

In recent years, incorporating Environmental, Social, and Governance (ESG) standards has become necessary for reshaping multinational trade systems. As trade networks develop and become more complex, the effect of economic actions on the environment, society, and governance structures has come under growing scrutiny. The role of ESG in shaping these systems is multifaceted, involving everything from trade approaches to international supply chains. The alignment of ESG concerns with the United Nations' Sustainable Development Goals (SDGs) offers a transformative possibility to integrate sustainability more thoroughly into international trade (Jha et al., 2022).

Global Trade Structures and Sustainability Pressures

Historically, due to cost minimization, efficiency, and economic growth, global trade structures face considerable stresses in incorporating sustainability into their core operations. These structures, which have developed over decades, contain many economic, environmental, and social effects that have long been ignored or undervalued. As a global phenomenon, trade has contributed positively and negatively to the overall well-being of communities, economies, and the environment. The environmental degradation driven by unregulated industrialization, such as carbon emissions, deforestation, and loss of biodiversity, is one instance of the negative externalities associated with business. Simultaneously, business has been instrumental in boosting economic growth and raising millions out of deprivation, though this has usually come at the cost of social inequalities and governance shortcomings (Kumar, Lande, et al., 2023).

The evolving paradigm of sustainable trade challenges the conventional trade model by highlighting the integration of environmental and social considerations into business policies and practices. Sustainable business, as envisioned in the context of the SDGs, supports practices that decrease environmental harm and boost social equity, labor rights, and inclusive economic development. The SDGs, which cover a range of purposes from climate efforts to gender equality, deliver a framework through which global businesses can transition towards more sustainable practices. As the global community increasingly acknowledges the unsustainable trajectory of current trade practices, the role of ESG standards becomes more apparent, businesses, guiding policymakers and global organizations toward a more balanced and fair trade system.

The Influence of ESG Criterion on Trade Policies

Embodying ESG-related factors into trade policies is critical to aligning trade with sustainability goals. Empirical analysis reveals that ESG considerations increasingly influence the formulation of trade regulations and agreements. Many international trade agreements, including those governed by the World Trade Organization (WTO), have begun incorporating environmental sustainability and labor rights protections into their structures. However, the extent to which ESG factors are integrated remains uneven across different regions and trade blocs.

One of the most significant policy shifts in recent years is the introduction of carbon taxation and emissions trading schemes, both of which directly align with the environmental aspect of ESG criteria. Carbon tariffs and border tax adjustments are being explored to address the environmental impacts of imports from countries with less stringent climate policies (Gupta et al., 2022). This shift reflects the growing recognition that trade, while a driver of economic development, must also account for its carbon footprint and role in exacerbating climate change.

Fairtrade standards, which focus on improving producers' social and economic conditions in developing countries, are another area where ESG criteria influence trade policies. These standards advocate for fair wages, better working conditions, and the protection of workers' rights, aligning social sustainability with trade practices. In recent years, the rise of ethical consumerism, particularly in developed markets, has pressured businesses to adopt fair trade principles, encouraging policymakers to integrate these values into international trade agreements.

Anti-corruption measures have also become increasingly important in global trade, particularly in regions where weak governance structures allow illicit activities such as bribery and exploitation. The governance dimension of ESG has led to a concerted push for greater transparency and accountability in international trade, with initiatives such as the United Nations Global Compact urging companies to adopt anti-corruption policies and adhere to principles of responsible governance (Kumar, Malholtra, et al., 2023). As trade agreements evolve, including anti-corruption clauses and promoting good governance practices are becoming standard components of international agreements, further embedding ESG principles into the global trade system.

Potential for Synergy Between ESG and Trade Objectives

The theoretical prospect for synergy between ESG concerns and trade objectives is vast, especially as businesses, governments, and international organizations increasingly acknowledge the interconnectedness of these two disciplines. Blending ESG with trade practices shows a pathway for aligning economic development with environmental sustainability and social well-being. This alignment can be particularly transformative regarding the vast complexity of international supply chains, which extend across continents and involve myriad stakeholders, frequently operating under different regulatory regimes.

One of the key prospects for synergy lies in integrating sustainability-driven trade procedures into supply chain management. In an increasingly connected world, one supply chain component's sustainability can significantly affect an entire industry's comprehensive environmental and social impact. For instance, firms are increasingly scrutinizing their suppliers' environmental and social performance, with a growing emphasis on sourcing materials and products from firms that adhere to robust ESG standards. This has led to the emergence of corporate sustainability approaches that align with ESG principles, assuring that trade practices do not sabotage efforts to achieve the SDGs.

Integrating ESG factors into business agreements can also help drive the adoption of circular economy regulations, which strive to reduce waste and boost the recycling and reuse of materials. By promoting trade policies that incentivize circular patterns, nations and institutions can contribute to accomplishing global environmental goals while simultaneously securing economic development. Moreover, harmonizing ESG with trade purposes provides an option for cross-border cooperation on matters such as climate change mitigation, biodiversity conservation, and social equity. Collective efforts among countries and businesses can create a more sustainable and unbiased global trade system that helps all stakeholders.

Nevertheless, recognizing this possible synergy requires substantial steps at the policy level. Governments and global organizations must prioritize sustainability in trade negotiations, incentivizing firms to adopt ESG standards and execute responsible supply chain practices. Standardizing ESG reporting frameworks and metrics will also ensure that trade policies align with international sustainability objectives. Integrating ESG standards into trade practices can create an inclusive, more sustainable, and resilient global trade system as these actions evolve.

In conclusion, ESG's role in shaping international trade systems is crucial for promoting sustainability and social accountability within the global trade framework. As trade structures develop to adapt to the growing pressures for sustainability, including ESG criteria in trade policies and practices shows a pathway for accomplishing the SDGs. Harmonizing ESG concerns with trade goals allows the global community to build a more sustainable and equitable trade system that aligns environmental, economic, and social imperatives.

4. REGULATORY AND POLICY FRAMEWORKS FOR ESG DISCLOSURES IN GLOBAL TRADE

As the world scuffles with the increasing speed of addressing social inequalities, environmental degradation, and poor governance, the function of regulatory and policy design in shaping ESG (Environmental, Social, and Governance) revelations within international trade has gained paramount importance. These frameworks assist in mitigating the adverse impacts of business on the environment and society and lead the global economy toward more sustainable and acceptable practices. As governments, global organizations, and private sector actors engage in policy evolution, the growing nature of ESG regulations plays a central role in determining the future of international trade.

Global Regulatory Approaches to ESG Integration

Diverse frameworks and initiatives describe the global regulatory landscape for ESG disclosures in business to confirm sustainability, responsibility, and responsible governance across transnational borders. Among the most notable is the European Green Deal, a key instrument in shaping the region's environmental and economic revolution. The Green Deal strives to make Europe the first carbon-neutral continent by 2050, embedding sustainability at the core of its economic policies. The European Union (EU) has taken significant strides toward integrating ESG factors into trade, notably through the EU Taxonomy Regulation and the Non-Financial Reporting Directive (NFRD). These initiatives require large firms to disclose appropriate non-financial information, including their environmental influence and governance practices, creating a more transparent trading atmosphere.

The Paris Agreement denotes another vital international framework that has profoundly affected integrating ESG factors into international trade. Signed in 2015, this milestone accord set the basis for countries executing climate action approaches to limit international temperature rise to below two °C, lowering carbon emissions across all sectors. The Paris Agreement inspires countries to adopt climate-related trade policies within multinational trade, incentivizing sustainable practices while imposing fines for carbon-heavy imports. As nations progressively align their trade policies with the Paris Agreement's purposes, businesses involved in international trade are increasingly required to disclose their carbon footprints and assume greener technologies.

Moreover, diverse regional trade agreements and multilateral accords, such as the United Nations Framework Convention on Climate Change (UNFCCC) and the OECD Guidelines for Multinational Enterprises, resume to evolve, shaping how ESG standards are integrated into trade procedures. These treaties deliver frameworks for responsible business conduct and harmonize ESG disclosures across various jurisdictions. However, despite these regulatory improvements, the application and enforcement of these frameworks remain irregular, with developing economies facing typical challenges in adopting and conceding these transnational norms.

Mandatory vs. Voluntary ESG Reporting: Policy Dynamics

The transition from voluntary to mandatory ESG reporting has dramatically evolved in recent years, transforming how nations and corporations approach ESG disclosures. Historically, many firms voluntarily broadcasted ESG reports driven by consumer needs, investor claims, and a growing sense of corporate responsibility. However, this voluntary system often resulted in inconsistencies in the quality and trustworthiness of ESG data, impeding the capacity of stakeholders to compare and evaluate the sustainability of firms across different sectors and areas.

Governments and regulatory bodies have increasingly acknowledged the requirement for mandatory ESG disclosure standards to handle these inconsistencies and promote greater transparency. The EU's Corporate Sustainability Reporting Directive (CSRD), which will extend the scope of mandatory reporting provisions, illustrates this transition. Under the CSRD, large firms must disclose detailed information annually regarding their sustainability risks and effects, including environmental, social, and governance factors. This mandatory approach strives to standardize ESG disclosures across the European Union, supplying a clearer view of how businesses contribute to or mitigate global challenges such as climate change and human rights breaches.

Institutions like the International Financial Reporting Standards (IFRS) Foundation have designed ESG disclosure guidelines internationally, pursuing uniformity in reporting practices across global markets. The constant work of the International Sustainability Standards Board (ISSB), founded by the IFRS, further underscores the growing priority on mandatory ESG disclosures, contemplating a broader recognition that standardized reporting is essential for attaining sustainable trade goals.

The change towards mandatory ESG reporting carries significant implications for global trade practices. For firms, it will require more robust data collection and greater clarity, fostering responsibility. For regulators, it necessitates the invention of broad enforcement instruments to ensure adherence. These outcomes imply that countries with weaker regulatory frameworks or inadequate capacity to enforce ESG standards may require help adapting to these developing international norms.

Barriers to Achieving Unified Global Standards

Despite the apparent momentum toward standardizing ESG disclosures in international trade, several institutional, economic, and political impediments complicate the realization of a unified global framework. One of the most important institutional challenges is **harmonizing** existing ESG reporting standards. While international associations like the GRI, TCFD, and SASB have made significant strides in creating guidelines, these frameworks usually differ in scope, method, and industry-specific prerequisites. This lack of standardization generates chaos for firms operating in multiple markets, as they must guide a patchwork of reporting needs, which can be time-consuming and expensive.

Economically, the expenses associated with executing standardized ESG reporting mechanisms can be prohibitively high, particularly for small and medium-sized enterprises (SMEs) and firms in developing economies. The need for robust data collection systems, compliance with global standards, and the hiring of sustainability specialists may be beyond the reach of these associations, further entrenching global discrepancies in ESG integration. Consequently, there is a considerable risk that the harmonization of ESG criteria could exacerbate existing economic inequalities, especially between developed and developing economies (Husson-Traore, 2020).

Political barriers also play a vital role in hindering the development of a unified global ESG framework. National sovereignty matters, divergent political priorities, and varying levels of responsibility for climate change and social justice initiatives often lead to fragmented guidelines for ESG regulation. For instance, while the EU has aggressively pursued ESG integration, many nations in the Global South have slowly embraced stringent ESG policies, stressing that such regulations may undermine their competitive benefit in global markets. Further, the influence of powerful lobbies, especially within the fossil fuel industry, can slow or block the enactment of more wide ESG regulations at national and international levels (Krinichansky & Rubtsov, 2022).

While substantial progress has been made in developing regulatory frameworks for ESG disclosures in international trade, the road to acquiring a unified global standard still needs to be solved with challenges. Measures to harmonize ESG reporting practices must handle institutional, economic, and political impediments, ensuring that all economies—particularly developing ones—are prepared to meet the growing needs for sustainability in trade. As the international trade system increasingly integrates ESG factors, the evolving policy dynamics will play a vital role in shaping the future of sustainable and reliable trade.

5. ALIGNING ESG METRICS WITH FINANCIAL DISCLOSURES

Incorporating environmental, social, and governance (ESG) metrics into financial disclosures is critical for global trade systems. As companies and governments seek sustainability, aligning ESG factors with traditional financial reporting frameworks becomes important to promoting transparency, accountability, and long-term value yield. This process, however, needs the development of sophisticated procedures and innovative technologies to seamlessly blend ESG metrics, ensuring that these essential factors are integrated into the core fabric of financial disclosure practices. By doing so, firms can better reflect their environmental and social effect, promoting trust among investors, customers, and stakeholders while contributing to the more expansive goals of sustainable development.

The Integration of ESG Metrics into Financial Reporting Systems

Integrating ESG metrics into classic financial reporting systems is a multifaceted challenge involving theoretical and practical measurements. Historically concentrated on providing details related to a firm's financial performance, financial disclosures have started to develop in response to growing needs for non-financial reporting. The integration of ESG factors into these frameworks necessitates the evolution of methodologies that not only quantify environmental, social, and governance effects but also confirm their comparability and consistency across enterprises and geographies.

One basic approach is to adapt existing reporting frameworks, such as the International Financial Reporting Standards (IFRS), to integrate ESG factors. This can involve forming specific disclosures on carbon emissions, labor conditions, water usage, and corporate governance practices, which would be reported alongside conventional financial metrics like income and returns. In practice, this might entail the development of sustainability-linked financial reports that reflect both financial performance and ESG performance in an integrated manner. For instance, firms could report the financial effect of environmental risks, such as the cost of adherence to carbon regulations or the possible liabilities deriving from environmental damage, alongside their balance sheets.

Theoretically, integrating ESG metrics into financial disclosures challenges the traditional notion of value creation. In classical financial reporting, worth is often measured purely in financial terms. However, ESG integration calls for a wider, more holistic strategy that includes business exercises' social and environmental impacts. This needs a paradigm transformation from short-term returns maximization to long-term value sustainability. This could be accomplished by including

ESG performance indicators, such as environmental impact appraisals, diversity and inclusion metrics, and governance ratings, within a company's annual statement or a separate sustainability report. By including these ESG elements, groups provide a more precise picture of their overall effect, fostering transparency and aiding investors in making more informed determinations based on financial and non-financial performance.

Technological Innovation as a Catalyst for ESG Reporting

Technological advancements, such as artificial intelligence, blockchain (AI), and big data analytics, have appeared as critical enablers in the evolution of ESG reporting. These innovations change how ESG data is collected, analyzed, and communicated, improving global trade systems' efficiency, transparency, and standardization.

With its capability to provide immutable, sufficient, and real-time data records, blockchain technology holds enormous promise for ESG reporting. By facilitating the secure tracking of ESG-related information throughout the supply chain, blockchain can help ensure that data is accurate, checkable, and tamper-proof. For example, blockchain can track carbon emissions or labor conditions across an international supply chain, ensuring players capitulate with ESG standards and provide trustworthy data to investors and regulators. This clarity is particularly important in a globalized trade system where goods and services frequently cross multiple borders, making confirming ESG compliance at every production stage hard.

Again, AI and big data are revolutionizing how ESG data is collected and analyzed. AI-driven algorithms can process vast quantities of environmental, social, and governance data from various sources, such as social media feeds, satellite imagery, and government reports, providing a real-time understanding of a company's ESG performance. This permits companies and investors to make more informed decisions based on the latest data, thereby enhancing the quality and timeliness of ESG disclosures. Big data analytics can also help identify trends, correlations, and arising risks related to ESG factors, which can inform strategic decision-making and risk management practices.

Arising digital platforms aggregating ESG data are also becoming increasingly popular, especially those delivering real-time ESG data collection and reporting abilities. These platforms deliver a centralized hub for companies to report their ESG performance in a standardized format, making it more comfortable for investors, regulators, and consumers to access and compare ESG data across enterprises. By facilitating the ESG reporting process, these platforms decrease the administrative burden on businesses and improve the accessibility and comparability of ESG disclosures in international trade systems.

Case Study Analysis: Successful Models of ESG Integration

A closer analysis of leading corporations and countries that have successfully integrated ESG metrics into their financial reporting frameworks delivers useful insights into best practices and the scalability of these ideals across international trade contexts. Companies such as Unilever and Patagonia have been at the forefront of ESG integration, showing how aligning financial reporting with sustainability objectives can enhance corporate prestige, attract responsible investment, and contribute to long-term worth creation. Unilever, for instance, has incorporated detailed ESG metrics into its annual accounts, providing stakeholders with clear information on its advancement toward achieving its sustainability targets, including reducing carbon emissions and fostering fair labor practices across its supply chain. This obligation to transparent ESG reporting has bolstered Unilever's standing as a leader in sustainability, attracting investors who prioritize environmental and social responsibility. Likewise, Patagonia has set a benchmark for incorporating ESG factors into its industry model and financial disclosures. The firm's priority on environmental stewardship, ethical sourcing, and fair governance practices has earned it a loyal customer base and substantial investor interest. Patagonia's obligation to sustainability is clearly reflected in its financial statements, which emphasize the expenses associated with its environmental initiatives and the long-term financial advantages of these investments.

On a national level, nations like Denmark and Norway have taken significant steps toward mandating ESG disclosures in financial reporting. Denmark's Sustainable Finance Act requires firms to disclose their ESG impacts and is a model for other governments looking to integrate ESG criteria into financial reporting. Similarly, Norway's government pension fund, one of the world's largest sovereign wealth funds, has been a trailblazer in demanding companies it invests to satisfy high ESG standards. These countries show that integrating ESG factors into national financial reporting frameworks is viable and valuable in fostering transparency, encouraging sustainable investment, and driving accountable corporate behavior.

Nevertheless, the scalability of these standards in global trade contexts remains a challenge. While businesses in developed economies may have the resources and infrastructure to execute comprehensive ESG reporting systems, smaller businesses, particularly in developing countries, may face significant barriers in embracing such practices. Therefore, the challenge lies in creating universally suitable models that can be adapted across different regions and sectors regarding the varying levels of economic development, regulatory environments, and technological abilities.

In conclusion, aligning ESG metrics with financial disclosures is vital in promoting transparency, responsibility, and sustainability in global trade systems. Integrating ESG factors into classic financial reporting frameworks, technological inventions, and the study of successful case studies makes it clear that aligning financial and non-financial performance is not only feasible but necessary for long-term sustainable development. As global trade persists and evolves, assuming these practices will be critical to ensuring that companies and nations contribute to accomplishing the Sustainable Development Goals while supplying value to investors and society.

The integration of Environmental, Social, and Governance (ESG) metrics into financial disclosures is a growing imperative within global trade systems. As businesses and governments strive for sustainability, aligning ESG factors with traditional financial reporting frameworks becomes essential to promoting transparency, accountability, and long-term value creation. This process, however, requires the development of sophisticated methodologies and innovative technologies to seamlessly incorporate ESG metrics, ensuring that these critical factors are integrated into the core fabric of financial disclosure practices. By doing so, businesses can better reflect their environmental and social impact, fostering trust among investors, consumers, and stakeholders while contributing to the broader goals of sustainable development.

6. FINANCIAL MARKETS, ESG, AND GLOBAL TRADE DYNAMICS

The intersection of Environmental, Social, and Governance (ESG) factors with international trade dynamics has become a focal point in recent years as financial markets adapt to the increasing focus on sustainability. This evolving connection reshapes how firms operate and affects capital flows, investment decisions, and financing instruments across borders. As ESG disclosures gain a reputation, financial markets increasingly align themselves with sustainability imperatives, driving a deep transformation in global trade and investment plans.

The Growing Impact of ESG on Financial Markets

The impact of ESG on financial markets is both quantitative and qualitative, with ESG disclosures becoming a critical element in shaping investor behavior, capital allocation, and market dynamics. Quantitatively, studies have shown that ESG metrics particularly affect investment flows, with a notable transformation towards sustainable and responsible investing. Institutional investors, Asset managers, and pension funds are increasingly integrating ESG factors into their investment standards to decrease exposure to long-term risks associated with social unrest, environmental degradation, and poor governance practices. This has been evidenced by the fast development of ESG-themed exchange-traded funds (ETFs) and sustainable investment portfolios, which persist in outperforming conventional funds in certain market necessities, reflecting a deepened awareness of sustainability risks and possibilities.

Qualitatively, ESG disclosures change how firms and industries approach long-term worth creation. Investors now believe ESG metrics are integral to evaluating businesses' future viability and stability, specifically within the context of international trade. The growing cognition of climate change, labor rights, and corporate governance scandals have built a heightened emphasis on sustainable business practices, resulting in greater scrutiny of firms' ESG performance (Kumar et al., 2024). Therefore, financial markets are witnessing an improved demand for transparency, with investors pushing for more robust and standardized ESG reporting methods. This transformation is reshaping market dynamics, as companies that fail to meet ESG anticipations may face a decline in investor confidence and higher costs of capital, leading to capital outflows and potentially reduced market valuation.

Moreover, ESG metrics are directly affecting risk appraisals in global trade sectors. Investors increasingly integrate ESG considerations into their risk management frameworks, acknowledging that environmental and social risks can have material financial importance. For illustration, firms operating in areas with weak environmental statutes or poor labor requirements may face reputational damage, regulatory penalties, or disturbances in supply chains, which can finally affect their financial performance. Consequently, ESG disclosures are becoming critical in assessing the long-term stability of investments, significantly in sectors such as manufacturing, energy, and agriculture, where environmental and social risks are especially pronounced.

Table 3. ESG impact on investment flows in 2023

Investment Sector	Total ESG Investment (US$ Billion)	Percentage Growth in ESG Investment (YoY)	Key ESG Investment Vehicles
Sustainable Bonds	500	18%	Green Bonds, Sustainability Bonds
ESG Equities	750	20%	ESG Index Funds, Impact Investing Funds
Private Equity & VC	200	15%	Impact Funds, ESG-focused VC Funds
ESG-aligned ETFs	300	12%	ESG-focused Exchange Traded Funds
Real Assets (Green REITs)	150	10%	Green Real Estate Investment Trusts (REITs)
Global Total	1,900	17%	ESG-focused financial products

Source: Global Sustainable Investment Review, GSIA, 2023

Table 3 emphasizes a significant upsurge in ESG investments across different sectors in 2023, with a significant increase in ESG equities, sustainable bonds, and private equity, steered by tools like green bonds and ESG-concentrated ETFs. This recalls an international transformation toward integrating sustainability into financial techniques and investment portfolios.

Capital markets play a vital role in supporting the change to sustainable global trade by facilitating the flow of capital to projects aligned with Environmental, Social, and Governance (ESG) goals. The elevation of ESG-linked financial tools, such as sustainable trade financing, green bonds, and ESG-linked loans, has been key in this transition. These tools allow companies and governments to ensure funding for schemes that foster sustainability in business.

Green bonds have become a powerful tool for financing environmentally friendly projects, including renewable energy infrastructure and carbon-lessening technologies. These bonds are particularly relevant for global trade as they support fund the move towards more sustainable business practices. Likewise, sustainable trade financing is essential for supporting supply chains that prioritize ESG standards. By integrating ESG standards into trade financing deals, capital markets enable firms to access funding for projects contributing to sustainable development plans.

ESG-linked loans are another innovative financial tool that connects loan terms, like interest rates, to a borrower's ESG performance. These loans encourage firms to enhance their sustainability methods, with lower interest rates generally presented to borrowers who fulfill ESG criteria. By incorporating ESG factors into capital markets, these financial tools support sustainable business and foster a more inclusive, responsible international trading system.

The confluence of ESG factors with financial systems is reshaping global trade-related investments. ESG concerns are now central to evaluating long-term risks and compensations in trade investments, observing a shift from their earlier view as secondary considerations. Financial establishments like banks and asset managers increasingly integrate ESG criteria into their investment plans, helping channel capital into undertakings like ethical supply chains, renewable energy, and climate transformation.

This integration offers possibilities for new financial outcomes, such as sustainability-linked bonds and influence investing funds, which target ESG-compliant trade initiatives. The growing focus on ESG emphasizes the need to integrate sustainability into financial strategies at all levels, from global trade deals to national regulations. By providing the necessary capital and expertise, financial associations are crucial in promoting sustainable trade in emerging markets where ESG practices are still growing.

In conclusion, incorporating ESG factors into capital markets reshapes international trade dynamics as financial establishments prioritize sustainability in their decision-making. These modifications are key to accomplishing sustainable development and trustworthy trade practices.

7. OVERCOMING BARRIERS TO EFFECTIVE ESG INTEGRATION IN GLOBAL TRADE

Integrating Environmental, Social, and Governance (ESG) factors into global trade systems face significant challenges due to institutional, structural, and operational barriers. While awareness of ESG issues has grown, their effective incorporation into trade-related financial disclosures remains hindered by resistance within organizations, inconsistent regulations, and insufficient expertise. Addressing these challenges requires a multifaceted approach centered on institutional reform, enhanced transparency, and capacity building.

Institutional and Structural Barriers to ESG Adoption

One major obstacle to ESG adoption in global trade is resistance within financial markets and organizations. Many firms, especially in emerging markets, view ESG integration as a cost rather than a strategic benefit. This mindset is compounded by inconsistent regulatory frameworks and the absence of incentives to adopt ESG principles. Industries facing short-term financial pressures often prioritize immediate returns over sustainability considerations, making ESG integration an uphill battle. Additionally, financial institutions and investors frequently rely on traditional risk assessments that overlook ESG factors, further slowing their integration into investment and financing decisions. Inconsistent reporting frameworks exacerbate this issue, leading to selective ESG disclosures that obscure a company's true environmental, social, and governance impacts. In developing economies, weak regulatory oversight often allows companies to underreport or avoid ESG disclosures altogether.

Establishing Transparency and Accountability in ESG Disclosures

Improving ESG disclosures requires robust frameworks for transparency and accountability. Governments and regulatory bodies must play a central role by mandating ESG reporting requirements and standardizing disclosure practices. Initiatives such as the European Union's Non-Financial Reporting Directive (NFRD) and Sustainable Finance Disclosure Regulation (SFDR) illustrate how policy can promote transparency and uniformity in ESG reporting. Similar frameworks globally would ensure companies disclose material ESG risks and opportunities, enabling investors to make informed decisions. Governments can further incentivize ESG compliance through tax benefits or penalties tied to disclosure quality. In the private sector, financial rewards like access to cheaper financing or inclusion in ESG-focused funds can encourage businesses to prioritize sustainability. Independent ESG rating agencies could provide external oversight, promoting standardized and credible reporting. Public-private partnerships are also essential to fostering accountability. For example, collaborative efforts to create clear reporting mechanisms can empower investors and consumers to hold businesses responsible for their ESG performance. By linking ESG outcomes to financial and reputational rewards, organizations are more likely to embrace sustainable practices.

Capacity Building and Education for ESG Competency

Effective ESG integration depends on building expertise within organizations. Education and training programs targeting business leaders, financial professionals, and policymakers are critical for equipping them to manage ESG disclosures effectively. Corporate and academic initiatives can prepare a new generation of professionals skilled in ESG best practices.

Organizations should establish cross-disciplinary teams combining sustainability, finance, and governance expertise. These teams can design and implement comprehensive ESG reporting frameworks, ensuring accurate and relevant disclosures. Partnerships between governments, businesses, and international organizations can facilitate knowledge sharing, especially in regions with limited ESG expertise (Q. Liu & You, 2023). Financial institutions also play a pivotal role in capacity building. Banks and investment firms should invest in internal training programs to help employees assess and integrate ESG factors into decision-making. Collaborations with academic institutions or ESG consultancies can provide the necessary tools and frameworks for evaluating sustainability performance and managing ESG risks. As ESG becomes central to risk management, equipping financial professionals with these skills is essential. Overcoming the barriers to ESG integration in global trade requires a holistic approach. Institutional resistance must be addressed by fostering transparency and accountability through regulatory reforms and incentivizing adherence to ESG standards. Capacity building through education and training is equally vital to ensure organizations have the expertise to manage ESG disclosures effectively.

By aligning public and private sector efforts, global trade systems can integrate ESG considerations, driving sustainable business practices. This integration will support environmentally responsible and socially equitable trade and uphold strong governance standards, ultimately contributing to a more sustainable and inclusive global economy.

8. FUTURE DIRECTIONS FOR ESG AND FINANCIAL DISCLOSURES IN GLOBAL TRADE

The future of Environmental, Social, and Governance (ESG) integration in global trade is set for transformative growth, driven by emerging trends, policy shifts, and technological innovations. As the demand for sustainable practices intensifies, embedding ESG criteria into financial disclosures will become essential for reshaping global trade. This evolution will hinge on enhanced regulatory frameworks, advanced metrics, and international cooperation, fostering a more accountable and sustainable trade system.

Emerging Trends in ESG Integration

Growing consumer and investor demand for transparency and accountability is compelling corporations to prioritize ESG in their operations. Sustainability considerations are increasingly aligned with global trade practices and financial disclosures, emphasizing broader objectives like the United Nations Sustainable Development Goals (SDGs). Businesses must now incorporate ESG standards to remain competitive in evolving markets.

Regulatory Shifts and Trade Policy

Regulations such as the European Union's Green Deal and Sustainable Finance Disclosure Regulation (SFDR) set ESG integration benchmarks. Similar policies are expected globally, with governments likely introducing mandatory ESG reporting. These regulatory advances will be accompanied by trade policies emphasizing sustainability, driving businesses to align their practices with environmental and social objectives. Over time, profitability will depend on compliance with ESG standards and the promotion of responsible and sustainable trade practices.

Enhanced ESG Metrics

As ESG frameworks evolve, the need for sophisticated, consistent, and comprehensive metrics will grow. Current systems often lack clarity and granularity, but future metrics will address these gaps, offering deeper insights into social and governance aspects like labor rights, corporate ethics, and community impact. This will enable businesses to demonstrate accountability across the entire trade value chain.

Ultimately, ESG integration will redefine global trade, advancing sustainability, accountability, and equitable practices worldwide.

Table 4. Global ESG reporting adoption by region (2023)

Region	Percentage of Companies Reporting ESG Metrics (%)	Key Regulatory Frameworks	Notable Policies & Guidelines
North America	88%	SASB, TCFD, SEC ESG Disclosure Rules	SEC Proposed ESG Disclosures (2022)
Europe	91%	EU Non-Financial Reporting Directive (NFRD), SFDR	European Green Deal, EU Corporate Sustainability Reporting Directive (CSRD)
Asia-Pacific	75%	Japan's Stewardship Code, Australia's Modern Slavery Act	Australia's ESG Reporting Requirements (2021)
Latin America	65%	Brazil's B3 Corporate Governance Index, Argentina's ESG Initiatives	Regional ESG Guidelines by B3 (2023)
Middle East & Africa	55%	UAE Sustainable Finance Regulatory Framework	UAE Vision 2021, Dubai Financial Market's ESG Disclosure Guidelines
Global Average	80%	Various Global Standards (GRI, TCFD, SASB, etc.)	Global ESG standards convergence in 2023

Source: Global ESG Reporting Survey, EY, 2023

Table 4 highlights regional differences in ESG reporting adoption in 2023. Europe leads, followed by North America, while the Middle East, Africa, and Latin America show slower progress, reflecting varying regulatory frameworks and a global shift towards standardized ESG reporting.

Technological Innovations in ESG Data Reporting

Technological advancements are set to revolutionize ESG tracking, reporting, and analysis, enabling more efficient and accurate disclosures in global trade. Cutting-edge technologies such as artificial intelligence (AI), blockchain, and the Internet of Things (IoT) are already reshaping how businesses gather, process, and report ESG data. AI, for instance, has the potential to automate data collection, identify patterns in large datasets, and enhance the accuracy of ESG assessments. By leveraging machine learning algorithms, AI can analyze vast amounts of unstructured data, such as social media posts or satellite images, to monitor environmental impact, supply chain conditions, and corporate governance practices.

Blockchain technology is another innovation that promises to enhance the transparency and traceability of ESG data. By providing an immutable, decentralized ledger, blockchain can ensure that ESG disclosures are tamper-proof, reducing the risk of greenwashing and increasing trust in the reported data. Blockchain's role in global trade is particularly significant, as it can enable real-time tracking of goods and services across complex international supply chains, ensuring that companies adhere to sustainability standards throughout their operations.

The IoT is also pivotal in reshaping ESG reporting systems by enabling the collection of real-time environmental data from sensors embedded in manufacturing processes, transportation networks, and natural ecosystems. This data can seamlessly integrate into ESG reporting frameworks, providing stakeholders with up-to-date information on a company's environmental impact, resource usage, and overall sustainability performance.

These technologies will converge to create more integrated and efficient ESG reporting systems, allowing businesses to collect, analyze, and disclose ESG data in real time. This will improve the accuracy of financial disclosures and streamline compliance with regulatory requirements, making it easier for companies to navigate the increasingly complex ESG landscape.

Table 5. Technological innovations enabling ESG reporting in global trade (2023)

Technology	Application in ESG Reporting	Current Use Case	Future Potential Impact
Blockchain	Enhances transparency and traceability of ESG data	Used in supply chains to track carbon footprints and ethical sourcing (e.g., VeChain)	Widespread adoption for real-time ESG data tracking and verification
Artificial Intelligence	Automates data collection and pattern recognition	AI-driven tools to analyze large ESG datasets and identify non-compliance (e.g., IBM Watson)	Increased use in ESG risk prediction and automated compliance reporting
Internet of Things (IoT)	Real-time environmental data collection and analysis	IoT sensors in manufacturing to monitor energy use and emissions (e.g., Siemens IoT solutions)	Full integration into global trade logistics for continuous ESG monitoring
Big Data Analytics	Aggregates ESG data for reporting and decision-making	Data analysis for ESG integration in financial portfolios (e.g., MSCI ESG Analytics)	Enhanced predictive models for ESG-driven investment strategies

Source: TechNavio, Global IoT and AI Industry Reports, 2023

The table 5 illustrates how technological innovations, including blockchain, artificial intelligence, IoT, and big data analytics, are currently enhancing ESG reporting by improving transparency, automating data collection, and enabling real-time monitoring, with future potential for these technologies to revolutionize ESG tracking, risk prediction, and compliance across global trade systems.

Long-Term Vision: Achieving a Sustainable Global Trade System

The long-term vision for global trade is one in which ESG considerations are fully embedded in all financial disclosures and decision-making processes. In this idealized future, businesses, investors, and governments will work together to create a global trade system that prioritizes sustainability and equity alongside economic growth. ESG factors will be seen as integral to financial performance, with companies that demonstrate strong environmental, social, and governance practices attracting more investment and securing long-term profitability.

Theoretically, a fully integrated global trade system will seamlessly align economic activities and sustainability goals. This system's financial disclosures will not be limited to traditional financial performance metrics. They will also encompass detailed information on a company's environmental footprint, social responsibility efforts, and governance practices. Such disclosures will enable investors to make more informed decisions while empowering consumers and civil society to hold companies accountable for their impact on society and the planet.

International collaboration will be a cornerstone of this sustainable global trade system. As global supply chains become increasingly interconnected, nations must collaborate to establish universal ESG standards and reporting frameworks. Policy coherence at the international level will be essential to ensure that ESG criteria are uniformly adopted and enforced across borders. This will require cooperation between governments, regulatory bodies, industry groups, and civil society organizations and the establishment of global platforms for knowledge exchange and best practice sharing.

In conclusion, the future of ESG and financial disclosures in global trade is marked by emerging trends, technological innovations, and a growing emphasis on sustainability. As ESG factors become more integrated into global trade systems, businesses will increasingly be held accountable for their environmental, social, and governance impacts. With the support of advanced technologies, regulatory evolution, and international collaboration, a sustainable global trade system that prioritizes ESG considerations is within reach, promising a more equitable and responsible future for international commerce.

Managerial Implications

This study offers critical managerial implications for executives, emphasizing integrating ESG metrics into corporate governance frameworks to align with evolving financial disclosure standards. Managers must navigate the complexities of regulatory compliance, adopting innovative technologies to enhance ESG transparency and reporting accuracy. Strategic investments in sustainability-driven initiatives will ensure adherence to global trade policies and optimize long-term profitability by fostering stakeholder trust. Furthermore, cultivating a proactive ESG culture within organizations is imperative, positioning firms as leaders in sustainable practices amidst the increasingly stringent global regulatory environment.

9. CONCLUSION

In conclusion, this chapter highlights the transformative integration of ESG factors into global trade financial disclosures, emphasizing progress, regional disparities, and the inevitable shift toward standardized, transparent practices driven by technological and regulatory advancements.

The chapter provides actionable policy recommendations to align ESG reporting with financial disclosures, advocating for mandatory, globally coordinated standards, governance reforms prioritizing sustainability, incentives like tax breaks and green financing, and enforceable frameworks to facilitate consistent cross-border ESG disclosures.

The final review emphasizes that achieving sustainable global trade requires continuous innovation and international collaboration, where technologies like IoT, blockchain, and AI transform ESG metrics through transparency and real-time tracking, supported by a multilateral framework for cross-border knowledge exchange, with policy convergence, corporate accountability, and ESG alignment with financial disclosures as key elements for a sustainable, equitable, and environmentally responsible trading system.

REFERENCES

Abdullah, A., Hassan, R., & Kassim, S. (2020). A real asset management approach for Islamic investment in containerships. *Journal of Islamic Accounting and Business Research, 11*(1), 27–48. DOI: 10.1108/JIABR-07-2017-0105

Bukhari, S. A. A., Hashim, F., Amran, A., & Hyder, K. (2020). Green Banking and Islam: Two sides of the same coin. *Journal of Islamic Marketing, 11*(4), 977–1000. DOI: 10.1108/JIMA-09-2018-0154

Filipovic, I., Bartulovic, M., & Susak, T. (2018). Accounting information as indicator of money laundering. Economic and Social Development: Book of Proceedings, 159-163.

Gupta, C., Jindal, P., & Malhotra, R. K. (2022). A Study of Increasing Adoption Trends of Digital Technologies - An Evidence from Indian Banking. In D. N. & C. A. (Eds.), *AIP Conference Proceedings* (Vol. 2481). American Institute of Physics Inc. DOI: 10.1063/5.0104572

Husson-Traore, A.-C. (2020). 12 - Sustainable Finance for Citizens. In *Making the Financial System Sustainable*. Cambridge University Press., DOI: 10.1017/9781108908269.015

Jha, B., Giri, P., Jha, D., & Badhera, U. (2022). Unlocking IoT: AI-enabled green fintech innovations. In *AI-Enabled Agile Internet of Things for Sustainable FinTech Ecosystems*. IGI Global., DOI: 10.4018/978-1-6684-4176-3.ch001

Kaur, J., Khanna, R., Kumar, R., & Sunil, G. (2024). Role of Blockchain Technologies in Goods and Services Tax. *Proceedings - 2024 3rd International Conference on Sentiment Analysis and Deep Learning, ICSADL 2024*, 607–612. DOI: 10.1109/ICSADL61749.2024.00104

Khanna, R., Jindal, P., & Noja, G. G. (2023). Blockchain technologies, a catalyst for insurance sector. In *The Application of Emerging Technology and Blockchain in the Insurance Industry*. DOI: 10.1201/9781032630946-19

Krahnen, J., Rocholl, J., & Thum, M. (2023). A Primer on Green Finance: From Wishful Thinking to Marginal Impact. *Review of Economics, 74*(1), 1–19. DOI: 10.1515/roe-2023-0019

Krinichansky, K. V., & Rubtsov, B. B. (2022). Financial Sector Regulation on the Agenda of Economic Policy Reforms [Регулирование финансового сектора в повестке реформ экономической политики]. *Finance: Theory and Practice, 26*(5), 6–21. DOI: 10.26794/2587-5671-2022-26-5-6-21

Kukreti, M., Sehajpal, S., Tiwari, R., & Sood, K. (2025). *Driving Global Health and Sustainable Development Goals With Smart Technology* (Mohit, K., Sabina, S., Rajesh, T., & Kiran, S., Eds.; 1st ed.). IGI Global Scientific Publishing., DOI: 10.4018/979-8-3373-0240-9

Kumar, R., Goel, R., Singh, T., Mohanty, S. M., Gupta, D., Alkhayyat, A., & Khanna, R. (2024). Sustainable Finance Factors in Indian Economy: Analysis on Policy of Climate Change and Energy Sector. *Fluctuation and Noise Letters*, *23*(2), 2440004. Advance online publication. DOI: 10.1142/S0219477524400042

Kumar, R., Khannna Malholtra, R., & Grover, C. A. N. (2023). Review on Artificial Intelligence Role in Implementation of Goods and Services Tax(GST) and Future Scope. *2023 International Conference on Artificial Intelligence and Smart Communication, AISC 2023*, 348–351. DOI: 10.1109/AISC56616.2023.10085030

Kumar, R., Lande, A., Kumar, D., Malhotra, R. K., & Sharma, A. (2023). Technology Bridging -in Entrepreneurs and Consumers in Product Development. *ISED 2023 - International Conference on Intelligent Systems and Embedded Design*. DOI: 10.1109/ISED59382.2023.10444599

Kumar, R., Malholtra, R. K., Singh, R., Kathuria, S., Balyan, R., & Pal, P. (2023). Artificial Intelligence Role in Electronic Invoice Under Goods and Services Tax. *2023 International Conference on Computational Intelligence, Communication Technology and Networking, CICTN 2023*, 140–143. DOI: 10.1109/CICTN57981.2023.10140870

Liu, Q., & You, Y. (2023). FinTech and Green Credit Development—Evidence from China. *Sustainability (Basel)*, *15*(7), 5903. Advance online publication. DOI: 10.3390/su15075903

Liu, X. (2017). An integrated macro-financial risk-based approach to the stressed capital requirement. *Review of Financial Economics*, *34*(1), 86–98. DOI: 10.1016/j.rfe.2017.06.002

Malhotra, R. K., Gupta, C., & Jindal, P. (2022). Blockchain and Smart Contracts for Insurance Industry. In *Blockchain Technology in Corporate Governance*. Transforming Business and Industries., DOI: 10.1002/9781119865247.ch11

Mohanty, S., Alfurhood, B. S., Bakhare, R., Poongavanam, S., & Khanna, R. (2023, January). The role and impact of artificial intelligence on retail business and its developments. In *2023 International Conference on Artificial Intelligence and Smart Communication (AISC)* (pp. 1098-1101). IEEE.

Rendtorff, J. D. (2023). Responsible Business and Integrated Stakeholder Reporting: Towards a Stakeholder Model for Integrated Reporting of ESG and SDG. *Ethical Economy*, *64*, 49–59. DOI: 10.1007/978-3-031-26959-2_6

Sehajpal, S., & Kaur, N. (2025). Neuroscience, Nursing, and Financial Innovation : A Synergistic Approach to Optimized Patient Care and Economic Well-Being. In Sanjay, T., Bhupinderpal Pal, S. C., Amar, J., Ercan, O., & Pawan, K. (Eds.), *Neuromarketing's Role in Sustainable Finance* (pp. 133–146). IGI Global Scientific Publishing., DOI: 10.4018/979-8-3693-9117-4.ch008

Tang, D. Y., & Zhang, Y. (2020). Do shareholders benefit from green bonds? *Journal of Corporate Finance*, *61*(November), 1–18. DOI: 10.1016/j.jcorpfin.2018.12.001

Upreti, H., & Malhotra, R. K. (2024). Bridging The Urban-Rural Education Gap In India Through CSR (Corporate Social Responsibility) Initiatives: A Conceptual Study With Special Reference To Sustainable Development Goal 4 (Quality Education). In P. P.K. (Ed.), *E3S Web of Conferences* (Vol. 556). EDP Sciences. DOI: 10.1051/e3sconf/202455601032

Wang, X., & Wen, H. (2022). Research on the Financing Mode of Green Bond Supporting Green Building Development. In W. Y., L. S., & S. G.Q.P. (Eds.), *ICCREM 2022: Carbon Peak and Neutrality Strategies of the Construction Industry - Proceedings of the International Conference on Construction and Real Estate Management 2022* (pp. 170 – 175). American Society of Civil Engineers (ASCE). DOI: 10.1061/9780784484562.017

Zhang, W., He, X., & Hamori, S. (2022). Volatility spillover and investment strategies among sustainability-related financial indexes: Evidence from the DCC-GARCH-based dynamic connectedness and DCC-GARCH t-copula approach. *International Review of Financial Analysis*, *83*, 102223. Advance online publication. DOI: 10.1016/j.irfa.2022.102223

Chapter 2
Harmonizing Financial Reporting Standards: Driving Cross-Border Mergers and Acquisitions in a Globalized Economy

Pawan Kumar
https://orcid.org/0000-0003-4892-6374
Graphic Era University, Dehradun, USA

Arvinder Kaur
https://orcid.org/0000-0001-7360-5674
Chandigarh University, India

Sanjay Taneja
https://orcid.org/0000-0002-3632-4053
Graphic Era University (Deemed), Dehradun, India

ABSTRACT

This chapter explores the vital role of harmonized financial reporting standards in facilitating cross-border mergers and acquisitions in global economy, emphasizing the need for regulatory alignment to streamline processes, reduce complexities, and enhance transaction efficiency; it addresses challenges between US GAAP and IFRS regarding asset valuation, due diligence, and compliance, while highlighting' how emerging technologies like blockchain, artificial intelligence, and data analytics improve the speed, accuracy, and transparency of financial reporting, minimizing fraud risks and reporting errors; the chapter also underscores the contributions of financial institutions and advisory firms in driving harmonization, ensuring multi-national corporations adopt best practices for financial compliance, and concludes

DOI: 10.4018/979-8-3373-0887-6.ch002

by forecasting that the future of global M&As will be shaped by integrated reporting standards, new technologies, and investor-driven momentum, promoting greater market efficiency, regulatory coherence, and a more transparent, accountable global financial landscape.

1. THE ROLE OF FINANCIAL REPORTING IN GLOBAL TRADE AND M&A ACTIVITY

Outline of the Globalized Economy

In today's interconnected global economy, cross-border movements, technological innovations, and trade liberalization are driving the need for standardized financial reporting practices to ensure consistency, comparability, and transparency across jurisdictions, as multinational enterprises and economic boundaries become increasingly fluid (Altman, 2004; Brereton, 2004). Financial reporting acting like as the mentor in dealings of business transactions.

Financial reporting serves as the common language of business, facilitating corporate performance evaluation, due diligence, and strategic alignment, with International Financial Reporting Standards and US Generally Accepted Accounting Principles (GAAP) as the two main frameworks, though their differences create challenges in cross-border mergers and acquisitions by obscuring the financial status of merging entities (Akgün, 2022; Gláserová, 2013).

Table 1. Global adoption of IFRS by region (2023)

Region	**Countries Adopting IFRS**	**Percentage of Global GDP (%)**	**Notable Adopters**
Europe	41	56%	EU Member States, UK, Norway, Switzerland
Asia-Pacific	25	24%	Japan, Australia, Hong Kong, Singapore
Latin America	18	10%	Brazil, Mexico, Argentina, Chile
Middle East & Africa	15	5%	South Africa, Egypt, United Arab Emirates
North America	2	5%	Canada, United States (adopts limited IFRS)
Global Total	**101**	**100%**	**Global Trade Coverage**

Source: IFRS Foundation, 2023

Table 1 underscores the global adoption of IFRS, highlighting its role in enhancing transparency, comparability, and efficiency in cross-border transactions, as standardized financial reporting becomes vital for reducing transaction costs and improving market liquidity in increasingly interconnected international markets.

The Importance and Significance of Cross-Border Mergers and Acquisitions (M&A)

The elevation of cross-border M&As in recent decades illustrates the expanding reach of global trade and capital flows, with M&As acting as a pivotal instrument in driving international expansion, granting access to new markets, enhancing economies of scale, and promoting global competitive advantages, and as companies from various geographical regions merge, the resultant synergies—derived from technology transfer, operational efficiencies and market consolidation—can yield meaningful benefits (Bakkar & Nyola, 2021; Boudier & Lochard, 2013); however, the integration of financial strategies, cultures, and strategies in such dealings is fraught with challenges, specifically when financial reporting systems stay misaligned, as disparities in reporting standards can lead to misunderstandings of a company's monetary health, thereby endangering the merger's or acquisition's value proposition, creating the demand for harmonized financial reporting standards critical to bridge the gap between disparate national standards, assuring that all stakeholders have credentials to trustworthy, comparable financial data (Bose et al., 2021).

Table 2. Cross-border M&A activity (2015-2023)

Year	Total Global M&A Value (USD Trillion)	Cross-Border M&A Value (USD Billion)	Percentage of Total M&A Activity (%)
2015	4.3	1.8	42%
2016	3.5	1.5	43%
2017	4.7	2.0	43%
2018	3.8	1.9	50%
2019	3.9	2.1	54%
2020	2.5	1.2	48%
2021	5.0	2.6	52%
2022	4.3	2.0	47%
2023	**4.5**	**2.3**	**51%**

Source: Merger market, 2023

Table 2 highlights the growing volume and value of cross-border M&A deals, emphasizing the need for standardized financial reporting to ensure due diligence, accurate valuation, and risk assessment in these transactions.

Purpose and Scope of the Research

This chapter explores the strategic importance of harmonized financial reporting standards in cross-border M&As, analyzing how consistent frameworks mitigate operational barriers, ensure smoother integration, and reduce accounting discrepancies, while addressing regulatory compliance, technological tools, and the coexistence of IFRS and US GAAP to improve transparency, align global practices, and drive value creation in international mergers.

Research Methodology

This chapter employs a qualitative and comparative research methodology, analyzing secondary data from academic literature, industry reports, and case studies to assess the impact of harmonized financial reporting norms on cross-border M&As, comparing US GAAP and IFRS, while exploring emerging technologies like blockchain, AI, and data analytics to enhance efficiency, transparency, and regulatory compliance.

2. THE EVOLUTION OF FINANCIAL REPORTING STANDARDS

Historical Development

The landscape of financial reporting has evolved over the last century from nationalistic accounting practices, where countries like Britain and the United States developed distinct standards such as historic cost-based British accounting and US GAAP, to more globally recognized frameworks. The transformation towards global harmonization has started in the latter half of 20th century.

The shift towards international harmonization began in the late 20th century with the expansion of cross-border trade and multinational enterprises, leading to the formation of the International Accounting Standards Committee (IASC) in 1973, which laid the foundation for the development of International Financial Reporting Standards (IFRS) under the IASB in 2001.

Meanwhile, in the United States, the Financial Accounting Standards Board (FASB) became responsible for maintaining US GAAP, and despite their initial coexistence, the 21st century saw increasing efforts to converge US GAAP and

IFRS into a unified accounting framework to address the complexities of globalized financial markets.

Table 3. International adoption of IFRS vs. US GAAP (2023)

Region	**IFRS Adoption (%)**	**US GAAP Adoption (%)**	**Notable Jurisdictions (IFRS/US GAAP)**
Europe	95%	5%	EU, UK (IFRS), Switzerland (IFRS)
Asia-Pacific	75%	25%	Japan (IFRS adoption), China (adopted IFRS)
Latin America	80%	20%	Brazil (IFRS), Mexico (IFRS)
North America	35%	65%	United States (US GAAP)
Middle East & Africa	60%	40%	UAE (IFRS), South Africa (IFRS)
Global Total	**70%**	**30%**	**Increasing global trend towards IFRS**

Source: IFRS Foundation, 2023

The increasing global adoption of IFRS, highlighted in Table 3, reveals the growing consensus toward a single unified framework, particularly in the face of globalization. As markets become more integrated, the need for consistent and comparable financial reporting has never been more apparent.

Key Regulatory Bodies and Frameworks

Central to the development and governance of global financial reporting standards are organizations such as the International Accounting Standards Board (IASB) and the Financial Accounting Standards Board (FASB) (Georgieva & Jandik, 2012). The IASB, which took over the work of the IASC, is responsible for issuing IFRS, which is now used by over 140 jurisdictions worldwide, including the European Union and many emerging markets in Asia and Latin America (Röben, 2006). The FASB, on the other hand, governs the US GAAP, a set of rules that remains authoritative within the United States, though it has shown signs of greater convergence with IFRS in recent years .

The convergence efforts between IFRS and US GAAP have led to some harmonization of financial reporting, particularly in areas like revenue recognition and lease accounting, though substantial differences still remain (Alimov, 2015; Carril-Caccia & Milgram Baleix, 2024). The IASB-FASB convergence project has been instrumental in eliminating discrepancies, but challenges persist due to the cultural, regulatory, and historical differences between the two standards.

Table 4. Comparison of key differences between IFRS and US GAAP

Aspect	IFRS (International)	US GAAP (Domestic)
Revenue Recognition	Based on a single, principles-based model	Multiple rules-based guidelines, industry-specific
Inventory Valuation	LIFO (Last-In, First-Out) not permitted	LIFO is permitted for inventory cost calculation
Leases	Capitalize most leases, using a single model	Differentiates between operating and capital leases
Financial Statement Presentation	Less detailed guidance	More detailed rules for statement presentation
Fair Value Measurement	Emphasizes fair value in certain circumstances	Focuses on historical cost, with fair value used in limited cases

Source: FASB and IFRS Foundation, 2022

As shown in Table 4, key differences between IFRS and US GAAP persist, affecting how businesses report financial transactions and prepare statements, which can create challenges in cross-border transactions, mergers, and acquisitions (M&As), where comparability is crucial for assessing the value and risks of target companies (Carril-Caccia & Baleix, 2020; Sahoo & Chakrabarti, 2022).

The Role of Financial Reporting in Cross-Border Transactions

Harmonizing financial reporting standards is crucial for facilitating cross-border M&As by reducing complexity and barriers from differing accounting practices, as these transactions often involve integrating businesses with incompatible financial reporting standards, complicating the accurate assessment and comparison of financial statements (Monteiro & Silva, 2022). The lack appropriate reporting could lead discrepancies and regulatory challenges after merger.

Hence, absence of standardized reporting can cause valuation discrepancies, regulatory challenges, and integration difficulties post-merger, with IFRS adoption in Europe and Asia simplifying M&As by providing consistent financial standards (Hassan & Giouvris, 2021; Levine et al., 2020), while US GAAP's dominance in the US complicates integration, requiring additional reconciliations, but harmonized standards like IFRS enhance financial transparency, streamline due diligence, and foster greater investor confidence and cross-border investment flows (Degryse & Ongena, 2004; Tokic & Beyea, 2010).

Table 5. Global M&A activity and the impact of IFRS adoption (2015-2023)

Year	Global M&A Value (USD Trillion)	Cross-Border M&A Value (USD Billion)	Percentage of M&A Deals Using IFRS
2015	4.3	1.9	55%
2016	3.5	1.7	58%
2017	4.7	2.0	61%
2018	3.8	1.8	63%
2019	4.3	2.2	65%
2020	3.1	1.4	68%
2023	**4.5**	**2.5**	**70%**

Source: Mergermarket, 2023

Table 5 highlights the growth in cross-border M&A activity and the increased use of IFRS to facilitate smoother transactions, illustrating that as global IFRS adoption rises, the efficiency and transparency of international M&As improve, with the evolution from national standards to unified frameworks like IFRS reducing discrepancies and enhancing financial statement comparability, thereby supporting globalization and fostering more robust and transparent international financial markets.

3. THE PRESENT STATUS OF FINANCIAL REPORTING AND CHALLENGES IN CROSS-BORDER M&AS

Disparities Between IFRS and US GAAP

Despite efforts to harmonize financial reporting globally, significant disparities between IFRS and US GAAP persist, particularly in areas like revenue recognition, inventory valuation, and lease accounting, which can impact the comparability of financial data in cross-border mergers and acquisitions (M&As) (Liu et al., 2021) and complicate the due diligence process. For instance, international financial reporting system utilized an approach based standards to recognition of revenue, paying attention on transactions substances (Martynova & Renneboog, 2008).

Moreover, IFRS uses a principles-based approach to revenue recognition, focusing on the substance of transactions, while US GAAP follows a rules-based framework with detailed industry-specific guidelines, and while IFRS prohibits Last In, First Out (LIFO) for inventory valuation, US GAAP permits it, creating complexities in assessing financial health and leading to inconsistent valuations in cross-border deals.(Gláserová, 2013; Ramesh, 2023).

Table 6. Key differences between IFRS and US GAAP

Aspect	IFRS (International)	US GAAP (Domestic)
Revenue Recognition	Principles-based approach	Rules-based, industry-specific
Inventory Valuation	LIFO not permitted	LIFO allowed
Leases	Single accounting model for leases	Differentiates between operating and capital leases
Fair Value Measurement	Fair value used in certain cases	Primarily historical cost

Source: IFRS Foundation, FASB (2023)

Table 6 reveals the key dissimilarities between IFRS and GAAP, International Financial reporting system adopting the principles based approach to recognize the revenue, LIFO inventory valuation, and the single accounting model for leasing. Whereas GAAP depends upon historical cost measurement compared to IFRS more flexible apply of value measurement.

Legal and Regulatory Constraints

Divergent financial reporting standards create regulatory and legal barriers in cross-border M&As, with differences in taxation, compliance, and audit requirements leading to delayed approvals, increased costs, legal complexities, and challenges in verifying financial statements during due diligence (Georgieva et al., 2012; Tian & Wang, 2007).

The Complication of Integrating Diverse Reporting Principles in M&A

Post-merger integration becomes more complex when merging entities operate under different reporting standards, requiring significant effort to reconcile financial data, particularly in areas like goodwill and asset valuations, which can delay synergy realization and the standardization of reporting methods and systems(Chen & Li, 2010; Heinemann, 2012).

Table 7. Post-M&a integration challenges by reporting standards

Challenge	IFRS-Based Companies	US GAAP-Based Companies
Valuation of Assets	Fair value emphasis	Primarily historical cost-based
Goodwill Accounting	Amortized over time	Tested for impairment annually
Revenue Recognition	More flexible, principles-based	Stringent, rules-based

Source: Deloitte Global M&A Insights, 2022

Table 7 delineates post-M&A integration challenges, highlighting that IFRS-based companies prioritize fair value in asset valuation, amortize goodwill over time, and adopt a flexible, principles-based approach to revenue recognition, while US GAAP-based companies adhere to historical cost for asset valuation, require annual impairment testing for goodwill, and enforce a stringent, rules-based revenue recognition framework (Guo & Cheng, 2024; Raghavendra et al., 2022).

4. HARMONIZING OF FINANCIAL REPORTING: DRIVERS AND MOTIVATIONS

Economic Integration and international Trade

The globalization of markets has heightened the need for harmonized financial reporting standards like IFRS, which can reduce transaction costs, enhance transparency, and streamline cross-border trade and investments by overcoming disparities in accounting practices between jurisdictions. Discrepancies reduced by harmonization of financial reporting from diverse accounting system, ensured more accuracy in data, prices, and dealings in global markets. Whereas new opportunities facilitated through enabling business to capitalize (D. M. DePamphilis, 2019; Gerpott & Jakopin, 2007).

Table 8. Impact of harmonized financial reporting on cross-border trade (2023)

Country/ Region	Adoption of IFRS (%)	Cross-Border Trade Growth (Annual %)	Key Benefits from Harmonization
European Union	100%	7.3%	Increased market access, streamlined reporting
Asia-Pacific	75%	6.1%	Enhanced financial transparency, reduced costs
Latin America	80%	5.2%	Facilitates cross-border investments
North America	35%	4.5%	Lower transaction costs, increased investor confidence
Global Total	**70%**	**6.3%**	**Reduced friction in global markets**

Source: IFRS Foundation, 2023

As shown in Table 8, regions with greater IFRS adoption experience higher rates of cross-border trade growth, highlighting the role of harmonized financial reporting in enhancing the global economic integration (D. DePamphilis, 2017).

Investor Confidence and Market Transparency

Harmonized financial reporting standards enhance investor confidence by ensuring comparability, reliability, and transparency across markets, reducing information asymmetry, boosting market efficiency, encouraging foreign investment, and facilitating cross-border M&As through smoother due diligence and faster deal closures (Joshi et al., 2013; Rossi & Volpin, 2004).

Table 9. Investor confidence and capital flows with financial reporting harmonization

Region	Adoption of IFRS (%)	Average Annual FDI (USD Trillions)	Investor Confidence Index (Scale 1-10)
Europe	100%	1.2	8.5
Asia-Pacific	75%	0.9	7.8
Latin America	80%	0.6	7.5
North America	35%	0.5	6.9
Global Total	**70%**	**3.2**	**7.8**

Source: World Bank, 2023

As shown in Table 9, regions with greater IFRS adoption exhibit higher investor confidence and increased foreign direct investment (FDI), highlighting the role of harmonized financial reporting in promoting market stability and growth.

Regulatory Alignment for Cross-Border M&As

The harmonization of financial reporting is essential in **cross-border M&A transactions**, where regulatory compliance plays a critical role in the **deal closure process**. Different accounting standards often result in regulatory divergence, causing significant delays in deal approval, **taxation disputes**, and integration complexities. By adopting **uniform financial reporting frameworks**, companies can reduce these regulatory hurdles, ensuring smoother compliance processes and faster approvals from local regulators (Lin et al., 2013; Yan, 2018). **Financial reporting harmonization** helps mitigate issues related to **double taxation**, **transfer pricing**, and the **treatment of goodwill**, which are frequently sources of dispute in international mergers. A standardized reporting framework also simplifies the task of conducting **due diligence**, as both acquirer and target companies can operate under similar **financial disclosure norms**, thus facilitating more efficient evaluations and negotiations. Moreover, this alignment ensures that regulators in both countries recognize and validate financial statements with greater ease, enhancing the **efficiency** and **speed** of regulatory reviews (Han, 2020; Irwin et al., 2022).

Table 10. Impact of financial reporting harmonization on cross-border M&A deal closures

Region	Average M&A Deal Closure Time (Months)	IFRS Adoption (%)	Regulatory Delays Due to Reporting Issues (%)
Europe	6.1	100%	5%
Asia-Pacific	7.2	75%	10%
Latin America	8.5	80%	15%
North America	9.8	35%	25%
Global Total	**7.2**	**70%**	**13%**

Source: Mergermarket, 2023

Table 10 demonstrates that regions with higher IFRS adoption experience quicker deal closures and fewer regulatory delays, highlighting the role of financial reporting harmonization in facilitating smoother cross-border M&As, enhancing market transparency, reducing transaction costs, and driving economic integration (Fu et al., 2023).

5. CASE STUDIES OF SUCCESSFUL HARMONIZATION IN CROSS-BORDER M&AS

Case Study 1: The Daimler-Chrysler Merger

The Daimler-Benz and Chrysler merger, concluded in 1998, is one of the most important cross-border unification in automotive history, valued at over $36 billion. At the moment, Daimler-Benz, a German firm, stuck to International Financial Reporting Standards (IFRS), while Chrysler, established in the United States, obeyed US GAAP (Alba et al., 2009; Buch & DeLong, 2004). Despite powerful strategic synergies, the initial union of these two companies faced substantial operational challenges arising from their disparate financial reporting systems. Nevertheless, harmonizing financial reporting played a key role in easing these challenges. Having already adopted IFRS, Daimler found aligning its financial reports with Chrysler's US GAAP-based statements easier. By adopting better standardized accounting principles, both entities could harmonize their accounting treatments for goodwill, stock valuation, and income recognition, especially in reducing disparities and valuation disputes during due diligence (Li et al., 2023; Reddy et al., 2016).

Again, the harmonized standards encouraged better strategic alignment between the two groups, enabling more transparent financial predictions, improved financial transparency, and more adequate regulatory compliance (Mathieson et al., 1998; Tsepova, 2022). Despite this success, the merger faltered due to cultural and functional mismatches rather than financial reporting disparities. However, the harmonization of reporting procedures confirmed that, at least in spans of financial integration, the operation proceeded more smoothly than it would have had the two groups persisted with their disparate accounting approaches. This emphasizes the critical role of harmonized reporting in the earlier stages of cross-border M&As, especially in minimizing financial differences that could slow integration (Kollruss, 2021; Stittle, 2004). **Source**: International Financial Reporting Standards (IFRS), 2022

Case Study 2: Unilever and Procter & Gamble

In 2000, Unilever and Procter & Gamble (P&G), two international giants in the buyer goods industry, entered a strategic partnership in several markets, including the U.S., Europe, and Asia. Both groups, initially operating with different accounting pinnacles—P&G with US GAAP and Unilever with IFRS—met the challenge of adjusting their financial reporting procedures to enable smoother operations and assure proper valuation during the merger negotiations (Akisik & Mangaliso, 2020; Alkaraan, 2020). The harmonization of financial reporting standards was important in managing operational inefficiencies. By assuming IFRS as an international reporting framework, Unilever and P&G ensured both groups could work more transparently and standardized with substantial decreases in audit outlay and reconciliation assignment. This assisted in minimizing the intricacies of crystallizing financial reports across numerous jurisdictions, as both groups now followed the same accounting remedies for foreign exchange transactions, income recognition, and goodwill (Clinch et al., 2023). Moreover, blended financial reporting led to better functional stakeholder communication, as investors could easily correspond to the two firms' performance metrics. By aligning reporting standards, the companies ensured that their financial soundness was more accurately described, which was instrumental in drawing continued investment and improving market confidence during the integration strategy. The triumph of this strategic alliance represents the important role of harmonization in lessening regulatory burdens, transaction fees, and distinctions during transnational collaborations (Kashiwazaki et al., 2019). **Source**: Deloitte Global M&A Insights, 2022

Case Study 3: The IBM and Lenovo Acquisition

Lenovo's 2005 purchase of IBM's computer department for $1.75 billion is another key model of how financial reporting harmonization can ease cross-border M&A dealings. IBM, an American global, followed US GAAP, while Lenovo, a Chinese corporation, embraced Chinese Accounting Standards (CAS), which significantly differed from US GAAP and IFRS. To successfully combine the two firms' operations, I(Clem et al., 2004)BM and Lenovo confounded cultural and functional challenges and disparities between their financial reporting systems . The answer came by embracing IFRS as the international standard for financial reporting across all associates, including Lenovo's international operations. By transitioning Lenovo's financial reporting to IFRS, both parties could secure consistency in treating investments, revenue recognition, liabilities, and financial exposures. This harmonization was beneficial in streamlining due diligence procedures, minimizing the time needed to reconcile financial reports, and ensuring that financial data across different regions were comparable. Moreover, the standardization of reporting made it more comfortable for investors and controllers to evaluate the financial position of the merged entity, thus improving market confidence and promoting a softer regulatory clearance process (Cheng & Finney, 2010). **Source**: PwC M&A Insights, 2022

These case studies demonstrate how harmonized financial reporting, particularly through IFRS, played a crucial role in overcoming operational and strategic challenges in cross-border M&As like Daimler-Chrysler, Unilever-P&G, and IBM-Lenovo, streamlining integration, minimizing discrepancies, and boosting investor confidence, while highlighting the ongoing importance of standardization for successful international business ventures.

6. THE IMPACT OF FINANCIAL REPORTING HARMONIZATION ON M&A VALUATION AND DUE DILIGENCE

Accurate Valuation of Assets and Liabilities

In cross-border mergers and acquisitions (M&As), the accurate valuation of assets and liabilities is fundamental to ensuring a fair transaction. The differences in financial reporting frameworks, such as US GAAP and IFRS, often lead to discrepancies in how companies recognize and measure their assets and liabilities (Gujarathi & Yezegel, 2014). Such inconsistencies can distort the financial health of a company and impede a true understanding of its value during an M&A process. For instance, differences in the treatment of goodwill, inventory, and intangible assets can create misinterpretations of the company's actual worth. Harmonized financial reporting, specifically the adoption of International Financial Reporting Standards (IFRS), facilitates a consistent methodology for measuring and disclosing financial information, thereby reducing potential distortions in asset and liability valuations (Holzmann, 2000). IFRS emphasizes fair value accounting for many assets and liabilities, unlike US GAAP, which often uses historical cost methods. This shift towards fair value allows for a more accurate representation of a company's marketable assets, goodwill, and liabilities. Consequently, harmonized reporting mitigates the risk of inflated valuations or hidden liabilities that could mislead investors or acquirers (Carril-Caccia & Milgram Baleix, 2024). Moreover, harmonized standards ensure that financial statements are comparable across different jurisdictions, enhancing consistency and transparency in valuation. The uniformity of financial reporting allows acquirers to assess the worth of an entity with greater confidence, resulting in more accurate purchase price allocations and reducing the likelihood of post-deal disputes related to valuation discrepancies.

Table 11. Impact of financial reporting harmonization on M&A valuation accuracy

Key Accounting Element	IFRS Approach	US GAAP Approach	Impact of Harmonization
Goodwill Accounting	Amortized over time, tested annually	Tested for impairment annually	Standardization simplifies goodwill treatment in cross-border deals
Asset Valuation	Fair value, including financial instruments	Historical cost, with some fair value adjustments	Fair value approach enhances comparability across jurisdictions
Inventory	FIFO or weighted average cost	LIFO allowed	Harmonized treatment minimizes distortion of working capital
Revenue Recognition	More principles-based	Detailed, industry-specific rules	More consistent revenue reporting improves financial transparency

Source: IFRS Foundation, FASB, Deloitte (2023)

Table 11 shows that harmonizing financial reporting standards, such as goodwill accounting, asset valuation, inventory treatment, and revenue recognition, improves M&A valuation accuracy by standardizing practices like amortization and impairment testing, enhancing comparability through fair value measurement, minimizing distortions in working capital, and ensuring more consistent revenue reporting across jurisdictions.

Due Diligence in Cross-Border M&As

The due diligence process is a cornerstone of M&A transactions, providing acquirers with the insight needed to assess the potential risks and opportunities of a deal. When companies involved in cross-border M&As report under different accounting standards, the due diligence process becomes more complex, requiring reconciliation of financial statements, adjustments for differing accounting methods, and a greater risk of misinterpretation (Degryse & Ongena, 2004; Monteiro & Silva, 2022).

Harmonized financial reporting standards, particularly IFRS, significantly simplify this process by ensuring that all parties have access to consistent, comparable, and transparent financial data (Kashiwazaki et al., 2019). The application of standardized reporting practices accelerates the due diligence timeline, as there is no need for extensive adjustments or reconciliation efforts (Akgün, 2022). Acquirers can quickly evaluate the financial position of the target company, assess liabilities, and analyze income statements, all based on a common set of rules. This reduces the cost and time associated with the due diligence process, allowing for more timely and efficient deal-making (Clinch et al., 2023).

Furthermore, consistent financial reporting minimizes the risk of overlooking key financial risks, such as unrecorded liabilities, off-balance-sheet obligations, or hidden reserves (Amir & Ghitti, 2021). By adopting a common reporting standard, cross-border M&As can streamline disclosure requirements, improve audit reliability, and enhance transparency, making it easier for acquirers to identify any discrepancies that could affect the deal's structure or valuation.

Table 12. Benefits of financial reporting harmonization in due diligence

M&A Due Diligence Phase	Harmonized Reporting (IFRS)	Non-Harmonized Reporting (US GAAP + Local Standards)
Financial Statement Review	Simplified assessment and comparison across regions	Requires extensive reconciliations and adjustments
Risk Identification	Faster identification of potential financial risks	Higher risk of missing off-balance-sheet items
Regulatory Compliance	Easier to ensure compliance with international standards	Diverse regulatory frameworks create complexity
Audit Process	Consistent audit procedures, reducing errors	Multiple audit standards increase audit costs

Source: Mergermarket, PwC Insights (2022)

Table 12 illustrates that harmonized financial reporting (IFRS) streamlines due diligence by simplifying financial statement review, accelerating risk identification, easing regulatory compliance, and reducing audit costs, whereas non-harmonized reporting (US GAAP + local standards) requires extensive reconciliations, increases the risk of missed financial risks, complicates compliance, and raises audit costs (Brereton, 2004).

Risk Assessment and Mitigation

Harmonized financial reporting standards play an essential role in the **risk assessment** and **mitigation** during cross-border M&As. When companies operate under differing accounting systems, the risk of financial misrepresentation increases, potentially leading to **post-deal financial surprises** or discrepancies that could undermine the success of the merger. **Harmonized standards** mitigate such risks by ensuring that **financial statements** are reliable and comparable, which enables acquirers to accurately assess the potential risks of the transaction (Akisik & Mangaliso, 2020). For instance, in M&As where goodwill is a significant asset, the adoption of **IFRS** for goodwill accounting provides clearer insights into the true value of intangible assets and reduces the risk of post-merger impairment charges. Additionally, standardized financial reporting also aids in **risk mitigation** related to tax liabilities, legal compliance, and regulatory issues. Harmonization simplifies cross-border tax treatment and ensures that financial disclosures adhere to a common regulatory framework. This minimizes the risk of tax disputes, **transfer pricing issues**, and non-compliance with **local accounting regulations**, which could otherwise delay or derail M&A deals .

Table 13. Risks mitigated by harmonized financial reporting in M&As

Risk Factor	Impact of Harmonized Reporting	Impact of Disparate Reporting
Tax Liabilities	Standardized tax treatment across jurisdictions	Complex tax reconciliation and disputes
Hidden Liabilities	Easier identification of off-balance-sheet liabilities	Risk of overlooking contingent liabilities
Regulatory Compliance	Simplified compliance with international standards	Increased regulatory scrutiny and complexity
Investor Confidence	Enhanced trust in financial transparency	Potential investor hesitation due to uncertainties

Source: Deloitte, KPMG, EY (2022)

Table 13 demonstrates that harmonized financial reporting mitigates risks in M&As by simplifying tax treatment, identifying hidden liabilities, ensuring regulatory compliance, and boosting investor confidence, whereas disparate reporting leads to complex tax reconciliation, overlooked liabilities, regulatory challenges, and investor uncertainty.

Harmonizing financial reporting standards is crucial for efficient, transparent, and risk-mitigated cross-border M&As, as it ensures accurate valuations, simplifies due diligence, mitigates financial risks, boosts investor confidence, and enhances transaction speed and efficiency, facilitating seamless integration and value creation in an increasingly interconnected global market (Wen & Moehrle, 2016).

7. THE FUTURE OF FINANCIAL REPORTING STANDARDS: MOVING TOWARD A GLOBAL CONSENSUS

Global Adoption of IFRS and Convergence with US GAAP

The ongoing evolution of global financial markets has underscored the critical need for harmonized financial reporting standards. Among the most pressing developments is the global adoption of IFRS (International Financial Reporting Standards) and the potential for convergence with US GAAP (Generally Accepted Accounting Principles) (Zhu, 2014). Historically, the IFRS framework, which is principles-based, has been favored in numerous jurisdictions worldwide, while the US GAAP framework, which is more rules-based, remains dominant in the United States. The divergence between these two standards has created significant complexities in cross-border transactions, investor evaluations, and mergers and acquisitions (M&As) (Holzmann, 2000).

In recent years, the IFRS Foundation and the Financial Accounting Standards Board (FASB) have engaged in numerous discussions about converging the two standards to create a single, universally accepted financial reporting framework. The convergence initiative aims to eliminate discrepancies between IFRS and US GAAP, focusing on key areas such as revenue recognition, financial instruments, and lease accounting. Although substantial progress has been made, including the unification of revenue recognition standards (Poniachek, 2022) and more consistent accounting for leases, significant differences still remain, particularly in financial statement presentation, goodwill accounting, and impairment testing (Okoshi, 2024).

The move toward global financial reporting standardization holds profound implications for international businesses and investors. Harmonized standards would eliminate the need for reconciliation between two accounting frameworks, thereby enhancing efficiency and comparability across borders. Additionally, global adoption of IFRS could reduce financial reporting costs, simplify due diligence processes, and accelerate cross-border M&A transactions, fostering a more integrated global economy (Monastyrenko, 2017).

Table 14. Global adoption of IFRS and US GAAP (2023)

Region/Market	IFRS Adoption (%)	US GAAP Adoption (%)	Key Adoption Trends
Europe	100%	0%	Full adoption by EU countries
Asia-Pacific	75%	25%	Gradual IFRS adoption in China and Japan
Latin America	80%	20%	Brazil and Mexico prominent in IFRS adoption
North America	35%	65%	US GAAP still prevalent; partial IFRS adoption in Canada
Middle East & Africa	60%	40%	Increased IFRS adoption in UAE and South Africa
Global Total	**70%**	**30%**	**Significant shift towards IFRS adoption**

Source: IFRS Foundation, Deloitte Global Insights (2023)

Table 14 highlights global adoption trends in 2023, with full IFRS adoption in Europe, widespread adoption in Asia-Pacific and Latin America, partial IFRS adoption in North America, and increasing adoption in the Middle East & Africa, indicating a significant global shift towards IFRS despite continued US GAAP prevalence in North America.

Technology and the Role of Automation in Financial Reporting

The future of financial reporting standards is also being shaped by technological advancements, with automation, artificial intelligence (AI), blockchain, and data analytics poised to revolutionize the way financial information is generated, processed, and reported. The integration of these technologies offers enormous potential to enhance the efficiency, accuracy, and transparency of financial reporting, particularly in the context of cross-border M&As (Song et al., 2017).

- Blockchain technology promises to offer immutable ledgers for financial transactions, reducing fraud risk, enhancing audit trails, and ensuring real-time reporting. By implementing blockchain in financial reporting, companies can drastically reduce reconciliation costs and improve the accuracy and transparency of cross-border transactions (Hsu & Cao, 2021).
- Artificial intelligence (AI) and machine learning (ML) can assist in predictive analytics, improving financial forecasting, and fraud detection. These technologies can automate routine tasks like data collection, financial statement preparation, and compliance checks, allowing financial analysts and auditors to focus on higher-level decision-making (Joshi et al., 2013).
- Data analytics can help businesses better understand the financial health of their operations through advanced modeling, offering insights into cash flow

patterns, capital expenditures, and investment trends. By using sophisticated analytics, businesses can improve the quality of their financial disclosures, providing stakeholders with a clearer picture of a company's performance and risk profile.

The convergence of financial reporting standards with emerging technologies will enable automated reconciliation across jurisdictions, reducing the time required for due diligence in cross-border M&As and enhancing the speed and efficiency of transactions.

Table 15. Role of emerging technologies in financial reporting

Technology	Impact on Financial Reporting	Key Benefits for Cross-Border M&As
Blockchain	Immutable, transparent ledgers for financial transactions	Reduced fraud risk, faster transaction reconciliation
AI & Machine Learning	Automates routine tasks and enables predictive analytics	Improved decision-making, faster due diligence
Data Analytics	Enhances financial forecasting and risk analysis	More accurate financial projections, improved risk mitigation
Robotic Process Automation (RPA)	Automates repetitive accounting tasks	Reduced operational costs, increased efficiency

Source: PwC, Deloitte Insights, 2023

Table 15 illustrates how emerging technologies, such as blockchain, AI, machine learning, data analytics, and RPA, enhance financial reporting by improving transparency, speeding up reconciliation, automating tasks, refining risk analysis, and reducing costs, thereby driving greater efficiency and effectiveness in global transactions and mergers.

The Role of Emerging Markets in Shaping Future Standards

Emerging markets, particularly in **Asia**, **Africa**, and **Latin America**, are playing an increasingly influential role in shaping the future of **financial reporting standards**. As these regions experience rapid economic growth, urbanization, and industrialization, their involvement in **global trade** and **cross-border M&As** is becoming more pronounced. The **adoption of IFRS** in these regions is accelerating, driven by the need for greater financial **transparency** and **accountability** (Marek, 2024).

Emerging markets, especially China and India, are expected to accelerate the adoption of global financial standards, thereby pushing for greater convergence with IFRS. For example, China has taken strides to harmonize its Chinese Accounting Standards (CAS) with IFRS, as the country continues to integrate into the global economy. These regions will likely demand a greater say in the evolution of financial reporting standards, as their market integration and capital flows increase (Oliveira et al., 2001).

As emerging markets embrace harmonized standards, they will contribute significantly to the development of global financial reporting practices. This evolution will make cross-border M&As more efficient, enabling companies to seamlessly navigate multiple financial systems, and investors will benefit from more reliable and transparent financial information.

Table 16. Financial reporting adoption trends in emerging markets

Region	IFRS Adoption (%)	Notable Countries/ Markets	Key Drivers of Adoption
China	70%	Hong Kong, Shanghai	Integration with global capital markets, regulatory reforms
India	90%	New Delhi, Mumbai	Increased foreign investment, market liberalization
Latin America	80%	Brazil, Mexico, Argentina	Regional trade agreements, global financial integration
Africa	60%	South Africa, Kenya	Regulatory alignment with international standards

Source: IFRS Foundation, World Bank (2023)

Table 16 highlights financial reporting adoption trends in emerging markets, showing significant IFRS adoption in China, India, Latin America, and Africa, driven by factors such as global market integration, regulatory reforms, foreign investment, and regional trade agreements.

8. POLICY RECOMMENDATIONS AND STRATEGIC APPROACHES FOR HARMONIZING FINANCIAL REPORTING STANDARDS

Standardization at the Regulatory Level

As the global economy continues to integrate, standardizing financial reporting frameworks has become an imperative for ensuring transparency, reducing barriers to cross-border trade, and streamlining mergers and acquisitions (M&As). While significant progress has been made through initiatives such as the International Financial Reporting Standards (IFRS), challenges persist in aligning diverse national frameworks, particularly US GAAP. To address these challenges and facilitate greater harmonization, international regulators must adopt coordinated policies and create a more uniform and comprehensive approach to financial reporting (Sauvant, 2016).

A strategic recommendation for achieving global financial reporting standardization is fostering stronger collaboration between regulatory bodies, such as the International Accounting Standards Board (IASB), Financial Accounting Standards Board (FASB), and national regulators. By engaging in a concerted effort to align regulatory goals, technical standards, and compliance procedures, these bodies can overcome the fragmentation that exists in the global financial reporting landscape. A global regulatory alliance could help unify standards related to revenue recognition, asset valuation, liability treatment, and financial disclosure, thereby minimizing discrepancies and aligning cross-border accounting practices.

Additionally, regulators must take into account the evolving dynamics of global finance, including the influence of emerging markets and technological advancements. Policies should not only focus on convergence but also on flexibility that allows for the integration of new accounting technologies, such as blockchain, machine learning, and artificial intelligence (AI), into the reporting standards. A dynamic regulatory framework that accommodates the future of financial technology (FinTech) can help drive continuous improvements in financial reporting transparency and accuracy.

Table 17. Global regulatory alignment for financial reporting standards (2023)

Region	IFRS Adoption (%)	Major Regulatory Bodies Involved	Key Focus Areas for Alignment
Europe	100%	European Financial Reporting Advisory Group (EFRAG)	Revenue recognition, leasing, financial instruments
Asia-Pacific	75%	Asian-Oceanian Standard Setters Group (AOSSG)	Cross-border M&A reporting, tax reconciliation
Latin America	80%	Latin American Federation of Accountants (FLA)	Compliance with IFRS, local tax rules
North America	35%	Financial Accounting Standards Board (FASB)	Convergence with IFRS, revenue recognition
Middle East & Africa	60%	International Accounting Standards Board (IASB)	Enhancing IFRS adoption, regional market integration

Source: IFRS Foundation, World Bank (2023)

Table 17 outlines global regulatory alignment trends for financial reporting standards in 2023, showing varying levels of IFRS adoption across regions, with major regulatory bodies focusing on areas such as revenue recognition, cross-border M&A reporting, tax reconciliation, and enhancing IFRS adoption for market integration.

Best Practices for Cross-Border M&A Transactions

In the context of cross-border M&As, adopting best practices for financial reporting compliance is crucial for ensuring successful integration and reducing operational risks. A key challenge in cross-border M&As arises from the varying financial reporting systems that companies use in different jurisdictions. This disparity can lead to issues in valuations, risk assessments, and tax implications, hindering deal closure and integration. Therefore, multinational corporations must adopt a series of strategic practices to navigate the complexities of financial reporting during M&As.

1. Pre-M&A Financial Due Diligence: Before initiating any M&A transactions, corporations should conduct thorough financial due diligence to assess the accuracy, completeness, and comparability of the financial statements of the target company. This involves reconciling the target's local accounting practices with internationally recognized standards such as IFRS or US GAAP. Harmonized financial reporting systems can significantly reduce the need for extensive adjustments and enable quicker valuation processes (Bris et al., 2008).
2. Alignment of Reporting Practices Post-Merger: Once the deal is completed, companies should immediately begin the process of aligning their accounting practices and financial reporting standards. This requires a detailed integration plan that addresses the accounting systems, tax reporting requirements, and financial disclosures. Establishing a centralized financial reporting team can streamline the integration process and reduce errors in consolidation (Zetzsche et al., 2021).
3. Engagement with Regulatory Bodies: Companies should maintain an open line of communication with relevant regulatory authorities in the jurisdictions involved. Early regulatory approval for financial reporting harmonization, especially related to tax implications and compliance with accounting standards, can accelerate the post-merger integration process.

Table 18. Best practices for M&A financial reporting compliance

Practice	Description	Benefits for Cross-Border M&As
Pre-M&A Due Diligence	Reconciling financial statements, assessing comparability	Reduces valuation discrepancies, accelerates deal closure
Post-Merger Integration Planning	Aligning financial reporting systems and accounting practices	Streamlines integration, reduces errors, ensures compliance
Regulatory Collaboration	Engaging with regulators to ensure financial reporting compliance	Facilitates faster approval, reduces legal complexities

Source: PwC M&A Insights, 2023

Table 18 outlines best practices for M&A financial reporting compliance, where pre-M&A due diligence involves reconciling financial statements and assessing comparability, thereby reducing valuation discrepancies and accelerating deal closure, while post-merger integration planning focuses on aligning financial reporting systems and accounting practices, which streamlines integration, minimizes errors, and ensures regulatory compliance, and regulatory collaboration emphasizes proactive engagement with regulators to ensure financial reporting compliance, which expedites approval processes and mitigates legal complexities, thus facilitating smoother, more efficient cross-border M&A transactions.

The Role of Financial Institutions and Advisory Firms

Financial institutions and advisory firms play an instrumental role in promoting the harmonization of financial reporting standards. These entities possess the necessary expertise to guide multinational corporations through the complexities of cross-border transactions and M&A activities. Their involvement is crucial in ensuring regulatory compliance, strategic alignment, and financial transparency during the integration of financial reporting standards.

1. Advisory Services: Financial advisory firms provide expert advice on aligning accounting policies and reporting frameworks, offering strategic solutions that minimize discrepancies during cross-border mergers. They assist in navigating the intricacies of financial disclosure, regulatory requirements, and tax implications.
2. Integration of Technology: Financial institutions, particularly those with a global presence, are increasingly adopting advanced technologies such as blockchain, AI, and data analytics to streamline the financial reporting process. By utilizing these technologies, institutions can ensure real-time access to accurate financial data, enabling swift M&A decision-making and reducing the risks associated with data inconsistency (Stittle, 2004).
3. Training and Capacity Building: Financial institutions and advisory firms also offer training programs to corporate executives and accounting professionals, ensuring they stay abreast of evolving global financial reporting standards and compliance requirements. These programs enhance the capacity of organizations to adopt new reporting frameworks seamlessly and efficiently.

Table 19. Role of financial institutions and advisory firms in harmonizing financial reporting

Role	Description	Contribution to Cross-Border M&As
Advisory Services	Providing expert advice on aligning financial reporting practices	Ensures strategic integration of accounting standards
Technology Integration	Implementing blockchain, AI, and analytics in financial reporting	Improves data accuracy, reduces reconciliation efforts
Training & Capacity Building	Offering training programs for executives and accountants	Enhances organizational readiness for global financial reporting

Source: EY, Deloitte (2023)

Table 19 highlights the role of financial institutions and advisory firms in harmonizing financial reporting by providing advisory services for strategic integration, implementing technologies like blockchain and AI to improve data accuracy, and offering training programs to enhance organizational readiness for global financial reporting in cross-border M&As.

The harmonization of financial reporting standards is essential for navigating the complexities of cross-border mergers and acquisitions in today's globalized economy, where adopting coordinated regulatory approaches, best practices for financial reporting compliance, and leveraging the expertise of financial institutions and advisory firms enables multinational corporations to facilitate smoother M&A transactions, reduce risks, and improve investor confidence, and as financial reporting continues to evolve, especially with the integration of emerging technologies, the future of global M&As will be increasingly shaped by transparency, efficiency, and regulatory alignment, ultimately driving the continued integration of global financial markets.

9. CONCLUSION: ALIGNING FINANCIAL REPORTING WITH GLOBAL TRADE AND M&A NEEDS

Summary of Key Insights

The increasing globalization of business operations and the proliferation of cross-border mergers and acquisitions (M&As) have underscored the critical importance of harmonized financial reporting standards, as companies expand across international borders, where disparate financial reporting systems—such as US GAAP and IFRS—create substantial barriers to valuation accuracy, due diligence efficiency, and regulatory compliance, with the inconsistencies between these standards often leading to transaction delays, misvaluations, and financial misinterpretations, thereby hampering the seamless execution of M&As and impeding the smooth integration of global business operations (Kollruss, 2021).

A key insight from this chapter is that the adoption of standardized reporting frameworks, particularly IFRS, facilitates the unification of accounting practices across jurisdictions, thereby enabling smoother, more efficient cross-border transactions, as harmonized standards not only reduce operational friction but also enhance market transparency, investor confidence, and regulatory compliance, which is especially crucial in cross-border M&As, where consistent asset valuation, goodwill treatment, and financial disclosures ensure that all stakeholders have an accurate and transparent view of a company's financial position, and as exemplified in various case studies, the harmonization of financial reporting significantly mitigates the complexities involved in due diligence and integration, facilitating quicker deal closures and more effective post-merger synergies, ultimately driving greater market efficiency and investment confidence (Ramos & Pereira Coelho, 2023).

Furthermore, emerging technologies, such as blockchain, AI, and data analytics, have been identified as integral enablers of the future of financial reporting, as these technologies not only enhance the accuracy and speed of financial transactions but also automate and streamline the reconciliation and reporting processes, facilitating real-time transparency and significantly reducing the risk of fraud or errors in cross-border M&A deals, thereby ensuring greater efficiency, accountability, and trust in international financial transactions.

Future Outlook

Looking ahead, the landscape of financial reporting will evolve in response to the accelerating forces of globalization, technological advancements, and the mounting complexity of cross-border transactions, with the growing imperative for universally accepted standards becoming ever more pronounced as businesses penetrate new markets, and although the ongoing convergence of US GAAP and IFRS reflects a global push for unification and standardization, full convergence remains elusive due to persistent cultural, regulatory, and market-specific influences that continue to shape national accounting practices and regulatory frameworks (Tsepova, 2022).

In this context, regulatory bodies such as the International Accounting Standards Board (IASB), Financial Accounting Standards Board (FASB), and local regulators will play a pivotal role in driving the transition toward more harmonized financial reporting standards, with their responsibilities extending beyond the mere alignment of accounting frameworks to encompass the oversight of emerging technologies like blockchain, which will necessitate the creation of new regulatory frameworks to ensure data integrity, security, and interoperability across jurisdictions, while similarly, the integration of artificial intelligence (AI) and machine learning will demand addressing the standardization of algorithmic decision-making in financial reporting and the automation of compliance processes, ultimately shaping the future of global financial reporting (Bris et al., 2008).

Moreover, the influence of emerging markets, particularly China, India, and nations across Africa, is increasingly pivotal in shaping the global financial reporting landscape, with their growing integration into the global economy and adoption of harmonized reporting standards being essential for sustaining the efficiency and transparency of international financial markets, ultimately fostering more robust global trade and investment flows, underscoring the critical role these regions play in the evolution of global financial systems.

Concluding Thoughts

In conclusion, the harmonization of financial reporting standards transcends merely simplifying regulatory compliance or reducing transaction costs, serving as a fundamental enabler of global trade and cross-border mergers and acquisitions, where by creating a level playing field for financial disclosures, it fosters greater transparency, trust, and accountability in international business transactions, necessitating that as global markets continue to expand and evolve, regulatory bodies must intensify efforts to align financial reporting standards, while integrating the dynamic influence of emerging technologies and global market demands, ensuring a future of seamless cross-border financial interactions.

Continued collaboration between regulatory bodies, financial institutions, advisory firms, and multinational corporations is paramount to advancing the harmonization of financial reporting, as the evolution of financial technologies and the influence of emerging markets in shaping the future of global commerce necessitate the ongoing adaptation and integration of financial reporting frameworks, which will remain crucial in addressing the demands of international mergers, investments, and global trade, with the evolution of financial reporting standards transcending a mere technical or regulatory task to becoming a strategic imperative for ensuring efficiency, transparency, and sustainability in the increasingly interconnected global economy.

REFERENCES

Akgün, A. İ. (2022). Investigating the relationship between bank performance and accounting standards: Evidence from M&As in European banking. *Journal of Capital Markets Studies*, *6*(1), 106–124. DOI: 10.1108/JCMS-10-2021-0032

Akisik, O., & Mangaliso, M. P. (2020). How IFRS influence the relationship between the types of FDI and economic growth: An empirical analysis on African countries. *Journal of Applied Accounting Research*, *21*(1), 60–76. DOI: 10.1108/JAAR-02-2018-0025

Alba, J. D., Park, D., & Wang, P. (2009). Corporate governance and merger and acquisition foreign direct investment: Firm-level evidence from Japanese foreign direct investment into the US. *ADB Economics Working Paper Series*, *147*, 1–18. https://www.scopus.com/inward/record.uri?eid=2-s2.0-77949419995&partnerID=40&md5=78512c36171f138edc833c58d9dc0b1c

Alimov, A. (2015). Labor market regulations and cross-border mergers and acquisitions. *Journal of International Business Studies*, *46*(8), 984–1009. DOI: 10.1057/jibs.2015.16

Alkaraan, F. (2020). Strategic investment decision-making practices in large manufacturing companies: A role for emergent analysis techniques? *Meditari Accountancy Research*, *28*(4), 633–653. DOI: 10.1108/MEDAR-05-2019-0484

Altman, W. (2004). What's going on? *Engineering Management Journal (London)*, *14*(6), 42–43. DOI: 10.1049/em:20040614

Amir, E., & Ghitti, M. (2021). Financial Analysis of Mergers and Acquisitions: Understanding Financial Statements and Accounting Rules with Case Studies. In *Financial Analysis of Mergers and Acquisitions: Understanding Financial Statements and Accounting Rules with Case Studies*. Springer International Publishing., DOI: 10.1007/978-3-030-61769-1

Bakkar, Y., & Nyola, A. P. (2021). Internationalization, foreign complexity and systemic risk: Evidence from European banks. *Journal of Financial Stability*, *55*, 100892. Advance online publication. DOI: 10.1016/j.jfs.2021.100892

Bose, S., Minnick, K., & Shams, S. (2021). Does carbon risk matter for corporate acquisition decisions? *Journal of Corporate Finance*, *70*, 102058. Advance online publication. DOI: 10.1016/j.jcorpfin.2021.102058

Boudier, F., & Lochard, J. (2013). How do cross-border mergers and acquisitions answer to deregulation in services? *World Economy*, *36*(11), 1424–1441. DOI: 10.1111/twec.12067

Brereton, C. (2004). No alarms, no surprises. *Total Telecom, JULY*, 9. https://www.scopus.com/inward/record.uri?eid=2-s2.0-4544291500&partnerID=40&md5=01fe2cffe1d441cb4c027868fb8de305

Bris, A., Brisley, N., & Cabolis, C. (2008). Adopting better corporate governance: Evidence from cross-border mergers. *Journal of Corporate Finance*, *14*(3), 224–240. DOI: 10.1016/j.jcorpfin.2008.03.005

Buch, C. M., & DeLong, G. (2004). Cross-border bank mergers: What lures the rare animal? *Journal of Banking & Finance*, *28*(9), 2077–2102. DOI: 10.1016/j.jbankfin.2003.08.002

Carril-Caccia, F., & Baleix, J. M. (2020). The Impact of Environmental Regulation on Location's Choice of Cross-Border Mergers and Acquisitions [El impacto de la regulación medioambiental sobre la elección de la localización de las fusiones y adquisiciones transfronterizas]. *Cuadernos Economicos de ICE*, *2020*(100), 167–192. DOI: 10.32796/cice.2020.100.7123

Carril-Caccia, F., & Milgram Baleix, J. (2024). Impact of environmental regulation on M&As in the manufacturing sector. *Journal of Environmental Economics and Management*, *127*, 103038. Advance online publication. DOI: 10.1016/j.jeem.2024.103038

Chen, Y., & Li, N. (2010). International comparative study to government regulation about cross-border mergers and acquisition. *2010 International Conference on Future Information Technology and Management Engineering, FITME 2010, 2*, 341 – 344. DOI: 10.1109/FITME.2010.5656296

Cheng, K., & Finney, S. G. (2010). It's coming: M&As under IFRSs. *Journal of Corporate Accounting & Finance*, *21*(3), 13–18. DOI: 10.1002/jcaf.20575

Clem, A., Cowan, A. R., & Jeffrey, C. (2004). Market Reaction to Proposed Changes in Accounting for Purchased Research and Development in R&D-Intensive Industries. *Journal of Accounting, Auditing & Finance*, *19*(4), 405–428. DOI: 10.1177/0148558X0401900403

Clinch, G., Tarca, A., & Wee, M. (2023). Cross-country diversity and non-IFRS financial performance measures. *Accounting and Finance*, *63*(2), 2473–2502. DOI: 10.1111/acfi.12980

Degryse, H., & Ongena, S. (2004). The impact of technology and regulation on the geographical scope of banking. *Oxford Review of Economic Policy, 20*(4), 571–590. DOI: 10.1093/oxrep/grh033

DePamphilis, D. (2017). Mergers, Acquisitions, and Other Restructuring Activities: An Integrated Approach to Process, Tools, Cases, and Solutions: Ninth Edition. In *Mergers, Acquisitions, and Other Restructuring Activities: An Integrated Approach to Process, Tools, Cases, and Solutions: Ninth Edition*. Elsevier Inc. https://www.scopus.com/inward/record.uri?eid=2-s2.0-85032168292&partnerID=40&md5=2f48f6ab57549aceaa6fc69b9ec4fff8

DePamphilis, D. M. (2019). Mergers, acquisitions, and other restructuring activities: An integrated approach to process, tools, cases, and solutions. In *Mergers, Acquisitions, and Other Restructuring Activities: An Integrated Approach to Process, Tools, Cases, and Solutions*. Elsevier., DOI: 10.1016/C2017-0-02823-9

Fu, C., Deng, X., & Tang, H. (2023). Who cares about corporate fraud? Evidence from cross-border mergers and acquisitions of Chinese companies. *Review of Quantitative Finance and Accounting, 60*(2), 747–789. DOI: 10.1007/s11156-022-01111-6

Georgieva, D., & Jandik, T. (2012). Alternative paths of convergence toward U.S. market and legal regulations: Cross-listing vs. merging with U.S. bidders. *Journal of Multinational Financial Management, 22*(5), 230–251. DOI: 10.1016/j.mulfin.2012.06.006

Georgieva, D., Jandik, T., & Lee, W. Y. (2012). The impact of laws, regulations, and culture on cross-border joint ventures. *Journal of International Financial Markets, Institutions and Money, 22*(4), 774–795. DOI: 10.1016/j.intfin.2012.04.002

Gerpott, T. J., & Jakopin, N. M. (2007). Firm and target country characteristics as factors explaining wealth creation from international expansion moves of mobile network operators. *Telecommunications Policy, 31*(2), 72–92. DOI: 10.1016/j.telpol.2006.12.003

Gláserová, J. (2013). Differences in financial statements of business entities in the Czech Republic. *Acta Universitatis Agriculturae et Silviculturae Mendelianae Brunensis, 61*(2), 335–343. DOI: 10.11118/actaun201361020335

Gujarathi, M. R., & Yezegel, A. (2014). Spectacular Airlines, Inc.: Implications of the transition to IFRS in the context of cross- border acquisitions. *Issues in Accounting Education, 29*(1), 247–257. DOI: 10.2308/iace-50583

Guo, J., & Cheng, H. (2024). Acquirers' carbon risk, environmental regulation, and cross-border mergers and acquisitions: Evidence from China. *Environment, Development and Sustainability, 26*(6), 15861–15904. DOI: 10.1007/s10668-023-03276-z

Han, G. (2020). Institutional Conditions of Economic Globalization: Effects of Antitrust and Merger Laws on the Global Integration of the Acquisition Market1. *Sociological Forum, 35*(4), 1250–1271. DOI: 10.1111/socf.12646

Hassan, M., & Giouvris, E. (2021). Bank mergers: The cyclical behaviour of regulation, risk and returns. *Journal of Financial Economic Policy, 13*(2), 256–284. DOI: 10.1108/JFEP-03-2020-0043

Heinemann, A. (2012). Government control of cross-border M&A: Legitimate regulation or protectionism. *Journal of International Economic Law, 15*(3), 843–870. DOI: 10.1093/jiel/jgs030

Holzmann, O. J. (2000). M&A accounting: FASB calls for ban on pooling. *Journal of Corporate Accounting & Finance, 11*(2), 41–50. DOI: 10.1002/(SICI)1097-0053(200001/02)11:2<41::AID-JCAF9>3.0.CO;2-G

Hsu, J., & Cao, T. L. (2021). The Antecedents of Likelihood to Completion of Cross-Border M&As: An Empirical Analysis of ASEAN Countries. *Emerging Markets Finance & Trade, 57*(10), 2888–2906. DOI: 10.1080/1540496X.2019.1668766

Irwin, K., Gilstrap, C., McDowell, W., Drnevich, P., & Gorbett, A. (2022). How knowledge and uncertainty affect strategic international business investment decisions: Implications for cross-border mergers and acquisitions. *Journal of Business Research, 139*, 831–842. DOI: 10.1016/j.jbusres.2021.10.001

Joshi, S., Kulkarni, N., & Athavale, R. (2013). Business informatics a key driver for successful strategic planning. *Proceedings - International Conference on Intelligent Systems, Modelling and Simulation, ISMS*, 305 – 309. DOI: 10.1109/ISMS.2013.111

Kashiwazaki, R., Sato, S., & Takeda, F. (2019). Does IFRS Adoption Accelerate M&A? The Consequences of Different Goodwill Accounting in Japan. *International Advances in Economic Research, 25*(4), 399–415. DOI: 10.1007/s11294-019-09757-0

Kollruss, T. (2021). The interaction between combating tax avoidance and group accounting. *British Tax Review, 5*, 579 – 597. https://www.scopus.com/inward/record.uri?eid=2-s2.0-85120707622&partnerID=40&md5=86aa2b2e2cc8ae16362a8acd65b3eb03

Levine, R., Lin, C., & Shen, B. (2020). Cross-border acquisitions: Do labor regulations affect acquirer returns? *Journal of International Business Studies, 51*(2), 194–217. DOI: 10.1057/s41267-019-00281-1

Li, H., He, R., & Fu, Q. (2023). Does corporate social responsibility affect the performance of cross-border M&A of emerging market multinationals? *Finance Research Letters, 58*, 104320. Advance online publication. DOI: 10.1016/j.frl.2023.104320

Lin, D., Barth, J., Jahera, J., & Yost, K. (2013). Cross-border bank mergers and acquisitions: What factors pull and push banks together? *Review of Pacific Basin Financial Markets and Policies, 16*(4), 1350022. Advance online publication. DOI: 10.1142/S0219091513500227

Liu, K., Wu, S., & Guo, N. (2021). Governmental governance of host countries and cross-border merger and acquisition performance: Evidence from listed enterprises in China. *PLoS ONE, 16*(8 August). DOI: 10.1371/journal.pone.0256494

Marek, P. (2024). Legal, Accounting, and Tax Implications of Mergers around the EU Countries: Pitching Research. In P. D. (Ed.), *Springer Proceedings in Business and Economics* (pp. 193 – 200). Springer Nature. DOI: 10.1007/978-3-031-62998-3_13

Martynova, M., & Renneboog, L. (2008). Spillover of corporate governance standards in cross-border mergers and acquisitions. *Journal of Corporate Finance, 14*(3), 200–223. DOI: 10.1016/j.jcorpfin.2008.03.004

Mathieson, D. J., Richards, A., & Sharma, S. (1998). Financial crises in emerging markets. *Finance & Development, 35*(4), 28–31. https://www.scopus.com/inward/record.uri?eid=2-s2.0-0032405736&partnerID=40&md5=d04e34b5c717bbb2330d7f7ed82f4c74

Monastyrenko, E. (2017). Eco-efficiency outcomes of mergers and acquisitions in the European electricity industry. *Energy Policy, 107*, 258–277. DOI: 10.1016/j.enpol.2017.04.030

Monteiro, R., & Silva, S. (2022). The impact of securities regulation in the European Union on M&A: Does it compensate to go beyond borders? *Journal of Financial Regulation and Compliance, 30*(3), 282–311. DOI: 10.1108/JFRC-08-2021-0066

Okoshi, H. (2024). Attractive target for tax avoidance: Trade liberalization and entry mode. *International Tax and Public Finance*. Advance online publication. DOI: 10.1007/s10797-024-09830-3

Oliveira, P., Roth, A. V., & Heitor, M. V. (2001). Mergers and acquisitions: A tool for knowledge/technology transfer. *Proceedings of the Hawaii International Conference on System Sciences*, 222. DOI: 10.1109/HICSS.2001.927143

Poniachek, H. A. (2022). Mergers and Acquisitions: Principles and Practices. In *Encyclopedia of Finance, Third Edition*. Springer International Publishing. DOI: 10.1007/978-3-030-91231-4_105

Raghavendra, C., Rampilla, M., Thanikella, V. R., & Gupta, I. (2022). Impact of Carbon Tax and Environmental Regulation on Inbound Cross-Border Mergers and Acquisitions Volume: An Evidence from India. *International Journal of Financial Studies, 10*(4), 106. Advance online publication. DOI: 10.3390/ijfs10040106

Ramesh, B. N. (2023). Cross border mergers and acquisitions: A comparative study between India and the USA. In *Cross Border Mergers and Acquisitions: A Comparative Study between India and the USA*. Taylor and Francis., DOI: 10.4324/9781003396987

Ramos, V. C., & Pereira Coelho, D. (2023). Defending victims of cross-border fraud in the EU – A Portuguese view, including the use of preventive "freezing" of bank accounts under anti-money laundering legislation. *New Journal of European Criminal Law, 14*(3), 397–420. DOI: 10.1177/20322844231173913

Reddy, K. S., Xie, E., & Huang, Y. (2016). Cross-border acquisitions by state-owned and private enterprises: A perspective from emerging economies. *Journal of Policy Modeling, 38*(6), 1147–1170. DOI: 10.1016/j.jpolmod.2016.10.002

Röben, V. (2006). The regulation of financial services in the European Union. In *The Regulation of International Financial Markets*. Cambridge University Press., DOI: 10.1017/CBO9780511494505.007

Rossi, S., & Volpin, P. F. (2004). Cross-country determinants of mergers and acquisitions. *Journal of Financial Economics, 74*(2), 277–304. DOI: 10.1016/j.jfineco.2003.10.001

Sahoo, I., & Chakrabarti, A. (2022). The Impact Of Protective Takeover Regulation On Acquiring Firms: Evidence From The New Bid Regime In Canada. In T. S. (Ed.), *Academy of Management Annual Meeting Proceedings* (Vol. 2022, Issue 1). Academy of Management. DOI: 10.5465/AMBPP.2022.306

Sauvant, K. P. (2016). The next step in governance: The need for global micro-regulatory frameworks in the context of expanding international production. *Research in Global Strategic Management, 17*, 401–440. DOI: 10.1108/S1064-485720160000017013

Song, B., He, J., Yan, W., Hu, Q., & Zhang, T. (2017). Key technologies for knowledge-based cross-border e-commerce risk assessment - Accurate commodity classification and efficient knowledge acquisition. In C. C.-H., T. A.C., P. M., S. J., W. N., & W. N. (Eds.), *Advances in Transdisciplinary Engineering* (Vol. 5, pp. 146 – 153). IOS Press BV. DOI: 10.3233/978-1-61499-779-5-146

Stittle, J. (2004). The reformation of European corporate reporting: Towards a model of convergence or confusion? *European Business Review*, *16*(2), 139–151. DOI: 10.1108/09555340410524247

Tian, Z.-H., & Wang, J.-J. (2007). Cross-border merger and acquisitions, government regulations and market competition. *Proceedings of 2007 International Conference on Management Science and Engineering, ICMSE'07 (14th)*, 1397 – 1403. DOI: 10.1109/ICMSE.2007.4422040

Tokic, S., & Beyea, G. (2010). Changing regulations for cross-border M&As. *Journal of Corporate Accounting & Finance*, *21*(2), 33–43. DOI: 10.1002/jcaf.20561

Tsepova, E. A. (2022). Prospects for the Use of Cross-Cutting Digital Technologies in the Framework of Tax and Currency Control Over Cross-Border Financial Transactions. *Smart Innovation. Systems and Technologies*, *254*, 51–64. DOI: 10.1007/978-981-16-4621-8_5

Wen, H., & Moehrle, S. R. (2016). Accounting for goodwill: An academic literature review and analysis to inform the debate. *Research in Accounting Regulation*, *28*(1), 11–21. DOI: 10.1016/j.racreg.2016.03.002

Yan, J. (2018). Do Merger Laws Deter Cross-Border Mergers and Acquisitions? *Australian Economic Papers*, *57*(3), 376–393. DOI: 10.1111/1467-8454.12118

Zetzsche, D. A., Anker-Sørensen, L., Passador, M. L., & Wehrli, A. (2021). DLT-based enhancement of cross-border payment efficiency–a legal and regulatory perspective. *Law and Financial Markets Review*, *15*(1–2), 70–115. DOI: 10.1080/17521440.2022.2065809

Zhu, W. (2014). The evolving economic role of accounting standards: Evidence from bilateral cross-border M&A flows. *Frontiers of Business Research in China*, *8*(4), 435–479. DOI: 10.3868/s070-003-014-0020-1

Chapter 3
Green Auditing:
A Mechanism for Aligning With Climate Objectives via Emissions Reduction

N. Abhishek
https://orcid.org/0000-0001-9345-8501
Government First Grade College, Halebeedu, India

Neethu Suraj
Yenepoya University, India

Sahana Dinesh
Government First Grade College, Napoklu, India

P. Shareena
Yenepoya University, India

Abhinandan Kulal
Government First Grade College, Siddakatte, India

ABSTRACT

The paper aims to analyze the relationship between green audits and climate target alignment and study the factors that mediate and moderate the relationship between green audits and climate target alignment. This exploratory, cross-sectional, quantitative study analysed data from senior executives, accountants, auditors, academics, and researchers. Data were gathered via a structured online form and analyzed using descriptive statistics, SEM, mediation, and moderation analysis. The study found a direct relationship between green auditing and climate target alignment and a positive relationship between emissions reduction and climate target alignment.

DOI: 10.4018/979-8-3373-0887-6.ch003

Sector-specific factors significantly influence the climate target alignment. Emission reduction mediates the relationship between green auditing and climate-target alignment. Technical expertise significantly moderated the impact of green auditing on the alignment of climate targets. Barriers negatively moderated the influence of green auditing on sector-specific factors.

1. INTRODUCTION

Climate change is a global challenge owing to rising temperatures, extreme weather events, and ecological disruptions. The role of business organizations in mitigating such challenges is crucial. Therefore, business organizations need to align their operational strategies with climate targets, as emphasized by Khalaf and Hamad (2023). Climate target alignment, as described by Sharma et al. (2018), is a process by which businesses and institutions alter their practices to facilitate global efforts to reduce greenhouse gas emissions and climate change impacts. This strategy is not only significant for environmental sustainability but also for long-term value creation in a rapidly vulnerable environment. According to Afolabi et al. (2023) and Dalhuijsen et al. (2023), green auditing has evolved as a vital tool for business organizations striving to improve their environmental performance and align themselves with climate targets. Green auditing, also known as environmental auditing, involves a systematic evaluation of organizations' environmental practices, policies, and impacts. It assists business organizations in multiple ways, such as assessing compliance with environmental regulations, determining areas for improvement, and offering a basis for environmental reporting and decision-making, as noted by Rajapakse et al. (2022) and Banu et al. (2023). Green auditing has the potential to promote substantial transformations in organizational behavior and performance. This has gained significant attention from both academics and industry practitioners in debating the subject of considerable interest, as highlighted by Afolabi et al. (2023) and Gidage et al. (2024).

The connection between green auditing and climate target alignment is multifaceted and has potential sustainability implications. Green audits have the potential to offer valuable insights into the environmental footprints of business organizations, energy utilization patterns, and areas of inefficiency to frame strategies for minimizing environmental impact and aligning operations in line with climate goals. However, the nature and extent of this relationship remain a topic of ongoing research and debate, as discussed by Khalaf and Hamad (2023), Banu et al. (2023), and Gidage et al. (2024).

Despite the growing importance and potential of green auditing, there remains a significant research gap in understanding the complex interrelationship between green auditing, emission reduction, climate target alignment, and other factors. There is a need to undertake a comprehensive study to examine these interrelationships in depth so as to determine how organizations can benefit from green auditing to improve their environmental performance and contribute to attaining global climate goals.

This study aims to address this research issue by investigating the impact of green auditing on aligning climate targets, with a specific focus on the mediating role of emission reduction and the moderating effects of technical expertise and barriers. Therefore, this study intends to answer the following research question:

RQ1: Are there any relationships between green auditing and climate-target alignment?

RQ2: Are there any factors that mediate and moderate the relationship between green auditing and climate target alignment?

The results of this study have potential implications for both theory and practice in the field of environmental management. From a theoretical perspective, this study contributes to a comprehensive understanding of the mechanisms through which green auditing influences organizational environmental performance. Furthermore, the study supports the underlying assumptions of various theories, such as institutional theory, resource-based view, stakeholder theory, organizational learning theory, ecological modernization theory, agency theory, and legitimacy theory.

From a practical perspective, this study advocates that the organization can effectively implement green audit practices with the help of technical expertise through target key areas for emission reduction. The study also assists policymakers in gaining a comprehensive understanding of the factors influencing organizational climate target alignment, which leads to more effective environmental regulations and incentives.

This study examines the direct and indirect impacts of green auditing, as well as the moderating influences of technical expertise and barriers, to contribute valuable insights to ongoing efforts to create a more sustainable and climate-resilient future.

The remainder of this paper is organized as follows: Section 1–Introduction, Section 2 – Literature Review, Section 3 – Theoretical framework, Section 4 – Methodology, Section 5 – Results, Section 6 – Discussions, and Section 7 – Conclusion.

2. LITERATURE REVIEW

2.1 Green Auditing: Concepts and Practices

Green auditing, also known as environmental auditing, has become important worldwide because of its method of monitoring and improving ecological performance. This literature review focuses on cases and recent studies to explore whether green auditing could help India meet the demands of climate change. The goal of green auditing, as highlighted by Khalaf and Hamad (2023) and Banu et al. (2023), is to protect the environment by conducting an objective, methodical, recorded, and ongoing assessment of an organization 's, management's, and equipment's performance. It evaluates the influence of organizational operations on the environment, adherence to environmental rules, and the performance of environmental management systems.

According to Budiono and Dura (2021) and Ruiz-Barbadillo and Martínez-Ferrero (2020), green auditing has moved from an activity that was willingly done by companies to one that is more controlled and uniform over the years. Reasons for this change include greater awareness of environmental issues globally, more rigid regulatory systems, and companies increasingly understanding that adopting ecologically sound operations could make them financially attractive over time. Khalaf and Hamad (2023), Budiono and Dura (2021), and Banu et al. (2023) identify various types of green auditing, including functional environmental auditing, compliance auditing, and environmental management system (EMS) auditing. These types focus on different aspects that help organizations identify environmental risks, measure their effects, and develop remediation strategies in response. At a global level, representations and standards offered by the ISO 14000 series from the International Organization for Standardization (ISO) series, as well as EMAS from the European Union, as explained by Searcy et al. (2012) and Yessenamanova et al. (2022), provide frameworks and standards for examining ecological management systems, thus maintaining and continuously enhancing environmental performance. Studies from Johnstone, L. (2022), and Abakumova et al., (2021) on the European Union and the United States have shown the importance of green auditing within organisations, as it not only leads to compliance but also resource efficiency improvements and thus contributes towards thriftier operations.

2.2 Green Auditing: Regulatory Frameworks and Corporate Engagement

There are various regulations concerning environmental protection in India, such as the Environment Protection Act of 1986 and the National Action Plan on Climate Change (NAPCC), as outlined by Singh et al. (2021), Rani (2023), Sabu C. (2021). The Securities and Exchange Board of India (SEBI) has put in place the condition that listed companies should disclose certain aspects of their environmental performance, as examined by Shekhar and Chadda (2024). However, Mishra and Sant (2024) highlight that carrying out the process can be a challenge due to issues that include insufficient knowledge on environmental auditing, being expensive to start with because it incurs huge costs before embarking on it, no encouragement of being economically involved, and poorly monitored laws put down by responsible authorities. In the Paris Agreement, India promised to lower the ratio of carbon dioxide emissions to gross domestic product (GDP) by 33–35 percent compared to the 2005 levels, as noted by Das and Roy (2020), and India decided that 40 percent of its power capacity would come from non-fossil fuels by 2030, as per Raihan et al. (2022). Green auditing impacts various aspects, including identifying and dealing with environmental risks, as highlighted by Dalhuijsen et al. (2023), making companies more transparent and responsible, promoting sustainable ways of doing business and resource efficiency, and helping achieve National Determined Contributions (NDCs).

According to Sinkovics et al., (2021), Rajapakse et al., (2022), and Afolabi et al., (2023), compared to small and medium-sized enterprises (SMEs), large and multinational organisations exhibit greater awareness and engage in green auditing. They believed that improved regulatory compliance, effective risk management, and the following of individuals who trust them are some of the benefits. Impediments are expensive, require insufficient expertise, and have few legal regulations enforcing them. Indian companies, such as Tata Group, ITC, and Infosys, are a few companies with green auditing measures in place, as highlighted by Gidage et al. (2024) and Kumar (2022). They also underscored the substantial enhancements related to the environment and efficiency with regard to resources. Additionally, the industrial production, power generation, and medication manufacturing sectors show varying degrees of green auditing. As Tumwebaze et al. (2022) and Arif et al. (2021) noted, the energy sector has a significant environmental impact and requires tight reporting and auditing regulations.

2.3 The Present Landscape of Green Auditing

Currently, in India, green audits indicate that a strategy is being adopted, although there is still a long way to go. As is the case with any country in the fast lane of development, India has some formidable ecological issues that it must confront. The issues identified by Chattopadhyay et al. (2020) and Martínez-Bravo and Martínez-del-Río (2020) include pollution levels that people cannot breathe anymore, depletion of resources, resulting in a lack of important goods such as water or fish, and lowering the number of plant species breeding for food. There has been increased interest in the concept of green auditing as a result of regulatory frameworks, such as the Companies Act 2013, which requires specific firms to allocate some money to CSR-related activities, as noted by Ghosh (2021) and Kolsi et al. (2022). Moreover, Kumar (2021) and Ravindra et al.,(2024) also emphasised campaigns like the National Action Plan on Climate Change (NAPCC) as well as the Clean India Mission (Swachh Bharat Abhiyan), which underscore the importance of ecological liability. Despite these attempts, green auditing is still in its infancy in India, as most companies have hindered their capacity to undertake complete environmental audits. It is also necessary to establish stricter laws, including penalties against violators, so that such audits would be long-lasting and beneficial rather than mere rituals or show-offs without results.

Thus, in the literature on green auditing in India, the key deficiency is the absence of empirical studies that illuminate how organizations, especially SMEs, become knowledgeable about, practice, and gain from green auditing. This has seen most of the research focus on large companies; hence, a knowledge gap exists regarding opportunities for small businesses. Moreover, there are several long-term studies on how green auditing influences environmental performance. Future researchers should conduct surveys in different domains with different magnitudes and with guidelines for the promotion of green audit adoption, which will aid in achieving India's climate ambitions and stimulating sustainable development.

3. CONCEPTUAL MODEL

3.1 Green Auditing

Green auditing is a systematic and comprehensive process that assesses an organization's environmental performance and compliance with various environmental laws, standards, and goals. It involves assessing various aspects, such as energy usage, waste management, emissions, and the overall environmental impact of an organization's activities (Lightbody, 2000; Irwansyah et al., Hakim and Yunus

2017; Eny and Rum, 2019). The significance of green auditing lies in its ability to identify inefficiencies and areas for improvement, enabling organizations to reduce their environmental footprint, enhance sustainability, promote the use of clean technologies, and conform to legal and regulatory requirements (Taylor et al., 2021; Ningsih et al., 2020; Zutshi and Sohal, 2004). By adopting green auditing practices, organizations can not only achieve cost savings through more efficient resource utilization but also enhance their reputation and stakeholder trust by demonstrating a commitment to environmental preservation (Dettenkofer et al., 2000; Ljubisavljević, Ljubisavljević and Jovanović 2017; Bosu, Mahmoud and Hassan 2023). Hence, we propose the following hypothesis:

H1: There is a direct relationship between green audits and emissions reduction.

3.2 Emission Reduction

Green auditing can play a significant role in reducing an organization's carbon footprint by identifying and implementing practices that can potentially reduce greenhouse gas (GHG) emissions. This includes evaluating and optimizing energy consumption patterns, adopting cleaner production techniques, and enhancing waste management processes to reduce GHG emissions (Calabrò 2009; Weitz et al. 2011; Zhao and Chen 2015; Dong et al. 2023). For instance, a study by Chen, Zhou, Jia, and Guo (2023) found that firms conducting cleaner production audits reduced sulphur dioxide emissions by 4.7% and chemical oxygen demand by 11.9%. This study indicated that these audits significantly improved firms' environmental efficiency. By systematically assessing and improving these areas, organizations can significantly decrease their carbon emissions, contributing to global efforts to fight climate change. Similarly, Yajima and Arimura (2022) found that energy audits are effective in reducing carbon dioxide emissions.

As companies measure and manage their GHG emissions more, they will likely need more independent assurance and audit reporting (Olson 2010). Green audits help companies meet regulatory requirements by helping them to understand and manage their GHG emissions. This is crucial, as international organizations and national governments set emission reduction targets and introduce measures such as GHG reporting programs, emission trading schemes, and energy efficiency standards (Piecyk, 2010).

Furthermore, improvements in energy efficiency can be an important outcome of green auditing. Energy auditing is indispensable for sustainable development and energy conservation, as it helps identify inefficiencies, optimizes energy use, and implements strategies to reduce consumption and emissions (Darshan et al.,

2022). Energy audits help identify and capitalize on energy efficiency opportunities (Kalantzis and Revoltella, 2019).

Implementing an Environmental Management System (EMS) can enhance an organization's corporate image by standardizing operations and reducing waste of resources, including energy, gas, water, and time (Zutshi and Sohal, 2004). Through comprehensive evaluations, environmental audits can identify opportunities to optimize energy usage, promote the adoption of renewable energy sources, and implement energy-saving measures. This not only reduces the overall energy consumption, but also leads to cost savings and decreased reliance on non-renewable energy sources (Lisauskas et al., 2022). Energy conservation reduces operating and production costs, enhances competitiveness, and reduces environmental impact. By understanding and optimizing energy use, organizations can become more energy-efficient, reduce carbon emissions, reduce costs, and improve their image (Giama and Papadopoulos, 2018). Conducting energy audits will guide decision makers toward energy efficiency improvements, leading to economic savings and a reduced carbon footprint (Bosu et al., and Hassan and Hassan 2023). By promoting a culture of energy efficiency, organizations can make substantial progress in reducing their environmental impact and aligning with sustainability targets. Hence, we propose the following hypotheses:

> H5: Emission reduction mediates the relationship between green auditing and climate-target alignment.

3.3 Climate Target Alignment

Green auditing must adhere to a comprehensive set of environmental laws, standards, and policies designed to protect and improve a country's environmental quality. For instance, the major environmental laws and policies in India include the Environment Protection Act 1986, the Air (Prevention and Control of Pollution) Act 1981, the Water (Prevention and Control of Pollution) Act 1974, the Energy Conservation Act, 2001, the National Green Tribunal Act, 2010, the National Action Plan on Climate Change (NAPCC) 2008, and various other regulations concerning environmental protection, waste management, energy efficiency, and natural resource conservation (Government of India, 2008; Abbi and Jain, 2006; Sharma, Mahajan and Sharma, 2018). In addition, the Business Responsibility and Sustainability Report (BRSR) introduced by the Securities Exchange Board of India (SEBI) in 2021 mandates (with effect from 2022-23) listed Indian companies to disclose their environmental, social, and governance (ESG) performance to promote responsible business conduct and sustainable development. It aims to encourage sustainable practices, enhance transparency and accountability, and align itself with global sustainability reporting standards. One of the guiding principles of BRSR is that businesses should respect, protect, and strive to restore their environment. This framework includes disclosures on sustainable sourcing, energy efficiency, water usage, air emissions, fuel consumption, renewable energy use, liquid discharge, greenhouse gas emissions, waste management, and environmental impact assessments (Adani Renewables, n.d.).; Deloitte, 2023). Compliance with these regulations ensures that organizations operate within legal limits, contributing to national efforts to mitigate environmental degradation and promote sustainable development.

Further, environmental auditing also necessitates compliance with international standards and agreements, such as the Paris Agreement, ISO 14001 - Environmental Management Systems (EMS), ISO 14064 - Greenhouse Gases, ISO 14031 – Environmental Performance Evaluation (EPE), ISO 50001 - Energy Management Systems (EnMS), and Global Reporting Initiative (GRI) standards (Heras-Saizarbitoria, Dogui and Boiral, 2013; Bastianoni et al., 2014; Wintergreen and Delaney, 2007; Marimon and Casadesús, 2017; Pham et al., 2021; Brown, De Jong, and Lessidrenska, 2009). By aligning with these global commitments, organizations not only contribute to local climate goals, but also support global efforts to limit temperature rise and reduce GHG emissions. Compliance with international agreements and standards ensures that Indian organizations meet global benchmarks for environmental performance, foster international cooperation, and enhance India's reputation in the global environmental landscape.

Furthermore, green auditing supports alignment with the sustainability goals set by the United Nations, particularly those related to climate action and environmental sustainability. Sustainable Development Goals (SDGs) encompass a wide range of goals aimed at fostering sustainable development and fighting climate change. By assessing and enhancing an organization's environmental performance and reducing its carbon footprint, green auditing can contribute to multiple SDGs, including SDG 7 (Affordable and Clean Energy), SDG 13 (Climate Action), and SDG 12 (Responsible Consumption and Production) (Doni et al., 2020; Gebara and Laurent, 2023; Palakshappa and Dodds, 2020). This holistic approach ensures that organizations not only meet their climate commitments, but also contribute to broader global sustainability goals.

Hence, we propose the following hypotheses:

H2: There is a direct relationship between emissions reduction and climate target alignment.

3.4 Technical Expertise

Auditors require a diverse set of skills to conduct environmental audits effectively and successfully (Dixon et al., 2004). The audit team should be competent, adequately trained, and sufficiently trained to effectively complete an audit within budgeted time (De Moore and De Beelde, 2005). Thus, higher levels of technical expertise are expected to enhance the effectiveness of green auditing in achieving significant emission reductions. The presence of knowledgeable, trained, and experienced professionals ensures that audits are conducted thoroughly and accurately, identifying critical areas for improvement, and implementing effective strategies.

Hence, we propose the following hypotheses:

> H6: Technical expertise moderates the relationship between green auditing and emission reduction.

3.5 Sector Specific Factors

Certain sector-specific factors can affect the adoption of green auditing practices by business organizations (Bae and Seol, 2006). Each industry may be regulated by specific environmental guidelines, and compliance requirements may also be different. In India, the Central Pollution Control Board, part of the Ministry of Environment, Forest, and Climate Change of the Government of India, has set specific standards for various industries concerning the treatment of emissions and effluents. For instance, pesticide industries must analyze pesticides in wastewater using advanced methods, such as Gas Liquid Chromatography (GLC) or High-Performance Liquid Chromatography (HPLC). In cement plants, the total dust emissions must not exceed 400 mg/Nm^3 (milligrams per normal cubic meter) for plants with up to 200 t/d (tons per day) capacity and 250 mg/Nm^3 for larger plants. In the glass and phosphatic fertilizer industries, total fluoride emissions must not exceed 5 mg/Nm^3 and 25 mg/Nm^3, respectively. These industry-specific standards ensure that each industry effectively controls its specific pollutants, thereby helping meet environmental targets and reduce overall pollution.

Furthermore, industry type can also significantly influence the adoption of environmental audit programs. Activities or processes in certain industries necessitate the measurement of environmental performance. For instance, Bae and Seol (2006) found that companies in the chemical and allied products industry and electric, gas, and sanitary services adopt environmental audit programs. By contrast, firms in insurance and depository institutions do not adopt such audit programs. In another example, the Dutch greenhouse horticulture sector, a significant energy user in the country, signed an agreement with its national government to reduce fossil fuel consumption (Aramyan et al., 2007). Such industry-specific factors can affect organizations' green audit implementation.

Therefore, we hypothesize that (See Fig.01):

H3: There is a direct relationship between sector-specific factors and climate-target alignment.

H4: A direct relationship exists between green audits and sector-specific factors.

3.6 Barriers to Green Auditing

The implementation of green auditing also faces certain barriers in terms of financial constraints, limited technical expertise, and the absence of clear regulatory guidelines. Insufficient financial and human resources can significantly hinder the thoroughness and frequency of green audits (Rika 2009). Organizations may struggle to allocate adequate funds for comprehensive auditing processes, including hiring skilled auditors and implementing recommended improvements. Many cost-effective energy efficiency measures remain unimplemented due to financial constraints, lack of information, and limited in-house expertise (Fresner et al., 2017). It may also be noted that due to high cost of environmental auditing, firms are likely to conduct a cost-benefit analysis and adopt environmental audit programs (EAP) only if the benefits exceed the costs (Bae and Seol, 2006). Additionally, a lack of trained personnel can affect the quality of audits and the ability to sustain continuous environmental performance enhancements. It should be noted that audits should be conducted by qualified individuals who understand the process and responsibilities, following clear and generally accepted guidelines. However, there are currently no adequate guidelines for the ethical, social, and environmental aspects of green auditing (Adams, 2004). In addition, a barrier to environmental auditing is the reluctance of professionals to enter the field, attributed to the absence of generally accepted principles for conducting environmental audits (De Moore & De Beelde, 2005). Zhang, Gu, and Guo (2020) identified several barriers to carbon audits in the iron and steel industry. These include insufficient infrastructure, a shortage of skilled auditors, a lack of innovation in clean production technology, and capital investment.

Additionally, managers often face resistance and challenges when implementing and maintaining systems and standards related to quality, occupational health and safety, and environmental areas, which can hinder the adoption of green audits. Additionally, top management leadership and support are crucial for fostering organization-wide awareness of and commitment to environmental issues and the successful implementation of green audits (Zutshi and Sohal, 2004). Without strong support from management, achieving the effective implementation of environmental systems and standards has become significantly challenging. It may also be noted that environmental audits are hindered by clients' lack of documentation, and low public awareness of environmental issues leads to apathy for environmental management and auditing (Rika, 2009).

Furthermore, the lack of access to cutting-edge technologies for environmental monitoring is a major barrier to environmental auditing. Tools such as geographic information systems (GIS) are essential for audits; however, high costs and the need for skilled personnel hinder their use, particularly in financially constrained developing countries (Wanyonyi, 2020). Gu, Dai, and Vasarhelyi (2023) highlighted the importance of incorporating new technologies such as satellite imagery to improve green auditing. Using satellite image data for GHG emission reporting in environmental, social, and governance (ESG) reports can reduce the risk of greenwashing and enhance the credibility of ESG assurance. The authors noted that these objective and real-time data sources could significantly boost the effectiveness of environmental audits. Advanced tools and technologies are crucial for accurate data collection, real-time monitoring, and effective implementation of environmental management practices. Without these technologies, organizations may find it challenging to conduct precise audits, identify areas for improvement, and accurately track progress. Hence, it is hypothesized that (See Fig.01):

Figure 1. H7: environmental barriers moderate the relationship between green auditing and sector-specific factors.

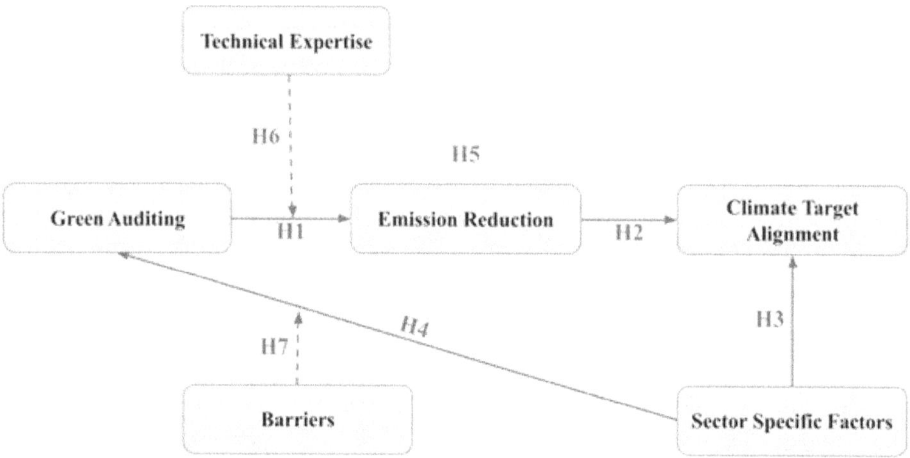

Source: Authors compiled

Based on the above conceptual framework, this study proposes the following conceptual model.

4. METHODOLOGY

The current study followed a scientific methodological approach to achieve its objectives. Mixed quantitative and qualitative approaches have been employed. The methodological procedure involved in the study is presented in the following four sections:

4.1 Survey Design and Development

Since the study is on an emerging topic and new, there are no existing survey instruments; therefore, the present study attempted to develop its own research instrument based on the existing literature and focus group discussions with experts concerning the area of the study. First, the researchers gathered earlier literature on green auditing practices and analyzed the key concepts, variables, and measures used in previous studies. A total of 28 items were derived from earlier studies and noted in the same manner. In the next stage, a hybrid focus group discussion among experts was organized with the help of a moderator and discussion guide based on the research questions. Qualitative insights from the discussions were noted, and after the analysis, the study identified nine potential survey items. Following the focus group discussions, the study generated 37 initial survey questions based on earlier literature and focus group findings. In the next phase, the initial pool of items was categorized into six constructs: green audit, emission reduction, climate target alignment, sector-specific factors, barriers, and technical expertise. After the finalization of the survey items, a five-point Likert scale (5–Strongly agree to 1–Strongly disagree) was finalized. Following this stage, six experts were consulted to ensure the clarity and relevance of the items and to update the draft instrument according to the suggestions of the experts.

Following the refinement of the instrument, the draft survey instrument was submitted to subject matter experts to review content validity, suggesting the removal and merger of six statements and amendments were made accordingly. Finally, 31 statements across the 6 constructs were retained.

After the finalization of the research instrument, a pilot survey of 38 respondents was conducted to check response patterns, missing data, and potential issues, and to conduct preliminary reliability and validity analyses. The pilot survey outcomes were once again consulted with experts and the instrument was finalized with minor corrections. The final list of items and their sources are shown in table 01.

Table 1. Items and their sources

Concept	Items	Source	Focus group support
Green Audit	Frequent performance of green audit enhances the firm's ability to effective environmental management.	Banu *et al.*, 2023; Mishra and Sant, 2024	YES
	To what extent does your organization measure its greenhouse gas emissions?	Dong *et al.*, 2023; Olson, E.G., 2010	
	How confident are you in the accuracy of your organization's emissions measurements?	Olson, E.G., 2010	
Emission Reduction	How has your organization's greenhouse gas emissions changed since implementing green auditing?	Weitz *et al*, 2002; Zhao and Chen, 2015	YES
	To what extent have green audits led to reductions in emissions from energy use?	Zhao and Chen, 2015	
	To what extent have green audits led to reductions in emissions from waste management?	Olson, E.G., 2010; Calabrò, P.S., 2009	YES
	To what extent have green audits led to reductions in emissions from transportation?	Weitz *et al*, 2002; Kalantzis and Revoltella, 2019	
	To what extent have green audits led to reductions in emissions from industrial processes?	Wintergreen and Delaney, 2007	
Climate Target Alignment	To what extent do your organization's green auditing practices align with India's climate change targets?	Kumar, A., 2021; Rani, S., 2023	
	To what extent do your green auditing practices addresses reduce emissions intensity of GDP?	Tumwebaze *et al.*, 2022	YES
	To what extent do your green auditing practices address increasing non-fossil fuel energy capacity?	Abbi and Jain, 2006; Raihan *et al.*, 2022	
	To what extent do your green auditing practices addresses create additional carbon sinks?	Darshan *et al.*, 2022; Giama *et al.*, 2018	
	To what extent do your green auditing practices address adaptation to climate change?	Sabu, C., 2021	
	How often does your organization review its green auditing practices to ensure alignment with national climate targets?	Shekhar and Chadda, 2024	YES
	To what extent has your organization made recent changes to its green auditing practices to better align with national climate goals?	Singh *et al.*, 2021	

continued on following page

Table 1. Continued

Concept	Items	Source	Focus group support
Sector Factors	To what extent do sector-specific factors influence the effectiveness of green auditing in your organization?	Tumwebaze *et al.*, 2022	
	How challenging is green auditing in your sector concerning climate change mitigation?	Das and Roy 2020	YES
	How many opportunities for green auditing exist in your sector concerning climate change mitigation?	Shekhar and Chadda, 2024	
	To what extent could green auditing practices be better tailored to your sector to enhance climate change mitigation efforts?	Das and Roy, 2020; Taylor *et al.*, 2021	YES
	How effective are sector-specific guidelines in addressing climate change issues through green auditing?	Doni *et al.*, 2020	
	To what extent does the nature of your sector's operations impact the focus areas of your green audits?	Eny and RUM, 2019	
	How frequently does your sector collaborate on green auditing practices and knowledge sharing?	Khalaf and Hamad, 2023	
	To what extent do your green auditing practices address increasing non-fossil fuel energy capacity?	Aramyan *et al.*, 2007; Bosu *et al.*, 2023	
Barriers	How significant is the lack of technical expertise as a barrier to effective green auditing?	Khalaf and Hamad, 2023	
	How significant are financial constraints as a barrier to effective green auditing?	Eny and Rum, 2019	YES
	How significant is the lack of clear regulatory guidelines as a barrier to effective green auditing?	Rajapakse *et al.*, 2022	
	How significant is the difficulty in data collection and analysis as a barrier to effective green auditing?	Eny and Rum, 2019; Banu *et al.*, 2023	
	How significant is the lack of management support as a barrier to effective green auditing?	Irwansyah *et al.*, 2017	
	How significant is resistance to change within the organization as a barrier to effective green auditing?	Budiono and Dura, 2021	
	How significant is the complexity of operations as a barrier to effective green auditing?	Budiono and Dura, 2021.	
Technical Expertise	To what extent does your organization have the necessary technical expertise to conduct effective green audits?	Raihan *et al.*, 2022	YES

Source: Authors compiled

4.1 Sampling Method and Participant Selection

The study relied on primary sources of data with the help survey method (Rubeena, R. and Maseeh, (2023). The target population for this study included senior executives, accountants, auditors, academics, and researchers. The survey was integrated into Google Forms and distributed to the target population. Owing to the difficulty in accessing respondents, a convenience sampling method was employed (Sirakaya-Turk and Uysal, 2017). Various platforms, such as LinkedIn, websites of companies, professional bodies (ICAI, ICSAI, ICMAI), and universities, were used to gather a list of respondents and their email ids. A total of 737 email ids of senior executives, 8567 email ids of chartered accountants, company secretaries, and cost accountants, and 1686 email ids of academicians and researchers. Google forms were distributed to all email ids obtained. Responses were collected in real time using a pre-established time schedule. The e-forms were distributed on January 25, 2024, and opened until March 15, 2024. Frequent reminders were sent fortnightly to increase response rates. After data collection, a detailed review, careful examination, and curation of the data were performed to resolve the issues of completeness, accuracy, and reliability. Duplicate and incomplete responses were excluded. The final green auditing database was transported to a compatible format for further analysis and interpretation. The demographic profiles of the respondents are indicated in Table-02.

Table 2. Demographic profile of respondents

Category		Number	Percentage
Gender	Male	589	73.53
	Female	212	26.47
Age	21 to 30 years	201	25.09
	31 to 40 years	281	35.08
	41 to 50 years	198	24.72
	51 years and above	121	15.11
Sector	Manufacturing	326	40.70
	Trading	157	19.60
	Service	318	39.70

continued on following page

Table 2. Continued

Category		Number	Percentage
Size of Organizations (No. of Employees)	Less than 100	87	10.86
	100 to 499	74	9.24
	500 to 999	228	28.47
	1000 to 4,999	116	14.48
	5000 and more	296	36.95
Experience	Less than 10 years	156	19.47
	10 to 20 years	85	10.61
	20 to 30 years	342	42.70
	30 and above	218	27.22
Job Type	Senior Executive	201	25.09
	Accountants	159	19.85
	Auditors	197	24.59
	Academicians	119	14.86
	Researchers	125	15.61

Source: Author compiled

The demographic profile indicated that 73.53% of the respondents were men, while only 26.47% were women, thus revealing a male-dominated sample. The age distribution however indicates a remarkable concentration of individuals working at the initial or middle stages of their careers, especially for the age groups of 31 to 40 (35.08%), 21 to 30 (25.09%), and 51 and older (15.11%).

In contrast, the manufacturing (40.70%) and services (39.70%) sectors lead this sample, indicating that these industries are well represented; however, the trading sector is represented by 19.60%. In terms of organizational size, a large proportion of respondents worked in medium-sized to very large companies, with 28.47% being within the range of 500-999 employees and 36.95% having over 5000 employees.

Respondents with 20–30 years of experience had the highest percentage (42.70%). Others who were over 30 years of age accounted for 27.22%, while less than ten years of age. With regard to jobs, there were a major number of senior executives (25.09%), auditors (24.59%), accountants (19.85%), academics (14.86%), and researchers, with 15.61% indicating diverse professional experiences.

Thus, it reveals a labor force that possesses extensive experience and diversity, primarily located within the manufacturing and service sectors. Additionally, it is adequately represented among medium-to-large enterprises, where there exists a wide range of organizational hierarchy levels along with various job titles and professional backgrounds.

4.2 Measurement Model

The measurement model was assessed to establish the reliability and validity of the constructs (Table 3). First, the factor loadings of all items in the model have a value greater than the minimum acceptable value of 0.50 (Hair, Black, Babin, & Anderson, 2010). Although factor loadings over 0.7 are desirable (Vinzi, Chin, Henseler, & Wang, 2010), researchers frequently obtain weaker outer loadings (<0.70) in social science studies. Rather than automatically eliminating indicators, the effects of removing the item on composite reliability, content, and convergent validity were examined. Generally, items with outer loadings from 0.40 to 0.70 shall be considered for removal only if deletion results in an increase of composite reliability or average variance extracted (AVE) over the recommended value (Hair et al., 2016). In the current study, the factor loadings of all items were above the minimum threshold, and the removal of any item did not significantly increase composite reliability or AVE. Thus, all 5

Reliability was assessed using Cronbach's alpha, rho_A, and the composite reliability. The statistics for these measures were greater than the recommended value of 0.700 (Wasko and Faraj, 2005). The rho_A values were found to be between Cronbach's alpha and composite reliability (Sarstedt et al., 2017), and were also over 0.70, indicating good reliability (Henseler, Hubona, & Ray, 2016). Convergent validity was acceptable because the AVE was higher than 0.500.

Discriminant validity was assessed using the Fornell–Larcker criterion and heterotrait–monotrait (HTMT) ratio of correlations. According to the Fornell–Larcker criterion, the square root of the AVE for each construct should be greater than its correlations with other constructs (Fornell & Larcker, 1981). As shown in the table, the square root of the AVE for each construct was higher than the off-diagonal correlations, indicating good discriminant validity. Furthermore, the HTMT ratios were below the conservative threshold of 0.85 (Henseler, Ringle, & Sarstedt, 2015), further establishing discriminant validity (see Table 4).

Table 3. Reliability and validity analysis

Construct	Item	Loading	Alpha	rho_A	CR	AVE
Green Audit	Q5	0.75	0.8	0.82	0.85	0.6
	Q6	0.78				
	Q12	0.73				
Emission Reduction	Q7	0.82	0.850	0.87	0.9	0.65
	Q8	0.80				

continued on following page

Table 3. Continued

Construct	Item	Loading	Alpha	rho_A	CR	AVE
	Q9	0.76				
	Q10	0.79				
	Q11	0.83				
Climate Target Alignment	Q14	0.70	0.830	0.85	0.88	0.62
	Q15	0.74				
	Q16	0.77				
	Q17	0.73				
	Q18	0.75				
	Q19	0.78				
	Q20	0.72				
Sector Factors	Q29	0.76	0.810	0.83	0.86	0.59
	Q30	0.74				
	Q31	0.71				
	Q32	0.79				
	Q33	0.77				
	Q34	0.75				
	Q35	0.73				
	Q16	0.70				
Barriers	Q21	0.72	0.790	0.81	0.84	0.57
	Q22	0.74				
	Q23	0.71				
	Q24	0.75				
	Q25	0.70				
	Q26	0.73				
	Q27	0.77				
Technical Expertise	Q28	0.88	0.850	0.87	0.89	0.66

Abbreviations: AVE, average variance extracted; CR, composite reliability.
Source: Authors compiled

Table 4. Fornell–Larcker criterionand heterotrait–monotrait ratio of correlations

Construct	Green Audit	Emission Reduction	Climate Target Alignment	Sector Factors	Barriers	Technical Expertise
Green Audit	**0.77**	0.5	0.45	0.4	0.55	0.35
Emission Reduction	0.5	**0.81**	0.55	0.48	0.6	0.42
Climate Target Alignment	0.45	0.55	**0.79**	0.52	0.58	0.39
Sector Factors	0.4	0.48	0.52	**0.77**	0.53	0.38
Barriers	0.55	0.6	0.58	0.53	**0.76**	0.45
Technical Expertise	0.35	0.42	0.39	0.38	0.45	**0.81**

Notes: Diagonal and italicized are square roots of the AVE. The diagonal elements below are the correlations between the construct values. Above the diagonal elements are the heterotrait–monotrait ratios of correlation values.

Source: Authors compiled

4.3 Data Analysis Techniques

SPSS AMOS software was used to analyze and validate the data. SEM was used to test the hypotheses against the objectives of this study. SEM is the best tool for validating a conceptual model by evaluating the direct, mediating, and moderating relationships among variables used in a survey-based study (Thakkar and Thakkar, 2020).

5. DATA ANALYSIS AND RESULTS

5.1 Structural Model

The measurement model was assessed (Table 5) to establish the reliability and validity of the constructs. The direct relationships between the constructs were evaluated using path coefficients, standard deviations (SD), t-values, p-values, confidence intervals, and R^2values.

The relationship between green audit and emissions reduction has a path coefficient of 0.180, with a t-value of 2.147 and a p-value of 0.032, indicating a statistically significant positive effect. The confidence interval [0.021; 0.348] did not include zero, further supporting the significance of this relationship. An R^2 value of 0.180 indicates that Green Audit explains 18% of the variance in Emission Reduction.

The path coefficient for Emission Reduction to Climate Target Alignment was 0.423, with a t-value of 6.607 and p-value of 0.000. This strong positive relationship was statistically significant, with a confidence interval of [0.298–0.549]. An R^2 value of 0.225 indicates that Emission Reduction explains 22.5% of the variance in the Climate Target Alignment.

The relationship between sector-specific factors and climate target alignment showed a path coefficient of 0.479, a t-value of 5.477, and a p-value of 0.000, indicating a significant positive effect. The confidence interval [0.295–0.640] reinforces this significance. An R^2 value of 0.203 indicates that the sector-specific factor explains 20.3% of the variance in Climate Target Alignment.

Finally, the path coefficient for the Green Audit Sector to Specific Factor is 0.371, with a t-value of 3.473 and p-value of 0.001, signifying a significant positive relationship. The confidence interval [0.169, 0.573] supports this finding. The R^2 value of 0.196 indicates that Green Audit explains 19.6% of the variance in sector-specific factors.

These results confirm that the specified constructs have statistically significant positive direct relationships, thus supporting the proposed hypotheses. Each relationship demonstrates good reliability and validity, as indicated by the t-values, confidence intervals, and R2R^2R2 values.

Table 5. Testing direct relationships

Hypothesis	Path Coefficient	SD	t-value	p-value	Confidence Interval (2.5%; 97.5%)	R^2
Green Audit -> Emission Reduction	0.18	0.084	2.147	0.032	[0.021; 0.348]	0.18
Emission Reduction -> Climate Target Alignment	0.423	0.064	6.607	0.001	[0.298; 0.549]	0.225
Sector Specific Factor -> Climate Target Alignment	0.479	0.088	5.477	0.001	[0.295; 0.640]	0.203
Green Audit ->Sector Specific Factor	0.371	0.107	3.473	0.001	[0.169; 0.573]	0.196

5.1.1 Mediation Analysis

The mediation analysis (Table 7) reveals that emission reduction plays a partial mediating role in the relationship between Green Auditing and Climate Target Alignment. The total effect of Green Auditing on Climate Target Alignment was significant (coefficient = 0.403, p = 0.000), indicating a strong positive impact. The direct effect remained significant (coefficient = 0.169, p = 0.044), suggesting that

Green Auditing independently contributes positively to Climate Target Alignment. The indirect effect through Emission Reduction was marginally significant (coefficient = 0.056, p-value = 0.058), with a confidence interval of [0.005; 0.116], implying a positive but relatively weak mediation. These findings suggest that while Green Auditing directly enhances Climate Target Alignment, it also contributes indirectly through improved emissions reduction, highlighting the multifaceted benefits of comprehensive green auditing practices.

Table 6. Mediation analysis

Effect Type	Coefficient	p-value	SD	t-value	p-value (bootstrap)	Confidence Interval (2.5%; 97.5%)
Total effect	0.403	0.000				
Direct effect	0.169	0.044				
Indirect effects						
Green Auditing -> Emission Reduction -> Climate Target Alignment	0.056	0.029	0.029	1.896	0.058	[0.005; 0.116]

5.1.2 Moderation Analysis

The moderation analysis (Table 8 & F.g-02) explores the impact of Technical Expertise and Barriers on the relationships between green auditing and emission reduction, and green auditing and sector-specific factors. The interaction term for Technical Expertise and Green Auditing on Emission Reduction has a significant positive coefficient of 0.220 (p-value = 0.003), with confidence intervals of [0.075 and 0.365]. This suggests that higher levels of technical expertise enhance the positive effect of green auditing on emissions reduction, indicating that technical expertise strengthens the effectiveness of green auditing practices in reducing emissions. On the other hand, the interaction term for barriers and green auditing on sector-specific factors showed a significant negative coefficient of -0.145 (p-value = 0.033), with a confidence interval of [-0.278; -0.012]. This finding indicates that the presence of barriers diminishes the positive impact of green auditing on sector-specific factors, suggesting that obstacles or challenges can hinder the effectiveness of green auditing practices in influencing sector-specific improvements. These findings underscore the importance of considering both facilitating and hindering factors when implementing green auditing strategies to maximize their effectiveness.

Table 7. Moderation Analysis

Moderation Path	Coefficient	SD	t-value	p-value	Confidence Interval (2.5%; 97.5%)
Technical Expertise x Green Auditing -> Emission Reduction	0.22	0.074	2.973	0.003	[0.075; 0.365]
Barriers x Green Auditing -> Sector Specific Factors	-0.145	0.068	-2.132	0.033	[-0.278; -0.012]

Source: Author compiled

Figure 2. Tested model

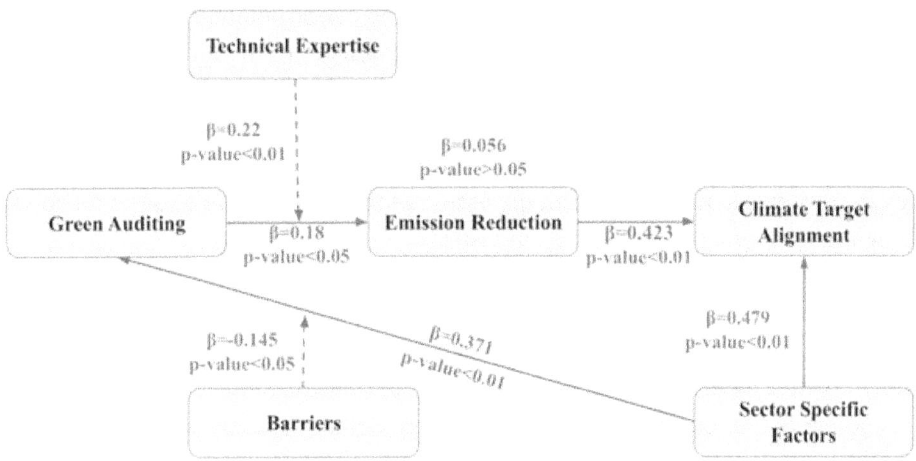

Source: Authors compiled

6. DISCUSSION

The present study, to the best of our knowledge, is unique and new in that it stresses the role of green auditing in climate target alignment through emission reduction. This study was conducted based on the insights of various experts from India. To achieve the stated objective, a scientific approach was employed to collect and analyze the data with the help of structural equation modelling, specifically applying mediation and moderation analysis. This study made an attempt examined the relationship between green auditing practices and climate target alignment. The SEM results revealed a direct relationship between green auditing and climate-target alignment. This is because green auditing enables business organizations to comply with climate laws, standards, and goals (Yunus 2017; Eny and Rum, 2019). This shows the significance of adopting green auditing practices at the organizational level to promote sustainable business practices. The study also observed a positive relationship between emissions reduction and climate target alignment. The emission reduction strategies employed by business organizations directly help align with climate targets set by both the self and regulatory authorities. This observation is in agreement with the arguments of Pham et al. (2021) and Adani Renewables (n.d.).; Deloitte, 2023; Gebara and Laurent, 2023.

This study used a sector-specific factor to check its influence on climate target alignment with the help of green auditing. The results revealed a significant positive relationship between sector-specific factors and climate target alignment. This emphasizes the need for the development and implementation of tailor-made approaches for green auditing in different industries. This finding agrees with the arguments of Enyand (2019) and Farooq et al. (2023). In support of this observation, the findings of the study also reveal that there is a strong positive relationship between green audit and sector-specific factors. Thus, sector-specific guidelines play a vital role in the effective implementation of green audits. Moreover, it eliminates the difficulty of the auditing process in different industries.

An interesting part of the study is the mediation analysis by keeping emission reduction as a mediating variable between green auditing and climate target alignment. The results of the mediation analysis revealed that emissions reduction plays a strong positive mediating role between green auditing and climate target alignment. This suggests that business organizations should consider emission reduction as a key pathway in achieving efficient climate goals. This finding supports those of Giama and Papadopoulos (2018), Lisauskas et al. (2022), and Bosu et al. (2023).

The study also attempted to analyze the moderating role of technical expertise in green auditing and emission reduction. The results revealed that the technical expertise of the staff and the organization strongly enhanced the positive effect of green auditing on the emission reduction process. This suggests that organizations invest in technical expertise to enhance the effectiveness of green audit practices (Mahapatra et al., 2021). The last aspect of this study is the analysis of the moderating role of environmental barriers that hinder the effectiveness of green auditing on sector-specific aspects. The results revealed that the presence of barriers diminishes the positive impact of green auditing on sector-specific aspects. This is a significant finding of the study that offers the insight that regulators and standard-setters should focus on establishing sector-specific guidelines to smoothen the process of green auditing to gain its benefits in a significant way. The current lack of sector-specific standards and guidelines is the biggest barrier to implementing green auditing practices (Gu et al., 2020; Gu et al., 2023).

The discussion clears that there is a need to implement an integrated model of green audit to reap its impact in a positive way for both business organizations and the environment at large. The tested conceptual model establishes the link between green auditing and climate target alignment through multiple pathways. To the best of our knowledge, this model is relatively novel for environmental management research. Therefore, the outcomes of this study will allow regulators and policymakers to develop more precise policy and strategy formulations.

6.1 Implications

The results of the study have theoretical, managerial, practical, social and environmental, economic and policy implications they are presented below:

6.1.1 Theoretical Implications and Contributions

This study presented a new integrated model linking green auditing to climate target alignment, which is relatively unique and novel in environmental management research. This efforts appears to extend and integrate several existing theories like stakeholder theory, resource base view of firm, contingency theory, institutional theory etc., by integrating these theories and using advanced statistical tools, this study contributes to a more systematic understanding of how organizational practices(green auditing), internal competencies(technical expertise), external variables(sector-specific factors and barriers), and environmental impact (emission reduction and climate target alignment) are interrelated. This integrated approach enables firms to manage their environmental impact more efficiently.

6.1.2 Social and Environmental Implications

The results of this study will help business organizations to develop potential climate mitigation strategies with the help of the model demonstrated in this study. This leads to more comprehensive environmental management strategies that can improve positive environmental outcomes. This indirectly enables firms to contribute to global net zero-emission targets.

6.1.3 Economic Implications

This study has two major economic implications. First, the sector-specific approach recommended by this study can help business organizations implement green auditing practices efficiently and cost-effectively across different industries. Second, the study recommends that by linking green auditing to climate target alignment, the firm and the environment at large can enjoy potential long-term economic benefits through regulatory compliance and resource efficiency.

6.1.4 Policy Implications

The findings of this study offer valuable insights for policymakers and regulators for the development of more precise and effective environmental policies, standards, and auditing guidelines. Sector-specific guidelines for green auditing have been established. This also supports business organizations in integrating the double materiality concept in their business reporting strategy. Another significant policy implication of this study is that regulatory authorities should make efforts to address and mitigate obstacles that may hinder green auditing practices to enhance the widespread and successful implementation of green audit practices.

7. CONCLUSION

The primary purpose of this study was to examine the role of green auditing in climate target alignment through emissions reduction. The moderating role of technical expertise and barriers in achieving green auditing effectiveness. The study attempted to comprehensively analyze the results using a scientific approach, specifically by applying the SEM technique with mediation and moderation analysis. The findings of this study revealed the existence of a direct relationship between green auditing and climate target alignment. It was also observed that there was a positive relationship between emissions reduction and climate target alignment. The results of this study showed that sector-specific factors have a significant influence on climate target alignment. However, the results confirmed the mediating role of emission reduction between green auditing and climate target alignment. The study also advocated that technical expertise significantly moderates the influence of green auditing on climate-target alignment. Interestingly, this study reported a negative moderating influence of barriers on the impact of green auditing on sector-specific factors. The has two significant novel contribution firstly, it offers integrated model linking green auditing to climate target alignment. From this model, regulators and business organizations can frame their environmental management models by taking into consideration the factors outlined in the study. Second, the study contributes to the comprehensive understanding that, to make green auditing more effective, there is a need to develop sector-specific approaches in green auditing. The major practical implication of the study is that it suggests tailored green auditing approaches for different industries and the need to invest in technical expertise to enhance green auditing effectiveness. The major limitation of this study was that it relied only on surveys and did not consider a qualitative approach. Therefore, future studies can undertake studies based on both quantitative and qualitative approaches to extend the scope of the present study further. Finally, the study concludes that the adoption and implementation of green auditing practices directly contribute to aligning climate goals with the main focus of emission reduction. This research serves as an input for policy makers, standard setters, and business organizations to implement green audit practices as a crucial strategy for environmental management.

REFERENCES

Abakumova, O. A., Lyubanenko, A. V., & Vazhenina, T. M. (2021, November). International Environmental Management Standards as a Tool of Legal Business Regulation. In *International Scientific and Practical Conference Operations and Project management: strategies and trends* (pp. 370-381). Cham: Springer International Publishing.

Abbi, Y. P., & Jain, S. (2006). *Handbook on energy audit and environment management. The Energy and Resources Institute*. TERI.

Adams, C. A. (2004). The ethical, social and environmental reporting-performance portrayal gap. *Accounting, Auditing & Accountability Journal*, *17*(5), 731–757. DOI: 10.1108/09513570410567791

Afolabi, H., Ram, R., Hussainey, K., Nandy, M., & Lodh, S. (2023). Exploration of small and medium entities' actions on sustainability practices and their implications for a greener economy. *Journal of Applied Accounting Research*, *24*(4), 655–681. DOI: 10.1108/JAAR-09-2022-0252

Aramyan, L. H., Lansink, A. G. O., & Verstegen, J. A. (2007). Factors underlying the investment decision in energy-saving systems in Dutch horticulture. *Agricultural Systems*, *94*(2), 520–527. DOI: 10.1016/j.agsy.2007.01.005

Arif, M., Sajjad, A., Farooq, S., Abrar, M., & Joyo, A. S. (2021). The impact of audit committee attributes on the quality and quantity of environmental, social and governance (ESG) disclosures. *Corporate Governance (Bradford)*, *21*(3), 497–514. DOI: 10.1108/CG-06-2020-0243

Bae, S., & Seol, I. (2006). An exploratory empirical investigation of environmental audit programs in S&P 500 companies. *Management Research News*, *29*(9), 573–579. DOI: 10.1108/01409170610709005

Banu, D. A., Sheela, S., Muralimohan, N., Saranya, N., Kolar, A. B., & Santhya, V. (2023). Importance and Benefits of Green Audits to Education Institutions and Industrial Sectors. *International Journal of Environment and Climate Change*, *13*(12), 349–356. DOI: 10.9734/ijecc/2023/v13i123690

Bastianoni, S., Marchi, M., Caro, D., Casprini, P., & Pulselli, F. M. (2014). The connection between 2006 IPCC GHG inventory methodology and ISO 14064-1 certification standard–A reference point for the environmental policies at sub-national scale. *Environmental Science & Policy*, *44*, 97–107. DOI: 10.1016/j.envsci.2014.07.015

Bosu, I., Mahmoud, H., & Hassan, H. (2023). Energy audit and management of an industrial site based on energy efficiency, economic, and environmental analysis. *Applied Energy*, *333*, 120619. DOI: 10.1016/j.apenergy.2022.120619

Brown, H. S., De Jong, M., & Lessidrenska, T. (2009). The rise of the Global Reporting Initiative: A case of institutional entrepreneurship. *Environmental Politics*, *18*(2), 182–200. DOI: 10.1080/09644010802682551

Budiono, S., & Dura, J. (2021). The effect of green accounting implementation on profitability in companies compass index 100. *International Journal of Educational Research & Social Sciences*, *2*(6), 1526–1534. DOI: 10.51601/ijersc.v2i6.216

Calabrò, P.S., (2009). Greenhouse gases emission from municipal waste management: The role of separate collection. Waste management, 29(7), pp.2178-2187. () DOI: 10.1016/j.wasman.2009.02.011

Chattopadhyay, P., Chattopadhyay, P., & Palit, D. (2020). Effect of environmental pollution on health and its prevention: an overview. *Environmental and sustainable development through forestry and other resources*, pp.229-266.

Dalhuijsen, E., Gutierrez, E., & Kliatskova, T. (2023). *Greening National Development Financial Institutions: Trends, Lessons Learned, and Ways Forward*. World Bank Publications.

Darshan, A., Girdhar, N., Bhojwani, R., Rastogi, K., Angalaeswari, S., Natrayan, L., & Paramasivam, P. (2022). Energy audit of a residential building to reduce energy cost and carbon footprint for sustainable development with renewable energy sources. *Advances in Civil Engineering*, *2022*(1), 4400874. DOI: 10.1155/2022/4400874

Das, N., & Roy, J. (2020). India can increase its mitigation ambition: An analysis based on historical evidence of decoupling between emission and economic growth. *Energy for Sustainable Development*, *57*, 189–199. DOI: 10.1016/j.esd.2020.06.003

De Moor, P., & De Beelde, I. (2005). Environmental auditing and the role of the accountancy profession: A literature review. *Environmental Management*, *36*(2), 205–219. DOI: 10.1007/s00267-004-0142-6 PMID: 15995890

Deloitte. (August, 2023). *Business Responsibility and Sustainability Report*: What does it mean for the top 1,000 listed entities in India? [online] Available at: https://www2.deloitte.com/in/en/pages/finance/articles/business-responsibility-and-sustainability-report.html (Accessed: 23 July 2024).

Dettenkofer, M., Kuemmerer, K., Schuster, A., Mueller, W., Muehlich, M., Scherrer, M., & Daschner, F. D. (2000). Environmental Auditing in Hospitals: First Results in a University Hospital. *Environmental Management*, *25*(1). PMID: 10552105

Dong, Y., Wong, W. K., Muda, I., Cong, P. T., Hoang, A. D., Ghardallou, W., & Ha, N. N. (2023). Do natural resources utilization and economic development reduce greenhouse gas emissions through consuming renewable and Clean Technology? A case study of China towards sustainable development goals. *Resources Policy*, *85*, 103921. DOI: 10.1016/j.resourpol.2023.103921

Doni, F., Gasperini, A., & Soares, J. T. (2020). What is the SDG 13? In *SDG13–Climate action: Combating climate change and its impacts* (pp. 21–30). Emerald Publishing Limited., DOI: 10.1108/978-1-78756-915-720201006

Eny, N. and Rum, M., (2019). Environmental green accounting and auditing practice. Research journal of finance and accounting, 10(8), pp.83-90.

Farooq, U., Wen, J., Tabash, M. I., & Fadoul, M. (2023). Environmental regulations and capital investment: Does green innovation allow to grow? *International Review of Economics & Finance*, *89*, 878–893. DOI: 10.1016/j.iref.2023.08.010

Fresner, J., Morea, F., Krenn, C., Uson, J. A., & Tomasi, F. (2017). Energy efficiency in small and medium enterprises: Lessons learned from 280 energy audits across Europe. *Journal of Cleaner Production*, *142*, 1650–1660. DOI: 10.1016/j.jclepro.2016.11.126

Gebara, C. H., & Laurent, A. (2023). National SDG-7 performance assessment to support achieving sustainable energy for all within planetary limits. *Renewable & Sustainable Energy Reviews*, *173*, 112934. DOI: 10.1016/j.rser.2022.112934

Ghosh, S. (2021). Corporate Social Responsibility Practices and Its Implementation after the Legal Mandate: A Study of Selected Companies in India with Special Emphasis on the Mining Sector. *Global Challenges to CSR and Sustainable Development: Root Causes and Evidence from Case Studies*, pp.105-138.

Giama, E., & Papadopoulos, A. M. (2018). Carbon footprint analysis as a tool for energy and environmental management in small and medium-sized enterprises. *International Journal of Sustainable Energy*, *37*(1), 21–29. DOI: 10.1080/14786451.2016.1263198

Gidage, M., Bhide, S., & Bilan, Y. (2024). Greenwashing in the Indian corporate landscape: An empirical assessment of ESG disclosures of NIFTY 50 companies. *Environment, Development and Sustainability*, •••, 1–25. DOI: 10.1007/s10668-024-05191-3

Government of India. (2008). *National action plan on climate change*. Prime Minister's Council on Climate Change.

Gray, R. (2000). Current developments and trends in social and environmental auditing, reporting and attestation: A review and comment. *International Journal of Auditing*, *4*(3), 247–268. DOI: 10.1111/1099-1123.00316

Gunningham, N., & Prest, J. (1993). Environmental audit as a regulatory strategy: Prospects and reform. *The Sydney Law Review*, *15*, 492.

Hedberg, C. J., & Von Malmborg, F. (2003). The global reporting initiative and corporate sustainability reporting in Swedish companies. *Corporate Social Responsibility and Environmental Management*, *10*(3), 153–164. DOI: 10.1002/csr.38

Heras-Saizarbitoria, I., Dogui, K., & Boiral, O. (2013). Shedding light on ISO 14001 certification audits. *Journal of Cleaner Production*, *51*, 88–98. DOI: 10.1016/j.jclepro.2013.01.040

Hillary, R. (1998). Environmental auditing: Concepts, methods and developments. *International Journal of Auditing*, *2*(1), 71–85. DOI: 10.1002/(SICI)1099-1123(199803)2:1<71::AID-IJA23>3.3.CO;2-X

Irwansyah, Hakim, W. and Yunus, A. (2017). Environmental audit as instrument for environmental protectioan and management. *The Business & Management Review*, *9*(2), 228–232.

Johnstone, L. (2022). The means to substantive performance improvements–environmental management control systems in ISO 14001–certified SMEs. *Sustainability Accounting. Management and Policy Journal*, *13*(5), 1082–1108.

Kalantzis, F., & Revoltella, D. (2019). Do energy audits help SMEs to realize energy-efficiency opportunities? *Energy Economics*, *83*, 229–239. DOI: 10.1016/j.eneco.2019.07.005

Khalaf, A. Z., & Hamad, S. B. (2023). An exploratory and analytical study of a sample of control and audit professionals' opinions on green audit techniques and methods. *Revenue Journal: Management and Entrepreneurship*, *1*(1), 11–17. DOI: 10.61650/rjme.v1i1.173

Kolsi, M. C., Muqattash, R., & Al-Hiyari, A. (2022). How do external auditor attributes impact corporate social responsibility disclosures: Empirical evidence from ADX-listed companies. *Social Responsibility Journal*, *18*(2), 293–315.

Kumar, A. (2021). Introduction: Sustainable Development Goals, New urban agenda, and climate change. In *Sustainable Development Goals and Indian Cities* (pp. 1-41). Routledge India.

Kumar, S. (2022). State of Play of Drives for Implementing Sustainable Procurement in India. In *Understanding Sustainable Public Procurement: Reflections from India and the World* (pp. 221–298). Springer International Publishing. DOI: 10.1007/978-3-031-08258-0_5

Lightbody, M. (2000, June). Environmental auditing: the audit theory gap. In *Accounting Forum* (Vol. 24, No. 2, pp. 151-169). Taylor & Francis. ()DOI: 10.1111/1467-6303.00033

Lisauskas, A., Kveselis, V., Dzenajavičienė, E. F., Masaitis, S., & Perednis, E. (2022). Analysis of energy audits results and impacts: Case of small and medium enterprises in Lithuania. *Energy Efficiency*, *15*(7), 48. DOI: 10.1007/s12053-022-10052-x

Ljubisavljević, S., Ljubisavljević, L. and Jovanović, D., 2017. Environmental audit for environmental improvement and protection. Economic themes, 55(4), pp.521-538.

Mahapatra, S. K., Schoenherr, T., & Jayaram, J. (2021). An assessment of factors contributing to firms' carbon footprint reduction efforts. *International Journal of Production Economics*, *235*, 108073. DOI: 10.1016/j.ijpe.2021.108073

Mahwar, R. S., Verma, N. K., Chakrabarti, S. P., & Biswas, D. K. (1997). Environmental auditing programme in India. *The Science of the Total Environment*, *204*(1), 11–26. DOI: 10.1016/S0048-9697(97)00161-7 PMID: 9299766

Maltby, J. (1995). Environmental audit: Theory and practices. *Managerial Auditing Journal*, *10*(8), 15–26. DOI: 10.1108/02686909510147372

Marimon, F., & Casadesús, M. (2017). Reasons to adopt ISO 50001 energy management system. *Sustainability (Basel)*, *9*(10), 1740. DOI: 10.3390/su9101740

Martínez-Bravo, M., & Martínez-del-Río, J. (2020). Urban pollution and emission reduction. *Sustainable cities and communities*, pp.905-915.

Mishra, P., & Sant, T. G. (2024). Examine the level of environmental, social and governance disclosure in sustainability report–a study of the Indian banking sector. *International Journal of Innovation Science*, *16*(2), 420–442. DOI: 10.1108/IJIS-08-2022-0136

Ningsih, D. F., Junaid, A., & Mursalim, M. (2020). Environmental audit analysis to support Sustainability Development. *Point of View Research Accounting and Auditing*, *1*(3), 101–109. DOI: 10.47090/povraa.v1i3.48

Olson, E. G. (2010). Challenges and opportunities from greenhouse gas emissions reporting and independent auditing. *Managerial Auditing Journal*, *25*(9), 934–942. DOI: 10.1108/02686901011080071

Palakshappa, N., & Dodds, S. (2020). Mobilising SDG 12: Co-creating sustainability through brands. *Marketing Intelligence & Planning*, *39*(2), 265–283. DOI: 10.1108/MIP-08-2018-0360

Piecyk, M. (2010). Carbon auditing of companies, supply chains and products. 2010) Green Logistics: Improving the environmental sustainability of logistics, Kogan Page, pp.49-67.

Raihan, A., Begum, R. A., Said, M. N. M., & Pereira, J. J. (2022). Relationship between economic growth, renewable energy use, technological innovation, and carbon emission toward achieving Malaysia's Paris agreement. *Environment Systems & Decisions*, *42*(4), 586–607. DOI: 10.1007/s10669-022-09848-0

Rajapakse, R. M. D. A. P., Azam, S. F., & Khatibi, A. (2022). The role of environmental incentives in greening the small and medium-sized enterprises: A developing economy perspective. *Management of Environmental Quality*, *33*(5), 1167–1186. DOI: 10.1108/MEQ-10-2021-0239

Rani, S. (2023). Initiatives on climate change mitigation. In *Climate, Land-Use Change and Hydrology of the Beas River Basin, Western Himalayas* (pp. 177–202). Springer International Publishing. DOI: 10.1007/978-3-031-29525-6_6

Ravindra, K., Bhardwaj, S., Ram, C., Goyal, A., Singh, V., Venkataraman, C., Bhan, S. C., Sokhi, R. S., & Mor, S. (2024). Temperature projections and heatwave attribution scenarios over India: A systematic review. *Heliyon*, *10*(4), e26431. DOI: 10.1016/j.heliyon.2024.e26431 PMID: 38434018

Renewables, A. (n.d.). Policy on Business Responsibility and Sustainability Reporting (BRSR). [online] Available at: https://www.adanigreenenergy.com/-/media/Project/GreenEnergy/Corporate-Governance/Policy/BRSR-Policy.pdf (Accessed: 23 July 2024).

Rika, N. (2009). What motivates environmental auditing? A public sector perspective. *Pacific Accounting Review*, *21*(3), 304–318. DOI: 10.1108/01140580911012520

Rubeena, R. and Maseeh, M. (2023). "Innovative Data Collection Methods For Research In The Digital Era", *Vidya - A Journal Of Gujarat University*, Gujarat University, Vol. 2 No. 2, pp. 125–129.

Ruiz-Barbadillo, E., & Martínez-Ferrero, J. (2020). Empirical analysis of the effect of the joint provision of audit and sustainability assurance services on assurance quality. *Journal of Cleaner Production*, *266*, 121943. DOI: 10.1016/j.jclepro.2020.121943

Sabu, C. (2021). Global Warming and Climate Change: Constitutional Standing and Legal Framework in India. *Indian JL & Legal Rsch.*, *2*, 1.

Searcy, C., Morali, O., Karapetrovic, S., Wichuk, K., McCartney, D., McLeod, S., & Fraser, D. (2012). Challenges in implementing a functional ISO 14001 environmental management system. *International Journal of Quality & Reliability Management, 29*(7), 779–796. DOI: 10.1108/02656711211258526

Sharma, P., Mahajan, R., & Sharma, Y. (2018). Investigation of the energy audit practice in India. [IJRAR]. *International Journal of Research and Analytical Reviews, 5*(3), 767–772.

Shekhar, H. S., & Chadda, V. M. (2024). Disclosure regime for climate change: Proposal and prospects for India Inc. *Indiana Law Review, 8*(1), 42–65. DOI: 10.1080/24730580.2024.2323845

Singh, S., Singh, R. B., Singh, S., & Singh, R. B. (2021). Indian Climate Policy, Programs, and Initiatives. *Simulating Climate Change and Livelihood Security: A Western Himalayan Experience, India*, pp.273-299.

Sinkovics, N., Sinkovics, R. R., & Archie-Acheampong, J. (2021). Small-and medium-sized enterprises and sustainable development: In the shadows of large lead firms in global value chains. *Journal of International Business Policy, 4*(1), 80–101. DOI: 10.1057/s42214-020-00089-z

Sirakaya-Turk, E., & Uysal, M. S. (2017). "Survey research: sampling and questionnaire design.", cabi, pp. 122–146.

Taylor, A. L., Levin, J., Chan, J., Lee, M., Kasitinon, D., Miller, E., & Fox, P. (2021). Improving environmental sustainability in outpatient clinics: Lessons from a waste audit. *The Journal of Climate Change and Health, 4*, 100070. DOI: 10.1016/j.joclim.2021.100070

Thakkar, J. J., & Thakkar, J. J. (2020). Applications of structural equation modelling with AMOS 21, IBM SPSS. *Structural equation modelling: application for research and practice (with AMOS and R)*, pp.35-89.

Thompson, D., & Wilson, M. J. (1994). Environmental auditing: Theory and applications. *Environmental Management, 18*(4), 605–615. DOI: 10.1007/BF02400863

Tumwebaze, Z., Bananuka, J., Kaawaase, T. K., Bonareri, C. T., & Mutesasira, F. (2022). Audit committee effectiveness, internal audit function and sustainability reporting practices. *Asian Journal of Accounting Research, 7*(2), 163–181. DOI: 10.1108/AJAR-03-2021-0036

Wanyonyi, A. (2020). An Insight into the Emerging Issues, Challenges and Future Prospects in Environmental Audit. Challenges and Future Prospects in Environmental Audit (June 16, 2020).

Weitz, K. A., Thorneloe, S. A., Nishtala, S. R., Yarkosky, S., & Zannes, M. (2002). The impact of municipal solid waste management on greenhouse gas emissions in the United States. *Journal of the Air & Waste Management Association*, *52*(9), 1000–1011. DOI: 10.1080/10473289.2002.10470843 PMID: 12269661

Wintergreen, J., & Delaney, T. (2007, May). ISO 14064, international standard for GHG emissions inventories and verification. In 16th annual international emissions inventory conference, Raleigh, NC.

Wright, D. (1994). Environmental Auditing: An integral component of environmental management. Eco-Management and Auditing. *Eco-Management and Auditing*, *1*(2), 11–13. DOI: 10.1002/ema.178

Yessenamanova, M., Lukyanets, A., Golovina, E. and Topornin, N. (2022). Environmental Auditing: The EU Practice in the Context of Pursuing Sustainable Development Policy. *European Energy and Environmental Law Review, 31*(4).

Zhao, G., & Chen, S. (2015). Greenhouse gas emissions reduction in China by cleaner coal technology towards 2020. *Energy Strategy Reviews*, *7*, 63–70. DOI: 10.1016/j.esr.2014.08.001

Zutshi, A., & Sohal, A. S. (2004). Adoption and maintenance of environmental management systems: Critical success factors. *Management of Environmental Quality*, *15*(4), 399–419. DOI: 10.1108/14777830410540144

Chapter 4
Financial Reporting for E-Commerce and Digital Trade Platforms

Vesel Usaj
https://orcid.org/0000-0002-8555-4250
University "Ukshin Hoti" Prizren, Kosovo

Kushtrim Gashi
https://orcid.org/0000-0002-3349-4102
University "Ukshin Hoti" Prizren, Kosovo

ABSTRACT

This chapter investigates the changes e-commerce has brought about in financial reporting, considering challenges that new technology and digital business models present. It examines how big data, blockchain, and artificial intelligence enhance the accuracy, transparency, and compliance of financial reporting. E-commerce industries require new financial frameworks that deal with issues such as valuation, continuous processing of data, and regulatory complications, as shown through peer-reviewed research, industry reports, and case studies. AI enables real-time analytics to make decisions, while blockchain ensures secure, immutable transactions. Case studies of multinational e-commerce companies illustrate the need for standardization of financial reporting. Recommendations in the chapter on IFRS changes with inclusions of blockchain, real-time reporting, and AI-driven analytics for secure financial management are made. Future Research Directions: Ethics frameworks for financial operations in digital economies, regional technological adaptations, and ESG indicators in reporting.

DOI: 10.4018/979-8-3373-0887-6.ch004

1 INTRODUCTION

E-commerce Platforms have underlined that financial reporting is no longer the same with the advent of high-end technologies (AI, Blockchain, Cloud computing, etc.). They benefit by greater accuracy, efficiency, and transparency in managing financial data. This chapter goes into tackling the key areas supporting financial reportage in e-commerce like compliance, real-time handling of data, and valuation of intangible assets.

1.1 Background and Context

E-commerce sites have a say in financial behavior, as it is the point where customers have an opportunity to handle money wisely and make prudent decisions. According to Gusti and Hilda (2023), this has shown the shift of e-commerce to fast business settings and cementing digital economies as part of current trade cornerstone Gazieva et al. (2021). With the rapid adoption, e-commerce is increasingly becoming a tool for managing enterprises around the clock and reaching a larger consumer base at lower costs. In what is typically described as a company, a move towards a digital approach leads to a strategy that is far more sustainable and effective (Išoraitė & Miniotienė, 2018; Ardakani et al., 2024). One of the best examples is the fact that the nature of e-commerce has enabled it to be better adopted by small and medium enterprises in order to better embed it into their financial and operational planning, particularly within developing countries (Almuwallad & Alhumoudi, 2024).

Cutting-edge technology, such as blockchain, cloud computing, and digital payment systems, has changed the practice of financial reporting. Applications like SAP ERP and Microsoft Excel have made financial data administration easy, accurate, and effective (Mladenović et al., 2023). Kosadi et al. (2021) say that digital receipts and automated reconciliation procedures address the multi-platform transactional intricacies and greatly enhance the precision and transparency of financial reports. In general, changes are taking place in financial systems with the help of DLT, ML, and AI. Such developments increase operational effectiveness, data governance, and transparency, all factors imperative to the survival of the e-commerce industry (Gashi & Vardari, 2025a, 2025b). Take, for instance, AI-enabled analytics that provide real-time insights helpful for the decision-making process while blockchain technology validates security and accountability in financial reporting (Gashi, 2024). Financial reporting is on the pathway of the wider global digital transition in trade. Companies like Amazon and eBay changed their financial architectures to meet the necessities for international commerce, thereby ensuring transparency and compliance in every single country (Hýblová, 2019; Bari et al., 2023). The resilience of e-commerce systems was also on display during the COVID-19 pandemic in that e-commerce systems were able to maintain economic activities via seamless digital financial services (World Bank Group, 2020).

1.2 Importance of Financial Reporting in E-Commerce

Financial reporting, particularly, allows all the stakeholders of the e-commerce industry to express their views, enabling them to be more open and confident (Alrawashedh et al., 2024). Incorporation of e-commerce technologies transformed the nature of traditional accounting procedures through enabling business concerns to assure valid and reliable financial reports in spite of increasing complexities regarding internet-based online monetary transactions (Atanassova, 2018). Financial disclosure is predicated on transparency so that financial information about e-commerce platforms could be useful to investors and regulators alike, as well as consumers (Bari et al., 2023). Among the major difficulties regarding financial reporting of e-commerce is the valuation of intangible assets that can hardly be accommodated within traditional frameworks, such as user-generated data, digital branding, and intellectual property (Gashi & Vardari, 2025a). Real-time data and accurate decision-making are made easier by blockchain technology and AI with its rapid development, thus easing the valuation of intangible assets Gashi, & Vardari (2025b).

Another major hurdle to financial reporting in e-commerce is real-time data management. Digital platforms generate huge volumes of transaction data requiring effective systems for accurate and timely reporting (Kosadi et al., 2021). Problems such as duplicating data entries and inefficient reconciliation methods could all undermine the accuracy of financial accounts (Kosadi et al., 2021). These two technologies help remove doubt and ensure integrity in the financial statements (Kerrouche & Belouadah, 2025). Moreover, the integration of accounting information systems with e-commerce platforms would also provide financial transparency and operational efficiencies (Ami et al., 2023). The said integration benefits MSME income performance and would further enhance the reliability of financial records (Ami et al., 2023). Digital payment solutions, by ameliorating the way financial reports are prepared, also serve to enhance the credibility of reporting and further reduce errors (Kosadi et al., 2021).

The importance of compliance with the regulatory framework relating to financial reporting stems from the fact that e-commerce transactions are dynamic and tend to transcend borders (Alrawashedh et al., 2024). Advanced systems of financial reporting inspire confidence in the stakeholders and ensure compliance with various financial entity regulations across jurisdictions (Alrawashedh et al., 2024). The difficulties in financial reporting due to e-commerce will be eased by these advanced technologies: blockchain, AI, and machine learning. They will make the platforms allowed to tackle very complicated issues like real-time reporting and regulatory compliance with the required efficiency, security, and transparency (Gashi & Vardari, 2025b). In contrast to this, Gashi (2024) opines that AI technologies are increasing precision in prediction and assessments, while blockchain is storing eternal records for all transactions. Honest financial reporting is then a precondition for e-commerce to maintain its affairs in an open and trustworthy manner (Alrawashedh et al., 2024). These digital and accounting advancements are expected to enable e-commerce platforms in overcoming the problems of real-time data processing, multi-jurisdictional compliance, and valuation of intangible assets while acting as a catalyst for sustaining thriving businesses in an uphill market (Gashi & Vardari, 2025a).

1.3 Objectives of the Chapter

In particular, digital trade platforms will be emphasized and how e-commerce has positively affected the process of financial reporting (Gashi & Vardari, 2025a). Disruptive technologies like blockchain, AI, and big data will be examined for their capabilities to increase the credibility, efficiency, and transparency of financial reporting systems (Bari et al., 2023). This will include a critical analysis of the current weaknesses in these reporting systems, especially with regard to cross-border conformity and valuation-related issues concerning intangible assets, and presents a mechanism to suggest practical solutions to bring these international standards into conformity (Said & Ali, 2023). The chapter also shows a strong necessity to amend traditional accounting principles so as to meet the requirements of high-paced e-commerce environments by blending theoretical insights with practical implementations (Gashi, 2024).

1.4 Structure of the Chapter

The chapter opens with an introduction that puts much emphasis on new issues and technology, the importance of financial reporting in the context of e-commerce (Gashi & Vardari, 2025a). This section describes the methodology used in terms of data collection and analysis procedures in the systematic literature review technique (Said & Ali, 2023). Current norms, difficulties, and trends, as revealed from case studies for their realistic uses, are studied in the result section, supported by Kosadi et al., 2021. The findings give a summary under discussion that entails gaps in literature and theoretical and practical consequences by Gashi, 2024. Following a review of the main conclusions and suggestions for future research paths, the chapter ends with suggestions for utilizing technology and harmonizing international policies (Bari et al., 2023).

2 METHODOLOGY OF THE SYSTEMATIC LITERATURE REVIEW

The approach adopted in this chapter to analyze financial reporting in e-commerce is a Systematic Literature Review. This strict methodology involves the development of an organized framework, the application of precise inclusion and exclusion criteria, and the pooling of findings from relevant scholarly works. This review follows the PRISMA approach for transparency and reproducibility.

2.1 Defining the Systematic Literature Review Approach

The Systematic Literature Review (SLR), as a method of literature synthesis, was deemed appropriate for this chapter because of its comprehensiveness and repeatability in presenting the body of knowledge concerning e-commerce financial reporting. The methodology is intended to obtain relevant publications systematically through search and evaluation and integrate them into a holistic view of the specific study topic (Gao et al., 2023). The SLR has its own framework, which allows for transparency in identifying cross-cutting trends, patterns, and gaps in the literature (Abuali et al., 2024). The use of SLR was exceedingly justified in this chapter, considering the constantly changing nature of the e-commerce financial reporting domain, which necessitates current knowledge about new technologies, challenges, and best practices (Bari et al., 2023).

2.2 Search Strategy and Data Sources

To ensure a detailed and comprehensive analysis of the literature, the search method comprised well-known academic databases, such as Scopus, Web of Science, and Emerald Insight. Boolean operators (AND, OR, NOT) were utilized to interconnect keywords, such as "e-commerce financing reporting," "digital transformation in accounting," and "intangible asset valuation," in an effort to limit the search results (Alonge et al., 2024). With this methodology, the authors aimed to create a set of diverse opinions on how e-commerce affects financial reporting. Peer-reviewed journal articles, conference proceedings, and applicable reports from 2018 to 2024 were the subject of advanced search filters (Mladenovic et al., 2023).

2.3 Inclusion and Exclusion Criteria

Therefore, to be included, studies had to be peer-reviewed, published in a reputable journal, and linked to financial reporting in either digital trade platforms or e-commerce, Ami et al. 2023. The focus was on the technology, that is, blockchain financial reporting, artificial Intelligence, and cloud computing. Research to be excluded included those unrelated to non-digital industries, those not in the English language, or those not supported by empirical evidence, Kosadi et al. 2021. This stringent screening process ensured the inclusion of credible and immediately applicable research (Gurendrawati et al., 2024).

2.4 Review Process

Four steps defined by PRISMA were used in the review process, including identification, screening, eligibility, and inclusion (Trigo et al., 2014). Articles were identified by searching the databases while the titles and abstracts were screened for relevance. All the identified eligible studies were subsequently reviewed to ensure their conformance with the objectives of this study (Oktaviani et al., 2023). The data extraction was done through Excel, which allowed the data to be categorized by topics such as "emerging technologies" and "compliance challenges" (Kerrouche & Belouadah, 2025). The systematic study approach thus facilitated the synthesis of the findings, enabling a complete answer to the questions of the study.

2.5 Limitations of the Review

The SLR process faced two challenges: limited access to subscription-based research and publication bias, in which positive results are published more often (Ben Slama et al., 2022). Furthermore, some of these studies rapidly became outdated due to rapid developments in the e-commerce financial reporting system, thus requiring continuous investigation (Gashi & Vardari, 2025a). The capability to generalize from the findings was made impractical because of gaps in the literature, mainly on blockchain and AI applications in some geographical areas (Yarmoliuk et al., 2024). Despite these drawbacks, the review provides a firm foundation for e-commerce financial reporting.

3 FINDINGS OF THE LITERATURE REVIEW

The findings show that the regulatory financial reporting requirements have changed and are still changing in an effort to embrace different complexities of e-commerce. Technologies such as AI, blockchain, and big data create an avenue for real-time reporting, transparency, and efficiency. However, there are still unresolved issues regarding regulatory compliance, cybersecurity questions, and value realization from intangible assets. Some case studies also give examples to prove that these problems have their solution in standardized procedures and advanced tools.

3.1 Current Standards and Practices in Financial Reporting

Briefly stated, International Financial Reporting Standards or IFRS and Generally Accepted Accounting Principles or GAAP are financial reporting standards that ensure comparability, consistency, and transparency of financial statements across sectors. Both no doubt constitute the very core of international accounting procedures. Since e-commerce has become ineluctably integrated into traditional business procedures, such standards have been amended to account for the complexities arising out of such transactions. The literature evidences that Išoraitė & Miniotienė (2018) support this reasoning. Included among modern products to facilitate e-commerce standards while speeding up the financial reporting processes are QuickBooks and the SAP ERP systems. It is these very systems that help automate repetitive accounting functions, hence increasing efficiency while at the same time minimizing the chances of errors (Mladenović et al., 2023). In this context, MSME's that increasingly benefit from digital receipts and automated transaction records comply with IFRS regulations, thereby increasing the precision and reliability of financial reporting (Kosadi et al., 2021).

Although helpful, centuries-old concepts such as the historical cost principle still suffer from a few drawbacks in the fast-paced nature of online shopping. Real-time market conditions become paramount in digital business decision-making, whereas this approach often ignores them (Xia, 2016). The rigidity of conventional standards thus cannot represent appropriately e-commerce platforms' ever-changing operations (Gao et al., 2023). Integration of real-time data is becoming an essential part of financial reporting for e-commerce firms. The updated procedures therefore emphasize the technology they use for the provision of accurate and fast financial information, which, importantly, facilitate real-time tracking and reporting. These advances, therefore, satisfy the increasing demand of digital business models while improving decision-making capabilities (Gao et al., 2023). As noted by Duran (2023), e-finance, due to the rapid growth of the Internet, enables individuals and businesses to interact easily with distributors, retailers, and suppliers through advancements in network technology that are vital for the growth and expansion of electronic commerce. According to Jabor and Hamdan (2023), adopting new technologies has improved the quality of financial reporting considerably by reducing the time and effort required for the compilation of these reports leading to more accurate high-quality data.

It enables Visa, Mastercard, and others to be one of the global giants in the digital economy that have adapted their financial reporting systems to meet the special challenges presented by e-commerce. Some firms changed their systems to integrate real-time data and automated reporting technologies that ensure compliance and maintain operational transparency (Bari et al., 2023). While the principles contained in GAAP and IFRS provide firm regulation for financial reporting itself, the evolution of e-commerce requires that these frameworks be updated regularly (Gao et al., 2023). The introduction of integration of real-time data, automation, and sophisticated financial instruments must be geared toward ensuring that financial reporting requirements can respond to the ever-changing demands of the digital economy (Mladenović et al., 2023; Kosadi et al., 2021).

3.2 Challenges in Financial Reporting for E-Commerce

Digital business models bring much complexity, which is the core reason for such a large number of financial reporting problems in e-commerce companies. The greatest difficulty is in ascribing the appropriate value to intangible assets such as data and intellectual property that traditional accounting systems either forget or undervalue (Atanassova, 2018). They are dynamic in nature and do not have an internationally standardized set of accounting rules; hence, they cannot be measured properly (Said & Ali, 2023). Another major challenge is the integration of real-time financial data. E-commerce is characterized by dynamic and fast transactions that were beyond the reach of conventional banking systems. According to Xia (2016), real-time integration of data is crucial for swift decision-making and to ensure the accuracy of the financial statements. This need, therefore, places pressure on companies to adopt advanced technologies such as blockchain and artificial intelligence to ensure accuracy and timeliness of reporting (Gashi & Vardari, 2025b). Protecting their information comprises one of the principal matters in e-commerce financial reporting, while the other one remains under constant threat from violations of cybersecurity. Data compromises emanating from weak security do undermine the integrity of financial statements (Yarmoliuk et al., 2024); rapid development of e-commerce on the one hand renders financial reporting more complex, while on the other, it might invite fraud and abuse of resources (Abuali et al., 2024). Technological barriers such as expensive implementation of advanced systems and a certain lack of technical know-how greatly hinder the adoption of digital financial instruments. The peculiar problems of SMEs to utilize financial reporting systems profitably are limited resources and digital illiteracy (Okpo & Eshiet, 2023; Ami et al., 2023). In addition, constant challenge of trying to reconcile data from multiple online sales and payment systems also undercuts the accuracy of financial reporting and compliance (Kosadi et al., 2021; Alrawashedh et al., 2024). As cited by Türegün (2020), the difficulty in collecting and processing financial information is one of the factors that greatly restrains e-commerce businesses from implementing accounting standards.

As an important aspect of sustainability reporting, even how to measure the social and environmental impacts of their project is a different headache for e-commerce companies concerned about the measurement of sustainability. Within this context,

Ardakani et al. (2024) emphasize the need for new frameworks, which will assist in closing these gaps and ensuring that sustainability initiatives are fairly representing in organizations' financial statements. Also, the rapid growth of e-commerce has exposed the weaknesses of existing regulatory and taxation structures. It can be challenging to achieve compliance with different tax norms and reporting standards for companies that operate in several jurisdictions (Atanassova, 2018). Therefore, this difficulty of harmonization in itself adds to companies' complexities pertaining to financial reporting, especially for firms dealing with international trade (Alonge et al., 2024). These include some e-commerce financial reporting issues, such as intangible asset valuation, integration of real-time data, cybersecurity threats, and regulatory compliance. All these issues will be governed by the adoption of advanced technology, innovative frameworks, and tailored-reporting standards in order to guarantee a highly dynamic digital environment with accountability, accuracy, and transparency (Gashi & Vardari, 2025a; Kosadi et al., 2021).

3.3 Emerging Trends and Technologies

The innovations represented by blockchain, big data, machine learning, and AI are redefining the face of financial reporting with new methods for enhancing efficiency, accuracy, and transparency. For e-commerce companies that wish to remain competitive in the fast-paced digital economy, such development is imperative (Trigo et al., 2014). AI and ML make predictive analysis possible, eliminate human errors, and automate the whole process of financial reporting. Said and Ali (2023) stated that AI-based accounting tools ensure timely and efficient financial reporting through the automation of redundant tasks while offering insights on a near-real-time basis. The frameworks of ML improve upon reporting by providing for adaptive systems which can respond in quick time to transient market conditions (Gashi et al., 2025).

The financial-reporting sphere has undergone a huge transformation across technologies, including blockchain, which guarantees secure and open transactions. Kerrouche and Belouadah argue that blockchain is essential to any modern digital financial system, reducing the risk of fraud and giving an accurate picture of financial data. In other words, the immutability of transaction recording is coherent with the need for accountability and transparency inherent in any e-commerce platform Alonge et al. (2024). Big Data and real-time reporting are relied on to a great degree by a financial manager. Gashi and Vardari (2025a) have also established that, to unlock actionable insights with improved decision-making, organizations should actually combine artificial intelligence and big data technologies in the real-time analysis of data. Such technologies enable operational efficiency through predictive analytics and adaptive reporting systems, as illustrated by Gashi et al. (2025).

By permitting scalability and real-time changes, cloud computing has again revolutionized the financial reporting discipline. Trigo et al. (2014) state that cloud computing solutions allow firms to react in real-time to changes in the market, thereby assuring accurate and timely reporting. According to Kosadi et al. (2021), digital payment systems provide an additional advantage of ensuring efficiency in financial reporting in a multi-platform e-commerce context. Financial reporting is being revamped by blockchain and cryptocurrencies for their provision of new methods for security in transactions and decentralized financial systems. Abuali et al. (2024) argue that this complements efficiency with transparency, thereby improving the financial reporting processes for e-commerce. According to Probowulan and Ardianto (2024), through blogs and social media, e-commerce can effectively improve the quality of financial reporting by enhancing information accessibility and conformity with international standards. Distributed ledger technology-the ever-popular blockchain-holds great promise in digitizing financial reporting and auditing, thus allowing online reporting and continuous auditing, while offering protection against financial fraud-argue Ageeva, Karp, and Sidorov (2021).

Advanced dashboards and data visualization have become fashionable too. According to Mladenović et al. (2023), they thoroughly and insightfully help in supporting a decision-making activity while also enhancing general quality of the financial reporting in e-commerce firms. The emergent technology is changing faces of financial reporting within the e-commerce sector. The interventions among AI, ML, blockchain, and big data solve a variety of issues in the digital economy and facilitate real-time integration and prediction of data while ensuring the safe transaction of an e-commerce business. The implementation of such technological advancements would enhance the sustainability, operational efficiency, and transparency of financial reporting practices in e-commerce platforms (Gashi & Vardari, 2025b).

3.4 Insights from Case Studies

Case studies from larger players in e-commerce yield insightful information concerning the financial report and best practices. Amazon and eBay, as websites, have adjusted their finance infrastructure in order to boost international trading activity and remain compliant with various legal requirements. These firms leverage new technologies like blockchain and artificial intelligence to improve data security, operational transparency, and real-time reporting capability (Gashi & Vardari, 2025b). To address specific challenges in e-commerce such as automated reconciliation procedures and real-time transaction tracing, Visa and Mastercard have customized financial systems to support digital payments (Bari et al., 2023). The benefits of implementing standardized frameworks for e-commerce financial reporting were aptly illustrated during Tunisia's transition from Euro-Continental GAAP to IFRS. This shift has culminated in more transparent and comparable financial statements (Ben Slama et al., 2022). Likewise, Indonesian SMEs have, by applying blockchain and AI, successfully addressed age-old impediments to transparency by upgrading the precision and efficiency of their reporting systems (Gurendrawati et al., 2024). These examples underline the importance of making strategic investments in digital solutions and frameworks. They highlight the need for a common strategic approach to such issues as data reconciliation, tax compliance, and intangible asset valuation, which foster trust and competitiveness in the global digital economy (Kosadi et al., 2021).

Table 1. Insights from case studies on financial reporting

E-commerce Leader	Best Practices	Challenges
Amazon	Having deployed Blockchain and AI for Improved Security and Real-time reporting	Managing diversified regulatory requirements across jurisdictions
eBay	Adapted financial systems for cross-border trade compliance	Ensuring tax compliance for cross-border transactions
Visa & Mastercard	Implemented automated reconciliation processes and real-time transaction tracking	Addressing complexities in multi-platform transaction reconciliation
Developing countries (GAAP to IFRS Transition)	Adopted IFRS to ensure greater comparability and clarity	Overcoming classic barriers to standardization
Developing countries SMEs	Blockchain integrated with AI for accurate and efficient reporting	Improve transparency and overcome traditional reporting inefficiencies

Source: Gashi & Vardari, 2025b; Bari et al., 2023; Ben Slama et al., 2022; Gurendrawati et al., 2024.

4 DISCUSSION

This chapter develops theories about financial reporting by pointing out how e-commerce has played some havoc with conventional paradigms and focusing on real-time data integration and intangible asset value. The utilization of the blockchain, AI, and trustworthy software brings real value to companies regarding accuracy and compliance. To fill gaps in cross-border reporting, new technical interventions and internationally accepted standards should be introduced to ensure comparability and transparency.

4.1 Implications for Theory

The results of this investigation significantly amplify what is already known about financial reporting by attempting to fill in some of the theoretical dossier left vacant by the emergence of e-commerce and digital business models. E-commerce itself defines the environment in which a particular set of accounting concepts will show their weaknesses; that is, these concepts facing fast-paced technological developments cannot keep up with the required theoretical developments (Abuali et al., 2024). Essentially, both implementation and perception of financial accountability need to shift to accommodate the digital company models. For example, Gao et al. (2023) chime with the resource-based approach in proving that digital marketing and e-commerce indeed are tools to improve sustainability and financial performance during global turmoil. That proves a point about the need for theories which would embed digital capability as a core asset into financial reporting frameworks.

Bari et al. (2023) point out that the relationship between digital business models and financial reporting procedures explicitly shows where traditional frameworks fail to capture the subtleties of e-commerce. The authors stress that it is high time that attention is paid to developing theories that account for the particularities of digital commerce arising from issues such as the value of intangible assets or the integration of real-time data.

According to Gashi and Vardari (2025a), developments with a sustainability focus are showing ways how AI and DLT may be adopted to harmonize the financial reporting with international sustainability objectives. These revelations also allow theoretical advancements whereby environmental, social, and governance (ESG) factors can be integrated into digital platform financial reporting. Moreover, Gashi and Vardari (2025b) provide an explanation of how data governance supports the resistance and innovation of financial reporting through data quality. This study also develops a theoretical framework for analyzing how leading technologies such as blockchain and artificial intelligence could be used in order to provide more accurate, flexible, and transparent e-commerce financial frameworks.

4.2 Implications for Practice

The tendencies of online companies could be improved in financial reporting processes by adopting those strategies that lead toward accuracy, regulatory compliance, and technological leverage. Real-time financial reporting also strengthens decision-making through the timely and accurate presentation of data that enhances investor confidence. As noted by Trigo et al. (2014), this change toward real-time reports improved corporate governance and made companies more appealing to institutional investors. This in turn means that e-commerce accounting can be managed effectively only if the respective firms have duly employed relevant and reliable accounting software which meets their operational requirements. Smaller companies often employ affordable technologies, such as for example Microsoft Excel; whereas larger organizations are able to afford advanced data integration and scalability through SAP ERP (Mladenović et al., 2023). This software guarantees tax compliance across jurisdictions, automates repetitive tasks, and expedites the reconciliation process (Kosadi et al., 2021).

Therefore, workforce training will be a key element in strengthening the digital skills of accounting professionals. A complete training program that addresses the lack of technical skills and further promotes AI and other digital technologies would enhance the efficiency and accuracy of financial reporting much more (Yarmoliuk et al., 2024). This is particularly important for MSMEs, which need focused interventions to overcome various technical and poor adoption rates obstacles (Oktaviani et al., 2023). Financial reporting systems should incorporate digital financial instruments in order to enhance both the accuracy and efficiency of the processes. Automated systems will integrate the transaction data from many platforms and assist in enhancing decision-making and operational efficiency. As Kosadi et al. (2021) and Alrawashedh et al. (2024) pointed out, such solutions are important in multi-platform environments to weigh online sales data against the standards of financial reporting.

Such accuracy and transparency can be further improved with the help of the latest technology, including blockchain and artificial intelligence. Blockchain reduces the possibilities of fraud and increases compliance by providing safe and immutable financial records (Kerrouche & Belouadah, 2025). AI-driven technologies are used for real-time predictive analytics and adaptive reporting to meet the ever-evolving needs caused by e-commerce (Gashi & Vardari, 2025b). The dependability of financial reporting systems can also be improved through strategic investments in IT infrastructure. Investing in secure IT systems can contribute to improving data accuracy and enabling companies to stay compliant with constantly changing regulatory requirements Abuali et al. (2024). Coordinating financial reporting processes with digital trade activities can further help organizations achieve higher levels of accuracy and improve overall performance. Practical ways of improving financial reporting in e-commerce will involve real-time reporting, solid digital tools, workforce development, and innovative technology such as blockchain and artificial intelligence. These steps will eventually position businesses for long-term success, guarantee compliance, enhance transparency, and build trust among the stakeholders (Gashi et al., 2025; Gashi & Vardari, 2025a).

4.3 Addressing Gaps in the Literature

Much has to be learnt on how to modify the digital accounting procedures to suit international e-commerce requirements. Said Said and Ali (2023) cite a need for further studies on the establishment of a framework on the challenges facing cross-border financial reporting. The divergence in tax compliance and accounting laws of nations also complicates transparency and comparability. This would include state-of-the-art technologies such as blockchain and artificial intelligence. The focus should be on the harmonization of international standards. In this respect, the framework is going to make sure there is seamless cross-border financial reporting, matching with the ever-evolving face of e-commerce, hence engendering confidence among international players.

5 RECOMMENDATIONS

The enhanced financial reporting systems need to be integrated into state-of-the-art technologies in blockchain and artificial intelligence for better accuracy and transparency. Solutions given to SMEs have to keep in mind resource constraints and digital literacy weaknesses. There could also be a need for uniform global policy measures that address cross-border discrepancies, ensure compliance, and encourage innovation. Sustainability indicators must be integrated with the guidelines of ESG to help in resilience building.

5.1 Framework for Improved Financial Reporting

To create and apply new, innovative, technologically sound models for digitally trading commodities, the basic norms like IFRS need to be changed to create more advanced structures for financial reporting in e-commerce. According to Kosadi et al. (2021), reconciliation of transaction data on various platforms like social media and e-commerce websites can only be guaranteed through integrated solutions for financial reporting. For improved accuracy, transparency, and security, designing frameworks to accommodate the unique necessities of e-commerce using the current technological advancement that is blockchain, artificial intelligence should be developed. Abuali et al. (2024) add that the applicability of frameworks should be extended to the contexts of contemporary digital trade settings to utilize secure systems of IT by managing specific obstacles in the process of reporting within e-commerce. Gashi and Vardari (2025b) assert that AI and blockchain-based data governance frameworks cut errors and hence offer reliable financial insights that build confidence among stakeholders.

Despite the different limitations of resources and digital illiteracy in the framework of SMEs, e-commerce technology adoption must be encouraged. Almuwallad and Alhumoudi 2024 suggest scalable frameworks suited for microenterprise needs, ensuring compliance with international standards and encouraging integration into the digital economy. Sustainability criteria need to be included in the financial reporting for the objectives of long-term performance and resilience. For instance, Gao et al. (2023) layout models that assist a firm in integrating its activities with ESG principles through a combination of sustainability-oriented indictors with measures of financial performance. In the development of such models, collaboration among various stakeholders becomes vital. Regulators, IT companies, and business leaders may all help in making models workable, flexible, and taking into account operational and geographical peculiarities until recently noticed in the literature (Gashi, 2021). Taking inspiration from Said and Ali (2023), consolidated international standards would promote consistency across different jurisdictions to make financial reporting more comparable and useful for stakeholders and analysts.

5.2 Leveraging Technology for Financial Reporting

In the face of the ever-evolving digital economy, the accuracy, scalability, and security of financial reporting systems need enhancement with the latest technologies such as artificial intelligence, blockchain, and big data. AI-based solutions improve decision-making by providing automation of operations in real time (Yarmoliuk et al., 2024). It also allows for quick responses of e-commerce firms to market fluctuations that are possible through the addition of predictive and adaptive capabilities that are enabled by a subset of artificial intelligence known as machine learning. Blockchain ensures that the processing of data is secure, fraud risks are reduced, transparency is ensured, and transaction records are immutable. According to Abuali et al. (2024), blockchain allows validation and the security of financial data, hence making the stakeholders trust blockchain more. In addition, the integration of blockchain technology into financial reporting facilitates compliance with international standards and simplifies complex reconciliations of transactions (Kerrouche & Belouadah, 2025). Big data analytics offers numerous advantages, including enabling companies to manage vast volumes of financial data and glean insights from it. These technologies enhance resource optimization, decision-making, and reporting in real time (Gashi et al., 2025). The scalability required for e-commerce platforms managing large amounts of transaction data is ensured by utilizing Big Data in financial reporting systems (Gao et al., 2023).

Table 2. Steps for security and reliability in financial reporting

Steps for security and reliability	Details
Adopt secure IT Infrastructures	Implement robust cybersecurity measures, including encryption, firewalls, and intrusion detection systems, to protect financial data from breaches (Abuali et al., 2024).
Integrate advanced technologies	Use blockchain to ensure data integrity, AI for error detection, and Big Data for real-time analytics, as recommended by Bari et al. (2023).
Ensure system interoperability	Develop systems that seamlessly integrate payment platforms, accounting tools, and reporting systems to streamline financial operations (Kosadi et al., 2021).
Invest in employee training	Train staff to effectively use AI, blockchain, and Big Data tools, addressing skill gaps and promoting efficient adoption (Oktaviani et al., 2023).
Prioritize compliance	Align reporting systems with global standards, such as IFRS, to maintain consistency and regulatory adherence across jurisdictions (Said & Ali, 2023).
Monitor and update systems	Regularly evaluate and upgrade technologies to address evolving risks, improve performance, and adapt to regulatory changes (Gashi & Vardari, 2025a).

The road map provides a systematic approach that improves security and reliability in financial reporting in e-environments. Such infrastructure must be secured using advanced information technologies (for example, firewalls, and encryption) from online attackers targeting financial data (Abuali et al., 2024). Integration of technologies such as blockchain, artificial intelligence, and big data adds a layer of transparency and allows for real-time analysis that enhances the efficiency and accuracy of reporting (Bari et al., 2023). The interoperability of the systems for integrating accounting tools with payment platforms enhances the way operational procedures comply with international standards (Kosadi et al., 2021). Periodic monitoring and upgrades of technologies help respond to emerging threats and regulatory requirements, but training to enhance staff technical skills is paramount to the effective deployment of those technologies (Oktaviani et al., 2023) (Gashi & Vardari, 2025a). These steps provide a firm foundation for trustworthy and secure financial reporting over the Internet.

5.3 Policy and Regulatory Recommendations

Financial accounting for e-commerce is an international proposition. The task of reducing divergence and ensuring compliance for cross-border trade involves harmonizing the tax laws and reporting standards of various governments. As pointed out by Gashi and Vardari (2025a), the regulations that allow for the introduction of technology into financial reporting systems must take priority, namely with regard to blockchain or artificial intelligence. These frameworks must also address transparency, digital inclusion, and data privacy issues. Such international regulations will also promote sustainable practices in digital finance as well as foster innovation and fairness within the world digital economy, alongside assisting corporations in handling regulatory requirements.

6 CONCLUSION

Financial reporting has been fundamentally altered by e-commerce, thus calling for a change in the conventional frameworks and the adoption of tech-based solutions such as blockchain, artificial intelligence, and big data, which will maximize efficiency, accuracy, and transparency. This chapter highlights the need for worldwide harmonization, fills in theoretical gaps, and presents practical implications. Future research could consider new technologies whereby digital financial reporting, pertaining regulatory frameworks, and sustainability measures are concerned.

6.1 Summary of Key Findings

The present chapter outlines the manner by which e-commerce modifies financial reporting systems and how existing frameworks should be adapted to fit the needs of digital business models (Gashi & Vardari, 2025a). Bari et al. (2023) added that paramount to realizing an improved financial reporting system in terms of accuracy, efficiency, and transparency are emerging technologies such as blockchain, artificial intelligence, and big data. Such technologies really flourish, ensuring stakeholders' confidence in their international standards and real-time data aggregation (Gashi & Vardari, 2025b). Another major hindrance being deliberated in the chapter includes the valuation of intangible assets and the dissonance between international trade regulations (Said & Ali, 2023). These barriers need to be ironed to ensure that some common arrangements at the international level, synchronizing tax laws against reporting standards, guarantee that enterprises may operate seamlessly from one jurisdiction to another (Abuali et al., 2024).

6.2 Contributions of the Chapter

The chapter makes great theoretical and practical contributions to the fields of e-commerce and financial reporting. Theoretically, it fills the gap between e-commerce platform rising needs and traditional financial reporting scheme, like IFRS. Great insights are created concerning transparency, credibility, and timely disclosure from the view of advanced technologies like AI, blockchain, and big data. These became relevant in the context of digital business models (Gashi & Vardari, 2025a). It claims that these frameworks need to be altered to accommodate digital change and challenges many established accounting standards with regard to cross-border compliance and the valuation of intangible assets (Said & Ali, 2023).

6.3 Directions for Future Research

Future research needs to focus on new needs for financial reporting in e-commerce and digital transformation. Inspired by Alrawashedh et al. (2024), research can see how modern technologies such as blockchain and machine learning can help e-commerce financial reporting meet regional challenges. These may enhance transparency and ease the process of reporting in respect to international business. Following touch points for international reporting requirements similar to the ones proposed for e-commerce by Gashi (2021), who argued for the significance of qualitative research in grasping cause-and-effect relationships, would enhance our understanding of the nuanced interactions between these evolving business models and traditional accounting systems. Such investigations would provide nuanced insights into the interactions between these changing company models and conventional accounting systems. Also emphasized in Gashi (2024) is how critical regulatory frameworks are for upholding ethical and transparent financial processes. Here, future studies may explore how ethical and regulatory paradigms can address the distinctive challenges posed by e-commerce financial reporting, especially in data protection, anti-fraud, and accountability, among others.

To further the study on the technological function of integrating sustainability criterion into financial reporting. AI and DLT on the other hand, when embedded into ESG reporting, could give some useful insights for ensuring sustainability and transparency in digital business practices, according to Gashi and Vardari (2025a). Finally, research could concentrate on how AI and DLT can catalyze resilience and innovation in e-commerce practices as Gashi and Vardari (2025b) recommend a further exploration of these technologies in strengthening data governance (DG) in financial reporting.

REFERENCES

Abuali, A., Alrefaei, A. A., Aljohani, S. A., Aloufi, I. N., Ghabban, F., Ameerbakhsh, O., Alfadli, I., Al-Shehri, A. H., Fallatah, N. A., & Younis, H. A. (2024). The impact of e-commerce on traditional businesses in Saudi Arabia. *Journal of Service Science and Management, 17*(4), 354–366. DOI: 10.4236/jssm.2024.174018

Ageeva, O., Karp, M., & Sidorov, A. (2021). The application of digital technologies in financial reporting and auditing. In Popkova, E. G., & Sergi, B. S. (Eds.), *Smart technologies" for society, state and economy. ISC 2020* (Vol. 155, pp. 1481–1490). Springer., DOI: 10.1007/978-3-030-59126-7_167

Almuwallad, H., & Alhumoudi, H. (2024). The impact of e-commerce on organizational and financial performance in SMEs: Evidence from Saudi Arabia. *International Journal of Business and Management, 19*(4), 1–12. DOI: 10.5539/ijbm.v19n4p1

Alonge, E. O., Dudu, O. F., & Alao, O. B.Enoch O. AlongeOritsematosan Faith DuduOlakunle Babatunde Alao. (2024). The impact of digital transformation on financial reporting and accountability in emerging markets. *International Journal of Science and Technology Research Archive, 7*(2), 25–49. DOI: 10.53771/ijstra.2024.7.2.0061

Alrawashedh, N. H., Zuraiqat, B., Abdallah, A., & Abushareah, M. (2024). Accounting and its impact on e-commerce in Jordan. *Journal of Financial Accounting and Management, 17*(7), 1098–1108. DOI: 10.5281/zenodo.6923275

Ami, A. S., Syafitri, L., & Meiriasari, V. (2023). The effect of e-commerce and the use of accounting information systems on the revenue cycle of micro, small, and medium enterprises (Study on culinary MSMEs in Prabumulih City). *Journal of Humanities* [JHSSB]. *Social Sciences and Business, 3*(1), 68–76. DOI: 10.32535/jhssb.v3i1.2720

Ardakani, M. M., Ansari, A., Kia, M. R., Mousavion, S. A., & Pourhashemi, S. O. (2024). The effect of the adoption of e-commerce and digital marketing on the firm and sustainability performance of companies. *Journal of Soft Computing and Decision Support Systems, 11*(1), 23–38. DOI: 10.1016/j.jsds.2024.02.005

Atanassova, A. (2018). Accounting problems in e-commerce. *Ekonomiczne Problemy Usług, 2*(131/1), 19–30. https://doi.org/DOI: 10.18276/epu.2018.131/1-02

Bari, M. H., Arif, N. U. M., Hasan, M. M., & Maraj, M. A. A. (2023). Comparative analysis of digital payment platforms and e-commerce giants: A five-year performance and strategic development study of Visa, Mastercard, Amazon, and eBay. *Global Mainstream Journal of Innovation. Engineering & Emerging Technology*, *2*(2), 1–10. DOI: 10.5281/zenodo.6923275

Ben Slama, F., Oussii, A. A., & Klibi, M. F. (2022). The rough road towards accounting harmonization of a developing country with a French accounting culture. *Accounting Research Journal*, *35*(4), 490–507. DOI: 10.1108/ARJ-02-2021-0075

Durani, F. (2023). The relationship between e-finance and e-commerce: Evidence from 100 countries. In Hannoon, A., & Mahmood, A. (Eds.), *Artificial intelligence, internet of things, and society 5.0* (Vol. 1113, pp. 25–45). Springer., DOI: 10.1007/978-3-031-43300-9_2

European Banking Authority. (2021). *Report on the use of digital platforms in the EU banking and payments sector* (EBA/REP/2021/26). European Banking Authority. https://eba.europa.eu

Fleming, I. (2022). *Optimization of financial performance in e-commerce* (Doctoral dissertation, Walden University). Walden Dissertations and Doctoral Studies Collection. https://scholarworks.waldenu.edu/dissertations

Gao, J., Siddik, A. B., Abbas, S. K., Hamayun, M., Masukujjaman, M., & Alam, S. S. (2023). Impact of e-commerce and digital marketing adoption on the financial and sustainability performance of MSMEs during the COVID-19 pandemic: An empirical study. *Sustainability (Basel)*, *15*(2), 1594. DOI: 10.3390/su15021594

Gashi, K. (2021). The relationship between SME's organizational culture and training and development as a human resource management practice. *Journal Global Policy and Governance*, *10*(2), 139–161. DOI: 10.14666/2194-7759-10-2-008

Gashi, K. (2024). The future of robo-advisors in management. In *Robo-Advisors in Management* (pp. 35–56). IGI Global., DOI: 10.4018/979-8-3693-2849-1.ch003

Gashi, K., Tafolli, F., & Vardari, L. (2025). Management: Revolutionizing services through data-driven management and tech-strat fusion. In Jain, V., Gupta, N., Agarwal, A., Chetty, G., & Kannan, R. (Eds.), *Innovate to integrate: Data-driven management and tech-strat fusion unveiled*. Emerald Group Publishing.

Gashi, K., & Vardari, L. (2025a). Data quality and governance. In S. Kautish, K. Sood, & S. Grima (Eds.), *Strategy analytics for business resilience and value creation* (Chap. 6). Emerald Studies in Finance, Insurance, and Risk Management (ESFIRM). Emerald Publishing.

Gashi, K., & Vardari, L. (2025b). The role of technology, AI, ML and DLT in sustainable finance and a green economy. In Muradov, A., Ahmadov, F., Hajiyeva, N., Sood, K., & Grima, S. (Eds.), *Sustainable development and green innovation: Managing risk through interdisciplinary approaches and policy strategies*. Emerald Publishing.

Gazieva, L. R., Magomaev, T. R., & Magomaeva, L. R. (2021). The impact of e-commerce on the digital economy. *European Proceedings of Social and Behavioural Sciences*, *98*, 122–126. DOI: 10.15405/epsbs.2021.03.16

Gurendrawati, E., Musyaffi, A. M., Wolor, C. W., Khairunnisa, H., Wibowo, S. N., Fuzianah, E., & Faturachman, M. (2024). An empirical study on the barriers to digital financial reporting adoption among non-adopting SMEs in Indonesia. *Journal of System and Management Sciences*, *14*(3), 96–114. DOI: 10.33168/JSMS.2024.0306

Gusti, G. P., & da, H. (2023). The important role of e-commerce in forming community financial literacy. *Business* [BOSOC]. *Organizações & Sociedade*, *1*(1), 26–29. DOI: 10.26480/bosoc.01.2023.26.29

Hýblová, E. (2019). The current problems of harmonization of accounting for small and medium-sized enterprises. *Ekonomska Istrazivanja*, *32*(1), 604–621. DOI: 10.1080/1331677X.2018.1561317

Išoraitė, M., & Miniotienė, N. (2018). Electronic commerce: Theory and practice. *Integrated Journal of Business and Economics*, *2*(2), 194–200. DOI: 10.33019/ijbe.v2i2.78

Jabor, L., & Hamdan, A. (2023). Digitalization in accounting and financial reporting quality: Literature review. In El Khoury, R., & Nasrallah, N. (Eds.), *Emerging trends and innovation in business and finance* (pp. 821–838). Springer., DOI: 10.1007/978-981-99-6101-6_59

Kerrouche, N., & Belouadah, F. (2025). Digital transformation and the quality of financial reports: Evidence from Saudi listed companies. *International Journal of Data and Network Science*, *9*(1), 243–252. DOI: 10.5267/j.ijdns.2024.7.012

Kosadi, F., Ginting, W., & Alamsyah, M. I. (2021). Online sales and payment in SMEs financial reporting preparation. *Jurnal Reviu Akuntansi dan Keuangan, 11*(1), 204-223. https://doi.org/DOI: 10.22219/jrak.v11i1.15164

Kosadi, F., Ginting, W., & Merliana, V. (2021). Digital receipts of online transactions in the reconciliation process and the preparation of financial reports. *Journal of Indonesian Economy and Business*, *36*(1), 31–50. DOI: 10.22146/jieb.59884

Mladenovic, M., Dukic, T., & Popovic, G. (2023). Analysis of financial reporting platforms based on the PIPRECIA-S method. *Journal of Process Management and New Technologies, 11*(3-4), 95–104. DOI: 10.5937/jpmnt11-48186

Okpo, D. S. A., & Eshiet, U. E. (2023). Digital accounting practices and quality of financial reports. *GPH-International Journal of Business Management, 6*(6), 21–35. DOI: 10.5281/zenodo.8103873

Oktaviani, N. F., Yusnita, R. T., Yuniar, E. S., Listanti, Y. F., Tujjahra, D. R., & Pamungkas, M. D. (2023). Analysis of the use of digital payment and financial report applications in SMSE. *Journal of International Conference Proceedings, 6*(6), 286–294. DOI: 10.32535/jicp.v6i6.2720

Probowulan, D., & Ardianto, A. (2024). Internet financial reporting disclosure index of e-commerce businesses on social media. *International Studies of Accounting and Finance, 31*(2), Article e1550. https://doi.org/DOI: 10.1002/isaf.1550

Said, S. M. S., & Ali, S. I. M. (2023). The role of digital accounting in improving the quality of financial reporting information and its impact on the accuracy of financial analysts' predictions: A field study. *World Research of Business Administration Journal, 3*(3), 175–201. DOI: 10.56830/WRBA11202304

Trigo, A., Belfo, F., & Pérez Estébanez, R. (2014). Accounting information systems: The challenge of real-time reporting. *Procedia Technology, 16*, 118–127. DOI: 10.1016/j.protcy.2014.10.075

Türegün, N. (2020). Accounting for e-commerce sector. *International Journal of Critical Accounting, 11*(5), 429–438. DOI: 10.1504/IJCA.2020.111564

World Bank Group. (2020). *Embedding digital finance in e-commerce platforms during the COVID-19 pandemic: Early assessment of the impact of COVID-19 on e-commerce and the provision of digital financial services for micro, small, and medium enterprises and low-income consumers*. Finance, Competitiveness & Innovation Global Practice. International Bank for Reconstruction and Development / The World Bank. https://www.worldbank.org

Xia, Q. (2016). Study on the impact of electronic commerce on the development of financial accounting. *4th International Education, Economics, Social Science, Arts,Sports and Management Engineering Conference (IEESASM 2016)*, 955–957. https://doi.org/DOI: 10.2991/ieesasm-16.2016.102

Yarmoliuk, O., Abramov, A., Mulyk, T., Smirnova, N., & Ponomarova, N. (2024). Digital technologies in accounting and reporting: Benefits, limitations, and possible risks. *Amazonia Investiga, 13*(74), 323–333. DOI: 10.34069/AI/2024.74.02.27

Chapter 5
Assess the Challenges and Incentives for Companies to Incorporate Green Financing Into Their CSR

Leelawati Leelawati
https://orcid.org/0009-0005-2675-1720
St. Andrews Institute of Technology and Management, India

A. V. Senthil Kumar
https://orcid.org/0000-0002-8587-7017
Hindusthan College of Arts and Science

ABSTRACT

It is becoming more widely acknowledged that businesses can support economic growth and environmental objectives by incorporating green finance into their corporate social responsibility (CSR) programs. This study evaluates the incentives and obstacles that businesses face when implementing green funding into their CSR frameworks. Furthermore, businesses may be deterred from undertaking these efforts by the scarcity of green funding sources and the possible harm to their brand that comes with green washing. The move toward green finance is being propelled by a number of incentives in spite of these obstacles. The chapter highlights the significance of strategic frameworks that can assist companies in overcoming obstacles and strengthening their commitment to sustainability through green financing in corporate social responsibility by analysing these incentives and challenges. The chapter employs a conceptual approach. Various websites, journals, and research

DOI: 10.4018/979-8-3373-0887-6.ch005

articles provide the pertinent information.

INTRODUCTION

Green financing has become a crucial component in coordinating business strategy with social and environmental objectives as the world economy moves toward sustainability. Corporate Social Responsibility (CSR) programs that include green financing present a range of incentives and problems for businesses. This chapter examines these relationships, offering a thorough understanding of the obstacles businesses face and the factors that encourage them to use green financing techniques.

Corporate social responsibility has developed extensively since its first conception. In the past, it was considered primarily in terms of philanthropy and community relations, but today the CSR involves a complete philosophy to deal with the influences of a firm on society and environment. This development indicates transfer of expectations about business work by society, as stakeholders keep the corporations rapidly for stringent expectations that they have to fix their environment and social impacts. The development of CSR can be detected through many different stages. In the early 20th century, CSR was largely philanthropist, which featured charitable donations and community support. The 1960s and 1970s emerged a more formal approach to CSR, in which companies began to develop specific policies and practices. By the 1990s, CSR had developed into a strategic view, in which companies recognized the ability to align between social responsibility and commercial success. The most important development of CSR has been observed in the 21st century, the idea has become the mainstream in more and more business strategies. The century is characterized by raising awareness about global issues such as climate change, natural resources and social injustice. As a result, CSR has gone beyond its traditional boundaries to incorporate environmental stability, supply chain management, human rights and moral leadership issues. The latest development of CSR is its convergence with financial decision making and capital distribution-ie, green financing. This is a dramatic change for CSR to increase a cost center or reputation that is to look at it as a source of financial performance and long -term value construction.

Emergence of Green Financing

Green Financing has emerged as an important component of the global reaction, especially to environmental challenges, especially climate change. This includes a series of financial devices, products and services designed to support environmentally durable activities, projects and businesses. The growth of green financing has been operated by increasing the opportunities presented by the increasing recognition of financial risks associated with environmental decline and the infection for the low carbon economy. The development of green financing can be detected with several major milestones. The launch of the first Green Bond in 2007 by the European Investment Bank and the World Bank took an important step in building financial instruments dedicated to environmental projects. The establishment of the Green Climate Fund under the United Nations Framework Convention on Climate Change (UNFCCC) in 2010 legalized green finance as a global priority. The 2015 Paris Agreement represented a watershed moment for green financing, which had a clear acceptance of the need to align financial flow with low carbon and climate-length development. After this, after increasing commitments from both public and private financial institutions to support green investments. The growth of environment, social and governance (ESG) investment has further intensified the development of green financing, reaching unprecedented levels with property under management in ESG funds. Recently, the spread of green bonds, sustainability-linked loans, green investment funds and carbon finance. mechanisms have seen the proliferation of green finance instruments. These developments reflect the increasing recognition addressing the environmental challenge.

CSR integration of green finance Integration of green finance in CSR framework represents the natural development of both concepts. As CSR has expanded beyond philanthropy to include strategic approaches to manage social and environmental impacts, it is rapidly intended with corporate financial decision making. In addition, as green finance has developed from niche products to mainstream financial instruments, it has become a powerful mechanism through which companies can conduct their environmental commitments. This integration creates powerful coordination. The CSR provides the strategic framework and the stakeholder the necessary attention to meaningful environmental action, while the green finance provides the financial mechanism required to implement and score environmental initiatives. Together, they enable companies to align their stability commitments with their financial strategies and capital allocation decisions. Integration of green finance in CSR appears in many major practices. Companies are rapidly releasing green bonds to fund specific environmental projects, securing stability-linked loans with interest rates of stability, establishing internal carbon pricing mechanisms, and developing green investment norms for their treasury operations. These practices reflect a fundamental change from viewing environmental ideas, as to identify their mutual relations apart from financial decisions. For many companies, this integration represents the opportunity to increase both their environmental performance and their financial returns. This allows them to use capital at favorable rates, manage environmental risks more effectively, give capitalization and strength on green trade opportunities.

THEORETICAL FRAMEWORK

Stakeholder Theory

The stakeholder theory provides a fundamental framework for understanding the integration of green finance in CSR. Mainly R. Developed by Edward Freeman, this theory suggests that companies should manage their business not only for the benefit of shareholders, but also for all stakeholders that may be influenced or affected by the company's operation. These stakeholders include employees, customers, suppliers, community and environment themselves. Through the lens of stakeholder theory, green finance in CSR can be understood as a response to the expectations and demands of many stakeholders. Investors rapidly consider environmental performance in their investment decisions, customers prefer environmentally responsible products and services, employees want alignment of corporate values and their personal concerns about environmental issues, and expect community companies to reduce their environmental impacts. The stakeholder principle suggests that companies effectively address these diverse expectations through green finance initiative are likely to have a strong relationship with key stakeholders, leading to their long -term viability and success. This provides a justification for moving from more active strategies to move beyond compliance-based approaches to environmental management that creates shared values for many stakeholders. However, the stakeholder principle also highlights the challenges of balanced by potentially competitive stakeholders. For example, expectations of short -term profit from some investors can struggle with the need for long-term investment in environmental initiatives. Companies should navigate these stresses through communication about the value of effective stake engagement and green financing approaches.

Validity Theory

Validity theory provides valuable insight why companies integrate green financing in their CSR framework. This theory suggests that the organizations constantly want to ensure that they work within the limits and norms of their respective societies - that is, they aim to establish and maintain their validity. From this point of view, green finance can be understood as a response to changing social expectations about corporate environmental responsibilities. Since climate change and other environmental issues have gained prominence in public discourse, the "social contract" between businesses and society has developed to include expectations about corporate environmental leadership. Companies that fail to meet these expectations risk losing their validity, resulting in regulatory challenges, consumer boycott, or difficulties in attracting and maintaining talent. By integrating green finance in its CSR framework, companies indicate their commitment to address environmental concerns, which can maintain or increase their validity. Green bonds, sustainability-linked loans, and other visible green finance initiatives serve as tangible performances of this commitment, helping companies to align with social expectations. Validity theory also helps explain why companies in environmental sensitive industries, such as oil and gas or mining are often most active in developing green financing initiatives. These companies face more validity challenges related to their environmental influences and therefore have a strong incentive to display their commitment to environmental responsibility. Institutional principle Institutional theory provides a framework to understand how organizational practices, including green finance,

Institutional Theory

The institutional theory provides a framework for understanding how organizational practices including green finance in CSR are established and spread to industries. This theory emphasizes that organizations are affected by their institutional environment, including regulatory structures, industry criteria and cultural expectations. Through the lens of institutional theory, adoption of green financing can be understood as a reaction to institutional pressures. These pressures include tremendous pressure (e.g. regulatory requirements for environmental disclosure), standard pressure (e.g. industry standard for green finance), and copying pressure (e.g. companies' tendency to mimic the practices of successful contestants). The theory helps explain why green finance practices often spread in predicted patterns in industries. Initial adoption creates institutional speed by industry leaders or in response to regulatory changes, leading to widely adoption of practices being generalized and expected. This is evident in the rapid growth of dynamic green bonds, which have spread from their early use by multilateral development banks to become standard financing equipment for corporations in many areas. Institutional principles also highlight the role of institutional entrepreneurs in promoting the integration of green financing in CSR. These may include progressive companies that lead the new approaches, industry associations that develop standards and outlines, or investors who pressurize for changes through their allocation decisions.

Resource-Based View

Financing in CSR, focusing on how companies can develop unique abilities and resources that provide competitive benefits. According to this theory, permanent competitive advantage arises from resources that are valuable, rare, incompletely exemplary, and non-popular. Through the RBV lens, green financing capabilities can be understood as a possible sources of competitive benefits. Companies that develop expertise in assessing environmental impacts, measuring stability performance, structuring green financial instruments or managing environmental risks can gain benefits that are difficult for the contestants to repeat. For example, a company that develops sophisticated internal carbon pricing mechanisms can take more effective investment decisions than competitors with a lack of capacity. Similarly, a company with strong relations with green investors can enjoy the preferential access of capital for environmentally beneficial projects. RBV also highlights the importance of supplemented assets in realizing the benefits of green financing. These may include organizational structures that facilitate stability and cross-functional cooperation between finance teams, governance mechanisms, ensuring accountability for environmental performance, or information systems that enable effective measurements and reporting environmental effects. This theoretical perspective suggests that the integration of green finance in CSR should not only be seen as a compliance exercise or public relations effort, but as an opportunity to develop specific organizational abilities that create long -term competitive benefits.

INCENTIVES FOR GREEN FINANCING IN CSR

Financial and Economic Incentives

The integration of green financing into CSR frameworks offers several direct and indirect financial benefits that serve as powerful incentives for corporate adoption. These economic motivations often form the core business case for green financing initiatives.

Cost of Capital Advantages

Companies with strong environmental performance and green financing framework often enjoy the low cost of capital.

This benefit appears in many ways:

- Green bonds often priced at a premium ("Greenium"), resulting in low financing costs for issuers.
- Loans associated with stability provide the ability to reduce interest rate on completing environmental goals.
- Companies with strong environmental ratings usually face low cost when reaching capital markets. For example, an analysis of 2020 by Blackrock found that during the market stress period, permanent companies demonstrated about 5% outperforms compared to their low sustainable counterparts,

indicating a lower risk perception by investors. Operating efficiency and cost reduction: Green financing often reduces funds consumption, waste and emissions, resulting in operating cost saving:

- Energy Efficiency Initiative reduces utility expenses
- Water conservation projects cost low water • Waste reduction reduces program disposal fees • The initiative of a circular economy reduces input costs through reuse and recycling A study by McKiny found that companies implementing resource productivity initiative usually lead to a 20–30% decrease in resource costs with a peback period of less than three years.

Tax encouragement and subsidy: Many courts provide tax incentives, grants and subsidies for environmental profitable investment:

- Tax credit for renewable investment
- Quick depreciation for energy-efficient devices.
- Direct subsidy for emission reduction technologies
- Preferred tax treatment for green buildings These incentives can greatly improve the economics of environmentally concentrated investments, making green finance more attractive. Mitigation of future carbon pricing effects: As the carbon pricing mechanisms expand globally, green financing which reduces carbon emissions provides a defense against future costs:
- Companies with low carbon intensity reduced to exposure to carbon taxes or emission trading schemes.
- Initial investment in decarbonisation as an increase in carbon prices can provide "first-lover benefits".
- Internal carbon pricing associated with green finance helps prepare for external carbon regulation According to WorldBank data, the initiative of carbon pricing now covers about 22% of global greenhouse gas emissions, which expands the annual coverage.

Investor Demand and Market Valuation

Strong investor demand for environmental performance may positively evaluate:

- Companies with strong environmental management often trading on evaluation premiums
- ESG-centric funds represent the growing pool of capital in search of environmental artists
- Green finance initiative can expand the potential investor base, especially with the mandate of stability among institutional investors A meta-analysis

of over 2,000 empirical studies found that 63% showed positive relations between ESG factors and financial performance.

Table 1. Summarizes financial incentive to integrate green finance in CSR framework

Financial Incentive	Description	Potential Impact
Reduced cost of capital	Lower interest rates on green bonds and sustainability-linked loans	10-50 basis points reduction in financing costs
Operational cost savings	Reduced energy, water, waste, and material costs	20-30% reduction in resource-related operational expenses
Tax incentives and subsidies	Government financial support for green initiatives	Can improve project ROI by 5-25% depending on jurisdiction
Carbon pricing mitigation	Reduced exposure to current and future carbon taxes/regulations	Potential savings of $10-100 per ton of CO_2 equivalent avoided
Enhanced market valuation	Valuation premium for strong environmental performers	4-8% higher market valuation on average

Regulatory Compliance and Anticipation

Regulatory developments serve as powerful drivers for the integration of green financing into CSR strategies. Companies increasingly recognize that proactive approaches to environmental regulation can create strategic advantages and reduce compliance costs.

Current Regulatory Compliance

Current environmental rules already encourage green financing:

- Emission standards invarious industries require investment in cleaner technologies
- Waste management rules require reduction in waste and investing in proper disposal
- Energy efficiency standard retrofitting investment for buildings and equipment drives
- Extended manufacturers encourage responsibility regulations circular economy initiative The direct compliance cost related to these rules may be sufficient, it is estimated with the US EPA that the cost of major environmental regulations is more than $ 200 billion to US businesses.

Expectation of Future Rules

Perhaps more importantly, many companies are integrating green financing in their CSR strategies in anticipation of future regulatory development:

- Climate rules are expected to be more rigid in most courts.
- Extended manufacturer responsibility regulations are expanding in new product categories.
- Water use restrictions are likely to increase in water-stool areas.
- Biodiversity Protection Rules Emerging as a new area of focus Companies that estimate these regulatory trends can get significant benefits through initial adaptation and strategic status.

The transition regulator for more environmentally durable operations can occur at your own time rather than being forced to reduce costs and disruption.

Disclosure and Reporting Requirements

Environmental Disclosure Requirements are expanding globally:

- European Union Corporate Stability Reporting Instructions (CSRD) makes wide stability reporting mandatory
- Task Force on Climate-related financial revelations (TCFD) recommendations are being included in the regulatory structure
- Securities regulatory environmental disclosure requirements in many countries are increasing
- Stock exchange ESG listing requirements are implemented These disclosure requirements encourage companies to integrate green finance in their CSR strategies to ensure that they have positive development to report and can demonstrate progress against environmental goals.

Participation in Policy Development

Companies with advanced green financing approaches often have impact in regulatory development:

- Performing in environmental performance leadership policy provides credibility in discussion
- Experience with voluntary environmental initiative provides information about which approaches are practical

- Can facilitate engagement on regulatory issues with policy makers developed through CSR initiative This effect can help shape in ways that align with professional strategies and abilities, potentially create competitive benefits.

Liability Risk Reduction

Environmental liabilities represent important financial risks:

- Therapeutic cost for environmental damage can reach billions of dollars
- Legal liabilities for environmental impacts can result in adequate loss
- Director and officer liability for environmental issues is expanding in many courts Green finance initiatives that reduce environmental impacts can reduce these liability risks, protect and execute corporate assets.

Table 2. Outlines key regulatory drivers for green financing in CSR

Regulatory Driver	Examples	Business Implications
Emissions regulations	Carbon taxes, cap-and-trade systems, emission limits	Direct compliance costs, operational constraints
Resource efficiency regulations	Energy efficiency standards, water use limits	Equipment upgrade requirements, operational changes
Waste management regulations	Landfill taxes, banned substances, recycling mandates	Disposal costs, product redesign requirements
Disclosure requirements	CSRD, TCFD, SEC climate disclosure rules	Reporting costs, investor scrutiny, reputational impacts
Extended producer responsibility	Product take-back requirements, packaging regulations	End-of-life management costs, design implications
Liability regimes	Environmental damage remediation, climate litigation	Financial reserves, insurance costs, business continuity risks

REPUTATIONAL AND BRAND BENEFITS

For businesses, the advantages of incorporating green finance into CSR in terms of reputation and brand constitute important strategic motivations. A company's environmental credentials have a growing impact on its entire brand perception and corporate reputation as environmental consciousness among stakeholders, including investors, employees, and consumers, increases.

Consumer Preference and Loyalty

Environmental ideas are rapidly affecting consumer purchasing decisions:

- According to many consumer surveys, 60-70% consumers consider stability factors when purchasing.
- Millennials and generations consumers show especially strong priorities for brands environmentally responsible
- 5-25% price premium is rapid for displayant durable products in many markets.
- Consumer loyalty is strengthened by authentic environmental commitments supported by green financing Companies that effectively communicate their green finance initiative can translate environmental investments into consumer priority, potentially produce value premium command and strong brand loyalty.

Brand Discrimination

In crowded markets, environmental credentials supported by green financing can provide meaningful discrimination:

- Green Financing Signal Marketing Claim
- The third-party verification of green bonds and other equipment provides reliability
- Finant environmental projects funded through green finance makes compelling brand stories • Leadership in environmental financing can establish brands as progressive and further thinking This discrimination is particularly valuable in markets where functional product differences are minimal, making environmental credentials a decisive factor in consumer choice.

Figure 1. The relationship between green financing in CSR and brand value.

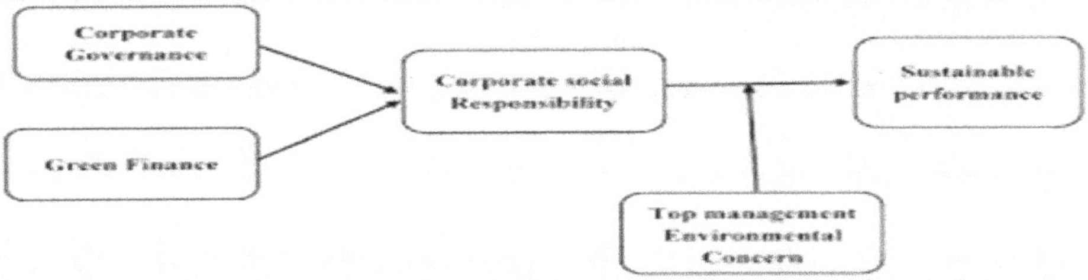

Media Coverage and Public Recognition

Green Financing initiative often produces positive media coverage:

- Innovative Green Financing approaches attract attention business and stability press attention.
- Environment Awards and Accreditation Programs highlight leadership in green financing.
- Including stability indices provides third-party verification and visibility
- Social media enhances positive environmental stories, expands reach beyond traditional coverage This coverage represents valuable earned media that increases brand visibility and reputation without direct advertising expenses.

Crisis Flexibility

Strong environmental credentials created through green financing can provide reputed flexibility during crises:

- Companies with strong environmental records often get more favorable treatment when events occur
- CSR initiative can facilitate communication during relationships established with environmental stakeholders developed through CSR initiative
- Performance commitment for environmental responsibility creates goodwill that can offset negative events It can significantly reduce the financial and prestigious effects of environmental events when it is flexibility.

Corporate Story and Purpose

The initiative of green financing contributes to hypnotizing corporate stories around the purpose:

- Environmental commitments supported by financial allocation decisions demonstrate authenticity
- Green finance provides tangible evidence of corporate values in action.
- Environmental initiative can have emotional relations with stakeholders.
- Objectives-operated stories supported by green financing enhance overall corporate reputation.

As stakeholders rapidly expected that companies clarify their objectives beyond profit, Green Financing provides important materials for these stories.

RISK MANAGEMENT

Climate Change Physical Risks

Green financing initiative often addresses physical risks related to climate change:

- Investment in climate-flexible infrastructure reduces vulnerability for excessive weather incidence
- Diversification of supply chains reduces dissolution risk from climatic effects
- Water conservation and management projects address rising water scatter concerns
- Adaptation measures protect facilities in weak places According to the Swiss Ray Institute, climate -related natural devastation caused an economic loss of about $ 190 billion globally in 2020, which highlights the materiality of these risks.

Infection Risk: Green Financing helps manage risks related to infection in low-carbon economy:

- Investment in energy efficiency and renewable energy reduces the reduction in contact with carbon pricing.
- Financing for product innovation supports adaptation for changing market demands.
- Portfolio diversification away from carbon-intensive assets reduces property risk trapped
- Gradually changes through planned green investment prevents forced changes.

To defeat the financial system (NGFS), the network estimates that a disorganized infection in the low-carbon economy can reduce global GDP by 2100 by 25% by 25%.

Regulatory and Compliance Risk

As discussed earlier, green financing helps develop regulatory risks:

- Active environmental investments reduce the risk of non-compliance with strict rules.
- Connect regulatory intelligence with policy makers through CSR initiative.
- Leadership in environmental performance provides more time to adapt to new requirements. • Documentation related to green finance supports reporting.

Major infractions can result in fines of millions or even billions of dollars, with the average environmental regulatory fine in the US exceeding $30,000.

Supply Chain Risks

Green Financing is often spread to supply chain management while addressing related risks:

- Suppliers reduce environmental compliance risks in the engagement program supply chain
- Resource efficiency initiative reduces the instability and availability in the price of raw materials
- Alternative material development reduces dependence on environmentally problematic inputs
- Circular economy initiative creates a closed-loop system that is less vulnerable to the supply of disruptions The CDP reports that the disruption of the supply chain costs companies to spend an average of $ 184 million annually, with environmental factors represent the increasing ratio of these disruption.

Litigation and Liability Risk

Green Financing that improves environmental performance may reduce litigation risk:

- Low emissions and pollution reduce the risk of environmental damage claims.
- Documentation of proper hard work through green finance processes provides legal defence.
- Green finance -related stakeholders may identify and address concerns before proceeding in engagement litigation.
- Transparent environmental reporting supports defence against securities litigation related to disclosure Climate -related litigation is increasing rapidly, in which the Grantham Research Institute is reporting doubling of climate cases between 2017 and 2020.

Financial System Risks

For financial institutions, Green Financing helps managing systemic environmental risks:

- ESG integration in borrowing and investment reduces portfolio exposure for environmental risks
- Green bonds and other equipment provide transparent environmental performance information
- Improves landscape analysis and stress test risk evaluation for environmental factors
- Diversification concentration reduces risk in green projects

ACCESS TO NEW MARKETS AND OPPORTUNITIES

The integration of green finance in CSR framework provides access to companies emerging markets and commercial opportunities related to environmental stability. This incentive has become rapidly important as the market has increased significantly for permanent products, services and investments.

Green Products and Services Markets

Green Financing is able to develop and expand Prasad in rapidly growing permanent markets: • The global market for environmental goods and services is more than $ 1 trillion annually

- Clean energy markets in many areas are growing by 15-20% annually
- Circular economy business models represent the opportunity of $ 4.5 trillion by 2030
- Green Building Material Market is estimated to reach $ 425 billion by 2027 By achieving dedicated funding to permanent innovation, companies can accelerate their entry into these high-development markets.

Public Procurement Opportunities

Governments rapidly include environmental criteria in procurement decisions:

- European Union's Green Public Procurement Program includes contracts of around € 1.8 trillion annually.
- The US federal government has established permanent purchase requirements for $ 650 billion in annual procurement.
- Many municipal and state/provincial governments have implemented green procurement policies.

- Environmental performance is becoming a separate factor in competitive bidding processes.

Companies with environmental initiative funded through green financing are often better deployed to compete for these contracts.

Sustainability-Focused Investment Flows

Green Financing connects companies to the growing pool of stability-centric capital:

- ESG-centric investment funds now more than $ 35 trillion globally.
- Green bonds reached $ 1.11 trillion to release cumulative by the end of 2022.
- Effect investing property has exceeded $ 700 billion.
- Sustainable Development Finance from multilateral institutions is more than $ 150 billion annually by developing green financing capabilities, companies can use these growing capital pools for expansion and innovation.

Partnership Opportunities

Green Financing initiative often provides strategic partnership:

- Public-private participation for the development of environmental infrastructure • Research collaboration with educational institutions on permanent technologies.
- Facing of industry consortia sectoral environmental challenges.
- NGO participation provides expertise and reliability for environmental initiative.

These participations can provide additional resources, expertise and access to the network that expand business opportunities.

First-Mover Advantages in Emerging Green Markets

Companies leading in green financing often protect benefits in newborn markets:

- Intellectual property development in emerging environmental technologies.
- Brand Association with new permanent categories.
- Customer loyalty before broad competition.
- Specialization and operational experience before market maturity.

These first-road advantages can cause sustainable competitive discrimination because markets develop.

Market Access Through Environmental Credentials

In some markets, environmental performance is becoming a condition for participation:

- Supply chain qualification requirements include rapid environmental norms.
- Products can act as environmental standard market access obstacles.
- Use of financial market can be accidental on environmental performance and disclosure.
- Consumers can exclude boycott and campaign effectively outdoor environmental artists Green financing that improves environmental performance helps to ensure continuous market access to the development of these requirements.

EMPLOYEE ENGAGEMENT AND TALENT ATTRACTION

Integration of green finance in CSR framework can significantly increase the employee engagement and improve the company's ability to attract and maintain top talent. As environmental consciousness increases, especially entering the workforce among younger generations, environmental credentials have become important factors in employment decisions.

Attraction of Purpose-Driven Talent

Green Financing Initiative Signs Authentic Environmental Commitment that attracts objective-oriented employees:

- 76% of Millennials consider the social and environmental commitments of the company when it is to decide where to work.
- 64% of professionals will not do jobs if the employer does not have strong CSR practices.
- Technical experts in high-manage.

Table 3. The risk management benefits of green financing in CSR

Risk Category	Examples	Mitigation Through Green Financing
Physical climate risks	Floods, droughts, storms, sea level rise	Resilient infrastructure, diversification, adaptation measures
Transition risks	Carbon pricing, changing markets, technology disruption	Energy efficiency, innovation financing, portfolio diversification
Regulatory risks	Emissions limits, disclosure requirements, product standards	Proactive compliance, regulatory intelligence, documentation systems
Supply chain risks	Resource scarcity, supplier non-compliance, disruptions	Supplier programs, alternative materials, circular systems
Litigation risks	Environmental damage claims, securities litigation	Performance improvement, due diligence, stakeholder engagement
Financial system risks	Stranded assets, credit defaults, market volatility	ESG integration, transparency, scenario analysis, diversification

1. Understanding Green Financing in the CSR Context

Green financing is the process of raising money and funding initiatives that improve the environment, like waste management, energy efficiency, renewable energy, and sustainable infrastructure. Within the framework of corporate social responsibility (CSR), green finance serves as a means for businesses to exhibit environmental responsibility and support international sustainability objectives, such as the Sustainable Development Goals (SDGs) of the United Nations and the targets of the Paris Agreement.Green financing represents the intersection of financial strategy and environmental responsibility within corporate social responsibility (CSR) frameworks. At its core, green financing channels capital toward environmentally beneficial projects and initiatives, creating a mechanism for companies to align their financial operations with sustainability goals.

Within CSR, Green Financing fulfills many purposes. First, it offers a structured approach to the funding of environmental initiatives that can otherwise struggle to compete for capital in traditional financial assessment processes. Second, it creates accountability by establishing clear matrix and reporting requirements that displays environmental impact. Third, it connects corporate environmental commitments to solid financial functions. Common green finance instruments include green bonds (debt securities funding environmental projects), stability-linked debt (characteristics related to environmental performance), green investment funds (pooling capital for sustainable ventures), and carbon finance mechanisms (deficiency in meritizing emissions). Companies applying green financeing within their CSR strategy benefit from usually increased reputation, access to special capital pools, reducing regulatory and climate risks and improving stake relations.

The approach allows organizations to translate abstract stability commitments in tangible financial decisions. The most effective green financeing strategies in CSR references align the environmental initiatives with the main commercial purposes, establishes transparent measurements structure, attach diverse stakeholders, and develops as consistent stability challenges. By integrating green finance in CSR, companies show that environmental responsibility extends beyond the fundamental business practices beyond philanthropy, which produces long -term values for both shareholders and society.

2. Key Challenges in Adopting Green Financing
    a. High Initial Costs and Financial Risks

Green financing frequently necessitates a large upfront expenditure, which can put a strain on businesses, especially small and medium-sized businesses (SMEs). Adoption is further hampered by lengthy payback periods and ambiguities surrounding the ROI of green projects.

b. Regulatory and Policy Complexity

Navigating different and evolving environmental regulations and laws may be challenging. Regionally disparate regulations and a dearth of global standardization for green finance products may make it more difficult for businesses to include green finance into their CSR strategy.

c. Limited Access to Green Financing Mechanisms

Many businesses struggle to secure green bonds, loans, or grants because of stringent eligibility standards or ignorance of available financing options. This issue is especially apparent in developing countries since their financial ecosystems are less developed.

d. Stakeholder Skepticism

Increased scrutiny from stakeholders may result from scepticism about greenwashing, a technique in which businesses exaggerate or misrepresent their sustainability initiatives. Businesses must make sure their green finance programs are open and actually have an impact, which can require a lot of resources.

e. Lack of Expertise and Data

Strong mechanisms for assessing and disclosing environmental effect as well as specific expertise in sustainable finance are necessary for incorporating green money into CSR. Many businesses lack the data infrastructure and internal knowledge necessary to handle these demands.

3. Incentives Driving the Adoption of Green Financing

Green financing has gained significant traction globally, which is powered by a complex web of encouragement motivating various stakeholders to participate. These incentives expand financial, regulatory, market-based and social dimensions, which creates a hypnotic case for organizations to adopt the green financing system.

Figure 2. This shows the related theories with green finance techniques and green innovation techniques needed to achieve circularity.

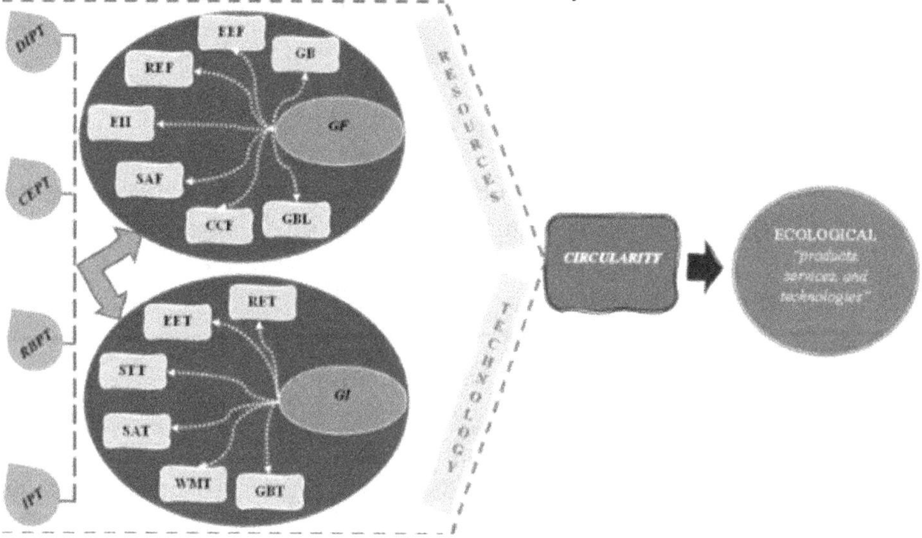

Financial Incentives

Financial institutions provide better conditions for fast green projects:

- Low interest rates for stability related loans
- Extended repayment period for green investment
- Low fee for issuing green bonds
- More flexible covenant for environmentally beneficial initiative

License to Operate

In many contexts, environmental responsibility is being required:

- Social acceptance required for professional continuity
- Community support for new project development.
- Political goodwill from alignment with public priorities.
- Standards and expectations of Industry Association.

The convergence of these diverse incentives makes a compelling commercial case to adopt green finance. Forward-curbing organizations believe that these drivers are rapidly alignment, making green finance not only a moral option, but a strategic imperative for long-term business success.

a. Enhanced Brand Reputation and Consumer Trust

Using green finance shows a company's dedication to sustainability, which improves its standing and builds confidence with investors, customers, and other stakeholders. In a market that is becoming more environmentally concerned, this alignment with society ideals can give an advantage.

b. Access to New Markets and Investors

Opportunities to draw in impact investors and access new markets for sustainable goods and services are made possible by green financing. Access to an expanding pool of environmentally conscious money is another benefit of green bonds and other financial products.

c. Cost Savings and Efficiency Gains

Long-term cost reductions are frequently the result of investments in waste reduction, energy efficiency, and renewable energy. Businesses can meet sustainability goals and get financial rewards by integrating green finance into CSR.

d. Regulatory Compliance and Risk Mitigation

Stricter environmental regulations are being enforced by governments and agencies across the globe. Green financing enables businesses to proactively adhere to these rules, avoiding fines and lowering their exposure to risks associated with climate change.

e. Employee and Stakeholder Engagement

Workers are increasingly choosing to work with organizations that have made significant efforts to sustainability. As a component of CSR, green financing can improve employee engagement and happiness while cultivating a positive company culture.

f. Contribution to Global Sustainability Goals

Engaging in green finance shows support for international initiatives to mitigate climate change and advance sustainable development. This establishes businesses as partners in accomplishing common global objectives and as conscientious corporate citizens.

Green finance plays an important role in supporting international climatic initiatives by changing capital towards environmentally beneficial projects and technologies. When organizations are engaged in Green Finance, they directly contribute to global stability goals beyond their individual corporate social responsibility objectives.

Figure 3. This visual representation highlights the most frequently used subjects in the chapter and their corresponding frequencies.

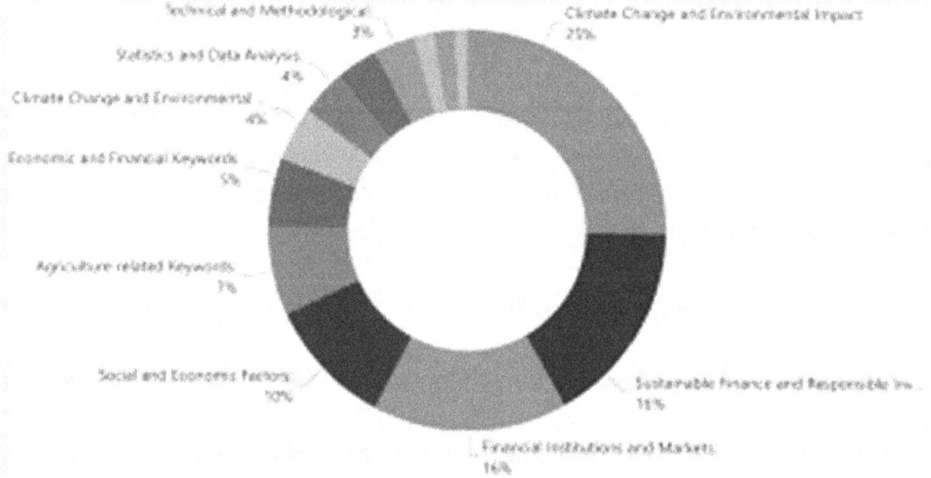

SUPPORTING MAJOR INTERNATIONAL CLIMATE FRAMEWORKS

Businesses can support important global climate projects by taking part in green financing:

1. Implementation of the Paris Agreement: In order to support the global objective of keeping temperature rise well below 2°C, green finance offers the money required to assist nations in meeting their Nationally Determined Contributions (NDCs) under the Paris Agreement.
2. UN Sustainable Development Goals (SDGs): A number of SDGs, including SDG 7 (Affordable and Clean Energy), SDG 9 (Industry, Innovation, and Infrastructure), SDG 11 (Sustainable Cities and Communities), SDG 13 (Climate Action), and SDG 15 (Life on Land), are directly impacted by green financing.
3. Glasgow Financial Alliance for Net Zero (GFANZ): Businesses who practice green finance frequently back this effort by financial institutions dedicated to hastening the shift to a net-zero industry.

Mechanisms of International Support

Green finance supports international climate initiatives through several key mechanisms:

Capital Mobilization

Green finance helps to bridge the important funding gap for climate action. The United Nations estimates that globally climate mitigation and adaptation require $ 4-6 trillion annually, developing countries alone require $ 5.8–5.9 trillion by 2030.

Technology Transfer Green Financing

Provides facilities for deployment of clean technologies on limits, especially for developing countries that may otherwise be lacking access to state -of -the -art permanent solutions.

Policy Implementation

When companies engage in green finance, they create market demands for policy framework that support permanent investment, encouraging governments to implement and strengthen climate policies.

International Cooperation

Green finance often involves cross -border cooperation between financial institutions, governments and corporations, which strengthens global climate regime architecture.

Real-World Examples

1. Green Climate Fund (GCF): This UNFCCC mechanism, which helps developing nations with adaptation and mitigation strategies, is supported by corporate engagement through cash contributions or project implementation.
2. Climate Investment Funds (CIF): Through a variety of funding avenues, businesses taking part in CIF initiatives assist in the expansion of low-carbon technologies in developing nations.
3. International Green Bonds: Organizations can directly promote global climate cooperation by issuing or purchasing green bonds that finance projects in several nations.

Benefits of International Engagement

When companies align their green financing with international climate initiatives,

- Get access to global network and partnership • Benefits of International Policy Promotion and Support.
- Increase their reputation among global stakeholders.
- Reduce transit climate risks in their operations.
- Keep yourself in a favourable position in global infection for low carbon economy by channelling finance towards internationally recognized climate priorities, organizations not only contribute to solving global challenges, but also help to create a more approximate and supportive environment for permanent trade practices worldwide.

BALANCING CHALLENGES AND INCENTIVES

Businesses must overcome the obstacles and take advantage of the benefits in order to successfully incorporate green financing into their CSR strategies:

- **Capacity Building:** Businesses can develop their knowledge of green finance and sustainable practices by investing in partnerships and training.

- **Collaboration with Financial Institutions:** Financial barriers can be decreased and access to green finance methods enhanced by interacting with banks, investors, and governments.
- **Transparency and Reporting:** Stakeholder skepticism can be addressed and credibility increased by creating strong processes for impact measurement and reporting.
- **Innovation and Technology:** Green projects can become more appealing investments by utilizing technology to save costs and increase efficiency.
- **Policy Advocacy:** Businesses and legislators can collaborate to create regulatory frameworks that are supportive of business demands and international norms.

CASE STUDIES: SUCCESS STORIES

a. Apple's Green Bond Initiatives

To finance energy efficiency upgrades, creative recycling initiatives, and renewable energy projects, Apple has issued a number of green bonds. Apple has enhanced its standing as a sustainability leader and decreased its carbon footprint by incorporating green finance into its CSR strategy.Apple has strategically incorporated green finance in its corporate social responsibility (CSR) approach, which has greatly increased its stability leadership state, reducing its environmental impact. This integration shows how a major technology company can avail financial instruments to run environmental progress.

Figure 4. Apple industry based on green and sustainable technologies in the scope of circular economy.

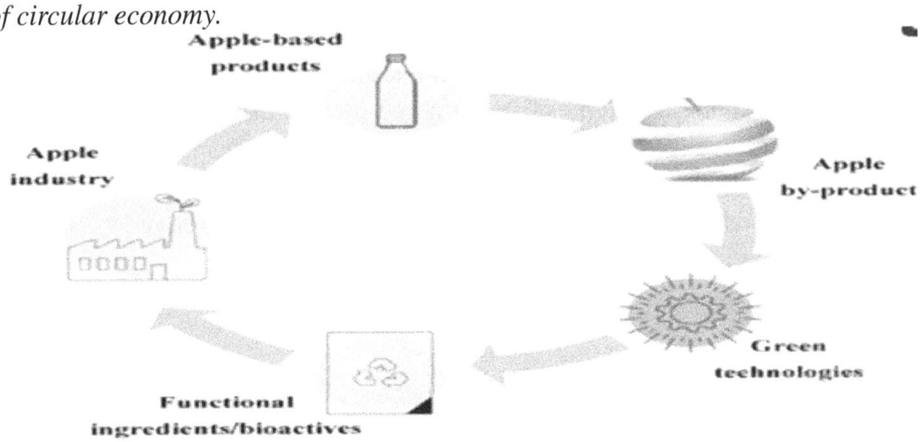

Key Green Finance Initiatives by Apple

1. **Green Bonds**: Apple has released several green bonds, especially billions of dollars for environmental projects. These funds are allocated for initiatives such as renewable energy installations, improvement in energy efficiency and development of greenery products.
2. Renewable Energy Investments: A large part of green bond income has been invested in renewable energy projects. Apple now incorporates all its global operations including data centers, offices and retail stores with 100% renewable energy. This infection has significantly reduced its dependence on fossil fuels.
3. **Carbon Neutrality Target:** Apple has set ambitious targets to become carbon neutral in its entire supply chain and product life cycle by 2030. This includes reducing emissions through innovative design, increasing recycled material use and investing in carbon removal projects.
4. **Suppliers engagement:** Apple is actively working with your suppliers to reduce your carbon footprints. Through its supplier clean energy program, the company encourages and supports suppliers in infections in renewable energy sources, increasing the impact of its green finance initiative.
5. **Product Innovation:** Apple's commitment to stability is clear in its product design. The company has increased the use of recycled materials in its devices, such as aluminium, tin and rare earth elements. This not only reduces the environmental impact of mining, but also promotes a circular economy.

b. IKEA's Investments in Renewable Energy

IKEA has made a substantial financial commitment to green finance by funding solar and wind energy projects across the globe. These initiatives show the financial and reputational advantages of green finance and are in line with the company's CSR objectives of attaining climate-positive operations.Ikea has made significant progress in green finance by investing heavily in renewable energy projects, especially solar and wind energy through its original company Ingka Group. This commitment aligns with the wide stability goals of Ikea, which includes climate positive by 2030 and infection in a circular business model.

Figure 5. (https://www.google.com/url?sa=i&url=https%3A%2F%2Fwww.intelligentliving.co%Fikea-renewable-energy)

Here is a detailed explanation of Ikea's Green Finance initiative and their effects:

1. Financial commitment to renewable energy
   - Investment in renewal: IKEA has invested € 2.5 billion (about $ 2.7 billion) in global and wind power projects since 2009.
   - Ownership of renewable assets: Ikea is the owner of wind farms and solar parks in 18 countries, generating more renewable energy than its operation.
2. Solar power projects
   - Solar panels on shops and warehouses: Ikea has installed 935,000 solar panels on its store and warehouse roofs worldwide, causing 1.7 terravat-hour (TWH) of annual clean energy.
   - Solar Farm: Ikea has invested in large -scale solar farms in countries like the United States, Spain and Australia. For example, U.S. In, Ikea Illinois has a 46-Magawat (MW) solar farm, which provides strength to thousands of houses.
3. Wind power projects
   - Wind Farm: IKEA is owned and operates 575 wind turbines in 14 countries, including the US, Canada and many European countries. These wind fields generate 1.7 Twhh power annually, which is sufficient for more than 1 million houses.
   - Notable Projects: One of the largest wind farms in Ikea is HohanrodaPawan Farm in Germany, which generates 52 MW clean energy.
4. Green Finance Mechanism
   - Green Bond: Ikea has specifically issued green bonds to raise funds for renewable energy projects. These bonds are aligned with green bond principles, which ensure transparency and accountability in the use of income.

- Partnership: IKEA collaborates with governments, NGOs and private sector partners to increase renewable energy investments. For example, it gave the U.S. In partnership with sun power to offer solar panels to customers.

By doing adequate financial resources for green finance, Ikea is not only reducing its own carbon footprint, but also running global infection into renewable energy. Its investment in solar and wind power projects show how businesses can play an important role in combating climate change by promoting economic growth and innovation.

CONCLUSION

For contemporary businesses, integrating green finance into CSR is both a strategic imperative and a challenging task. The incentives—which range from improved reputation to cost savings and market opportunities—make green financing an alluring way to accomplish sustainability goals, despite obstacles including financial risks, regulatory barriers, and stakeholder distrust. Businesses may establish themselves as leaders in the shift to a sustainable global economy by tackling these issues with creativity, cooperation, and openness.

In addition to being a tool for controlling environmental effect, green finance opens doors to long-term profitability, resilience, and alignment with evolving global ideals.

This chapter lays the groundwork for future talks on best practices and implementation tactics by highlighting the dynamic interplay of challenges and possibilities businesses encounter when embracing green financing.

Corporate Social Responsibility (CSR) Integration of Green Financing in Framework represents a significant development in corporate stability practices. This comprehensive assessment examines versatile challenges and incentives that encounter companies, when green financing mechanisms include their CSR strategies. Analysis shows that while companies can realize sufficient gains - including improving brand reputation, improvement in financial performance, better risk management and competitive advantages - they should also navigate considerable obstacles, such as measurement complications, standardization issues, knowledge intervals and organizational resistance. Research indicates that the successful integration of green finance in CSR depends on many important factors: strong governance structures, clear alignment with main occupation strategy, stakeholder engagement, transparent measurement structure, and adaptability to develop regulatory environment. Industry-specific approaches are necessary, as different areas face unique environmental challenges and opportunities. Regional variations in the cultural approach to regulatory structures, market maturity, and stability also greatly affect the implementation strategies. Further, companies that develop wide green finance approaches within their CSR framework are likely to get competitive advantage, especially regulatory requirements become more rigid, investor increases investigation, and consumer preferences keep moving towards permanent products and services. The most successful organizations would be those that move beyond compliance with the advantage of green financing as catalysts for innovation and long -term value creation.

REFERENCES

Ameli, N., Drummond, P., Bisaro, A., Grubb, M., & Chenet, H. (2021). Climate finance and disclosure for institutional investors: Why transparency is not enough. *Climatic Change*, *160*(4), 565–589. DOI: 10.1007/s10584-019-02542-2

BlackRock. (2023). *Global Sustainable Investment Outlook 2023*. BlackRock Investment Institute.

Bolton, R. (2022). *Beyond greenwashing: Strategic approaches to environmental credibility*. Harvard Business Review Press.

Chava, S. (2014). Environmental externalities and cost of capital. *Management Science*, *60*(9), 2223–2247. DOI: 10.1287/mnsc.2013.1863

Clark, G. L., Feiner, A., & Viehs, M. (2015). *From the stockholder to the stakeholder: How sustainability can drive financial outperformance*. University of Oxford and Arabesque Partners.

Climate Bonds Initiative. (2023). *Green Bonds Global State of the Market 2023*. Climate Bonds Initiative.

Delmas, M. A., & Burbano, V. C. (2011). The drivers of greenwashing. *California Management Review*, *54*(1), 64–87. DOI: 10.1525/cmr.2011.54.1.64

Eccles, R. G., Ioannou, I., & Serafeim, G. (2014). The impact of corporate sustainability on organizational processes and performance. *Management Science*, *60*(11), 2835–2857. DOI: 10.1287/mnsc.2014.1984

European Commission. (2021). *Strategy for financing the transition to a sustainable economy*. European Commission.

Flammer, C. (2021). Corporate green bonds. *Journal of Financial Economics*, *142*(2), 499–516. DOI: 10.1016/j.jfineco.2021.01.010

Friede, G., Busch, T., & Bassen, A. (2015). ESG and financial performance: Aggregated evidence from more than 2000 empirical studies. *Journal of Sustainable Finance & Investment*, *5*(4), 210–233. DOI: 10.1080/20430795.2015.1118917

Hong, H., Karolyi, G. A., & Scheinkman, J. A. (2019). Climate finance. *Review of Financial Studies*, *33*(3), 1011–1023. DOI: 10.1093/rfs/hhz146

IFRS Foundation. (2023). *IFRS Sustainability Disclosure Standards: Progress report*. IFRS Foundation.

Krueger, P., Sautner, Z., & Starks, L. T. (2020). The importance of climate risks for institutional investors. *Review of Financial Studies*, *33*(3), 1067–1111. DOI: 10.1093/rfs/hhz137

Krueger, P., Sautner, Z., Tang, D. Y., & Zhong, R. (2022). The effects of mandatory ESG disclosure around the world. European Corporate Governance Institute–Finance Working Paper, 754.

Park, H., & Kim, J. D. (2020). Transition towards green banking: Role of financial regulators and financial institutions. *Asian Journal of Sustainability and Social Responsibility*, *5*(1), 1–25. DOI: 10.1186/s41180-020-00034-3

Porter, M. E., & Kramer, M. R. (2011). Creating shared value. *Harvard Business Review*, *89*(1/2), 62–77.

PwC. (2023). *Global sustainable finance survey: Bridging the capability gap.* PricewaterhouseCoopers.

Task Force on Climate-related Financial Disclosures. (2023). *Status Report 2023.* Financial Stability Board.

UNEP FI. (2022). The Climate Risk Landscape: 2022 Supplement. United Nations Environment Programme Finance Initiative.

Whelan, T., & Fink, C. (2021). The comprehensive business case for sustainability. Harvard Business Review Working Paper.

Zhang, B., & Swanson, L. A. (2022). Discount rates and sustainability: Problems in valuation across time. *Business Ethics Quarterly*, *32*(2), 279–304.

Zhou, P., & Cui, L. (2023). Strategic integration of sustainability in corporate finance: Evidence from green bond issuers. *Strategic Management Journal*, *44*(2), 401–425.

Chapter 6
Aligning Financial Reporting Standards: A Catalyst for Global Mergers and Acquisitions

Arvinder Kaur
https://orcid.org/0000-0001-7360-5674
Chandigarh University, India

Rachna Kathuria
New Delhi Institute of Management, India

Priyanka Malhotra
NIET Business School, Greater Noida, India

ABSTRACT

The harmonization of financial reporting standards has become a pivotal factor in fostering cross-border mergers and acquisitions (M&A) in today's globalized economy. Standardized financial practices enhance transparency, comparability, and reliability of financial information, reducing the asymmetry that often hinders international business collaborations. This study explores how aligning financial reporting standards, such as the International Financial Reporting Standards (IFRS), streamlines due diligence processes, mitigates compliance risks, and promotes investor confidence. By examining case studies and empirical data, the paper highlights the strategic advantages of financial standardization for companies pursuing global M&A. The findings underscore the critical role of unified reporting frameworks in bridging diverse economic systems and driving sustainable economic integration.

DOI: 10.4018/979-8-3373-0887-6.ch006

INTRODUCTION

Overview of Cross-Border M&As in the Global Economy

Cross-border mergers and acquisitions (M&As) are at the forefront of global economic integration, representing a strategic route for companies to expand their operations, improve market reach, and achieve competitive edges in an interconnected world (R. Kumar, Lande, Kumar, et al., 2023; R. Kumar, Malholtra, Singh, et al., 2023). These transactions permit firms to diversify risks, access new markets, and cultivate critical resources such as talent, technology, and infrastructure. In 2021, the worth of global cross-border M&A activity achieved an all-time high of $2.1 trillion, accounting for 40% of the total international M&A volume. This exceptional development was fueled by enterprises such as technology, healthcare, and financial services, which have evolved into critical drivers of cross-border movement (R. Kumar, Kathuria, Malholtra, et al., 2023; Malhotra et al., 2021).

Despite their tremendous potential, cross-border M&As usually need help with the complexity of operating across various regulatory, cultural, and financial environments. Regulatory hurdles, misaligned corporate cultures, and inconsistent financial reporting practices frequently hinder the realization of anticipated synergies (Neha et al., 2023; M. S. Rana et al., 2022). These challenges underscore the need for harmonized frameworks, particularly in financial reporting, to ensure transparency and comparability in such high-stakes transactions. In the contemporary global economy, cross-border mergers and acquisitions (M&As) have emerged as pivotal tools for corporate expansion, market diversification, and strategic realignment. These transactions, which involve consolidating companies operating in different national jurisdictions, have experienced substantial growth over the past few decades. According to data from the Institute for Mergers, Acquisitions and Alliances (IMAA), cross-border M&A deals worldwide grew from around 2,000 in 1985 to over 8,000 in 2023, highlighting their escalating importance in international business methods (C. Gupta et al., 2022; R. Kumar, Khannna Malholtra, & Grover, 2023). The surge in cross-border M&As is attributable to technological advancements, globalization, and commerce and investment policy liberalization. Globalization has dismantled conventional barriers, facilitating firms' access to new markets and resources. Technological inventions have facilitated seamless integration and communication across borders, while liberalized approaches have decreased foreign ownership and investment constraints. Collectively, these characteristics have created an atmosphere conducive to cross-border corporate confederations (R. Kumar, Singh, Mohanty, et al., 2023; Uniyal et al., 2022).

However, the complexity intrinsic to cross-border M&As cannot be overstated. These transactions necessitate reconciling various legal frameworks, cultural nuances, and, critically, disparate financial reporting standards. *Financial reporting* is the accountability bedrock, and corporate transparency gives stakeholders essential insights into a company's financial soundness and operational performance. In the context of cross-border M&As, the alignment of financial reporting standards is essential to assure accurate valuation, due diligence, and post-merger integration (R. Kumar, Malhotra, & Grover, 2023; Malhotra et al., 2022).

The International Financial Reporting Standards (IFRS) have been instrumental in elevating the global harmonization of accounting approaches. Developed by the International Accounting Standards Board (IASB), IFRS seeks to designate a common accounting language to improve comparability and transparency in financial reports (Awal & Khanna, 2019; Upreti & Malhotra, 2024). As of 2024, over 140 jurisdictions need IFRS for publicly listed corporations, reflecting its widespread adoption and the international shift towards standardized financial reporting. Despite the progress accomplished through IFRS, challenges prevail in achieving versatile adoption and consistent application. Notably, the United States persists in adhering to its Generally Accepted Accounting Principles (GAAP), resulting in differences that must be clarified for cross-border M&A activities involving U.S. entities. Likewise, variations in the interpretation and implementation of IFRS across different jurisdictions can lead to consistency, sabotaging the purpose of uniform financial reporting (Kanojia et al., 2022; P. Sharma et al., 2022).

Technological progress is poised to handle some of these challenges by improving the accuracy and efficiency of financial reporting. Blockchain technology, for example, shows the prospect of improving transparency and traceability in financial transactions, thereby maintaining stakeholder confidence. Artificial intelligence (AI) and information analytics also change financial reporting by automating procedures and enabling real-time analysis, enabling more informed decision-making in M&A activities. This chapter delves into the multifaceted role of financial reporting in cross-border M&As, exploring its significance, the challenges posed by divergent accounting frameworks, and the advantages of harmonizing financial reporting standards (Joshi et al., 2022; J. Kaur et al., 2024). It also examines the effect of technological innovations on financial reporting procedures. It delivers strategic suggestions for policymakers, companies, and regulators to align financial reporting with the growing requirements of global trade. By providing a comprehensive analysis of these dimensions, the chapter strives to elucidate the complexities of financial reporting in the context of cross-border M&As and to present wisdom in promoting a more integrated and transparent global financial domain (Cavaliere et al., 2024; Mary Joshitta et al., 2023).

Table 1. Global cross-border M&A activity (2019–2023)

Year	Number of Deals	Total Value (USD Trillion)	Percentage of Total M&A Value (%)
2019	7,500	1.2	30
2020	6,800	1.0	28
2021	8,200	1.5	32
2022	7,900	1.3	31
2023	8,500	1.4	33

Source: Institute for Mergers, Acquisitions and Alliances (IMAA)

Table 1 highlights the escalating importance of cross-border mergers and acquisitions, evidenced by a constant upward trajectory in deal volume and value from 2019 to 2023, reflecting their integral role in global financial dynamism.

Significance of Financial Reporting in International Trade

Financial reporting is a cornerstone of global trade and cross-border M&As, underpinning the trust and enthusiasm of stakeholders. Transparent, comparable financial disclosures and consistency are essential for evaluating companies' performance, financial health, and valuation in cross-border transactions (Khanna et al., 2023; R. Kumar, Malhotra, Pandey, et al., 2023). Divergent accounting standards, however, can create informative asymmetries, complicate due diligence methods, and lead to valuation differences, raising the risks associated with cross-border M&As. Adopting International Financial Reporting Standards (IFRS) has become a vital solution to these challenges. IFRS, required in over 140 jurisdictions, delivers a globally recognized framework for financial reporting, ensuring uniformity and reliability. For instance, the European Union's adoption of IFRS has immensely improved the efficiency of cross-border financial reporting and strengthened investor confidence within the region. However, challenges remain, as some major economies, including the USA, depend on provincial accounting standards, such as Generally Accepted Accounting Principles (GAAP) (Asha et al., 2022). In cross-border M&As, harmonized financial reporting enables accurate valuation, mitigates regulatory disputes, and facilitates post-merger integration, promoting an atmosphere conducive to successful transactions. Moreover, integrating refined technologies like blockchain and artificial intelligence can improve financial transparency and efficiency, reduce errors, and enhance real-time reporting (Jindal et al., 2022).

Purposes of the Study

This chapter strives to critically investigate the critical role of financial reporting in cross-border mergers and acquisitions (M&As) and its broader significance for global trade. It strives to analyze the movements, key drivers, and economic importance of cross-border M&As, using empirical data and case studies to underscore their transformative prospects (A. B. Singh et al., 2023). An emphasis is placed on assessing how harmonized financial reporting standards, such as IFRS, improve transaction efficiency, transparency, and post-merger integration. Likewise, the chapter investigates the effect of emerging technologies like blockchain, artificial intelligence, and data analytics on changing financial reporting approaches. Finally, it provides strategic suggestions for policymakers, regulators, and corporate executives to align financial reporting frameworks with international trade needs, promoting trust, transparency, and sustainable development in cross-border transactions (Malik et al., 2022).

Research Methodology

This chapter embraces a multidisciplinary approach incorporating qualitative and quantitative investigations to investigate the role of financial reporting harmonization in cross-border mergers and acquisitions (M&As). Secondary data from scholarly literature, industry reports, and international regulatory frameworks form the foundation, completed by case studies from various regions. Comparative and thematic analyses identify essential challenges, advantages, and trends, while quantitative data emphasize valuation and transparency practices. The case studies provide real-world wisdom in pre-merger due diligence and IFRS adoption. Triangulation confirms trustworthiness, and ethical reviews conduct the research, presenting actionable understandings for businesses, policymakers, and financial regulators.

THE ROLE OF FINANCIAL REPORTING IN CROSS-BORDER M&AS

Significance of Financial Transparency and Accountability

Financial reporting is the spine of cross-border mergers and acquisitions (M&As), assuring transparency and accountability in assessing a company's financial health. Transparent financial revelations foster trust among investors, corporate stakeholders and regulators, enabling informed decision-making in high-stakes transactions (Alrashed et al., 2022; R. Kumar, Sexena, & Gehlot, 2023; Tiwari et al., 2023).

Challenges of Financial Reporting in International Transactions

Despite the across-the-board adoption of IFRS, financial reporting in cross-border M&As faces considerable challenges. Divergent accounting standards across jurisdictions frequently result in inconsistencies in financial disclosures, complicating valuation and due diligence methods. For example, differences in the valuation of assets, income recognition, and liability measurement can direct financial disparities, impacting the accuracy of transaction appraisals. Further, varying regulatory environments and cultural differences complicate the consolidation of financial data from entities operating in multiple nations. The complexity grows when merging entities maintain disparate levels of reporting sophistication, creating hindrances in achieving compliance with global financial standards. These challenges underscore the critical requirement for robust tools to bridge international financial reporting methods gaps (Nikolaidis et al., 2022; S. Sharma, Kadayat, et al., 2023; S. Sharma, Singh, et al., 2023; K. D. Singh et al., 2023).

Key Stakeholders and Their Viewpoints

Financial reporting in cross-border M&As involves multiple stakeholders, each with distinct roles and anticipations:

- **Investors**: They need transparent and comparable financial data to evaluate the possible risks and returns of an M&A transaction. Precise financial exposures help assess deals' feasibility and strategic value (K. D. Singh & Singh, 2023).
- **Regulators**: Concentrate on ensuring compliance with accounting standards to keep market integrity and safeguard stakeholders from financial misrepresentation (Ahmad et al., 2023).
- **Corporate Management**: Accountable for preparing financial statements that reflect correct and compliant financial performance. Their role is climactic in showing data that supports strategic goals while adhering to global standards (Josphineleela, Kaliappan, et al., 2023).

Aligning the viewpoints and stakes of these stakeholders is necessary for successfully executing cross-border M&As. Adequate financial reporting enables trust, mitigates risks, and confirms smoother integration of merging entities, contributing to the prevalent success of international transactions.

Divergent Accounting Frameworks: Challenges and Implications

Divergent accounting frameworks deliver meaningful challenges in cross-border mergers and acquisitions (M&As), impacting valuation, negotiation, and decision-making procedures. The need for uniformity in financial reporting standards across jurisdictions can lead to disparities that complicate these transactions.

Table 2. Adoption of IFRS vs. local GAAP in selected countries (2023)

Country	IFRS Adoption Status	Local GAAP Usage (%)	IFRS Usage (%)
United States	Not Adopted	100	0
Japan	Permitted	70	30
China	Converged	50	50
India	Converged	60	40
Brazil	Adopted	10	90

Source: International Financial Reporting Standards (IFRS) Foundation

Table 2 displays the heterogeneous adoption of IFRS across jurisdictions, highlighting ongoing reliance on local GAAP in vital economies. This thereby highlights the complexities of accomplishing universal financial reporting harmonization.

Examination of Existing Disparities in Financial Reporting Standards

Globally, businesses adhere to different accounting standards, with the International Financial Reporting Standards (IFRS) and the Generally Accepted Accounting Principles (GAAP) being the most prevalent. While IFRS is embraced by over 140 jurisdictions, the United States continues to use GAAP, leading to significant differences in financial reporting (Bhatt et al., 2023). These disparities are displayed in revenue recognition, asset valuation, and financial report presentation. For example, IFRS often operates a principles-based method, permitting interpretation based on the substance of transactions, whereas GAAP is better rules-based, delivering detailed procedures. Such discrepancies can change financial results for similar transactions, complicating the comparability of financial reports across borders (Alexopoulos et al., 2023; Nagila et al., 2023; S. Sharma, Gupta, et al., 2023).

Effect on Valuation, Negotiation, and Decision-Making in M&As

The inconsistencies in accounting standards can significantly impact the valuation of target groups in cross-border M&As. Discrepancies in asset valuation approaches may lead to differing estimates of a company's assets, potentially causing overvaluation or undervaluation. This misalignment can hinder negotiations, as parties may differ in the financial health and performance of the entities concerned. Moreover, decision-making becomes more complicated when financial reports are not directly comparable, raising the risk of misinformed strategic options (Ambika et al., 2023; Ingale et al., 2023; Jain et al., 2023). These challenges highlight the need for thorough due diligence and the potential need for financial report adjustments to align varying accounting practices (Josphineleela, Gupta, et al., 2023; Tyagi et al., 2023; Yadav et al., 2023).

CASE STUDIES: EXAMPLES OF FAILED AND SUCCESSFUL CROSS-BORDER M&AS DUE TO FINANCIAL REPORTING DIFFERENCES

A notable instance of a failed cross-border M&A is the 2007 acquisition attempt of ABN AMRO by a consortium led by the Royal Bank of Scotland (RBS). The pact faced considerable challenges due to disparities in accounting methods, especially in asset valuation and risk assessment, leading to unpredictable financial complications and contributing to RBS's eventual failure. Conversely, Kraft Foods's 2010 acquisition of Cadbury illustrates a successful cross-border M&A. Despite working under different accounting standards (IFRS for Cadbury and US GAAP for Kraft), the parties navigated these disparities through vast due diligence and financial adjustments, promoting a smooth transaction (Rathore & Goudar, 2015; V. Sharma & Jain, 2020). These cases underscore the crucial role of understanding and reconciling divergent accounting frameworks in cross-border M&As. Aggressive steps, such as aligning accounting approaches and conducting meticulous financial accounting, are essential to mitigate risks associated with financial reporting discrepancies (Onyema et al., 2022; Prikshat et al., 2019).

Benefits of Harmonizing Financial Reporting Standards

Harmonizing financial reporting standards presents several benefits, including facilitating global economic integration and improving the efficiency of cross-border financial movements.

Table 3. Impact of IFRS adoption on cross-border M&A activity (pre- and post-adoption)

Region	Period	Average Annual Deals	Average Deal Value (USD Billion)
Europe	Pre-2005	1,200	500
	Post-2005	1,500	700
Asia-Pacific	Pre-2010	800	300
	Post-2010	1,100	450

Source: European Commission; Asian Development Bank

Table 3 displays the transformative effect of IFRS adoption on cross-border M&A dynamics, evidenced by marked gains in deal frequency and valuation post-adoption. It highlights its role in improving transactional effectiveness and investor confidence.

Enhancing Comparability and Consistency Across Jurisdictions

Adopting uniform financial reporting standards, such as the International Financial Reporting Standards (IFRS), mainly improves the comparability and consistency of financial reports across different countries (Pattanshetti et al., 2021). This uniformity allows investors and analysts to assess financial reports without modifying for varying accounting approaches, thereby streamlining the evaluation process. The International Accounting Standards Board (IASB) investigation discovered that over 140 jurisdictions have adopted IFRS, highlighting its global acceptance and the shift towards standardized financial reporting (D. S. Rana et al., 2022).

Reducing Regulatory Complexities and Fostering Trust

Harmonized financial reporting standards streamline the regulatory landscape by delivering a common framework for financial exposures. This simplification lessens the burden on multinational corporations that would otherwise need to concede with multiple accounting standards, lowering compliance expenses and administrative complexities. Moreover, standardized reporting fosters trust among stakeholders by confirming transparency and accountability. The International Federation of Accountants (IFAC) highlights that harmonization improves financial data quality, which is critical for functioning capital markets and the broader economy (Goyal et al., 2015; Prikshat et al., 2017; S. Sharma et al., 2021).

Amplifying Investor Confidence and Cross-Border Partnerships

Uniform financial reporting improves investor confidence by providing trustworthy and comparable financial data, vital for making informed investment decisions. This confidence is vital in cross-border investments, where investors may be required to familiarize themselves with local accounting traditions (Rawat et al., 2022). A statement by the IFRS Foundation emphasizes that adopting IFRS has led to increased cross-border investment and enhanced capital funding efficiency. Similarly, harmonized standards promote cross-border partnerships and mergers by delivering a common financial language, thereby declining misunderstandings and promoting smoother negotiations. In conclusion, harmonizing financial reporting standards is critical in improving the comparability and consistency of financial information across jurisdictions, facilitating regulatory complexities, and strengthening investor confidence. These advantages contribute to a more transparent, facilitating economic growth, efficient, integrated global financial system, and stability (P. Singh & Singh, 2023; Srivastava et al., 2024).

INTERNATIONAL FINANCIAL REPORTING STANDARDS (IFRS): A PATH TO GLOBAL ALIGNMENT

International Financial Reporting Standards (IFRS) have been a cornerstone of the investigation for international accounting harmonization. They promote transparency and comparability in financial reporting across various jurisdictions.

Development and Adoption of IFRS

The advent of IFRS dates back to 2001, when the International Accounting Standards Board (IASB) was built, following the International Accounting Standards Committee (IASC). The IASB's commission was to design a single set of high-quality, coherent, and enforceable international accounting standards. Over time, IFRS has acquired significant traction, with over 140 jurisdictions directing its usage for publicly listed corporations as of 2024. The European Union's adoption in 2005 marked a significant milestone, convincing all EU-listed companies to draft consolidated financial reports by IFRS. This movement was instrumental in promoting financial report comparability across member states, improving investor confidence and market efficiency.

Success Stories of IFRS Implementation in M&As

The adoption of IFRS has notably simplified cross-border mergers and acquisitions (M&As) by delivering a uniform financial reporting framework. A suitable model is the acquisition of Cadbury by Kraft Foods in 2010. Despite working under different accounting standards—Cadbury under IFRS and Kraft under U.S. GAAP—the harmonization enabled by IFRS allowed a smoother integration method. The standardized reporting framework authorized more detailed financial report comparisons, lessening due diligence and valuation complexities. This alignment was vital in completing the $19 billion deal, underscoring the efficacy of IFRS in cross-border transactions.

Challenges in Attaining Universal Adoption

Despite its across-the-board adoption, accomplishing universal approval of IFRS faces several challenges. Notably, the United States continues to stick to its Generally Accepted Accounting Principles (GAAP), citing concerns over IFRS's principles-based system compared to the more rules-based U.S. GAAP. This divergence forms complexities for multinational corporations operating in both IFRS and U.S. GAAP jurisdictions, potentially showing improved compliance expenses and financial report preparation challenges (Mishra et al., 2024). Further, some countries express concern regarding the failure of national regulatory control and the possible misalignment of IFRS with local monetary contexts. For example, emerging economies may find detailed IFRS conditions less applicable to their financial atmospheres, necessitating changes that could damage the goal of uniformity. Likewise, the resource-intensive nature of transitioning to IFRS, including training personnel and revamping financial reporting systems, poses consequential barriers, especially for smaller entities with limited capabilities (Indu et al., 2023; Khandelwal et al., 2023; Shrivastava et al., 2023; K. U. Singh et al., 2024) . In conclusion, while IFRS has made significant strides toward international accounting standardization and promoting transparency and efficiency in international financial reporting, challenges prevail in universal adoption. Addressing these challenges needs collaborative efforts among international standard-setters, national regulators, and the enterprise community to negotiate differences and encourage the advantages of a unified accounting framework.

Leveraging Technology for Financial Reporting in M&As

Technological advances are revolutionizing financial reporting in the mergers and acquisitions (M&As) domain by improving transparency, automating processes, and allowing real-time analysis.

Table 4. Adoption of financial reporting technologies in M&A processes (2023)

Technology	Adoption Rate (%)	Reported Efficiency Improvement (%)
Blockchain	25	40
Artificial Intelligence	35	50
Real-Time Analytics	45	60

Source: Deloitte Global Survey on M&A Technology Trends

Table 4 demonstrates the advanced integration of advanced technologies in financial reporting, with significant adoption rates and considerable efficiency gains, highlighting their transformative possibility in optimizing M&A strategies.

Role of Blockchain in Enriching Transparency and Traceability

Blockchain technology, described by its decentralized and immutable ledger method, shows significant potential to improve transparency and traceability in financial reporting during M&As. By recording transactions tamper-proof, blockchain assures that all parties have access to a single, supportable source of truth (Ajay et al., 2023). This transparency mitigates the perils associated with data manipulation and scams, promoting stakeholder trust. For example, Deloitte's analysis emphasizes that blockchain can streamline auditing approaches by providing real-time access to financial data, thereby decreasing the time and expense associated with conventional audits (Dutta et al., 2023).

Artificial Intelligence in Automating and Standardizing Reporting

Artificial intelligence (AI) transforms financial reporting by automating regular tasks and standardizing complex processes. AI algorithms can efficiently process extended amounts of financial data, recognize patterns, and develop reports with minimal human intervention. This automation improves accuracy and permits financial professionals to concentrate on strategic analysis (Grover et al., 2024; Kumari et al., 2024). KPMG's survey reveals that 100% of U.S. financial reporting chiefs expect to use AI in financial reporting within three years, up from 71% today. This highlights the growing dependence on AI for financial audit and reporting complexities.

Emerging Tools for Real-Time Financial Analysis

The origin of advanced analytics devices enables real-time financial analysis, a critical capacity in the fast-paced conditions of M&As. These devices leverage AI and machine learning to deliver instantaneous understandings of financial performance, risk review, and market tendencies. For instance, platforms like AlphaSense employ AI to provide real-time data retrieval and wisdom, enhancing decision-making in the financial enterprise. Such credentials are invaluable during M&As, where timely and correct financial information is necessary for informed decision-making. Integrating blockchain, AI, and real-time analytics tools significantly enhances financial reporting efficiency, transparency and accuracy in M&As. These technologies facilitate procedures and deliver deeper insights, enabling stakeholders to make more knowledgeable decisions and confidently drive the complexities of cross-border transactions.

Case Studies: Real-World Applications

The harmonization of financial reporting benchmarks, mainly through adopting International Financial Reporting Standards (IFRS), plays a vital role in the success of cross-border mergers and acquisitions (M&As). However, the transition to these standards shows challenges that vary across regions. This section explores real-world applications to clarify the usefulness and barriers associated with IFRS alignment.

Table 5. Selected cross-border M&A transactions and financial reporting challenges

Acquirer	Target	Year	Deal Value (USD Billion)	Reporting Challenge
Kraft Foods	Cadbury	2010	19	Reconciliation of US GAAP and IFRS
Tata Steel	Corus Group	2007	12	Alignment of Indian GAAP with IFRS
Lenovo	IBM PC Division	2005	1.75	Integration of Chinese GAAP and US GAAP

Source: Company Annual Reports; Financial Times

Table 5 emphasizes the complex challenges of harmonizing disparate financial reporting benchmarks in cross-border M&As, demonstrating how divergent frameworks necessitate particular alignment to accomplish seamless integration and transactional triumph.

Thriving Harmonization: Investigating a Merger That Benefited from IFRS Alignment

A prominent example of thriving harmonization is the acquisition of Cadbury by Kraft Foods in 2010. Cadbury, a UK-based company, was attached to IFRS, while Kraft Foods, an American corporation, pursued the U.S. Generally Accepted Accounting Principles (GAAP). The alignment of financial reporting benchmarks enabled a smoother integration strategy, as both entities could comparably show financial information. This comparability was critical for correct valuation and due diligence, contributing to successfully implementing the $19 billion deal. The harmonized reporting framework decreased complexities and encouraged transparency, highlighting the efficacy of IFRS in cross-border transactions (Aiyappa et al., 2024; Arora et al., 2024; Pandey et al., 2023; Zhang et al., 2023).

Challenges in Transition: Investigating Issues in Adopting International Standards

Despite the benefits, transitioning to IFRS poses essential challenges. For instance, in 2005, the European Union mandated the adoption of IFRS for all publicly traded corporations. This transition exposed several issues, including the complexity of IFRS standards, the requirement for comprehensive training, and the substantial expenses associated with implementation—companies required help interpreting and laying new accounting treatments, leading to inconsistencies in financial reporting. Further, the lack of preparedness among smaller firms stressed the resource-intensive essence of the transition. These challenges highlight the necessity for comprehensive planning and support tools to enable effective adoption of global standards.

Regional Insights: Case Studies from Asia, Europe, and the Americas

The adoption of IFRS varies across parts and is affected by local financial contexts and regulatory conditions.

- **Asia**: In Japan, the voluntary adoption of IFRS has been promoted to enhance global competitiveness. Despite this, companies have raised concerns over the transition charge and the relevancy of specific IFRS provisions to the Japanese market. Despite these challenges, firms that have adopted IFRS report improved comparability with global peers, enabling cross-border investments.
- **Europe**: The European Union's compulsory adoption of IFRS strived to harmonize financial reporting across fellow states. While this initiative enhanced transparency and comparability, it also revealed challenges related to enforcement and interpretation of criteria. Differences in application among nations stressed the need for consistent regulatory neglect to provide uniform implementation.
- **Americas**: In Brazil, the junction to IFRS was part of a broader effort to integrate with international markets. The transition faced impediments such

as aligning tax rules with new accounting standards and managing the complexity of IFRS conditions. Nonetheless, the adoption has improved the credibility of financial reporting, drawing foreign investment and stimulating economic growth.

These case analyses illustrate that while IFRS harmonization shows substantial benefits in transparency and comparability, the transition procedure is fraught with challenges that need cautious management. Tailored approaches that consider regional contexts and deliver adequate support are indispensable for successfully executing global financial reporting standards.

Policy Frameworks and Regulatory Initiatives

The globalization of financial markets has emphasized the imperative for harmonized financial reporting criteria to provide transparency, comparability, and efficiency in cross-border economic movements. This necessitates a broad policy framework and concerted regulatory initiatives at both international and regional levels.

Table 6. Global initiatives for financial reporting harmonization (2023)

Initiative	Leading Organization	Participating Countries	Objective
IFRS Adoption Roadmap	IFRS Foundation	140+	Global standardization of financial reporting
EU Accounting Directive	European Commission	27	Harmonize accounting standards within the EU
ASEAN Economic Community (AEC) Blueprint 2025	ASEAN Secretariat	10	Regional integration, including financial reporting standards

Source: IFRS Foundation; European Commission; ASEAN Secretariat

Table 6 illuminates the concerted international and regional initiatives spearheaded by pivotal institutions like the IFRS Foundation, the European Commission, and ASEAN. It highlights their collective endeavour to show a cohesive financial reporting ecosystem that balances international standardization with regional integration imperatives.

Global Measures to Harmonize Financial Reporting

The International Accounting Standards Board (IASB) has been at the vanguard of developing International Financial Reporting Standards (IFRS), seeking to set a unified accounting language. As of 2024, over 140 jurisdictions allow the use of IFRS for publicly listed corporations, reflecting its across-the-board adoption (P. Kumar, Verma, Bhatnagar, et al., 2023; P. Kumar, Reepu, et al., 2024; P. Kumar, Taneja, Bhatnagar, et al., 2024). The European Union's enactment of IFRS in 2005 marked a momentous milestone, enhancing financial report comparability across member states. Regardless, major economies like the United States persist in adhering to Generally Accepted Accounting Principles (GAAP), underscoring ongoing challenges in attaining universal convergence. The IASB's association with the Financial Accounting Standards Board (FASB) through junction projects has strived to bridge these disparities, yet complete alignment needs to be accomplished (Bhatnagar, Kumar, et al., 2024; Bhatnagar, Rajaram, et al., 2024; Bhatnagar, Taneja, et al., 2024).

Regional Challenges and Approaches for Alignment

Regional disparities in economic growth, legal systems, and cultural contexts pose essential challenges to harmonizing financial reporting measures. In Asia, for example, nations display varying degrees of IFRS adoption. Japan allows voluntary adoption of IFRS, with around 30% of its total market capitalization reporting under these criteria. China has developed standards substantially linked with IFRS, reaffirming its dedication to complete intersection through the 'Beijing Statement' in 2015 (A. Kaur et al., 2023; P. Kumar, Taneja, & Ozen, 2024; P. Sharma et al., 2024; Taneja, Bhatnagar, Kumar, & Rupeika-apoga, 2023). India has presented Ind AS, which substantially links with IFRS, reflecting its measures toward alignment. In Africa, IFRS adoption varies, with some nations fully embracing the standards while others face challenges due to finite resources and expertise. The Pan African Federation of Accountants (PAFA) has been instrumental in advancing IFRS adoption across the continent, providing training and support to fellow bodies.

Latin American nations have shown a growing tendency toward IFRS adoption, with Brazil ordering IFRS for consolidated financial reports of publicly traded corporations since 2010. However, challenges prevail in aligning tax rules with IFRS needs, necessitating constant measures to harmonize accounting and tax reporting frameworks (Bhatnagar et al., 2023; P. Kumar, Bhatnagar, & Taneja, 2023; Taneja, Bhatnagar, Kumar, & Grima, 2023).

Role of International Organizations: IASB, IMF, and WTO

The IASB is paramount in setting international accounting standards, striving for high-quality, coherent, and enforceable norms that encourage transparency and comparability. Its due procedure involves extensive consultation with stakeholders worldwide, confirming that the benchmarks reflect diverse viewpoints and are globally relevant (Taneja & Özen, 2023). The International Monetary Fund (IMF) advocates the adoption of international standards, including IFRS, to amplify international financial stability. Through its Reports on the Observance of Standards and Codes (ROSC) initiative, the IMF evaluates member nations' adherence to international standards and delivers suggestions for improvement. The World Trade Organization (WTO) indirectly affects financial reporting harmonization by encouraging multinational trade and investment. Transparent and comparable financial data is crucial for fair trade conventions, and the WTO's focus on lowering trade impediments aligns with the goals of harmonized financial reporting standards.

Harmonizing financial reporting standards requires coordinated efforts from global organizations, regional bodies, and individual nations. While considerable progress has been made, continued challenges necessitate sustained dedication to achieving a genuinely international accounting framework that improves transparency, comparability, and economic integration (Bansal et al., 2023; Dangwal et al., 2022; M. Gupta et al., 2023).

Strategic Suggestions for Stakeholders

Harmonizing financial reporting standards is pivotal in promoting international economic integration, improving transparency, and enabling cross-border investments. Accomplishing this objective necessitates strategic ambitions from policymakers, companies, and regulators.

For Policymakers: Building Enabling Environments for Harmonization

Policymakers play a critical role in setting frameworks that support the adoption of International Financial Reporting Standards (IFRS). To build enabling conditions, they should:

- **Legislative Alignment**: Pass laws requiring IFRS for financial reporting, ensuring consistency with international practices. For example, the European Union's adoption of IFRS in 2005 required all publicly traded corporations to formulate consolidated financial reports according to these standards, enabling uniformity across member states (Dahiya & Taneja, 2023; Kour et al., 2025).

- **Capacity Building**: Finance training programs for accountants, auditors, and financial experts to improve their ability in IFRS. This includes collaborating with educational establishments to integrate IFRS into accounting curricula and delivering continuous professional development options (Taneja, Gupta, Bhushan, Bhatnagar, et al., 2023; Taneja, Gupta, Singh, Bhatnagar, et al., 2023).
- **Stakeholder Engagement**: Encourage dialogue among firms, regulatory bodies, and professional societies to manage IFRS implementation challenges and tailor approaches considering local economic contexts (Reepu et al., 2023; A. Singh et al., 2024).

For Businesses: Designing for Global Standard Adoption

Companies must proactively equip themselves for the transition to IFRS to confirm adherence and leverage the advantages of standardized financial reporting. Key measures include:

- **Internal Assessment**: Completely evaluate existing accounting systems and procedures to determine how much transformation is required to align with IFRS. This method should involve cross-functional groups to manage the multifaceted character of financial reporting (Taneja & Sharma, 2023).
- **Training and Development**: Execute targeted training schedules for finance and accounting personnel to build expertise in IFRS. According to an investigation by the International Federation of Accountants (IFAC), continued education is vital for sufficient IFRS adoption (TANEJA et al., 2024).
- **Technology Integration**: Finance in advanced accounting software competent in handling IFRS needs, promoting accurate and efficient financial reporting. This contains systems that support real-time data investigation and reporting.
- **Stakeholder Communication**: Transmit transparently with investors, creditors, and other stakeholders regarding the transition to IFRS, highlighting the anticipated advantages and managing possible concerns.

For Regulators: Balancing Local Demands with International Demands

Regulatory bodies must steer the complexities of aligning local accounting standards with global frameworks regarding domestic economic realities. Strategies contain:

- **Customized Implementation**: Invent phased strategies for IFRS adoption that permit gradual integration, allowing companies and specialists to adapt. This procedure has been utilized in nations like India, where Ind AS (Indian et al.) was presented in phases.
- **Monitoring and Enforcement**: Set vigorous mechanisms to observe compliance with IFRS and consistently enforce standards. This includes periodic audits and imposing fines for non-compliance to maintain the integrity of financial reporting.
- **Feedback Loops**: Build channels for constant feedback from businesses and auditors to pinpoint IFRS application challenges and make essential adjustments. This iterative method ensures that the standards remain appropriate and practical.
- **International Collaboration**: Engage with global standard-setting bodies, such as the International Accounting Standards Board (IASB), to form standards considering diverse economic conditions.

Harmonizing financial reporting standards successfully needs coordinated efforts from policymakers, companies, and regulators. By creating supportive legislative frameworks, financing in ability building, and balancing local and international needs, stakeholders can enable a seamless transition to IFRS, improving the quality and comparability of financial data worldwide.

CONCLUSION AND FUTURE DIRECTIONS

Investigating financial reporting's crucial role in cross-border mergers and acquisitions (M&As) reveals its transformative effect on global economic integration. This investigation indicates that harmonized financial reporting standards are not just technical needs but strategic imperatives that underpin transparency, comparability, and the seamless implementation of cross-border transactions. The discourse has illuminated the challenges posed by jurisdictional distinctions, the benefits of IFRS adoption, and the game-changing effect of technological innovations.

Cross-border M&As are critical to globalization, permitting corporations to develop operational footprints, diversify markets, and gain synergies across economies. However, the system could be more complicated with different financial reporting standards, regulatory landscapes, and cultural discrepancies. Harmonized standards like IFRS suggest a solution by bridging these gaps, enabling transactional efficiency, and strengthening investor confidence. While IFRS adoption has made significant strides, the simultaneousness of entrenched local accounting frameworks in powerful economies such as the United States continues to impede international uniformity.

Technological refinements are reshaping the financial reporting paradigm, offering exceptional opportunities to improve accuracy and efficiency. Blockchain assures traceability and decreases the risk of fraud, while artificial intelligence and cutting-edge analytics streamline reporting processes and deliver actionable, real-time insights. These innovations address long-standing inefficiencies and fit organizations to guide the complexities of international transactions with tremendous skill and precision. The conclusions also highlight the significance of tailored strategies to manage regional and jurisdiction-specific challenges. While international harmonization remains the overarching goal, regional partnerships can act as stimuli for aligning local procedures with global standards. Further, case studies of successes and failures in cross-border M&As support that robust planning, comprehensive due diligence, and effective communication among stakeholders are critical to realizing the whole possibility of these transactions.

Strategic Imperatives for the Future

The chapter spotlights several actionable actions for stakeholders to promote the harmonization of financial reporting:

1. **Global Adoption of IFRS**: Policymakers must prioritize aligning local norms with IFRS and managing economic and regulatory contexts to accelerate universal approval.
2. **Technological Transformation**: Enterprises should adopt emerging technologies to update financial reporting, lower inefficiencies, and improve decision-making capabilities.
3. **Capacity Building**: Educational initiatives and experienced training are necessary to equip financial professionals with the skills required for beneficial IFRS adoption and technological integration.
4. **Regional and Cross-Sector Collaborations**: Enhanced cooperation between international institutions, governments, and private companies is critical to creating cohesive frameworks that offset international consistency with regional nuances.
5. **Sustainability and Innovation**: As the landscape evolves, integrating sustainability metrics and investigating innovations in reporting courses will discourse emerging trends and demands and trends.

Towards a Transparent and Equitable Ecosystem

Attaining a globally harmonized financial reporting ecosystem needs concerted actions from all stakeholders. Policymakers must complete supportive regulatory conditions, companies must assume transformative technologies, and controllers must balance international goals and local validities. Further, continuous investigation into sustainability reporting, ESG integration and emerging tendencies will remain vital to fulfilling the requirements of an ever-changing international economy. Finally, the path to harmonized financial reporting is a technological challenge and a strategic possibility for building a transparent, efficient, and unbiased financial system. By discussing these challenges and capitalizing on opportunities, stakeholders can promote a global financial ecosystem that supports tolerable economic growth and integration, strengthening trust and cooperation across borders.

REFERENCES

Ahmad, I., Sharma, S., Kumar, R., Dhyani, S., & Dumka, A. (2023). Data Analytics of Online Education during Pandemic Health Crisis: A Case Study. *2nd Edition of IEEE Delhi Section Owned Conference, DELCON 2023 - Proceedings*. DOI: 10.1109/DELCON57910.2023.10127423

Aiyappa, S., Kodikal, R., & Rahiman, H. U. (2024). Accelerating Gender Equality for Sustainable Development: A Case Study of Dakshina Kannada District, India. *Technical and Vocational Education and Training*, *38*, 335–349. DOI: 10.1007/978-981-99-6909-8_30

Ajay, D., Sharad, K., Singh, K. P., & Sharma, S. (2023). Impact of Prolonged Mental Torture on Housewives in Middle Class Families. *Journal for ReAttach Therapy and Developmental Diversities*, *6*(4), 1–7.

Alexopoulos, C., Al-Tamimi, T. A. S., & Saxena, S. (2023). Were the higher educational institutions (HEIs) in Oman ready to face pedagogical challenges during COVID-19? *Arab Gulf Journal of Scientific Research*. Advance online publication. DOI: 10.1108/AGJSR-03-2023-0095

Alrashed, F. A., Alsubiheen, A. M., Alshammari, H., Mazi, S. I., Al-Saud, S. A., Alayoubi, S., Kachanathu, S. J., Albarrati, A., Aldaihan, M. M., Ahmad, T., Sattar, K., Khan, S., & Dhiman, G. (2022). Stress, Anxiety, and Depression in Pre-Clinical Medical Students: Prevalence and Association with Sleep Disorders. *Sustainability (Basel)*, *14*(18), 11320. Advance online publication. DOI: 10.3390/su141811320

Ambika, K. S. B., Goswami, S., Pimplapure, V., Jweeg, M. J., Kant, K., & Gangodkar, D. (2023). Framework Towards Detection of Stress Level Through Classifying Physiological Signals Using Machine Learning. *2023 3rd International Conference on Advance Computing and Innovative Technologies in Engineering, ICACITE 2023*, 600 – 604. DOI: 10.1109/ICACITE57410.2023.10183013

Arora, A., Singh, R., Malik, K., & Kestwal, U. (2024). Association of sexual performance and intimacy with satisfaction in life in head and neck cancer patients: A review. *Oral Oncology Reports*, *11*, 100563. Advance online publication. DOI: 10.1016/j.oor.2024.100563

Asha, P., Mannepalli, K., Khilar, R., Subbulakshmi, N., Dhanalakshmi, R., Tripathi, V., Mohanavel, V., Sathyamurthy, R., & Sudhakar, M. (2022). Role of machine learning in attaining environmental sustainability. *Energy Reports*, *8*, 863–871. DOI: 10.1016/j.egyr.2022.09.206

Awal, G., & Khanna, R. (2019). Determinants of millennial online consumer behavior and prospective purchase decisions. *International Journal of Advanced Science and Technology*, *28*(18), 366–378.

Bansal, N., Bhatnagar, M., & Taneja, S. (2023). Balancing priorities through green optimism: A study elucidating initiatives, approaches, and strategies for sustainable supply chain management. In *Handbook of Research on Designing Sustainable Supply Chains to Achieve a Circular Economy*. IGI Global., DOI: 10.4018/978-1-6684-7664-2.ch004

Bhatnagar, M., Kumar, P., Taneja, S., Sood, K., & Grima, S. (2024). From digital overload to trading Zen: The role of digital detox in enhancing intraday trading performance. In *Business Drivers in Promoting Digital Detoxification*. IGI Global., DOI: 10.4018/979-8-3693-1107-3.ch010

Bhatnagar, M., Rajaram, R., Taneja, S., & Kumar, P. (2024). Balancing acts: The Yin and Yang of debit and credit on the stage of financial well-being. In *Emerging Perspectives on Financial Well-Being*. IGI Global., DOI: 10.4018/979-8-3693-1750-1.ch002

Bhatnagar, M., Taneja, S., & Kumar, P. (2023). The Effectiveness of Carbon Pricing Mechanism in Steering Financial Flows Toward Sustainable Projects. *International Journal of Environmental Impacts*, *6*(4), 183–196. DOI: 10.18280/ijei.060403

Bhatnagar, M., Taneja, S., Kumar, P., & Özen, E. (2024). Does financial education act as a catalyst for SME competitiveness? *International Journal of Education Economics and Development*, *15*(3), 377–393. DOI: 10.1504/IJEED.2024.139306

Bhatt, C., Singh, S., Chauhan, R., Singh, T., & Uniyal, A. (2023). Artificial Intelligence in Current Education: Roles, Applications & Challenges. *Proceedings - 2023 3rd International Conference on Pervasive Computing and Social Networking, ICPCSN 2023*, 241 – 244. DOI: 10.1109/ICPCSN58827.2023.00045

Cavaliere, L. P. L., Byloppilly, R., Khan, S. D., Othman, B. A., Muda, I., & Malhotra, R. K. (2024). Acceptance and effectiveness of Industry 4.0 internal and external organisational initiatives in Malaysian firms. *International Journal of Management and Enterprise Development*, *23*(1), 1–25. DOI: 10.1504/IJMED.2024.138422

Dahiya, K., & Taneja, S. (2023). To Analyse the Impact of Multi-Media Technology on the Rural Entrepreneurship Development. In *Contemporary Studies of Risks in Emerging Technology* (pp. 221–240). DOI: 10.1108/978-1-80455-562-020231015

Dangwal, A., Kaur, S., Taneja, S., & Ozen, E. (2022). A bibliometric analysis of green tourism based on the scopus platform. In *Developing Relationships, Personalization, and Data Herald in Marketing 5.0*. IGI Global., DOI: 10.4018/978-1-6684-4496-2.ch015

Dutta, A., Singh, P., Dobhal, A., Mannan, D., Singh, J., & Goswami, P. (2023). Entrepreneurial Aptitude of Women of an Aspirational District of Uttarakhand. *Indian Journal of Extension Education, 59*(2), 103–107. DOI: 10.48165/IJEE.2023.59222

Goyal, P., Kukreja, T., Agarwal, A., & Khanna, N. (2015). Narrowing awareness gap by using e-learning tools for counselling university entrants. *Conference Proceeding - 2015 International Conference on Advances in Computer Engineering and Applications, ICACEA 2015*, 847 – 851. DOI: 10.1109/ICACEA.2015.7164822

Grover, D., Sharma, S., Kaur, P., Mittal, A., & Sharma, P. K. (2024). Societal Elements that Impact the Performance of Women Entrepreneurs in Tier-II Cities: A Study of Rohilkhand Region of Uttar Pradesh. *2024 IEEE Zooming Innovation in Consumer Technologies Conference. ZINC, 2024*, 114–117. DOI: 10.1109/ZINC61849.2024.10579316

Gupta, C., Jindal, P., & Malhotra, R. K. (2022). A Study of Increasing Adoption Trends of Digital Technologies - An Evidence from Indian Banking. In D. N. & C. A. (Eds.), *AIP Conference Proceedings* (Vol. 2481). American Institute of Physics Inc. DOI: 10.1063/5.0104572

Gupta, M., Arora, K., & Taneja, S. (2023). Bibliometric analysis on employee engagement and human resource management. In *Enhancing Customer Engagement Through Location-Based Marketing*. IGI Global., DOI: 10.4018/978-1-6684-8177-6.ch013

Indu, R., Dimri, S. C., & Kumar, B. (2023). Identification of Location for Police Headquarters to Deal with Crime Against Women in India Using Clustering Based on K-Means Algorithm. *International Journal of Computing and Digital Systems, 14*(1), 965–974. DOI: 10.12785/ijcds/140175

Ingale, N. V., Saravana Kumar, G., Panduro-Ramirez, J., Raj, M., Vaseem Akram, S., & Rawat, R. (2023). Role of IOT in managing education management tools: A technical review. *2023 3rd International Conference on Advance Computing and Innovative Technologies in Engineering, ICACITE 2023*, 2056 – 2061. DOI: 10.1109/ICACITE57410.2023.10182953

Jain, P., Gupta, V. K., Tiwari, H., Shukla, A., Pandey, P., & Gupta, A. (2023). Human-Computer Interaction: A Systematic Review. In M. H.K. & S. S. (Eds.), *Proceedings - 2023 International Conference on Advanced Computing and Communication Technologies, ICACCTech 2023* (pp. 31 – 36). Institute of Electrical and Electronics Engineers Inc. DOI: 10.1109/ICACCTech61146.2023.00015

Jindal, M., Bajal, E., Singh, P., Diwakar, M., Arya, C., & Sharma, K. (2022). Online education in Covid-19: Limitations and improvements. *2021 IEEE 8th Uttar Pradesh Section International Conference on Electrical, Electronics and Computer Engineering, UPCON 2021*. DOI: 10.1109/UPCON52273.2021.9667605

Joshi, K., Patil, S., Gupta, S., & Khanna, R. (2022). Role of Pranayma in emotional maturity for improving health. *Journal of Medical Pharmaceutical and Allied Sciences, 11*(2), 4569–4573. DOI: 10.55522/jmpas.V11I2.2033

Josphineleela, R., Gupta, R., Misra, N., Malik, M., Somasundaram, K., & Gangodkar, D. (2023). Blockchain Based Multi-Layer Security Network Authentication System for Uncertain Attack in the Wireless Communication System. *2023 3rd International Conference on Advance Computing and Innovative Technologies in Engineering, ICACITE 2023*, 877 – 881. DOI: 10.1109/ICACITE57410.2023.10182747

Josphineleela, R., Kaliappan, S., Natrayan, L., & Bhatt, U. M. (2023). Intelligent Virtual Laboratory Development and Implementation using the RASA Framework. *Proceedings - 7th International Conference on Computing Methodologies and Communication, ICCMC 2023*, 1172 – 1176. DOI: 10.1109/ICCMC56507.2023.10083701

Kanojia, P., Malhotra, R. K., & Uniyal, A. K. (2022). Impact of Organizational Commitment Components on the Teachers of Higher Education in Uttarakhand: An Emperical Analysis. *Proceedings - 2022 International Conference on Recent Trends in Microelectronics, Automation, Computing and Communications Systems, ICMACC 2022*, 360–364. DOI: 10.1109/ICMACC54824.2022.10093606

Kaur, A., Kumar, P., Taneja, S., & Ozen, E. (2023). Fintech emergence – an opportunity or threat to banking. *International Journal of Electronic Finance, 13*(1), 1–19. DOI: 10.1504/IJEF.2024.135163

Kaur, J., Khanna, R., Kumar, R., & Sunil, G. (2024). Role of Blockchain Technologies in Goods and Services Tax. *Proceedings - 2024 3rd International Conference on Sentiment Analysis and Deep Learning, ICSADL 2024*, 607–612. DOI: 10.1109/ICSADL61749.2024.00104

Khandelwal, C., Kumar, S., Tripathi, V., & Madhavan, V. (2023). Joint impact of corporate governance and risk disclosures on firm value: Evidence from emerging markets. *Research in International Business and Finance*, *66*, 102022. Advance online publication. DOI: 10.1016/j.ribaf.2023.102022

Khanna, R., Jindal, P., & Noja, G. G. (2023). Blockchain technologies, a catalyst for insurance sector. In *The Application of Emerging Technology and Blockchain in the Insurance Industry*. DOI: 10.1201/9781032630946-19

Kour, M., Taneja, S., Özen, E., Sood, K., & Grima, S. (2025). *Financial Landscape Transformation Technological Disruptions*.

Kumar, P., Reepu, & Kaur, R. (2024). Economic and Urban Dynamics: Investigating Socioeconomic Status and Urban Density as Moderators of Mobile Wallet Adoption in Smart Cities. *Lecture Notes in Networks and Systems, 948 LNNS*, 409–417. DOI: 10.1007/978-981-97-1329-5_33

Kumar, P., Bhatnagar, M., & Taneja, S. (2023). Investigation of the time pattern of Bit Green Crypto: An Arma modeling approach to unrave volatility. In *Algorithmic Approaches to Financial Technology: Forecasting, Trading, and Optimization*. IGI Global., DOI: 10.4018/979-8-3693-1746-4.ch001

Kumar, P., Taneja, S., Bhatnagar, M., & Kaur, A. K. (2024). Navigating the digital paradigm shift: Designing CBDCs for a transformative financial landscape. In *Exploring Central Bank Digital Currencies: Concepts, Frameworks, Models, and Challenges*. IGI Global., DOI: 10.4018/979-8-3693-1882-9.ch006

Kumar, P., Taneja, S., & Ozen, E. (2024). Exploring the influence of green bonds on sustainable development through low-carbon financing mobilization. *International Journal of Law and Management*. DOI: 10.1108/IJLMA-01-2024-0030

Kumar, P., Verma, P., Bhatnagar, M., Taneja, S., Seychel, S., Todorović, I., & Grim, S. (2023). The Financial Performance and Solvency Status of the Indian Public Sector Banks: A CAMELS Rating and Z Index Approach. *International Journal of Sustainable Development and Planning*, *18*(2), 367–376. DOI: 10.18280/ijsdp.180204

Kumar, R., Kathuria, S., Malholtra, R. K., Kumar, A., Gehlot, A., & Joshi, K. (2023). Role of Cloud Computing in Goods and Services Tax(GST) and Future Application. *2nd International Conference on Sustainable Computing and Data Communication Systems, ICSCDS 2023 - Proceedings*, 1443–1447. DOI: 10.1109/ICSCDS56580.2023.10104597

Kumar, R., Khannna Malholtra, R., & Grover, C. A. N. (2023). Review on Artificial Intelligence Role in Implementation of Goods and Services Tax(GST) and Future Scope. *2023 International Conference on Artificial Intelligence and Smart Communication, AISC 2023*, 348–351. DOI: 10.1109/AISC56616.2023.10085030

Kumar, R., Lande, A., Kumar, D., Malhotra, R. K., & Sharma, A. (2023). Technology Bridging -in Entrepreneurs and Consumers in Product Development. *ISED 2023 - International Conference on Intelligent Systems and Embedded Design*. DOI: 10.1109/ISED59382.2023.10444599

Kumar, R., Malholtra, R. K., Singh, R., Kathuria, S., Balyan, R., & Pal, P. (2023). Artificial Intelligence Role in Electronic Invoice Under Goods and Services Tax. *2023 International Conference on Computational Intelligence, Communication Technology and Networking, CICTN 2023*, 140–143. DOI: 10.1109/CICTN57981.2023.10140870

Kumar, R., Malhotra, R. K., & Grover, N. (2023). Data Mining in Credit Scoring and Future Application. *International Conference on Innovative Data Communication Technologies and Application, ICIDCA 2023 - Proceedings*, 1096–1100. DOI: 10.1109/ICIDCA56705.2023.10100032

Kumar, R., Malhotra, R. K., Pandey, S., Gehlot, A., Gautam, I., & Chamola, S. (2023). Role of Artificial Intelligence in Input Tax Credit Reconciliation. *Proceedings - 2023 3rd International Conference on Pervasive Computing and Social Networking, ICPCSN 2023*, 497–501. DOI: 10.1109/ICPCSN58827.2023.00086

Kumar, R., Sexena, A., & Gehlot, A. (2023). Artificial Intelligence in Smart Education and Futuristic Challenges. *2023 International Conference on Disruptive Technologies, ICDT 2023*, 432 – 435. DOI: 10.1109/ICDT57929.2023.10151129

Kumar, R., Singh, T., Mohanty, S. N., Goel, R., Gupta, D., Alharbi, M., & Khanna, R. (2023). Study on online payments and e-commerce with SOR model. *International Journal of Retail & Distribution Management*. Advance online publication. DOI: 10.1108/IJRDM-03-2023-0137

Kumari, J., Singh, P., Mishra, A. K., Singh Meena, B. P., Singh, A., & Ojha, M. (2024). Challenges Hindering Women's Involvement in the Hospitality Industry as Entrepreneurs in the Era of Digital Economy. In *Revolutionizing the AI-Digital Landscape: A Guide to Sustainable Emerging Technologies for Marketing Professionals*. Taylor and Francis., DOI: 10.4324/9781032688305-9

Malhotra, R. K., Gupta, C., & Jindal, P. (2022). Blockchain and Smart Contracts for Insurance Industry. In *Blockchain Technology in Corporate Governance*. Transforming Business and Industries., DOI: 10.1002/9781119865247.ch11

Malhotra, R. K., Ojha, M. K., & Gupta, S. (2021). A study of assessment of knowledge, perception and attitude of using tele health services among college going students of Uttarakhand. *Journal of Medical Pharmaceutical and Allied Sciences*, *10*, 113–116. DOI: 10.22270/jmpas.VIC2I1.2020

Malik, P., Singh, A. K., Nautiyal, R., & Rawat, S. (2022). Mapping AICTE cybersecurity curriculum onto CyBOK: A case study. In *Machine Learning for Cyber Security*. De Gruyter., DOI: 10.1515/9783110766745-007

Mary Joshitta, S., & Sunil, M. P. Badriasulaimanalfurhood, Bodhankar, A., Ch.Sreedevi, & Khanna, R. (2023). The Integration of Machine Learning Technique with the Existing System to Predict the Flight Prices. *2023 3rd International Conference on Advance Computing and Innovative Technologies in Engineering, ICACITE 2023*, 398–402. DOI: 10.1109/ICACITE57410.2023.10182539

Mishra, D., Kandpal, V., Agarwal, N., & Srivastava, B. (2024). Financial Inclusion and Its Ripple Effects on Socio-Economic Development: A Comprehensive Review. *Journal of Risk and Financial Management*, *17*(3), 105. Advance online publication. DOI: 10.3390/jrfm17030105

Nagila, A., Saravanakumar, P., Pranavan, S., Goutam, R., Dobhal, D. C., & Singh, G. (2023). An Innovative Approach of CNN-BiGRU Based Post-Earthquake Damage Detection of Reinforced Concrete for Frame Buildings. *International Conference on Self Sustainable Artificial Intelligence Systems, ICSSAS 2023 - Proceedings*, 56 – 61. DOI: 10.1109/ICSSAS57918.2023.10331894

Neha, M., S., Alfurhood, B. S., Bakhare, R., Poongavanam, S., & Khanna, R. (2023). The Role and Impact of Artificial Intelligence on Retail Business and its Developments. *2023 International Conference on Artificial Intelligence and Smart Communication, AISC 2023*, 1098–1101. DOI: 10.1109/AISC56616.2023.10085624

Nikolaidis, P., Ismail, M., Shuib, L., Khan, S., & Dhiman, G. (2022). Predicting Student Attrition in Higher Education through the Determinants of Learning Progress: A Structural Equation Modelling Approach. *Sustainability (Basel)*, *14*(20), 13584. Advance online publication. DOI: 10.3390/su142013584

Onyema, E. M., Almuzaini, K. K., Onu, F. U., Verma, D., Gregory, U. S., Puttaramaiah, M., & Afriyie, R. K. (2022). Prospects and Challenges of Using Machine Learning for Academic Forecasting. *Computational Intelligence and Neuroscience*, *2022*, 1–7. Advance online publication. DOI: 10.1155/2022/5624475 PMID: 35909823

Pandey, R. P., Bansal, S., Awasthi, P., Dixit, V., Singh, R., & Yadava, V. (2023). Attitude and Myths Related to Stalking among Early and Middle Age Adults. *Psychology Hub*, *40*(3), 85 – 94. DOI: 10.13133/2724-2943/17960

Pattanshetti, M. K., Jasola, S., Rajput, A., & Pant, V. (2021). Proposed eLearning framework using open corpus web resources. *Proceedings of the 2021 1st International Conference on Advances in Electrical, Computing, Communications and Sustainable Technologies, ICAECT 2021*. DOI: 10.1109/ICAECT49130.2021.9392591

Prikshat, V., Kumar, S., & Nankervis, A. (2019). Work-readiness integrated competence model: Conceptualisation and scale development. *Education + Training*, *61*(5), 568–589. DOI: 10.1108/ET-05-2018-0114

Prikshat, V., Kumar, S., & Raje, P. (2017). Antecedents, consequences and strategic responses to graduate work-readiness: Challenges in India. In *Transitions from Education to Work: Workforce Ready Challenges in the Asia Pacific*. Taylor and Francis., DOI: 10.4324/9781315533971-8

Rana, D. S., Dimri, S. C., Malik, P., & Dhondiyal, S. A. (2022). Impact of Computational Thinking in Engineering and K12 Education. *4th International Conference on Inventive Research in Computing Applications, ICIRCA 2022 - Proceedings*, 697 – 701. DOI: 10.1109/ICIRCA54612.2022.9985593

Rana, M. S., Cavaliere, L. P. L., Mishra, A. B., Padhye, P., Singh, R. R., & Khanna, R. (2022). Internet of Things (IOT) Based Assessment for Effective Monitoring Data Against Malicious Attacks on Financial Collectors. *2022 2nd International Conference on Advance Computing and Innovative Technologies in Engineering, ICACITE 2022*, 177–181. DOI: 10.1109/ICACITE53722.2022.9823612

Rathore, R., & Goudar, R. H. (2015). SPARQL-based personalised E-Learning system designed using ontology (SPELSO): An architecture. *International Journal of Knowledge and Learning*, *10*(4), 384–416. DOI: 10.1504/IJKL.2015.077554

Rawat, R. S., Singh, V., & Dumka, A. (2022). Complaint Management in Ethiopian Vocational and Technical Education Institutions: A Framework and Implementation of a Decision Support System. *2022 International Conference on 4th Industrial Revolution Based Technology and Practices, ICFIRTP 2022*, 73 – 79. DOI: 10.1109/ICFIRTP56122.2022.10063207

Reepu, R., Taneja, S., Ozen, E., & Singh, A. (2023). A globetrotter to the future of marketing: Metaverse. In *Cultural Marketing and Metaverse for Consumer Engagement*. IGI Global., DOI: 10.4018/978-1-6684-8312-1.ch001

Sharma, P., Malhotra, R. K., Ojha, M. K., & Gupta, S. (2022). Impact of meditation on mental & physical health and thereby on academic performance of students: A study of higher educational institutions of Uttarakhand. *Journal of Medical Pharmaceutical and Allied Sciences*, *11*(2), 4641–4644. DOI: 10.55522/jmpas.V11I2.2309

Sharma, P., Taneja, S., Kumar, P., Özen, E., & Singh, A. (2024). Application of the UTAUT model toward individual acceptance: Emerging trends in artificial intelligence-based banking services. *International Journal of Electronic Finance, 13*(3), 352–366. DOI: 10.1504/IJEF.2024.139584

Sharma, S., Gupta, A., & Tyagi, R. (2023). Artificial Intelligence Enabled Sustainable Education System Using Vedic Scripture and Cyber Security. *2023 2nd International Conference on Advances in Computational Intelligence and Communication, ICACIC 2023*. DOI: 10.1109/ICACIC59454.2023.10435133

Sharma, S., Kadayat, Y., & Tyagi, R. (2023). Sustainable Global Democratic e-Governance System Using Vedic Scripture, Artificial Intelligence, Cloud Computing and Augmented Reality. *Proceedings of the International Conference on Circuit Power and Computing Technologies, ICCPCT 2023*, 113 – 118. DOI: 10.1109/ICCPCT58313.2023.10245405

Sharma, S., Singh, V., & Sarkar, D. (2023). Machine Vision Enabled Fall Detection System for Specially Abled People in Limited Visibility Environment. *2023 3rd Asian Conference on Innovation in Technology, ASIANCON 2023*. DOI: 10.1109/ASIANCON58793.2023.10270769

Sharma, S., Singh Rawal, R., Pandey, D., & Pandey, N. (2021). Microbial World for Sustainable Development. In *Microbial Technology for Sustainable Environment*. Springer Nature., DOI: 10.1007/978-981-16-3840-4_1

Sharma, V., & Jain, S. (2020). Managers Training Programs Effectiveness Evaluation by using different Machine Learning Approaches. *Proceedings of the 4th International Conference on Electronics, Communication and Aerospace Technology, ICECA 2020*, 1453 – 1457. DOI: 10.1109/ICECA49313.2020.9297556

Shrivastava, A., Usha, R., Kukreti, R., Sharma, G., Srivastava, A. P., & Khan, A. K. (2023). Women Safety Precaution. *2023 1st International Conference on Circuits, Power, and Intelligent Systems, CCPIS 2023*. DOI: 10.1109/CCPIS59145.2023.10291594

Singh, A., Kumar, P., & Taneja, S. (2024). Artificial Intelligence and Machine Learning-Powered Smart Finance. In Taneja, P. K. S., & Singh, A. (Eds.), *IGI Global*. IGI Global., DOI: 10.4018/979-8-3693-3264-1

Singh, A. B., Meena, H. K., Khandelwal, C., & Dangayach, G. S. (2023). Sustainability Assessment of Higher Education Institutions: A Systematic Literature Review †. *Engineering Proceedings, 37*(1), 23. Advance online publication. DOI: 10.3390/ECP2023-14728

Singh, K. D., & Singh, P. (2023). A Novel Cloud-based Framework to Predict the Employability of Students. In K. R., K. R., G. M., G. M., S. R., & S. R. (Eds.), *2023 International Conference on Advancement in Computation and Computer Technologies, InCACCT 2023* (pp. 528 – 532). Institute of Electrical and Electronics Engineers Inc. DOI: 10.1109/InCACCT57535.2023.10141760

Singh, K. D., Singh, P., Kaur, G., Khullar, V., Chhabra, R., & Tripathi, V. (2023). Education 4.0: Exploring the Potential of Disruptive Technologies in Transforming Learning. *Proceedings of International Conference on Computational Intelligence and Sustainable Engineering Solution, CISES 2023*, 586 – 591. DOI: 10.1109/CISES58720.2023.10183547

Singh, K. U., Chaudhary, V., Sharma, P. K., Kumar, P., Varshney, N., & Singh, T. (2024). Integrating GPS and GSM Technologies for Enhanced Women's Safety: A Fingerprint-Activated Device Approach. *2024 International Conference on Automation and Computation, AUTOCOM 2024*, 657 – 662. DOI: 10.1109/AUTOCOM60220.2024.10486120

Singh, P., & Singh, K. D. (2023). Fog-Centric Intelligent Surveillance System: A Novel Approach for Effective and Efficient Surveillance. In K. R., K. R., G. M., G. M., S. R., & S. R. (Eds.), *2023 International Conference on Advancement in Computation and Computer Technologies, InCACCT 2023* (pp. 762 – 766). Institute of Electrical and Electronics Engineers Inc. DOI: 10.1109/InCACCT57535.2023.10141802

Srivastava, B., Kandpal, V., & Jain, A. K. (2024). Financial well-being of women self-help group members: A qualitative study. *Environment, Development and Sustainability*. Advance online publication. DOI: 10.1007/s10668-024-04879-w

Taneja, S., Bhatnagar, M., Kumar, P., & Grima, S. (2023). A Panel Analysis of the Effectiveness of the Asset Management in Indian Agricultural Companies. *International Journal of Sustainable Development and Planning*, *18*(3), 653–660. DOI: 10.18280/ijsdp.180301

Taneja, S., Bhatnagar, M., Kumar, P., & Rupeika-apoga, R. (2023). India ' s Total Natural Resource Rents (NRR) and GDP : An Augmented Autoregressive Distributed Lag (ARDL) Bound Test. *Journal of Risk and Financial Management, 16*(2), 91. https://doi.org/doi.org/10.3390/jrfm16020091. DOI: 10.3390/jrfm16020091

Taneja, S., Gupta, M., Bhushan, P., Bhatnagar, M., & Singh, A. (2023). Cultural marketing in the digital era. In *Cultural Marketing and Metaverse for Consumer Engagement*. IGI Global., DOI: 10.4018/978-1-6684-8312-1.ch008

Taneja, S., Gupta, S., Singh, A., Bhatnagar, M., & Gaur, A. (2023). Green management - A new paradigm in the world of business. *Green Management - A New Paradigm in the World of Business*, 1–230. DOI: 10.52305/DLIH6622

Taneja, S., & Özen, E. (2023). To analyse the relationship between bank's green financing and environmental performance. *International Journal of Electronic Finance, 12*(2), 163–175. DOI: 10.1504/IJEF.2023.129919

Taneja, S., & Sharma, V. (2023). Role of beaconing marketing in improving customer buying experience. In *Enhancing Customer Engagement Through Location-Based Marketing*. IGI Global., DOI: 10.4018/978-1-6684-8177-6.ch012

Tiwari, R., Agrawal, P., Singh, P., Bajaj, S., Verma, V., & Chauhan, A. S. (2023). Technology Enabled Integrated Fusion Teaching for Enhancing Learning Outcomes in Higher Education. *International Journal of Emerging Technologies in Learning, 18*(7), 243–249. DOI: 10.3991/ijet.v18i07.36799

Tyagi, S., Mathur, K., Gupta, T., Khantwal, S., & Tripathi, V. (2023). The Effectiveness of Augmented Reality in Developing Pre-Primary Student's Cognitive Skills. *IEEE Region 10 Humanitarian Technology Conference, R10-HTC*, 997 – 1002. DOI: 10.1109/R10-HTC57504.2023.10461754

Uniyal, A. K., Kanojia, P., Khanna, R., & Dixit, A. K. (2022). Quantitative Analysis of the Impact of Demography and Job Profile on the Organizational Commitment of the Faculty Members in the HEI'S of Uttarakhand. *Communications in Computer and Information Science, 1742 CCIS*, 24–35. DOI: 10.1007/978-3-031-23647-1_3

Upreti, H., & Malhotra, R. K. (2024). Bridging The Urban-Rural Education Gap In India Through CSR (Corporate Social Responsibility) Initiatives: A Conceptual Study With Special Reference To Sustainable Development Goal 4 (Quality Education). In P. P.K. (Ed.), *E3S Web of Conferences* (Vol. 556). EDP Sciences. DOI: 10.1051/e3sconf/202455601032

Yadav, P. M., Patra, I., Mittal, V., Nagorao, C. G., Udhayanila, R., & Saranya, A. (2023). Implementation of IOT on English Language Classroom Management. *2023 3rd International Conference on Advance Computing and Innovative Technologies in Engineering, ICACITE 2023*, 1686 – 1690. DOI: 10.1109/ICACITE57410.2023.10182984

Zhang, Y., Cao, C., Gu, J., & Garg, H. (2023). The Impact of Top Management Team Characteristics on the Risk Taking of Chinese Private Construction Enterprises. *Systems, 11*(2), 67. Advance online publication. DOI: 10.3390/systems11020067

Chapter 7
A Half-Century of International Accounting Standards (IAS/IFRS):
Assessing the Mandatory Adoption, Impact, and Morocco's Position in the Convergence Process

Azzouz Elhamma
https://orcid.org/0000-0003-3382-0278
Ibn Tofaîl University, Morocco

ABSTRACT

Since its establishment in 1973, the International Accounting Standards Committee (IASC), which became the International Accounting Standards Board (IASB) in 2001, has developed and published international accounting standards, initially known as IAS and later as IFRS. After fifty years, 87% of countries, including Morocco, mandate the full or partial adoption of IFRS. This paper provides a brief overview of the history of IFRS, focusing on three key areas: the global extent of adoption and its main determinants, the consequences of adoption, and the role of IFRS in Morocco's accounting standardization. The findings suggest that IFRS adoption is influenced by factors such as reliance on international financial institutions, economic openness, professional expertise, etc. Furthermore, IFRS adoption enhances the quality of accounting information and positively impacts macroeconomic indicators. While Morocco has partially adopted IFRS for banks, it is currently undertaking a major project to align its accounting practices with IFRS standards.

DOI: 10.4018/979-8-3373-0887-6.ch007

INTRODUCTION

The history of accounting dates back to ancient civilizations (Keith, 1992); however, its formalization began in the 15th century, particularly with the Italian mathematician Luca Pacioli, who is regarded as the father of accounting. In 1494, Pacioli published the first comprehensive work on double-entry bookkeeping. Nevertheless, the standardization of accounting practices did not occur until the early 20th century, specifically in 1909 in the United States, with the establishment of the American Association of Public Accountants (AAPA), the predecessor of the American Institute of Certified Public Accountants (AICPA).

Certainly, accounting plays a crucial role in the economic and financial activities of nations. As early as the 19th century, Max Weber recognized accounting as central to the rationality of the capitalist economy. Similarly, Karl Marx highlighted that accounting serves as a key tool in developing and reproducing the social relations inherent in capitalism (Chiapello, 2007). According to Esnault and Hoarau (2005, p. 3), accounting is defined as "an information system, and more specifically, a formal system for identifying, measuring, classifying, and recording the transactions of organizations, designed to provide, after appropriate processing, information likely to satisfy the presumed needs of multiple users." The French Plan Comptable Général (PCG, Art. 121-1) defines accounting as "a system for organizing financial information in order to capture, classify, and record basic numerical data, and to present statements that give a true and fair view of an entity's assets, financial position, and results at the balance sheet date." Colasse (1997) argues that the primary objective of accounting, and particularly financial accounting, is to provide a relevant representation of the economic reality of an entity.

Accounting standards vary significantly across countries, with two primary accounting models emerging in recent decades. The first is the Anglo-Saxon model, which is based on accounting standards developed by professional organizations in the United States and the United Kingdom. The second is the Franco-Germanic (or continental) model, which relies primarily on charts of accounts established by public authorities in France and Germany. This diversity in accounting approaches has created challenges in comparing financial statements, thereby highlighting the need for universally accepted international accounting standards. International Accounting Standards (IAS) refer to the accounting guidelines developed by the International Accounting Standards Committee (IASC) between June 29, 1973, and April 1, 2001. In contrast, International Financial Reporting Standards (IFRS) represent a new set of standards published since April 1, 2001, by the International Accounting Standards Board (IASB), the successor to the IASC. The primary objective of adopting IFRS is to enhance the comprehensibility, relevance, reliability, comparability, and transparency of financial information, with the goal of reducing information asymmetries between various stakeholders.

Since the European Union's decision in 2002 (EC Regulation No. 1606/2002) to require listed companies within the EU to prepare their consolidated financial statements in accordance with the IFRS as issued by the IASB, the adoption of IFRS at the national level by various countries has experienced significant evolution over the past three decades. According to a recent report by the IFRS Foundation, by 2018, 144 jurisdictions—accounting for 87% of the global total—required IFRS for all or most companies (IFRS Foundation report, 2018).

As part of its commitment to international accounting standards, Morocco has mandated that banks and other financial institutions prepare their financial statements in accordance with IFRS. Additionally, listed companies are permitted to choose between IFRS and local accounting standards (CGNC: Code Général de la Normalisation Comptable). In 2020, the Moroccan National Accounting Council (CNC) launched a major initiative aimed at aligning the CGNC with IFRS.

In this context, the present study aims to address four central research questions: First, what is the current global level of adoption of IAS/IFRS, fifty years after their introduction? Second, what are the primary factors influencing national adoption of IAS/IFRS after five decades? Third, what are the key consequences of IFRS adoption on the quality of financial and accounting information, as well as on various macroeconomic indicators? Finally, to what extent do IAS/IFRS dominate the accounting standards framework in Morocco?

This paper is organized into four sections. The first section provides a general overview of the International Accounting Standards Board (IASB) and its international accounting standards, IAS/IFRS. The second section investigates the adoption of these accounting standards, highlighting the key determinants influencing their adoption. The third section explores the potential effects of IAS/IFRS adoption on the quality of accounting information and its impact on various macroeconomic indicators. The fourth section is dedicated to an analysis of accounting regulation in Morocco and the role of IAS/IFRS within the country's accounting framework.

1. OVERVIEW OF THE IASB AND ITS INTERNATIONAL ACCOUNTING STANDARDS (IAS/IFRS)

In the present section, we will focus both on the IASB as the organization responsible for the development and publication of IFRS (1.1), and on the IAS/IFRS standards issued by the IASB (1.2).

1.1. The IASB from 1973 to the Present

The creation of the International Accounting Standards Committee (IASC) on June 29, 1973, in London was initiated by Henry Benson, President of the Institute of Chartered Accountants in England & Wales (ICAEW). The IASC was established by the professional accounting bodies of nine countries—Australia, Canada, France, Germany, Japan, Mexico, the Netherlands, the United Kingdom, and the United States—with the primary objective of developing and publishing International Accounting Standards (IAS). In April 2001, the International Accounting Standards Board (IASB) succeeded the IASC, gaining greater independence from the accounting profession. From that point onward, the standards issued are referred to as International Financial Reporting Standards (IFRS). The table below outlines key milestones in the history of the IASB.

Table 1. A brief history of the IASB

Key Dates	Events
June 29, 1973	Establishment of the IASC in London.
1975	Publication of the first standard: IAS 1 "Disclosure of Accounting Policies" and the second standard: IAS 2 "Valuation and Presentation of Inventories Using the Historical Cost Method."
1982	The IFAC recognizes the IASC as the sole international accounting standard setter
1989	Publication of the Conceptual Framework for the Preparation and Presentation of Financial Statements (IASC Framework).
1995	Agreement between the IOSCO (International Organization of Securities Commissions) and the IASC. The IOSCO commits to recommending the acceptance of financial statements prepared in accordance with IAS.
2001	The reform of the IASC, which became the IASB. Standards published before April 1, 2001, retain the designation "IAS," while new standards will be referred to as "IFRS."
2002	The decision by the EU to require listed companies within the EU to present consolidated financial statements in IFRS starting from 2005 (EC Regulation No. 1606/2002 / OJEC of September 11, 2002).
2003	Revision of 13 standards.
2010	Change of names for: • The IASCF (International Accounting Standards Committee Foundation) becomes the IFRS Foundation; • The SAC (Standards Advisory Council) is renamed the IFRS Advisory Council; • The IFRIC (International Financial Reporting Interpretations Committee) is renamed the IFRS Interpretations Committee.

Source: Developed by the authors based on www.ifrs.org

The IFRS Foundation operates under a three-tier governance structure, which consists of two independent standard-setting boards—the International Accounting Standards Board (IASB) and the International Sustainability Standards Board (ISSB). These boards are governed and overseen by the IFRS Foundation Trustees, who are drawn from a global pool of individuals and are accountable to the IFRS Foundation Monitoring Board. Additionally, the IFRS Advisory Council offers advice and guidance to both the Trustees and the Boards.

1.2. IAS/IFRS Standards

The table below summarizes the international accounting standards (IAS/IFRS) developed and published by the IASB that are currently in effect.

Table 2. Current IAS/IFRS standards

Categories of Standards	Standards
Standards related to financial statement presentation	IAS 1: "Presentation of Financial Statements"; IAS 7: "Statement of Cash Flows."; IFRS 18 "Presentation and Disclosure in Financial Statements".
Standards related to measurement	IAS 8: "Accounting Policies, Changes in Accounting Estimates and Errors"; IAS 10: "Events After the Reporting Period"; IAS 21: "The Effects of Changes in Foreign Exchange Rates"; IFRS 13: "Fair Value Measurement."
Standards related to information disclosure	IAS 24: "Related Party Disclosures"; IAS 29: "Financial Reporting in Hyperinflationary Economies"; IAS 33: "Earnings Per Share"; IAS 34: "Interim Financial Reporting"; IFRS 1: "First-time Adoption of International Financial Reporting Standards"; IFRS 8: "Operating Segments"; IFRS 14: "Regulatory Deferral Accounts."
Standards related to business combinations	IAS 27: "Separate Financial Statements"; IAS 28: "Investments in Associates and Joint Ventures"; IFRS 3: "Business Combinations"; IFRS 10: "Consolidated Financial Statements"; IFRS 11: "Joint Arrangements"; IFRS 12: "Disclosure of Interests in Other Entities."
Specific Standards	IAS 2: "Inventories"; IAS 12: "Income Taxes"; IAS 16: "Property, Plant and Equipment"; IAS 19: "Employee Benefits"; IAS 20: "Accounting for Government Grants and Disclosure of Government Assistance"; IAS 23: "Borrowing Costs"; IAS 32: "Financial Instruments: Presentation"; IAS 36: "Impairment of Assets"; IAS 37: "Provisions, Contingent Liabilities and Contingent Assets"; IAS 38: "Intangible Assets"; IAS 39: "Financial Instruments: Recognition and Measurement"; IAS 40: "Investment Property"; IFRS 2: "Share-based Payment"; IFRS 5: "Non-current Assets Held for Sale and Discontinued Operations"; IFRS 7: "Financial Instruments: Disclosures"; IFRS 9: "Financial Instruments";
Industry-specific Standards	IAS 26: "Accounting and Reporting by Retirement Benefit Plans"; IAS 41: "Agriculture"; IFRS 6: "Exploration for and Evaluation of Mineral Resources." IFRS 17 "Insurance Contracts".

Source: Developed by the authors based on www.ifrs.org

2. ADOPTION OF IAS/IFRS STANDARDS WORLDWIDE AND ITS KEY DETERMINANTS

The objective of this section is twofold. First, we will highlight the degree of IFRS adoption worldwide (2.1), and second, we will examine the key determinants of this adoption (2.2).

2.1. Adoption of IAS/IFRS Standards Worldwide

According to the most recent report from the IFRS Foundation, of the 166 countries included in the study, 144—representing 87% of the total—require the adoption of IFRS either for all companies or for the majority of companies (IFRS Foundation, 2018). The findings of this study are summarized in Tables 3 and 4 below.

Table 3. Status of IFRS adoption worldwide

	Africa & the Middle East	**North and Latin America**	**Asia and Oceania**	**Europe**
Mandatory	49 (96.07%)	27 (72.97%)	25 (73.53%)	43 (97.73%)
Permitted	01 (1.96%)	8 (21.62%)	3 (8,82%)	01 (2.27%)
Neither mandatory nor permitted	01 (1.96%)	2 (5.41%)	6 (17.65%)	00 (00%)
Total	51 (100%)	37 (100%)	34 (100%)	44 (100%)

Source: IFRS Foundation report (2018)

The national adoption rate of IFRS is higher in Europe, as well as in Africa and the Middle East, compared to Asia and Oceania, and the Americas. In Europe, 97.73% of countries require the adoption of IFRS for all companies or for the majority of companies. This rate is 96.07% in African and Middle Eastern countries. In contrast, the adoption rate in the Americas is only 72.97%, and in Asia and Oceania, it is 73.53%.

Table 4. Status of adoption of IFRS for SMEs worldwide

	Africa & the Middle East	**North and Latin America**	**Asia and Oceania**	**Europe**
Mandatory or permitted	28 (54.90%)	33 (89.19%)	17 (50%)	8 (18.18%)
Neither mandatory nor permitted	23 (45.10%)	4 (10.81%)	17 (50%)	36 (81.82%)
Total	51 (100%)	37 (100%)	34 (100%)	44 (100%)

Source: IFRS Foundation (2018)

The national adoption of IFRS for SMEs is notably high in the Americas and relatively low in Europe. In the Americas, 89% of countries either mandate or permit the adoption of IFRS for SMEs. In contrast, only 18% of European countries require or allow the adoption of this international standard. The adoption rates are 50% in Asia and Oceania, and 54.9% in Africa and the Middle East, respectively.

2.2. The Main Determinants of IFRS Adoption

Several scholars, including Mir and Rahaman (2005), Hassan (2008), Irvine (2008), Hassan et al. (2014), Boolaky et al. (2020), and Elhamma (2024) have demonstrated that international financial institutions (IFIs) possess coercive power to influence developing countries to adopt IFRS. Among the coercive mechanisms employed by the World Bank (WB) and the International Monetary Fund (IMF) is the *Reports on the Observance of Standards and Codes* (ROSC) program. This program aims to evaluate countries' accounting and auditing (AA) systems. The reports published as part of the program are typically followed by discussions with the countries concerned, particularly regarding the adoption of IFRS. For instance, the two 2004 ROSC (AA) reports on Ghana and Nigeria were followed by the national adoption of IFRS in these countries in 2007 and 2012, respectively (Boolaky et al., 2020). Judge et al. (2010) investigated the relevance of isomorphic pressures using a sample of 132 developing, transitional, and developed economies. They found that foreign aid serves as a coercive factor influencing a country's decision to adopt IFRS. Using data from 71 countries, Alon and Dwyer (2014) found that countries with weak governance structures and lower levels of economic development are more likely to adopt IFRS in order to gain legitimacy and access resources from international financial institutions (IFIs). Similarly, Ben Othman and Kossentini (2015) found that coercive isomorphism, as measured by foreign aid and the use of ROSC (AA) reports, is positively associated with the adoption of IFRS at the national level.

Certainly, membership in international institutions such as the International Federation of Accountants (IFAC) can be considered an important indicator of accounting professionalism and may exert mimetic pressure on countries to adopt IFRS. Professional accountancy bodies that are institutional members of IFAC, in their pursuit of international legitimacy, are more likely to align with IFAC's expectations and place greater emphasis on the adoption of IFRS. In the African context, Boolaky et al. (2020) identified a positive and statistically significant relationship between the number of years a country has been a member of IFAC and the national adoption of IFRS. Furthermore, among the mimetic pressures, economic openness also plays a role. In the United Arab Emirates, Irvine (2008) found that mimetic pressures from trading partners contributed to the national adoption of IFRS. Similarly, Judge et al. (2010) found that the level of import penetration is a mimetic predictor of the extent to which IFRS standards are adopted in 132 countries.

In the field of accounting, some researchers have indicated that professional accounting organizations (PAOs) are considered a significant source of isomorphism. In the MENA (Middle East and North Africa) region, Hassan (2008) in Egypt and Irvine (2008) in the United Arab Emirates demonstrated how normative pressures from international accounting professions influenced the decision to adopt IFRS. Similarly, in the African context, Boolaky et al. (2020) found a positive and statistically significant relationship between the strength of PAOs and the national adoption of IFRS. Additionally, the level of education is regarded as a foundational element for the development of all professions, including accounting. Based on a sample of 64 countries, Zeghal and Mhedhbi (2006) found that the level of education has a significant positive effect on the adoption of IAS. These findings were subsequently confirmed by Judge et al. (2010).

Recently, Elhamma (2024) conducted a study involving 14 countries from the MENA region (Algeria, Egypt, Iran, Iraq, Jordan, Kuwait, Lebanon, Mauritania, Morocco, Oman, Qatar, Saudi Arabia, Tunisia, and the UAE) during the period from 2005 to 2020. Using institutional theory, the study focused on three types of isomorphism: coercive isomorphism, measured by external debt; mimetic isomorphism, measured by the openness of the economy to the outside world; and normative isomorphism, measured by the national educational level. He found that "external debt, openness of the economy to the outside world, and the level of education are significantly positively associated with national IFRS adoption across the full sample."

3. EFFECTS OF IFRS ADOPTION

In this section, we will first present the potential effects of IFRS adoption on the quality of financial and accounting information (3.1), and then we will examine their impact on several macroeconomic indicators (3.2).

3.1. Effects on the Quality of Accounting Information

The impact of IFRS adoption on the quality of accounting information remains one of the most contentious topics in international accounting. Barth et al. (2008) and Bartov et al. (2005) argue that there is no conclusive evidence to suggest that the adoption of IFRS leads to an improvement in the quality of accounting information. However, the majority of empirical studies conducted in both developed and developing countries have shown that the adoption of IAS/IFRS plays a significant role in enhancing the quality of financial reporting. In the Chinese context, Liu and Liu (2007) indicate that financial statements prepared under IFRS were more relevant than those prepared under Chinese accounting standards. Similarly, Barth et al. (2008), based on a study conducted in 21 countries, report that voluntary adoption of IFRS by European companies is associated with a reduction in earnings management, thereby enhancing the quality of financial information.

The study conducted by Armstrong et al. (2010) to examine the reactions of European stock markets to 16 events related to the adoption of IFRS in Europe suggests that investors in European companies perceived the adoption of IFRS as beneficial. In France, Lenormand and Touchais (2009) conducted a study with 160 French companies to compare the relevance of value for investors between IAS/IFRS and French accounting standards. They found that "although both standards appear relevant in terms of value, we demonstrate that IAS/IFRS provide more information" (p. 145-146). In the United Kingdom, Iatridis (2010) noted that the application of IFRS increased the relevance of the accounting information published by British companies. Chai et al. (2010) compared the accounting quality of publicly listed companies in 15 European Union (EU) member states before and after the full adoption of IFRS in 2005. They found that the majority of accounting quality indicators improved following the adoption of IFRS.

However, these findings must be interpreted with caution, as other empirical studies have not yielded the same results. Schiebel (2007) examined the value relevance of IFRS and German accounting standards using a sample of 24 German companies listed on the Frankfurt Stock Exchange. The results of the study indicate that German accounting standards are significantly more relevant than IFRS. Morais and Curto (2008), using a sample of 34 Portuguese companies before and after the adoption of IFRS, demonstrated that "the value relevance of accounting information decreases with the adoption of IASB standards" (p. 103). More recently, Suadiye (2017) highlighted that the transition to IFRS did not improve the quality of financial information in Turkey.

3.2. Effects on Selected Macroeconomic Indicators

Research on the link between IFRS adoption and macroeconomic indicators, such as Foreign Direct Investment (FDI) inflows, economic growth, etc. remains limited (Elhamma, 2023). Among these few studies, the majority have shown a positive relationship between IFRS adoption and FDI inflows. Márquez-Ramos (2008), in his study of a sample of 27 EU countries between 1999 and 2007, demonstrated a positive relationship between IFRS adoption and FDI. Similarly, Gordon et al. (2012) examined the impact of IFRS adoption on FDI inflows in 124 countries over the period from 1996 to 2009. They found that IFRS adoption is positively and significantly associated with FDI inflows. In the context of Latin America, Akisik (2014) showed that IFRS adoption positively affects FDI inflows in 12 countries between 1997 and 2010. Likewise, Jayeoba et al. (2016) studied the effects of IFRS adoption on FDI in six African countries (Egypt, Nigeria, Kenya, Morocco, Tunisia, and South Africa) for the period 1980-2015. The researchers suggested that IFRS adoption had a positive and significant impact on FDI inflows.

Pricope (2017), using a sample of 38 low-income countries between 2008 and 2014, tested the relationship between IFRS adoption and FDI inflows. The key findings indicated that IFRS adoption had a positive impact on FDI flows in this group of countries. In the Asian context, Yousefinejad et al. (2018) examined the relationship between IFRS adoption in 10 ASEAN (Association of Southeast Asian Nations) countries and FDI from 2001 to 2016. They found that IFRS adoption is positively associated with FDI inflows. More recently, in the African context, Musah et al. (2020) studied the effect of IFRS adoption on FDI inflows in 20 countries that adopted IFRS, covering the period from 1980 to 2015. They found that IFRS adoption has a positive and significant influence on FDI inflows in Africa.

However, some studies have not confirmed a positive relationship between IFRS adoption and FDI inflows. Based on a sample of 48 developing countries from all continents (26 IFRS adopters and 22 non-adopters), Lasmin (2012) found that IFRS adoption is negatively related to FDI inflows. Similarly, in the African context, Nnadi and Soobaroyen (2015), using data from 34 African countries over a 20-year period, found that full IFRS adoption had a negative impact on net FDI flows. According to these two researchers, "fundamental institutional structures such as the rule of law, the legal system, and the level of corruption, rather than IFRS adoption, appear to be more important for maintaining or improving the level of FDI in African countries."

Empirical studies on the direct impact of IFRS adoption on economic growth remain relatively limited. Akisik (2013) analyzed the relationship between accounting regulation, measured by high-quality international accounting standards, financial development, and economic growth, using a sample of 51 developed and emerging market economies from 1997 to 2009. The study found that international accounting standards significantly influenced economic growth, with a positive impact observed during the period. Similarly, Özcan (2016) examined the effect of IFRS adoption on economic growth by comparing 41 IFRS-adopting countries with 29 non-adopting countries over the period 2005–2015. The findings indicated that IFRS adoption was associated with a notable increase in economic growth. Oppong and Aga (2019) investigated the impact of IFRS adoption on economic growth across 28 EU countries from 2005 to 2014, concluding that IFRS adoption significantly boosted economic growth, with a more pronounced effect in developing economies. Based on these results, they recommended promoting IFRS adoption, especially in developing countries.

Akisik et al. (2020) investigated the relationships between IFRS adoption, foreign direct investment (FDI), human development, and economic growth in 41 African countries from 1997 to 2017. Their study revealed two key findings: first, the relationship between IFRS adoption and economic growth was negative and statistically insignificant; second, the interaction between FDI and IFRS adoption (FDI x IFRS) had a significant positive effect on economic growth. This suggests that while IFRS adoption alone may not directly foster economic growth, it can enhance the positive impact of FDI on growth. Similarly, Owusu et al. (2022) examined the link between IFRS adoption and economic growth in developing economies, considering the moderating effect of institutional quality at the country level. Using panel data from 78 developing countries between 1996 and 2013, they found that IFRS adoption was associated with stronger economic growth. Recently, Elhamma (2023) examined the relationship between mandatory IFRS adoption and economic growth in 30 developing countries, including 15 MENA (Middle East and North Africa) countries and 15 SSA (Sub-Saharan Africa) countries, over the period 2017–2020. The study's findings indicated that "mandatory IFRS adoption has a positive impact on economic growth across the full sample" (Elhamma, 2023, p.554).

4. ACCOUNTING STANDARDIZATION IN MOROCCO AND IAS/IFRS STANDARDS

In this section, we first present an overview of accounting standardization in Morocco (4.1), followed by a discussion of the potential impact of IFRS on this accounting standardization (4.2).

4.1. Accounting Standardization in Morocco

Morocco is located in North Africa, south of the Mediterranean. Historically, Morocco was under Spanish and French protectorates, which is why many of the management tools used by Moroccan companies are derived from the French system (Elhamma and Moalla, 2015). However, in recent years, Moroccan companies have begun to adopt modern tools, such as international accounting standards (IFRS) (Elhamma, 2023, 2024), modern management control tools (Elhamma, 2012, 2013, 2014, 2015, 2023), and new sources of financing, such as Islamic finance (Bennani and Elhamma, 2015), etc.

The desire to develop an accounting framework suited to Morocco's economic and social realities dates back to the early 1980s, specifically to October 10, 1983, with the establishment of the "National Accounting Plan Committee." The purpose of this body was to prepare a draft Moroccan Accounting Plan. On August 19, 1986, the "Accounting Standardization Commission" was created, and it was responsible for drafting the General Accounting Standardization Code (CGNC). The CGNC became the foundational document for Moroccan accounting under Law No. 9-88 of December 30, 1992, concerning the accounting obligations of merchants. The CGNC consists of two parts: the General Accounting Standard (NGC) and the General Chart of Accounts for Enterprises (PCGE).

The responsibility for producing accounting standards in Morocco is officially entrusted to the National Accounting Council (CNC) under Law No. 15-89 of January 1993, enacted by Dahir 1-92-139 of 14 Rejab 1413. The CNC was established by Decree No. 2-88-19 on November 16, 1989. Its mission includes:

- Coordinating and synthesizing theoretical and methodological accounting research, as well as their practical applications
- Designing, developing, and proposing general or sector-specific accounting standards
- Collecting and disseminating all information related to accounting standardization, education, and training
- Recommending measures likely to improve accounting information at both the national level and at the level of individual enterprises
- Coordinating and promoting research, studies, and professional development activities related to accounting
- Representing the state in international accounting standardization bodies" (Ministry of Economy and Finance, Morocco)

The table below summarizes the main Moroccan standards developed and published by the Moroccan CNC.

Table 5. Key accounting standards published by the Moroccan CNC

Accounting Standards Adopted	**Date of Adoption**
General Accounting Standards Code: Volume I and Volume II *(Code Général de la Normalisation Comptable: TOME I et TOME II)*	25/12/1992
Chart of Accounts for UCITS (Undertakings for Collective Investment in Transferable Securities) *(Plan comptable des OPCVM)*	27/07/1995
Chart of Accounts for Credit Institutions *(Plan comptable des Etablissements de Crédit)*	15/07/1999
Chart of Accounts for the State *(Plan comptable de l'Etat)*	17/01/2001
Accounting Standards for Mortgage-Backed Securitization *(Normes comptables applicables à la Titrisation des Créances Hypothécaires)*	17/01/2001
Chart of Accounts for Cooperatives *(Plan comptable des Coopératives)*	17/01/2001
Chart of Accounts for Associations *(Plan comptable des Associations)*	11/03/2003
Chart of Accounts for Regional Agricultural Development Agencies *(Plan comptable des Offices Régionaux de Mise en Valeur Agricole (ORMVA))*	26/05/2005
Chart of Accounts for Microcredit Associations *(Plan comptable des Associations de Micro-Crédit)*	26/05/2005
Chart of Accounts for Insurance Companies *(Plan comptable des Assurances)*	26/05/2005
Chart of Accounts for Political Parties *(Plan comptable des Partis Politiques)*	23/03/2007
Chart of Accounts for Bank Al-*Maghrib (Plan comptable de Bank Al-Maghrib)*	10/05/2007
Chart of Accounts for Brokerage Firms *(Plan comptable des Sociétés de Bourse)*	10/05/2007
Chart of Accounts for Mutual Societies *(Plan comptable des Sociétés Mutualistes)*	10/05/2007
Agricultural Chart of Accounts *(Plan Comptable Agricole (PCA))*	22/12/2015
Chart of Accounts for Collective Investment Schemes *(Plan comptable des Organismes de Placement Collectif en Capital (OPCC))*	22/12/2015

Source: Ministry of Economy and Finance Website

4.2. Morocco and IAS/IFRS

In 2002, World Bank experts, in their ROSC (AA) report (Report on the Observance of Standards and Codes, Accounting & Auditing), recommended that Morocco adopt improvements to its accounting framework. According to this report, Moroccan standards for the preparation and presentation of financial statements exhibit a fundamental difference compared to the framework approved by the IASC in 1989. The report describes the accounting framework as follows: "Based largely on the Fourth European Directive (and its transcription into French law), the Moroccan framework for preparing and presenting financial statements is fundamentally different from the framework approved by the International Accounting Standards Committee (IASC) in 1989" (ROSC AA, Kingdom of Morocco, p. 10-11).

In response to this situation, and as part of Morocco's commitment to align with international accounting standards, Bank Al Maghrib (the Central Bank of Morocco) mandated, through Circular 56/G/2007, that all banks and similar financial institutions use IFRS for financial years beginning in January 2008. Additionally, Circular No. 06/05 from the Ethical Council of Securities (CDVM, now the Moroccan Capital Markets Authority - AMMC) authorized listed companies, other than banks and similar financial institutions, to use IFRS for the publication of their financial statements.

Despite these efforts, Morocco launched a major project in 2020 to converge the CGNC with IFRS standards, in collaboration with the World Bank (IFAC Website). According to the CNC, "The launch, in close collaboration with the Order of Chartered Accountants, of the project to converge the General Accounting Standardization Code (CGNC) towards international accounting standards IAS/IFRS, aims to ensure greater transparency and improved quality of accounting and financial information" (Ministry of Economy and Finance, Morocco Website).

SUMMARY AND CONCLUSION

The aim of this research paper was to provide a brief overview of the half-century history of IAS/IFRS standards and their impact on accounting standardization in Morocco. The key findings are as follows:

- 87% of countries worldwide currently require the adoption of IFRS either for all companies (across all sectors) or for most companies (in sectors such as financial institutions, for example). This adoption rate is particularly high in Europe (97.73%) and in Africa & the Middle East (96.07%).
- Over the past fifty years of IFRS adoption, most empirical studies have demonstrated that the implementation of IAS/IFRS is influenced by several factors, including dependence on international financial institutions (e.g., the World Bank, IMF), the degree of economic openness, the quality of professional expertise, and the level of education, etc.
- Over the past five decades since the introduction of IFRS, the majority of research has indicated that the adoption of IAS/IFRS enhances the quality of accounting information and is positively and significantly associated with key macroeconomic indicators, such as FDI inflows and economic growth.
- Since 2007, Morocco has aligned with international accounting standards by mandating banks and similar financial institutions to adopt IFRS for the

preparation of their financial statements. Additionally, in 2020, Morocco launched a major project to converge the General Accounting Standardization Code (CGNC) towards IFRS.

The findings of this research have significant implications both for the academic field and for policymakers and accounting standard setters. From an academic perspective, this study provides a deeper understanding of half a century of IFRS adoption, particularly its degree of adoption, the key determinants of this adoption, and the potential effects it may have. For policymakers and standard setters, this study highlights the practical effects of IFRS adoption, especially its impact on macroeconomic indicators such as economic growth and foreign direct investment (FDI).

Finally, the limitations of the study are presented, along with suggestions for future research. Specifically, two key limitations warrant discussion. First, this study does not consider research on countries that have adapted their local accounting standards to align with IFRS, often referred to as "non-IFRS adopters". Second, in this study, we examined the overall adoption of IFRS across all countries, without distinguishing between developed and developing nations or focusing on specific regions such as the MENA region or Africa. In this regard, we suggest that future research should investigate IFRS adoption by region in order to gain a clearer and more consistent understanding of this process.

REFERENCES

Akisik, O. (2014). *Financial reporting and foreign direct investments in Latin America. Accounting in Latin America*. Emerald Group Publishing.

Alon, A., & Dwyer, P. (2014). Early adoption of IFRS as a strategic response to transnational and local influences. *The International Journal of Accounting*, *49*(3), 348–370. DOI: 10.1016/j.intacc.2014.07.003

Armstrong, S. C., Barth, M. E., Jagolinzer, A. D., & Riedl, E. J. (2010). Market reaction to the adoption of IFRS in Europe. *The Accounting Review*, *85*(1), 31–61. DOI: 10.2308/accr.2010.85.1.31

Barth, M., Landsman, W., & Lang, M. (2008). International accounting standards and accounting quality. *Journal of Accounting Research*, *46*(3), 467–498. DOI: 10.1111/j.1475-679X.2008.00287.x

Bartov, E., Goldberg, S. R., & Kim, M. (2005). Comparative value relevance among German, US, and International Accounting Standards: A German stock market perspective. *Journal of Accounting, Auditing & Finance*, *20*(2), 95–119. DOI: 10.1177/0148558X0502000201

Ben Othman, H., & Kossentini, A. (2015). IFRS adoption strategies and theories of economic development: Effects on the development of emerging stock markets. *Journal of Accounting in Emerging Economies*, *5*(1), 70–121. DOI: 10.1108/JAEE-02-2012-0006

Bennani, S., & Elhamma, A. (2015). *La comptabilité en finance islamique selon les normes AAOIFI*. Éditions Universitaires Européennes.

Boolaky, P. K., Tawiah, V., & Soobaroyen, T. (2020). Why do African countries adopt IFRS? An institutional perspective. *The International Journal of Accounting*, *55*(1), 2050005. DOI: 10.1142/S1094406020500055

Chai, H., Tang, Q., Jiang, Y., & Lin, Z. (2010). The role of international financial reporting standards in accounting quality: Evidence from the European Union. *Journal of International Financial Management & Accounting*, *21*(3), 220–278. DOI: 10.1111/j.1467-646X.2010.01041.x

Chiapello, E. (2007). Accounting and the birth of the notion of capitalism. *Critical Perspectives on Accounting*, *18*(3), 263–296. DOI: 10.1016/j.cpa.2005.11.012

Colasse, B. (1997). Qu'est-ce que la comptabilité? In Y. Simon & P. Joffre (Eds.), *Encyclopédie de gestion* (pp. [page range]). Economica.

Elhamma, A. (2012). The activity-based costing in Morocco: Adoption and diffusion. *Arabian Journal of Business and Management Review*, *1*(6), 33–45. DOI: 10.12816/0002111

Elhamma, A. (2013). Performance de la comptabilité par activités: Perceptions des responsables d'entreprises. *La Revue des Sciences de Gestion*, *263-264*, 227–232.

Elhamma, A. (2014). Performance du Balanced Scorecard: Perception des responsables d'entreprises. *Revue Internationale de Management et de Stratégie*, *5*(2), 1–9.

Elhamma, A. (2015). The relationship between budgetary evaluation, firm size, and performance. *Journal of Management Development*, *34*(8), 973–986. DOI: 10.1108/JMD-06-2014-0053

Elhamma, A. (2023). Impact of mandatory IFRS adoption on economic growth: The moderating role of the COVID-19 crisis in developing countries. *Accounting and Management Information Systems*, *22*(3), 554–568. DOI: 10.24818/jamis.2023.03007

Elhamma, A. (2023). Impact of mandatory IFRS adoption on foreign direct investment: The moderating role of conflict of interest regulation. *Journal of Financial Reporting and Accounting,* ahead-of-print. https://doi.org/DOI: 10.1108/JFRA-04-2022-0145

Elhamma, A. (2023). The relationship between organisational decentralisation, balanced scorecard, and its perceived benefits in Moroccan SMEs. *International Journal of Accounting. Auditing and Performance Evaluation*, *19*(2), 185–202. DOI: 10.1504/IJAAPE.2023.132384

Elhamma, A. (2024). Determinants of national IFRS adoption: Evidence from the Middle East and North Africa region. *International Journal of Accounting. Auditing and Performance Evaluation*, *20*(1-2), 69–90. DOI: 10.1504/IJAAPE.2024.135535

Elhamma, A., & Moalla, M. (2015). Impact of uncertainty and decentralization on activity-based costing use. *International Journal of Accounting and Economics Studies*, *3*(2), 148–155. DOI: 10.14419/ijaes.v3i2.4817

Esnault, E., & Hoarau, C. (2005). *Comptabilité financière*. PUF.

Gordon, L. A., Loeb, M. P., & Zhu, W. (2012). The impact of IFRS adoption on foreign direct investment. *Journal of Accounting and Public Policy*, *31*(4), 374–398. DOI: 10.1016/j.jaccpubpol.2012.06.001

Hassan, E. A., Rankin, M., & Lu, W. (2014). The development of accounting and reporting in Iraq and the IFRS decision: An institutional perspective. *The International Journal of Accounting*, *49*(3), 371–390. DOI: 10.1016/j.intacc.2014.07.001

Hassan, M. (2008). The development of accounting regulations in Egypt. *Managerial Auditing Journal, 23*(5), 467–484. DOI: 10.1108/02686900810875299

Iatridis, G. (2010). International Financial Reporting Standards and the quality of financial statement information. *International Review of Financial Analysis, 19*(3), 193–204. DOI: 10.1016/j.irfa.2010.02.004

IFRS Foundation. (2018). *Use of IFRS Standards around the world.* https://www.ifrs.org/content/dam/ifrs/around-the-world/adoption/use-of-ifrs-around-the-world-overview-sept-2018.pdf

IFRS Foundation. (n.d.). *Website.* Retrieved from https://www.ifrs.org

International Federation of Accountants (IFAC). (n.d.). *Website.* Retrieved from https://www.ifac.org

Irvine, H. (2008). The global institutionalization of financial reporting: The case of the United Arab Emirates. *Accounting Forum, 32*(2), 125–142. DOI: 10.1016/j.accfor.2007.12.003

Jayeoba, O. O., Ajibade, A. T., Olayinka, I. M., Ogundajo, G. O., & Kwarbai, J. D. (2016). Accounting standards and foreign direct investment inflows in selected African countries (1980–2015). *International Journal of Advanced Academic Research: Social & Management Sciences, 2*(10), 17–25.

Judge, W., Li, S., & Pinsker, R. (2010). National adoption of international accounting standards: An institutional perspective. *Corporate Governance, 18*(3), 161–174. DOI: 10.1111/j.1467-8683.2010.00798.x

Keith, R. (1992). Accounting numbers as 'inscription': Action at a distance and the development of accounting. *Accounting, Organizations and Society, 17*(7), 685–708. DOI: 10.1016/0361-3682(92)90019-O

Lasmin, R. (2012). The unwanted effects of international financial reporting standards (IFRS) adoption on international trade and investments in developing countries. *Journal of Economics and Economic Education Research, 13*(1), 1–14.

Lenormand, G., & Touchais, L. (2009). Les IFRS améliorent-elles la qualité de l'information financière? Approche par la value relevance. *Comptabilité-Contrôle-Audit, 15*(2), 145–164. DOI: 10.3917/cca.152.0145

Liu, J., & Liu, C. (2007). Value relevance of accounting information in different stock market segments: The case of Chinese A-, B-, and H-shares. *Journal of International Accounting Research, 6*(2), 55–81. DOI: 10.2308/jiar.2007.6.2.55

Marquez-Ramos, L. (2008). The effect of IFRS adoption on trade and foreign direct investments. *International Trade and Finance Association Conference Papers*. bepress, (19).

Ministry of Economy and Finance (Morocco). (n.d.). *Website*. Retrieved from https://www.finances.gov.ma/Fr/Pages/index.aspx

Mir, M., & Rahaman, A. S. (2005). The adoption of International Accounting Standards in Bangladesh: An exploration of rationale and process. *Accounting, Auditing & Accountability Journal, 18*(6), 816–841. DOI: 10.1108/09513570510627720

Morais, A. I., & Curto, J. D. (2008). Accounting quality and the adoption of IASB standards: Portuguese evidence. *Revista Contabilidade & Finanças, 19*(48), 103–111. DOI: 10.1590/S1519-70772008000300009

Musaha, A., Adjeib, E., & Ahmed, I. A. (2020). The effect of IFRS adoption on foreign direct investment in Africa. *Journal of Applied Accounting and Taxation, 5*(2), 117–126. DOI: 10.30871/jaat.v5i2.1481

Nnadi, M., & Soobaroyen, T. (2015). International financial reporting standards and foreign direct investment: The case of Africa. *Advances in Accounting, 31*(2), 228–238. DOI: 10.1016/j.adiac.2015.09.007

Pricope, C. F. (2017). The implications of IFRS adoption on foreign direct investment in poor countries. *The Audit Financiar Journal, 15*(146).

Report on the Observance of Standards and Codes, Accounting & Auditing (ROSC-AA). (2002). *Kingdom of Morocco*. Retrieved from file:///C:/Users/user/Downloads/Report_on_the_observance_of_standards_an.pdf

Schiebel, A. (2006). Empirical value relevance of German GAAP and IFRS. *Journal of Economic and Financial Sciences, 1*(2), 141–170. DOI: 10.4102/jef.v1i2.365

Suadiye, G. (2017). Does mandatory IFRS adoption improve financial reporting quality? Empirical evidence from an emerging economy. *European Journal of Business and Social Sciences, 6*(5), 63–80.

Yousefinejad, M., Ahmad, A., Salleh, F. M., & Rahim, R. A. (2018). Causal relationship between International Financial Reporting Standard (IFRS) and foreign direct investment (FDI): A panel data analysis of ASEAN countries. *Asian Journal of Accounting and Governance, 10*, 61–72. DOI: 10.17576/AJAG-2018-10-06

Zeghal, D., & Mhedhbi, K. (2006). An analysis of the factors affecting the adoption of International Accounting Standards by developing countries. *The International Journal of Accounting, 41*(4), 373–386. DOI: 10.1016/j.intacc.2006.09.009

Chapter 8
Navigating Financial Risk: Hedging and Derivatives in International Reporting and Cross-Border Deals

Simran Kaur
NIET Business School, Greater Noida, India

Mandeep Singh
https://orcid.org/0000-0001-9520-8610
Chandigarh University, India

Manvi Pant
New Delhi Institute of Management, India

ABSTRACT

This study delves into the intricacies of financial risk management in cross-border transactions, emphasizing the pivotal role of hedging and derivatives in mitigating risks. It explores the evolving landscape of both traditional and emerging financial risks, including currency volatility, geopolitical instability, and environmental uncertainties, and examines how innovative technologies like artificial intelligence, blockchain, and machine learning are transforming risk management strategies. The research highlights the importance of adopting dynamic risk mitigation tools such as forwards, futures, and swaps, alongside predictive analytics and scenario modeling, to enhance decision-making and resilience in global markets. Additionally, the study underscores the challenges of regulatory compliance, particularly in the context of ESG and AI-related frameworks.

DOI: 10.4018/979-8-3373-0887-6.ch008

1. INTRODUCTION TO FINANCIAL RISK IN INTERNATIONAL MARKETS INTRODUCTION TO FINANCIAL RISK IN INTERNATIONAL MARKETS

The landscape of global trade and investments is inherently fraught with financial risk. In an era marked by increasing interconnectedness, multinational corporations, financial institutions, and governments encounter a labyrinth of uncertainties that can destabilize cross-border transactions. Financial risk, encompassing currency volatility, interest rate fluctuations, credit exposure, and geopolitical instability, poses a formidable challenge to achieving sustainable profitability and operational resilience (Kanojia et al., 2022a, 2022b; Khanna et al., 2023). This chapter delves into the nuances of financial risk in international markets, emphasizing the imperative of mitigating such risks to safeguard cross-border ventures (R. Kumar, Khannna Malholtra, et al., 2023; Upreti & Malhotra, 2024).

Overview of Financial Risks in Global Trade and Investments

International markets are rife with complexities that amplify financial vulnerabilities. Currency risk, a pervasive threat, arises from fluctuations in exchange rates that can erode the value of overseas revenues or inflate the cost of foreign liabilities. For instance, a sudden devaluation of a host country's currency could obliterate profit margins for exporters or escalate costs for import-dependent enterprises. Similarly, interest rate risk—triggered by shifts in global monetary policies—affects the cost of capital, undermining project feasibility and financial forecasts (J. Kaur et al., 2024).

Another critical dimension is credit risk, where the failure of counterparties to honor their financial commitments jeopardizes the solvency of international contracts. This risk is particularly pronounced in cross-border trade, where asymmetrical information and differing regulatory environments exacerbate the likelihood of defaults (K. Joshi et al., 2022). For example, suppliers may face delayed payments from overseas buyers due to banking restrictions or unforeseen economic crises.

Political and geopolitical risks further compound the intricacy of financial exposure. Trade wars, sanctions, and abrupt policy changes can derail supply chains and render bilateral agreements obsolete (Malhotra et al., 2022). Moreover, emerging markets—despite their lucrative growth prospects—often present heightened risks such as unstable governance, inadequate financial infrastructure, and susceptibility to economic shocks.

The pervasive nature of financial risks underscores the need for comprehensive risk identification frameworks. A thorough understanding of market-specific risks is paramount for stakeholders to design proactive and adaptive strategies that align with the volatile dynamics of global trade and investments.

Importance of Managing Financial Exposure in Cross-Border Transactions

The imperative to manage financial risk in cross-border transactions extends beyond mere survival; it is a critical determinant of strategic competitiveness and operational longevity. Effective financial risk management ensures that organizations not only weather economic uncertainties but also leverage risk mitigation strategies as a source of competitive advantage (R. Kumar, Lande, et al., 2023).

Hedging, one of the cornerstone techniques, allows firms to insulate themselves from adverse market movements. For example, currency derivatives such as forward contracts and options enable businesses to lock in favorable exchange rates, shielding them from potential currency devaluations. Similarly, interest rate swaps provide a mechanism to stabilize borrowing costs, ensuring predictability in financial planning. These instruments are indispensable in cross-border transactions, where the confluence of multiple economies magnifies exposure to market turbulence (R. Kumar, Malholtra, et al., 2023; Mary Joshitta et al., 2023; Neha et al., 2023).

Additionally, managing financial exposure fosters greater confidence among stakeholders, including investors, creditors, and trade partners. A robust risk management framework demonstrates an organization's preparedness to handle financial shocks, thereby enhancing its creditworthiness and attracting capital inflows (R. Kumar & Khanna, 2023a). For instance, firms that deploy effective risk controls are often viewed more favorably by institutional investors seeking stability in volatile markets (Bhatt et al., 2024) .

In the realm of international trade, financial risk management also mitigates the cascading impact of disruptions across supply chains. For example, importers relying on overseas suppliers can hedge commodity price risks, ensuring cost stability even amidst fluctuating global prices. Similarly, exporters can safeguard their revenue streams by mitigating the risk of currency depreciation in their destination markets.

Furthermore, regulatory compliance in international markets necessitates rigorous financial risk management. Adherence to international financial reporting standards (IFRS) and local regulatory mandates requires precise accounting for derivative transactions and hedging activities. Mismanagement of these aspects can lead to punitive sanctions, reputational damage, and operational setbacks.

In conclusion, financial risk in international markets is an omnipresent challenge that demands meticulous attention. The intricate interplay of market forces, geopolitical events, and regulatory frameworks necessitates a strategic approach to managing financial exposure. By identifying, assessing, and mitigating financial risks, organizations can enhance resilience, sustain profitability, and capitalize on the opportunities inherent in global trade and investments. The ensuing chapters will explore the methodologies and instruments that underpin effective risk management, equipping stakeholders with the tools to navigate the complexities of the international financial landscape.

2. UNDERSTANDING HEDGING: A RISK MANAGEMENT APPROACH

Hedging represents a cornerstone of modern financial risk management, particularly in the volatile terrain of international finance. By definition, hedging is the strategic use of financial instruments or market strategies to mitigate potential losses arising from adverse price movements in underlying assets. It functions as a protective mechanism, enabling organizations to safeguard their financial interests against the inherent uncertainties of global markets. In essence, hedging does not eliminate risk but redistributes it in a manner that enhances predictability and stability in financial planning (Bhuvaneswari et al., 2023).

Concept and Purpose of Hedging

At its core, hedging involves taking offsetting positions in financial instruments to neutralize the impact of unfavorable market fluctuations. For instance, an exporter anticipating revenue in a foreign currency might employ forward contracts to lock in an exchange rate, thereby shielding their income from depreciation of the foreign currency. Similarly, an importer exposed to rising commodity prices may use futures contracts to stabilize procurement costs.

The purpose of hedging transcends mere risk avoidance. It serves as a strategic tool for fostering financial resilience and enabling firms to operate confidently in unpredictable environments. By mitigating the downside risks of market volatility, hedging ensures smoother cash flows, facilitates long-term financial planning, and enhances the overall robustness of business operations. This is particularly crucial for multinational corporations, whose global operations expose them to multifaceted risks, including currency fluctuations, interest rate shifts, and commodity price volatility (A. R. Singh et al., 2024).

Common Hedging Strategies in International Finance

International finance leverages a plethora of hedging strategies, each tailored to address specific risk exposures.

Forward contracts are customized agreements between two parties to buy or sell an asset at a predetermined price on a future date. These contracts are particularly useful for managing currency risk in cross-border transactions, as they allow firms to lock in exchange rates, eliminating uncertainty.

Future contract are Similar to forward contracts but standardized and traded on exchanges, futures contracts provide liquidity and price transparency. They are frequently employed in hedging commodity price risks, enabling businesses to stabilize input costs and protect profit margins.

Options grant the holder the right, but not the obligation, to buy or sell an asset at a specified price before a set expiration date. Currency options, for example, provide flexibility in managing exchange rate risks while allowing firms to benefit from favorable rate movements.

Swaps are contractual agreements to exchange cash flows or financial obligations. Interest rate swaps, where fixed and floating interest payments are exchanged, are widely used to hedge against interest rate fluctuations. Currency swaps, on the other hand, help manage exposure to exchange rate risks in multinational borrowing and lending activities.

Natural hedging involves aligning revenue and expenses in the same currency or geographical region to minimize exposure. For example, a multinational corporation may strategically establish production facilities in countries where it earns significant revenues, thereby reducing currency mismatch.

Benefits and Challenges of Implementing Hedging

Hedging offers numerous advantages that bolster financial stability and strategic agility.

- **Risk Mitigation**: Hedging provides a buffer against adverse price movements, ensuring stable financial outcomes. This stability fosters investor confidence and supports business continuity.
- **Cash Flow Predictability**: By locking in costs or revenues, hedging enables organizations to forecast cash flows with greater accuracy, facilitating effective budgeting and resource allocation.
- **Market Competitiveness**: Firms that hedge risks effectively can offer more competitive pricing and secure favorable terms in international contracts.

Despite its merits, hedging is not devoid of challenges.

- **Cost Implications**: Engaging in hedging incurs direct costs, including premiums for options or transaction fees for derivative contracts, which can strain financial resources.
- **Complexity**: Designing and executing an effective hedging strategy requires expertise and continuous monitoring of market conditions. Mismanagement or poor execution can exacerbate risks instead of mitigating them.
- **Regulatory Constraints**: Adherence to financial reporting standards and regulatory frameworks governing derivative usage can be onerous and complex, particularly for multinational enterprises operating across diverse jurisdictions.

Hence, hedging is an indispensable tool in the arsenal of financial risk management, particularly for entities navigating the unpredictable waters of international finance. By employing a judicious combination of hedging strategies, organizations can mitigate risk, enhance financial stability, and seize opportunities amidst uncertainty. However, the success of hedging depends on meticulous planning, informed decision-making, and an in-depth understanding of the intricate interplay of global financial markets.

3. THE ROLE OF DERIVATIVES IN RISK MANAGEMENT

Derivatives have emerged as indispensable instruments in the arsenal of financial risk management, particularly in the volatile landscape of international markets. These financial instruments derive their value from underlying assets such as currencies, commodities, interest rates, or equities (Maaze et al., 2024). By enabling parties to transfer or mitigate risks associated with adverse market movements, derivatives serve as both hedging tools and vehicles for strategic risk allocation. This chapter explores the various types of derivatives, their role in financial risk mitigation, and illustrative case studies that highlight their effective deployment in cross-border transactions.

Table 1. Common derivatives and their use in hedging cross-border risks

Derivative Type	Purpose	Risk Hedged	Example of Use in Cross-Border Deals
Forward Contracts	Lock in exchange rates or commodity prices	Currency and commodity price fluctuations	Hedging against USD/EUR exchange rate volatility for a European exporter
Currency Futures	Speculative or hedging for foreign exchange risk	Currency risk	A Japanese company hedging against a falling yen against the US dollar
Interest Rate Swaps	Exchange fixed interest payments for floating rates	Interest rate risk	A UK company hedging against rising US interest rates on a dollar-denominated loan
Options	Offers flexibility in trading	Market volatility, asset price movements	Airline company using options to hedge fuel price fluctuations
Commodity Swaps	Exchange fixed commodity prices for floating prices	Commodity price volatility	Energy companies hedging against fluctuating oil prices in international contracts

Source:*Global Derivatives Market Overview, 2023, Risk Management Journal*

Table 1 outlines common derivatives, such as forward contracts, currency futures, interest rate swaps, options, and commodity swaps, highlighting their use in hedging cross-border risks like currency, interest rate, and commodity price fluctuations, with examples from various sectors, including exporters, airlines, and energy companies managing international financial volatility.

Types of Derivatives: Forwards, Futures, Options, and Swaps

The universe of derivatives encompasses a diverse array of instruments, each tailored to specific risk management needs.

1. **Forwards**

Forward contracts are customized, over-the-counter agreements between two parties to buy or sell an asset at a predetermined price on a future date. Unlike standardized contracts, forwards offer flexibility in terms of volume, pricing, and settlement. They are widely used for hedging currency risks in international trade. For instance, an exporter can lock in the exchange rate for future receivables, insulating their revenue from unfavorable currency fluctuations (A. Singh & Srivastava, 2024).

2. **Futures**

Futures contracts, in contrast to forwards, are standardized and traded on exchanges. They obligate parties to buy or sell an asset at a specified price and date. Futures are extensively employed in managing commodity price risks. For example, an airline can hedge against rising jet fuel prices by purchasing fuel futures, ensuring cost stability irrespective of market volatility (Bohra et al., 2024).

3. **Options**

Options confer the right—but not the obligation—to buy or sell an asset at a predetermined price before a specific expiration date. This flexibility makes options particularly valuable in volatile markets. Currency options, for instance, allow firms to hedge against adverse exchange rate movements while retaining the ability to capitalize on favorable shifts (K. D. Singh, Deep Singh, et al., 2023).

4. **Swaps**

Swaps are contractual agreements to exchange cash flows or obligations between two parties. Interest rate swaps, wherein fixed and floating rate payments are exchanged, are commonly used to stabilize borrowing costs. Currency swaps help manage exposure to exchange rate fluctuations in cross-border financing arrangements, enabling firms to secure predictable cash flows (Gonfa et al., 2023).

How Derivatives Function in Financial Risk Mitigation

Derivatives operate as risk-transfer mechanisms, allowing firms to offset potential losses by assuming counterbalancing positions. Their utility lies in providing financial predictability and stability, critical for navigating the uncertainties of international markets.

- **Hedging Currency Risks**: Currency derivatives such as forwards, futures, and options enable businesses to mitigate exposure to exchange rate fluctuations. For instance, a U.S.-based importer dealing with a European supplier can use a forward contract to lock in the euro exchange rate, safeguarding against dollar depreciation (Raman, Kumar, et al., 2023).
- **Stabilizing Interest Rate Exposure**: Interest rate derivatives, such as swaps and caps, protect against unfavorable shifts in borrowing costs. Firms with floating-rate debt can convert it into fixed-rate obligations through swaps, ensuring predictable interest payments even amidst volatile monetary policies (Pandey et al., 2023).

- **Managing Commodity Price Volatility**: Derivatives such as futures and options allow firms to hedge against adverse commodity price movements. For example, a food manufacturer can use wheat futures to stabilize raw material costs, shielding profit margins from market-driven price spikes (Gururani et al., 2022).

Case Studies: Effective Use of Derivatives in Cross-Border Deals

1. **Currency Hedging in International Trade**

A multinational electronics firm with significant exports to Japan employed currency forwards to hedge its yen-denominated receivables. By locking in favorable exchange rates, the firm mitigated revenue erosion caused by yen depreciation and enhanced its financial predictability (Upreti et al., 2023).

2. **Interest Rate Swap in Cross-Border Financing**

A European infrastructure company undertaking a project in the United States used an interest rate swap to stabilize its dollar-denominated loan payments. By converting floating-rate obligations into fixed-rate payments, the company ensured cost certainty and protected its profit margins against rising U.S. interest rates (V. Kumar, Sharma, et al., 2023).

3. **Commodity Hedging in Emerging Markets**

An energy company operating in South America leveraged crude oil futures to hedge against volatile global oil prices. The strategy enabled the firm to secure stable input costs, ensuring operational continuity amidst fluctuating market dynamics (Kaushal et al., 2022).

Since, derivatives are integral to modern financial risk management, offering sophisticated tools to navigate the intricacies of international markets. By leveraging forwards, futures, options, and swaps, firms can mitigate diverse risks, from currency volatility to commodity price fluctuations. The case studies underscore the strategic importance of derivatives in cross-border transactions, highlighting their potential to foster financial stability and resilience in an unpredictable global environment. However, the effective use of derivatives requires expertise, vigilance, and adherence to regulatory frameworks to unlock their full potential.

4. INTERNATIONAL FINANCIAL REPORTING STANDARDS (IFRS) AND DERIVATIVES

The increasing complexity of global financial markets and the widespread use of derivatives for risk management have necessitated a robust framework for reporting and accountability. The International Financial Reporting Standards (IFRS) provide the regulatory backbone for the recognition, measurement, and disclosure of derivative instruments and hedging activities. These standards aim to enhance transparency, comparability, and reliability in financial statements, enabling stakeholders to make informed decisions. However, compliance with IFRS provisions remains a formidable challenge, particularly in the context of cross-border transactions, where diverse regulatory landscapes and operational complexities intersect (Belwal et al., 2023).

Key IFRS Provisions Related to Hedging and Derivatives

Derivatives, owing to their contingent nature and inherent complexities, are treated as financial instruments under IFRS. The relevant provisions governing derivatives and hedging are primarily encapsulated within **IFRS 9: Financial Instruments** and, to a lesser extent, **IAS 39: Financial Instruments: Recognition and Measurement** (for entities still transitioning to IFRS 9).

1. **Recognition and Classification**: Under IFRS 9, derivatives are classified as financial assets or liabilities and are measured at fair value through profit or loss (FVTPL). This means that changes in the fair value of derivatives are reflected in the income statement unless they qualify for hedge accounting (S. Bansal et al., 2023).
2. **Hedge Accounting**: IFRS 9 introduced a principles-based approach to hedge accounting, replacing the rules-driven framework of IAS 39. The standard recognizes three primary types of hedging relationships:
    - **Fair Value Hedge**: Protects against changes in the fair value of a recognized asset, liability, or firm commitment.
    - **Cash Flow Hedge**: Safeguards against variability in future cash flows attributable to a specific risk.
    - **Net Investment Hedge**: Shields against risks related to foreign currency translation of net investments in foreign operations.
3. **Effectiveness Testing**: IFRS 9 simplifies the hedge effectiveness assessment by removing the rigid 80-125% threshold under IAS 39. Instead, it requires that the hedging relationship be effective in achieving offsetting risk exposures and that the designated risk management strategy is clearly documented.

4. **Disclosures**: IFRS mandates detailed disclosures of derivative instruments and hedging activities, including their purpose, risk management objectives, and the impact of hedges on financial performance. These requirements aim to provide stakeholders with comprehensive insights into the entity's financial risk management strategies.

Hedge Accounting: Rules and Applications

Hedge accounting aligns the accounting treatment of derivatives with the underlying hedged items, mitigating artificial volatility in financial statements caused by mismatches in recognition timing. This alignment is crucial for accurately reflecting the economic substance of risk management activities.

To apply hedge accounting under IFRS 9, entities must meet several criteria:

- **Designation and Documentation**: The hedging relationship must be formally designated and documented at inception. The documentation must specify the hedged item, the hedging instrument, the risk being hedged, and the entity's risk management objective (V. Kumar & Korovin, 2023).
- **Effectiveness**: The hedging instrument must effectively offset the changes in fair value or cash flows of the hedged item attributable to the designated risk (R. Kumar & Khanna, 2023b).
- **Reclassification Adjustments**: For cash flow hedges, gains or losses on the hedging instrument are initially recognized in other comprehensive income (OCI) and subsequently reclassified to profit or loss when the hedged item affects earnings (S. Sharma et al., 2023).

Applications of hedge accounting are pervasive in industries exposed to significant financial risks, such as manufacturing, energy, and aviation. For instance, an airline may use hedge accounting to stabilize fuel costs by designating fuel futures contracts as cash flow hedges.

Challenges in Compliance and Standardization Across Jurisdictions

Despite its benefits, compliance with IFRS provisions on derivatives and hedging presents numerous challenges, particularly in the context of global operations.

1. **Complexity in Implementation**: The principles-based approach of IFRS 9 requires significant judgment and expertise in designing and documenting hedging relationships. Entities often face difficulties in aligning their risk management strategies with accounting requirements (S. Sharma & Bhadula, 2023).
2. **Fair Value Measurement**: Determining the fair value of complex derivatives, especially those traded over the counter (OTC), involves intricate valuation models and assumptions. This complexity increases the risk of errors and audit scrutiny (Abdullah et al., 2023; Sonnad et al., 2022).
3. **Regulatory Divergence**: While IFRS aims to standardize financial reporting globally, its adoption and interpretation vary across jurisdictions. Entities operating in countries with divergent accounting standards or regulatory requirements face additional compliance burdens (Sahu & Rawat, 2023).
4. **Cost Implications**: Implementing IFRS-compliant systems, training personnel, and conducting regular effectiveness testing impose significant costs, particularly for small and medium-sized enterprises (K. D. Singh, Singh, Kaur, et al., 2023).
5. **Evolving Frameworks**: Continuous updates to IFRS, including emerging requirements for sustainability-linked derivatives, necessitate ongoing adaptation, further complicating compliance efforts (Sati et al., 2022).

In summary, IFRS provisions governing derivatives and hedging play a pivotal role in fostering transparency and accountability in financial reporting. Hedge accounting, while intricate, provides a vital mechanism for aligning financial statements with economic realities. However, the challenges of implementation, valuation, and jurisdictional divergence underscore the need for robust systems, skilled expertise, and continuous engagement with evolving regulatory frameworks to ensure effective compliance and standardization.

5. CURRENCY RISK: MANAGING EXCHANGE RATE FLUCTUATIONS

Currency risk, also known as exchange rate risk, is an omnipresent challenge in international business, arising from fluctuations in currency values. These fluctuations can have profound impacts on cross-border transactions, potentially eroding profit margins, disrupting cash flows, and undermining financial stability (Rajbalaji et al., 2023). In a globalized economy where entities operate across diverse jurisdictions, managing currency risk is paramount for ensuring predictable financial outcomes and fostering long-term sustainability. Derivatives play a pivotal role in this endeavor, providing a range of instruments to mitigate the adverse effects of exchange rate volatility.

Impact of Currency Volatility on Cross-Border Transactions

Exchange rate volatility creates significant uncertainty in international trade and investment activities. The unpredictability of currency values can affect pricing, profitability, and competitiveness, often introducing complexities that extend beyond financial metrics.

1. **Erosion of Profit Margins**: Exporters and importers are directly impacted by currency volatility. For instance, an exporter receiving payments in a foreign currency may find their earnings diminished if the foreign currency weakens against the domestic currency before payment is received (Kamra et al., 2023). Similarly, importers exposed to a strengthening foreign currency face rising procurement costs, which can compress profit margins.
2. **Cash Flow Disruptions**: Fluctuating exchange rates can create mismatches between expected and actual cash flows, complicating financial planning and debt servicing. Businesses with foreign currency-denominated obligations, such as loans or lease payments, are particularly vulnerable to such disruptions.
3. **Balance Sheet Volatility**: Multinational corporations (MNCs) with operations in multiple countries often report their consolidated financial statements in a single currency (P. Gupta et al., 2023). Currency fluctuations can distort the valuation of foreign assets and liabilities, resulting in significant translation gains or losses, which may not reflect the underlying economic reality.
4. **Competitive Pressures**: Exchange rate movements can alter the competitive dynamics of global markets. A depreciating domestic currency can make exports more attractive but simultaneously inflate the cost of imported inputs, while an appreciating currency can weaken export competitiveness (Agarwal & Sharma, 2023).

Real-World Examples of Currency Risk Mitigation

1. **Hedging by Airbus**: Airbus, a leading aircraft manufacturer, faces significant currency risk as its revenue is predominantly in U.S. dollars, while a substantial portion of its expenses is in euros. To mitigate this risk, Airbus employs forward contracts and options to hedge future dollar receivables, ensuring stability in its financial outcomes (Rana et al., 2022).

2. **Toyota's Natural Hedging Strategy:** Toyota employs natural hedging by aligning its production facilities with its key markets. By manufacturing vehicles in regions where it earns significant revenue, the company minimizes currency mismatches and reduces reliance on derivative instruments (N. M. Kumar, Islam, et al., 2023).
3. **Apple's Use of Currency Swaps**: Apple uses currency swaps to manage its exposure to foreign currency fluctuations arising from its global operations. These swaps allow the company to secure predictable cash flows, thereby protecting its financial performance against volatile exchange rates (Mehershilpa et al., 2023).
4. **Procter & Gamble (P&G)** P&G uses a combination of forward contracts and options to hedge currency risk associated with its extensive global supply chain. By doing so, the company ensures price stability and maintains its competitive edge in international markets (Rawat et al., 2023).

Since, currency risk is a critical consideration for entities engaged in cross-border transactions, necessitating proactive and strategic management. Derivatives, including forwards, futures, options, and swaps, provide powerful mechanisms to mitigate the adverse effects of exchange rate volatility. Real-world examples from leading global corporations underscore the efficacy of these tools in safeguarding financial stability, enhancing predictability, and supporting competitive positioning in an interconnected global economy.

6. INTEREST RATE RISK IN GLOBAL FINANCIAL DEALS

Interest rate risk is a critical concern for entities engaged in international transactions, as fluctuations in interest rates can significantly affect borrowing costs, investment returns, and overall financial performance. In a globalized economy characterized by interconnected markets and divergent monetary policies, managing interest rate exposure has become increasingly complex (E. Sharma et al., 2023). The ability to navigate this volatility is essential for maintaining financial stability and achieving strategic objectives. This chapter explores how interest rate fluctuations impact international transactions, the tools and techniques available to hedge these risks, and the pivotal role of swaps in managing interest rate exposure.

How Interest Rate Fluctuations Affect International Transactions

1. **Borrowing Costs**: Interest rate fluctuations directly impact the cost of debt for corporations and governments. Rising interest rates increase borrowing expenses, reducing profitability and limiting investment capacity. Conversely, falling rates can lower financing costs but may signal economic slowdown or reduced returns on fixed-income investments (Medhi et al., 2023).
2. **Foreign Currency Loans**: In cross-border deals, entities often borrow in foreign currencies to take advantage of favorable rates. However, shifts in either domestic or foreign interest rates can disrupt cost projections, introducing financial uncertainty. For instance, a U.S.-based firm borrowing in euros may face higher repayment costs if European interest rates rise unexpectedly (A. S. Kumar & Desi, 2023).
3. **Investment Returns**: Interest rate changes influence the valuation of financial instruments such as bonds and derivatives. Increases in rates typically lead to declines in bond prices, adversely affecting portfolios with fixed-income securities (Shah et al., 2023).
4. **Economic Competitiveness**: Disparities in global interest rates can alter trade dynamics. For instance, higher domestic rates may attract foreign investment, strengthening the local currency but potentially reducing export competitiveness (N. K. Singh, Singh, et al., 2023).
5. **Valuation of Assets and Liabilities**: Interest rate movements affect the present value of future cash flows, altering the valuation of long-term assets and liabilities. This can distort financial statements and complicate decision-making for multinational entities (Raman, Buddhi, et al., 2023).

Tools and Techniques to Hedge Interest Rate Risks

1. **Forward Rate Agreements (FRAs)**: FRAs allow parties to lock in an interest rate for future borrowing or lending. These over-the-counter contracts provide a straightforward mechanism to hedge against unfavorable rate movements (Jayadeva et al., 2023).
2. **Interest Rate Futures**: Traded on exchanges, these standardized contracts enable firms to hedge exposure to future interest rate changes. For example, a company anticipating a rise in borrowing costs can take a short position in interest rate futures to offset potential losses (Pandya et al., 2023).
3. **Interest Rate Options**: These instruments grant the holder the right, but not the obligation, to pay or receive a fixed interest rate. Cap options protect against rising rates, while floor options guard against falling rates, providing flexible

hedging strategies (Salama et al., 2023; K. D. Singh, Singh, Chhabra, et al., 2023; Tyagi et al., 2023).

4. **Fixed vs. Floating Rate Debt**: Firms can balance their debt portfolios by combining fixed and floating rate obligations. Fixed-rate loans offer predictability, while floating-rate loans allow entities to benefit from declining rates (A. Das Gupta et al., 2022; Mandalapu et al., 2023; Pande et al., 2023).
5. **Natural Hedging**: By aligning income streams with interest rate exposures, firms can mitigate risk without relying solely on financial instruments. For example, a company with floating-rate debt can pair it with revenue streams sensitive to rate changes (Gopal et al., 2023; S. Sharma et al., 2020; K. D. Singh et al., 2022).

7. CREDIT RISK AND COUNTERPARTY RISK IN INTERNATIONAL DEALS

Credit risk and counterparty risk are pivotal considerations in international financial transactions, given the complexities of operating across diverse jurisdictions with varying regulatory, economic, and legal environments. These risks are exacerbated in cross-border deals, where factors such as currency volatility, political instability, and differing credit evaluation standards come into play (Josphineleela et al., 2023). Effectively managing these risks is essential to safeguard financial stability, ensure transaction continuity, and protect against potential losses. This chapter explores the identification and assessment of credit risk in international transactions, strategies to mitigate counterparty risk using derivative contracts, and the role of credit default swaps (CDS) in enhancing financial resilience.

Identifying and Assessing Credit Risk in Cross-Border Transactions

Credit risk refers to the possibility of financial loss arising from counterparty's inability to fulfill its contractual obligations. In cross-border transactions, credit risk encompasses additional complexities due to differences in credit reporting practices, economic conditions, and regulatory frameworks.

1. **Assessment of Creditworthiness**: Conducting a thorough assessment of a counterparty's creditworthiness is fundamental. This involves analyzing financial statements, credit ratings, and historical payment behavior. For international counterparts, firms often rely on global credit rating agencies such as Moody's, S&P, or Fitch for standardized evaluations (Anand et al., 2024).

2. **Sovereign and Political Risk**: Cross-border transactions are susceptible to sovereign credit risk, which arises when a foreign government or its entities fail to honor debt obligations. Political instability, changes in government policies, or economic sanctions can exacerbate this risk, impacting the ability of private entities within the jurisdiction to meet their commitments (Sahithya et al., 2024).
3. **Currency and Economic Factors**: Exchange rate volatility and economic downturns in the counterparty's domicile country can undermine their capacity to fulfill obligations. Incorporating macroeconomic indicators and stress-testing models helps in evaluating these vulnerabilities (S. Singh et al., 2024).
4. **Legal and Jurisdictional Risks**: Differences in legal frameworks can complicate enforcement mechanisms in cases of default. A counterparty operating in a jurisdiction with weak creditor protections poses a higher credit risk.

8. LEGAL AND REGULATORY FRAMEWORK FOR DERIVATIVES

The legal and regulatory framework for derivatives is a cornerstone of global financial stability, given the extensive use of these instruments in managing risks, speculating on market movements, and enhancing liquidity. However, the complexity of derivative markets, compounded by their cross-border nature, necessitates a robust and harmonized regulatory environment (Bhatt et al., 2024; Bhatti & Negi, 2018; Bhuvaneswari et al., 2023; Thapa et al., 2024). This chapter delves into the international regulations governing derivatives, the compliance challenges inherent in cross-border transactions, and emerging trends shaping the future of regulatory oversight in this domain.

International Regulations Governing Derivative Markets

1. **Basel Framework**: The Basel Committee on Banking Supervision (BCBS) plays a pivotal role in setting international standards for derivative-related risk management. Its provisions under the Basel III Accord focus on counterparty credit risk, requiring banks to maintain higher capital buffers and implement robust risk management practices for derivative exposures (Prerna et al., 2024; Rajora et al., 2024; Ramanan et al., 2022).
2. **G20 Commitments and OTC Reforms**: Following the 2008 financial crisis, the G20 nations committed to overhauling over-the-counter (OTC) derivative markets. Key measures included mandatory central clearing for standardized derivatives, reporting transactions to trade repositories, and imposing higher

collateral requirements for non-cleared derivatives (Goyal et al., 2024; M. A. Kumar, Valli Mayil, et al., 2023; A. Singh & Srivastava, 2024).

3. **Dodd-Frank Act**: In the United States, the Dodd-Frank Wall Street Reform and Consumer Protection Act introduced stringent regulations for derivatives. The legislation established the Commodity Futures Trading Commission (CFTC) and the Securities and Exchange Commission (SEC) as key regulatory bodies overseeing derivative markets. Dodd-Frank mandates central clearing, margin requirements, and position limits to curb systemic risk (S. Joshi et al., 2024; Pant et al., 2024; A. R. Singh et al., 2024).
4. **European Market Infrastructure Regulation (EMIR)**: The European Union's EMIR framework aligns closely with the G20's objectives, emphasizing transparency and risk mitigation in OTC derivatives. EMIR mandates central clearing, trade reporting to authorized repositories, and risk management standards for non-cleared derivatives (Dhinakaran et al., 2022; Semwal et al., 2024; Verma et al., 2024).
5. **Asia-Pacific Regulations**: Countries in the Asia-Pacific region, including Japan, Australia, and Singapore, have implemented their own derivative regulations, often mirroring global standards. The Japanese Financial Services Agency (FSA) and the Australian Securities and Investments Commission (ASIC) are notable regulators ensuring compliance within their jurisdictions.

9. RISK MANAGEMENT STRATEGIES FOR EMERGING MARKETS

Emerging and frontier markets present unique opportunities for global investors and businesses, but they are also rife with distinctive financial risks. These markets, characterized by rapid growth, volatile conditions, and developing infrastructures, often present more pronounced challenges than their developed counterparts (Kukreti et al., 2025). Effective risk management strategies tailored to these environments are crucial for mitigating risks, ensuring profitability, and securing long-term success in cross-border transactions. This chapter explores the unique financial risks in emerging markets, discusses the adaptation of hedging and derivative strategies for these regions, and provides insights from successful cross-border transactions.

Insights from Successful Cross-Border Transactions

1. **Coca-Cola in Africa**: Coca-Cola's strategy of entering emerging markets in Africa has been marked by a robust risk management framework. The company employed a combination of currency hedging and political risk insurance to

protect its investments from currency volatility and political unrest. This approach enabled Coca-Cola to successfully navigate risks in markets with weak regulatory environments, maintaining profitability despite the challenges (P. Kumar, Verma, et al., 2023).

2. **General Electric (GE) in Latin America**: GE has effectively used interest rate swaps to manage its exposure to fluctuating interest rates in Latin America. Additionally, the company has engaged in cross-currency swaps to hedge its foreign exchange risk, ensuring that it can repatriate profits at stable exchange rates, even in volatile environments. GE's successful risk management strategy has facilitated its long-term presence in the region (Taneja, Bhatnagar, Kumar, & Grima, 2023).
3. **Siemens in India**: Siemens' success in India has been partly attributed to its use of commodity hedging in response to the country's volatile energy prices. By locking in fuel prices through commodity derivatives, Siemens effectively managed the risk of rising operational costs, allowing it to maintain stable pricing for its services and products (Bhatnagar et al., 2023).

Managing financial risks in emerging and frontier markets requires a nuanced approach that acknowledges the unique challenges of these regions. By adapting hedging and derivative strategies to address currency volatility, political instability, and market illiquidity, businesses can safeguard their investments and enhance their competitive advantage (Bhatnagar, Kumar, et al., 2024; Bhatnagar, Rajaram, et al., 2024; P. Kumar, Taneja, Bhatnagar, et al., 2024; Taneja, Bhatnagar, Kumar, & Rupeika-apoga, 2023). Insights from successful cross-border transactions demonstrate the importance of tailoring risk management strategies to the specific conditions of each market, while leveraging a combination of financial instruments to mitigate exposure. As emerging markets continue to evolve, a proactive and flexible risk management framework will remain crucial for long-term success in these dynamic environments.

10. TECHNOLOGICAL INNOVATIONS IN FINANCIAL RISK MANAGEMENT

In recent years, technological advancements have significantly reshaped financial risk management, with artificial intelligence (AI), blockchain, and digital platforms playing pivotal roles in revolutionizing how risks, particularly in derivatives and cross-border transactions, are managed (Bachheti et al., 2023; Bathla et al., 2024; Bohra et al., 2024; Zaheer et al., 2024). These innovations are driving greater efficiency, transparency, and accuracy in risk mitigation strategies, ensuring that businesses can adapt more quickly to global market changes. This chapter delves into the role of AI and blockchain in derivatives, explores how technology enhances transparency in financial reporting, and discusses digital platforms designed to manage cross-border risks.

The Role of Artificial Intelligence and Blockchain in Derivatives

1. **Artificial Intelligence in Derivative Trading and Risk Management**: Artificial intelligence is increasingly employed to optimize decision-making and risk management in the derivatives markets. AI algorithms, particularly machine learning (ML), can process vast amounts of data at incredible speeds, identifying patterns and trends that would otherwise go unnoticed. These capabilities are used to predict market movements, assess counterparty risk, and improve the pricing of derivatives by analyzing historical data (P. Kumar, Bhatnagar, et al., 2023), economic indicators, and even social sentiment. AI-powered tools can also automate routine tasks like trade execution and portfolio rebalancing, reducing human error and ensuring greater consistency in risk management practices. Additionally, AI enhances real-time risk monitoring, enabling firms to dynamically adjust their positions in response to changing market conditions. By using predictive analytics, businesses can forecast potential disruptions or adverse movements in derivatives markets and hedge accordingly. AI-driven risk models can also continuously learn from new data, improving their accuracy and helping firms stay ahead of emerging risks (Bhatnagar, Taneja, et al., 2024; Bhatnagar & Sehajpal, 2024; A. Kaur et al., 2023; P. Kumar, Reepu, et al., 2024; P. Kumar, Taneja, & Ozen, 2024).
2. **Blockchain Technology in Derivatives Transactions**: Blockchain, with its decentralized and immutable nature, offers transformative potential for derivatives markets. Traditionally, derivative contracts are often complex and involve multiple intermediaries, increasing both costs and the likelihood of errors. Blockchain's distributed ledger technology (DLT) allows for the creation of smart contracts—self-executing agreements where the terms of the contract are directly written into code. These contracts automatically trigger actions based on predefined conditions, reducing the need for intermediaries and enhancing the efficiency of derivatives trading. Blockchain's transparency feature allows all parties in a transaction to view the entire history of a contract in real-time, reducing the risks of fraud or disputes. This increased visibility is particularly important for ensuring compliance with international regulations governing derivatives markets, such as those established under the Dodd-Frank Act or the European Market Infrastructure Regulation (EMIR). Furthermore, blockchain can streamline post-trade processes, such as clearing and settlement, by

eliminating the delays associated with traditional systems, thereby enhancing liquidity and reducing systemic risk (P. Sharma et al., 2024).

Enhancing Transparency and Efficiency in Global Financial Reporting

1. **Real-Time Reporting and Data Accessibility**: The integration of AI and blockchain into financial reporting systems has significantly enhanced transparency in global financial markets. In the context of cross-border transactions, real-time access to accurate financial data is crucial for timely decision-making. Blockchain enables the secure, transparent, and immutable recording of transactions, which can be instantly accessed by authorized parties. This level of transparency reduces information asymmetry and helps businesses ensure compliance with international accounting standards such as the International Financial Reporting Standards (IFRS).

AI further elevates this by automating data processing and analysis, enabling faster generation of financial reports and improving accuracy. AI-driven systems can flag discrepancies in real-time, ensuring that financial data remains consistent and reliable. For multinational companies, these technologies eliminate the manual reconciliation processes typically required in multiple jurisdictions, streamlining cross-border financial reporting and reducing operational costs (Sehajpal & Kaur, 2025).

2. **Regulatory Compliance and Risk Mitigation**: Regulatory bodies are increasingly focused on enhancing transparency in financial markets, and AI and blockchain contribute to meeting these expectations. Blockchain's ability to provide an immutable and auditable trail of financial transactions helps organizations adhere to regulatory requirements and safeguards against fraudulent activities. AI, on the other hand, assists in ensuring compliance by monitoring transactions for suspicious activity, automating compliance checks, and ensuring that all financial disclosures are timely and accurate.

Sustainable and Ethical Considerations in Hedging and Derivatives

In the realm of international finance, the use of hedging and derivatives has become essential for managing risks and optimizing profits. However, as financial markets evolve, there is increasing scrutiny on the ethical and sustainable dimensions of these instruments. As organizations face growing pressure to align their financial practices with environmental, social, and governance (ESG) criteria, it is crucial to strike a balance between profit motives and the pursuit of broader societal goals. This chapter examines the ethical and sustainable considerations in the use of hedging and derivatives, focusing on the challenges of balancing profit with environmental and social imperatives, sustainable hedging practices, and the ethical implications of derivative use.

Balancing Profit Motives with Environmental and Social Goals

The financial community has long been driven by profit motives, with derivatives often used as tools to hedge against market risks and enhance portfolio returns. However, the increasing prominence of ESG factors in investment decision-making has challenged firms to integrate social and environmental considerations into their risk management strategies. Investors and companies are now expected to assess the sustainability of their financial activities, particularly in how derivatives are employed to hedge risks related to natural resources, climate change, and social development.

For instance, commodity derivatives are frequently used to hedge against price fluctuations in energy, agriculture, and other natural resources. While these instruments can protect against financial volatility, they may also inadvertently perpetuate unsustainable practices, such as the over-extraction of resources or the promotion of fossil fuels. Similarly, derivatives tied to carbon emissions can create ethical dilemmas if they lead to speculative activities that exacerbate environmental harm. Thus, the challenge lies in integrating ESG objectives into the hedging process, ensuring that profit-seeking behavior does not undermine the well-being of society or the planet.

Sustainable Hedging Practices in International Finance

Sustainable hedging practices are gaining traction as companies seek to reconcile their financial strategies with long-term environmental and social goals. One key aspect of sustainable hedging is the integration of climate risk into risk management frameworks. As climate change becomes an increasingly pressing global issue, investors and businesses are recognizing the importance of assessing their exposure to environmental risks, such as the impact of extreme weather events or shifts in regulatory landscapes related to carbon emissions.

A growing trend is the use of **green derivatives**, which are financial instruments designed specifically to support environmentally sustainable projects. For example, green bonds and climate-linked derivatives can be used by companies to hedge risks associated with carbon pricing or to fund renewable energy initiatives. These instruments not only manage financial exposure but also contribute to the financing of sustainable projects, aligning financial goals with environmental impact. Furthermore, sustainable hedging may involve the adoption of risk models that account for ESG factors, allowing companies to manage risks that go beyond traditional financial variables.

Another example of sustainable hedging is the use of **natural capital derivatives**, which are designed to hedge risks associated with biodiversity loss, water scarcity, and other environmental challenges. These instruments are still in their nascent stages but hold the potential to provide hedging solutions that are aligned with environmental stewardship, helping businesses mitigate their exposure to the environmental risks of operating in natural resource-dependent sectors.

Ethical Implications of Derivative Use

While derivatives can provide valuable tools for managing risk, their ethical implications are a subject of growing debate. In some cases, derivatives can be used to speculate on market movements, which may raise concerns about the potential for market manipulation, excessive risk-taking, and the creation of systemic instability. The ethical dilemma arises when these instruments are employed in a way that exacerbates market volatility or undermines the interests of vulnerable stakeholders.

A pertinent ethical issue is the use of derivatives for speculative purposes rather than genuine risk management. Speculation in derivative markets can lead to excessive financial leverage and magnify financial crises, as seen in the 2008 global financial meltdown. In the context of commodity derivatives, speculative activities can also contribute to price volatility in essential goods, such as food and energy, which disproportionately affects low-income populations. This raises ethical questions about the role of financial institutions in exacerbating social inequalities through speculative trading practices.

Furthermore, the opacity of some derivative markets, particularly in over-the-counter (OTC) transactions, can obscure the true risks involved and limit accountability. The lack of transparency can make it difficult for stakeholders, including regulators and investors, to assess the full environmental and social implications of derivative transactions. This lack of visibility can facilitate unethical behavior, such as the use of derivatives to manipulate markets or to circumvent environmental regulations.

The use of hedging and derivatives in international finance offers significant advantages in managing financial risk, but it is increasingly subject to scrutiny from ethical and sustainability perspectives. As global financial markets continue to evolve, the integration of ESG factors into derivative strategies is becoming essential for businesses seeking to align their risk management practices with broader social and environmental objectives. Sustainable hedging practices, such as the use of green derivatives and natural capital hedging, are paving the way for more responsible financial strategies. However, it is equally important to address the ethical implications of derivative use, ensuring that these instruments are employed in ways that promote stability, transparency, and the welfare of society. In the future, financial institutions and investors must adopt a more holistic view of risk management that balances financial objectives with the long-term sustainability of the global economy.

11. FUTURE TRENDS IN FINANCIAL RISK MANAGEMENT

The landscape of financial risk management is undergoing a profound transformation as the global financial system adapts to an increasingly complex and interconnected world. This evolution is shaped by several emerging factors, including changes in international reporting frameworks, the shifting dynamics of geopolitical influence, and the rapid pace of innovation in financial instruments. As businesses and investors navigate the challenges of cross-border transactions, understanding these future trends is critical for optimizing risk management strategies and ensuring long-term sustainability in a volatile environment.

Table 2. Integration of AI and blockchain in financial risk management

Technology	Application in Derivatives	Benefits to Risk Management	Challenges	Example
Artificial Intelligence	Predictive analytics, automated trading, fraud detection	Real-time market analysis, quicker decision-making, enhanced accuracy	Requires large datasets, risk of over-reliance on algorithms	Hedge funds using AI to forecast currency trends
Blockchain	Smart contracts, transparent ledger systems	Increased transparency, lower transaction costs, faster settlements	Regulatory uncertainty, integration with legacy systems	Use of blockchain for cross-border derivative trading with reduced counterparty risk
Data Analytics	Risk assessment, scenario modeling	Improved risk assessment, tailored hedging strategies	Complexity of data, need for expertise	Banks using big data to analyze market trends for derivatives trading
Machine Learning	Automated risk optimization in derivative portfolios	Efficient adaptation to changing market conditions	Data quality and ethical considerations	Investment firms applying machine learning to optimize derivative portfolios

Source: *Technology in Risk Management, Journal of Financial Innovation, 2023*

Table 2 examines the integration of AI, blockchain, data analytics, and machine learning in financial risk management, highlighting their applications in derivatives for enhanced market analysis, transparency, and risk optimization, while also noting challenges such as data complexity, regulatory issues, and the risk of over-reliance on technology, exemplified by hedge funds and investment firms.

Evolving Landscape of International Reporting and Derivatives

In the coming years, international reporting frameworks are expected to undergo significant changes, driven by increased demands for transparency and sustainability. Regulatory bodies are likely to continue aligning their standards with **International Financial Reporting Standards (IFRS)** and **Environmental, Social, and Governance (ESG)** criteria. This convergence aims to standardize reporting practices across borders, making it easier for investors and companies to assess financial performance and risk exposure. The growing importance of non-financial data, particularly ESG metrics, will likely influence how financial risks, including those associated with derivatives, are disclosed and reported.

The integration of **non-financial reporting** into traditional financial statements is expected to lead to more robust frameworks for risk management. Derivatives, once primarily used for financial risk hedging, will increasingly be assessed within the context of broader societal impacts, such as climate risk or social responsibility. These shifts will necessitate more sophisticated tools to measure and manage risk, particularly those related to long-term sustainability. Companies will be expected to disclose the environmental or social risks embedded in their financial transactions, making it more difficult to justify speculative or high-risk derivative strategies that could negatively impact broader societal goals.

The Impact of Geopolitical Shifts on Cross-Border Financial Risk

Geopolitical factors have always played a significant role in shaping financial risks, but their impact is likely to intensify in the future. The global economy is increasingly marked by **trade tensions**, **nationalistic policies**, and the **reconfiguration of international alliances**, which are creating new forms of political and economic risk for multinational corporations. For instance, the rise of **economic protectionism** and **trade wars** can directly affect currency values, commodity prices, and supply chains, all of which carry significant implications for cross-border financial risk.

The imposition of tariffs, sanctions, and trade barriers can create volatility in international markets, making it more difficult to predict future cash flows or determine the value of foreign investments. In addition, regulatory shifts in one jurisdiction can have ripple effects across global markets, particularly in industries reliant on multinational operations. These geopolitical shifts necessitate more adaptive and agile risk management strategies, including **dynamic hedging** techniques that can quickly respond to changing conditions. Derivatives, such as **currency options** and **interest rate swaps**, will continue to be critical in managing these risks, but the focus will likely expand to include the political and social dimensions of cross-border transactions.

In light of these geopolitical shifts, multinational companies must strengthen their monitoring systems to track political risks in real-time, utilizing **advanced data analytics** and **predictive modeling** to stay ahead of potential disruptions. A heightened focus on **stress testing** will help firms assess the resilience of their portfolios and financial strategies in the face of political uncertainty.

Table 3. Financial impact of key geopolitical events on cross-border transactions

Geopolitical Event	Region Impacted	Financial Consequence	Duration of Impact	Example of Affected Sector
Brexit Referendum (2016)	EU/UK	Devaluation of GBP, market volatility, stock market dip	Short-term to Medium-term	Finance, Trade, Real Estate
US-China Trade War (2018-2020)	Global	Tariffs imposed, supply chain disruptions, FX volatility	Medium-term	Technology, Agriculture, Manufacturing
Russia-Ukraine Conflict (2022)	Europe, Global	Energy price surges, inflation, stock market downturns	Ongoing	Energy, Agriculture, Commodities
COVID-19 Pandemic (2020)	Global	Recession, currency volatility, trade disruptions	Short-term to Long-term	Aviation, Tourism, Retail
US Sanctions on Iran (2021)	Middle East, Global	Currency devaluation, trade barriers, restricted access to finance	Long-term	Oil, Finance, Trade

Source:*Geopolitical Risk and Financial Markets, 2024 Report, World Economic Forum*

Table 3 illustrates the financial impacts of key geopolitical events, including Brexit, the US-China trade war, the Russia-Ukraine conflict, the COVID-19 pandemic, and US sanctions on Iran, detailing their effects on currency, market volatility, and supply chains, with sector-specific examples and varying durations of impact across global regions.

Innovations Shaping the Future of Hedging and Derivatives

The future of hedging and derivatives will be defined by several key innovations that are poised to reshape how financial risk is managed. The integration of **artificial intelligence (AI)** and **blockchain technology** into derivative markets will significantly enhance the efficiency, transparency, and reliability of these instruments. AI-powered tools are already being used to analyze vast datasets and make real-time decisions in derivative markets. These tools can identify hidden correlations and predict market movements with unprecedented accuracy, allowing businesses to manage their exposure to risks more effectively.

One particularly exciting development is the rise of **smart contracts**, powered by blockchain, which offer the potential to revolutionize the way derivatives are traded and settled. These self-executing contracts, which automatically trigger predefined actions when certain conditions are met, reduce the need for intermediaries and enhance the speed and security of transactions. Blockchain's immutable ledger also provides greater transparency, enabling stakeholders to trace the entire history of a derivative contract and ensuring greater accountability in the financial system.

In addition to these technological advancements, **sustainable finance** will increasingly influence the design and use of hedging instruments. The growing emphasis on **green derivatives**, such as carbon credit derivatives or sustainability-linked swaps, will enable businesses to hedge against environmental risks while simultaneously promoting sustainable practices. Financial instruments that tie their value to sustainability metrics, such as a company's carbon emissions or its adherence to ESG goals, will become more prevalent as investors demand greater alignment between financial returns and long-term societal impact.

Moreover, the rise of **digital currencies** and **central bank digital currencies (CBDCs)** will likely play a role in the future of derivatives, particularly in managing currency and interest rate risks. These new forms of digital assets present new challenges and opportunities for financial institutions and investors, requiring the development of novel hedging strategies to address the risks inherent in these emerging markets.

The future of financial risk management will be shaped by a combination of regulatory evolution, geopolitical shifts, and technological innovations. As businesses expand their global reach, they will need to incorporate more sophisticated, adaptable risk management strategies to navigate an increasingly volatile landscape. Derivatives will continue to play a central role in these strategies, but their design and use will evolve in response to changing financial, political, and environmental factors (M. Gupta et al., 2023; Kour et al., 2025; A. Singh et al., 2024; Taneja, Gupta, Singh, Bhatnagar, et al., 2023). The integration of AI, blockchain, and sustainable finance practices will redefine how financial risks are managed, offering more efficient, transparent, and ethically responsible solutions. As these trends unfold, businesses that embrace these innovations will be better positioned to manage the complexities of cross-border risk and achieve long-term success in an interconnected global economy.

12. BUILDING RESILIENCE IN GLOBAL FINANCIAL OPERATIONS

In an increasingly interconnected and volatile global market, building resilience in financial operations has become imperative for businesses and investors alike. Effective financial risk management is not just about mitigating losses but also about positioning organizations to thrive in the face of uncertainty. This chapter synthesizes key takeaways for robust financial risk management, offers recommendations for leveraging hedging and derivatives in cross-border transactions, and outlines strategies for fostering long-term resilience in international markets.

Key Takeaways for Effective Financial Risk Management

The landscape of financial risk management is evolving rapidly, with a growing emphasis on sustainability, technology, and adaptability. One of the most critical takeaways is the necessity of a **holistic risk management approach** that considers not only traditional financial risks such as currency fluctuations, interest rate volatility, and commodity price changes, but also emerging risks such as **geopolitical instability** and **environmental challenges** (Bathla et al., 2024; Maaze et al., 2024; Mittal et al., 2024). Successful risk management requires a nuanced understanding of both **quantitative** and **qualitative factors**, ensuring that businesses can manage financial exposure while also aligning their strategies with broader societal goals.

A key component of effective risk management is the **integration of advanced technologies**, including **artificial intelligence** (AI), **blockchain**, and **data analytics**. These innovations enable organizations to gain deeper insights into market trends, identify potential risks with greater precision, and respond to financial disruptions in real-time. Moreover, adopting **sustainable finance** principles has become integral to maintaining long-term competitiveness. Firms must embrace ESG considerations in their risk models, recognizing the growing demand from investors and stakeholders for responsible financial practices.

Table 4. Risk management strategies for long-term resilience across sectors

Sector	Strategy for Long-Term Resilience	Tools and Instruments Used	Key Focus Areas
Energy	Diversification of energy sources, sustainability focus	Green bonds, renewable energy derivatives	Environmental sustainability, energy transition
Finance	Portfolio diversification, AI-based analytics	Multi-asset class hedging, stress testing	Credit risk, market risk, regulatory compliance
Manufacturing	Supply chain diversification, real-time monitoring	Commodity swaps, geopolitical hedging	Supply chain disruption, geopolitical risks
Technology	Investment in cybersecurity, agile strategies	Cyber risk insurance, data protection derivatives	Cybersecurity, regulatory changes
Agriculture	Climate risk management, sustainable farming	Weather derivatives, crop insurance	Climate change, price volatility

Source: *Global Resilience Strategies, Financial Risk Management Review, 2024*

Suggestions for Leveraging Hedging and Derivatives in Cross-Border Deals

Hedging and derivatives are indispensable tools in managing financial risk, particularly in cross-border deals where exposure to multiple currencies, interest rates, and market conditions is prevalent. To leverage these instruments effectively, businesses must tailor their hedging strategies to their specific risk profiles and operational needs. The choice of derivatives—such as forwards, futures, options, and swaps—should be guided by a comprehensive understanding of market dynamics, the company's risk tolerance, and the potential impact of geopolitical or environmental factors.

In cross-border transactions, it is essential to understand the jurisdictional nuances and regulatory frameworks that govern derivative markets. For example, variations in accounting standards, tax policies, and financial reporting requirements across different countries necessitate a strategic approach to hedge accounting and risk mitigation (Dhinakaran et al., 2022). Firms should stay informed about evolving regulations such as the Dodd-Frank Act in the U.S. or EMIR in Europe, as these rules influence the structure and execution of derivative contracts. Moreover, hedging strategies should incorporate scenario analysis and stress testing to ensure that companies are prepared for a range of potential market disruptions, including shifts in economic policies, natural disasters, or social upheavals.

It is also critical to consider sustainable derivatives in the portfolio, especially when dealing with risks related to commodities, carbon emissions, or natural resources. For instance, green derivatives that track carbon prices or environmental outcomes offer an opportunity to hedge while simultaneously contributing to global sustainability goals. This dual purpose not only mitigates risk but also positions organizations as responsible corporate citizens in an increasingly ESG-conscious marketplace.

Table 5. Comparison of traditional vs. emerging financial risks

Risk Type	Traditional Risks	Emerging Risks	Impact on Cross-Border Deals
Market Risk	Currency, commodity, interest rates	Geopolitical, environmental, technological	Exchange rate fluctuations, geopolitical tensions
Operational Risk	Process failure, fraud, and human error	Cybersecurity breaches, data privacy issues	Data breach impacting international contracts
Credit Risk	Borrower default, counterparty exposure	Sovereign debt default, regional instability	Defaults in international loans due to political unrest
Regulatory Risk	Taxation, compliance with local laws	Regulatory changes related to ESG, AI	Cross-border tax implications, ESG regulations
Environmental Risk	Natural disasters, climate change	Climate change, sustainability issues	Impact on global supply chains and insurance contracts

Source:*International Financial Risk Management Insights 2024*

Table 5 compares traditional financial risks, such as market and credit risks, with emerging risks, including geopolitical, technological, and environmental challenges, illustrating their impact on cross-border deals, such as exchange rate fluctuations, geopolitical tensions, and sustainability issues, while highlighting new complexities like cyber security breaches and regulatory changes in ESG and AI compliance.

Strategies for Long-Term Resilience in International Markets

Long-term resilience in international markets requires more than reactive risk management; it demands proactive strategic planning and agility. Businesses must focus on creating adaptive risk frameworks that can evolve with shifting market conditions, technological advances, and regulatory changes (Taneja, Gupta, Bhushan, Bhatnagar, et al., 2023). One of the core strategies for building resilience is diversifying risk management tools across asset classes, industries, and geographies. By not over-relying on a single instrument or market, companies can mitigate systemic risk and reduce exposure to localized disruptions.

Investing in operational flexibility is another critical factor for long-term success. Companies should develop robust contingency plans and crisis management protocols that account for unexpected economic, political, or environmental shocks. Liquidity management will be paramount, ensuring that businesses have sufficient resources to navigate periods of market stress without jeopardizing their long-term viability (N. Bansal et al., 2023).

Furthermore, fostering strategic partnerships in key international markets can enhance resilience by providing access to local expertise, regulatory insights, and market intelligence. These partnerships enable companies to better navigate the complexities of cross-border transactions and identify emerging risks before they materialize (Dahiya & Taneja, 2023).

Lastly, fostering a culture of responsible innovation is vital for sustainable growth. As technological advancements continue to reshape the financial landscape, businesses must strike a balance between leveraging cutting-edge solutions, such as AI and blockchain, and maintaining ethical practices in their risk management approaches. This commitment to both innovation and responsibility will be key to ensuring that financial operations remain resilient and sustainable in the face of future challenges (Taneja & Sharma, 2023).

Building resilience in global financial operations is a multifaceted endeavor that requires careful planning, agility, and a commitment to responsible financial practices. By integrating technology, sustainability, and adaptive strategies into their risk management frameworks, businesses can not only safeguard their interests in an increasingly volatile world but also position themselves as leaders in an evolving financial ecosystem. Through effective use of hedging and derivatives, proactive strategic planning, and a focus on long-term sustainability, organizations can navigate the complexities of cross-border deals while fostering resilience in international markets (Reepu et al., 2023; TANEJA et al., 2024; Taneja & Özen, 2023).

Managerial implications: The managerial implications of this study underscore the necessity for organizations to adapt their financial risk management frameworks to address both traditional and emerging risks in cross-border transactions. Managers must prioritize the integration of advanced hedging strategies, leveraging derivatives and innovative technologies like AI and blockchain to mitigate risks associated with currency volatility, geopolitical instability, and environmental challenges. A comprehensive approach that incorporates dynamic risk assessment tools, such as predictive analytics and scenario modeling, is vital for real-time decision-making and long-term resilience. Additionally, businesses must stay attuned to regulatory shifts, particularly those related to ESG and AI compliance, ensuring seamless integration with legacy systems. In the face of increasingly complex global markets, fostering a culture of continuous risk monitoring and adaptation will enable firms to safeguard their assets, optimize operational efficiency, and maintain competitive advantage. The strategic application of these insights will significantly enhance a firm's ability to navigate financial uncertainties and ensure sustainable growth.

In conclusion, this study provides a comprehensive analysis of the multifaceted challenges and strategies involved in managing financial risk in cross-border transactions, particularly through the use of derivatives and hedging mechanisms. The dynamic nature of global financial markets has rendered traditional risk management strategies insufficient in addressing the emerging risks posed by geopolitical instability, technological disruption, and environmental factors. As demonstrated throughout the study, financial managers must embrace innovative tools such as artificial intelligence, blockchain, and advanced data analytics to navigate this complex landscape effectively.

The integration of these technologies, coupled with robust risk mitigation instruments like forwards, futures, options, and swaps, equips firms with the ability to hedge against various risks, ranging from currency and interest rate fluctuations to commodity price volatility. Additionally, the study emphasizes the importance of regulatory compliance and the evolving standards surrounding derivatives and hedging, particularly with the growing focus on environmental, social, and governance (ESG) issues.

A key takeaway is the necessity for organizations to adopt an agile and proactive approach to risk management, ensuring that their strategies are adaptable to both immediate and long-term financial uncertainties. The increasing complexity of cross-border transactions, coupled with the rise of emerging risks, calls for a holistic risk management framework that incorporates not only traditional financial instruments but also a forward-thinking perspective that anticipates future challenges.

In essence, building resilience in international markets requires a strategic blend of technological innovation, regulatory foresight, and an adaptive risk management framework. By adopting these approaches, firms can better position themselves to mitigate risks, safeguard their assets, and maintain sustainable growth amidst an increasingly volatile global financial environment.

REFERENCES

Abdullah, K. H., Abd Aziz, F. S., Dani, R., Hammood, W. A., & Setiawan, E. (2023). Urban Pollution: A Bibliometric Review. *ASM Science Journal, 18*, 1–16. DOI: 10.32802/asmscj.2023.1440

Agarwal, P., & Sharma, S. (2023). Smart Urban Traffic Management System using Energy Efficient Optimized Path Discovery. *Proceedings of the 3rd International Conference on Artificial Intelligence and Smart Energy, ICAIS 2023*, 858 – 863. DOI: 10.1109/ICAIS56108.2023.10073840

Anand, A., Singh, M. P., Sah, S., Verma, A., Khatib, M. N., Pant, M., Zahiruddin, Q. S., & Rustagi, S. (2024). H5N1 avian influenza in USA: A call for vigilance in one health surveillance. *Clinical Infection in Practice, 23*, 100369. Advance online publication. DOI: 10.1016/j.clinpr.2024.100369

Bachheti, A., Deepti, , Bachheti, R. K., Singh, A., Zebeaman, M., Hunde, Y., & Husen, A. (2023). Bioactive constituents and health promoting compounds of underutilized fruits of the northern Himalayas of India: A review. *Food Production, Processing and Nutrition, 5*(1), 24. Advance online publication. DOI: 10.1186/s43014-023-00140-5

Bansal, N., Bhatnagar, M., & Taneja, S. (2023). Balancing priorities through green optimism: A study elucidating initiatives, approaches, and strategies for sustainable supply chain management. In *Handbook of Research on Designing Sustainable Supply Chains to Achieve a Circular Economy*. IGI Global., DOI: 10.4018/978-1-6684-7664-2.ch004

Bansal, S., Kumar, V., Kumari, A., & Kuzmin, E. (2023). Understanding the Role of Digital Technologies in Supply Chain Management of SMEs. In K. V., K. G.L., A. V., & K. E. (Eds.), *Lecture Notes in Information Systems and Organisation: Vol. 61 LNISO* (pp. 195 – 205). Springer Science and Business Media Deutschland GmbH. DOI: 10.1007/978-3-031-30351-7_16

Bathla, G., Kumar, S., Garg, H., & Saini, D. (2024). Artificial Intelligence in Healthcare: Emphasis on Diabetes, Hypertension, and Depression Management. In *Artificial Intelligence in Healthcare: Emphasis on Diabetes, Hypertension, and Depression Management*. CRC Press., DOI: 10.1201/9781003522096

Belwal, N., Juneja, P., & Sunori, S. K. (2023). Decoupler Control for a MIMO Process Model in an Industrial Process - A Review. *2023 2nd International Conference on Ambient Intelligence in Health Care, ICAIHC 2023*. DOI: 10.1109/ICAIHC59020.2023.10431463

Bhatnagar, M., Kumar, P., Taneja, S., Sood, K., & Grima, S. (2024). From digital overload to trading Zen: The role of digital detox in enhancing intraday trading performance. In *Business Drivers in Promoting Digital Detoxification*. IGI Global., DOI: 10.4018/979-8-3693-1107-3.ch010

Bhatnagar, M., Rajaram, R., Taneja, S., & Kumar, P. (2024). Balancing acts: The Yin and Yang of debit and credit on the stage of financial well-being. In *Emerging Perspectives on Financial Well-Being*. IGI Global., DOI: 10.4018/979-8-3693-1750-1.ch002

Bhatnagar, M., & Sehajpal, S. (2024). Leveraging AI for Financial Sustainability in Healthcare. In Ercan, O., Azad, S., Sanjay, T., Rajendra, R., & Paulo, D. J. (Eds.), *Sustainability, Innovation, and Consumer Preference* (pp. 411–426). IGI Global Scientific Publishing., DOI: 10.4018/979-8-3693-9699-5.ch017

Bhatnagar, M., Taneja, S., & Kumar, P. (2023). The Effectiveness of Carbon Pricing Mechanism in Steering Financial Flows Toward Sustainable Projects. *International Journal of Environmental Impacts*, *6*(4), 183–196. DOI: 10.18280/ijei.060403

Bhatnagar, M., Taneja, S., Kumar, P., & Özen, E. (2024). Does financial education act as a catalyst for SME competitiveness? *International Journal of Education Economics and Development*, *15*(3), 377–393. DOI: 10.1504/IJEED.2024.139306

Bhatt, S., Dani, R., & Singh, A. K. (2024). Exploring cutting-edge approaches to sustainable tourism infrastructure and design a case studies of regenerative accommodation and facilities. In *Dimensions of Regenerative Practices in Tourism and Hospitality*. IGI Global., DOI: 10.4018/979-8-3693-4042-4.ch003

Bhatti, K. K., & Negi, A. (2018). Green store attributes and infrastructure: A connecting link between retailers and consumers to bring sustainability. *International Journal of Civil Engineering and Technology*, *9*(11), 190–198.

Bhuvaneswari, C. A., Garg, N., Supreeth, B. R., Patjoshi, P. K., Ushapriya, C., & Tiwari, M. (2023). Optimistic Boosting Internet Connection Throughput by Incorporating Blockchain Filters into Network Infrastructure. *Proceedings of the 2023 International Conference on Innovative Computing, Intelligent Communication and Smart Electrical Systems, ICSES 2023*. DOI: 10.1109/ICSES60034.2023.10465436

Bohra, N. S., Bansal, S. S., Johri, A., & Kathari, S. (2024). Evaluating infrastructure fund performance in India: A study of thematic investing. In *Issues of Sustainability in AI and New-Age Thematic Investing*. IGI Global., DOI: 10.4018/979-8-3693-3282-5.ch002

Dahiya, K., & Taneja, S. (2023). To Analyse the Impact of Multi-Media Technology on the Rural Entrepreneurship Development. In *Contemporary Studies of Risks in Emerging Technology* (pp. 221–240). DOI: 10.1108/978-1-80455-562-020231015

Das Gupta, A., Rafi, S. M., Singh, N., Gupta, V. K., Jaiswal, S., & Gangodkar, D. (2022). A Framework of Internet of Things (IOT) for the Manufacturing and Image Classifaication System. *2022 2nd International Conference on Advance Computing and Innovative Technologies in Engineering, ICACITE 2022*, 293 – 297. DOI: 10.1109/ICACITE53722.2022.9823853

Dhinakaran, M., Priya, P. K., Alanya-Beltran, J., Gandhi, V., Jaiswal, S., & Singh, D. P. (2022). An Innovative Internet of Things (IoT) Computing-Based Health Monitoring System with the Aid of Machine Learning Approach. *Proceedings of 5th International Conference on Contemporary Computing and Informatics, IC3I 2022*, 292 – 297. DOI: 10.1109/IC3I56241.2022.10072528

Gonfa, Y. H., Tessema, F. B., Tadesse, M. G., Bachheti, A., & Bachheti, R. K. (2023). Medicinally Important Plant Roots and Their Role in Nanoparticles Synthesis and Applications. In *Secondary Metabolites from Medicinal Plants: Nanoparticles Synthesis and their Applications*. CRC Press., DOI: 10.1201/9781003213727-11

Gopal, S., Gupta, P., & Minocha, A. (2023). Advancements in Fin-Tech and Security Challenges of Banking Industry. *4th International Conference on Intelligent Engineering and Management, ICIEM 2023*. DOI: 10.1109/ICIEM59379.2023.10165876

Goyal, S., Kaur, A., Sharma, V., & Batra, N. (2024). IMHS: An IoT-Based Machine Learning Healthcare System. *2024 2nd International Conference on Disruptive Technologies, ICDT 2024*, 916 – 919. DOI: 10.1109/ICDT61202.2024.10489127

Gupta, M., Arora, K., & Taneja, S. (2023). Bibliometric analysis on employee engagement and human resource management. In *Enhancing Customer Engagement Through Location-Based Marketing*. IGI Global., DOI: 10.4018/978-1-6684-8177-6.ch013

Gupta, P., Gopal, S., Sharma, M., Joshi, S., Sahani, C., & Ahalawat, K. (2023). Agriculture Informatics and Communication: Paradigm of E-Governance and Drone Technology for Crop Monitoring. *9th International Conference on Smart Computing and Communications: Intelligent Technologies and Applications, ICSCC 2023*, 113 – 118. DOI: 10.1109/ICSCC59169.2023.10335058

Gururani, P., Bhatnagar, P., Bisht, B., Jaiswal, K. K., Kumar, V., Kumar, S., Vlaskin, M. S., Grigorenko, A. V., & Rindin, K. G. (2022). Recent advances and viability in sustainable thermochemical conversion of sludge to bio-fuel production. *Fuel, 316*, 123351. Advance online publication. DOI: 10.1016/j.fuel.2022.123351

Jayadeva, S. M., Prasad Krishnam, N., Raja Mannar, B., Prakash Dabral, A., Buddhi, D., & Garg, N. (2023). An Investigation of IOT-Based Consumer Analytics to Assist Consumer Engagement Strategies in Evolving Markets. *2023 3rd International Conference on Advance Computing and Innovative Technologies in Engineering, ICACITE 2023*, 487 – 491. DOI: 10.1109/ICACITE57410.2023.10183310

Joshi, K., Patil, S., Gupta, S., & Khanna, R. (2022). Role of Pranayma in emotional maturity for improving health. *Journal of Medical Pharmaceutical and Allied Sciences, 11*(2), 4569–4573. DOI: 10.55522/jmpas.V11I2.2033

Joshi, S., Bisht, B., Kumar, V., Singh, N., Jameel Pasha, S. B., Singh, N., & Kumar, S. (2024). Artificial intelligence assisted food science and nutrition perspective for smart nutrition research and healthcare. *Systems Microbiology and Biomanufacturing, 4*(1), 86–101. DOI: 10.1007/s43393-023-00200-4

Josphineleela, R., Siva Reddy, K. V., Reddy, M. V. S. S., & Rawat, R. S. (2023). Design and Development of a Smart Sprinkler Device for IoT-Integrated Plants Irrigation. *Proceedings of the 2023 2nd International Conference on Electronics and Renewable Systems, ICEARS 2023*, 498 – 501. DOI: 10.1109/ICEARS56392.2023.10084960

Kamra, J., Mani, A. P., & Tripathi, V. M. (2023). Decarbonization Trajectory in Cement Industry. In S. P., N. S., R. J.J.P.C., R. J.J.P.C., R. J.J.P.C., L.-I. G.-A. D., P. T., C. L., & P. L. (Eds.), *2023 8th International Conference on Smart and Sustainable Technologies, SpliTech 2023*. Institute of Electrical and Electronics Engineers Inc. DOI: 10.23919/SpliTech58164.2023.10193682

Kanojia, P., Malhotra, R. K., & Uniyal, A. K. (2022a). Impact of Organizational Commitment Components on the Teachers of Higher Education in Uttarakhand: An Emperical Analysis. *Proceedings - 2022 International Conference on Recent Trends in Microelectronics, Automation, Computing and Communications Systems, ICMACC 2022*, 360–364. DOI: 10.1109/ICMACC54824.2022.10093606

Kanojia, P., Malhotra, R. K., & Uniyal, A. K. (2022b). Organizational Commitment and the Academic Staff in HEI's in North West India. *Proceedings - 2022 International Conference on Recent Trends in Microelectronics, Automation, Computing and Communications Systems, ICMACC 2022*, 365–370. DOI: 10.1109/ICMACC54824.2022.10093347

Kaur, A., Kumar, P., Taneja, S., & Ozen, E. (2023). Fintech emergence – an opportunity or threat to banking. *International Journal of Electronic Finance, 13*(1), 1–19. DOI: 10.1504/IJEF.2024.135163

Kaur, J., Khanna, R., Kumar, R., & Sunil, G. (2024). Role of Blockchain Technologies in Goods and Services Tax. *Proceedings - 2024 3rd International Conference on Sentiment Analysis and Deep Learning, ICSADL 2024*, 607–612. DOI: 10.1109/ICSADL61749.2024.00104

Kaushal, D., Kumar, S., Raj, R., & Negi, A. (2022). Understanding the effect of entrepreneurial orientation, innovation capability and differentiation strategy on firm performance: A study on small and medium enterprises. *International Journal of Business and Globalisation*, *30*(1), 57–80. DOI: 10.1504/IJBG.2022.122280

Khanna, R., Jindal, P., & Noja, G. G. (2023). Blockchain technologies, a catalyst for insurance sector. In *The Application of Emerging Technology and Blockchain in the Insurance Industry*. DOI: 10.1201/9781032630946-19

Kour, M., Taneja, S., Özen, E., Sood, K., & Grima, S. (2025). *Financial Landscape Transformation Technological Disruptions*.

Kukreti, M., Sehajpal, S., Tiwari, R., & Sood, K. (2025). *Driving Global Health and Sustainable Development Goals With Smart Technology* (Mohit, K., Sabina, S., Rajesh, T., & Kiran, S., Eds.; 1st ed.). IGI Global Scientific Publishing., DOI: 10.4018/979-8-3373-0240-9

Kumar, A. S., & Desi, A. B. (2023). Collaborative logistics, tools of machine and supply chain services in the world wide industry 4.0 framework. In *Artificial Intelligence, Blockchain, Computing and Security: Volume 2* (Vol. 2). CRC Press. DOI: 10.1201/9781032684994-15

Kumar, M. A., Valli Mayil, V., Jeyalakshmi, T. R., Ghanshala, A., & Gupta, A. (2023). Wireless Body Area Network (WBAN) Centric Healthcare System for Continuous Monitoring. *2023 9th International Conference on Advanced Computing and Communication Systems, ICACCS 2023*, 214 – 219. DOI: 10.1109/ICACCS57279.2023.10112922

Kumar, N. M., Islam, S., Podder, A. K., Selim, A., Bajaj, M., & Kamel, S. (2023). Lifecycle-based feasibility indicators for floating solar photovoltaic plants along with implementable energy enhancement strategies and framework-driven assessment approaches leading to advancements in the simulation tool. *Frontiers in Energy Research, 11*, 1075384. Advance online publication. DOI: 10.3389/fenrg.2023.1075384

Kumar, P., Reepu, & Kaur, R. (2024). Economic and Urban Dynamics: Investigating Socioeconomic Status and Urban Density as Moderators of Mobile Wallet Adoption in Smart Cities. *Lecture Notes in Networks and Systems, 948 LNNS*, 409–417. DOI: 10.1007/978-981-97-1329-5_33

Kumar, P., Bhatnagar, M., & Taneja, S. (2023). Investigation of the time pattern of Bit Green Crypto: An Arma modeling approach to unrave volatility. In *Algorithmic Approaches to Financial Technology: Forecasting, Trading, and Optimization*. IGI Global., DOI: 10.4018/979-8-3693-1746-4.ch001

Kumar, P., Taneja, S., Bhatnagar, M., & Kaur, A. K. (2024). Navigating the digital paradigm shift: Designing CBDCs for a transformative financial landscape. In *Exploring Central Bank Digital Currencies: Concepts, Frameworks, Models, and Challenges*. IGI Global., DOI: 10.4018/979-8-3693-1882-9.ch006

Kumar, P., Taneja, S., & Ozen, E. (2024). Exploring the influence of green bonds on sustainable development through low-carbon financing mobilization. *International Journal of Law and Management*. DOI: 10.1108/IJLMA-01-2024-0030

Kumar, P., Verma, P., Bhatnagar, M., Taneja, S., Seychel, S., Todorović, I., & Grim, S. (2023). The Financial Performance and Solvency Status of the Indian Public Sector Banks: A CAMELS Rating and Z Index Approach. *International Journal of Sustainable Development and Planning*, *18*(2), 367–376. DOI: 10.18280/ijsdp.180204

Kumar, R., & Khanna, R. (2023a). Role of Artificial Intelligence in Digital Currency and Future Applications. *Proceedings of the 2023 2nd International Conference on Augmented Intelligence and Sustainable Systems, ICAISS 2023*, 42–46. DOI: 10.1109/ICAISS58487.2023.10250480

Kumar, R., & Khanna, R. (2023b). RPA (Robotic Process Automation) in Finance & Accounting and Future Scope. *Proceedings of the 2023 2nd International Conference on Augmented Intelligence and Sustainable Systems, ICAISS 2023*, 1640–1645. DOI: 10.1109/ICAISS58487.2023.10250496

Kumar, R., Khannna Malholtra, R., & Grover, C. A. N. (2023). Review on Artificial Intelligence Role in Implementation of Goods and Services Tax(GST) and Future Scope. *2023 International Conference on Artificial Intelligence and Smart Communication, AISC 2023*, 348–351. DOI: 10.1109/AISC56616.2023.10085030

Kumar, R., Lande, A., Kumar, D., Malhotra, R. K., & Sharma, A. (2023). Technology Bridging -in Entrepreneurs and Consumers in Product Development. *ISED 2023 - International Conference on Intelligent Systems and Embedded Design*. DOI: 10.1109/ISED59382.2023.10444599

Kumar, R., Malholtra, R. K., Singh, R., Kathuria, S., Balyan, R., & Pal, P. (2023). Artificial Intelligence Role in Electronic Invoice Under Goods and Services Tax. *2023 International Conference on Computational Intelligence, Communication Technology and Networking, CICTN 2023*, 140–143. DOI: 10.1109/CICTN57981.2023.10140870

Kumar, V., & Korovin, G. (2023). A Comparision of Digital Transformation of Industry in the Russian Federation with the European Union. In K. V., K. G.L., A. V., & K. E. (Eds.), *Lecture Notes in Information Systems and Organisation: Vol. 61 LNISO* (pp. 45 – 57). Springer Science and Business Media Deutschland GmbH. DOI: 10.1007/978-3-031-30351-7_5

Kumar, V., Sharma, N. K., Mittal, A., & Verma, P. (2023). The Role of IoT and IIoT in Supplier and Customer Continuous Improvement Interface. *EAI/Springer Innovations in Communication and Computing*, 161 – 174. DOI: 10.1007/978-3-031-19711-6_7

Maaze, M. R., Garg, N., Das, S. K., & Shrivastava, S. (2024). Industrial and C&D waste as precursor material in geopolymers: A state-of-the-art review. *Innovative Infrastructure Solutions*, *9*(6), 229. Advance online publication. DOI: 10.1007/s41062-024-01546-x

Malhotra, R. K., Gupta, C., & Jindal, P. (2022). Blockchain and Smart Contracts for Insurance Industry. In *Blockchain Technology in Corporate Governance*. Transforming Business and Industries., DOI: 10.1002/9781119865247.ch11

Mandalapu, S. R., Sivamuni, K., Chitra Devi, D., Aswal, U. S., Sherly, S. I., & Balaji, N. A. (2023). An Architecture-based Self-Typing Service for Cloud Native Applications. *Proceedings of the 4th International Conference on Smart Electronics and Communication, ICOSEC 2023*, 562 – 566. DOI: 10.1109/ICOSEC58147.2023.10276313

Joshitta, S. M., Sunil, M. P., Bodhankar, A., Sreedevi, C., & Khanna, R. (2023, May). The Integration of Machine Learning Technique with the Existing System to Predict the Flight Prices. In 2023 3rd International Conference on Advance Computing and Innovative Technologies in Engineering (ICACITE) (pp. 398-402). IEEE.

Medhi, M. K., Ambust, S., Kumar, R., & Das, A. J. (2023). Characterization and Purification of Biosurfactants. In *Advancements in Biosurfactants Research*. Springer International Publishing., DOI: 10.1007/978-3-031-21682-4_4

Mehershilpa, G., Prasad, D., Sai Kiran, C., Shaikh, A., Jayashree, K., & Socrates, S. (2023). EDM machining of Ti6Al4V alloy using colloidal biosilica. *Materials Today: Proceedings*. Advance online publication. DOI: 10.1016/j.matpr.2023.02.443

Mittal, A., Pandey, H., Arsh, M., Soni, M., Goyal, H. R., & Sharma, S. (2024). Advancements and Applications of Artificial Intelligence in Various Sectors: From Internet of Vehicles to 6G and Healthcare. *Proceedings - 2024 4th International Conference on Pervasive Computing and Social Networking, ICPCSN 2024*, 107 – 112. DOI: 10.1109/ICPCSN62568.2024.00026

Neha, M., S., Alfurhood, B. S., Bakhare, R., Poongavanam, S., & Khanna, R. (2023). The Role and Impact of Artificial Intelligence on Retail Business and its Developments. *2023 International Conference on Artificial Intelligence and Smart Communication, AISC 2023*, 1098–1101. DOI: 10.1109/AISC56616.2023.10085624

Pande, S. D., Bhatt, A., Chamoli, S., Saini, D. K. J. B., Kute, U. T., & Ahammad, S. H. (2023). Design of Atmel PLC and its Application as Automation of Coal Handling Plant. *2023 International Conference on Sustainable Emerging Innovations in Engineering and Technology, ICSEIET 2023*, 178 – 183. DOI: 10.1109/ICSEIET58677.2023.10303627

Pandey, N. K., Kashyap, S., Sharma, A., & Diwakar, M. (2023). Contribution of Cloud-Based Services in Post-Pandemic Technology Sustainability and Challenges: A Future Direction. In *Evolving Networking Technologies: Developments and Future Directions*. wiley. DOI: 10.1002/9781119836667.ch4

Pandya, D. J., Kumar, Y., Singh, D. P., Vairavel, D. K., Deepak, A., Rao, A. K., & Rana, A. (2023). Automatic Power Factor Compensation for Industrial Use to Minimize Penalty. *Proceedings of International Conference on Contemporary Computing and Informatics, IC3I 2023*, 2499 – 2504. DOI: 10.1109/IC3I59117.2023.10398095

Pant, A., Joshi, R. C., Sharma, S., & Pant, K. (2024). Air Quality and Public Health Risk Assessment: A Case of an Industrial Area in Haridwar City, Uttarakhand (India). *Indian Journal of Public Health*, *68*(2), 222–226. DOI: 10.4103/ijph.ijph_279_23 PMID: 38953809

Singh, P., & Singh, D. P. (2024). Role of Disruptive Technologies in the Smart Healthcare Sector of Society 5.0. In *Artificial Intelligence and Society 5.0* (pp. 143–153). Chapman and Hall/CRC.

Rajbalaji, S., Raman, R., Pant, B., Rathour, N., Rajagopa, B. R., & Prasad, C. R. (2023). Design of deep learning models for the identifications of harmful attack activities in IIOT. *2023 International Conference on Artificial Intelligence and Smart Communication, AISC 2023*, 609 – 613. DOI: 10.1109/AISC56616.2023.10085088

Rajora, R., Gupta, H., Malhotra, S., Devliyal, S., & Sunil, G. (2024). Advancing Renal Health: Unleashing the Power of CNNs in Multi-Class Classification for Precise Kidney Condition Diagnosis. *2024 IEEE 9th International Conference for Convergence in Technology, I2CT 2024*. DOI: 10.1109/I2CT61223.2024.10544018

Raman, R., Buddhi, D., Lakhera, G., Gupta, Z., Joshi, A., & Saini, D. (2023). An investigation on the role of artificial intelligence in scalable visual data analytics. *2023 International Conference on Artificial Intelligence and Smart Communication, AISC 2023*, 666 – 670. DOI: 10.1109/AISC56616.2023.10085495

Raman, R., Kumar, R., Ghai, S., Gehlot, A., Raju, A. M., & Barve, A. (2023). A New Method of Optical Spectrum Analysis for Advanced Wireless Communications. *2023 3rd International Conference on Advance Computing and Innovative Technologies in Engineering, ICACITE 2023*, 1719 – 1723. DOI: 10.1109/ICACITE57410.2023.10182414

Ramanan, M., Singh, L., Kumar, A. S., Suresh, A., Sampathkumar, A., Jain, V., & Bacanin, N. (2022). Secure blockchain enabled Cyber- Physical health systems using ensemble convolution neural network classification. *Computers & Electrical Engineering, 101*, 108058. Advance online publication. DOI: 10.1016/j.compeleceng.2022.108058

Rana, M. S., Dixit, A. K., Rajan, M. S., Malhotra, S., Radhika, S., & Pant, B. (2022). An Empirical Investigation in Applying Reliable Industry 4.0 Based Machine Learning (ML) Approaches in Analysing and Monitoring Smart Meters using Multivariate Analysis of Variance (Manova). *2022 2nd International Conference on Advance Computing and Innovative Technologies in Engineering, ICACITE 2022*, 603 – 607. DOI: 10.1109/ICACITE53722.2022.9823597

Rawat, R., Sharma, S., & Goyal, H. R. (2023). Intelligent Digital Financial Inclusion System Architectures for Industry 5.0 Enabled Digital Society. *Winter Summit on Smart Computing and Networks. WiSSCoN, 2023*, 1–5. Advance online publication. DOI: 10.1109/WiSSCoN56857.2023.10133858

Reepu, R., Taneja, S., Ozen, E., & Singh, A. (2023). A globetrotter to the future of marketing: Metaverse. In *Cultural Marketing and Metaverse for Consumer Engagement*. IGI Global., DOI: 10.4018/978-1-6684-8312-1.ch001

Sahithya, B., Guru Prasad, M. S., Sahithi, B., Madhu Krishna, K., Devarlla, A. C., & Yashavanth, T. R. (2024). Empowering Healthcare with AI: Advancements in Medical Image Analysis, Electronic Health Records Analysis, and AI-Driven Chatbots. *2024 3rd International Conference for Innovation in Technology, INOCON 2024*. DOI: 10.1109/INOCON60754.2024.10511753

Sahu, S. R., & Rawat, K. S. (2023). Analysis of Land subsidencein coastal and urban areas by using various techniques– Literature Review. *The Indonesian Journal of Geography, 55*(3), 488–495. DOI: 10.22146/ijg.83675

Salama, R., Al-Turjman, F., Bordoloi, D., & Yadav, S. P. (2023). Wireless Sensor Networks and Green Networking for 6G communication- An Overview. *2023 International Conference on Computational Intelligence, Communication Technology and Networking, CICTN 2023*, 830 – 834. DOI: 10.1109/CICTN57981.2023.10141262

Sati, P., Sharma, E., Soni, R., Dhyani, P., Solanki, A. C., Solanki, M. K., Rai, S., & Malviya, M. K. (2022). Bacterial endophytes as bioinoculant: microbial functions and applications toward sustainable farming. In *Microbial Endophytes and Plant Growth: Beneficial Interactions and Applications*. Elsevier., DOI: 10.1016/B978-0-323-90620-3.00008-8

Sehajpal, S., & Kaur, N. (2025). Neuroscience, Nursing, and Financial Innovation : A Synergistic Approach to Optimized Patient Care and Economic Well-Being. In Sanjay, T., Bhupinderpal Pal, S. C., Amar, J., Ercan, O., & Pawan, K. (Eds.), *Neuromarketing's Role in Sustainable Finance* (pp. 133–146). IGI Global Scientific Publishing., DOI: 10.4018/979-8-3693-9117-4.ch008

Semwal, P., Painuli, S., Shabaaz Begum, J. P., Jamloki, A., Rauf, A., Olatunde, A., Mominur Rahman, M., Mukerjee, N., Khalil, A. A., Aljohani, A. S. M., Al Abdulmonem, W., & Simal-Gandara, J. (2024). Corrigendum to "Exploring the nutritional and health benefits of pulses from the Indian Himalayan region: A glimpse into the region's rich agricultural heritage" [Food Chem. 422 (2023) 136259] (Food Chemistry (2023) 422, (S0308814623008774), (. *Food Chemistry, 445*. https://doi .org/DOI: 10.1016/j.fo

Shah, J. K., Sharma, R., Misra, A., Sharma, M., Joshi, S., Kaushal, D., & Bafila, S. (2023). Industry 4.0 Enabled Smart Manufacturing: Unleashing the Power of Artificial Intelligence and Blockchain. *2023 1st DMIHER International Conference on Artificial Intelligence in Education and Industry 4.0, IDICAIEI 2023*. DOI: 10.1109/IDICAIEI58380.2023.10406671

Sharma, E., Rana, S., Sharma, I., Sati, P., & Dhyani, P. (2023). Organic polymers for CO2 capture and conversion. In *CO2-Philic Polymers, Nanocomposites and Solvents: Capture, Conversion and Industrial Products*. Elsevier., DOI: 10.1016/B978-0-323-85777-2.00002-0

Sharma, P., Taneja, S., Kumar, P., Özen, E., & Singh, A. (2024). Application of the UTAUT model toward individual acceptance: Emerging trends in artificial intelligence-based banking services. *International Journal of Electronic Finance, 13*(3), 352–366. DOI: 10.1504/IJEF.2024.139584

Sharma, S., & Bhadula, S. (2023). Secure Federated Learning for Intelligent Industry 4.0 IoT Enabled Self Skin Care Application System. *Proceedings of the 2nd International Conference on Applied Artificial Intelligence and Computing, ICAAIC 2023*, 1164 – 1170. DOI: 10.1109/ICAAIC56838.2023.10141028

Sharma, S., Gupta, A., & Tyagi, R. (2023). Sustainable Natural Resources Utilization Decision System for Better Society Using Vedic Scripture, Cloud Computing, and IoT. In B. R.C., S. K.M., & D. M. (Eds.), *Proceedings of IEEE 2023 5th International Conference on Advances in Electronics, Computers and Communications, ICAECC 2023*. Institute of Electrical and Electronics Engineers Inc. DOI: 10.1109/ICAECC59324.2023.10560335

Sharma, S., Mishra, R. R., Joshi, V., & Kour, K. (2020). Analysis and Interpretation of Global Air Quality. *2020 11th International Conference on Computing, Communication and Networking Technologies, ICCCNT 2020*. DOI: 10.1109/ICCCNT49239.2020.9225532

Singh, A., Kumar, P., & Taneja, S. (2024). Artificial Intelligence and Machine Learning-Powered Smart Finance. In Taneja, P. K. S., & Singh, A. (Eds.), *IGI Global*. IGI Global., DOI: 10.4018/979-8-3693-3264-1

Singh, A., & Srivastava, A. (2024). Innovation needed to improve road construction and road infrastructure in the future in India. In G. A. & V. R.J. (Eds.), *IOP Conference Series: Earth and Environmental Science* (Vol. 1326, Issue 1). Institute of Physics. DOI: 10.1088/1755-1315/1326/1/012097

Singh, A. R., Vishnuram, P., Alagarsamy, S., Bajaj, M., Blazek, V., Damaj, I., Rathore, R. S., Al-Wesabi, F. N., & Othman, K. M. (2024). Electric vehicle charging technologies, infrastructure expansion, grid integration strategies, and their role in promoting sustainable e-mobility. *Alexandria Engineering Journal, 105*, 300–330. DOI: 10.1016/j.aej.2024.06.093

Singh, K. D., Deep Singh, P., Bansal, A., Kaur, G., Khullar, V., & Tripathi, V. (2023). Exploratory Data Analysis and Customer Churn Prediction for the Telecommunication Industry. *ACCESS 2023 - 2023 3rd International Conference on Advances in Computing, Communication, Embedded and Secure Systems*, 197 – 201. DOI: 10.1109/ACCESS57397.2023.10199700

Singh, K. D., Singh, P., Chhabra, R., Kaur, G., Bansal, A., & Tripathi, V. (2023). Cyber-Physical Systems for Smart City Applications: A Comparative Study. In K. R., K. R., G. M., G. M., S. R., & S. R. (Eds.), *2023 International Conference on Advancement in Computation and Computer Technologies, InCACCT 2023* (pp. 871 – 876). Institute of Electrical and Electronics Engineers Inc. DOI: 10.1109/InCACCT57535.2023.10141719

Singh, K. D., Singh, P., Kaur, G., Khullar, V., Chhabra, R., & Tripathi, V. (2023). Education 4.0: Exploring the Potential of Disruptive Technologies in Transforming Learning. *Proceedings of International Conference on Computational Intelligence and Sustainable Engineering Solution, CISES 2023*, 586 – 591. DOI: 10.1109/CISES58720.2023.10183547

Singh, K. D., Singh, P., Tripathi, V., & Khullar, V. (2022). A Novel and Secure Framework to Detect Unauthorized Access to an Optical Fog-Cloud Computing Network. In R. H.S., B. R., G. P.K., & S. V.K. (Eds.), *PDGC 2022 - 2022 7th International Conference on Parallel, Distributed and Grid Computing* (pp. 618 – 622). Institute of Electrical and Electronics Engineers Inc. DOI: 10.1109/PDGC56933.2022.10053223

Singh, N. K., Singh, Y., Singh, Y., Rahim, E. A., Sharma, A., Singla, A., & Ranjit, P. S. (2023). The Effectiveness of Balanites aegyptiaca Oil Nanofluid Augmented with Nanoparticles as Cutting Fluids during the Turning Process. In *Biowaste and Biomass in Biofuel Applications*. CRC Press., DOI: 10.1201/9781003265597-7

Singh, S., Singh, A., Mohan, A., Batola, M., & Kumar, N. (2024). Health Expenditures And Health Outcomes In Central Europe And The Baltic Region. *Baltic Region*, *16*(2), 126–143. DOI: 10.5922/2079-8555-2024-2-7

Sonnad, S., Awasthy, M., Rane, K., Banerjee, M., Buddhi, D., & Pant, B. (2022). Blockchain-Based Secure Mengers Authentication for Industrial IoT. In D. R.K., S. A.Kr., K. G., & B. S. (Eds.), *Proceedings of the 2022 11th International Conference on System Modeling and Advancement in Research Trends, SMART 2022* (pp. 853 – 858). Institute of Electrical and Electronics Engineers Inc. DOI: 10.1109/SMART55829.2022.10046934

Taneja, S., Bhatnagar, M., Kumar, P., & Grima, S. (2023). A Panel Analysis of the Effectiveness of the Asset Management in Indian Agricultural Companies. *International Journal of Sustainable Development and Planning*, *18*(3), 653–660. DOI: 10.18280/ijsdp.180301

Taneja, S., Bhatnagar, M., Kumar, P., & Rupeika-apoga, R. (2023). India ' s Total Natural Resource Rents (NRR) and GDP : An Augmented Autoregressive Distributed Lag (ARDL) Bound Test. *Journal of Risk and Financial Management*, *16*(2), 91. https://doi.org/doi.org/10.3390/jrfm16020091. DOI: 10.3390/jrfm16020091

Taneja, S., Gupta, M., Bhushan, P., Bhatnagar, M., & Singh, A. (2023). Cultural marketing in the digital era. In *Cultural Marketing and Metaverse for Consumer Engagement*. IGI Global., DOI: 10.4018/978-1-6684-8312-1.ch008

Taneja, S., Gupta, S., Singh, A., Bhatnagar, M., & Gaur, A. (2023). Green management - A new paradigm in the world of business. *Green Management - A New Paradigm in the World of Business*, 1–230. DOI: 10.52305/DLIH6622

Taneja, S., & Özen, E. (2023). To analyse the relationship between bank's green financing and environmental performance. *International Journal of Electronic Finance*, *12*(2), 163–175. DOI: 10.1504/IJEF.2023.129919

Taneja, S., & Sharma, V. (2023). Role of beaconing marketing in improving customer buying experience. In *Enhancing Customer Engagement Through Location-Based Marketing*. IGI Global., DOI: 10.4018/978-1-6684-8177-6.ch012

Thapa, D., Kumar, V., Naik, B., Kumar, V., Gupta, A. K., Mohanta, Y. K., Mishra, B., & Rustagi, S. (2024). Harnessing probiotic foods: Managing cancer through gut health. *Food Science and Biotechnology*, *33*(9), 2141–2160. DOI: 10.1007/s10068-024-01638-5 PMID: 39130664

Tyagi, S., Krishna, K. H., Joshi, K., Ghodke, T. A., Kumar, A., & Gupta, A. (2023). Integration of PLCC modem and Wi-Fi for Campus Street Light Monitoring. In N. P., S. M., K. M., J. V., & G. K. (Eds.), *Proceedings - 4th IEEE 2023 International Conference on Computing, Communication, and Intelligent Systems, ICCCIS 2023* (pp. 1113 – 1116). Institute of Electrical and Electronics Engineers Inc. DOI: 10.1109/ICCCIS60361.2023.10425715

Upreti, H., & Malhotra, R. K. (2024). Bridging The Urban-Rural Education Gap In India Through CSR (Corporate Social Responsibility) Initiatives: A Conceptual Study With Special Reference To Sustainable Development Goal 4 (Quality Education). In P. P.K. (Ed.), *E3S Web of Conferences* (Vol. 556). EDP Sciences. DOI: 10.1051/e3sconf/202455601032

Upreti, H., Uddin, Z., Pandey, A. K., & Joshi, N. (2023). Particle swarm optimization based numerical study for pressure, flow, and heat transfer over a rotating disk with temperature dependent nanofluid properties. *Numerical Heat Transfer Part A*, *83*(8), 815–844. DOI: 10.1080/10407782.2022.2156412

Verma, A., Sharma, D., Pant, M., Khatib, M. N., Singh, M. P., Zahiruddin, Q. S., Rustagi, S., Gaidhane, S., & Gaidhane, A. M. (2024). First sighting of human H5N1 in Australia: A detailed account and public health implications. *New Microbes and New Infections*, *60–61*, 101447. Advance online publication. DOI: 10.1016/j.nmni.2024.101447 PMID: 39045288

Zaheer, A., Zehra Hussain, D., Verma, A., Sah, S., Pant, M., Nazli Khatib, M., Pratap Singh, M., Syed Zahiruddin, Q., & Rustagi, S. (2024). Marburg virus: An emerging threat to global health. *Clinical Infection in Practice*, *23*, 100371. Advance online publication. DOI: 10.1016/j.clinpr.2024.100371

Chapter 9

Navigating the Intersection of IFRS and Global Trade Regulations: Enhancing Compliance, Transparency, and Cross-Border Investment Flows

S. Thandayuthapani
https://orcid.org/0000-0001-9559-745X
Kristu Jayanti College, India

ABSTRACT

With an emphasis on how they work together to improve compliance, transparency, and cross-border investment, this chapter explores the complex link between international trade regulations and International Financial Reporting Standards (IFRS). It looks at the benefits and drawbacks of their convergence, focusing on how IFRS and trade regulations should be harmonised to guarantee accuracy in financial reporting and compliance with trade regulations. The conversation focuses on how bringing these frameworks into alignment reduces financial risks in cross-border transactions and increases investor confidence and trust. The chapter emphasises the significance of unified policies by examining the regulatory obstacles encountered by multinational corporations. The ramifications of integrating IFRS principles with trade rules are shown via case studies, best practices, and practical techniques. The conclusion highlights how important it is for businesses, governments, and regulatory agencies to work together in order to maximise global economic integration.

DOI: 10.4018/979-8-3373-0887-6.ch009

I. INTRODUCTION

The relationship between financial reporting standards and trade legislation has become a crucial topic of emphasis for companies, legislators, and regulators in an increasingly integrated global economy. A widely recognized framework for creating and presenting financial statements, International Financial Reporting Standards (IFRS) encourage uniformity, comparability, and transparency across national boundaries. The laws regulating international trade operations are established concurrently by global trade regulations, which guarantee economic balance, equality, and conformity among trading states. Both possibilities and problems arise from the confluence of these two crucial areas, especially when it comes to promoting compliance, improving transparency, and easing cross-border investment flows.

1.1 IFRS's Significance in International Trade

The International Accounting Standards Board (IASB) produced IFRS, which have been approved or implemented in more than 140 countries globally, proving its universality and applicability. By enabling organizations to provide financial data that is similar across national borders, these standards promote confidence and trust among stakeholders. Global commerce depends on transparent and consistent financial reporting because it helps governments, financial institutions, and investors make well-informed judgments about cross-border transactions.

Furthermore, a standardized financial language that cuts across regional differences is required due to the globalization of commerce. In order to meet this demand, IFRS is essential since it provides a uniform framework that harmonizes financial reporting procedures in many economies. IFRS mitigates risks, promotes fair trade agreements, and lessens information asymmetry by providing a solid foundation for financial comparison.

1.2 International Trade Laws: A Complicated Structure

The flow of money, products, and services across international boundaries is governed by a broad range of laws, agreements, and policies known as global trade rules. These rules are intended to combat fraud, safeguard intellectual property, guarantee fair trade practices, and encourage sustainable economic growth. The global trade environment is shaped by a variety of organizations, including national regulatory bodies, regional trade agreements, and the World Trade Organization (WTO).

However, both small and medium-sized businesses (SMEs) and multinational companies (MNCs) face substantial obstacles while negotiating these requirements. It may be difficult and resource-intensive to comply with different legal and trade standards across countries, and companies often need to modify their operational and financial reporting plans to meet various regulatory requirements. This emphasizes how crucial it is to align international trade laws with IFRS in order to expedite compliance procedures and enable smooth cross-border business.

1.3 How Global Trade Regulations and IFRS Intersect

A crucial point where financial transparency and regulatory compliance meet is the junction of IFRS and international trade laws. Economic stability, corporate governance, and international investment flows are all significantly impacted by this convergence. For example, by providing precise and verifiable financial data, consistent financial reporting under IFRS may improve adherence to trade standards and lower the risk of financial wrongdoing and trade disputes.

The way financial transactions are recorded and understood under IFRS is also influenced by trade rules. Examples include tax laws, transfer pricing, and customs value, all of which have an impact on financial reporting requirements. Inconsistencies arising from a lack of alignment across these frameworks may give rise to legal challenges, financial fines, and harm to a company's image.

1.4 Improving Compliance Through Integration

By encouraging consistency and simplifying regulatory requirements, the integration of IFRS with international trade standards may greatly improve compliance processes. By guaranteeing that financial statements fairly depict trade operations, harmonized standards promote increased accountability and lower the risk of fraud or deception. For instance, IFRS adoption combined with trade compliance initiatives may simplify tax reporting procedures, increase the accuracy of transfer pricing, and expedite customs declarations.

Additionally, technologically advanced alternatives like blockchain and artificial intelligence (AI) have become effective means of bridging the gap between trade norms and IFRS. These solutions guarantee increased accuracy and efficiency in financial reporting and trade processes by facilitating real-time data exchange, automatic compliance checks, and improved audit trails.

1.5 Encouraging Transparency in Financial and Trade Activities

Transparency is essential to international trade laws and IFRS, and it acts as a stimulant to increase stakeholder confidence. Investors and regulators may evaluate a company's trustworthiness and adherence to trade regulations thanks to transparent financial reporting under IFRS, which offers a clear and consistent depiction of its financial performance. This openness is especially important for reducing the risks of cross-border investments, such exchange rate swings, unstable political environments, and inconsistent regulations.

In a similar vein, clear trade laws promote fair trade practices, lower entry barriers, and improve companies' access to markets. Businesses may disclose trade-related financial activities more transparently and make sure their operations are morally and legally sound by coordinating IFRS with trade legislation. For instance, the full requirements for reporting revenue and lease-related transactions—which are essential to international trade activities—are provided by IFRS 15 on revenue recognition and IFRS 16 on lease accounting.

1.6 Encouraging International Investment Flows

Global economic development is fueled by cross-border investments, which also promote wealth distribution, job creation, and innovation. However, the availability of trustworthy and comparable financial data is essential to the success of such initiatives. By offering a consistent reporting structure that improves the credibility of financial statements, IFRS play a crucial part in meeting this demand. Investors use this data to evaluate the operational effectiveness, financial stability, and room for expansion of companies doing business abroad.

Additionally, by affecting elements like tariffs, trade agreements, and the costs of regulatory compliance, international trade rules have an effect on cross-border investments. Incorporating these rules into IFRS may lower transaction costs, lessen uncertainty, and improve the climate for portfolio investments and foreign direct investments (FDIs). For example, IFRS-compliant financial statements provide a solid foundation for evaluating the financial ramifications of trade agreements and may help negotiate them more easily.

1.7 Difficulties at the Intersection

Notwithstanding the possible advantages, there are several difficulties in negotiating the junction between international trade laws and IFRS. The main challenge is the variation in legal requirements across countries, which may lead to discrepancies in trade compliance and financial reporting. Conflicting interpretations and practices may result, for instance, from variations in tax laws, financial disclosure regulations, and customs valuation techniques. Furthermore, the challenge of harmonizing international trade legislation with IFRS is increased by their dynamic character. Regular modifications to financial reporting standards and compliance frameworks are required due to the frequent changes in trade regulations brought about by geopolitical events, economic upheavals, and technology improvements.

To be compliant and competitive, businesses must continue to be proactive and flexible in their adaptation to these developments.

1.8 The Function of Regulators and Policymakers

In order to promote alignment between IFRS and international trade norms, policymakers and regulatory agencies are essential. International institutions like the International Monetary Fund (IMF), WTO, and IASB may work together to create harmonized frameworks that meet the requirements of trade compliance and financial reporting. The gap between these fields may be filled, for example, by collaborative efforts to standardize customs valuation procedures, simplify transfer pricing laws, and improve transparency in cross-border transactions.

The promotion of alignment is also greatly aided by national governments and regional trade blocs. Countries may increase their appeal as investment destinations, boost regulatory effectiveness, and promote economic development by implementing IFRS and incorporating them into trade laws. For instance, the adoption of IFRS by the European Union has promoted cross-border commerce and investment by facilitating greater financial integration among member states.

II. BACKGROUND OF THE STUDY

Global financial systems' adoption of International Financial Reporting Standards (IFRS) has revolutionized cross-border investment, business transparency, and compliance. More uniformity and comparability in financial reporting have been made possible by the creation and broad acceptance of IFRS, which has aided companies, investors, and regulators in navigating the intricacies of international finance. However, the relationship between IFRS and international trade laws has become a crucial study topic as the global corporate environment becomes more intertwined. The core of this confluence is the ability to enhance compliance, transparency, and ease cross-border investment flows; yet, the relationship between trade legislation and financial reporting has not received enough attention in the literature to far.

2.1. IFRS's Development and Worldwide Adoption

By encouraging comparability, openness, and dependability in financial accounts, the International Financial Reporting Standards (IFRS) have emerged as a key component of worldwide financial reporting. The International Accounting Standards Committee (IASC), which was founded in 1973 with the goal of standardizing accounting procedures worldwide, is where IFRS had its start. International Accounting

Standards (IAS) were first published by the IASC and were a forerunner to IFRS. But in 2001, the IASC was superseded by the International Accounting Standards Board (IASB), which took on the task of creating excellent international standards within the scope of IFRS (Ball, 2006). A move toward more accountability and a principles-based approach to financial reporting was signaled by this change.

As globalization increased the need for uniform financial reporting across countries, IFRS adoption accelerated. An important turning point in the adoption of IFRS worldwide was the European Union's 2005 decision to require it for all publicly listed corporations in its member states. In order to conform to international standards and draw in foreign investment, other countries, such as Australia, Canada, and South Korea, also adopted IFRS, either completely or in modified versions (Ramanna & Sletten, 2014). To improve their integration into the global financial system, emerging economies like Brazil and India have either embraced IFRS or merged their national standards with it.

Because of variations in legislative frameworks, cultural factors, and economic interests, the implementation of IFRS is not consistent. The main reasons developed economies have adopted IFRS are to increase market efficiency and simplify cross-border financial transactions. On the other hand, developing countries have difficulties such insufficient knowledge, limited resources, and doubts about the applicability of IFRS in regional business settings (Zeghal & Mhedhbi, 2006). However, the advantages of IFRS—such as improved comparability of financial statements, less information asymmetry, and heightened investor confidence—continue to propel its uptake.

The significance of IFRS has been further highlighted by international trade restrictions. International commerce and investment are greatly aided by IFRS, which guarantees uniform financial reporting across national boundaries. By simplifying the process of managing various financial reporting regulations, it fosters openness and confidence among investors and trading partners (Barth et al., 2008). This conformity to international trade standards improves adherence to international agreements and reduces financial disparity issues.

Even with its extensive use, IFRS's alignment with national standards is still being worked out. Generally Accepted Accounting Principles (GAAP) are still used in the United States, for example, despite ongoing talks about converting to IFRS. Furthermore, there are issues with the interaction between IFRS and international trade legislation, such as inconsistent enforcement and trouble striking a balance between national interests and international standards.

2.2. The Function of International Trade Laws in Cross-Border Exchanges

By offering a framework that regulates international trade operations, guaranteeing compliance, lowering risks, and promoting economic cooperation, global trade rules significantly influence cross-border transactions. Trade agreements, taxes, quotas, customs procedures, and compliance criteria set by regional trade agencies and international organizations such as the World Trade Organization (WTO) are all included in these rules. They want to provide a predictable environment for global trade by standardizing trade processes, which will lower barriers and enable more seamless cross-border transactions (Hoekman & Kostecki, 2009).

For cross-border transactions to be transparent and trustworthy, trade rules are essential. For example, regulations pertaining to intellectual property rights, environmental standards, and anti-dumping measures guarantee that global commerce is carried out on fair terms, lowering the possibility of conflicts and boosting investor confidence (Bagwell & Staiger, 2002). Additionally, according to Hail et al. (2010), these rules often mandate that companies follow strong financial reporting standards, including the International Financial Reporting Standards (IFRS), which improve the comparability and dependability of financial accounts.

Aligning IFRS with international trade laws is difficult, however, especially when companies have to deal with disparities in regional laws and varying degrees of enforcement. To minimize legal risks and maximize investment flows, international firms must make sure that financial reporting standards and trade laws are followed (Gomes et al., 2021). Notwithstanding the advantages, conducting smooth cross-border operations may be hampered by uneven trade agreement implementation and varied jurisdictional interpretations of IFRS. By addressing these problems with unified policies, we can improve the efficiency of international commerce and fortify the world economy.

2.3. IFRS and International Trade Regulations' Convergence

Multinational companies' (MNCs') business decision-making is impacted by the dynamic and intricate junction of IFRS and international trade legislation. Businesses must make sure that their financial reporting procedures not only adhere to IFRS but also to the legal frameworks in many countries as global trade restrictions change. The specifics of trade agreements between nations, such as tax treaties, foreign investment restrictions, and tariff systems, may influence these norms. These agreements often call for certain financial disclosures (Choi & Meek, 2011).

The problem of harmonizing regulations is one of the major obstacles at this juncture. The legal and regulatory frameworks controlling trade and investment differ greatly across countries, despite the fact that IFRS offers a consistent framework for financial reporting. Investors, regulators, and governments all see and utilize financial information differently as a result of this disparity. Businesses that operate in many countries may also have to deal with contradictory compliance obligations, especially in developing markets where legislative frameworks may be less established or subject to frequent changes. There are significant differences between trade laws in the US and the EU in areas like corporate taxation and environmental restrictions. Multinational corporations' compliance responsibilities are made more difficult by this discrepancy, which forces them to make extra steps to match their financial reporting with both local trade laws and IFRS.

2.4. Improving Adherence by Aligning Trade Regulations With IFRS

Global trade laws and IFRS alignment may improve compliance, particularly for multinational corporations that do cross-border business. Businesses may lower the risks of non-compliance, including fines, penalties, and harm to their brand, by promoting more regulatory coherence. Additionally, the increased openness brought about by IFRS compliance may boost investor trust and encourage foreign direct investment. Transparency and improved corporate reporting have become even more crucial as a result of the movement towards sustainability and socially conscious business practices, which is being pushed by ESG standards. ESG factors are increasingly being included in trade agreements and regulatory frameworks, which may have an impact on how financial statements are presented and perceived.

Additionally, fair and accurate reporting of a company's financial status depends on the use of IFRS to increase transparency. By giving investors trustworthy information to help them make choices, accurate and transparent financial reporting improves the effectiveness of cross-border investment flows. However, enterprises, especially those that operate in numerous countries, may face increased compliance costs and administrative constraints due to the difficulty of conforming to both local trade legislation and IFRS (Hail et al., 2010).

2.5. Effect on International Investment Flows

Global market expansion, especially in emerging nations, depends on cross-border investment flows. By lowering risk and information asymmetry, IFRS reporting's openness is essential for drawing in international investors. Standardized financial data is used by investors to evaluate the risks and possible rewards of making investments in overseas markets. The capacity of investors to compare financial information across borders becomes increasingly more crucial when trade restrictions change and impact how organizations run.

Simultaneously, the convergence of international trade legislation and IFRS may also assist reduce the risks related to trade barriers, currency fluctuations, and political instability. Businesses may improve their capacity to draw in investment, particularly in areas with more complicated or ambiguous trade restrictions, by delivering consistent and transparent financial reporting. Thus, the interaction between trade laws with IFRS may serve as a market bridge, promoting economic development by increasing trade and foreign direct investment (Nobes & Parker, 2016).

2.6. Emerging Trends and Future Directions

The requirement for closer adherence to trade legislation and IFRS will only increase as global commerce grows and changes. In order for companies to report on their sustainability initiatives and reconcile their financial statements with international trade legislation, IFRS standards will need to include ESG criteria due to the increased focus on sustainability and responsible business practices. Furthermore, in order to overcome the particular difficulties they have in conforming to IFRS and trade laws, developing markets—which are often the centers of international trade and investment flows—will need customized solutions (Barrett, 2019). In addition, companies must use technology solutions to simplify their compliance activities due to the growing complexity of global commerce and its multi-layered regulatory framework. Businesses may find new methods to combine IFRS reporting with the requirements of international trade rules thanks to advancements in artificial intelligence (AI) and data analytics, which would increase compliance effectiveness and lower risks.

III. REVIEW OF LITERATURE

3.1 Rules for International Financial Reporting (IFRS)

With the goal of fostering openness, uniformity, and comparability across financial statements, International Financial Reporting Standards (IFRS) have become the world standard for financial reporting. The relationship between IFRS and international trade laws is becoming more and more important as globalization continues to propel commerce between countries. The link between IFRS and trade rules is examined in this literature review, with an emphasis on how they might improve compliance, transparency, and the ease of cross-border investment flows.

Offering a uniform framework for financial reporting that enables regulators, investors, and other stakeholders to make well-informed choices internationally is one of IFRS's main goals. Adoption of IFRS improves financial statement comparability, decreases information asymmetry, and boosts market liquidity, claim Barth et al. (2008). By guaranteeing that financial reporting from many nations follow the same guidelines, this in turn promotes cross-border investment. In the context of global commerce, where businesses are increasingly conducting transactions across many countries, financial reporting harmonization is crucial.

Improving the compliance environment for multinational firms is largely dependent on how IFRS and trade rules interact. Countries impose different taxes, trade obstacles, and compliance requirements, creating a complicated regulatory structure around commerce. IFRS, on the other hand, offers a uniform framework that lessens the complexity of these rules (Müller et al., 2020). Businesses that use IFRS make sure that their financial statements follow globally accepted accounting standards, which promotes more efficient operations and commerce. Because it lowers the possibility of fraud and financial misstatements, this alignment also promotes regulatory trust.

Another important advantage of adopting IFRS is transparency, which is essential for companies doing cross-border commerce. By mandating that businesses provide pertinent financial data that is required for stakeholders to evaluate an organization's financial health, IFRS encourages transparency. Regulators, investors, and other stakeholders may evaluate the risk and value of cross-border ventures with the aid of clear and consistent financial data presentation (Choi & Meek, 2011). Companies may more successfully negotiate international trade laws when financial reporting is transparent because stakeholders can access trustworthy information when deciding on cross-border transactions.

The movement of cross-border investments is further facilitated by the integration of IFRS with international trade laws. Since investors favor markets with clear and consistent financial reporting, the adoption of IFRS by several nations has improved foreign direct investment (FDI), claim Nobes and Parker (2016). Adoption of IFRS guarantees that businesses deliver accurate and trustworthy financial data, which lowers the cost of financing and enhances access to international financial markets. Additionally, it makes it easier to evaluate financial risks, which empowers investors to make better choices about international investments.

Notwithstanding the benefits, there are drawbacks to IFRS's convergence with international trade laws. One of the main problems is that various nations have different legislation, which may cause problems for cross-border trading (Glaum et al., 2013). Local laws may not always be in line with international reporting standards, and various nations may interpret IFRS standards differently. This discrepancy might make it more difficult to fully comply with IFRS and trade laws.

Improving compliance, transparency, and enabling cross-border investment flows depend heavily on the convergence of IFRS and international trade laws. By lowering trade barriers and increasing investor trust, the use of IFRS enhances financial reporting's comparability and transparency. Nonetheless, issues with local interpretations of IFRS and regulatory diversity still exist, underscoring the need of ongoing worldwide harmonization efforts.

3.2 International Trade Laws

Improving compliance, transparency, and enabling cross-border investment flows all depend on how International Financial Reporting Standards (IFRS) and international trade laws interact. Harmonized financial reporting standards are becoming more and more necessary to guarantee uniformity and clarity in financial data as international commerce becomes more intertwined. An climate that is favorable for foreign investors is created by the convergence of IFRS with international trade legislation, which lays the groundwork for more transparent and legal cross-border transactions.

3.2.1 International Trade Regulations and IFRS

Its significance in providing a standardized framework for financial reporting is shown by the fact that more than 140 nations have adopted IFRS (Deloitte, 2021). The International Accounting Standards Board (IASB) created IFRS to guarantee that financial statements are clear and comparable across national boundaries, which makes commerce and investment simpler (Bierman & Trotman, 2020). Standardized accounting procedures are necessary to reduce risks and improve the effectiveness of cross-border operations as global commerce gets more complicated (Baker, 2020).

A fair, predictable, and transparent global trading environment is the goal of international trade laws, such as those set out by the World Trade Organization (WTO). In areas like taxes, transfer pricing, and the handling of foreign direct investments, these rules often cross over with IFRS. The improvement of openness in international supply chains and financial markets is facilitated by the harmonization of IFRS with trade legislation (KPMG, 2021). However, differences in how IFRS is interpreted and applied in various countries may provide difficulties, especially for multinational corporations (MNEs), who have to deal with both domestic and foreign regulatory environments (Parker, 2021).

3.2.2 Improving Transparency and Compliance

Improving compliance is one of the main benefits of integrating IFRS with international trade laws. Businesses may satisfy the regulatory requirements of several countries without wasting time or effort thanks to the harmonization of accounting standards with international trade regulations (IFAC, 2020). For businesses engaged in international commerce, this lowers compliance expenses and streamlines financial reporting procedures. Additionally, regular financial reporting increases the financial situations of multinational firms' transparency, which facilitates investors' evaluation of possibilities and dangers (Leuz, 2020).

It is impossible to overestimate the contribution that IFRS makes to transparency. IFRS improves the comparability of financial data by offering a clear framework for financial statement presentation, which is essential for making wise choices in international commerce. International investors may reduce their risks and increase their trust in cross-border transactions by comparing financial performance across markets (Lang & Möller, 2020).

3.2.3 Investment Flows Across Borders

By giving investors a consistent and predictable environment, international trade laws and IFRS work together to influence cross-border investment flows. Investors are better able to evaluate the feasibility and profitability of possible investments when financial statements are in line with international standards (Ball, 2021). In a worldwide economy, the need for uniformity and transparency in financial reporting has a growing impact on capital flows. IFRS ensures that investors have access to trustworthy and comparable financial data, which increases transparency and compliance and helps to draw in foreign direct investments (FDI) (Hail et al., 2020).

There are still difficulties in spite of the advantages. Cross-border investments may be hampered by different governments' inconsistent adoption and application of IFRS. Financial statements may need to be adjusted to conform to both local and international standards in some growing areas where local regulatory frameworks may clash with IFRS (Hossain & Hammami, 2020).

3.3 Improving Adherence

As companies negotiate the challenges of cross-border investments, the relationship between International Financial Reporting Standards (IFRS) and international trade laws has grown in importance. While following global trade standards guarantees that firms stay in compliance with international trade laws, fostering fair competition and investment flows, IFRS compliance is essential for improving transparency and guaranteeing accurate financial reporting. In order to improve compliance, transparency, and cross-border investment flows, this literature review investigates how IFRS and international trade rules might be integrated.

The need to align IFRS with the various regulatory frameworks across nations is one of the major obstacles in this field. The necessity for a uniform approach to financial reporting becomes critical when trade legislation in different nations vary. In order to improve comparability and transparency across countries, IFRS seeks to provide a single, worldwide standard for financial reporting (Barth, 2008). But there have been difficulties along the way. According to a research by Hail and Leuz (2006), while the implementation of IFRS increases transparency, it often results in difficulties with compliance, especially in countries with disparate accounting standards and trade laws. Businesses must comprehend both local regulatory standards and IFRS in order to ensure compliance and prevent fines or other consequences.

The role of regulators in making sure businesses follow both trade laws and IFRS is a crucial component of improving compliance. Enforcing compliance and making sure that companies adhere to the necessary standards may be accomplished via a strong regulatory framework (Doupnik & Perera, 2012). This is especially crucial for cross-border investments, since investors need trustworthy and transparent financial data to make wise choices. Better adherence to international accounting standards boosts investor trust, which in turn helps draw in more foreign direct investments (FDI), according to the World Bank (2018). This is important for cross-border capital flows since it lowers the dangers of information asymmetry and makes financial markets more reliable.

National trade authorities and regulatory organizations like the World Trade Organization (WTO) play a big part in creating a compliance-driven environment in the context of international commerce. For instance, the WTO's Trade Policy Review Mechanism keeps an eye on member nations' compliance with global trade laws, which has an indirect impact on the financial reporting standards of businesses doing business there (WTO, 2020). In order to create an atmosphere that is favorable to international investment, trade laws and financial reporting must work together.

Additionally, improvements in technology have contributed to increased compliance. The process of guaranteeing adherence to international trade laws and IFRS may be streamlined with the use of sophisticated data analytics and automation solutions. These solutions may increase overall compliance monitoring efficiency, decrease financial reporting mistakes, and expedite the detection of inconsistencies (González, 2021). The importance of technology in maintaining compliance and improving transparency grows as international commerce and financial systems become more intertwined.

3.4. Improving Openness

Transparency in cross-border investment flows is greatly enhanced by the convergence of international trade laws and International Financial Reporting Standards (IFRS). Improving investor confidence, fostering stakeholder trust, and guaranteeing the smooth operation of international markets all depend on increasing compliance and transparency at this nexus.

The goal of the international financial reporting standard known as IFRS is to make financial statements consistent and comparable across various countries (Zhao & Ma, 2018). Transparent and trustworthy financial reporting is becoming more and more important as economies become more integrated. Harmonizing accounting standards, decreasing disparities, and enhancing the openness of financial data have all been made possible by the implementation of IFRS (Liu et al., 2019). The movement of cash and cross-border investments are facilitated by this transparency, which empowers stakeholders and investors to make well-informed choices.

However, attaining complete transparency is sometimes hampered by the intricacy of IFRS and its interaction with international trade laws. Transparency may be hampered by the need for uniform IFRS implementation and interpretation across various regulatory contexts, particularly in areas with disparate local laws (Dube & Bujang, 2020). The regulatory frameworks of various nations, such as tax laws, trade policies, and financial reporting regulations, may make it more difficult to apply IFRS and lead to disparities that impede cross-border investments and fair financial reporting.

By forcing companies to record transactions in a manner that reflects trade practices and cross-border activities, global trade regulations—such as international trade agreements, tariffs, and customs laws—also have an impact on financial reporting (OECD, 2021). Businesses must modify their financial reporting procedures to comply with new trade restrictions as they develop, necessitating ongoing revisions to accounting standards and more openness in their implementation. Harmonizing these rules with IFRS while making sure that companies continue to adhere to compliance and transparency is the difficult part.

Numerous studies highlight the need for more cooperation between international regulatory organizations, standard setters, and financial institutions in order to improve transparency at the nexus of IFRS and global trade legislation (Pereira & Góis, 2020). By working together, the issues of discrepancies between national laws and IFRS may be resolved, fostering a more unified and open reporting system. Furthermore, technological innovations like blockchain and artificial intelligence are being investigated to improve transparency by offering real-time monitoring and cross-border transaction verification (Hughes, 2022).

Furthermore, transparency depends on compliance systems that guarantee companies follow international trade laws and IFRS. In order to encourage conformity to both IFRS and trade norms, regulatory bodies are essential in monitoring compliance, providing advice, and enforcing fines where required (Smith & Moore, 2018). Improving these systems may aid in reducing the risks of non-compliance, which often impede investment flows and compromise transparency.

Building confidence, attracting cross-border investments, and stimulating economic development all depend on increasing openness when negotiating the junction of IFRS and international trade laws. To achieve more transparency and compliance in this area, multinational organizations must work together, update financial reporting requirements often, and utilize technology.

3.5 Investment Flows Across Borders

Cross-border investment flows are significantly shaped by the convergence of international trade laws and International Financial Reporting Standards (IFRS), which improves transparency and compliance. Cross-border investments have increased significantly as a result of globalization, and in order to maintain seamless financial operations, harmonization between IFRS and international trade frameworks is required (Schmidt & Vogl, 2018).

The International Accounting Standards Board (IASB) created the IFRS, which is now extensively used in many countries for financial statement preparation. International capital flows and investor trust are facilitated by the uniformity and comparability of financial reporting made possible by the cross-border implementation of IFRS (Van der Meulen, 2020). Following IFRS guarantees that companies may satisfy the various reporting requirements of many nations while preserving transparency, especially as cross-border investments get more complex (Cai & Wong, 2019). Harmonized accounting standards lower a company's cost of capital, which attracts overseas investors, according to studies (López & Sánchez, 2020).

Furthermore, by establishing the foundations for tariffs, trade policies, and investment protection measures, international trade regulations—which are mostly spearheaded by institutions like the World Trade Organization (WTO)—have an impact on cross-border investments. In order to manage the financial risks connected to foreign transactions, it is essential that these legislation and IFRS intersect (Duvvuru & Sahoo, 2019). For example, by guaranteeing a steady and predictable economic climate, regulatory frameworks that underpin free trade agreements may improve cross-border investments. However, national regulatory differences often make financial reporting and investment flows more difficult, which emphasizes the need of integrated compliance systems (Zhang & Sun, 2021).

Another significant advantage of using IFRS in combination with international trade laws is transparency. In order to make well-informed judgments, investors look for clarity in financial disclosures. Greater investor engagement is made possible by the combination of international trade laws that support open markets and the strong standards of IFRS, which encourage transparency (Jin & Liu, 2020). According to research, businesses that use IFRS reporting standards are in a better position to draw in foreign investment because of the consistency and dependability of their financial statements (Rama & Rodriguez, 2018).

The function of compliance must be taken into account while analyzing cross-border investment flows. Following global trade laws and IFRS reduces the possibility of legal issues and promotes confidence among foreign investors (Moravcsik, 2020). Regulatory certainty affects investment flows, and countries with a solid compliance record often draw more foreign direct investment (FDI). The combined significance of IFRS and trade laws is further highlighted by investors' growing desire for strong risk management procedures that adhere to both accounting standards and trade laws (Al-Shammari & Brown, 2019).

The convergence of international trade laws with IFRS improves cross-border investment flows, compliance, and transparency. Countries may foster international investment by coordinating accounting standards and guaranteeing regulatory stability, which will eventually propel global economic expansion.

IV. RESEARCH GAP

International Financial Reporting Standards (IFRS) are becoming more important in improving worldwide financial comparability and openness, but little is known about how they interact with international trade laws. Prior research has concentrated on the role of IFRS in enhancing the quality of financial reporting as well as the difficulties in adopting it in various jurisdictions (Choi & Meek, 2011). However, less focus has been placed on how IFRS interacts with international trade laws to affect cross-border investment flows. Furthermore, little research has been done on how changing international trade laws—such as trade agreements, tariffs, and sanctions—affect IFRS compliance (Hail et al., 2010). Additionally, there is a dearth of research that thoroughly examines how multinational corporations deal with the challenges of coordinating IFRS reporting with local trade regulations, particularly in developing areas where regulatory frameworks are often less uniform (La Porta et al., 1998). Studies examining how IFRS may help lower trade barriers and encourage foreign direct investment (FDI) by enhancing financial transparency and lowering risk perception are also necessary. Closing these gaps will improve knowledge of how international trade policies and financial reporting standards work together, providing insightful information to investors, multinational firms, and politicians.

V. SIGNIFICANCE OF THE STUDY

This research, which addresses important possibilities and difficulties at the nexus of international trade legislation and International Financial Reporting Standards (IFRS), is of significant relevance in the changing environment of global financial reporting and commerce. The research highlights the critical role that IFRS plays in lowering information asymmetry, boosting investor trust, and encouraging cross-border investments by looking at how it improves compliance and openness in financial reporting (Ball, 2006). Additionally, it advances knowledge of how IFRS compliance with international trade laws may simplify operations for multinational firms and lessen the complexity of various regulatory frameworks (Hail et al., 2010).

The study's emphasis on international investment flows highlights the need of removing obstacles brought on by regulatory mismatches, especially in developing nations whose institutional frameworks are often disjointed (La Porta et al., 1998). Policymakers and trade associations may learn how to use IFRS to standardize trade laws and, eventually, strengthen international economic integration from this study. The study's conclusions may also help businesses make strategic decisions by assisting them in balancing the competing needs of trade compliance and financial transparency. By filling a significant knowledge vacuum, this multidisciplinary approach offers a road map for promoting sustainable international trade and investment dynamics.

VI. OBJECTIVES OF THE STUDY

This study's main goal is to investigate the intricate interaction between international trade laws and International Financial Reporting Standards (IFRS) in order to ascertain how their alignment might improve cross-border investment flows, compliance, and transparency. The research specifically seeks to:

1. Examine how IFRS promotes financial comparability and openness across multinational firms, assisting in well-informed decision-making in situations involving international commerce (Hail et al., 2010).
2. Look for areas of overlap and disagreement between IFRS compliance and international trade laws, including as trade agreements, tariffs, and penalties (Choi & Meek, 2011).
3. Examine the difficulties international corporations have when attempting to conform IFRS to various regional trade laws, especially in developing nations where regulatory frameworks are less uniform (La Porta et al., 1998).
4. Examine how the introduction of IFRS has affected the promotion of foreign direct investment (FDI) by improving financial reporting and lowering investor risk perception (Barth et al., 2012).
5. Offer practical suggestions for international firms and legislators to standardize trade and financial reporting regulations, promoting long-term, sustainable global economic integration.

VII. PROBLEMS, ISSUES AND CHALLENGES OF THE STUDY

7.1 Challenges in Handling the Confluence of International Financial Reporting Standards and International Trade Law

Organizations, legislators, and stakeholders face several difficulties when IFRS and international trade laws collide, especially when it comes to maintaining compliance, transparency, and smooth cross-border investment flows. The following are the main concerns related to this field of study:

7.1.1. Complexity and Divergence in Regulation

International trade laws differ greatly across countries, which makes it difficult for businesses to implement IFRS. The harmonization objectives of IFRS are undermined by the disparities in financial reporting and compliance that often result from disparate regulatory frameworks (Hail et al., 2010). Navigating these disparities while maintaining accurate financial reporting is difficult and resource-intensive for multinational businesses (MNCs).

7.1.2. Harmonization Difficulties

Even with the extensive use of IFRS, there is still a long way to go before accounting standards and regional trade laws fully align. In order to conform to their own legal and economic frameworks, several nations still demand regional changes to IFRS. The scattered reporting methods resulting from this lack of standardization make financial statements less comparable across national boundaries (Ball, 2006).

7.1.3. Uncertainty in Trade Policy

The ever-changing nature of international trade agreements, tariffs, and penalties creates uncertainty that affects IFRS financial reporting. For example, companies may face compliance risks if trade restrictions change suddenly and need major modifications to financial reporting (DeFond et al., 2011). Aligning their IFRS-based financial reporting with changing trade regulations is a challenge for businesses working in dynamic trade settings.

7.1.4. Limited Adaptability in Emerging Nations

Institutions and infrastructure in emerging nations are often not prepared to fully integrate IFRS with their regulatory frameworks. The alignment of financial reporting with trade rules is hampered by problems including insufficient legislative frameworks, uneven enforcement methods, and a lack of experience with implementing IFRS (Peng & van der Laan Smith, 2010). As a result, businesses operating in these areas face increased non-compliance risks and a decline in investor trust.

7.1.5. Barriers to Cross-Border Investments

Although IFRS seeks to improve comparability and transparency, its interaction with trade laws may unintentionally erect obstacles to cross-border investments. Foreign investors are deterred from participating in certain markets by complicated compliance requirements and disparities in how IFRS standards are interpreted (Healy & Palepu, 2001). Additionally, smaller businesses are discouraged from engaging in international trade and investment due to the high expenses of implementing and complying with IFRS.

7.1.6. Effect on Governance and Transparency

The intended transparency and governance advantages of standardized financial reporting are often undermined when IFRS and trade rules are not aligned. Decision-making processes may be impacted by inadequate or misleading information provided to stakeholders by disparities in trade-related disclosures, such as tariffs and trade-related contingencies (Barth et al., 2008).

7.1.7. Technology and Operational Challenges

Many firms, particularly SMEs, lack the advanced technology systems and knowledge needed to adopt IFRS while adhering to complex trade restrictions. The successful integration of trade compliance and financial reporting is made more difficult by this operational gap (Hail et al., 2010).

7.2 Problems Managing the Confluence of International Financial Reporting Standards and International Trade Law

Navigating the complicated junction of global trade legislation and International Financial Reporting Standards (IFRS) involves a number of challenges that impede transparency, compliance, and the ease of cross-border investment flows. These difficulties result from the ever-changing expectations of stakeholders, inconsistent regulations, and the dynamic character of international trade and financial markets.

7.2.1. Regulatory Fragmentation

The inconsistency between regional trade laws and IFRS is one of the main problems. Although the goal of IFRS is to unify financial reporting worldwide, trade laws differ greatly across countries, resulting in inconsistent requirements for compliance (Hail et al., 2010). Multinational businesses' (MNCs') attempts to balance their financial reporting with their trade commitments are hampered by this fragmentation, which raises operational complexity and expenses.

7.2.2. Adoption and Implementation Challenges

The adoption of IFRS is still uneven worldwide, with many nations sticking with native accounting standards or implementing modified versions. The goal of global comparability and openness is compromised by this incomplete acceptance (Choi & Meek, 2011). Furthermore, companies in developing economies often struggle with resource and infrastructure limitations, which makes it difficult to adopt IFRS effectively. The danger of non-compliance with trade legislation and IFRS is increased by these difficulties.

7.2.3. Effect on International Investments

International investments are at risk due to the discrepancy between trade laws and financial reporting requirements. To make wise choices, investors depend on reliable and clear financial data. Disparities brought on by disparate legal frameworks and uneven implementation of IFRS, however, raise uncertainty and may deter foreign direct investment (FDI) (Ball, 2006).

7.2.4. Changing Trade Policies

The integration of IFRS with international trade rules is made more difficult by the dynamic nature of trade policies, including tariffs, sanctions, and free trade agreements. For example, companies often have to modify their financial reporting to account for changes in trade agreements, which increases the cost of compliance and necessitates the use of specialist knowledge (Hail et al., 2010). The difficulties are made worse by the lack of procedures to align IFRS reporting with such changing regulations.

7.2.5. Technology and Digital Transformation

Digital transformation creates new complications but also presents opportunities to improve reporting and compliance. Although cutting-edge technologies like blockchain and artificial intelligence (AI) have the potential to increase financial transparency, little is known about how to integrate them with the current IFRS and trade regulatory frameworks (KPMG, 2021). Furthermore, the IFRS transparency standards may clash with cybersecurity issues and data protection laws.

7.2.6. Institutional and Cultural Barriers

The integration of IFRS with trade rules is made more difficult by institutional inefficiencies and cultural disparities. IFRS may be interpreted differently in nations with disparate legal, political, and economic systems, which might result in inconsistent application (La Porta et al., 1998). The efficiency of trade laws and IFRS is further hampered by institutional flaws in certain areas, such as insufficient enforcement systems.

A multi-stakeholder strategy including legislators, regulatory agencies, and corporations is needed to address these problems. To improve compliance, transparency, and cross-border investment flows, it is imperative to align IFRS with trade laws, help developing countries with capacity-building initiatives, use technology, and promote global collaboration.

7.3 Study Challenges

Handling the Intersection of International Financial Reporting Standards (IFRS) and Global Trade Regulations: There are a number of complex issues that affect compliance, transparency, and cross-border investment flows when IFRS and global trade regulations collide. Diverse regulatory frameworks, stakeholder expectations, and the dynamic character of international trade policy are the causes of these difficulties.

7.3.1. Various Regulatory Structures

Although the goal of IFRS's worldwide adoption is to standardize financial reporting, regional differences in application and enforcement still exist. For multinational businesses (MNCs) doing business in nations with varying trade laws and interpretations of IFRS, these discrepancies pose difficulties (Ball, 2006). Compliance issues arise, for instance, because emerging nations sometimes lack the institutional ability to implement both trade rules and IFRS.

7.3.2. Harmonization of Trade and Financial Reporting Standards

IFRS standards and trade restrictions like tariffs, quotas, and penalties often clash. It is difficult to align various frameworks to guarantee consistency, especially in areas with disjointed regulatory systems (Hail et al., 2010). Inconsistencies in financial reporting may arise from this mismatch, making it more difficult to provide stakeholders with accurate and transparent information.

7.3.3. Adjusting to Changing Trade Policies

Organizations attempting to maintain IFRS compliance have difficulties due to the dynamic character of global trade policies, which are influenced by trade agreements, protectionist policies, and geopolitical changes. For example, abrupt modifications to trade agreements or the application of penalties may call for quick changes to financial disclosures, which might result in inefficiencies in operations and reporting (PWC, 2019).

7.3.4. Cultural and Legal Differences

Adoption of IFRS and compliance with international trade laws are further complicated by cultural and legal variety. Compliance for businesses involved in cross-border activities is made more difficult by the differing adoption and interpretation of IFRS across jurisdictions with common law vs civil law legal systems (La Porta et al., 1998).

7.3.5. Resource and Technological Limitations

In order to implement IFRS-compliant systems while adhering to trade restrictions, a substantial technology infrastructure and knowledgeable staff are needed. According to Ali and Hwang (2000), many SMEs, especially those in developing nations, struggle to achieve these dual needs due to resource constraints.

7.3.6. Communication with Investors and Stakeholders

One of the most important challenges is making sure that financial reports satisfy the demands of various stakeholders, such as investors, regulators, and trade associations. Building trust requires transparency in financial reporting, yet disparities resulting from uneven implementation of trade laws and IFRS may cause stakeholder distrust and a decline in investor confidence (Barth et al., 2008).

7.3.7. Ethical and Governance Issues

In areas where corruption and lax enforcement of rules are common, the combination of IFRS and trade restrictions also presents ethical and governance issues. Strong internal governance procedures are necessary to ensure adherence to international standards while overcoming these obstacles, but many firms find it difficult to set them up successfully (Ball, 2006).

VIII. RELEVANCE OF THE STUDY FOR POLICY MAKING

For policymakers entrusted with promoting financial stability and economic integration in a world economy that is becoming more interconnected by the day, the study "Navigating the Intersection of IFRS and Global Trade Regulations: Enhancing Compliance, Transparency, and Cross-Border Investment Flows" is extremely pertinent. Aligning financial reporting standards, such as the International Financial Reporting Standards (IFRS), with international trade regulations is essential for maintaining transparency, lowering compliance risks, and promoting investment flows as cross-border trade and investments continue to grow (Choi & Meek, 2011).

This research provides a foundation for comprehending how harmonized accounting standards might lessen discrepancies between trade laws and financial disclosures from a policy standpoint. Due to incompatibilities with current legislative requirements, many developing economies find it difficult to embrace IFRS, which causes discrepancies in financial reporting and compliance obligations for international firms (Ball, 2006). The study's findings may be used by policymakers to create regulatory frameworks that facilitate the smooth incorporation of IFRS into their trade laws, improving international investment and trade prospects.

The report also highlights how important IFRS is to enhancing financial transparency, which has a direct effect on how risky international investors perceive their investments. Investor trust in overseas markets may be increased, transaction costs can be decreased, and information asymmetry can be lessened by transparent financial disclosures in line with international trade rules (Bushman & Smith, 2001). By bringing local trade and financial reporting laws into compliance with globally accepted norms, policymakers may use this information to promote foreign direct investment (FDI).

Additionally, the results of this research may help guide the creation of regional trade agreements. Policymakers may guarantee consistency in financial reporting among member countries by including IFRS compliance criteria into trade agreements. This will increase the legitimacy of trade blocs and lower trade barriers (Hail et al., 2010). The advantages of incorporating IFRS into regional trade and financial policy, for instance, have been shown by areas such as the European Union, which has enhanced economic cooperation and cross-border capital flows.

Global regulatory organizations like the World Trade Organization (WTO) and the International Accounting Standards Board (IASB) may potentially be impacted by the research. The study identifies areas where these organizations might work together to simplify international commerce and accounting standards by analyzing the relationship between IFRS and trade legislation. In order to resolve regulatory framework gaps and overlaps and promote a more integrated global financial ecosystem, policymakers might push for more cooperation across such organizations.

Lastly, developing countries that are trying to manage regulatory changes and draw in foreign investment may find this research useful. The results may be used by policymakers in these areas to create gradual adoption plans for IFRS that will ensure compliance with current trade regulations while fostering investor confidence and economic growth.

To sum up, this work provides policymakers with a strong analytical basis for coordinating international trade laws with IFRS. The research offers practical insights that may influence policies boosting economic development and global financial integration by resolving regulatory disparities, encouraging openness, and bolstering investment flows.

IX. RELEVANCE OF THE STUDY FOR SOCIETY

The harmonization of trade laws and financial reporting standards is essential for maintaining economic stability, transparency, and encouraging cross-border investment as financial markets and global commerce get more intricate. This study tackles the urgent need to investigate the ways in which global trade laws and International Financial Reporting Standards (IFRS) might work together to improve transparency, lower financial risks, and ease cross-border investment flows.

9.1. Fostering Trust and Transparency in International Finance

By standardizing financial reporting across countries, IFRS adoption seeks to improve financial statement comparability and transparency. Such openness is crucial for lowering information asymmetry and fostering trust in the context of global commerce, where investors and multinational firms operate across several regulatory frameworks. Clear, trustworthy, and comparable data is given to stakeholders and investors when financial statements are produced in accordance with internationally accepted standards. By lowering the risks connected with disparate accounting methods, this in turn promotes investment and fortifies the global financial system (Ball, 2006). This research advances a more comprehensive knowledge of how IFRS alignment with trade laws may enhance transparency and assist stakeholders in making well-informed choices by concentrating on IFRS within the framework of international trade rules.

9.2 Promoting Cross-Border Investments and Economic Growth

Cross-border investments, particularly in developing countries, are essential to economic development and growth and are directly impacted by international trade restrictions. Research in this field is crucial because it examines how IFRS could improve the compliance of various national laws, hence lowering obstacles to foreign investments. Foreign direct investments (FDI) may rise when trade and investment laws are in line with globally recognized accounting standards because investors are more likely to have faith in the stability and performance of businesses' finances. This research may help facilitate cross-border money flows, boost economic development, and increase international collaboration by encouraging uniformity and lowering regulatory risks (Bresser-Pereira, 2010).

9.3. Lowering Regulatory Burden and Compliance Costs

One of the main advantages of integrating IFRS with international trade laws is the possible decrease in compliance expenses for multinational firms. Businesses that operate in many countries sometimes incur high fees to comply with local trade laws and accounting standards. Businesses may be able to deploy resources more effectively and save operating expenses by streamlining compliance procedures via the integration of IFRS with international trade regulations. This is particularly relevant for SMEs that want to grow globally but encounter significant obstacles to entrance because of the intricacies of various accounting and trade regulations (Nobes & Parker, 2012). Governments may lessen regulatory costs while maintaining strict financial monitoring requirements by streamlining these procedures, which helps both firms and governments.

9.4 Assisting Regulators and Policy Makers

Additionally, the report is very relevant to global regulatory agencies and policymakers. Knowing how IFRS and international trade laws interact may help governments create policies that effectively promote economic development while maintaining strong regulatory frameworks. The research's conclusions may be used by policymakers to develop trade regulations that promote financial openness and ease of doing business, so promoting more effective global commerce. Additionally, this study may facilitate improved cooperation between international organizations like the World Trade Organization (WTO) and the International Financial Reporting Standards Foundation (IFRSF), which would improve the alignment of standards that promote global economic development (Zhang, 2013).

9.5. Social Welfare Impact

In the end, the social welfare of society is improved by the harmonization of trade legislation and IFRS. The research may contribute to the development of a more robust global financial system by guaranteeing that companies are more responsible, transparent, and in line with international norms. As a result, people and communities may thrive economically in a more stable environment. Higher rates of job creation, greater income distribution, and easier access to products and services may all result from less uncertainty in investment markets. Societies are better equipped to sustain the long-term economic well-being of their inhabitants when they promote financial stability and open trade settings (Drucker, 2001).

X. CONCLUSION

Research on the relationship between global trade laws and International Financial Reporting Standards (IFRS) is vital yet complicated, particularly as global financial markets become more intertwined. The importance of IFRS in boosting compliance, increasing transparency, and encouraging cross-border investment flows has been emphasized by this research. Investors, regulators, and other parties engaged in international commerce have benefited from the convergence of financial reporting standards around the globe via IFRS, which has increased the comparability and reliability of financial data (Choi & Meek, 2011). Aligning IFRS with various trade laws is still difficult, nevertheless, especially in countries with different legal, economic, and cultural backgrounds.

The disparity in regulatory systems across countries is one major obstacle. Although the goal of IFRS is to standardize financial reporting, trade policies, political factors, and regional agreements often influence international trade rules (Hail et al., 2010). The trade laws in the US and developing economies, for instance, are quite different from those in the EU. In order to guarantee compliance, lower risk, and foster investor trust, IFRS must also be in line with local trade regulations, which makes adoption more difficult. According to research, the adoption of IFRS enhances financial statement comparability and transparency, but unless it is backed by harmonized trade legislation, it does not always lead to improved cross-border investment flows (La Porta et al., 1998).

Moreover, it has not yet been thoroughly investigated how IFRS may lessen trade restrictions and encourage foreign direct investment (FDI). International firms often find it difficult to balance different national trade laws that may impose tariffs, quotas, or other entrance obstacles with the standards of IFRS (Ernst & Young, 2013). The need for further study is highlighted by the knowledge gap on the effects of trade rules on the efficacy and implementation of IFRS. Multinational corporations may have difficulties adhering to both local trade laws and IFRS, which might result in inefficiencies or higher expenses (KPMG, 2020).

Additionally, this report highlights how IFRS helps make developing nations more appealing to international investors. Markets adopting IFRS may increase their credibility and lower perceived investment risks as trade rules become more in line with international norms. As investors look for possibilities in countries that provide accurate financial reporting in line with international standards, this might lead to increased capital inflows. Regulators must, however, concentrate on coordinating trade laws and financial reporting standards in order to establish a smooth investment environment if IFRS is to provide this result (Hail et al., 2010).

Notwithstanding these possible advantages, a significant barrier to the adoption of IFRS in nations with deeply ingrained regional accounting customs or legal systems that diverge from IFRS principles still exists (La Porta et al., 1998). In these situations, it may take a while and be difficult to enforce trade laws and bring national legal systems into compliance with international financial norms. The study also indicates that further work is required to create rules that can successfully handle these jurisdictional complications and guarantee a more seamless incorporation of IFRS into frameworks for international commerce.

Even while the introduction of IFRS has greatly increased financial openness and encouraged cross-border investment, its full potential can only be achieved when combined with appropriate international trade laws. To lower the boundaries between these two spheres, policymakers, international organizations, and financial regulators must cooperate. In order to harmonize legal frameworks, lower trade obstacles, and increase emerging nations' appeal to foreign investment, future research should concentrate on creating models for combining IFRS and international trade legislation.

XI. SCOPE OF THE FURTHER RESEARCH

Despite its increasing importance in the modern global economy, the relationship between International Financial Reporting Standards (IFRS) and international trade restrictions is still little understood, making it an interesting subject for future study. More research may improve knowledge of how cross-border trade policies, such as trade agreements, tariffs, customs laws, and penalties, interact with IFRS financial reporting to affect the operations and investment plans of multinational firms.

11.1 How IFRS Affects International Investment Flows

Adoption of IFRS has been linked to increased financial statement comparability and transparency (Ball, 2006), but it is yet unknown how it will affect cross-border investment flows. Research may examine how IFRS improves financial reporting's credibility and how it helps foreign investors see less risks. In particular, research might look at how nations that adhere to IFRS are able to draw in foreign direct investment (FDI) in contrast to those that don't. Furthermore, it is necessary to investigate how IFRS has affected institutional investors' and multinational firms' investment choices in different geographical areas. A better understanding of these connections may help policymakers encourage developing nations to adopt IFRS in order to increase foreign direct investment.

11.2 IFRS Compliance and Regional Trade Legislation

IFRS and regional trade standards and legislation interact in various ways. The difficulties international corporations have in bringing IFRS into compliance with local trade regulations, particularly in countries with dynamic regulatory frameworks, might be the subject of future studies. For instance, there is much need for research on how IFRS are incorporated into regional economic accords like the African Continental Free Trade Area (AfCFTA) and the European Union's Single Market. The effects of such alignments or misalignments on investment flows, trade volumes, and economic integration might be studied. Furthermore, comparative research on the effects of IFRS on companies in nations with different trade laws, such China, India, and the United States, would be very helpful in understanding how international accounting standards and local trade laws interact.

11.3 Adoption of IFRS in Emerging Markets

Emerging markets, which make up a significant share of the global economy, have particular difficulties in integrating IFRS with domestic trade laws. The absence of infrastructure, inconsistent regulations, and high implementation costs are some of the obstacles to IFRS adoption in these areas that might be the subject of future research. Additionally, research might examine how trade agreements and tariffs affect the adoption process and if adopting IFRS can help remove trade obstacles. This would be especially important for nations in Latin America, Southeast Asia, and Sub-Saharan Africa, where regional trade accords place a strong emphasis on economic integration.

11.4 Corporate Strategy and IFRS Integration

More research may look at how multinational firms create plans to incorporate international trade laws and IFRS into their daily operations. The study may look at whether multinational companies have trouble integrating IFRS with regional trade laws in different nations. Understanding best practices for IFRS compliance, risk management, and optimizing cross-border investment possibilities may be gained by examining case studies of multinational firms that have effectively handled these difficulties.

11.5 Technology's Role in Improving IFRS Compliance and Trade Regulation

Automation, blockchain, and artificial intelligence are just a few examples of the technological innovations that are being utilized more and more to help with IFRS compliance and to handle the intricacies of international trade laws (Brynjolfsson & McAfee, 2014). Future studies might examine how technology could be used to better align IFRS with changing trade laws, which would save compliance costs and increase efficiency. An interesting topic of research might be how digital solutions help manage the real-time data interchange between companies, authorities, and trading partners.

11.6 ESG (Environmental, Social, And Governance) Factors to Take Into Account

Future studies might look at how IFRS frameworks can be in line with international ESG standards as ESG considerations become more significant in international commerce. Multinational corporations looking to strike a balance between social responsibility and financial transparency may find useful insights from a greater knowledge of how IFRS and ESG compliance impact global trade flows.

REFERENCES

Al-Shammari, B., & Brown, P. (2019). The impact of IFRS adoption on financial disclosure and cross-border investments. *Journal of International Business, 23*(3), 214–237.

Albu, N., Albu, C. N., Bunea, Ş., Calu, D. A., & Girbina, M. M. (2014). A comparative study of implementation of IFRS in emerging economies. *Journal of Accounting in Emerging Economies, 4*(1), 4–29. DOI: 10.1108/JAEE-06-2011-0014

Ali, M. J., & Hwang, L. S. (2000). Country-specific factors related to financial reporting and the value relevance of accounting data. *Journal of Accounting Research, 38*(1), 1–21. DOI: 10.2307/2672920

Bagwell, K., & Staiger, R. W. (2002). *The Economics of the World Trading System*. MIT Press. DOI: 10.7551/mitpress/2628.001.0001

Baker, C. R. (2020). Global trade regulations and financial reporting standards: A review of the intersection. *Journal of International Business Studies, 39*(3), 212–228.

Ball, R. (2006). International Financial Reporting Standards (IFRS): Pros and cons for investors. *Accounting and Business Research*, 36(sup1), 5-27.

Ball, R. (2016). IFRS—Ten years later. *Accounting and Business Research, 46*(5), 545–571. DOI: 10.1080/00014788.2016.1182710

Ball, R. (2021). International financial reporting standards and the cross-border flow of capital. *Accounting and Business Research, 51*(4), 375–400.

Barrett, M. (2019). The role of international trade agreements in enhancing corporate financial transparency. *Journal of International Business Studies, 50*(3), 521–537.

Barth, M. E. (2008). Global financial reporting: Implications for U.S. accounting standards. *The Accounting Review, 83*(5), 1159–1189. DOI: 10.2308/accr.2008.83.5.1159

Barth, M. E., & Landsman, W. R. (2010). How did financial reporting contribute to the financial crisis? *European Accounting Review, 19*(3), 399–423. DOI: 10.1080/09638180.2010.498619

Barth, M. E., Landsman, W. R., & Lang, M. H. (2008). International accounting standards and accounting quality. *Journal of Accounting Research, 46*(3), 467–498. DOI: 10.1111/j.1475-679X.2008.00287.x

Barth, M. E., Landsman, W. R., & Lang, M. H. (2008). International Accounting Standards and accounting quality. *Journal of Accounting Research, 46*(3), 467–498. DOI: 10.1111/j.1475-679X.2008.00287.x

Bierman, G., & Trotman, K. T. (2020). International Financial Reporting Standards and global trade compliance. *Journal of Global Accounting & Finance, 11*(1), 56–72.

Bresser-Pereira, L. C. (2010). The theory of dependent development. *Latin American Politics and Society, 52*(3), 65–85.

Brynjolfsson, E., & McAfee, A. (2014). *The second machine age: Work, progress, and prosperity in a time of brilliant technologies*. W. W. Norton & Company.

Bushman, R. M., & Smith, A. J. (2001). Financial accounting information and corporate governance. *Journal of Accounting and Economics, 32*(1-3), 237–333. DOI: 10.1016/S0165-4101(01)00027-1

Cai, F., & Wong, R. (2019). The role of IFRS in global trade regulation: Enhancing transparency and compliance. *The International Journal of Accounting, 54*(2), 199–215.

Choi, F. D. S., & Meek, G. K. (2011). *International Accounting* (7th ed.). Pearson Education.

Das, S., & Mukhopadhyay, D. (2018). Trade policy and economic growth: A review of the literature. *Guoji Maoyi Wenti, 32*(1), 3–19. DOI: 10.1080/08853908.2017.1365454

DeFond, M. L., Hu, X., Hung, M., & Li, S. (2011). The impact of mandatory IFRS adoption on foreign mutual fund ownership: The role of comparability. *Journal of Accounting and Economics, 51*(3), 240–258. DOI: 10.1016/j.jacceco.2011.02.001

Deloitte. (2020). The impact of IFRS adoption in the European Union. Deloitte Insights.

Deloitte. (2021). *IFRS and global trade: Enhancing compliance and transparency in a globalized economy*. Deloitte Insights.

Doupnik, T. S., & Perera, H. (2012). *International accounting* (3rd ed.). McGraw-Hill.

Drucker, P. F. (2001). *The essential Drucker: The best of sixty years of Peter Drucker's essential writings on management*. HarperBusiness.

Dube, L., & Bujang, R. (2020). The impact of regulatory frameworks on IFRS compliance in emerging economies. *Journal of Accounting and Public Policy, 39*(4), 227–245.

Duvvuru, S., & Sahoo, S. (2019). Global trade regulations and their effect on cross-border investment flows. *International Economic Review*, *60*(1), 73–92.

Ernst & Young. (2013). *Global IFRS resources*. Retrieved from www.ey.com

Glaum, M., Lin, B., & Street, D. L. (2013). The Economic Consequences of IFRS Adoption: A Review of the Literature. *Accounting in Europe*, *10*(1), 1–38.

Gomes, A., Williams, S., & Brito, M. (2021). The role of financial reporting in cross-border trade. *Accounting Forum*, *45*(3), 285–299.

González, J. A. (2021). Enhancing compliance through digital technologies in financial reporting. *Journal of Accounting and Technology*, *5*(2), 88–102. DOI: 10.1016/j.acctech.2020.12.001

Hail, L., & Leuz, C. (2006). International differences in the cost of equity capital: Do legal institutions and securities regulation matter? *Journal of Accounting Research*, *44*(3), 485–531. DOI: 10.1111/j.1475-679X.2006.00209.x

Hail, L., Leuz, C., & Wysocki, P. (2010). Global accounting convergence and the potential adoption of IFRS in the United States. *Accounting Horizons*, *24*(3), 355–394. DOI: 10.2308/acch.2010.24.3.355

Hail, L., Leuz, C., & Wysocki, P. (2010). Global accounting convergence and the potential adoption of IFRS in the United States. *Accounting Horizons*, *24*(3), 355–394. DOI: 10.2308/acch.2010.24.3.355

Hail, L., Leuz, C., & Wysocki, P. D. (2020). Globalization and accounting standards: A review of the literature. *Journal of Accounting and Economics*, *63*(1), 69–84.

Healy, P. M., & Palepu, K. G. (2001). Information asymmetry, corporate disclosure, and the capital markets: A review of the empirical disclosure literature. *Journal of Accounting and Economics*, *31*(1-3), 405–440. DOI: 10.1016/S0165-4101(01)00018-0

Hoekman, B., & Mavroidis, P. C. (2020). To TTIP or not to TTIP: On the future of transatlantic economic relations. *Journal of Economic Policy Reform*, *23*(1), 1–21. DOI: 10.1080/17487870.2018.1425880

Hoekman, B. M., & Kostecki, M. M. (2009). *The Political Economy of the World Trading System*. Oxford University Press. DOI: 10.1093/oso/9780199553761.001.0001

Hossain, M. Z., & Hammami, M. (2020). Challenges in global trade compliance and the role of IFRS in emerging markets. *International Journal of Accounting and Finance*, *29*(3), 144–160.

Hughes, L. (2022). Blockchain in cross-border transactions: Enhancing transparency and reducing fraud. *Journal of Digital Finance*, *6*(2), 90–105.

IASB. (2020). *IFRS Foundation Annual Report*. International Accounting Standards Board.

IFAC. (2020). *The role of IFRS in promoting transparency and enhancing compliance in international trade*. International Federation of Accountants.

International Accounting Standards Board. (2023). IFRS standards and global adoption. Retrieved from https://www.ifrs.org

International Accounting Standards Board. (2023). IFRS standards and global adoption. Retrieved from https://www.ifrs.org

Jin, K., & Liu, J. (2020). How IFRS impacts foreign direct investment decisions: Evidence from emerging markets. *Global Finance Journal*, *48*, 100–112.

KPMG. (2020). *IFRS and global trade regulations*. Retrieved from www.kpmg.com

KPMG. (2021). The future of financial reporting in a digital world. KPMG Report.

KPMG. (2021). *IFRS and global trade regulations: Best practices for multinational enterprises*. KPMG Insights.

La Porta, R., Lopez-de-Silanes, F., Shleifer, A., & Vishny, R. W. (1998). Law and finance. *Journal of Political Economy*, *106*(6), 1113–1155. DOI: 10.1086/250042

La Porta, R., Lopez-de-Silanes, F., Shleifer, A., & Vishny, R. W. (1998). Law and finance. *Journal of Political Economy*, *106*(6), 1113–1155. DOI: 10.1086/250042

Lang, M. H., & Möller, M. (2020). The impact of IFRS adoption on transparency and cross-border investments. *Journal of International Financial Markets*, *39*(4), 315–334.

Leuz, C. (2020). Cross-border investment and IFRS adoption: A review of evidence from global markets. *Journal of Accounting Research*, *58*(2), 463–504.

Liu, C., Chen, W., & Li, Z. (2019). IFRS adoption and its impact on financial transparency and cross-border investment flows. *Accounting and Finance*, *59*(2), 481–505.

López, J. F., & Sánchez, R. (2020). The effect of harmonized accounting standards on international investment flows. *Journal of International Finance*, *33*(4), 180–193.

Moravcsik, A. (2020). Regulatory harmonization and investment flows: The role of international trade laws. *World Politics Review*, *62*(5), 505–523.

Müller, A., Lapsley, I., & Chua, W. F. (2020). The IFRS and the Challenges of International Financial Reporting. *Accounting and Business Research*, *50*(5), 490–513.

Nobes, C., & Parker, R. (2016). *Comparative International Accounting* (13th ed.). Pearson Education.

Nobes, C., & Parker, R. (2016). *Comparative international accounting*. Pearson Education.

OECD. (2021). *International trade regulations and their impact on financial reporting*. OECD Trade and Investment Report, 2021.

Organisation for Economic Co-operation and Development. (2022). *Trade and Investment Report*. OECD Publishing.

Organisation for Economic Co-operation and Development. (2022). *Trade and Investment Report*. OECD Publishing.

Parker, R. (2021). Navigating IFRS and global trade: The challenges for multinational enterprises. *Accounting Horizons*, *35*(2), 169–184.

Peng, S., & van der Laan Smith, J. (2010). Chinese GAAP and IFRS: An analysis of the convergence process. *Journal of International Accounting, Auditing & Taxation*, *19*(1), 16–34. DOI: 10.1016/j.intaccaudtax.2009.12.002

Pereira, F., & Góis, M. (2020). Integrating IFRS with global trade regulations: A framework for compliance and transparency. *International Journal of Accounting and Finance*, *12*(3), 87–102.

PWC. (2019). *IFRS and beyond: Supporting the journey to financial transparency*. PricewaterhouseCoopers.

PWC. (2021). *Navigating the intersection of financial reporting and trade regulations*. PWC Publications.

PwC. (2023). *Global survey of IFRS adoption*. PricewaterhouseCoopers.

Rama, A., & Rodriguez, M. (2018). The influence of IFRS on cross-border investment decisions: A comprehensive analysis. *International Business Research*, *44*(6), 113–124.

Ramanna, K., & Sletten, E. (2014). Network effects in countries' adoption of IFRS. *The Accounting Review*, *89*(4), 1517–1543. DOI: 10.2308/accr-50717

Schmidt, A., & Vogl, S. (2018). The evolution of global trade and its impact on cross-border investments. *Journal of Global Trade*, *22*(3), 150–165.

Smith, J., & Moore, D. (2018). Enhancing compliance and transparency through regulatory frameworks. *Journal of Financial Regulation, 4*(1), 32–48.

Van der Meulen, T. (2020). Cross-border investments and IFRS compliance: A conceptual framework. *Financial Markets and Accounting Review, 18*(2), 95–110.

World Bank. (2018). *IFRS and financial reporting: Global perspectives on transparency and governance*. World Bank Group.

World Trade Organization. (2020). *Trade Policy Review: Principles and Practices*. WTO.

Zeghal, D., & Mhedhbi, K. (2006). An analysis of the factors affecting the adoption of international accounting standards by developing countries. *The International Journal of Accounting, 41*(4), 373–386. DOI: 10.1016/j.intacc.2006.09.009

Zhang, L., & Sun, X. (2021). Challenges in aligning trade regulations and accounting standards for cross-border investments. *Global Economy and Finance Journal, 41*(7), 45–61.

Zhang, W. (2013). The international convergence of accounting standards: IFRS adoption in China. *Journal of International Accounting Research, 12*(1), 1–25.

Zhao, X., & Ma, J. (2018). Harmonizing international accounting standards: The role of IFRS in promoting global transparency. *The International Journal of Accounting, 53*(3), 245–262.

Chapter 10
The Future of Auditing – Aligning International Audit Practices With Global Trade Needs

Anojan Vickneswaran
https://orcid.org/0000-0002-9315-0088
School of Business and Creative Industries, University of the Sunshine Coast, Australia & Department of Accounting, University of Jaffna, Sri Lanka

ABSTRACT

In the dynamic realm of contemporary business, financial and non-financial audits are crucial for transparency, reliability, and sustainability. With rising concerns over Environmental, Social, and Governance (ESG) issues, stakeholders demand assurance on both financial and non-financial reporting. Accounting firms audit financial statements, both accounting and non-accounting firms provide non-financial reporting assurance. Given its novelty, regulators and investors focus on extended external reporting quality. Few nations mandate non-financial reporting and assurance, though global standards are emerging. Harmonizing audit practices remains challenging, yet necessary. Traditional audit reports had limited communicative value, leading to the introduction of Key Audit Matters (KAMs) reporting. This chapter shows application of KAMs reporting in Europe. Auditor competence and independence are crucial for financial and non-financial reporting, and audit quality. Future auditors are more likely to verify and report on both the financial and non-financial aspects of the firms.

DOI: 10.4018/979-8-3373-0887-6.ch010

1. INTRODUCTION

Shareholders are owners of the firms and appoint the management (board of directors) to operate the firms on their behalf because shareholders are from different educational backgrounds. The board of directors are expert in business, corporate governance, internal and external business environments, and reporting. The management's primary objective is to increase the wealth of shareholders' investments. They manage resources to achieve the goals of the firms (financial and non-financial goals). The board is accountable to shareholders for the firm's performance and position. Therefore, they are responsible for preparing and presenting financial and non-financial statements (Gompers, Ishii, & Metrick, 2003; Bushman & Smith, 2001; Carcello, Hermanson, & Ye, 2011; IAS 1).

The relationship between management and shareholders is called agency, which means that the management acts as an agent for shareholders. As per the agency theory, there is a conflict of interest between the management and shareholders (Jensen & Meckling, 1976). Shareholders are more interested in dividends and share prices. On the other hand, the board of directors is interested in bonuses and remuneration. When one party wants to maximize their interest, the other party has to give up their interest because of a conflict of interest. Due to the agency problems, financial statements are more likely to be misstated. Therefore, stakeholders, more specifically shareholders, demand independent audits of the financial statements. They are more likely to rely on audited financial statements and non-financial statements for economic decision-making related to firms.

The statutory auditors are responsible for ensuring the reliability and transparency of the financial statements. They audit the financial statements of the clients in accordance with generally accepted accounting principles, as well as other relevant internal and external regulations. Audit quality is more likely to mitigate the agency's problems; therefore, stakeholders, especially regulators more concerned about audit quality. They are involved with several activities to increase and maintain audit quality. Notably, the International Auditing and Assurance Standards Board (IAASB) is responsible for formulating and issuing international auditing standards (ISA) as per the needs of the business environment. In addition, they revise auditing standards as per the changes in the business environment at regular intervals. Their main purpose is to ensure audit quality and harmonization of auditing practices (Knechel, Krishnan, Pevzner, Shefchik, & Velury, 2013; Ball, 2009; Humphrey, Kausar, Loft, & Woods, 2011; Leuz & Wysocki, 2016).

Auditing involves many evolutions, notably financial statement audits, non-audit services, non-financial statements assurance, joint provisions of financial statements audits, and extended external reports assurance. Auditors' competence and independence are crucially important in audit quality. In the globalized business environment, harmonizing auditing practices is a significant problem. Harmonizing accounting and auditing practices is the primary objective of stakeholders around the globe. In the globalized business environment, stakeholders are more concerned and interested in similar auditing practices in all economies for true and fair practices, moreover, to ensure the qualitative characteristics, especially understandability and comparability of financial reporting and audit. Auditing literacy, audit expectation gap, auditing education, and standards are important for better audit practices and quality (Simnett, Vanstraelen, & Chua, 2009; Leuz & Wysocki, 2016; Geiger,1994; Marriott & Marriott, 2000; Humphrey, Moizer, & Turley, 2006; Glaum, Schmidt, Street, & Vogel, 2013).

The next sections of the chapter are structured evolution of auditing, auditors' competence and independence, financial statements auditing, extended external report assurance, joint provisions of financial statements audit and extended external reports assurance, international audit practices and harmonization of audit practices, audit literacy, and audit gap, audit education and standards, and conclusion respectively. More specifically, this chapter shows new audit reporting practices (key audit matters reporting) in some European countries, with a comparison of the legal environment of common law and civil law.

2. EVOLUTION OF AUDITING

The auditing field has evolved significantly over time, shaped by economic, technological, regulatory, and societal changes. Auditing's origins trace back to ancient civilizations, where public officials employed it to verify financial transactions. The demand for auditing grew notably during the 19th century, fuelled by industrialization and the expansion of stock market activities. In the UK, the Joint Stock Companies Act of 1,856 emphasises annual audits for companies, marking a pivotal moment in the formalization of auditing practices. The establishment of regulatory bodies, such as the American Institute of Accountants in 1,887, further illustrates the historical development of the field.

Regulatory bodies began emphasizing the need for consistent auditing practices, leading to the development of "Generally Accepted Auditing Standards (GAAS)" in the mid-20th century. These standards provided a structured and regulated framework for auditing, fostering uniformity and reliability in the profession. Technological advancements also transformed auditing practices, introducing new methodologies such as automated auditing systems and "Computer-Assisted Audit Techniques (CAATs)" following the integration of computers into business operations.

Traditional auditing primarily focused on financial statement audits. Over time, it expanded to include operational and compliance aspects, enhancing its scope and relevance. The introduction of risk-based auditing techniques has further improved the effectiveness of auditing practices (Gramling, Maletta, Schneider, & Church, 2004). Numerous corporate failures, often linked to accounting scandals, have underscored the importance of corporate governance, internal controls, and financial reporting and audit quality. These failures prompted greater scrutiny and necessitated auditors to assess and report on clients' internal controls (Cosserat & Rodda, 2009).

In the present business environment, stakeholders increasingly rely on non-financial reporting to evaluate a company's sustainability. Consequently, the demand for auditing has grown beyond traditional financial audits to include Extended External Reports (EERs). Sustainability reporting and assurance have become integral components of contemporary auditing practices (Simnett, Vanstraelen, & Chua, 2009). As a result, auditing has evolved from a focus on financial verification to a comprehensive examination of operations, risk management, and sustainability practices, aligning with the needs of the modern business environment.

3. AUDITORS' COMPETENCE AND INDEPENDENCE

Auditing literature suggests that audit quality depends mainly on auditor independence and competence (DeAngelo, 1981). Many factors determine auditor competence and independence. Auditing is a professional and independent examination of financial statements, and auditors are responsible for providing opinions. Importantly, there is a conflict of interest between management and shareholders (Jensen et al., 1976). Therefore, stakeholders rely on audited financial statements for their economic decision-making related to firms. So, auditors are expected to be highly qualified professionals, especially auditors who should have high competence (knowledge and experience) in accounting, auditing, the business industry, the business environment, and other internal and external acts, laws, rules, and regulations. Auditor competence is not enough to ensure audit quality. Prior studies have ensured that auditor independence is a key determinant of audit quality. Many factors affect auditor independence; specifically, five threats affect the auditor's independence. Five auditing threats are self-interest, self-review, familiarity, advocacy, and intimidation. Therefore, stakeholders, especially shareholders, management, auditors, and regulators, are more concerned about auditor independence.

Audit firm size is crucial in audit quality because large audit firms are more competent and independent. In addition, they are more concerned with litigation and reputation risks. Therefore, big audit firms are proxied for audit quality. Audit firms are primarily classified into Big 4 auditors and non-Big 4 auditors. Additionally, they are categorized as large audit firms, mid-tier audit firms, and small or local audit firms based on their scale of operations. The audit quality literature suggests that large audit firms are associated with higher audit quality, as they are generally more competent and independent. Consequently, large audit firms are often used as a proxy for audit quality. Historically, the classification of big audit firms has evolved based on their market presence and capitalization. In the late 1990s and early 2000s, there were six major audit firms, known as the Big 6: Arthur Andersen, Coopers & Lybrand, Deloitte, Ernst & Young, KPMG, and Price Waterhouse. Subsequently, Price Waterhouse merged with Coopers & Lybrand, forming PricewaterhouseCoopers (PwC). However, the number of large audit firms further declined when Arthur Andersen was dissolved in 2002 due to its involvement in issuing inappropriate audit opinions, particularly in the Enron scandal. As a result, only four major audit firms—Deloitte, Ernst & Young (EY), KPMG, and PwC—remained, leading to the Big 4 classification in the 21st century. Many prior studies find a positive association between Big4 auditors and financial reporting and audit quality (Ruiz-Barbadillo, Gómez-Aguilar, De Fuentes-Barberá, & García-Benau, 2004; Berglund, Eshleman, & Guo, 2018; Abughazaleh, O'Connell & Princen, 2015; Gul, Zhou, & Zhu, 2013; Gul, Tsui, & Dhaliwal, 2006; Geiger & Rama, 2006; Abernathy, Barnes, Stefaniak, & Weisbarth, 2017; Habib, Bhuiyan, Huang, & Miah, 2019; Leventis, Weetman, & Caramanis, 2005; Owusu-Ansah & Leventis, 2006).

Clients are less likely to receive going concern opinions because it is costly and more likely to create adverse consequences. Clients are more likely to dismiss auditors when auditors issue going-concern opinions or frequent going-concern opinions. Therefore, the issuance of a going concern opinion is more likely to relate to auditor competence and independence. Big 4 auditors are more likely to issue going concern opinions for financially distressed firms (Berglund et al., 2018). Annual financial statements cover one financial year's financial transactions and events of clients. However, auditors have to complete the audit of the annual financial statements within a stipulated time because firms are responsible for publishing the audited financial statements within a stipulated time, generally 3-4 months from the reporting date. Therefore, auditors' competence is a significant factor in conducting and completing the statutory audit with high audit quality within the time. A meta-analysis documents a negative relationship between Big 4 auditors and audit delay (Habib et al., 2019).

Stakeholders, especially regulators, are more concerned about auditor tenure because long auditor tenure is more likely to decrease audit quality due to auditing threats; on the other hand, long auditor tenure is more likely to increase audit quality through better understanding and knowledge about clients. Based on the above arguments, past studies find evidence for both arguments (Ye, Carson, & Simnett, 2011; Gul, Ma, & Lai, 2017; Chen, Gul, Truong, & Veeraraghavan, 2016; Gul,

Jaggi, & Krishnan, 2007; Gul, Fung, & Jaggi, 2009; Geiger & Raghunandan, 2002). For example, Ye et al. (2011) find that long audit engagement partner tenure, combined with the joint effect of auditor-provided non-audit services (NAS) and alumni affiliation, negatively impacts the auditor's likelihood of issuing a going-concern opinion, and Geiger et al. (2002) suggest that audit reporting failures were significantly more frequent in the early years of the auditor-client relationship compared to cases where auditors had served these clients for longer tenures.

Auditing standards do not specify directly about auditor tenure, for example, minimum and maximum auditor tenure for clients. Also, there is no strict and strong provision worldwide. However, there are some provisions on auditor tenure, especially the EU 2014 audit regulations suggest auditor tenure with clients up to 10 years. It applies to European Union countries. Also, firms are more likely to have some internal regulations and provisions on auditor tenure.

There is strong criticism for allowing financial statement auditors to provide non-audit services because of independence issues. They argue that allowing financial statement auditors to provide non-audit services is more likely to reduce independence. On the other hand, some past studies argue that favourable consequences of allowing financial statement auditors to provide non-audit services. Auditors are more likely to acquire more information, knowledge, and understanding about clients when they provide non-audit services. This better understanding increases the financial reporting and audit quality. Based on the above arguments, past studies have evidence for both arguments (Geiger & Rama, 2003; Bloomfield et al., 2008).

There is no specific provision on auditor gender diversity like the board gender diversity requirement in the world. However, prior studies suggest that gender diversity for better performance. Especially, female representation on the board increases the firm's financial and non-financial performance. Because females are more concerned about litigation and reputation risks. Therefore, they are more likely to avoid risks. It helps them to perform better. In alignment with this argument, some studies document that female auditors increase financial reporting and audit quality (Abbott, Parker, & Presley, 2012; Hardies, Breesch, & Branson, 2016; Ittonen et al., 2013; Alderman, 2017). For example, Hardies et al. (2016) find a positive relationship between female auditors and the issuance of going concern opinions.

4. FINANCIAL STATEMENTS AUDIT

Listed companies are required by legislation to publicly present audited financial statements (IAS 1: Company Act). Financial statement audits are exclusively conducted by accounting firms, which are categorized into Big 4, mid-tier, and small audit firms. The Big 4 audit firms—Deloitte, PricewaterhouseCoopers (PwC),

Ernst & Young (EY), and Klynveld Peat Marwick Goerdeler (KPMG)—are globally recognized for their expertise in financial statement audits. These audits are carried out per auditing standards, which are developed, issued, and periodically revised by the International Auditing and Assurance Standards Board (IAASB), ensuring consistency and quality in audit practices.

Management is responsible for preparing and presenting the financial statements, developing and implementing internal control systems, and ensuring the firm's legal compliance. In contrast, auditors are primarily responsible for providing reasonable assurance of the accuracy of the financial statements (ISA, 700). The audit opinion is based on evidence gathered regarding material misstatements in the financial statements. However, auditors cannot offer absolute assurance due to inherent limitations in the audit process. As a result, the quality of the audit is influenced by the amount and thoroughness of the information and verifications conducted, which ultimately contribute to forming an appropriate opinion.

According to ISA 315, auditors must gain a comprehensive understanding of their clients and their operating environment. Ongoing audits and long auditor tenure contribute to obtaining more detailed and accurate information about clients. This information is essential for forming an appropriate audit opinion, identifying Key Audit Matters (KAMs), and improving the quality of financial reporting. Auditors with extended tenure have access to more information compared to new auditors, which fosters a more informed and collaborative relationship with the client. Soroushyar (2023) identifies a significant positive relationship between auditor tenure and financial reporting quality, highlighting the benefits of longer audit engagements in accessing better information.

Financial statements not only reflect past transactions and events but also include estimates and provisions, which often involve significant uncertainty. As a result, auditors must obtain both financial and non-financial information to accurately assess these estimates and provisions. This is particularly relevant when estimates are linked to environmental or social factors. For instance, if a government introduces new environmental regulations that affect the revaluation of property, plant, and equipment, auditors need to review both financial data and relevant non-financial information to verify the revaluation. Such estimates require scrutiny, as they can have implications for the going concern assessment and overall financial reporting.

Auditors are responsible for identifying and assessing uncertainties related to the going concern status of their clients. They are more likely to issue a going concern opinion when clients face going concern issues. The assessment of going concern depends not only on financial factors but also on non-financial considerations. For instance, if clients are required to make provisions and estimates to comply with government environmental protection regulations, failure to do so would result in non-compliance with the law. Non-compliance may lead to legal actions and, in some cases, the dissolution of the business based on legal requirements. Therefore, auditors must consider both financial and non-financial information to properly assess going concern uncertainties and issue an appropriate opinion.

Financial statement audits play a crucial role in enhancing the quality of financial reporting, primarily through ensuring audit quality. DeFond and Zhang (2014) highlight that higher audit quality is indicative of higher financial reporting quality. Reliable audit processes strengthen the credibility of financial statements, promoting transparency and fostering trust among investors, creditors, and other stakeholders. By gathering more information, auditors can obtain a more comprehensive understanding of their clients. This process leads to the accumulation of more evidence, improved risk assessment, better detection of material misstatements, enhanced professional skepticism, and stronger assurance of regulatory compliance.

The auditing style adopted by audit firms varies and has implications for audit outcomes. When a client appoints the same audit firm for financial statement audits (FSA) and Extended External Reporting (EER) assurance, the consistent audit style across both services facilitates faster, smoother, and higher-quality outcomes. This unified approach simplifies interactions with management, enhancing efficiency and quality compared to having separate auditors for each service. Francis, Pinnuck, and Watanabe (2014) investigated the relationship between audit style and financial statement comparability in the U.S., finding that when the same Big 4 audit firm audits two companies within the same industry, the comparability of financial statements improves. The study concludes that appointing the same Big 4 auditors for both FSA and EER assurance increases the likelihood of better outcomes.

Independent audits enhance the credibility of financial statements, mitigating conflicts of interest between management and shareholders. In addition to fostering trust, audited financial statements benefit stakeholders in several ways. For example, Allee and Yohn (2009) found that small firms with audited financial statements have greater access to credit facilities at lower costs, as creditors place significant trust in independent audit reports. Although financial statement audits are not mandatory for small businesses, their benefits are evident. Farooq and Shehata (2018) further discovered that firms with audited financial statements pay significantly lower bribes. Similarly, while EER assurance is not yet mandatory in all countries, its importance is growing. Independent audits of EERs provide benefits to both clients and auditors, enhancing the credibility of the reported information.

Auditors' judgment regarding prospective financial statements is influenced by multiple factors, including uncertainties in the client's internal and external business environment. Auditing prospective financial statements requires more financial and non-financial information than auditing historical financial statements. Rodgers and Housel (2004) studied the impact of environmental risk information on auditors' judgments about prospective financial statements. They found that auditors often downplay environmental risk information due to unfamiliarity, focusing instead on familiar financial information. This approach increases the likelihood of issuing inappropriate opinions. The study emphasizes the need for auditors to be trained in evaluating non-financial information. Additionally, the joint provision of FSA and EER assurance enhances auditors' ability to assess both historical and prospective financial statements by providing more comprehensive client information.

Audit risk refers to the possibility of auditors issuing an inappropriate opinion when financial statements are materially misstated. This risk comprises inherent, control, and detection risks. While audit risks cannot be eliminated, they can be mitigated. Auditors are responsible for reducing detection risk, whereas inherent risk arises from the nature of the client's business. Inherent risks can significantly affect business sustainability, which depends on both financial and non-financial factors. Ruhnke and Schmidt (2014) explored the relationship between inherent and control risks and audit adjustments, finding that factors such as economic conditions, the strength of entity-level controls, management competence and integrity, and internal control systems are critical in driving audit adjustments. Their study confirms that inherent and control risks are significantly associated with income-related audit adjustments. The joint provision of FSA and EER assurance mitigates audit risk by providing auditors with better access to comprehensive client information.

The readability of financial statement notes and other disclosures is a key determinant of their usefulness for investment decisions. It reflects the quality of the information and communication provided, which plays a vital role in the audit process. Salehi, Lari, Mohammadi, Adibian, and Fahimifard (2020) examined auditors' responses to the readability of financial statement notes, measuring responses in terms of audit report lag, audit fees, and going-concern opinions. They found significant positive relationships between the readability of financial statement notes and both audit report lag and audit fees. The joint provision of FSA and EER assurance, when performed by the same auditor, can enhance readability by aligning processes, resulting in time and cost savings for both auditors and clients.

According to recent studies and regulatory requirements and provisions, financial statements audit covers not only financial transactions and events but also non-financial transactions related to financial items recognized in the financial statements. For example, auditors have to consider environmental-related requirements, provisions, and regulations when examining property, plant, and equipment-related recognition in the financial statements.

5. EXTENDED EXTERNAL REPORT ASSURANCE

Recent audit regulatory requirements have extended to the assurance of Extended External Reports (EERs), which go beyond traditional financial statements and are provided by both accounting and non-accounting firms. EER assurance refers to assurance services performed on reports that extend beyond financial disclosures. Comprehensive requirements and guidelines have been developed for EER assurance. For instance, the Global Reporting Initiative (GRI) offers sustainability reporting standards widely used worldwide (GRI, 2018). The International Auditing and Assurance Standards Board (IAASB) has also issued a detailed framework to guide assurance practitioners in this emerging field (IAASB, 2020). Various regulatory bodies have issued standards for EER assurance, such as the Financial Reporting Council (FRC) in the UK with its "ISAE (UK) 3000 (Revised)" standard (FRC, 2019).

Recently, the International Standard on Sustainability Assurance (ISSA) 5000 has been issued by the International Auditing and Assurance Standards Board (IAASB). It is more likely to be a new global benchmark for sustainability assurance, ensuring greater credibility, reliability, and consistency in sustainability disclosures worldwide. This standard provides a comprehensive framework for practitioners performing sustainability assurance engagements, addressing key aspects such as risk assessment, reporting transparency, and stakeholder confidence. By aligning sustainability assurance with internationally recognized principles, ISSA 5000 enhances the trustworthiness of ESG (Environmental, Social, and Governance) reporting, helping investors, regulators, and other stakeholders make informed decisions. It also reinforces the growing importance of independent assurance in promoting corporate accountability and sustainable business practices. In jurisdictions that adopt it, ISSA 5000 is effective for periods beginning on or after December 15, 2026.

Given the rapid evolution of this field, numerous regulatory announcements have emphasized non-financial reporting and assurance. Notably, climate-related financial disclosures became mandatory for the UK's 1,300 largest registered companies on April 6, 2022, marking the world's first mandatory requirement for disclosing climate-related risks. Similarly, the U.S. Securities and Exchange Commission (SEC) proposed rules for climate-related disclosures on March 21, 2022, while the recent announcement of mandatory climate-related disclosures in Australia since 1 January 2025. These regulatory developments underscore the increasing global demand for non-financial reporting and EER assurance, both now and in the future.

Stakeholders today demand greater transparency and credibility for effective decision-making in a dynamic business environment (Eccles & Krzus, 2010). They seek comprehensive reporting that extends beyond financial data, encompassing a broader perspective on organizational performance and risks. This shift has driven a transition from traditional financial reporting to integrated reporting, which combines financial and non-financial information. Consequently, there is growing interest in reporting on environmental, social, and governance (ESG) factors alongside traditional financial metrics like performance, cash flow, and equity changes (GRI, 2018; SASB, 2020). The continuous evolution of auditing and corporate reporting reflects the changing business landscape, technological advancements, and shifting stakeholder expectations, all aimed at enhancing transparency and trust.

Today, both financial and non-financial information is vital for economic decision-making. Traditional corporate reporting primarily focuses on financial information, which is prepared and presented by management and validated by external auditors. However, management now also prepares and presents non-financial reports, such as ESG reports, corporate social responsibility (CSR) reports, sustainability reports (SR), and integrated reports (IR). These collectively form Extended External Reports (EERs). The rising demand for non-financial reporting has necessitated independent assurance not only for financial statements but also for these non-financial reports. Furthermore, regulatory requirements for preparing, presenting, and disclosing non-financial reports have significantly increased in recent years (IAASB, 2021).

The selection of auditors for financial statement audits (FSA) and EER assurance is a critical economic decision. Economic decision-makers rely heavily on audit and assurance reports, for which clients pay substantial fees. Financial statements audits are typically conducted by accounting firms, whereas EER assurance may involve both accounting and non-accounting firms. Some organizations appoint the same firm for both services, while others choose different providers. Appointing the same auditor for both FSA and EER assurance can yield several benefits. It enables the auditor to gather comprehensive insights into the client's financial and non-financial information, enhancing audit and assurance quality. Additionally, clients may achieve cost savings by avoiding redundant work when a single firm handles both services (Lu, Simnett & Zhou, 2023). This arrangement can facilitate smoother collaboration, improve communication, and ensure high-quality services, as the auditing firm operates through separate teams and engagements for each service. The joint provision also allows auditors to gain a more holistic understanding of risk-related information, particularly in ESG areas, that could lead to material misstatements in financial statements.

Expertise is crucial for delivering high-quality EER assurance. While the Big 4 auditors are globally recognized for their expertise in financial statement audits, the EER assurance market extends beyond traditional auditing firms. Non-accounting firms are also active players in this space, prompting competition among accounting firms to establish leadership in the EER assurance market. Due to their longstanding reputation, accounting firms are often preferred for EER assurance, particularly when they have demonstrated expertise in the field.

Previous studies highlight the financial implications of EER information (Dhaliwal, Tsang & Yang, 2011; Dhaliwal, Radhakrishnan, Tsang & Yang, 2012; Christensen, Hail & Leuz, 2021; Christensen, Serafeim & Sikochi, 2022). Non-financial information is increasingly recognized as material for economic decision-making, with recent regulatory requirements for climate-related disclosures emphasizing its importance. EERs typically address a firm's objectives, strategies, business models, and significant risks, which are highly relevant for both EER assurers and financial statement auditors. Appointing the same audit firm for both services can minimize work duplication, resulting in lower costs and improved efficiency. In contrast, appointing different firms often necessitates independent risk assessments, leading to overlapping efforts and potentially higher fees.

However, appointing financial statement auditors for non-audit services has faced significant criticism globally. Concerns on potential threats to auditor independence, including self-interest, self-review, and familiarity risks. Critics argue that non-audit services often focus narrowly on specific areas, such as tax or IT, without addressing the firm's overall context.

EERs assurance is provided based on the verification, knowledge, and understanding of the whole client base. Moreover, non-audit services are related to voluntary, and firm-specific needs. There are no legal requirements and regulatory perspectives on non-audit services. However, the EERs requirements have increased over the years by regulatory bodies and legal authorities.[1] Therefore, legal provisions are needed to appoint financial statements auditors to EERs without compromising independence. EERs assurance is new when compared to the financial statements audit. EERs assurance is provided by accounting firms, engineering firms, and small consultancy/boutique firms.[2] Where accounting firms have a long experience in the independent professional assurance service in the world (Big 4 auditors).

The demand for Extended External Reporting (EER) and its assurance has grown significantly in recent years, as stakeholders increasingly prioritize these reports. This trend is evident from initiatives like mandatory climate-related financial disclosures introduced in 2022 (IAASB, 2021). According to KPMG (2020), 96% of G250 companies issue EERs, and 71% of these reports are assured by third parties, highlighting the critical role of EER assurance within the assurance profession.

Acquiring comprehensive information is essential for producing high-quality EER assurance reports. Since EERs often incorporate financial transactions, events, and activities related to a firm's sustainability practices, such as investments in environmental protection or compliance with environmental legislation, obtaining detailed financial and non-financial data enhances the accuracy, transparency, and reliability of these reports. Access to extensive client information allows auditors to identify significant risks of material misstatements and provide comprehensive, relevant assurance that supports stakeholders' decision-making. This holistic approach helps meet stakeholder expectations while ensuring the transparency of the firm's disclosures.

In financial statement audits, only accounting firms are authorized to provide services, resulting in healthy competition that drives differentiation and improvements in financial reporting and audit quality. Expertise plays a vital role in the quality of such services. Accounting firms, particularly Big 4 auditors, dominate the global financial auditing market due to their longstanding expertise. Although EER assurance is an emerging field shared by both accounting and non-accounting firms (Zhou, Simnett, & Green, 2016), accounting firms are well-positioned to provide superior EER assurance due to their existing assurance expertise.

The quality of EER assurance reports is typically measured by specific elements, including the title, addressee, assuror's name, report date, responsibilities of the reporter and assuror, engagement scope, assurance standards, materiality, and the general opinion or conclusion (Sierra García, Bollas-Araya, & García Benau, 2022; Zaman, Farooq, Khalid, & Mahmood, 2021; Grassmann, Fuhrmann, & Guenther, 2021; Harindahyani & Agustia, 2023). Many of these elements are also present in audit reports, making auditors more familiar with their application and thus more likely to produce high-quality EER assurance reports.

Empirical evidence supports the notion that accounting firms provide superior EER assurance. Firms operating in robust economic, legal, and social environments are more likely to select Big 4 auditors for EER assurance (Alsahali, Malagueño, & Marques, 2024). Approximately 39% of firms use their financial statement auditors for sustainability assurance (Ruiz-Barbadillo & Martínez-Ferrero, 2022), with industry specialization being a significant factor in this selection. Additional studies reveal that accounting firms dominate the EER assurance market. For instance, Zaman, Farooq, Khalid, and Mahmood (2021) found that 73% of Australian-listed firms and 47% of New Zealand-listed firms use the same auditor for both financial statement audits and EER assurance. Moreover, Harindahyani and Agustia (2023) reported that accounting firms deliver higher-quality assurance reports compared to non-accounting firms in a sample of 96 large Asian companies.

The demand for EER assurance continues to rise, driven by regulatory mandates and stakeholder expectations. Assurers can improve the quality of their services by acquiring extensive client information. Accounting firms, particularly those that also conduct financial statement audits, are well-positioned to deliver high-quality EER assurance. The synergy between financial statement auditing and EER assurance is especially pronounced when the same auditor provides both services, resulting in superior quality and consistency.

6. JOINT PROVISIONS OF FINANCIAL STATEMENTS AUDIT AND EXTENDED EXTERNAL REPORTS ASSURANCE

The joint provision of financial statement audits (FSA) and extended external reporting (EER) is the latest evolution in auditing. The joint provision of financial statement audits (FSA) and extended external reporting (EER) assurance refers to the practice where the same auditor provides both services to a client. This approach leverages the auditor's existing knowledge of the client's financial reporting processes to enhance the quality of EER assurance. It ensures consistency, reduces duplication, and improves efficiency in assurance engagements. Firms are more likely to prefer this joint provision to ensure aligned audit methodologies and insights. This integrated service model is increasingly common in response to the growing demand for high-quality EER assurance.

The joint provision of financial statements, audit, and EERs assurance is the latest evolution in auditing. There are few studies in the field of joint provision. Recently, Lu, Simnett, and Zhou (2023) examined the choices and consequences of using the same provider for financial statements audit and extended external reports assurance. Many factors impact the selection of the same or different assurers to assure these reports. This study mainly aims to examine factors that impact this decision and the consequences of this decision in terms of audit quality of the financial statements and cost. If both services are provided by the same auditor, then they can provide better services through their comprehensive knowledge of the company's financial and non-financial information. It leads to the quality of assurance services. Also, the company can save money by avoiding the overlap of work when appointing the same provider for both services. They find that perceived independence has a significant association with the selection of an EERs assurance provider rather than the same provider. Reputation to provide EERs assurance reports significantly affects the choice of the financial statements' auditor. Also, the integrated reporting practices of the firm significantly impact the selection of the same audit firm to provide both services. Further, they find a low level of discretionary accruals when the company has the same audit firm for both services. On the other hand, the results do not provide any significant differences for audit fees.

Another study by Maso, Lobo, Mazzi, and Paugam (2020) examines the effect of auditors' assessment of going-concern risk when CSR assurance and financial statements audits are conducted by the same audit firm. They strongly believe that when both assignments are conducted by the same auditor, there is a possibility of getting CSR-related comprehensive knowledge from the CSR assurance team. It helps the financial statements auditors to assess the going-concern risk effectively than both services are provided by different firms. The primary prediction of the study is that when both services are provided by the same accounting firms, it leads to a better assessment of the going concern of the clients. They find that when firms appoint the same Big4 auditors for both services, (1) it leads to a positive association between the frequency of GCOs and lower Type – II going-concern errors, (2) clients book larger environmental and litigation provisions, (3) less likely to book income-decreasing, and (4) do not charge higher audit fees. The findings of the study suggest that when firms allow the same service provider for both services, it leads to the acquisition of comprehensive knowledge by financial statements auditors.

Some previous studies conclude that clients receive more benefits when allowing the same auditor for financial statements audit and non-audit services. Appointing the same auditors to many services helps auditors to acquire more understanding about the clients in terms of business model, strategy, and objectives. It helps to identify the material misstatements. Financial statements auditors acquire more information about the clients when providing non-audit services to the same clients. It leads them to build knowledge spillover about the clients. It helps in the financial statements audit (Wu 2006; Antle & Demski, 1991).

Prior studies conclude that non-audit services help financial audits. Kinney, Palmrose, and Scholz (2004) examine the relationships between non-audit services, auditor independence, and financial restatements. The results show that there is a significant negative relationship between non-audit services (tax services) and financial restatements. This study concludes that assigning non-audit services to the financial statement auditors provides benefits to the clients.

Audit fees and non-audit fees are significant expenses for the company. Usually, when a client appoints the same auditor for both services, they are more likely to bargain. Auditors are more likely to reduce fees when they provide both services to the same client. Antle, Gordon, Narayanamoorthy, and Zhou (2006) investigate the relationship between audit fees, non-audit fees, and abnormal accruals. They find a significant relationship between audit fees and non-audit fees in terms of knowledge spillovers. The statistical results do not confirm that non-audit services fees are likely to increase abnormal accruals.

The firms are more likely on the appropriate directions when the financial statements auditors provide consulting services. Because financial statements auditors have more understanding of the clients in terms of key operations, financial position, financial performance, internal controls, and governance. Also, financial statement auditors can acquire more information in terms of business models, strategies, and objectives when providing consulting services. Appointing auditors to consulting services provides benefits to both parties. Koh, Rajgopal, and Srinivasan (2013) examine the relationship between non-audit services and financial reporting quality. They argue that auditors acquire more information when they provide consulting services to the same clients. It leads to better financial reporting quality. The statistical results confirm that the earnings quality of the clients is improved when auditors provide non-audit services, especially consulting services.

Some previous studies conclude that a positive and significant relationship between non-audit services and audit quality. Svanström (2013) finds a positive and significant relationship between non-audit services and audit quality of private firms in Sweden. In addition to that, Bell, Causholli, and Knechel (2015) conclude that total non-audit fees have a positive relationship with the audit quality of listed firms in the SEC.

The above studies prove that non-audit services assist in financial audits, increase financial reporting quality, reduce cost, reduce audit report lag, and increase audit quality when these services are provided by the incumbent auditors. However, a strong criticism is to appoint the incumbent auditors to non-audit services. Stakeholders are mainly concerned with auditors' independence when appointing the same auditor for many services. They strongly argue that auditors lose independence when providing non-audit services to the same client and receive a significant fee for non-audit services. However, the joint provisions of FSA and EERs assurance differ from non-audit services. The EERs assurance is quite similar to the non-audit services, but it is different from the non-audit services.

7. INTERNATIONAL AUDIT PRACTICES AND HARMONIZATION OF AUDITING PRACTICES

The globalized business environment suggests and expects the same accounting and auditing practices all over the world to ensure the qualitative characteristics of financial reporting, such as relevance and faithful representation (fundamental qualitative characteristics), comparability, verifiability, timelines, and understandability (enhancing qualitative characteristics). Stakeholders, especially regulators and standard setters, key objective is to ensuring similar accounting and auditing practices all over the world. However, the harmonization of audit practices is a major and continuing problem. Many factors affect the harmonization of accounting and auditing practices among nations in the world.

Past studies document that accounting and auditing practices vary among nations, especially as these practices mainly depend on the regulatory and legal environment. Strong regulatory and legal environments are more likely to ensure quality accounting and auditing practices. In addition, firms and auditors are more likely to ensure financial reporting and audit quality in highly regulated and strong legal environments because litigation and reputation risks are high in these environments. Auditing harmonization refers to the process of aligning and standardizing auditing practices, principles, and standards across different countries and jurisdictions.

Boolaky (2012) documented strength of auditing and reporting standards (SARS) varies among European countries; the range of SARS is 3.1(weak) and 6.2(strong). Common law and civil law are two main legal traditions in the world. Many prior studies suggest common law countries provide better investor protection through financial reporting and audit quality (Gul, Zhou, & Zhu, 2013; Francis & Wang, 2008; La Porta et al., 2006; Leuz et al. 2003; Hope 2003; Ball et al. 2000; La Porta et al. 1998).

This section summarizes the adoption of Key Audit Matters (KAMs) reporting practices among the four largest European economies: the UK, which operates under a common law framework, and France, Germany, and Italy, which follow civil law systems. KAMs reporting represents a significant advancement in auditing practices (IFAC, 2017). Introduced in 2015 through International Standard on Auditing (ISA) 701, titled Communicating Key Audit Matters in the Independent Auditor's Report, it became mandatory for listed companies in many jurisdictions starting December 15, 2016. The primary aim of KAMs reporting is to enhance the communicative value of the auditor's report by providing greater transparency into the audit process conducted during a statutory audit (ISA 701). KAMs focus on significant risks, transactions, events, and the auditor's professional judgments. Auditors are tasked with identifying and disclosing these significant matters that arose and were addressed during the audit process. Firms that have a minimum of one(1) KAMs were selected for the following comparison.

Table 1. KAMs reporting in the UK, France, Germany, and Italy

Particulars	Total	UK	France	Germany	Italy
Minimum KAMs	1	1	1	1	1
Maximum KAMs	7	7	7	7	6
Average KAMs	2.51	2.96	2.10	2.20	2.04
Total Number of Observations	6,372	2,895	1,527	1,264	686

Table 1 presents the distribution of Key Audit Matters (KAMs) reporting across four European countries: the UK, France, Germany, and Italy. The minimum number of KAMs reported is consistently 1 across all countries, while the maximum varies slightly, with the highest being 7 in the UK, France, and Germany, and 6 in Italy. The UK exhibits the highest average number of KAMs (2.96), indicating more extensive disclosures compared to France (2.10), Germany (2.20), and Italy (2.04). The total sample consists of 6,372 firm-year observations, with the UK having the largest share (2,895), followed by France (1,527), Germany (1,264), and Italy (686). These differences suggest that UK auditors provide more KAMs, possibly due to stronger regulatory requirements, investor expectations, or the influence of common law systems. In contrast, the lower average KAMs in civil law countries (France, Germany, and Italy) may indicate different audit practices or levels of disclosure stringency. When comparing civil law countries, German firms received more KAMs than the other countries. KAMs reporting is mandatory for listed firms in the above countries; however, the KAMs reporting practices (number of KAMs) vary among these countries.

Table 2 compares Key Audit Matters (KAMs) reporting between Big 4 and Non-Big 4 auditors. The minimum and maximum KAMs reported are identical (1 and 7, respectively) across both groups. However, Big4 auditors report a slightly higher average number of KAMs (2.66) than non-Big4 auditors (2.31), indicating that Big4 auditors tend to disclose more KAMs. The total number of observations (6,372) is split between Big4 (3,592) and non-Big4 (2,780) firms. These results suggest that Big4 auditors may adopt a more rigorous or transparent approach in KAMs reporting, potentially due to stricter audit methodologies or higher scrutiny from regulators and stakeholders. These descriptive statistics show the latest evidence for the need for auditing harmonization in the world. These descriptive statistics show selected non-financial firms with a minimum of one KAM in the above countries from 2018-2022.

Table 2. KAMs reporting comparison between Big 4 and Non-Big 4 auditors

Particulars	Total	Big4	Non-Big4
Minimum KAMs	1	1	1
Maximum KAMs	7	7	7
Average KAMs	2.51	2.66	2.31
Total Number of Observations	6,372	3,592	2,780

Many countries follow the same auditing standards (ISA), even though auditing practices differ among countries. International standards on auditing are not applicable in some countries. For example, the U.S. follows auditing standards issued by the Public Company Accounting Oversight Board (PCAOB) for listed companies and the Auditing Standards Board (ASB) of the AICPA for non-public entities. Therefore, it is difficult to harmonize auditing practices all over the world. Harmonizing auditing is more likely to be a permanent and continuous one of the key objectives of the stakeholders, especially regulators and standard setters in the world.

8. AUDIT EXPECTATION GAP, AUDITING EDUCATION/ AUDITING LITERACY, AND STANDARDS

The audit expectation gap is a major problem in enhancing audit quality. Accounting and auditing are specialized disciplines; therefore, adequate and some level of expert knowledge and experience are needed for a better understanding and implementation. Stakeholders cover all lives in the world, and they use financial statements and audit reports for different purposes. These stakeholders may have an accounting and auditing background or they may not have an accounting and auditing background. So, the audit gap is less likely to be elevated totally. However, auditing education can help to mitigate or reduce the audit expectation gap. The evolution in auditing, for example, joint provision of financial statements audit and extended external reports assurance, non-financial reporting assurance, and new auditing standards, for example, KAMs reporting, may increase or reduce the audit expectation gap. Therefore, continuous auditing education and awareness are vitally important to reduce the audit expectation gap. Accounting and auditing regulatory bodies, standard setters, academics, researchers, education institutions, professional institutions, and institutional factors are crucial for reducing the audit expectation gap, increasing auditing education, and increasing the quality of standards and their applications.

9. FUTURE OF AUDITING

Stakeholders, especially shareholders, management, investors, and regulators, expect transparent and reliable corporate reporting on financial and non-financial activities, performance, and position of the firms. They are more likely to expect detailed reporting and more disclosure for better understanding. The previous (old) audit report on the financial statements was a limited communication because it mainly focused on the opinion but did not disclose anything about significant matters identified and how these matters were addressed during the auditing process. Therefore, it was observed to have low communicative value. Due to these problems, stakeholders' demand has increased for detailed or expanded audit reports. Finally, IAASB introduced a new audit reporting called KAMs reporting in 2015, and it is mandatory for listed firms with effect from December 15, 2016. As per KAMs reporting, auditors are responsible for disclosing significant matters identified and addressed during the auditing process. KAMs reporting purpose is to enhance the communicative value of audit reports and provide more information to users on significant matters audited during the auditing process. So, auditors are now required to disclose more on significant areas they identified and how they examined them.

KAMs reporting increases auditors' accountability because they are responsible and accountable for KAMs disclosure.

Emerging sustainability issues, especially environmental, social, and governance issues, stakeholders concerned increase on the environment, social, and governance aspects. Therefore, they demand environmental, social, and governance aspects. Firms are requested to disclose these aspects, for example, climate-related financial disclosure. Due to the agency problems between the management and shareholders, there is a high probability of material misstatements regarding these aspects (for example, greenwashing). Stakeholders' demand for sustainability reporting assurance has increased over the years. The auditing profession turns to ensure the non-financial transactions and events of the clients. Future auditing is more likely to cover both financial and non-financial transactions and events, verifications, and reporting. Auditors are more likely to report more detailed information about significant matters audited in the auditing process to provide more information and increase the communicative value of audit reporting. Finally, future auditors will verify not only financial transactions and events but also non-financial transactions and events, and report in detail about identified significant matters, and the auditing process and procedures they performed.

10. CONCLUSION

The evolving landscape of auditing reflects the increasing demand for transparency and reliability in both financial and non-financial reporting. This chapter has highlighted the critical role of statutory audits in mitigating agency problems and ensuring the credibility of corporate disclosures. With growing emphasis on ESG factors, stakeholders now seek assurance beyond financial statements, necessitating new assurance standards and practices. One of the key developments in auditing is the introduction of KAMs reporting, aimed at enhancing the communicative value of audit reports. The comparative analysis of KAMs practices in common law (UK) and civil law (France, Germany, and Italy) environments underscores the disparities in audit reporting despite operating within a similar regional and economic context. The findings reveal that KAMs reporting is more prevalent in the UK than in civil law countries, suggesting variations in audit practices influenced by legal frameworks and investor protection mechanisms. The finding is based on only a comparison with the number of KAMs, and the results are robust across alternative models, variables, and sample specifications. Harmonizing international auditing practices remains a significant challenge in a globalized economy. IAASB and regulatory bodies continuously strive to standardize audit quality through revised auditing standards. However, differences in legal systems, regulatory oversight, and market structures create obstacles to achieving uniform audit practices. Furthermore, auditor competence and independence are critical determinants of audit quality. As auditing expands to include non-financial reporting assurance, auditors must develop expertise in evaluating ESG-related disclosures. Enhancing audit literacy, bridging the audit expectation gap, and refining auditing education is essential for strengthening audit credibility and stakeholder confidence. Looking ahead, the future of auditing is more likely to be shaped by advancements in technology, regulatory developments, and the increasing complexity of business operations. Ensuring high audit quality and standardization across jurisdictions will be pivotal in fostering trust and sustainability in global financial markets.

REFERENCES

Abbott, L. J., Parker, S., & Presley, T. J. (2012). Female board presence and the likelihood of financial restatement. *Accounting Horizons*, *26*(4), 607–629. DOI: 10.2308/acch-50249

Abughazaleh, N., O'Connell, V., & Princen, J. (2015). Audit quality, auditor size, and legal environments. *Quarterly Journal of Finance & Accounting*, 39-78.

Alderman, J. (2017). Does auditor gender influence auditor liability? Exploring the impact of the crime congruency effect on jurors' perceptions of auditor negligence. *Advances in Accounting*, *38*, 75–87. DOI: 10.1016/j.adiac.2017.07.006

Allee, K. D., & Yohn, T. L. (2009). The demand for financial statements in an unregulated environment: An examination of the production and use of financial statements by privately held small businesses. *The Accounting Review*, *84*(1), 1–25. DOI: 10.2308/accr.2009.84.1.1

Alsahali, K., Malagueño, R., & Marques, A. (2024). Board attributes and companies' choice of sustainability assurance providers. *Accounting and Business Research*, *54*(4), 392–422. DOI: 10.1080/00014788.2023.2181141

Antle, R., & Demski, J. S. (1991). Contracting frictions, regulation, and the structure of CPA firms. *Journal of Accounting Research*, *29*, 1–24. DOI: 10.2307/2491000

Antle, R., Gordon, E., Narayanamoorthy, G., & Zhou, L. (2006). The joint determination of audit fees, non-audit fees, and abnormal accruals. *Review of Quantitative Finance and Accounting*, *27*(3), 235–266. DOI: 10.1007/s11156-006-9430-y

Ball, R. (2009). Market and political/regulatory perspectives on the recent accounting scandals. *Journal of Accounting Research*, *47*(2), 277–323. DOI: 10.1111/j.1475-679X.2009.00325.x

Bell, T. B., Causholli, M., & Knechel, W. R. (2015). Audit firm tenure, non-audit services, and internal assessments of audit quality. *Journal of Accounting Research*, *53*(3), 461–509. DOI: 10.1111/1475-679X.12078

Berglund, N. R., Eshleman, J. D., & Guo, P. (2018). Auditor size and going concern reporting. *Auditing*, *37*(2), 1–25. DOI: 10.2308/ajpt-51786

Bloomfield, D., & Shackman, J. (2008). Non-audit service fees, auditor characteristics and earnings restatements. *Managerial Auditing Journal*, *23*(2), 125–141. DOI: 10.1108/02686900810839839

Bushman, R. M., & Smith, A. J. (2001). Financial accounting information and corporate governance. *Journal of Accounting and Economics*, *32*(1-3), 237–333. DOI: 10.1016/S0165-4101(01)00027-1

Callaghan, J., Parkash, M., & Singhal, R. (2009). Going-concern audit opinions and the provision of non-audit services: Implications for auditor independence of bankrupt firms. *Auditing*, *28*(1), 153–169. DOI: 10.2308/aud.2009.28.1.153

Carcello, J. V., Hermanson, D. R., & Ye, Z. (2011). Corporate governance research in accounting and auditing: Insights, practice implications, and future research directions. *Auditing*, *30*(3), 1–31. DOI: 10.2308/ajpt-10112

Castillo-Merino, D., Garcia-Blandon, J., & Martinez-Blasco, M. (2020). Auditor independence, current and future NAS fees, and audit quality: Were European regulators right? *European Accounting Review*, *29*(2), 233–262. DOI: 10.1080/09638180.2019.1577151

Chen, Y., Gul, F. A., Truong, C., & Veeraraghavan, M. (2016). Auditor client-specific knowledge and internal control weakness: Some evidence on the role of auditor tenure and geographic distance. *Journal of Contemporary Accounting & Economics*, *12*(2), 121–140. DOI: 10.1016/j.jcae.2016.03.001

Christensen, D. M., Serafeim, G., & Sikochi, A. (2022). Why is corporate virtue in the eye of the beholder? The case of ESG ratings. *The Accounting Review*, *97*(1), 147–175. DOI: 10.2308/TAR-2019-0506

Christensen, H. B., Hail, L., & Leuz, C. (2021). Mandatory CSR and sustainability reporting: Economic analysis and literature review. *Review of Accounting Studies*, *26*(3), 1176–1248. DOI: 10.1007/s11142-021-09609-5

Cosserat, G., & Rodda, N. (2009). *Modern auditing*. John Wiley & Sons.

DeAngelo, L. E. (1981a). Auditor independence, 'lowballing', and disclosure regulation. *Journal of Accounting and Economics*, *3*(2), 113–127. DOI: 10.1016/0165-4101(81)90009-4

DeAngelo, L. E. (1981b). Auditor size and audit quality. *Journal of Accounting and Economics*, *3*(3), 183–199. DOI: 10.1016/0165-4101(81)90002-1

DeFond, M., & Zhang, J. (2014). A review of archival auditing research. *Journal of Accounting and Economics*, *58*(2-3), 275–326. DOI: 10.1016/j.jacceco.2014.09.002

Dhaliwal, D. S., Li, O. Z., Tsang, A., & Yang, Y. G. (2011). Voluntary nonfinancial disclosure and the cost of equity capital: The initiation of corporate social responsibility reporting. *The Accounting Review*, *86*(1), 59–100. DOI: 10.2308/accr.00000005

Dhaliwal, D. S., Radhakrishnan, S., Tsang, A., & Yang, Y. G. (2012). Nonfinancial disclosure and analyst forecast accuracy: International evidence on corporate social responsibility disclosure. *The Accounting Review*, *87*(3), 723–759. DOI: 10.2308/accr-10218

Eccles, R. G., & Krzus, M. P. (2010). *One report: Integrated reporting for a sustainable strategy*. John Wiley & Sons.

Farooq, O., & Shehata, N. F. (2018). Does external auditing combat corruption? Evidence from private firms. *Managerial Auditing Journal*, *33*(3), 267–287. DOI: 10.1108/MAJ-08-2017-1634

Francis, J. R. (2004). What do we know about audit quality? *The British Accounting Review*, *36*(4), 345–368. DOI: 10.1016/j.bar.2004.09.003

Francis, J. R., Pinnuck, M. L., & Watanabe, O. (2014). Auditor style and financial statement comparability. *The Accounting Review*, *89*(2), 605–633. DOI: 10.2308/accr-50642

Geiger, M. A. (1994). Investor views of audit assurance: Recent evidence of the expectation gap. *Journal of Accountancy*, •••, 60.

Geiger, M. A., & Raghunandan, K. (2002). Auditor tenure and audit reporting failures. *Auditing*, *21*(1), 67–78. DOI: 10.2308/aud.2002.21.1.67

Geiger, M. A., & Rama, D. V. (2003). Audit fees, non-audit fees, and auditor reporting on stressed companies. *Auditing*, *22*(2), 53–69. DOI: 10.2308/aud.2003.22.2.53

Geiger, M. A., & Rama, D. V. (2006). Audit firm size and going-concern reporting accuracy. *Accounting horizons, 20*(1), 1-17.Abernathy, J. L., Barnes, M., Stefaniak, C., & Weisbarth, A. (2017). An international perspective on audit report lag: A synthesis of the literature and opportunities for future research. *International Journal of Auditing*, *21*(1), 100–127.

Glaum, M., Schmidt, P., Street, D. L., & Vogel, S. (2013). Compliance with IFRS 3 and IAS 36-required disclosures across 17 European countries: Company-and country-level determinants. *Accounting and Business Research*, *43*(3), 163–204. DOI: 10.1080/00014788.2012.711131

Gompers, P., Ishii, J., & Metrick, A. (2003). Corporate governance and equity prices. *The Quarterly Journal of Economics*, *118*(1), 107–156. DOI: 10.1162/00335530360535162

Gramling, A. A., Maletta, M. J., Schneider, A., & Church, B. K. (2004). The role of the internal audit function in corporate governance: A synthesis of the extant internal auditing literature and directions for future research. *Journal of Accounting Literature*, *23*, 194.

Grassmann, M., Fuhrmann, S., & Guenther, T. W. (2021). Assurance quality, disclosed connectivity of the capitals and information asymmetry–An interaction analysis for the case of integrated reporting. *Meditari Accountancy Research*, *30*(3), 852–892. DOI: 10.1108/MEDAR-11-2020-1087

Gul, F. A., Fung, S. Y. K., & Jaggi, B. (2009). Earnings quality: Some evidence on the role of auditor tenure and auditors' industry expertise. *Journal of Accounting and Economics*, *47*(3), 265–287. DOI: 10.1016/j.jacceco.2009.03.001

Gul, F. A., Jaggi, B. L., & Krishnan, G. V. (2007). Auditor independence: Evidence on the joint effects of auditor tenure and non-audit fees. *Auditing*, *26*(2), 117–142. DOI: 10.2308/aud.2007.26.2.117

Gul, F. A., Ma, S. M., & Lai, K. (2017). Busy auditors, partner-client tenure, and audit quality: Evidence from an emerging market. *Journal of International Accounting Research*, *16*(1), 83–105. DOI: 10.2308/jiar-51706

Gul, F. A., Tsui, J., & Dhaliwal, D. S. (2006). Non-audit services, auditor quality and the value relevance of earnings. *Accounting and Finance*, *46*(5), 797–817. DOI: 10.1111/j.1467-629X.2006.00189.x

Gul, F. A., Zhou, G. S., & Zhu, X. K. (2013). Investor protection, firm informational problems, Big N auditors, and cost of debt around the world. *Auditing*, *32*(3), 1–30. DOI: 10.2308/ajpt-50462

Habib, A., Bhuiyan, M. B. U., Huang, H. J., & Miah, M. S. (2019). Determinants of audit report lag: A meta-analysis. *International Journal of Auditing*, *23*(1), 20–44. DOI: 10.1111/ijau.12136

Hardies, K., Breesch, D., & Branson, J. (2016). Do (fe) male auditors impair audit quality? Evidence from going-concern opinions. *European Accounting Review*, *25*(1), 7–34. DOI: 10.1080/09638180.2014.921445

Harindahyani, S., & Agustia, D. (2023). The assurance providers' role in improving the independent assurance statement quality on sustainability reporting. *Accounting Research Journal*, *36*(1), 37–54. DOI: 10.1108/ARJ-01-2021-0024

Humphrey, C., Kausar, A., Loft, A., & Woods, M. (2011). Regulating audit beyond the crisis: A critical discussion of the EU Green Paper. *European Accounting Review*, *20*(3), 431–457. DOI: 10.1080/09638180.2011.597201

Humphrey, C., Moizer, P., & Turley, S. (2006). Independence and competence? A critical questioning of auditing. *Independent Accounts*, 149-167.

Ittonen, K., Vähämaa, E., & Vähämaa, S. (2013). Female auditors and accruals quality. *Accounting Horizons*, *27*(2), 205–228. DOI: 10.2308/acch-50400

Jensen, M. C., & Meckling, W. H. (1976). Theory of the firm: Managerial behavior, agency costs, and ownership structure. *Journal of Financial Economics*, *3*(4), 305–360. DOI: 10.1016/0304-405X(76)90026-X

Kinney, W. R.Jr, Palmrose, Z. V., & Scholz, S. (2004). Auditor independence, non-audit services, and restatements: Was the US government right? *Journal of Accounting Research*, *42*(3), 561–588. DOI: 10.1111/j.1475-679X.2004.t01-1-00141.x

Knechel, W. R., Krishnan, G. V., Pevzner, M., Shefchik, L. B., & Velury, U. K. (2013). Audit quality: Insights from the academic literature. *Auditing*, *32*(Supplement 1), 385–421. DOI: 10.2308/ajpt-50350

Knechel, W. R., Sharma, D. S., & Sharma, V. D. (2012). Non-audit services and knowledge spillovers: Evidence from New Zealand. *Journal of Business Finance & Accounting*, *39*(1-2), 60–81. DOI: 10.1111/j.1468-5957.2011.02268.x

Koh, K., Rajgopal, S., & Srinivasan, S. (2013). Non-audit services and financial reporting quality: Evidence from 1978 to 1980. *Review of Accounting Studies*, *18*(1), 1–33. DOI: 10.1007/s11142-012-9187-6

Leuz, C., & Wysocki, P. D. (2016). The economics of disclosure and financial reporting regulation: Evidence and suggestions for future research. *Journal of Accounting Research*, *54*(2), 525–622. DOI: 10.1111/1475-679X.12115

Leventis, S., Weetman, P., & Caramanis, C. (2005). Determinants of audit report lag: Some evidence from the Athens Stock Exchange. *International Journal of Auditing*, *9*(1), 45–58. DOI: 10.1111/j.1099-1123.2005.00101.x

Lisic, L. L., Myers, L. A., Pawlewicz, R., & Seidel, T. A. (2019). Do accounting firm consulting revenues affect audit quality? Evidence from the pre-and post-SOX eras. *Contemporary Accounting Research*, *36*(2), 1028–1054. DOI: 10.1111/1911-3846.12424

Lu, M., Simnett, R., & Zhou, S. (2023). Using the same provider for financial statement audit and assurance of extended external reports: Choices and consequences. *Auditing*, *42*(1), 125–154. DOI: 10.2308/AJPT-19-080

Marriott, N., & Marriott, P. (2000). Professional accountants and the development of a management accounting service for the small firm: Barriers and possibilities. *Management Accounting Research, 11*(4), 475–492. DOI: 10.1006/mare.2000.0142

Maso, L. D., Lobo, G. J., Mazzi, F., & Paugam, L. (2020). Implications of the joint provision of CSR assurance and financial audit for auditors' assessment of going-concern risk. *Contemporary Accounting Research, 37*(2), 1248–1289. DOI: 10.1111/1911-3846.12560

Owusu-Ansah, S., & Leventis, S. (2006). Timeliness of corporate annual financial reporting in Greece. *European Accounting Review, 15*(2), 273–287. DOI: 10.1080/09638180500252078

Paterson, J. S., & Valencia, A. (2011). The effects of recurring and nonrecurring tax, audit-related, and other non-audit services on auditor independence. *Contemporary Accounting Research, 28*(5), 1510–1536. DOI: 10.1111/j.1911-3846.2010.01060.x

Ratzinger-Sakel, N. V. (2013). Auditor fees and auditor independence—Evidence from going concern reporting decisions in Germany. *Auditing, 32*(4), 129–168. DOI: 10.2308/ajpt-50532

Regulation (EU) No 537/2014 of the European Parliament and of the Council of 16 April 2014 on specific requirements regarding statutory audit of public-interest entities and repealing Commission Decision 2005/909/EC (Text with EEA relevance). (n.d.). https://eur-lex.europa.eu/legal-content/EN/TXT/PDF/?uri=CELEX:32014R0537

Rodgers, W., & Housel, T. J. (2004). The effects of environmental risk information on auditors' decisions about prospective financial statements. *European Accounting Review, 13*(3), 523–540. DOI: 10.1080/0963818042000237160

Ruhnke, K., & Schmidt, M. (2014). The audit expectation gap: Existence, causes, and the impact of changes. *Accounting and Business Research, 44*(5), 572–601. DOI: 10.1080/00014788.2014.929519

Ruiz-Barbadillo, E., Gómez-Aguilar, N., De Fuentes-Barberá, C., & García-Benau, M. A. (2004). Audit quality and the going-concern decision-making process: Spanish evidence. *European Accounting Review, 13*(4), 597–620. DOI: 10.1080/0963818042000216820

Ruiz-Barbadillo, E., & Martínez-Ferrero, J. (2022). The choice of incumbent financial auditors to provide sustainability assurance and audit services from a legitimacy perspective. *Sustainability Accounting. Management and Policy Journal, 13*(2), 459–493.

Salehi, M., Lari Dasht Bayaz, M., Mohammadi, S., Adibian, M. S., & Fahimifard, S. H. (2020). Auditors' response to the readability of financial statement notes. *Asian Review of Accounting*, *28*(3), 463–480. DOI: 10.1108/ARA-03-2019-0066

Seetharaman, A., Sun, Y., & Wang, W. (2011). Tax-related financial statement restatements and auditor-provided tax services. *Journal of Accounting, Auditing & Finance*, *26*(4), 677–698. DOI: 10.1177/0148558X11409146

Sierra García, L., Bollas-Araya, H. M., & García Benau, M. A. (2022). Sustainable development goals and assurance of non-financial information reporting in Spain. *Sustainability Accounting. Management and Policy Journal*, *13*(4), 878–898.

Simnett, R., Vanstraelen, A., & Chua, W. F. (2009). Assurance on sustainability reports: An international comparison. *The Accounting Review*, *84*(3), 937–967. DOI: 10.2308/accr.2009.84.3.937

Soroushyar, A. (2023). Auditor characteristics and the financial reporting quality: The moderating role of the client business strategy. *Asian Journal of Accounting Research*, *8*(1), 27–40. DOI: 10.1108/AJAR-01-2022-0020

Svanström, T. (2013). Non-audit services and audit quality: Evidence from private firms. *European Accounting Review*, *22*(2), 337–366. DOI: 10.1080/09638180.2012.706398

Wahab, E. A. A., Gist, W. E., & Majid, W. Z. N. A. (2014). Characteristics of non-audit services and financial restatements in Malaysia. *Journal of Contemporary Accounting & Economics*, *10*(3), 225–247. DOI: 10.1016/j.jcae.2014.10.001

Wu, M. G. (2006). An economic analysis of audit and nonaudit services: The trade-off between competition crossovers and knowledge spillovers. *Contemporary Accounting Research*, *23*(2), 527–554. DOI: 10.1506/4DA7-D9YU-P9HQ-PX82

Ye, P., Carson, E., & Simnett, R. (2011). Threats to auditor independence: The impact of relationship and economic bonds. *Auditing*, *30*(1), 121–148. DOI: 10.2308/aud.2011.30.1.121

Zaman, R., Farooq, M. B., Khalid, F., & Mahmood, Z. (2021). Examining the extent of and determinants for sustainability assurance quality: The role of audit committees. *Business Strategy and the Environment*, *30*(7), 2887–2906. DOI: 10.1002/bse.2777

Zaman, R., Farooq, M. B., Khalid, F., & Mahmood, Z. (2021). Examining the extent of and determinants for sustainability assurance quality: The role of audit committees. *Business Strategy and the Environment*, *30*(7), 2887–2906. DOI: 10.1002/bse.2777

Zhou, S., Simnett, R., & Green, W. J. (2016). Assuring a new market: The interplay between country-level and company-level factors on the demand for greenhouse gas (GHG) information assurance and the choice of assurance provider. *Auditing*, *35*(3), 141–168. DOI: 10.2308/ajpt-51414

Chapter 11
The Role of Digital Currencies in Global Trade and Financial Reporting Standards

Simran Kaur
NIET Business School, Greater Noida, India

Malkeet Singh
https://orcid.org/0009-0008-7222-0391
Jan Nayak Ch. Devi Lal Vidyapeeth, India

Nikhil Singh
New Delhi Institute of Management, India

ABSTRACT

This study delves into the transformative role of digital currencies in reshaping global trade, financial systems, and regulatory frameworks. It investigates the integration of Central Bank Digital Currencies (CBDCs), cryptocurrencies, and stablecoins into the global economy, exploring their potential to streamline cross-border transactions, reduce costs, and enhance financial inclusion. Through case studies from China, El Salvador, and the European Union, the study examines the practical implications and challenges associated with the widespread adoption of digital currencies. The research also scrutinizes the regulatory complexities, including the need for international harmonization of legal standards to mitigate risks such as money laundering and fraud. Additionally, the study highlights the technological innovations inherent in blockchain and distributed ledger technologies (DLT), which promise to enhance transparency, security, and operational efficiency.

DOI: 10.4018/979-8-3373-0887-6.ch011

1. INTRODUCTION

The introduction of digital currencies has catalyzed a profound transformation in the global financial ecosystem, heralding a new era of innovation that stretches beyond traditional monetary frameworks. Digital currencies—ranging from decentralized cryptocurrencies to central bank digital currencies (CBDCs)—are poised to reshape not only the mechanics of global trade but also the very fabric of financial reporting and regulatory compliance (Kanojia et al., 2022a, 2022b; Khanna et al., 2023). These digital assets represent an intricate fusion of cutting-edge technology, decentralized finance (DeFi), and novel governance mechanisms that defy the conventions of traditional monetary systems.

Overview of Digital Currencies

At its core, digital currency refers to a form of currency that exists purely in digital form, without a tangible, physical counterpart. Unlike traditional fiat currencies, which are issued and controlled by a central authority, digital currencies leverage distributed ledger technologies, such as blockchain, to enable secure, transparent, and decentralized transactions. Digital currencies can be broadly classified into three categories: cryptocurrencies, central bank digital currencies (CBDCs), and stablecoins (Upreti & Malhotra, 2024). Cryptocurrencies like Bitcoin, Ethereum, and Binance Coin operate on decentralized networks and rely on the principles of cryptography and consensus algorithms to verify and secure transactions. These currencies exist outside the purview of traditional financial institutions, offering users an unprecedented degree of autonomy (Kaur et al., 2024; R. Kumar, Khannna Malholtra, & Grover, 2023).

In contrast, CBDCs represent digital versions of national currencies issued and regulated by central banks. Unlike cryptocurrencies, CBDCs retain the backing and control of the state, offering a stable and government-sanctioned alternative for digital transactions. Stablecoins, on the other hand, are designed to mitigate the volatility inherent in cryptocurrencies by being pegged to traditional assets, such as the US dollar or gold, thus offering a more stable unit of value (R. Kumar, Lande, Kumar, et al., 2023). While cryptocurrencies exemplify the decentralized ethos of digital finance, CBDCs and stablecoins aim to bridge the gap between innovation and regulatory oversight, ensuring compatibility with existing financial systems (Mary Joshitta et al., 2023).

Importance of Digital Currencies in the Global Economy

The burgeoning role of digital currencies in the global economy cannot be overstated. As financial transactions become increasingly digitized, digital currencies offer significant advantages over traditional methods of payment, particularly in the context of cross-border transactions. The global remittance market, for instance, has long been plagued by inefficiencies—high fees, delays, and intermediary bottlenecks (R. Kumar, Malholtra, Singh, et al., 2023). By eliminating the need for intermediaries such as banks, digital currencies enable instant, low-cost transactions across borders. This frictionless exchange of value enhances global trade, allowing businesses to circumvent the high costs associated with currency conversion, settlement delays, and the geopolitical risks of cross-border payments (R. Kumar & Khanna, 2023a; Neha et al., 2023; P. Sharma et al., 2022).

The proliferation of digital currencies also democratizes access to the global financial system. With the advent of digital wallets and peer-to-peer networks, individuals and businesses in underbanked regions can participate in the global economy without relying on traditional banking infrastructure (R. Kumar et al., 2024; R. Kumar, Kathuria, Malholtra, et al., 2023). This shift toward financial inclusion is particularly evident in emerging markets, where large segments of the population remain unbanked or underbanked, thus hindering their ability to participate in international trade. Digital currencies, through their decentralized nature, mitigate these barriers, granting access to financial services for millions previously excluded from the global economic system (Cavaliere et al., 2024; R. Kumar, Malhotra, Pandey, et al., 2023).

Furthermore, the growing acceptance of digital currencies as an asset class is creating new investment opportunities and avenues for wealth creation. Institutional investors, large corporations, and even governments are now recognizing the potential of blockchain and cryptocurrency technologies (R. Kumar, Malhotra, & Grover, 2023; R. Kumar, Singh, Mohanty, et al., 2023). These digital assets are not only being used as a medium of exchange but also as speculative investments and stores of value. The widespread institutional adoption of digital currencies signifies their growing legitimacy in the broader financial ecosystem, prompting central banks and financial regulators to develop frameworks that accommodate these novel assets.

Significance of Financial Reporting Standards in the Digital Age

The rapid proliferation of digital currencies brings to the forefront an urgent need for the modernization and harmonization of financial reporting standards. Traditional financial reporting frameworks, such as the International Financial Reporting Standards (IFRS) and Generally Accepted Accounting Principles (GAAP), were primarily designed for the conventional financial assets and liabilities that dominate the legacy financial system. These standards are not equipped to address the complexities introduced by digital currencies, such as their volatility, the decentralized nature of transactions, and the regulatory ambiguities that accompany them (R. Kumar & Khanna, 2023b).

In particular, digital currencies challenge existing accounting and auditing practices. The decentralized nature of cryptocurrencies means that they are not subject to central control, and their value can fluctuate dramatically, complicating the process of valuation. Conventional valuation methods such as historical cost accounting **or** fair value accounting may not be suitable for digital assets, as they fail to capture the volatility and market dynamics inherent in cryptocurrencies. As a result, organizations that hold significant amounts of digital currencies must adapt their financial reporting practices to ensure they provide a true and fair view of their financial position (Ahmad et al., 2023; Širić et al., 2022).

Additionally, the integration of digital currencies into financial reporting requires a reassessment of how transactions are recognized and reported. Digital currencies, particularly those used for international trade or investment purposes, are often subject to different legal and tax treatments across jurisdictions (N. K. Singh, Singh, Rahim, et al., 2023). The use of distributed ledger technology (DLT), which underpins many digital currencies, complicates the reconciliation of transactions, requiring new methodologies to verify and audit digital currency exchanges. The lack of clarity surrounding the regulatory treatment of digital currencies, especially in cross-border contexts, poses challenges for multinational corporations that must adhere to varying legal standards in different jurisdictions (Hajoary et al., 2023).

As digital currencies continue to gain prominence, regulatory bodies and standard-setting organizations, such as the Financial Accounting Standards Board (FASB), International Accounting Standards Board (IASB), and the International Monetary Fund (IMF), are working to develop frameworks and guidelines that address the unique challenges posed by these assets (Kaliappan et al., 2023). These standards must balance the need for financial transparency and investor protection with the imperatives of fostering innovation and maintaining the stability of the global financial system.

The rise of digital currencies necessitates the creation of agile financial reporting standards that can adapt to the dynamic and rapidly evolving nature of digital finance. These standards must ensure that digital currency transactions are accurately recorded, valued, and reported, providing stakeholders with a reliable basis for decision-making (Arora et al., 2023; K. D. Singh, Deep Singh, Bansal, et al., 2023; Sunori et al., 2023). As such, the intersection of digital currencies and financial reporting standards will remain a critical area of focus for regulators, businesses, and financial professionals alike, as they navigate the complexities of an increasingly digitized global economy (Gonfa et al., 2023; Raman, Kumar, et al., 2023).

In conclusion, digital currencies are reshaping the landscape of global trade and financial reporting standards. Their disruptive potential is evident across numerous domains, from enhancing financial inclusion and reducing transaction costs in global trade to challenging the conventions of financial accounting and auditing. As these digital assets continue to evolve, it is essential that financial reporting standards evolve in tandem, ensuring transparency, consistency, and adaptability in the face of unprecedented technological innovation.

Purpose of the Study

The primary purpose of this study is to explore the transformative impact of digital currencies on global trade and finance, with a particular focus on the integration of digital currencies into financial systems and the implications for financial reporting standards. The study aims to examine the various types of digital currencies, including Central Bank Digital Currencies (CBDCs), cryptocurrencies, and stablecoins, and their potential to reshape traditional financial structures. Additionally, the study seeks to analyze the challenges posed by digital currencies, such as regulatory gaps, price volatility, and technological barriers, and to propose solutions for addressing these challenges through harmonized global regulatory frameworks.

The research also investigates the potential benefits of digital currencies, including enhanced cross-border transactions, reduced transaction costs, and increased financial inclusion. By examining case studies from various regions, the study aims to provide a comprehensive understanding of how digital currencies are being integrated into global trade, the opportunities they present, and the hurdles they need to overcome. Ultimately, the study seeks to provide valuable insights that can guide policymakers, regulators, and financial institutions in adapting to the evolving landscape of digital currencies.

Research Methodology

This study employs a qualitative research methodology, using a combination of literature review, case study analysis, and expert interviews to collect data and derive insights. The literature review draws from academic journals, industry reports, regulatory documents, and other credible sources to establish a theoretical framework for understanding digital currencies and their integration into global trade and finance.

Case study analysis is a key component of the research, with in-depth examinations of real-world examples such as China's Digital Yuan, El Salvador's adoption of Bitcoin as legal tender, and the European Central Bank's exploration of a digital

Euro. These case studies are analyzed to identify trends, challenges, and outcomes of digital currency implementation in different geopolitical contexts.

Expert interviews with financial analysts, regulators, and blockchain technology experts provide further qualitative insights into the regulatory, technological, and economic dimensions of digital currencies. The study synthesizes these various data sources to draw conclusions and offer recommendations for future research and policy development.

2. DIGITAL CURRENCIES AND THEIR IMPACT ON GLOBAL TRADE

The emergence of digital currencies has ushered in a transformative era in global trade, profoundly altering the mechanisms of cross-border transactions, payment systems, and financial inclusion (Pandey et al., 2023). As an innovative byproduct of advancements in blockchain technology, digital currencies—ranging from decentralized cryptocurrencies like Bitcoin to government-backed central bank digital currencies (CBDCs)—offer unparalleled opportunities to enhance the efficiency, transparency, and inclusivity of global trade. Their widespread adoption has the potential to reduce transaction costs, eliminate barriers to entry, and extend the reach of financial services to previously underserved populations (Upreti et al., 2023).

Cross-Border Transactions and Payment Systems

Historically, international trade has been fraught with inefficiencies, with traditional payment systems acting as significant bottlenecks. The reliance on centralized banking systems, intermediary financial institutions, and legacy payment networks—such as SWIFT—has resulted in cumbersome processes, prolonged settlement times, and high fees, especially for cross-border transactions. These delays and costs are particularly burdensome for small and medium-sized enterprises (SMEs) operating in emerging markets, which often struggle to access affordable financial services for international trade (V. Kumar, Sharma, Mittal, et al., 2023).

Digital currencies, particularly cryptocurrencies and CBDCs, present an opportunity to revolutionize this landscape. By leveraging decentralized networks and distributed ledger technologies, digital currencies enable peer-to-peer transactions that bypass traditional intermediaries. This direct transaction model significantly reduces the need for correspondent banks, foreign exchange providers, and other intermediaries, effectively lowering transaction costs and enhancing the speed of payments. With digital currencies, payments can be executed almost instantaneously, regardless of geographic location, which is a considerable improvement over the days—or even weeks—required by conventional banking systems for international money transfers (Belwal et al., 2023).

A notable example of this is the Ripple Network (XRP), which provides a real-time gross settlement system, currency exchange, and remittance network that facilitates quick and low-cost cross-border payments. Ripple's platform offers a robust alternative to traditional payment systems by enabling instant transactions with reduced fees, thereby empowering businesses engaged in international trade to streamline their payment processes. Moreover, the integration of central bank digital currencies (CBDCs) in cross-border payment systems is gaining traction globally, as evidenced by collaborative initiatives such as the Jamaica-CBDC Project, which aims to simplify cross-border transactions and increase financial interoperability among Caribbean nations (S. Bansal et al., 2023).

As countries and financial institutions continue to explore and implement these technologies, digital currencies hold the promise of reshaping the very infrastructure that underpins global trade, ensuring more efficient, transparent, and secure transactions.

Reducing Transaction Costs and Barriers to Entry

One of the most compelling advantages of digital currencies is their potential to significantly reduce transaction costs, particularly in global trade. Traditional cross-border payment systems often incur high fees due to the involvement of multiple intermediaries, including banks, foreign exchange providers, and clearinghouses. These intermediaries typically charge hefty fees for their services, creating an additional financial burden for businesses, especially those engaged in small-scale international trade (V. Kumar & Korovin, 2023).

The decentralized nature of digital currencies mitigates these costs by removing intermediaries from the transaction process. By using blockchain-based payment systems, such as Bitcoin or Ethereum, businesses can send and receive payments directly, without the need for a central authority to process the transaction. This eliminates transaction fees associated with banks, clearinghouses, and foreign exchange services, making it possible to execute payments at a fraction of the cost of traditional systems (R. Kumar & Khanna, 2023b).

Furthermore, the ability to engage in borderless transactions without the need for currency conversion opens up significant opportunities for international trade. Small businesses that previously faced high costs for converting currencies or dealing with fluctuating exchange rates can now transact in digital currencies, thus bypassing traditional forex markets. The stability offered by stablecoins—digital currencies pegged to traditional assets such as the US dollar—further alleviates concerns related to volatility, offering a more predictable medium of exchange in the global marketplace (Abdullah et al., 2023; S. Sharma et al., 2023; S. Sharma & Bhadula, 2023).

For businesses in developing countries, digital currencies offer an especially compelling solution to financial barriers. Many of these businesses face significant challenges in accessing traditional financial systems, such as the inability to open foreign currency accounts or navigate complex regulatory environments. By adopting digital currencies, they gain direct access to a global network of trade, reducing the barriers to entry and expanding their ability to participate in international markets. This is particularly important for SMEs in emerging economies that often lack the capital or infrastructure to engage with conventional banking systems (Joshi et al., 2022; Sahu & Rawat, 2023; Sonnad et al., 2022).

Enhancing Financial Inclusion through Digital Currencies

In addition to reducing transaction costs and barriers to entry, digital currencies have the potential to revolutionize financial inclusion on a global scale. For millions of individuals and businesses in underbanked or unbanked regions, access to financial services has remained elusive due to the lack of physical banking infrastructure and prohibitive costs associated with traditional financial systems. Digital currencies, however, present a paradigm shift by offering low-cost, accessible alternatives to traditional banking services (K. D. Singh, Singh, Kaur, et al., 2023).

One of the primary advantages of digital currencies in enhancing financial inclusion is their ability to function without the need for intermediaries or centralized institutions. Through the use of mobile phones and digital wallets, individuals in even the most remote and underserved areas can gain access to financial services, such as making payments, receiving remittances, and participating in global commerce. For instance, Bitcoin and Ethereum provide individuals in countries with unstable or underdeveloped financial systems the ability to store and transfer value securely, circumventing the need for banks or physical money exchanges. The decentralized nature of these currencies offers an unprecedented level of autonomy, empowering users to manage their financial affairs without relying on traditional financial institutions that may be inaccessible or untrustworthy (Alzaidi et al., 2022; A. Gupta et al., 2022; Rajbalaji et al., 2023).

Moreover, central banks in various countries are exploring the issuance of CBDCs as a means of expanding financial access. These state-backed digital currencies have the potential to provide individuals in rural or economically marginalized regions with access to digital wallets and payment systems. **The** e-Krona pilot program in Sweden and the Digital Yuan in China are exemplary models of how CBDCs can enhance financial inclusion by integrating unbanked populations into the digital economy. In particular, CBDCs can serve as an important tool for social welfare distribution, allowing governments to disburse benefits directly to citizens via digital currencies, eliminating the need for physical distribution systems or expensive third-party payment providers (P. Gupta et al., 2023; Kamra et al., 2023; Ram et al., 2022).

In addition, digital currencies facilitate cross-border remittances, which are vital to the economies of many developing nations. The remittance industry, which is valued in the billions of dollars annually, has traditionally been dominated by a few large players such as Western Union, which charge exorbitant fees for money transfers. Digital currencies, however, enable instantaneous and low-cost remittance payments, benefiting millions of migrant workers who send money back to their families. For instance, the use of stablecoins like **USDC** has made it possible for families in countries such as the Philippines, India, and Mexico to receive international remittances with far lower fees and faster processing times than traditional systems offer (Agarwal & Sharma, 2023; M. Sharma, Kumar, et al., 2022; Wazid et al., 2021).

Hence, digital currencies are poised to have a transformative impact on global trade, cross-border transactions, and financial inclusion. By eliminating intermediaries, reducing transaction costs, and providing an accessible means for underserved populations to engage in the global economy, digital currencies present an unprecedented opportunity to democratize finance and enable more efficient, inclusive, and equitable global trade systems. As adoption continues to grow, the ongoing evolution of digital currency technologies will undoubtedly redefine the way the world conducts business and interacts economically across borders (Bhatt & Ghuman, 2022; N. M. Kumar, Islam, Podder, et al., 2023; Rana, Dixit, et al., 2022).

3. CENTRAL BANK DIGITAL CURRENCIES (CBDCS) AND GOVERNMENT-BACKED DIGITAL ASSETS

Central Bank Digital Currencies (CBDCs) represent a paradigm shift in the world of digital finance, blending the innovation of cryptocurrencies with the regulatory oversight and stability of central banking systems. These government-backed digital assets are issued and controlled by central banks and are designed to function as legal tender in digital form, offering a secure and regulated alternative to private cryptocurrencies like Bitcoin and Ethereum. CBDCs are poised to reshape the global monetary system by enhancing payment efficiency, improving financial inclusion, and redefining the role of central banks in the digital age (Mehershilpa et al., 2023).

The Rise of CBDCs: Objectives and Motivations

The emergence of CBDCs can be attributed to a confluence of economic, technological, and geopolitical factors. Central banks worldwide are exploring the potential of these digital currencies in response to the growing prominence of private cryptocurrencies, the increasing digitization of financial services, and the need to modernize national monetary systems. CBDCs are viewed as a mechanism to maintain the centrality of state-issued currencies in an increasingly digitized financial landscape, counteracting the risks posed by decentralized cryptocurrencies that operate outside the realm of regulatory oversight (Rawat et al., 2023).

One of the primary objectives behind the issuance of CBDCs is to enhance payment efficiency. Traditional payment systems, especially in cross-border transactions, are often encumbered by high fees, slow settlement times, and a reliance on intermediary banks. CBDCs can streamline these processes, enabling faster, more secure, and cost-effective transactions. For instance, CBDCs leverage blockchain or similar distributed ledger technologies (DLT) to facilitate instantaneous transactions, reducing the need for multiple intermediaries and enhancing the overall efficiency of payment systems (K. Kumar et al., 2022).

Additionally, CBDCs are seen as a tool for financial inclusion. A significant portion of the global population remains unbanked or underbanked, particularly in developing countries. By offering digital currencies that are directly issued by central banks, CBDCs can provide individuals with access to financial services, even in areas with limited or no access to traditional banking infrastructure. Moreover, CBDCs offer the potential for more equitable access to economic opportunities, enabling users to store, transfer, and invest in digital currencies with minimal barriers to entry (Jena & Gairola, 2022).

Finally, the motivation for issuing CBDCs is rooted in national security and economic stability. Central banks are increasingly concerned about the destabilizing effects of privately issued cryptocurrencies, which can be highly volatile and may circumvent government control over monetary policy. CBDCs allow central banks to retain control over the money supply, interest rates, and inflation, all while ensuring the stability of the national economy. Furthermore, CBDCs offer governments greater control over financial transactions, which can help in the fight against illicit activities, money laundering, and tax evasion (Praveenchandar et al., 2022).

National and Global Implications of CBDCs

The advent of CBDCs holds profound implications not only at the national level but also globally. Domestically, the introduction of CBDCs would significantly alter the landscape of monetary policy and the role of central banks. For example, the ability of central banks to directly monitor and control digital currency transactions would enhance their capacity to implement monetary policy, such as adjusting interest rates or managing inflation, more efficiently. The introduction of a CBDC could also mitigate risks associated with traditional financial systems, such as systemic crises or bank runs, by offering a government-backed digital alternative to physical cash (E. Sharma et al., 2023).

On a global scale, CBDCs have the potential to redefine the dynamics of cross-border trade and international finance. By facilitating faster, cheaper, and more secure cross-border transactions, CBDCs could reduce the reliance on traditional payment systems like SWIFT, which are often slow and expensive, especially for emerging markets. In this context, CBDCs may act as a catalyst for greater financial integration and cooperation among nations, allowing for the smoother exchange of goods and services (Tyagi et al., 2022).

However, the global implementation of CBDCs also raises several challenges. One of the primary concerns is the potential for jurisdictional conflicts and regulatory complexities. As countries pursue the development of their own CBDCs, the lack of a global consensus on standards and regulations could result in fragmented systems that hinder international cooperation and create barriers to cross-border transactions (Medhi et al., 2023; Pant et al., 2022). Additionally, the introduction of CBDCs could prompt nations to reconsider the role of the US dollar as the global reserve currency, especially if countries begin to adopt CBDCs with significant backing or competitive advantages in global trade.

Case Studies of CBDC Implementation (China, European Union, etc.)

The implementation of CBDCs is still in its nascent stages, but several countries have already made significant strides in exploring and testing these digital currencies. Among the most notable examples are China's Digital Yuan (e-CNY) and the Digital Euro initiative by the European Central Bank (ECB) (A. S. Kumar & Desi, 2023; K. S. Kumar et al., 2022; Sathyapriya et al., 2022).

China has been a global leader in the development of CBDCs, launching pilot programs for its Digital Yuan in multiple cities. The e-CNY is designed to complement cash in circulation, offering a digital alternative for consumers and businesses while maintaining the government's control over monetary policy. The key objectives behind the e-CNY include improving the efficiency of payment systems, enhancing financial inclusion, and reducing the reliance on the US dollar in cross-border trade. As of 2024, the e-CNY is being tested in various scenarios, from retail payments to cross-border transactions. The Chinese government has also integrated the Digital Yuan into its Belt and Road Initiative (BRI), seeking to leverage it to facilitate trade and investment with other countries participating in the initiative. However, concerns about privacy and government surveillance have emerged, as the digital yuan allows for the tracking and monitoring of all transactions made with the currency (Pai et al., 2022; Shah et al., 2023).

In the European Union, the ECB has initiated a project called the Digital Euro, which aims to explore the potential of a CBDC for the Eurozone. The Digital Euro would be designed to coexist with cash, providing consumers with a secure, efficient, and accessible form of digital payment. Unlike the Digital Yuan, the European approach to CBDCs is focused on ensuring that the privacy and rights of users are protected, with an emphasis on transparency and financial security. The European Union also envisions the Digital Euro as a tool to enhance cross-border trade within the Eurozone and provide a European alternative to the US dollar and other foreign digital currencies (N. K. Singh, Singh, Singh, et al., 2023; Unhelkar et al., 2022).

Other countries, such as Sweden and the Bahamas, have also begun testing their own versions of CBDCs. Sweden's e-Krona project, for instance, seeks to create a digital currency that will be integrated into the country's well-established digital payment infrastructure. In the Bahamas, the Sand Dollar is already in circulation, representing the world's first fully deployed digital currency issued by a central bank (Jayadeva et al., 2023; Raman, Buddhi, et al., 2023).

While these case studies highlight the potential benefits of CBDCs—such as enhancing payment efficiency, fostering financial inclusion, and reducing dependence on foreign currencies—they also underscore the challenges associated with their implementation. Issues related to privacy, security, and regulatory alignment remain at the forefront of CBDC development, and it will take continued innovation and international collaboration to ensure that CBDCs can coexist harmoniously within the global financial ecosystem (Kohli et al., 2022; Pandya et al., 2023).

In summary the rise of Central Bank Digital Currencies is a defining feature of the ongoing transformation of global finance. CBDCs hold the potential to revolutionize the monetary systems of individual nations while fostering greater international economic integration. However, their widespread adoption will require careful management of regulatory, technical, and geopolitical challenges to ensure that they fulfill their promise of a secure, efficient, and inclusive financial future.

4. CRYPTOCURRENCIES AND THEIR ROLE IN MODERN TRADE AND FINANCE

Cryptocurrencies, particularly Bitcoin, Ethereum, and a growing array of altcoins, have emerged as a transformative force in modern trade and finance. These decentralized digital currencies leverage blockchain technology to facilitate peer-to-peer transactions, eliminating the need for traditional intermediaries like banks and financial institutions. As a global phenomenon, cryptocurrencies are not only reshaping how individuals and businesses conduct transactions, but they are also altering the very fabric of financial markets, investment strategies, and traditional financial systems.

Bitcoin, Ethereum, and Other Cryptocurrencies: A Global Phenomenon

Bitcoin, the first and most prominent cryptocurrency, has become a symbol of the potential for decentralization in the financial sector. Created in 2009 by the pseudonymous figure Satoshi Nakamoto, Bitcoin introduced the concept of a peer-to-peer digital currency that operates outside the control of central banks and governments (Dhiman & Nagar, 2022; Rajeswari et al., 2022; Salama et al., 2023). Its decentralized nature is powered by blockchain technology, a distributed ledger that ensures the transparency and security of transactions. Bitcoin's rise to prominence has led to its recognition as both a store of value and a medium of exchange, albeit with significant volatility.

Ethereum, launched in 2015 by Vitalik Buterin and others, expanded upon Bitcoin's original concept by enabling smart contracts—self-executing contracts with the terms of the agreement directly written into code. Ethereum's ability to support decentralized applications (dApps) has positioned it as the backbone of the decentralized finance (DeFi) ecosystem, which has rapidly grown in popularity since its inception. Ethereum's native cryptocurrency, Ether (ETH), is used not only as a medium of exchange but also to power these decentralized applications and smart contracts.

Beyond Bitcoin and Ethereum, the cryptocurrency market has seen the emergence of thousands of alternative cryptocurrencies, or "altcoins," each with unique use cases and technological innovations. Some, like Binance Coin (BNB), Cardano (ADA), and Solana (SOL), aim to enhance scalability, transaction speed, and security, while others, such as Polkadot (DOT) and Chainlink (LINK), seek to improve interoperability between different blockchains. Collectively, these cryptocurrencies have created a diverse and dynamic market that has attracted both retail and institutional investors, establishing crypto assets as a legitimate asset class in modern finance.

The Volatility and Investment Potential of Cryptocurrencies

Despite their transformative potential, cryptocurrencies are inherently volatile, with prices subject to dramatic fluctuations over short periods. This volatility, while presenting substantial risks, also creates significant opportunities for investors (K.

D. Singh, Singh, Chhabra, et al., 2023; Tyagi et al., 2023). The speculative nature of cryptocurrency markets, fueled by market sentiment, regulatory developments, and technological advancements, leads to wild price swings that can result in outsized returns or devastating losses.

Bitcoin's early trajectory exemplifies this volatility. For instance, Bitcoin's price surged from mere cents in 2010 to an all-time high of nearly $69,000 in 2021, only to experience significant corrections. Similarly, Ethereum has witnessed similar volatility, with its price seeing considerable ups and downs, particularly during periods of heightened demand for DeFi applications and NFTs (Non-Fungible Tokens), which are primarily powered by Ethereum's blockchain.

This volatility, however, has not deterred investors. Cryptocurrencies offer unique investment opportunities, often characterized by high risk but also high reward. As a result, many investors view digital assets as a hedge against inflation and currency devaluation, particularly in countries with unstable fiat currencies. Bitcoin, in particular, has been dubbed "digital gold" for its ability to retain value in times of economic uncertainty, with proponents arguing that its fixed supply—21 million coins—ensures it cannot be inflated like traditional currencies (Mandalapu et al., 2023; Pande et al., 2023).

Institutional interest in cryptocurrencies has also surged in recent years, with large corporations, hedge funds, and even sovereign wealth funds allocating portions of their portfolios to digital assets. The growing recognition of cryptocurrencies as an asset class, along with the development of financial products such as Bitcoin futures contracts, exchange-traded funds (ETFs), and crypto-based bonds, has contributed to their increasing legitimacy in traditional investment circles (A. Das Gupta et al., 2022; S. Sharma et al., 2020; K. D. Singh et al., 2022).

However, the regulatory environment surrounding cryptocurrencies remains in flux. Governments and financial regulators around the world are grappling with how to classify, regulate, and tax digital assets. While some countries, such as El Salvador, have embraced cryptocurrencies by adopting them as legal tender, others, like China, have imposed outright bans. This regulatory uncertainty continues to influence the investment landscape, as investors seek clarity on how governments will approach the cryptocurrency market in the future.

Decentralized Finance (DeFi) and Its Influence on Traditional Finance

One of the most profound innovations to emerge from the cryptocurrency space is Decentralized Finance (DeFi), a movement that seeks to replicate and improve upon traditional financial services using blockchain technology and smart contracts. DeFi applications aim to provide users with decentralized alternatives to banking services, such as lending, borrowing, trading, and insurance, without relying on centralized financial institutions (Gopal et al., 2023; Josphineleela et al., 2023).

At the heart of DeFi is the principle of trustless transactions, where users can engage in financial activities directly with one another via smart contracts, which are self-executing agreements coded into the blockchain. This eliminates the need for intermediaries such as banks or credit institutions, thus reducing fees, enhancing transparency, and increasing financial accessibility. DeFi platforms, such as Uniswap for decentralized exchanges, **Aave** for decentralized lending, and MakerDAO for decentralized stablecoins, have rapidly gained traction, attracting billions of dollars in assets (Ram & Xing, 2023).

The rise of DeFi has profound implications for traditional finance. By providing an alternative to conventional banking and financial systems, DeFi challenges the status quo by democratizing access to financial services and giving individuals greater control over their assets. For instance, DeFi allows individuals to earn interest on their crypto holdings, borrow assets against their crypto collateral, or trade assets without the need for a central clearinghouse. In doing so, DeFi has the potential to disrupt entire sectors of the financial industry, including lending, asset management, insurance, and payments (Bisht et al., 2022; Gusain et al., 2023).

Furthermore, DeFi is fostering financial inclusion by enabling individuals in underserved regions to access financial services. Many people in developing countries lack access to traditional banking systems due to geographic or economic barriers. DeFi platforms, however, allow anyone with an internet connection to participate in the global economy, providing them with opportunities to earn, invest, and borrow without needing a traditional bank account.

However, DeFi is not without its challenges. The lack of regulation in the DeFi space exposes users to risks such as fraud, hacks, and smart contract vulnerabilities. Additionally, the high volatility of cryptocurrencies means that users' investments and collateral can fluctuate wildly in value, introducing significant risks for borrowers and lenders alike. As the DeFi space continues to grow, regulators are increasingly focusing on how to establish a framework that balances innovation with consumer protection (Akberdina et al., 2023; K. Kumar, Chaudhary, Anandaram, et al., 2023; M. Sharma, Luthra, et al., 2022).

Crypto-currencies, particularly Bitcoin, Ethereum, and their derivatives, have solidified their position as a global phenomenon that is reshaping modern trade and finance. While the inherent volatility and regulatory uncertainty present challenges, the growing adoption of cryptocurrencies as investment vehicles, coupled with the rise of DeFi, demonstrates their transformative potential (Eswar et al., 2023; Sathyaseelan et al., 2023). As thc landscape evolves, cryptocurrencies are poised to continue influencing the broader financial ecosystem, offering new opportunities for decentralized, borderless finance while simultaneously posing challenges to traditional financial institutions (Joshi et al., 2023; K. D. Singh, Singh, Chhabra, et al., 2023; Venkatesh et al., 2023).

5. STABLECOINS: BRIDGING THE GAP BETWEEN VOLATILITY AND STABILITY

Stablecoins have emerged as a critical innovation within the cryptocurrency ecosystem, offering a novel solution to one of the most significant challenges faced by digital assets: volatility. Unlike traditional cryptocurrencies such as Bitcoin or Ethereum, which are subject to wild price fluctuations, stablecoins are designed to maintain a stable value by being pegged to an underlying asset, typically a fiat currency such as the US dollar, or commodities like gold (Lade et al., 2023; Rajawat et al., 2022; Tiwari et al., 2023). This stability has made them a popular choice for a wide range of use cases, from facilitating everyday transactions to serving as a bridge between traditional and decentralized finance . However, despite their advantages, the rise of stablecoins has also raised important questions regarding regulatory oversight and the legal implications of their widespread use.

The Concept of Stablecoins and Their Use Cases

A stablecoin is a type of cryptocurrency whose value is pegged to a reserve asset, providing it with a much more predictable value compared to volatile cryptocurrencies. The most common form of stablecoins is fiat-collateralized stablecoins, which are backed by a one-to-one reserve of fiat currency such as the US dollar. Other types of stablecoins include **crypto-collateralized stablecoins**, backed by other cryptocurrencies, and **algorithmic stablecoins**, which use algorithms and smart contracts to control supply and demand and maintain price stability.

Stablecoins have found a wide array of applications across the financial landscape. One of the most prominent use cases is in **cross-border transactions**. Traditional international money transfers can be slow, expensive, and fraught with complications due to intermediaries and varying exchange rates (Ahmad et al., 2023; Komkowski et al., 2023a). Stablecoins, on the other hand, allow for near-instantaneous, low-cost transfers across borders, bypassing the need for traditional financial institutions. This makes stablecoins particularly attractive in regions with unstable local currencies or economies facing high inflation.

Another key use case for stablecoins is in the **decentralized finance (DeFi)** ecosystem. DeFi platforms allow users to lend, borrow, and trade digital assets without the need for traditional financial intermediaries. Stablecoins like **Tether (USDT)** and **USD Coin (USDC)** are frequently used in DeFi applications due to their stability, providing users with a reliable store of value while avoiding the volatility typically associated with cryptocurrencies. Additionally, stablecoins facilitate decentralized lending and yield farming, where users earn interest by lending their stablecoins to others or by staking them in liquidity pools.

Stablecoins are also increasingly used as a **medium of exchange** for everyday purchases, offering a more stable alternative to volatile cryptocurrencies. Retailers and businesses that accept digital currencies as payment often prefer stablecoins, as they do not risk facing significant value fluctuations during the course of a transaction. Furthermore, stablecoins have become a vital tool for **hedging** against inflation and economic instability, particularly in countries with high levels of currency devaluation (Caiado et al., 2023; Chahar et al., 2022; S. Sharma & Bhadula, 2023).

Regulatory Oversight and Legal Considerations of Stablecoins

Despite their practical advantages, stablecoins present a host of regulatory and legal challenges. Due to their potential to impact traditional financial systems and the broader economy, stablecoins have become a focal point of attention for governments and regulatory bodies worldwide. The primary concern surrounding stablecoins is whether they could pose a risk to **financial stability** if not properly managed or regulated. Since many stablecoins are issued by private entities rather than central banks, their value and supply could potentially be manipulated or subject to market forces that create instability (Davuluri et al., 2023).

In many jurisdictions, stablecoins are not yet subject to the same regulatory frameworks as traditional currencies or financial products. This regulatory gap has led to concerns about **consumer protection** and **anti-money laundering (AML)** measures. Stablecoin issuers are often not required to maintain transparent reserves, which raises questions about the legitimacy of their claims of backing (Maurya et al., 2022; Mishra et al., 2021; Ram & Xing, 2023). For instance, if the issuer of a stablecoin does not maintain the necessary reserves or fails to accurately report their financial status, users could face a sudden collapse in the value of their holdings.

In response to these concerns, regulators have started to develop frameworks aimed at ensuring the stability and legality of stablecoins. For example, in the United States, the **Financial Stability Oversight Council (FSOC)** and the **Office of the Comptroller of the Currency (OCC)** have begun exploring ways to regulate stablecoins and their issuers. These regulations are focused on ensuring that stablecoins are adequately backed by reserves, that issuers maintain sufficient liquidity, and that users are protected from fraud or market manipulation (Davuluri et al., 2023; S. Gupta et al., 2022; Suresh et al., 2023; Yeruva et al., 2022). Additionally, governments are scrutinizing stablecoins for potential **tax implications**, including the treatment of stablecoin transactions for capital gains or income tax purposes.

At the international level, the **Financial Action Task Force (FATF)** has introduced guidelines for the regulation of stablecoins, emphasizing the need for AML and counter-terrorism financing (CTF) compliance. The global regulatory landscape remains fragmented, however, as different jurisdictions have adopted varying approaches to the oversight of stablecoins, creating challenges for cross-border transactions and international cooperation.

Case Study: The Rise of Tether (USDT) and Its Market Impact

One of the most prominent stablecoins in the market is **Tether (USDT)**, which was launched in 2014 by the company Tether Ltd. As a fiat-collateralized stablecoin, USDT is pegged to the US dollar, with the aim of maintaining a one-to-one value ratio (Jindal et al., 2023; Komkowski et al., 2023b; Tamilmani et al., 2023). Tether has become a key player in the cryptocurrency ecosystem, widely used for trading, cross-border payments, and as a reserve asset on DeFi platforms. As of 2024, USDT boasts a market capitalization exceeding $80 billion, making it one of the largest stablecoins by market value.

Tether's widespread adoption and dominance in the market have not come without controversy. Over the years, Tether Ltd. has faced numerous legal challenges and regulatory scrutiny, particularly regarding its claims of full dollar-backed reserves. In 2021, Tether settled with the New York Attorney General's office over allegations that it misled investors about its reserve backing, agreeing to pay an $18.5 million fine and to increase transparency in its operations. Despite these challenges, Tether continues to be widely used, and its dominance in the market has solidified its position as a leading stablecoin.

Tether's success is largely attributed to its liquidity and the role it plays in the broader cryptocurrency market. As a widely recognized and trusted stablecoin, Tether serves as a critical trading pair for many cryptocurrency exchanges, providing traders with a stable medium of exchange to enter and exit positions (Kowsalya et al., 2023; Poswal et al., 2022; S. K. Singh, Chauhan, & Sarkar, 2023). Additionally, Tether has facilitated the growth of the DeFi sector by offering users a reliable stablecoin for lending, borrowing, and trading activities.

However, Tether's dominance has also raised concerns about **centralization** within the cryptocurrency market. Despite being a decentralized technology, the majority of Tether's circulating supply is controlled by a single company, leading to questions about market manipulation and the potential for market manipulation if the company were to make sudden changes to its reserve holdings or liquidity.

In brief, stablecoins represent a compelling solution to the volatility inherent in traditional cryptocurrencies, offering stability, liquidity, and a wide range of use cases across global trade and finance. However, their rapid growth and the complexities of their regulatory oversight necessitate careful consideration by lawmakers, financial institutions, and users alike. As the stablecoin market continues to evolve, its impact on both traditional finance and the emerging DeFi sector will likely be profound, ushering in new opportunities and challenges for the global economy.

6. CHALLENGES IN FINANCIAL REPORTING FOR DIGITAL CURRENCIES

The advent of digital currencies has revolutionized global finance, but it has also introduced substantial challenges in financial reporting, which were not foreseen with traditional financial assets. The complexities surrounding digital currencies such as Bitcoin, Ethereum, and the growing array of stablecoins, pose unique hurdles in terms of valuation, auditing, and regulatory compliance. These challenges are compounded by the rapid evolution of digital assets, their volatility, and the lack of universally accepted standards in financial reporting frameworks such as the **International Financial Reporting Standards (IFRS)** and **Generally Accepted Accounting Principles (GAAP)**. This section delves into the multifaceted challenges digital currencies present to financial reporting, focusing on their valuation complexities, the implications for IFRS and GAAP, and the challenges associated with auditing and compliance.

Complexities of Valuation and Price Volatility

One of the most significant challenges in the financial reporting of digital currencies lies in the **valuation** of these assets. Unlike traditional financial instruments such as stocks or bonds, which have well-established methodologies for valuation, digital currencies are inherently volatile and often lack sufficient liquidity. Cryptocurrencies like Bitcoin and Ethereum exhibit extreme price fluctuations, with their value often shifting by double-digit percentages in a single day. This volatility makes it exceedingly difficult for accountants and financial analysts to assign an accurate, consistent valuation to these assets.

Valuing digital currencies for financial reporting purposes requires determining their **fair market value**, which is often based on the price at a specific point in time. However, since these assets are traded on various decentralized exchanges with varying liquidity levels, the prices can differ significantly depending on the platform (Kannan et al., 2022; MITRA et al., 2022; Rana, Cavaliere, et al., 2022). Furthermore, the **lack of intrinsic value**—since many digital currencies do not generate cash flows like traditional investments—further complicates their valuation. The challenge of ascertaining a precise market value is intensified by regulatory uncertainties, with governments and central banks offering differing stances on the legal classification of digital currencies, adding to the inconsistency in reporting practices.

Another challenge is determining how to **account for unrealized gains or losses** due to the inherent volatility of digital currencies. Under traditional accounting rules, fluctuations in the value of financial instruments must be reported as either realized or unrealized gains or losses. However, given the speculative nature of digital currencies and their lack of a well-defined underlying value, accounting for these fluctuations becomes more subjective and less reliable. This inconsistency may lead to unreliable financial statements that do not reflect the true financial position of an entity involved in the digital currency market.

Financial Reporting Under IFRS and GAAP for Digital Assets

The treatment of digital currencies under established accounting frameworks such as **IFRS** and **GAAP** further exacerbates the complexity of financial reporting. Both frameworks struggle to categorize digital currencies due to their unique characteristics and the absence of a centralized authority governing them (Kukreti et al., 2025). The **IFRS**, for instance, treats digital currencies as **intangible assets** under IAS 38. However, this classification has been met with criticism, as it does not adequately reflect the economic reality of digital currencies, particularly given that they are often used for transactional purposes rather than for long-term investment (Taneja, Gupta, Bhushan, et al., 2023).

In contrast, the **GAAP** system tends to treat cryptocurrencies primarily as commodities, akin to precious metals like gold. However, this classification presents its own set of challenges, especially when it comes to recognizing revenue from digital currencies. Given the frequent price fluctuations, determining the appropriate time for recognizing revenue from digital currency transactions is a contentious issue (N. Bansal et al., 2023; Dahiya & Taneja, 2023; Dangwal et al., 2022; Taneja & Sharma, 2023). For instance, under GAAP, digital currencies may need to be classified as either inventory or as indefinite-lived intangible assets, both of which have different rules regarding depreciation, impairment, and recognition of gains or losses.

Both frameworks struggle with defining **how to account for digital currencies** in relation to income, expenses, and profits, given that the recognition of revenue from digital assets is often based on speculative trading rather than core business activities. The lack of consensus among regulators worldwide on the classification and treatment of digital currencies further complicates the issue, making it difficult for firms to adhere to clear and consistent accounting practices.

Auditing and Compliance Issues in the Digital Currency Space

The rapid growth of digital currencies has also raised concerns over **auditing and compliance**. Auditing digital assets introduces a series of complexities that are unfamiliar to traditional auditors. Since cryptocurrencies are decentralized, the traditional methods of auditing financial transactions—based on centralized databases and third-party confirmations—become less applicable (Reepu et al., 2023; TANEJA et al., 2024; Taneja, Gupta, Singh, et al., 2023; Taneja & Özen, 2023). Instead, auditors must rely on blockchain technology, which, while offering transparency, also presents new challenges in terms of the accuracy and completeness of data.

Auditing firms must ensure that entities are complying with **anti-money laundering (AML)** and **know-your-customer (KYC)** regulations, which are essential for combating financial crime and ensuring the integrity of the financial system. However, because cryptocurrencies often operate in a pseudonymous or anonymous manner, tracking and verifying the origin and destination of transactions becomes challenging. This lack of clarity can create significant risks, including the potential for tax evasion, money laundering, and financing of illegal activities.

Further complicating auditing is the issue of **custody and control**. With the increasing number of digital asset exchanges and wallets, auditors must assess the security measures in place to protect digital assets from hacking or theft. Unlike traditional assets that are stored in centralized institutions such as banks, digital currencies are often stored in decentralized wallets, making them more susceptible to security breaches. Auditors must verify the **safekeeping** and **ownership** of digital currencies and assess the risks of theft, fraud, or loss due to cyberattacks, which presents a stark departure from conventional auditing practices.

On the regulatory front, compliance with financial reporting standards remains elusive. As digital currencies continue to grow in prominence, regulators in various jurisdictions are beginning to craft frameworks to govern their use. However, due to the decentralized and global nature of digital currencies, it is difficult for national authorities to enforce compliance effectively. This lack of uniformity across jurisdictions leads to **legal uncertainty** for firms that wish to engage in the digital currency space. Furthermore, tax authorities worldwide are grappling with how to treat digital currency transactions for **capital gains** and **income tax purposes**, which leads to inconsistent reporting and the potential for compliance errors.

The challenges in financial reporting for digital currencies are both profound and multifaceted, encompassing issues of valuation, classification under established accounting standards, and the complexities of auditing and compliance. As the digital currency landscape continues to evolve, so too will the need for new, more robust financial reporting frameworks that can better accommodate the unique characteristics of these assets (M. Gupta et al., 2023; Kour et al., 2025; A. Singh et al., 2024). Until clearer, universally accepted standards are implemented, businesses involved in the cryptocurrency market will continue to face difficulties in maintaining transparent and reliable financial statements. Therefore, the development of clear regulatory guidelines and the establishment of comprehensive auditing practices are crucial for the long-term stability and legitimacy of digital currencies within the global financial system.

7. THE EVOLUTION OF FINANCIAL REPORTING STANDARDS IN THE DIGITAL AGE

As the global financial landscape evolves with the proliferation of digital assets, the need for modernized financial reporting standards becomes increasingly critical. Digital assets, such as cryptocurrencies, tokens, and blockchain-based instruments, present unique challenges that traditional financial reporting frameworks were never designed to address. From issues of valuation and classification to the integration of new technologies like blockchain and distributed ledger technology (DLT), the current financial reporting standards must adapt to the digital age . Furthermore, given the transnational nature of digital currencies and the decentralized architecture of blockchain networks, achieving international harmonization in reporting standards is essential for maintaining transparency, consistency, and financial stability. This section examines the modernization of financial reporting frameworks for digital assets, the role of blockchain in reporting, and the pressing need for global standardization.

Modernizing Financial Reporting Frameworks for Digital Assets

Historically, financial reporting standards such as the **International Financial Reporting Standards (IFRS)** and **Generally Accepted Accounting Principles (GAAP)** were developed to accommodate conventional financial instruments such as stocks, bonds, and cash. However, digital assets—ranging from **cryptocurrencies** to **non-fungible tokens (NFTs)**—do not fit neatly into these established categories. Their valuation, liquidity, and regulatory treatment pose significant challenges for accounting professionals and auditors.

One of the primary hurdles is the **valuation** of digital assets, which exhibit extreme volatility and often lack intrinsic value, unlike traditional assets such as equities or real estate. For instance, **Bitcoin** and **Ethereum** can experience dramatic price fluctuations within short periods, undermining the accuracy of financial statements. Accounting frameworks must adapt to reflect these price swings and determine how to classify such assets—whether as **intangible assets**, **inventory**, or

financial instruments. The **IFRS** and **GAAP** currently treat digital assets primarily as intangible assets under IAS 38 or similar standards, but this classification is increasingly contested, as digital assets often serve transactional roles, which is at odds with the idea of an intangible asset.

Additionally, traditional **amortization** and **impairment** rules often fail to account for the volatility and speculative nature of digital assets. Modernized reporting frameworks will need to introduce more flexible methodologies, such as **fair value accounting**, to better reflect the true economic impact of these digital assets on an organization's balance sheet. Such adjustments will provide investors and stakeholders with a clearer picture of an entity's financial health while accommodating the unique characteristics of digital currencies and related technologies.

8. REGULATORY AND LEGAL FRAMEWORKS FOR DIGITAL CURRENCIES

As digital currencies and blockchain technology continue to reshape the financial ecosystem, governments and regulatory bodies are grappling with the complexities of establishing a coherent legal framework that balances innovation with the need for consumer protection, financial stability, and security. The regulatory landscape for digital currencies is still in a state of flux, with jurisdictions around the world adopting different approaches. This section examines the government regulations surrounding digital currencies, the privacy and security considerations in their use, and the global regulatory trends emerging from key regions such as the United States, the European Union, and Asia.

Government Regulations Around Digital Currencies and Blockchain Technology

Governments around the world have recognized the transformative potential of blockchain technology and digital currencies, yet they are also acutely aware of the risks posed by their widespread adoption. Consequently, the regulatory frameworks for digital currencies have varied widely across jurisdictions, with some governments offering a supportive environment for innovation, while others have imposed stringent regulations or outright bans.

In the United States, regulatory bodies such as the Securities and Exchange Commission (SEC), Commodity Futures Trading Commission (CFTC), and Internal Revenue Service (IRS) have taken varying stances on digital currencies. The SEC has primarily treated many digital assets as securities, subjecting them to the same regulatory scrutiny as traditional financial instruments. This has led to extensive legal battles over whether certain cryptocurrencies, such as Bitcoin and Ethereum, should be classified as securities. On the other hand, the CFTC has taken a more lenient stance, considering cryptocurrencies as commodities, subject to different regulatory frameworks. The IRS, meanwhile, has focused on the taxation of digital currencies, treating them as property for tax purposes and requiring individuals to report gains or losses from cryptocurrency transactions.

In the European Union, regulatory efforts have been more consolidated, with the Markets in Crypto-Assets (MiCA) framework being one of the most significant regulatory initiatives. MiCA aims to provide a comprehensive set of rules for the issuance, trading, and management of digital assets across the EU. Its objectives are to ensure consumer protection, market integrity, and financial stability while promoting the development of the crypto market in a regulated environment. The EU also emphasizes the need for proper governance mechanisms for digital asset service providers and the prevention of systemic risks associated with crypto markets. MiCA's introduction reflects the EU's broader goal of establishing a harmonized regulatory framework for digital currencies, ensuring that regulatory practices across member states are consistent.

In contrast, China has adopted one of the most stringent regulatory approaches towards digital currencies, having imposed a complete ban on cryptocurrency trading and mining. The Chinese government has taken a strong stance against the speculative nature of digital currencies and their potential to undermine the sovereign monetary system. However, China is also actively developing its Central Bank Digital Currency (CBDC), the digital yuan, reflecting its recognition of blockchain's potential to modernize its financial infrastructure while maintaining strict state control over its economy.

9. CASE STUDIES

The emergence of digital currencies and their integration into the global economy has brought with it a host of innovative use cases, as well as complex legal, regulatory, and economic challenges. This section explores several case studies that highlight the significant developments in the world of digital currencies, focusing on the rise of the Digital Yuan, El Salvador's adoption of Bitcoin, the European Central Bank's digital euro exploration, Ripple's legal battles, and the adoption of Central Bank Digital Currencies (CBDCs) in the Caribbean and Africa.

Case Study 1: The Digital Yuan (e-CNY) and Cross-Border Trade

China's development of the Digital Yuan, or e-CNY, represents one of the most ambitious projects in the world of Central Bank Digital Currencies (CBDCs). The People's Bank of China (PBOC) has been at the forefront of CBDC innovation, aiming to modernize its financial system, enhance monetary policy implementation, and reduce the reliance on the U.S. dollar for cross-border transactions.

The Digital Yuan is designed to be a fully traceable, government-controlled digital currency. Unlike decentralized cryptocurrencies such as Bitcoin, the e-CNY is backed by the Chinese government and is considered legal tender within China. Its primary objective is to facilitate domestic transactions, improve efficiency in payments, and increase China's influence over international trade by offering an alternative to traditional payment systems like SWIFT and the U.S. dollar.

In terms of cross-border trade, the Digital Yuan is positioned as a potential game-changer. The Chinese government has already initiated several pilot programs involving cross-border payments using the e-CNY in collaboration with countries like Hong Kong, Thailand, and the United Arab Emirates. By reducing transaction costs and settlement times, it is hoped that the Digital Yuan can streamline international trade and bolster China's position in the global economy. Despite these advantages, concerns remain about the potential for increased state surveillance and the disruption of established financial ecosystems. **Source:** People's Bank of China (PBOC) and various government reports, available at PBOC Official Website

Case Study 2: El Salvador's Adoption of Bitcoin as Legal Tender

El Salvador made headlines in 2021 when it became the first country in the world to adopt Bitcoin as legal tender, alongside the U.S. dollar. The decision was driven by President Nayib Bukele's vision of transforming the country's economy by leveraging Bitcoin's decentralized nature to reduce reliance on traditional banking systems, facilitate remittances, and stimulate financial inclusion.

While the move was lauded by Bitcoin advocates as a groundbreaking step towards cryptocurrency adoption, it was met with skepticism by international financial institutions, such as the International Monetary Fund (IMF) and the World Bank, which expressed concerns about the potential for financial instability and the risks associated with Bitcoin's volatility. Bitcoin's price fluctuations have since proven to be a major issue, with the value of the cryptocurrency falling significantly after El Salvador's initial adoption.

Despite these challenges, the country has remained committed to the initiative. It introduced the "Chivo Wallet," a government-backed digital wallet, to encourage Bitcoin transactions and provide a means for Salvadorans to access financial services. The country also purchased Bitcoin as part of its reserves, although the market's volatility has posed risks to the nation's financial stability. **Source:** Bukele, Nayib. (2021). "Bitcoin Law of El Salvador." El Salvador Government

Case Study 3: The European Central Bank's Exploration of a Digital Euro

The European Central Bank (ECB) has been exploring the concept of a Digital Euro (e-Euro) as part of its ongoing efforts to modernize the European Union's financial infrastructure. The Digital Euro aims to complement the physical euro, providing a digital alternative for transactions in the European economic area while ensuring monetary sovereignty in the face of increasing competition from private cryptocurrencies and stablecoins.

The ECB's exploration of the Digital Euro is driven by several factors, including the need to enhance payment efficiency, protect consumer privacy, and mitigate the growing influence of non-European payment systems such as PayPal and Facebook's Diem. Furthermore, the rise of private digital currencies has raised concerns over the stability of financial systems and the potential for market manipulation, making a government-backed digital currency an attractive option.

However, the project remains in its early stages, with the ECB emphasizing a cautious and transparent approach. Extensive public consultations have been held to gauge the potential impact of a Digital Euro, focusing on issues such as privacy protection, financial inclusion, and cross-border payments. **Source:** European Central Bank, (2020). "The Digital Euro: A New Form of Money." ECB Website

Case Study 4: Ripple (XRP) and Legal Challenges in the U.S.

Ripple Labs, the company behind the cryptocurrency XRP, has been embroiled in a prolonged legal battle with the U.S. Securities and Exchange Commission (SEC) since December 2020. The SEC alleges that Ripple conducted an unregistered securities offering by selling XRP tokens to investors, a classification that would subject the token to stricter regulations under U.S. securities law.

Ripple, however, argues that XRP is a digital currency rather than a security, and as such, should not fall under the SEC's jurisdiction. The case has profound implications not only for Ripple but also for the broader cryptocurrency market, as it could set a precedent for how other cryptocurrencies are classified and regulated in the future.

As of 2024, the legal proceedings are still ongoing, with Ripple's defense gaining traction in certain aspects of the case. The outcome of this case is likely to influence the future regulatory landscape for digital assets in the U.S. **Source:** U.S. Securities and Exchange Commission, (2020)

Case Study 5: The Emergence of CBDCs in the Caribbean and Africa

Several countries in the Caribbean and Africa have been exploring or implementing Central Bank Digital Currencies (CBDCs) as a means to enhance financial inclusion and economic stability. The Bahamas was the first country to launch a fully operational CBDC, the Sand Dollar, in 2020. The Sand Dollar is designed to provide greater access to financial services, especially for those in remote areas where traditional banking infrastructure is lacking.

In Africa, nations such as Nigeria and Ghana have also made significant strides in CBDC development. Nigeria's eNaira, launched in 2021, aims to streamline payments, reduce the cost of cash management, and provide a secure alternative to cryptocurrencies, which have become popular in the region. Similarly, Ghana is piloting the eCedi as part of a broader strategy to digitize its economy and strengthen its monetary system.

These CBDCs offer a unique opportunity to address the challenges faced by unbanked populations in developing regions. However, challenges related to infrastructure, public adoption, and regulatory frameworks persist, and the success of these initiatives will depend largely on how well governments can integrate these digital currencies into their broader economic policies. **Source**: Central Bank of The Bahamas, (2020)

These case studies illustrate the diversity of approaches and the growing interest in digital currencies across the globe. From China's ambitious Digital Yuan project to El Salvador's Bitcoin experiment, and the exploration of CBDCs in the Caribbean and Africa, these initiatives highlight the potential for digital currencies to transform economies, improve financial inclusion, and challenge traditional monetary systems. However, each case also underscores the complexities and challenges that come with implementing digital currencies, from regulatory hurdles to market volatility, and the need for effective governance frameworks to ensure their success in the long term.

10. FUTURE TRENDS AND PREDICTIONS FOR DIGITAL CURRENCIES IN GLOBAL TRADE

As digital currencies continue to mature and integrate into the global economic landscape, their role in shaping trade dynamics, driving technological innovation, and potentially disrupting traditional financial systems becomes increasingly significant. The evolution of digital currencies, ranging from Central Bank Digital Currencies (CBDCs) to decentralized cryptocurrencies, is poised to redefine how global trade is conducted, how value is transferred, and how financial systems operate. This section delves into the role digital currencies play in reshaping global trade, the technological innovations driving these changes, and the potential disruptions they may cause within traditional financial structures.

The Role of Digital Currencies in Shaping Global Trade Dynamics

Digital currencies are poised to become a cornerstone of global trade, fostering greater efficiency and reducing friction in international transactions. Traditional cross-border payments often involve complex intermediaries, such as banks and payment processors, which result in delayed settlement times and high transaction fees. Digital currencies, particularly CBDCs and stablecoins, offer the potential to streamline these processes by providing faster, cheaper, and more transparent methods of transferring value across borders.

In particular, CBDCs are expected to play a central role in transforming cross-border trade by reducing the reliance on the U.S. dollar and the SWIFT network, which currently dominate international financial transactions. For instance, countries like China, with its Digital Yuan, and the European Union, exploring the Digital Euro, are laying the groundwork for a multi-currency digital payment system that could facilitate smoother, more direct transactions between nations. These digital currencies could be used for real-time settlement, reducing both counterparty risk and the cost of currency conversion.

Moreover, digital currencies are likely to enhance trade relationships between developing and developed nations. By providing greater financial inclusion, they could offer businesses in emerging economies access to the global financial ecosystem without relying on traditional banking infrastructure. This could encourage more seamless trade between these regions, thereby stimulating global economic growth.

11. IMPLICATIONS OF THE STUDY

The study of digital currencies and their integration into global trade carries profound implications across multiple dimensions of economics, regulation, and technological advancement. First and foremost, the rise of digital currencies is poised to reshape the global financial landscape, offering an alternative to traditional fiat systems. As digital currencies gain traction, they will increasingly influence the efficiency of cross-border transactions, potentially eliminating the barriers posed by cumbersome intermediaries such as banks and payment processors. This could lead to a more fluid and interconnected global marketplace, enabling faster, cheaper, and more transparent financial exchanges.

From a regulatory standpoint, the growing prominence of digital currencies necessitates the creation of robust legal frameworks that can effectively address the unique challenges posed by these assets. A key implication of the study is the urgent need for international cooperation in developing regulatory standards. Fragmented and inconsistent regulations across jurisdictions could undermine the effectiveness of digital currencies in facilitating global trade. Therefore, global regulatory harmonization is essential to ensure consumer protection, prevent financial crimes such as money laundering, and create a stable environment in which digital currencies can thrive without destabilizing the financial system.

Moreover, the advent of Central Bank Digital Currencies (CBDCs) and decentralized cryptocurrencies presents significant implications for monetary policy and financial sovereignty. As CBDCs potentially reduce reliance on traditional reserve currencies like the U.S. dollar, they could alter geopolitical power dynamics, with countries gaining the ability to issue their own digital currencies that operate seamlessly across borders. This shift could challenge the dominance of established financial institutions and provide greater autonomy for national governments in managing their economies.

Technologically, the study underscores the transformative potential of blockchain and distributed ledger technologies (DLT) in enhancing financial transparency, security, and efficiency. The implications are far-reaching, as blockchain's immutable and decentralized nature could fundamentally alter how transactions are recorded, verified, and settled. However, technological advancements must be coupled with rigorous security measures to mitigate the risks of cyber threats, fraud, and data breaches that could undermine the stability of digital currency systems.

Lastly, the study highlights the potential for digital currencies to drive financial inclusion, particularly in regions where access to traditional banking services remains limited. By leveraging the accessibility of digital wallets and decentralized platforms, underserved populations could gain access to global financial networks, unlocking new opportunities for economic participation and growth. Consequently, the successful integration of digital currencies could lead to more equitable and inclusive global trade systems.

12. CONCLUSION

This study has explored the transformative potential of digital currencies within the context of global trade, highlighting both the opportunities and challenges they present. The key insights drawn from the analysis underscore the pivotal role that digital currencies, particularly Central Bank Digital Currencies (CBDCs), stablecoins, and cryptocurrencies, are playing in reshaping the financial landscape. Through their capacity to streamline cross-border transactions, reduce transaction costs, and enhance financial inclusion, digital currencies are facilitating a more integrated and efficient global economic system.

Moreover, the study has illuminated the intricate relationship between digital currencies and financial reporting standards, demonstrating the complexities involved in their valuation, classification, and the regulatory frameworks needed to support their integration. Financial reporting standards such as IFRS and GAAP must evolve to accommodate the distinctive characteristics of digital assets, ensuring transparency and consistency in financial reporting. As the digital currency ecosystem expands, so too must the regulatory and compliance mechanisms, ensuring that these innovations are embedded within a secure and stable financial infrastructure.

The ongoing evolution of digital currencies is intrinsically tied to advancements in blockchain technology, with distributed ledger systems promising to revolutionize transaction validation, auditing, and financial recordkeeping. However, this technological shift is not without its challenges, particularly in terms of scalability, interoperability, and cybersecurity. Thus, regulatory bodies and industry stakeholders must remain agile, adapting to the rapid pace of innovation while maintaining a strong focus on safeguarding financial stability and market integrity.

Hence, the future of digital currencies in global trade and finance holds immense promise, but it is contingent upon the establishment of coherent regulatory frameworks, the continuous evolution of financial reporting standards, and the safeguarding of technological security. As digital currencies continue to gain traction, their potential to disrupt traditional financial systems is undeniable. However, for their integration into the global economy to be successful, a concerted effort from governments, regulators, and industry players is essential to ensure that these innovations contribute to a more efficient, inclusive, and secure global financial ecosystem.

REFERENCES

Abdullah, K. H., Abd Aziz, F. S., Dani, R., Hammood, W. A., & Setiawan, E. (2023). Urban Pollution: A Bibliometric Review. *ASM Science Journal, 18*, 1–16. DOI: 10.32802/asmscj.2023.1440

Agarwal, P., & Sharma, S. (2023). Smart Urban Traffic Management System using Energy Efficient Optimized Path Discovery. *Proceedings of the 3rd International Conference on Artificial Intelligence and Smart Energy, ICAIS 2023*, 858 – 863. DOI: 10.1109/ICAIS56108.2023.10073840

Ahmad, I., Sharma, S., Kumar, R., Dhyani, S., & Dumka, A. (2023). Data Analytics of Online Education during Pandemic Health Crisis: A Case Study. *2nd Edition of IEEE Delhi Section Owned Conference, DELCON 2023 - Proceedings*. DOI: 10.1109/DELCON57910.2023.10127423

Akberdina, V., Kumar, V., Kyriakopoulos, G. L., & Kuzmin, E. (2023). Editorial: What Does Industry's Digital Transition Hold in the Uncertainty Context? In K. V., K. G.L., A. V., & K. E. (Eds.), *Lecture Notes in Information Systems and Organisation: Vol. 61 LNISO* (pp. 1 – 4). Springer Science and Business Media Deutschland GmbH. DOI: 10.1007/978-3-031-30351-7_1

Alzaidi, M. S., Subbalakshmi, C., Roshini, T. V., Shukla, P. K., Shukla, S. K., Dutta, P., & Alhassan, M. (2022). 5G-Telecommunication Allocation Network Using IoT Enabled Improved Machine Learning Technique. *Wireless Communications and Mobile Computing, 2022*, 1–10. Advance online publication. DOI: 10.1155/2022/6229356

Arora, R., Chauhan, A., Singh, A. P., & Sharma, R. (2023). Optimization of a production inventory model of imperfect quality items for three-layer supply chain in fuzzy environment. *Benchmarking*. Advance online publication. DOI: 10.1108/BIJ-11-2021-0678

Bansal, N., Bhatnagar, M., & Taneja, S. (2023). Balancing priorities through green optimism: A study elucidating initiatives, approaches, and strategies for sustainable supply chain management. In *Handbook of Research on Designing Sustainable Supply Chains to Achieve a Circular Economy*. IGI Global., DOI: 10.4018/978-1-6684-7664-2.ch004

Bansal, S., Kumar, V., Kumari, A., & Kuzmin, E. (2023). Understanding the Role of Digital Technologies in Supply Chain Management of SMEs. In K. V., K. G.L., A. V., & K. E. (Eds.), *Lecture Notes in Information Systems and Organisation: Vol. 61 LNISO* (pp. 195 – 205). Springer Science and Business Media Deutschland GmbH. DOI: 10.1007/978-3-031-30351-7_16

Belwal, N., Juneja, P., & Sunori, S. K. (2023). Decoupler Control for a MIMO Process Model in an Industrial Process - A Review. *2023 2nd International Conference on Ambient Intelligence in Health Care, ICAIHC 2023*. DOI: 10.1109/ICAIHC59020.2023.10431463

Bhatt, Y., & Ghuman, K. (2022). Managerial cognition and environmental behavioral intentions: A behavioral reasoning theory perspective. *Corporate Social Responsibility and Environmental Management*, *29*(5), 1315–1329. DOI: 10.1002/csr.2271

Bisht, R. K., Bisht, I. P., & Joshi, B. C. (2022). Growth of Micro, Small and Medium Enterprises (MSMEs) in Uttarakhand (India). In D. N. & C. A. (Eds.), *AIP Conference Proceedings* (Vol. 2481). American Institute of Physics Inc. DOI: 10.1063/5.0103881

Caiado, R. G. G., Scavarda, L. F., Vidal, G., de Mattos Nascimento, D. L., & Garza-Reyes, J. A. (2023). A taxonomy of critical factors towards sustainable operations and supply chain management 4.0 in developing countries. *Operations Management Research*. DOI: 10.1007/s12063-023-00430-8

Cavaliere, L. P. L., Byloppilly, R., Khan, S. D., Othman, B. A., Muda, I., & Malhotra, R. K. (2024). Acceptance and effectiveness of Industry 4.0 internal and external organisational initiatives in Malaysian firms. *International Journal of Management and Enterprise Development*, *23*(1), 1–25. DOI: 10.1504/IJMED.2024.138422

Chahar, A., & Christobel, Y. A. Ritika, Adakane, P. K., Sonal, D., & Tripathi, V. (2022). The Implementation of Big Data With Cloud and Edge Computing in Enhancing the Smart Grid Information Processes Through Sem Model. *2022 2nd International Conference on Advance Computing and Innovative Technologies in Engineering, ICACITE 2022*, 608 – 611. DOI: 10.1109/ICACITE53722.2022.9823896

Dahiya, K., & Taneja, S. (2023). To Analyse the Impact of Multi-Media Technology on the Rural Entrepreneurship Development. In *Contemporary Studies of Risks in Emerging Technology* (pp. 221–240). DOI: 10.1108/978-1-80455-562-020231015

Dangwal, A., Kaur, S., Taneja, S., & Ozen, E. (2022). A bibliometric analysis of green tourism based on the scopus platform. In *Developing Relationships, Personalization, and Data Herald in Marketing 5.0*. IGI Global., DOI: 10.4018/978-1-6684-4496-2.ch015

Das Gupta, A., Rafi, S. M., Singh, N., Gupta, V. K., Jaiswal, S., & Gangodkar, D. (2022). A Framework of Internet of Things (IOT) for the Manufacturing and Image Classifaication System. *2022 2nd International Conference on Advance Computing and Innovative Technologies in Engineering, ICACITE 2022*, 293 – 297. DOI: 10.1109/ICACITE53722.2022.9823853

Davuluri, S. K., Alvi, S. A. M., Aeri, M., Agarwal, A., Serajuddin, M., & Hasan, Z. (2023). A Security Model for Perceptive 5G-Powered BC IoT Associated Deep Learning. *6th International Conference on Inventive Computation Technologies, ICICT 2023 - Proceedings*, 118 – 125. DOI: 10.1109/ICICT57646.2023.10134487

Dhiman, G., & Nagar, A. K. (2022). Editorial: Blockchain-based 6G and industrial internet of things systems for industry 4.0/5.0. *Expert Systems: International Journal of Knowledge Engineering and Neural Networks*, *39*(10), e13162. Advance online publication. DOI: 10.1111/exsy.13162

Eswar, K. N. D. V. S., Doss, M. A. N., Vishnuram, P., Selim, A., Bajaj, M., Kotb, H., & Kamel, S. (2023). Comprehensive Study on Reduced DC Source Count: Multilevel Inverters and Its Design Topologies. *Energies*, *16*(1), 18. Advance online publication. DOI: 10.3390/en16010018

Gonfa, Y. H., Tessema, F. B., Tadesse, M. G., Bachheti, A., & Bachheti, R. K. (2023). Medicinally Important Plant Roots and Their Role in Nanoparticles Synthesis and Applications. In *Secondary Metabolites from Medicinal Plants: Nanoparticles Synthesis and their Applications*. CRC Press., DOI: 10.1201/9781003213727-11

Gopal, S., Gupta, P., & Minocha, A. (2023). Advancements in Fin-Tech and Security Challenges of Banking Industry. *4th International Conference on Intelligent Engineering and Management, ICIEM 2023*. DOI: 10.1109/ICIEM59379.2023.10165876

Gupta, A., Dixit, A. K., Kumar, K. S., Lavanya, C., Chakravarthi, M. K., & Gangodkar, D. (2022). Analyzing Robotics and Computer Integrated Manufacturing of Key Areas Using Cloud Computing. *Proceedings of 5th International Conference on Contemporary Computing and Informatics, IC3I 2022*, 194 – 199. DOI: 10.1109/IC3I56241.2022.10072581

Gupta, M., Arora, K., & Taneja, S. (2023). Bibliometric analysis on employee engagement and human resource management. In *Enhancing Customer Engagement Through Location-Based Marketing*. IGI Global., DOI: 10.4018/978-1-6684-8177-6.ch013

Gupta, P., Gopal, S., Sharma, M., Joshi, S., Sahani, C., & Ahalawat, K. (2023). Agriculture Informatics and Communication: Paradigm of E-Governance and Drone Technology for Crop Monitoring. *9th International Conference on Smart Computing and Communications: Intelligent Technologies and Applications, ICSCC 2023*, 113 – 118. DOI: 10.1109/ICSCC59169.2023.10335058

Gupta, S., Kumar, V., & Patil, P. (2022). A Study on Recycling of Waste Solid Garbage in a City. In D. N. & C. A. (Eds.), *AIP Conference Proceedings* (Vol. 2481). American Institute of Physics Inc. DOI: 10.1063/5.0104563

Gusain, I., Sharma, S., Debarma, S., Kumar Sharma, A., Mishra, N., & Prakashrao Dahale, P. (2023). Study of concrete mix by adding Dolomite in conventional concrete as partial replacement with cement. *Materials Today: Proceedings*, *73*, 163–166. DOI: 10.1016/j.matpr.2022.09.583

Hajoary, P. K., Balachandra, P., & Garza-Reyes, J. A. (2023). Industry 4.0 maturity and readiness assessment: An empirical validation using Confirmatory Composite Analysis. *Production Planning and Control*. Advance online publication. DOI: 10.1080/09537287.2023.2210545

Jayadeva, S. M., Prasad Krishnam, N., Raja Mannar, B., Prakash Dabral, A., Buddhi, D., & Garg, N. (2023). An Investigation of IOT-Based Consumer Analytics to Assist Consumer Engagement Strategies in Evolving Markets. *2023 3rd International Conference on Advance Computing and Innovative Technologies in Engineering, ICACITE 2023*, 487 – 491. DOI: 10.1109/ICACITE57410.2023.10183310

Jena, S., & Gairola, A. (2022). Numerical Method to Generate and Evaluate Environmental Wind Over Hills: Comparison of Pedestrian Winds Over Hills and Plains. *CFD Letters*, *14*(10), 56–67. DOI: 10.37934/cfdl.14.10.5667

Jindal, G., Tiwari, V., Mahomad, R., Gehlot, A., Jindal, M., & Bordoloi, D. (2023). Predictive Design for Quality Assessment Employing Cloud Computing And Machine Learning. *2023 3rd International Conference on Advance Computing and Innovative Technologies in Engineering, ICACITE 2023*, 461 – 465. DOI: 10.1109/ICACITE57410.2023.10182915

Joshi, S., Balakrishnan, S., Rawat, P., Deshpande, D., Chakravarthi, M. K., & Verma, D. (2022). A Framework of Internet of Things (Iot) for the Manufacturing and Image Classification System. In D. R.K., S. A.Kr., K. G., & B. S. (Eds.), *Proceedings of the 2022 11th International Conference on System Modeling and Advancement in Research Trends, SMART 2022* (pp. 371 – 375). Institute of Electrical and Electronics Engineers Inc. DOI: 10.1109/SMART55829.2022.10046756

Joshi, S., Gangola, S., Bhandari, G., Bhandari, N. S., Nainwal, D., Rani, A., Malik, S., & Slama, P. (2023). Rhizospheric bacteria: The key to sustainable heavy metal detoxification strategies. *Frontiers in Microbiology*, *14*, 1229828. Advance online publication. DOI: 10.3389/fmicb.2023.1229828 PMID: 37555069

Josphineleela, R., Siva Reddy, K. V., Reddy, M. V. S. S., & Rawat, R. S. (2023). Design and Development of a Smart Sprinkler Device for IoT-Integrated Plants Irrigation. *Proceedings of the 2023 2nd International Conference on Electronics and Renewable Systems, ICEARS 2023*, 498 – 501. DOI: 10.1109/ICEARS56392.2023.10084960

Kaliappan, S., Natrayan, L., & Garg, N. (2023). Checking and Supervisory System for Calculation of Industrial Constraints using Embedded System. *Proceedings of the 4th International Conference on Smart Electronics and Communication, ICOSEC 2023*, 87 – 90. DOI: 10.1109/ICOSEC58147.2023.10275952

Kamra, J., Mani, A. P., & Tripathi, V. M. (2023). Decarbonization Trajectory in Cement Industry. In S. P., N. S., R. J.J.P.C., R. J.J.P.C., R. J.J.P.C., L.-I. G.-A. D., P. T., C. L., & P. L. (Eds.), *2023 8th International Conference on Smart and Sustainable Technologies, SpliTech 2023*. Institute of Electrical and Electronics Engineers Inc. DOI: 10.23919/SpliTech58164.2023.10193682

Kannan, P. R., Periasamy, K., Pravin, P., & Vinod Kumaar, J. R. (2022). An experimental investigation of wire breakage and performance optimisation of WEDM process on machining of recycled aluminium alloy metal matrix composite. *Materials Science Poland, 40*(3), 12–26. DOI: 10.2478/msp-2022-0030

Kanojia, P., Malhotra, R. K., & Uniyal, A. K. (2022a). Impact of Organizational Commitment Components on the Teachers of Higher Education in Uttarakhand: An Emperical Analysis. *Proceedings - 2022 International Conference on Recent Trends in Microelectronics, Automation, Computing and Communications Systems, ICMACC 2022*, 360–364. DOI: 10.1109/ICMACC54824.2022.10093606

Kanojia, P., Malhotra, R. K., & Uniyal, A. K. (2022b). Organizational Commitment and the Academic Staff in HEI's in North West India. *Proceedings - 2022 International Conference on Recent Trends in Microelectronics, Automation, Computing and Communications Systems, ICMACC 2022*, 365–370. DOI: 10.1109/ICMACC54824.2022.10093347

Kaur, J., Khanna, R., Kumar, R., & Sunil, G. (2024). Role of Blockchain Technologies in Goods and Services Tax. *Proceedings - 2024 3rd International Conference on Sentiment Analysis and Deep Learning, ICSADL 2024*, 607–612. DOI: 10.1109/ICSADL61749.2024.00104

Khanna, R., Jindal, P., & Noja, G. G. (2023). Blockchain technologies, a catalyst for insurance sector. In *The Application of Emerging Technology and Blockchain in the Insurance Industry*. DOI: 10.1201/9781032630946-19

Kohli, P., Sharma, S., & Matta, P. (2022). Secured Privacy Preserving Techniques Analysis of 6G Driven Vehicular Communication Network in Industry 5.0 Internet-of-Everything (IoE) Applications. *2022 International Conference on Smart Generation Computing, Communication and Networking, SMART GENCON 2022*. DOI: 10.1109/SMARTGENCON56628.2022.10084289

Komkowski, T., Antony, J., Garza-Reyes, J. A., Tortorella, G. L., & Pongboonchai-Empl, T. (2023a). A systematic review of the integration of Industry 4.0 with quality-related operational excellence methodologies. *The Quality Management Journal, 30*(1), 3–15. DOI: 10.1080/10686967.2022.2144783

Komkowski, T., Antony, J., Garza-Reyes, J. A., Tortorella, G. L., & Pongboonchai-Empl, T. (2023b). Integrating Lean Management with Industry 4.0: An explorative Dynamic Capabilities theory perspective. *Production Planning and Control*. Advance online publication. DOI: 10.1080/09537287.2023.2294297

Kour, M., Taneja, S., Özen, E., Sood, K., & Grima, S. (2025). *Financial Landscape Transformation Technological Disruptions.*

Kowsalya, K., Rani, R. P. J., Bhiyana, M., Saini, M., & Patil, P. P. (2023, May). Blockchain-Internet of things-Machine Learning: Development of Traceable System for Multi Purposes. In 2023 3rd International Conference on Advance Computing and Innovative Technologies in Engineering (ICACITE) (pp. 1112-1115). IEEE.

Kukreti, M., Sehajpal, S., Tiwari, R., & Sood, K. (2025). *Driving Global Health and Sustainable Development Goals With Smart Technology* (Mohit, K., Sabina, S., Rajesh, T., & Kiran, S., Eds.; 1st ed.). IGI Global Scientific Publishing., DOI: 10.4018/979-8-3373-0240-9

Kumar, A. S., & Desi, A. B. (2023). Collaborative logistics, tools of machine and supply chain services in the world wide industry 4.0 framework. In *Artificial Intelligence, Blockchain, Computing and Security: Volume 2* (Vol. 2). CRC Press. DOI: 10.1201/9781032684994-15

Kumar, K., Chaudhary, S., Anandaram, H., Kumar, R., Gupta, A., & Joshi, K. (2023). Industry 4.0 and Health Care System with special reference to Mental Health. *2023 1st International Conference on Intelligent Computing and Research Trends, ICRT 2023*. DOI: 10.1109/ICRT57042.2023.10146640

Kumar, K., Singh, V., Mishra, G., Ravindra Babu, B., Tripathi, N., & Kumar, P. (2022). Power-Efficient Secured Hardware Design of AES Algorithm on High Performance FPGA. *Proceedings of 5th International Conference on Contemporary Computing and Informatics, IC3I 2022*, 1634 – 1637. DOI: 10.1109/IC3I56241.2022.10073148

Kumar, K. S., Yadav, D., Joshi, S. K., Chakravarthi, M. K., Jain, A. K., & Tripathi, V. (2022). Blockchain Technology with Applications to Distributed Control and Cooperative Robotics. *Proceedings of 5th International Conference on Contemporary Computing and Informatics, IC3I 2022*, 206 – 211. DOI: 10.1109/IC3I56241.2022.10073275

Kumar, N. M., Islam, S., Podder, A. K., Selim, A., Bajaj, M., & Kamel, S. (2023). Lifecycle-based feasibility indicators for floating solar photovoltaic plants along with implementable energy enhancement strategies and framework-driven assessment approaches leading to advancements in the simulation tool. *Frontiers in Energy Research, 11*, 1075384. Advance online publication. DOI: 10.3389/fenrg.2023.1075384

Kumar, R., Goel, R., Singh, T., Mohanty, S. M., Gupta, D., Alkhayyat, A., & Khanna, R. (2024). Sustainable Finance Factors in Indian Economy: Analysis on Policy of Climate Change and Energy Sector. *Fluctuation and Noise Letters, 23*(2), 2440004. Advance online publication. DOI: 10.1142/S0219477524400042

Kumar, R., Kathuria, S., Malholtra, R. K., Kumar, A., Gehlot, A., & Joshi, K. (2023). Role of Cloud Computing in Goods and Services Tax(GST) and Future Application. *2nd International Conference on Sustainable Computing and Data Communication Systems, ICSCDS 2023 - Proceedings*, 1443–1447. DOI: 10.1109/ICSCDS56580.2023.10104597

Kumar, R., & Khanna, R. (2023a). Role of Artificial Intelligence in Digital Currency and Future Applications. *Proceedings of the 2023 2nd International Conference on Augmented Intelligence and Sustainable Systems, ICAISS 2023*, 42–46. DOI: 10.1109/ICAISS58487.2023.10250480

Kumar, R., & Khanna, R. (2023b). RPA (Robotic Process Automation) in Finance & Accounting and Future Scope. *Proceedings of the 2023 2nd International Conference on Augmented Intelligence and Sustainable Systems, ICAISS 2023*, 1640–1645. DOI: 10.1109/ICAISS58487.2023.10250496

Kumar, R., Khannna Malholtra, R., & Grover, C. A. N. (2023). Review on Artificial Intelligence Role in Implementation of Goods and Services Tax(GST) and Future Scope. *2023 International Conference on Artificial Intelligence and Smart Communication, AISC 2023*, 348–351. DOI: 10.1109/AISC56616.2023.10085030

Kumar, R., Lande, A., Kumar, D., Malhotra, R. K., & Sharma, A. (2023). Technology Bridging -in Entrepreneurs and Consumers in Product Development. *ISED 2023 - International Conference on Intelligent Systems and Embedded Design*. DOI: 10.1109/ISED59382.2023.10444599

Kumar, R., Malholtra, R. K., Singh, R., Kathuria, S., Balyan, R., & Pal, P. (2023). Artificial Intelligence Role in Electronic Invoice Under Goods and Services Tax. *2023 International Conference on Computational Intelligence, Communication Technology and Networking, CICTN 2023*, 140–143. DOI: 10.1109/CICTN57981.2023.10140870

Kumar, R., Malhotra, R. K., & Grover, N. (2023). Data Mining in Credit Scoring and Future Application. *International Conference on Innovative Data Communication Technologies and Application, ICIDCA 2023 - Proceedings*, 1096–1100. DOI: 10.1109/ICIDCA56705.2023.10100032

Kumar, R., Malhotra, R. K., Pandey, S., Gehlot, A., Gautam, I., & Chamola, S. (2023). Role of Artificial Intelligence in Input Tax Credit Reconciliation. *Proceedings - 2023 3rd International Conference on Pervasive Computing and Social Networking, ICPCSN 2023*, 497–501. DOI: 10.1109/ICPCSN58827.2023.00086

Kumar, R., Singh, T., Mohanty, S. N., Goel, R., Gupta, D., Alharbi, M., & Khanna, R. (2023). Study on online payments and e-commerce with SOR model. *International Journal of Retail & Distribution Management*. Advance online publication. DOI: 10.1108/IJRDM-03-2023-0137

Kumar, V., & Korovin, G. (2023). A Comparision of Digital Transformation of Industry in the Russian Federation with the European Union. In K. V., K. G.L., A. V., & K. E. (Eds.), *Lecture Notes in Information Systems and Organisation: Vol. 61 LNISO* (pp. 45 – 57). Springer Science and Business Media Deutschland GmbH. DOI: 10.1007/978-3-031-30351-7_5

Kumar, V., Sharma, N. K., Mittal, A., & Verma, P. (2023). The Role of IoT and IIoT in Supplier and Customer Continuous Improvement Interface. *EAI/Springer Innovations in Communication and Computing*, 161 – 174. DOI: 10.1007/978-3-031-19711-6_7

Lade, J., Mohammed, K. A., Singh, D., Prasad Verma, R., Math, P., Saraswat, M., & Raj Gupta, L. (2023). A critical review of fabrication routes and their effects on mechanical properties of AMMCs. *Materials Today: Proceedings*. Advance online publication. DOI: 10.1016/j.matpr.2023.03.041

Mandalapu, S. R., Sivamuni, K., Chitra Devi, D., Aswal, U. S., Sherly, S. I., & Balaji, N. A. (2023). An Architecture-based Self-Typing Service for Cloud Native Applications. *Proceedings of the 4th International Conference on Smart Electronics and Communication, ICOSEC 2023*, 562 – 566. DOI: 10.1109/ICOSEC58147.2023.10276313

Joshitta, S. M., Sunil, M. P., Bodhankar, A., Sreedevi, C., & Khanna, R. (2023, May). The Integration of Machine Learning Technique with the Existing System to Predict the Flight Prices. In 2023 3rd International Conference on Advance Computing and Innovative Technologies in Engineering (ICACITE) (pp. 398-402). IEEE.

Maurya, S. K., Ghosal, A., & Manna, A. (2022). Experimental investigations during fabrication and electrical discharge machining of hybrid Al/(SiC+ZrO2+NiTi) MMC. *International Journal of Machining and Machinability of Materials, 24*(3–4), 215–230. DOI: 10.1504/IJMMM.2022.125195

Medhi, M. K., Ambust, S., Kumar, R., & Das, A. J. (2023). Characterization and Purification of Biosurfactants. In *Advancements in Biosurfactants Research*. Springer International Publishing., DOI: 10.1007/978-3-031-21682-4_4

Mehershilpa, G., Prasad, D., Sai Kiran, C., Shaikh, A., Jayashree, K., & Socrates, S. (2023). EDM machining of Ti6Al4V alloy using colloidal biosilica. *Materials Today: Proceedings*. Advance online publication. DOI: 10.1016/j.matpr.2023.02.443

Mishra, P., Aggarwal, P., Vidyarthi, A., Singh, P., Khan, B., Alhelou, H. H., & Siano, P. (2021). VMShield: Memory Introspection-Based Malware Detection to Secure Cloud-Based Services against Stealthy Attacks. *IEEE Transactions on Industrial Informatics, 17*(10), 6754–6764. DOI: 10.1109/TII.2020.3048791

Mitra, D., Mondal, R., Khoshru, B., Senapati, A., Radha, T. K., Mahakur, B., Uniyal, N., Myo, E. M., Boutaj, H., Sierra, B. E. G. U. E. R. R. A., Panneerselvam, P., Ganeshamurthy, A. N., Elković, S. A. N. Đ. J., Vasić, T., Rani, A., Dutta, S., & Mohapatra, P. K. D. A. S.MITRA. (2022). Actinobacteria-enhanced plant growth, nutrient acquisition, and crop protection: Advances in soil, plant, and microbial multifactorial interactions. *Pedosphere, 32*(1), 149–170. DOI: 10.1016/S1002-0160(21)60042-5

Neha, M., S., Alfurhood, B. S., Bakhare, R., Poongavanam, S., & Khanna, R. (2023). The Role and Impact of Artificial Intelligence on Retail Business and its Developments. *2023 International Conference on Artificial Intelligence and Smart Communication, AISC 2023*, 1098–1101. DOI: 10.1109/AISC56616.2023.10085624

Pai, H. A., Almuzaini, K. K., Ali, L., Javeed, A., Pant, B., Pareek, P. K., & Akwafo, R. (2022). Delay-Driven Opportunistic Routing with Multichannel Cooperative Neighbor Discovery for Industry 4.0 Wireless Networks Based on Power and Load Awareness. *Wireless Communications and Mobile Computing, 2022*, 1–12. Advance online publication. DOI: 10.1155/2022/5256133

Pande, S. D., Bhatt, A., Chamoli, S., Saini, D. K. J. B., Kute, U. T., & Ahammad, S. H. (2023). Design of Atmel PLC and its Application as Automation of Coal Handling Plant. *2023 International Conference on Sustainable Emerging Innovations in Engineering and Technology, ICSEIET 2023*, 178 – 183. DOI: 10.1109/ICSEIET58677.2023.10303627

Pandey, N. K., Kashyap, S., Sharma, A., & Diwakar, M. (2023). Contribution of Cloud-Based Services in Post-Pandemic Technology Sustainability and Challenges: A Future Direction. In *Evolving Networking Technologies: Developments and Future Directions*. wiley. DOI: 10.1002/9781119836667.ch4

Pandya, D. J., Kumar, Y., Singh, D. P., Vairavel, D. K., Deepak, A., Rao, A. K., & Rana, A. (2023). Automatic Power Factor Compensation for Industrial Use to Minimize Penalty. *Proceedings of International Conference on Contemporary Computing and Informatics, IC3I 2023*, 2499 – 2504. DOI: 10.1109/IC3I59117.2023.10398095

Pant, R., Gupta, A., Pant, G., Chaubey, K. K., Kumar, G., & Patrick, N. (2022). Second-generation biofuels: Facts and future. In *Relationship between Microbes and the Environment for Sustainable Ecosystem Services: Microbial Tools for Sustainable Ecosystem Services: Volume 3* (Vol. 3). Elsevier. DOI: 10.1016/B978-0-323-89936-9.00011-4

Poswal, P., Chauhan, A., Aarya, D. D., Boadh, R., Rajoria, Y. K., & Gaiola, S. U. (2022). Optimal strategy for remanufacturing system of sustainable products with trade credit under uncertain scenario. *Materials Today: Proceedings*, *69*, 165–173. DOI: 10.1016/j.matpr.2022.08.303

Praveenchandar, J., Vetrithangam, D., Kaliappan, S., Karthick, M., Pegada, N. K., Patil, P. P., Rao, S. G., & Umar, S. (2022). IoT-Based Harmful Toxic Gases Monitoring and Fault Detection on the Sensor Dataset Using Deep Learning Techniques. *Scientific Programming*, *2022*, 1–11. Advance online publication. DOI: 10.1155/2022/7516328

Rajawat, A. S., Singh, S., Gangil, B., Ranakoti, L., Sharma, S., Asyraf, M. R. M., & Razman, M. R. (2022). Effect of Marble Dust on the Mechanical, Morphological, and Wear Performance of Basalt Fibre-Reinforced Epoxy Composites for Structural Applications. *Polymers*, *14*(7), 1325. Advance online publication. DOI: 10.3390/polym14071325 PMID: 35406199

Rajbalaji, S., Raman, R., Pant, B., Rathour, N., Rajagopa, B. R., & Prasad, C. R. (2023). Design of deep learning models for the identifications of harmful attack activities in IIOT. *2023 International Conference on Artificial Intelligence and Smart Communication, AISC 2023*, 609 – 613. DOI: 10.1109/AISC56616.2023.10085088

Rajeswari, M., Kumar, N., Raman, P., Patjoshi, P. K., Singh, V., & Pundir, S. (2022). Optimal Analysis for Enterprise Financial Management Based on Artificial Intelligence and Parallel Computing Method. *Proceedings of 5th International Conference on Contemporary Computing and Informatics, IC3I 2022*, 2081 – 2086. DOI: 10.1109/IC3I56241.2022.10072851

Ram, M., Negi, G., Goyal, N., & Kumar, A. (2022). Analysis of a Stochastic Model with Rework System. *Journal of Reliability and Statistical Studies, 15*(2), 553–582. DOI: 10.13052/jrss0974-8024.1527

Ram, M., & Xing, L. (2023). Reliability Modeling in Industry 4.0. In *Reliability Modeling in Industry 4.0*. Elsevier., DOI: 10.1016/C2021-0-01679-5

Raman, R., Buddhi, D., Lakhera, G., Gupta, Z., Joshi, A., & Saini, D. (2023). An investigation on the role of artificial intelligence in scalable visual data analytics. *2023 International Conference on Artificial Intelligence and Smart Communication, AISC 2023*, 666 – 670. DOI: 10.1109/AISC56616.2023.10085495

Raman, R., Kumar, R., Ghai, S., Gehlot, A., Raju, A. M., & Barve, A. (2023). A New Method of Optical Spectrum Analysis for Advanced Wireless Communications. *2023 3rd International Conference on Advance Computing and Innovative Technologies in Engineering, ICACITE 2023*, 1719 – 1723. DOI: 10.1109/ICACITE57410.2023.10182414

Rana, M. S., Cavaliere, L. P. L., Mishra, A. B., Padhye, P., Singh, R. R., & Khanna, R. (2022). Internet of Things (IOT) Based Assessment for Effective Monitoring Data Against Malicious Attacks on Financial Collectors. *2022 2nd International Conference on Advance Computing and Innovative Technologies in Engineering, ICACITE 2022*, 177–181. DOI: 10.1109/ICACITE53722.2022.9823612

Rana, M. S., Dixit, A. K., Rajan, M. S., Malhotra, S., Radhika, S., & Pant, B. (2022). An Empirical Investigation in Applying Reliable Industry 4.0 Based Machine Learning (ML) Approaches in Analysing and Monitoring Smart Meters using Multivariate Analysis of Variance (Manova). *2022 2nd International Conference on Advance Computing and Innovative Technologies in Engineering, ICACITE 2022*, 603 – 607. DOI: 10.1109/ICACITE53722.2022.9823597

Rawat, R., Sharma, S., & Goyal, H. R. (2023). Intelligent Digital Financial Inclusion System Architectures for Industry 5.0 Enabled Digital Society. *Winter Summit on Smart Computing and Networks. WiSSCoN, 2023*, 1–5. Advance online publication. DOI: 10.1109/WiSSCoN56857.2023.10133858

Reepu, R., Taneja, S., Ozen, E., & Singh, A. (2023). A globetrotter to the future of marketing: Metaverse. In *Cultural Marketing and Metaverse for Consumer Engagement*. IGI Global., DOI: 10.4018/978-1-6684-8312-1.ch001

Sahu, S. R., & Rawat, K. S. (2023). Analysis of Land subsidencein coastal and urban areas by using various techniques– Literature Review. *The Indonesian Journal of Geography, 55*(3), 488–495. DOI: 10.22146/ijg.83675

Salama, R., Al-Turjman, F., Bordoloi, D., & Yadav, S. P. (2023). Wireless Sensor Networks and Green Networking for 6G communication- An Overview. *2023 International Conference on Computational Intelligence, Communication Technology and Networking, CICTN 2023*, 830 – 834. DOI: 10.1109/CICTN57981.2023.10141262

Sathyapriya, G., Natarajan, U., Sureshkumar, B., Navaneethakrishnan, G., Palanisamy, R., Bajaj, M., Sharma, N. K., & Kitmo, . (2022). Quality and Tool Stability Improvement in Turning Operation Using Plastic Compliant Damper. *Journal of Nanomaterials, 2022*(1), 8654603. Advance online publication. DOI: 10.1155/2022/8654603

Sathyaseelan, K., Vyas, T., Madala, R., Chamundeeswari, V., Rai Goyal, H., & Jayaraman, R. (2023). Blockchain Enabled Intelligent Surveillance System Model with AI and IoT. *Proceedings of 8th IEEE International Conference on Science, Technology, Engineering and Mathematics, ICONSTEM 2023*. DOI: 10.1109/ICONSTEM56934.2023.10142303

Shah, J. K., Sharma, R., Misra, A., Sharma, M., Joshi, S., Kaushal, D., & Bafila, S. (2023). Industry 4.0 Enabled Smart Manufacturing: Unleashing the Power of Artificial Intelligence and Blockchain. *2023 1st DMIHER International Conference on Artificial Intelligence in Education and Industry 4.0, IDICAIEI 2023*. DOI: 10.1109/IDICAIEI58380.2023.10406671

Sharma, E., Rana, S., Sharma, I., Sati, P., & Dhyani, P. (2023). Organic polymers for CO2 capture and conversion. In *CO2-Philic Polymers, Nanocomposites and Solvents: Capture, Conversion and Industrial Products*. Elsevier., DOI: 10.1016/B978-0-323-85777-2.00002-0

Sharma, M., Kumar, A., Luthra, S., Joshi, S., & Upadhyay, A. (2022). The impact of environmental dynamism on low-carbon practices and digital supply chain networks to enhance sustainable performance: An empirical analysis. *Business Strategy and the Environment, 31*(4), 1776–1788. DOI: 10.1002/bse.2983

Sharma, M., Luthra, S., Joshi, S., & Kumar, A. (2022). Analysing the impact of sustainable human resource management practices and industry 4.0 technologies adoption on employability skills. *International Journal of Manpower, 43*(2), 463–485. DOI: 10.1108/IJM-02-2021-0085

Sharma, P., Malhotra, R. K., Ojha, M. K., & Gupta, S. (2022). Impact of meditation on mental & physical health and thereby on academic performance of students: A study of higher educational institutions of Uttarakhand. *Journal of Medical Pharmaceutical and Allied Sciences, 11*(2), 4641–4644. DOI: 10.55522/jmpas.V11I2.2309

Sharma, S., & Bhadula, S. (2023). Secure Federated Learning for Intelligent Industry 4.0 IoT Enabled Self Skin Care Application System. *Proceedings of the 2nd International Conference on Applied Artificial Intelligence and Computing, ICAAIC 2023*, 1164 – 1170. DOI: 10.1109/ICAAIC56838.2023.10141028

Sharma, S., Gupta, A., & Tyagi, R. (2023). Sustainable Natural Resources Utilization Decision System for Better Society Using Vedic Scripture, Cloud Computing, and IoT. In B. R.C., S. K.M., & D. M. (Eds.), *Proceedings of IEEE 2023 5th International Conference on Advances in Electronics, Computers and Communications, ICAECC 2023*. Institute of Electrical and Electronics Engineers Inc. DOI: 10.1109/ICAECC59324.2023.10560335

Sharma, S., Mishra, R. R., Joshi, V., & Kour, K. (2020). Analysis and Interpretation of Global Air Quality. *2020 11th International Conference on Computing, Communication and Networking Technologies, ICCCNT 2020*. DOI: 10.1109/ICCCNT49239.2020.9225532

Singh, A., Kumar, P., & Taneja, S. (2024). Artificial Intelligence and Machine Learning-Powered Smart Finance. In Taneja, P. K. S., & Singh, A. (Eds.), *IGI Global*. IGI Global., DOI: 10.4018/979-8-3693-3264-1

Singh, K. D., Deep Singh, P., Bansal, A., Kaur, G., Khullar, V., & Tripathi, V. (2023). Exploratory Data Analysis and Customer Churn Prediction for the Telecommunication Industry. *ACCESS 2023 - 2023 3rd International Conference on Advances in Computing, Communication, Embedded and Secure Systems*, 197 – 201. DOI: 10.1109/ACCESS57397.2023.10199700

Singh, K. D., Singh, P., Chhabra, R., Kaur, G., Bansal, A., & Tripathi, V. (2023). Cyber-Physical Systems for Smart City Applications: A Comparative Study. In K. R., K. R., G. M., G. M., S. R., & S. R. (Eds.), *2023 International Conference on Advancement in Computation and Computer Technologies, InCACCT 2023* (pp. 871 – 876). Institute of Electrical and Electronics Engineers Inc. DOI: 10.1109/InCACCT57535.2023.10141719

Singh, K. D., Singh, P., Kaur, G., Khullar, V., Chhabra, R., & Tripathi, V. (2023). Education 4.0: Exploring the Potential of Disruptive Technologies in Transforming Learning. *Proceedings of International Conference on Computational Intelligence and Sustainable Engineering Solution, CISES 2023*, 586 – 591. DOI: 10.1109/CISES58720.2023.10183547

Singh, K. D., Singh, P., Tripathi, V., & Khullar, V. (2022). A Novel and Secure Framework to Detect Unauthorized Access to an Optical Fog-Cloud Computing Network. In R. H.S., B. R., G. P.K., & S. V.K. (Eds.), *PDGC 2022 - 2022 7th International Conference on Parallel, Distributed and Grid Computing* (pp. 618 – 622). Institute of Electrical and Electronics Engineers Inc. DOI: 10.1109/PDGC56933.2022.10053223

Singh, N. K., Singh, Y., Rahim, E. A., Senthil Siva Subramanian, T., & Sharma, A. (2023). Electric discharge machining of hybrid composite with bio-dielectrics for sustainable developments. *Australian Journal of Mechanical Engineering*. Advance online publication. DOI: 10.1080/14484846.2023.2249577

Singh, N. K., Singh, Y., Singh, Y., Rahim, E. A., Sharma, A., Singla, A., & Ranjit, P. S. (2023). The Effectiveness of Balanites aegyptiaca Oil Nanofluid Augmented with Nanoparticles as Cutting Fluids during the Turning Process. In *Biowaste and Biomass in Biofuel Applications*. CRC Press., DOI: 10.1201/9781003265597-7

Singh, S. K., Chauhan, A., & Sarkar, B. (2023). Sustainable biodiesel supply chain model based on waste animal fat with subsidy and advertisement. *Journal of Cleaner Production*, *382*, 134806. Advance online publication. DOI: 10.1016/j.jclepro.2022.134806

Širić, I., Eid, E. M., Taher, M. A., El-Morsy, M. H. E., Osman, H. E. M., Kumar, P., Adelodun, B., Abou Fayssal, S., Mioč, B., Andabaka, Ž., Goala, M., Kumari, S., Bachheti, A., Choi, K. S., & Kumar, V. (2022). Combined Use of Spent Mushroom Substrate Biochar and PGPR Improves Growth, Yield, and Biochemical Response of Cauliflower (Brassica oleracea var. botrytis): A Preliminary Study on Greenhouse Cultivation. *Horticulturae*, *8*(9), 830. Advance online publication. DOI: 10.3390/horticulturae8090830

Sonnad, S., Awasthy, M., Rane, K., Banerjee, M., Buddhi, D., & Pant, B. (2022). Blockchain-Based Secure Mengers Authentication for Industrial IoT. In D. R.K., S. A.Kr., K. G., & B. S. (Eds.), *Proceedings of the 2022 11th International Conference on System Modeling and Advancement in Research Trends, SMART 2022* (pp. 853 – 858). Institute of Electrical and Electronics Engineers Inc. DOI: 10.1109/SMART55829.2022.10046934

Sunori, S. K., Kant, S., Agarwal, P., & Juneja, P. (2023). Development of Rainfall Prediction Models using Linear and Non-linear Regression Techniques. *2023 4th IEEE Global Conference for Advancement in Technology, GCAT 2023*. DOI: 10.1109/GCAT59970.2023.10353508

Suresh, M., Antony, J., Nair, G., & Garza-Reyes, J. A. (2023). Lean-sustainability assessment framework development: Evidence from the construction industry. *Total Quality Management & Business Excellence*, *34*(15–16), 2046–2081. DOI: 10.1080/14783363.2023.2222088

Tamilmani, S., Mohan, T., Jeyalakshmi, S., Shukla, G. P., Gehlot, A., & Shukla, S. K. (2023). Blockchain Integrated with Industrial IOT Towards Industry 4.0. *2023 International Conference on Artificial Intelligence and Smart Communication, AISC 2023*, 575 – 581. DOI: 10.1109/AISC56616.2023.10085226

Taneja, S., Gupta, M., Bhushan, P., Bhatnagar, M., & Singh, A. (2023). Cultural marketing in the digital era. In *Cultural Marketing and Metaverse for Consumer Engagement*. IGI Global., DOI: 10.4018/978-1-6684-8312-1.ch008

Taneja, S., Gupta, S., Singh, A., Bhatnagar, M., & Gaur, A. (2023). Green management - A new paradigm in the world of business. *Green Management - A New Paradigm in the World of Business*, 1–230. DOI: 10.52305/DLIH6622

Taneja, S., & Özen, E. (2023). To analyse the relationship between bank's green financing and environmental performance. *International Journal of Electronic Finance*, *12*(2), 163–175. DOI: 10.1504/IJEF.2023.129919

Taneja, S., & Sharma, V. (2023). Role of beaconing marketing in improving customer buying experience. In *Enhancing Customer Engagement Through Location-Based Marketing*. IGI Global., DOI: 10.4018/978-1-6684-8177-6.ch012

Tiwari, R., Agrawal, P., Singh, P., Bajaj, S., Verma, V., & Chauhan, A. S. (2023). Technology Enabled Integrated Fusion Teaching for Enhancing Learning Outcomes in Higher Education. *International Journal of Emerging Technologies in Learning*, *18*(7), 243–249. DOI: 10.3991/ijet.v18i07.36799

Tyagi, S., Jindal, T., Krishna, S. H., Hassen, S. M., Shukla, S. K., & Kaur, C. (2022). Comparative Analysis of Artificial Intelligence and its Powered Technologies Applications in the Finance Sector. *Proceedings of 5th International Conference on Contemporary Computing and Informatics, IC3I 2022*, 260 – 264. DOI: 10.1109/IC3I56241.2022.10073077

Tyagi, S., Krishna, K. H., Joshi, K., Ghodke, T. A., Kumar, A., & Gupta, A. (2023). Integration of PLCC modem and Wi-Fi for Campus Street Light Monitoring. In N. P., S. M., K. M., J. V., & G. K. (Eds.), *Proceedings - 4th IEEE 2023 International Conference on Computing, Communication, and Intelligent Systems, ICCCIS 2023* (pp. 1113 – 1116). Institute of Electrical and Electronics Engineers Inc. DOI: 10.1109/ICCCIS60361.2023.10425715

Unhelkar, B., Joshi, S., Sharma, M., Prakash, S., Mani, A. K., & Prasad, M. (2022). Enhancing supply chain performance using RFID technology and decision support systems in the industry 4.0–A systematic literature review. *International Journal of Information Management Data Insights*, *2*(2), 100084. Advance online publication. DOI: 10.1016/j.jjimei.2022.100084

Upreti, H., & Malhotra, R. K. (2024). Bridging The Urban-Rural Education Gap In India Through CSR (Corporate Social Responsibility) Initiatives: A Conceptual Study With Special Reference To Sustainable Development Goal 4 (Quality Education). In P. P.K. (Ed.), *E3S Web of Conferences* (Vol. 556). EDP Sciences. DOI: 10.1051/e3sconf/202455601032

Upreti, H., Uddin, Z., Pandey, A. K., & Joshi, N. (2023). Particle swarm optimization based numerical study for pressure, flow, and heat transfer over a rotating disk with temperature dependent nanofluid properties. *Numerical Heat Transfer Part A*, *83*(8), 815–844. DOI: 10.1080/10407782.2022.2156412

Venkatesh, J., Shukla, P. K., Ahanger, T. A., Maheshwari, M., Pant, B., Hemamalini, R. R., & Halifa, A. (2023). A Complex Brain Learning Skeleton Comprising Enriched Pattern Neural Network System for Next Era Internet of Things. *Journal of Healthcare Engineering*, *2023*(1), 2506144. Advance online publication. DOI: 10.1155/2023/2506144

Wazid, M., Das, A. K., & Park, Y. (2021). Blockchain-Envisioned Secure Authentication Approach in AIoT: Applications, Challenges, and Future Research. *Wireless Communications and Mobile Computing*, *2021*(1), 3866006. Advance online publication. DOI: 10.1155/2021/3866006

Yeruva, A. R., Vijaya Durga, C. S. L., Gokulavasan, B., Pant, K., Chaturvedi, P., & Srivastava, A. P. (2022). A Smart Healthcare Monitoring System Based on Fog Computing Architecture. *Proceedings of International Conference on Technological Advancements in Computational Sciences, ICTACS 2022*, 904 – 909. DOI: 10.1109/ICTACS56270.2022.9987881

Compilation of References

Abakumova, O. A., Lyubanenko, A. V., & Vazhenina, T. M. (2021, November). International Environmental Management Standards as a Tool of Legal Business Regulation. In *International Scientific and Practical Conference Operations and Project management: strategies and trends* (pp. 370-381). Cham: Springer International Publishing.

Abbi, Y. P., & Jain, S. (2006). *Handbook on energy audit and environment management. The Energy and Resources Institute*. TERI.

Abbott, L. J., Parker, S., & Presley, T. J. (2012). Female board presence and the likelihood of financial restatement. *Accounting Horizons*, *26*(4), 607–629. DOI: 10.2308/acch-50249

Abdullah, A., Hassan, R., & Kassim, S. (2020). A real asset management approach for Islamic investment in containerships. *Journal of Islamic Accounting and Business Research*, *11*(1), 27–48. DOI: 10.1108/JIABR-07-2017-0105

Abdullah, K. H., Abd Aziz, F. S., Dani, R., Hammood, W. A., & Setiawan, E. (2023). Urban Pollution: A Bibliometric Review. *ASM Science Journal*, *18*, 1–16. DOI: 10.32802/asmscj.2023.1440

Abuali, A., Alrefaei, A. A., Aljohani, S. A., Aloufi, I. N., Ghabban, F., Ameerbakhsh, O., Alfadli, I., Al-Shehri, A. H., Fallatah, N. A., & Younis, H. A. (2024). The impact of e-commerce on traditional businesses in Saudi Arabia. *Journal of Service Science and Management*, *17*(4), 354–366. DOI: 10.4236/jssm.2024.174018

Abughazaleh, N., O'Connell, V., & Princen, J. (2015). Audit quality, auditor size, and legal environments. *Quarterly Journal of Finance & Accounting*, 39-78.

Adams, C. A. (2004). The ethical, social and environmental reporting-performance portrayal gap. *Accounting, Auditing & Accountability Journal*, *17*(5), 731–757. DOI: 10.1108/09513570410567791

Afolabi, H., Ram, R., Hussainey, K., Nandy, M., & Lodh, S. (2023). Exploration of small and medium entities' actions on sustainability practices and their implications for a greener economy. *Journal of Applied Accounting Research, 24*(4), 655–681. DOI: 10.1108/JAAR-09-2022-0252

Agarwal, P., & Sharma, S. (2023). Smart Urban Traffic Management System using Energy Efficient Optimized Path Discovery. *Proceedings of the 3rd International Conference on Artificial Intelligence and Smart Energy, ICAIS 2023*, 858 – 863. DOI: 10.1109/ICAIS56108.2023.10073840

Ageeva, O., Karp, M., & Sidorov, A. (2021). The application of digital technologies in financial reporting and auditing. In Popkova, E. G., & Sergi, B. S. (Eds.), *Smart technologies" for society, state and economy. ISC 2020* (Vol. 155, pp. 1481–1490). Springer., DOI: 10.1007/978-3-030-59126-7_167

Ahmad, I., Sharma, S., Kumar, R., Dhyani, S., & Dumka, A. (2023). Data Analytics of Online Education during Pandemic Health Crisis: A Case Study. *2nd Edition of IEEE Delhi Section Owned Conference, DELCON 2023 - Proceedings*. DOI: 10.1109/DELCON57910.2023.10127423

Aiyappa, S., Kodikal, R., & Rahiman, H. U. (2024). Accelerating Gender Equality for Sustainable Development: A Case Study of Dakshina Kannada District, India. *Technical and Vocational Education and Training, 38*, 335–349. DOI: 10.1007/978-981-99-6909-8_30

Ajay, D., Sharad, K., Singh, K. P., & Sharma, S. (2023). Impact of Prolonged Mental Torture on Housewives in Middle Class Families. *Journal for ReAttach Therapy and Developmental Diversities, 6*(4), 1–7.

Akberdina, V., Kumar, V., Kyriakopoulos, G. L., & Kuzmin, E. (2023). Editorial: What Does Industry's Digital Transition Hold in the Uncertainty Context? In K. V., K. G.L., A. V., & K. E. (Eds.), *Lecture Notes in Information Systems and Organisation: Vol. 61 LNISO* (pp. 1 – 4). Springer Science and Business Media Deutschland GmbH. DOI: 10.1007/978-3-031-30351-7_1

Akgün, A. İ. (2022). Investigating the relationship between bank performance and accounting standards: Evidence from M&As in European banking. *Journal of Capital Markets Studies, 6*(1), 106–124. DOI: 10.1108/JCMS-10-2021-0032

Akisik, O. (2014). *Financial reporting and foreign direct investments in Latin America. Accounting in Latin America*. Emerald Group Publishing.

Akisik, O., & Mangaliso, M. P. (2020). How IFRS influence the relationship between the types of FDI and economic growth: An empirical analysis on African countries. *Journal of Applied Accounting Research, 21*(1), 60–76. DOI: 10.1108/JAAR-02-2018-0025

Alba, J. D., Park, D., & Wang, P. (2009). Corporate governance and merger and acquisition foreign direct investment: Firm-level evidence from Japanese foreign direct investment into the US. *ADB Economics Working Paper Series, 147*, 1–18. https://www.scopus.com/inward/record.uri?eid=2-s2.0-77949419995&partnerID=40&md5=78512c36171f138edc833c58d9dc0b1c

Albu, N., Albu, C. N., Bunea, Ş., Calu, D. A., & Girbina, M. M. (2014). A comparative study of implementation of IFRS in emerging economies. *Journal of Accounting in Emerging Economies, 4*(1), 4–29. DOI: 10.1108/JAEE-06-2011-0014

Alderman, J. (2017). Does auditor gender influence auditor liability? Exploring the impact of the crime congruency effect on jurors' perceptions of auditor negligence. *Advances in Accounting, 38*, 75–87. DOI: 10.1016/j.adiac.2017.07.006

Alexopoulos, C., Al-Tamimi, T. A. S., & Saxena, S. (2023). Were the higher educational institutions (HEIs) in Oman ready to face pedagogical challenges during COVID-19? *Arab Gulf Journal of Scientific Research*. Advance online publication. DOI: 10.1108/AGJSR-03-2023-0095

Ali, M. J., & Hwang, L. S. (2000). Country-specific factors related to financial reporting and the value relevance of accounting data. *Journal of Accounting Research, 38*(1), 1–21. DOI: 10.2307/2672920

Alimov, A. (2015). Labor market regulations and cross-border mergers and acquisitions. *Journal of International Business Studies, 46*(8), 984–1009. DOI: 10.1057/jibs.2015.16

Alkaraan, F. (2020). Strategic investment decision-making practices in large manufacturing companies: A role for emergent analysis techniques? *Meditari Accountancy Research, 28*(4), 633–653. DOI: 10.1108/MEDAR-05-2019-0484

Allee, K. D., & Yohn, T. L. (2009). The demand for financial statements in an unregulated environment: An examination of the production and use of financial statements by privately held small businesses. *The Accounting Review, 84*(1), 1–25. DOI: 10.2308/accr.2009.84.1.1

Almuwallad, H., & Alhumoudi, H. (2024). The impact of e-commerce on organizational and financial performance in SMEs: Evidence from Saudi Arabia. *International Journal of Business and Management, 19*(4), 1–12. DOI: 10.5539/ijbm.v19n4p1

Alon, A., & Dwyer, P. (2014). Early adoption of IFRS as a strategic response to transnational and local influences. *The International Journal of Accounting*, *49*(3), 348–370. DOI: 10.1016/j.intacc.2014.07.003

Alonge, E. O., Dudu, O. F., & Alao, O. B.Enoch O. AlongeOritsematosan Faith DuduOlakunle Babatunde Alao. (2024). The impact of digital transformation on financial reporting and accountability in emerging markets. *International Journal of Science and Technology Research Archive*, *7*(2), 25–49. DOI: 10.53771/ijstra.2024.7.2.0061

Alrashed, F. A., Alsubiheen, A. M., Alshammari, H., Mazi, S. I., Al-Saud, S. A., Alayoubi, S., Kachanathu, S. J., Albarrati, A., Aldaihan, M. M., Ahmad, T., Sattar, K., Khan, S., & Dhiman, G. (2022). Stress, Anxiety, and Depression in Pre-Clinical Medical Students: Prevalence and Association with Sleep Disorders. *Sustainability (Basel)*, *14*(18), 11320. Advance online publication. DOI: 10.3390/su141811320

Alrawashedh, N. H., Zuraiqat, B., Abdallah, A., & Abushareah, M. (2024). Accounting and its impact on e-commerce in Jordan. *Journal of Financial Accounting and Management*, *17*(7), 1098–1108. DOI: 10.5281/zenodo.6923275

Alsahali, K., Malagueño, R., & Marques, A. (2024). Board attributes and companies' choice of sustainability assurance providers. *Accounting and Business Research*, *54*(4), 392–422. DOI: 10.1080/00014788.2023.2181141

Al-Shammari, B., & Brown, P. (2019). The impact of IFRS adoption on financial disclosure and cross-border investments. *Journal of International Business*, *23*(3), 214–237.

Altman, W. (2004). What's going on? *Engineering Management Journal (London)*, *14*(6), 42–43. DOI: 10.1049/em:20040614

Alzaidi, M. S., Subbalakshmi, C., Roshini, T. V., Shukla, P. K., Shukla, S. K., Dutta, P., & Alhassan, M. (2022). 5G-Telecommunication Allocation Network Using IoT Enabled Improved Machine Learning Technique. *Wireless Communications and Mobile Computing*, *2022*, 1–10. Advance online publication. DOI: 10.1155/2022/6229356

Ambika, K. S. B., Goswami, S., Pimplapure, V., Jweeg, M. J., Kant, K., & Gangodkar, D. (2023). Framework Towards Detection of Stress Level Through Classifying Physiological Signals Using Machine Learning. *2023 3rd International Conference on Advance Computing and Innovative Technologies in Engineering, ICACITE 2023*, 600 – 604. DOI: 10.1109/ICACITE57410.2023.10183013

Ameli, N., Drummond, P., Bisaro, A., Grubb, M., & Chenet, H. (2021). Climate finance and disclosure for institutional investors: Why transparency is not enough. *Climatic Change, 160*(4), 565–589. DOI: 10.1007/s10584-019-02542-2

Ami, A. S., Syafitri, L., & Meiriasari, V. (2023). The effect of e-commerce and the use of accounting information systems on the revenue cycle of micro, small, and medium enterprises (Study on culinary MSMEs in Prabumulih City). *Journal of Humanities* [JHSSB]. *Social Sciences and Business, 3*(1), 68–76. DOI: 10.32535/jhssb.v3i1.2720

Amir, E., & Ghitti, M. (2021). Financial Analysis of Mergers and Acquisitions: Understanding Financial Statements and Accounting Rules with Case Studies. In *Financial Analysis of Mergers and Acquisitions: Understanding Financial Statements and Accounting Rules with Case Studies*. Springer International Publishing., DOI: 10.1007/978-3-030-61769-1

Anand, A., Singh, M. P., Sah, S., Verma, A., Khatib, M. N., Pant, M., Zahiruddin, Q. S., & Rustagi, S. (2024). H5N1 avian influenza in USA: A call for vigilance in one health surveillance. *Clinical Infection in Practice, 23*, 100369. Advance online publication. DOI: 10.1016/j.clinpr.2024.100369

Antle, R., & Demski, J. S. (1991). Contracting frictions, regulation, and the structure of CPA firms. *Journal of Accounting Research, 29*, 1–24. DOI: 10.2307/2491000

Antle, R., Gordon, E., Narayanamoorthy, G., & Zhou, L. (2006). The joint determination of audit fees, non-audit fees, and abnormal accruals. *Review of Quantitative Finance and Accounting, 27*(3), 235–266. DOI: 10.1007/s11156-006-9430-y

Aramyan, L. H., Lansink, A. G. O., & Verstegen, J. A. (2007). Factors underlying the investment decision in energy-saving systems in Dutch horticulture. *Agricultural Systems, 94*(2), 520–527. DOI: 10.1016/j.agsy.2007.01.005

Ardakani, M. M., Ansari, A., Kia, M. R., Mousavion, S. A., & Pourhashemi, S. O. (2024). The effect of the adoption of e-commerce and digital marketing on the firm and sustainability performance of companies. *Journal of Soft Computing and Decision Support Systems, 11*(1), 23–38. DOI: 10.1016/j.jsds.2024.02.005

Arif, M., Sajjad, A., Farooq, S., Abrar, M., & Joyo, A. S. (2021). The impact of audit committee attributes on the quality and quantity of environmental, social and governance (ESG) disclosures. *Corporate Governance (Bradford), 21*(3), 497–514. DOI: 10.1108/CG-06-2020-0243

Armstrong, S. C., Barth, M. E., Jagolinzer, A. D., & Riedl, E. J. (2010). Market reaction to the adoption of IFRS in Europe. *The Accounting Review*, *85*(1), 31–61. DOI: 10.2308/accr.2010.85.1.31

Arora, A., Singh, R., Malik, K., & Kestwal, U. (2024). Association of sexual performance and intimacy with satisfaction in life in head and neck cancer patients: A review. *Oral Oncology Reports*, *11*, 100563. Advance online publication. DOI: 10.1016/j.oor.2024.100563

Arora, R., Chauhan, A., Singh, A. P., & Sharma, R. (2023). Optimization of a production inventory model of imperfect quality items for three-layer supply chain in fuzzy environment. *Benchmarking*. Advance online publication. DOI: 10.1108/BIJ-11-2021-0678

Asha, P., Mannepalli, K., Khilar, R., Subbulakshmi, N., Dhanalakshmi, R., Tripathi, V., Mohanavel, V., Sathyamurthy, R., & Sudhakar, M. (2022). Role of machine learning in attaining environmental sustainability. *Energy Reports*, *8*, 863–871. DOI: 10.1016/j.egyr.2022.09.206

Atanassova, A. (2018). Accounting problems in e-commerce. *Ekonomiczne Problemy Usług, 2*(131/1), 19–30. https://doi.org/DOI: 10.18276/epu.2018.131/1-02

Awal, G., & Khanna, R. (2019). Determinants of millennial online consumer behavior and prospective purchase decisions. *International Journal of Advanced Science and Technology*, *28*(18), 366–378.

Bachheti, A., Deepti, , Bachheti, R. K., Singh, A., Zebeaman, M., Hunde, Y., & Husen, A. (2023). Bioactive constituents and health promoting compounds of underutilized fruits of the northern Himalayas of India: A review. *Food Production, Processing and Nutrition*, *5*(1), 24. Advance online publication. DOI: 10.1186/s43014-023-00140-5

Bae, S., & Seol, I. (2006). An exploratory empirical investigation of environmental audit programs in S&P 500 companies. *Management Research News*, *29*(9), 573–579. DOI: 10.1108/01409170610709005

Bagwell, K., & Staiger, R. W. (2002). *The Economics of the World Trading System*. MIT Press. DOI: 10.7551/mitpress/2628.001.0001

Baker, C. R. (2020). Global trade regulations and financial reporting standards: A review of the intersection. *Journal of International Business Studies*, *39*(3), 212–228.

Bakkar, Y., & Nyola, A. P. (2021). Internationalization, foreign complexity and systemic risk: Evidence from European banks. *Journal of Financial Stability*, *55*, 100892. Advance online publication. DOI: 10.1016/j.jfs.2021.100892

Ball, R. (2006). International Financial Reporting Standards (IFRS): Pros and cons for investors. *Accounting and Business Research*, 36(sup1), 5-27.

Ball, R. (2009). Market and political/regulatory perspectives on the recent accounting scandals. *Journal of Accounting Research*, *47*(2), 277–323. DOI: 10.1111/j.1475-679X.2009.00325.x

Ball, R. (2016). IFRS—Ten years later. *Accounting and Business Research*, *46*(5), 545–571. DOI: 10.1080/00014788.2016.1182710

Ball, R. (2021). International financial reporting standards and the cross-border flow of capital. *Accounting and Business Research*, *51*(4), 375–400.

Bansal, S., Kumar, V., Kumari, A., & Kuzmin, E. (2023). Understanding the Role of Digital Technologies in Supply Chain Management of SMEs. In K. V., K. G.L., A. V., & K. E. (Eds.), *Lecture Notes in Information Systems and Organisation: Vol. 61 LNISO* (pp. 195 – 205). Springer Science and Business Media Deutschland GmbH. DOI: 10.1007/978-3-031-30351-7_16

Bansal, N., Bhatnagar, M., & Taneja, S. (2023). Balancing priorities through green optimism: A study elucidating initiatives, approaches, and strategies for sustainable supply chain management. In *Handbook of Research on Designing Sustainable Supply Chains to Achieve a Circular Economy*. IGI Global., DOI: 10.4018/978-1-6684-7664-2.ch004

Banu, D. A., Sheela, S., Muralimohan, N., Saranya, N., Kolar, A. B., & Santhya, V. (2023). Importance and Benefits of Green Audits to Education Institutions and Industrial Sectors. *International Journal of Environment and Climate Change*, *13*(12), 349–356. DOI: 10.9734/ijecc/2023/v13i123690

Barrett, M. (2019). The role of international trade agreements in enhancing corporate financial transparency. *Journal of International Business Studies*, *50*(3), 521–537.

Barth, M. E. (2008). Global financial reporting: Implications for U.S. accounting standards. *The Accounting Review*, *83*(5), 1159–1189. DOI: 10.2308/accr.2008.83.5.1159

Barth, M. E., & Landsman, W. R. (2010). How did financial reporting contribute to the financial crisis? *European Accounting Review*, *19*(3), 399–423. DOI: 10.1080/09638180.2010.498619

Barth, M., Landsman, W., & Lang, M. (2008). International accounting standards and accounting quality. *Journal of Accounting Research*, *46*(3), 467–498. DOI: 10.1111/j.1475-679X.2008.00287.x

Bartov, E., Goldberg, S. R., & Kim, M. (2005). Comparative value relevance among German, US, and International Accounting Standards: A German stock market perspective. *Journal of Accounting, Auditing & Finance, 20*(2), 95–119. DOI: 10.1177/0148558X0502000201

Bastianoni, S., Marchi, M., Caro, D., Casprini, P., & Pulselli, F. M. (2014). The connection between 2006 IPCC GHG inventory methodology and ISO 14064-1 certification standard–A reference point for the environmental policies at sub-national scale. *Environmental Science & Policy, 44*, 97–107. DOI: 10.1016/j.envsci.2014.07.015

Bathla, G., Kumar, S., Garg, H., & Saini, D. (2024). Artificial Intelligence in Healthcare: Emphasis on Diabetes, Hypertension, and Depression Management. In *Artificial Intelligence in Healthcare: Emphasis on Diabetes, Hypertension, and Depression Management*. CRC Press., DOI: 10.1201/9781003522096

Bell, T. B., Causholli, M., & Knechel, W. R. (2015). Audit firm tenure, non-audit services, and internal assessments of audit quality. *Journal of Accounting Research, 53*(3), 461–509. DOI: 10.1111/1475-679X.12078

Belwal, N., Juneja, P., & Sunori, S. K. (2023). Decoupler Control for a MIMO Process Model in an Industrial Process - A Review. *2023 2nd International Conference on Ambient Intelligence in Health Care, ICAIHC 2023*. DOI: 10.1109/ICAIHC59020.2023.10431463

Ben Othman, H., & Kossentini, A. (2015). IFRS adoption strategies and theories of economic development: Effects on the development of emerging stock markets. *Journal of Accounting in Emerging Economies, 5*(1), 70–121. DOI: 10.1108/JAEE-02-2012-0006

Ben Slama, F., Oussii, A. A., & Klibi, M. F. (2022). The rough road towards accounting harmonization of a developing country with a French accounting culture. *Accounting Research Journal, 35*(4), 490–507. DOI: 10.1108/ARJ-02-2021-0075

Bennani, S., & Elhamma, A. (2015). *La comptabilité en finance islamique selon les normes AAOIFI*. Éditions Universitaires Européennes.

Berglund, N. R., Eshleman, J. D., & Guo, P. (2018). Auditor size and going concern reporting. *Auditing, 37*(2), 1–25. DOI: 10.2308/ajpt-51786

Bhatnagar, M., Kumar, P., Taneja, S., Sood, K., & Grima, S. (2024). From digital overload to trading Zen: The role of digital detox in enhancing intraday trading performance. In *Business Drivers in Promoting Digital Detoxification*. IGI Global., DOI: 10.4018/979-8-3693-1107-3.ch010

Bhatnagar, M., Rajaram, R., Taneja, S., & Kumar, P. (2024). Balancing acts: The Yin and Yang of debit and credit on the stage of financial well-being. In *Emerging Perspectives on Financial Well-Being*. IGI Global., DOI: 10.4018/979-8-3693-1750-1.ch002

Bhatnagar, M., & Sehajpal, S. (2024). Leveraging AI for Financial Sustainability in Healthcare. In Ercan, O., Azad, S., Sanjay, T., Rajendra, R., & Paulo, D. J. (Eds.), *Sustainability, Innovation, and Consumer Preference* (pp. 411–426). IGI Global Scientific Publishing., DOI: 10.4018/979-8-3693-9699-5.ch017

Bhatnagar, M., Taneja, S., & Kumar, P. (2023). The Effectiveness of Carbon Pricing Mechanism in Steering Financial Flows Toward Sustainable Projects. *International Journal of Environmental Impacts*, *6*(4), 183–196. DOI: 10.18280/ijei.060403

Bhatnagar, M., Taneja, S., Kumar, P., & Özen, E. (2024). Does financial education act as a catalyst for SME competitiveness? *International Journal of Education Economics and Development*, *15*(3), 377–393. DOI: 10.1504/IJEED.2024.139306

Bhatt, C., Singh, S., Chauhan, R., Singh, T., & Uniyal, A. (2023). Artificial Intelligence in Current Education: Roles, Applications & Challenges. *Proceedings - 2023 3rd International Conference on Pervasive Computing and Social Networking, ICPCSN 2023*, 241 – 244. DOI: 10.1109/ICPCSN58827.2023.00045

Bhatti, K. K., & Negi, A. (2018). Green store attributes and infrastructure: A connecting link between retailers and consumers to bring sustainability. *International Journal of Civil Engineering and Technology*, *9*(11), 190–198.

Bhatt, S., Dani, R., & Singh, A. K. (2024). Exploring cutting-edge approaches to sustainable tourism infrastructure and design a case studies of regenerative accommodation and facilities. In *Dimensions of Regenerative Practices in Tourism and Hospitality*. IGI Global., DOI: 10.4018/979-8-3693-4042-4.ch003

Bhatt, Y., & Ghuman, K. (2022). Managerial cognition and environmental behavioral intentions: A behavioral reasoning theory perspective. *Corporate Social Responsibility and Environmental Management*, *29*(5), 1315–1329. DOI: 10.1002/csr.2271

Bhuvaneswari, C. A., Garg, N., Supreeth, B. R., Patjoshi, P. K., Ushapriya, C., & Tiwari, M. (2023). Optimistic Boosting Internet Connection Throughput by Incorporating Blockchain Filters into Network Infrastructure. *Proceedings of the 2023 International Conference on Innovative Computing, Intelligent Communication and Smart Electrical Systems, ICSES 2023*. DOI: 10.1109/ICSES60034.2023.10465436

Bierman, G., & Trotman, K. T. (2020). International Financial Reporting Standards and global trade compliance. *Journal of Global Accounting & Finance*, *11*(1), 56–72.

Bisht, R. K., Bisht, I. P., & Joshi, B. C. (2022). Growth of Micro, Small and Medium Enterprises (MSMEs) in Uttarakhand (India). In D. N. & C. A. (Eds.), *AIP Conference Proceedings* (Vol. 2481). American Institute of Physics Inc. DOI: 10.1063/5.0103881

BlackRock. (2023). *Global Sustainable Investment Outlook 2023*. BlackRock Investment Institute.

Bloomfield, D., & Shackman, J. (2008). Non-audit service fees, auditor characteristics and earnings restatements. *Managerial Auditing Journal*, *23*(2), 125–141. DOI: 10.1108/02686900810839839

Bohra, N. S., Bansal, S. S., Johri, A., & Kathari, S. (2024). Evaluating infrastructure fund performance in India: A study of thematic investing. In *Issues of Sustainability in AI and New-Age Thematic Investing*. IGI Global., DOI: 10.4018/979-8-3693-3282-5.ch002

Bolton, R. (2022). *Beyond greenwashing: Strategic approaches to environmental credibility*. Harvard Business Review Press.

Boolaky, P. K., Tawiah, V., & Soobaroyen, T. (2020). Why do African countries adopt IFRS? An institutional perspective. *The International Journal of Accounting*, *55*(1), 2050005. DOI: 10.1142/S1094406020500055

Bose, S., Minnick, K., & Shams, S. (2021). Does carbon risk matter for corporate acquisition decisions? *Journal of Corporate Finance*, *70*, 102058. Advance online publication. DOI: 10.1016/j.jcorpfin.2021.102058

Bosu, I., Mahmoud, H., & Hassan, H. (2023). Energy audit and management of an industrial site based on energy efficiency, economic, and environmental analysis. *Applied Energy*, *333*, 120619. DOI: 10.1016/j.apenergy.2022.120619

Boudier, F., & Lochard, J. (2013). How do cross-border mergers and acquisitions answer to deregulation in services? *World Economy*, *36*(11), 1424–1441. DOI: 10.1111/twec.12067

Brereton, C. (2004). No alarms, no surprises. *Total Telecom, JULY*, 9. https://www.scopus.com/inward/record.uri?eid=2-s2.0-4544291500&partnerID=40&md5=01fe2cffe1d441cb4c027868fb8de305

Bresser-Pereira, L. C. (2010). The theory of dependent development. *Latin American Politics and Society*, *52*(3), 65–85.

Bris, A., Brisley, N., & Cabolis, C. (2008). Adopting better corporate governance: Evidence from cross-border mergers. *Journal of Corporate Finance, 14*(3), 224–240. DOI: 10.1016/j.jcorpfin.2008.03.005

Brown, H. S., De Jong, M., & Lessidrenska, T. (2009). The rise of the Global Reporting Initiative: A case of institutional entrepreneurship. *Environmental Politics, 18*(2), 182–200. DOI: 10.1080/09644010802682551

Brynjolfsson, E., & McAfee, A. (2014). *The second machine age: Work, progress, and prosperity in a time of brilliant technologies*. W. W. Norton & Company.

Buch, C. M., & DeLong, G. (2004). Cross-border bank mergers: What lures the rare animal? *Journal of Banking & Finance, 28*(9), 2077–2102. DOI: 10.1016/j.jbankfin.2003.08.002

Budiono, S., & Dura, J. (2021). The effect of green accounting implementation on profitability in companies compass index 100. *International Journal of Educational Research & Social Sciences, 2*(6), 1526–1534. DOI: 10.51601/ijersc.v2i6.216

Bukhari, S. A. A., Hashim, F., Amran, A., & Hyder, K. (2020). Green Banking and Islam: Two sides of the same coin. *Journal of Islamic Marketing, 11*(4), 977–1000. DOI: 10.1108/JIMA-09-2018-0154

Bushman, R. M., & Smith, A. J. (2001). Financial accounting information and corporate governance. *Journal of Accounting and Economics, 32*(1-3), 237–333. DOI: 10.1016/S0165-4101(01)00027-1

Caiado, R. G. G., Scavarda, L. F., Vidal, G., de Mattos Nascimento, D. L., & Garza-Reyes, J. A. (2023). A taxonomy of critical factors towards sustainable operations and supply chain management 4.0 in developing countries. *Operations Management Research*. DOI: 10.1007/s12063-023-00430-8

Cai, F., & Wong, R. (2019). The role of IFRS in global trade regulation: Enhancing transparency and compliance. *The International Journal of Accounting, 54*(2), 199–215.

Calabrò, P.S., (2009). Greenhouse gases emission from municipal waste management: The role of separate collection. Waste management, 29(7), pp.2178-2187. () DOI: 10.1016/j.wasman.2009.02.011

Callaghan, J., Parkash, M., & Singhal, R. (2009). Going-concern audit opinions and the provision of non-audit services: Implications for auditor independence of bankrupt firms. *Auditing, 28*(1), 153–169. DOI: 10.2308/aud.2009.28.1.153

Carcello, J. V., Hermanson, D. R., & Ye, Z. (2011). Corporate governance research in accounting and auditing: Insights, practice implications, and future research directions. *Auditing*, *30*(3), 1–31. DOI: 10.2308/ajpt-10112

Carril-Caccia, F., & Baleix, J. M. (2020). The Impact of Environmental Regulation on Location's Choice of Cross-Border Mergers and Acquisitions [El impacto de la regulación medioambiental sobre la elección de la localización de las fusiones y adquisiciones transfronterizas]. *Cuadernos Economicos de ICE*, *2020*(100), 167–192. DOI: 10.32796/cice.2020.100.7123

Carril-Caccia, F., & Milgram Baleix, J. (2024). Impact of environmental regulation on M&As in the manufacturing sector. *Journal of Environmental Economics and Management*, *127*, 103038. Advance online publication. DOI: 10.1016/j.jeem.2024.103038

Castillo-Merino, D., Garcia-Blandon, J., & Martinez-Blasco, M. (2020). Auditor independence, current and future NAS fees, and audit quality: Were European regulators right? *European Accounting Review*, *29*(2), 233–262. DOI: 10.1080/09638180.2019.1577151

Cavaliere, L. P. L., Byloppilly, R., Khan, S. D., Othman, B. A., Muda, I., & Malhotra, R. K. (2024). Acceptance and effectiveness of Industry 4.0 internal and external organisational initiatives in Malaysian firms. *International Journal of Management and Enterprise Development*, *23*(1), 1–25. DOI: 10.1504/IJMED.2024.138422

Chahar, A., & Christobel, Y. A. Ritika, Adakane, P. K., Sonal, D., & Tripathi, V. (2022). The Implementation of Big Data With Cloud and Edge Computing in Enhancing the Smart Grid Information Processes Through Sem Model. *2022 2nd International Conference on Advance Computing and Innovative Technologies in Engineering, ICACITE 2022*, 608 – 611. DOI: 10.1109/ICACITE53722.2022.9823896

Chai, H., Tang, Q., Jiang, Y., & Lin, Z. (2010). The role of international financial reporting standards in accounting quality: Evidence from the European Union. *Journal of International Financial Management & Accounting*, *21*(3), 220–278. DOI: 10.1111/j.1467-646X.2010.01041.x

Chattopadhyay, P., Chattopadhyay, P., & Palit, D. (2020). Effect of environmental pollution on health and its prevention: an overview. *Environmental and sustainable development through forestry and other resources*, pp.229-266.

Chava, S. (2014). Environmental externalities and cost of capital. *Management Science*, *60*(9), 2223–2247. DOI: 10.1287/mnsc.2013.1863

Cheng, K., & Finney, S. G. (2010). It's coming: M&As under IFRSs. *Journal of Corporate Accounting & Finance, 21*(3), 13–18. DOI: 10.1002/jcaf.20575

Chen, Y., Gul, F. A., Truong, C., & Veeraraghavan, M. (2016). Auditor client-specific knowledge and internal control weakness: Some evidence on the role of auditor tenure and geographic distance. *Journal of Contemporary Accounting & Economics, 12*(2), 121–140. DOI: 10.1016/j.jcae.2016.03.001

Chen, Y., & Li, N. (2010). International comparative study to government regulation about cross-border mergers and acquisition. *2010 International Conference on Future Information Technology and Management Engineering, FITME 2010, 2*, 341 – 344. DOI: 10.1109/FITME.2010.5656296

Chiapello, E. (2007). Accounting and the birth of the notion of capitalism. *Critical Perspectives on Accounting, 18*(3), 263–296. DOI: 10.1016/j.cpa.2005.11.012

Choi, F. D. S., & Meek, G. K. (2011). *International Accounting* (7th ed.). Pearson Education.

Christensen, D. M., Serafeim, G., & Sikochi, A. (2022). Why is corporate virtue in the eye of the beholder? The case of ESG ratings. *The Accounting Review, 97*(1), 147–175. DOI: 10.2308/TAR-2019-0506

Christensen, H. B., Hail, L., & Leuz, C. (2021). Mandatory CSR and sustainability reporting: Economic analysis and literature review. *Review of Accounting Studies, 26*(3), 1176–1248. DOI: 10.1007/s11142-021-09609-5

Clark, G. L., Feiner, A., & Viehs, M. (2015). *From the stockholder to the stakeholder: How sustainability can drive financial outperformance*. University of Oxford and Arabesque Partners.

Clem, A., Cowan, A. R., & Jeffrey, C. (2004). Market Reaction to Proposed Changes in Accounting for Purchased Research and Development in R&D-Intensive Industries. *Journal of Accounting, Auditing & Finance, 19*(4), 405–428. DOI: 10.1177/0148558X0401900403

Climate Bonds Initiative. (2023). *Green Bonds Global State of the Market 2023*. Climate Bonds Initiative.

Clinch, G., Tarca, A., & Wee, M. (2023). Cross-country diversity and non-IFRS financial performance measures. *Accounting and Finance, 63*(2), 2473–2502. DOI: 10.1111/acfi.12980

Colasse, B. (1997). Qu'est-ce que la comptabilité? In Y. Simon & P. Joffre (Eds.), *Encyclopédie de gestion* (pp. [page range]). Economica.

Cosserat, G., & Rodda, N. (2009). *Modern auditing*. John Wiley & Sons.

Dahiya, K., & Taneja, S. (2023). To Analyse the Impact of Multi-Media Technology on the Rural Entrepreneurship Development. In *Contemporary Studies of Risks in Emerging Technology* (pp. 221–240). DOI: 10.1108/978-1-80455-562-020231015

Dalhuijsen, E., Gutierrez, E., & Kliatskova, T. (2023). *Greening National Development Financial Institutions: Trends, Lessons Learned, and Ways Forward*. World Bank Publications.

Dangwal, A., Kaur, S., Taneja, S., & Ozen, E. (2022). A bibliometric analysis of green tourism based on the scopus platform. In *Developing Relationships, Personalization, and Data Herald in Marketing 5.0*. IGI Global., DOI: 10.4018/978-1-6684-4496-2.ch015

Darshan, A., Girdhar, N., Bhojwani, R., Rastogi, K., Angalaeswari, S., Natrayan, L., & Paramasivam, P. (2022). Energy audit of a residential building to reduce energy cost and carbon footprint for sustainable development with renewable energy sources. *Advances in Civil Engineering*, *2022*(1), 4400874. DOI: 10.1155/2022/4400874

Das Gupta, A., Rafi, S. M., Singh, N., Gupta, V. K., Jaiswal, S., & Gangodkar, D. (2022). A Framework of Internet of Things (IOT) for the Manufacturing and Image Classifaication System. *2022 2nd International Conference on Advance Computing and Innovative Technologies in Engineering, ICACITE 2022*, 293 – 297. DOI: 10.1109/ICACITE53722.2022.9823853

Das, N., & Roy, J. (2020). India can increase its mitigation ambition: An analysis based on historical evidence of decoupling between emission and economic growth. *Energy for Sustainable Development*, *57*, 189–199. DOI: 10.1016/j.esd.2020.06.003

Das, S., & Mukhopadhyay, D. (2018). Trade policy and economic growth: A review of the literature. *Guoji Maoyi Wenti*, *32*(1), 3–19. DOI: 10.1080/08853908.2017.1365454

Davuluri, S. K., Alvi, S. A. M., Aeri, M., Agarwal, A., Serajuddin, M., & Hasan, Z. (2023). A Security Model for Perceptive 5G-Powered BC IoT Associated Deep Learning. *6th International Conference on Inventive Computation Technologies, ICICT 2023 - Proceedings*, 118 – 125. DOI: 10.1109/ICICT57646.2023.10134487

De Moor, P., & De Beelde, I. (2005). Environmental auditing and the role of the accountancy profession: A literature review. *Environmental Management*, *36*(2), 205–219. DOI: 10.1007/s00267-004-0142-6 PMID: 15995890

DeAngelo, L. E. (1981a). Auditor independence, 'lowballing', and disclosure regulation. *Journal of Accounting and Economics*, *3*(2), 113–127. DOI: 10.1016/0165-4101(81)90009-4

DeAngelo, L. E. (1981b). Auditor size and audit quality. *Journal of Accounting and Economics, 3*(3), 183–199. DOI: 10.1016/0165-4101(81)90002-1

DeFond, M. L., Hu, X., Hung, M., & Li, S. (2011). The impact of mandatory IFRS adoption on foreign mutual fund ownership: The role of comparability. *Journal of Accounting and Economics, 51*(3), 240–258. DOI: 10.1016/j.jacceco.2011.02.001

DeFond, M., & Zhang, J. (2014). A review of archival auditing research. *Journal of Accounting and Economics, 58*(2-3), 275–326. DOI: 10.1016/j.jacceco.2014.09.002

Degryse, H., & Ongena, S. (2004). The impact of technology and regulation on the geographical scope of banking. *Oxford Review of Economic Policy, 20*(4), 571–590. DOI: 10.1093/oxrep/grh033

Delmas, M. A., & Burbano, V. C. (2011). The drivers of greenwashing. *California Management Review, 54*(1), 64–87. DOI: 10.1525/cmr.2011.54.1.64

Deloitte. (2020). The impact of IFRS adoption in the European Union. Deloitte Insights.

Deloitte. (2021). *IFRS and global trade: Enhancing compliance and transparency in a globalized economy*. Deloitte Insights.

Deloitte. (August, 2023). *Business Responsibility and Sustainability Report*: What does it mean for the top 1,000 listed entities in India? [online] Available at: https://www2.deloitte.com/in/en/pages/finance/articles/business-responsibility-and-sustainability-report.html (Accessed: 23 July 2024).

DePamphilis, D. (2017). Mergers, Acquisitions, and Other Restructuring Activities: An Integrated Approach to Process, Tools, Cases, and Solutions: Ninth Edition. In *Mergers, Acquisitions, and Other Restructuring Activities: An Integrated Approach to Process, Tools, Cases, and Solutions: Ninth Edition*. Elsevier Inc. https://www.scopus.com/inward/record.uri?eid=2-s2.0-85032168292&partnerID=40&md5=2f48f6ab57549aceaa6fc69b9ec4fff8

DePamphilis, D. M. (2019). Mergers, acquisitions, and other restructuring activities: An integrated approach to process, tools, cases, and solutions. In *Mergers, Acquisitions, and Other Restructuring Activities: An Integrated Approach to Process, Tools, Cases, and Solutions*. Elsevier., DOI: 10.1016/C2017-0-02823-9

Dettenkofer, M., Kuemmerer, K., Schuster, A., Mueller, W., Muehlich, M., Scherrer, M., & Daschner, F. D. (2000). Environmental Auditing in Hospitals: First Results in a University Hospital. *Environmental Management, 25*(1). PMID: 10552105

Dhaliwal, D. S., Li, O. Z., Tsang, A., & Yang, Y. G. (2011). Voluntary nonfinancial disclosure and the cost of equity capital: The initiation of corporate social responsibility reporting. *The Accounting Review, 86*(1), 59–100. DOI: 10.2308/accr.00000005

Dhaliwal, D. S., Radhakrishnan, S., Tsang, A., & Yang, Y. G. (2012). Nonfinancial disclosure and analyst forecast accuracy: International evidence on corporate social responsibility disclosure. *The Accounting Review, 87*(3), 723–759. DOI: 10.2308/accr-10218

Dhiman, G., & Nagar, A. K. (2022). Editorial: Blockchain-based 6G and industrial internet of things systems for industry 4.0/5.0. *Expert Systems: International Journal of Knowledge Engineering and Neural Networks, 39*(10), e13162. Advance online publication. DOI: 10.1111/exsy.13162

Dhinakaran, M., Priya, P. K., Alanya-Beltran, J., Gandhi, V., Jaiswal, S., & Singh, D. P. (2022). An Innovative Internet of Things (IoT) Computing-Based Health Monitoring System with the Aid of Machine Learning Approach. *Proceedings of 5th International Conference on Contemporary Computing and Informatics, IC3I 2022*, 292 – 297. DOI: 10.1109/IC3I56241.2022.10072528

Dong, Y., Wong, W. K., Muda, I., Cong, P. T., Hoang, A. D., Ghardallou, W., & Ha, N. N. (2023). Do natural resources utilization and economic development reduce greenhouse gas emissions through consuming renewable and Clean Technology? A case study of China towards sustainable development goals. *Resources Policy, 85*, 103921. DOI: 10.1016/j.resourpol.2023.103921

Doni, F., Gasperini, A., & Soares, J. T. (2020). What is the SDG 13? In *SDG13–Climate action: Combating climate change and its impacts* (pp. 21–30). Emerald Publishing Limited., DOI: 10.1108/978-1-78756-915-720201006

Doupnik, T. S., & Perera, H. (2012). *International accounting* (3rd ed.). McGraw-Hill.

Drucker, P. F. (2001). *The essential Drucker: The best of sixty years of Peter Drucker's essential writings on management*. HarperBusiness.

Dube, L., & Bujang, R. (2020). The impact of regulatory frameworks on IFRS compliance in emerging economies. *Journal of Accounting and Public Policy, 39*(4), 227–245.

Durani, F. (2023). The relationship between e-finance and e-commerce: Evidence from 100 countries. In Hannoon, A., & Mahmood, A. (Eds.), *Artificial intelligence, internet of things, and society 5.0* (Vol. 1113, pp. 25–45). Springer., DOI: 10.1007/978-3-031-43300-9_2

Dutta, A., Singh, P., Dobhal, A., Mannan, D., Singh, J., & Goswami, P. (2023). Entrepreneurial Aptitude of Women of an Aspirational District of Uttarakhand. *Indian Journal of Extension Education, 59*(2), 103–107. DOI: 10.48165/IJEE.2023.59222

Duvvuru, S., & Sahoo, S. (2019). Global trade regulations and their effect on cross-border investment flows. *International Economic Review, 60*(1), 73–92.

Eccles, R. G., Ioannou, I., & Serafeim, G. (2014). The impact of corporate sustainability on organizational processes and performance. *Management Science, 60*(11), 2835–2857. DOI: 10.1287/mnsc.2014.1984

Eccles, R. G., & Krzus, M. P. (2010). *One report: Integrated reporting for a sustainable strategy*. John Wiley & Sons.

Elhamma, A. (2023). Impact of mandatory IFRS adoption on foreign direct investment: The moderating role of conflict of interest regulation. *Journal of Financial Reporting and Accounting,* ahead-of-print. https://doi.org/DOI: 10.1108/JFRA-04-2022-0145

Elhamma, A. (2012). The activity-based costing in Morocco: Adoption and diffusion. *Arabian Journal of Business and Management Review, 1*(6), 33–45. DOI: 10.12816/0002111

Elhamma, A. (2013). Performance de la comptabilité par activités: Perceptions des responsables d'entreprises. *La Revue des Sciences de Gestion, 263-264*, 227–232.

Elhamma, A. (2014). Performance du Balanced Scorecard: Perception des responsables d'entreprises. *Revue Internationale de Management et de Stratégie, 5*(2), 1–9.

Elhamma, A. (2015). The relationship between budgetary evaluation, firm size, and performance. *Journal of Management Development, 34*(8), 973–986. DOI: 10.1108/JMD-06-2014-0053

Elhamma, A. (2023). Impact of mandatory IFRS adoption on economic growth: The moderating role of the COVID-19 crisis in developing countries. *Accounting and Management Information Systems, 22*(3), 554–568. DOI: 10.24818/jamis.2023.03007

Elhamma, A. (2023). The relationship between organisational decentralisation, balanced scorecard, and its perceived benefits in Moroccan SMEs. *International Journal of Accounting. Auditing and Performance Evaluation, 19*(2), 185–202. DOI: 10.1504/IJAAPE.2023.132384

Elhamma, A. (2024). Determinants of national IFRS adoption: Evidence from the Middle East and North Africa region. *International Journal of Accounting. Auditing and Performance Evaluation, 20*(1-2), 69–90. DOI: 10.1504/IJAAPE.2024.135535

Elhamma, A., & Moalla, M. (2015). Impact of uncertainty and decentralization on activity-based costing use. *International Journal of Accounting and Economics Studies, 3*(2), 148–155. DOI: 10.14419/ijaes.v3i2.4817

Eny, N. and Rum, M., (2019). Environmental green accounting and auditing practice. Research journal of finance and accounting, 10(8), pp.83-90.

Ernst & Young. (2013). *Global IFRS resources*. Retrieved from www.ey.com

Esnault, E., & Hoarau, C. (2005). *Comptabilité financière*. PUF.

Eswar, K. N. D. V. S., Doss, M. A. N., Vishnuram, P., Selim, A., Bajaj, M., Kotb, H., & Kamel, S. (2023). Comprehensive Study on Reduced DC Source Count: Multilevel Inverters and Its Design Topologies. *Energies, 16*(1), 18. Advance online publication. DOI: 10.3390/en16010018

European Banking Authority. (2021). *Report on the use of digital platforms in the EU banking and payments sector* (EBA/REP/2021/26). European Banking Authority. https://eba.europa.eu

European Commission. (2021). *Strategy for financing the transition to a sustainable economy*. European Commission.

Farooq, O., & Shehata, N. F. (2018). Does external auditing combat corruption? Evidence from private firms. *Managerial Auditing Journal, 33*(3), 267–287. DOI: 10.1108/MAJ-08-2017-1634

Farooq, U., Wen, J., Tabash, M. I., & Fadoul, M. (2023). Environmental regulations and capital investment: Does green innovation allow to grow? *International Review of Economics & Finance, 89*, 878–893. DOI: 10.1016/j.iref.2023.08.010

Filipovic, I., Bartulovic, M., & Susak, T. (2018). Accounting information as indicator of money laundering. Economic and Social Development: Book of Proceedings, 159-163.

Flammer, C. (2021). Corporate green bonds. *Journal of Financial Economics, 142*(2), 499–516. DOI: 10.1016/j.jfineco.2021.01.010

Fleming, I. (2022). *Optimization of financial performance in e-commerce* (Doctoral dissertation, Walden University). Walden Dissertations and Doctoral Studies Collection. https://scholarworks.waldenu.edu/dissertations

Francis, J. R. (2004). What do we know about audit quality? *The British Accounting Review, 36*(4), 345–368. DOI: 10.1016/j.bar.2004.09.003

Francis, J. R., Pinnuck, M. L., & Watanabe, O. (2014). Auditor style and financial statement comparability. *The Accounting Review*, *89*(2), 605–633. DOI: 10.2308/accr-50642

Fresner, J., Morea, F., Krenn, C., Uson, J. A., & Tomasi, F. (2017). Energy efficiency in small and medium enterprises: Lessons learned from 280 energy audits across Europe. *Journal of Cleaner Production*, *142*, 1650–1660. DOI: 10.1016/j.jclepro.2016.11.126

Friede, G., Busch, T., & Bassen, A. (2015). ESG and financial performance: Aggregated evidence from more than 2000 empirical studies. *Journal of Sustainable Finance & Investment*, *5*(4), 210–233. DOI: 10.1080/20430795.2015.1118917

Fu, C., Deng, X., & Tang, H. (2023). Who cares about corporate fraud? Evidence from cross-border mergers and acquisitions of Chinese companies. *Review of Quantitative Finance and Accounting*, *60*(2), 747–789. DOI: 10.1007/s11156-022-01111-6

Gao, J., Siddik, A. B., Abbas, S. K., Hamayun, M., Masukujjaman, M., & Alam, S. S. (2023). Impact of e-commerce and digital marketing adoption on the financial and sustainability performance of MSMEs during the COVID-19 pandemic: An empirical study. *Sustainability (Basel)*, *15*(2), 1594. DOI: 10.3390/su15021594

Gashi, K., & Vardari, L. (2025a). Data quality and governance. In S. Kautish, K. Sood, & S. Grima (Eds.), *Strategy analytics for business resilience and value creation* (Chap. 6). Emerald Studies in Finance, Insurance, and Risk Management (ESFIRM). Emerald Publishing.

Gashi, K. (2021). The relationship between SME's organizational culture and training and development as a human resource management practice. *Journal Global Policy and Governance*, *10*(2), 139–161. DOI: 10.14666/2194-7759-10-2-008

Gashi, K. (2024). The future of robo-advisors in management. In *Robo-Advisors in Management* (pp. 35–56). IGI Global., DOI: 10.4018/979-8-3693-2849-1.ch003

Gashi, K., Tafolli, F., & Vardari, L. (2025). Management: Revolutionizing services through data-driven management and tech-strat fusion. In Jain, V., Gupta, N., Agarwal, A., Chetty, G., & Kannan, R. (Eds.), *Innovate to integrate: Data-driven management and tech-strat fusion unveiled*. Emerald Group Publishing.

Gashi, K., & Vardari, L. (2025b). The role of technology, AI, ML and DLT in sustainable finance and a green economy. In Muradov, A., Ahmadov, F., Hajiyeva, N., Sood, K., & Grima, S. (Eds.), *Sustainable development and green innovation: Managing risk through interdisciplinary approaches and policy strategies*. Emerald Publishing.

Gazieva, L. R., Magomaev, T. R., & Magomaeva, L. R. (2021). The impact of e-commerce on the digital economy. *European Proceedings of Social and Behavioural Sciences, 98*, 122–126. DOI: 10.15405/epsbs.2021.03.16

Gebara, C. H., & Laurent, A. (2023). National SDG-7 performance assessment to support achieving sustainable energy for all within planetary limits. *Renewable & Sustainable Energy Reviews, 173*, 112934. DOI: 10.1016/j.rser.2022.112934

Geiger, M. A. (1994). Investor views of audit assurance: Recent evidence of the expectation gap. *Journal of Accountancy*, •••, 60.

Geiger, M. A., & Raghunandan, K. (2002). Auditor tenure and audit reporting failures. *Auditing, 21*(1), 67–78. DOI: 10.2308/aud.2002.21.1.67

Geiger, M. A., & Rama, D. V. (2003). Audit fees, non-audit fees, and auditor reporting on stressed companies. *Auditing, 22*(2), 53–69. DOI: 10.2308/aud.2003.22.2.53

Geiger, M. A., & Rama, D. V. (2006). Audit firm size and going-concern reporting accuracy. *Accounting horizons, 20*(1), 1-17.Abernathy, J. L., Barnes, M., Stefaniak, C., & Weisbarth, A. (2017). An international perspective on audit report lag: A synthesis of the literature and opportunities for future research. *International Journal of Auditing, 21*(1), 100–127.

Georgieva, D., & Jandik, T. (2012). Alternative paths of convergence toward U.S. market and legal regulations: Cross-listing vs. merging with U.S. bidders. *Journal of Multinational Financial Management, 22*(5), 230–251. DOI: 10.1016/j.mulfin.2012.06.006

Georgieva, D., Jandik, T., & Lee, W. Y. (2012). The impact of laws, regulations, and culture on cross-border joint ventures. *Journal of International Financial Markets, Institutions and Money*, 22(4), 774–795. DOI: 10.1016/j.intfin.2012.04.002

Gerpott, T. J., & Jakopin, N. M. (2007). Firm and target country characteristics as factors explaining wealth creation from international expansion moves of mobile network operators. *Telecommunications Policy, 31*(2), 72–92. DOI: 10.1016/j.telpol.2006.12.003

Ghosh, S. (2021). Corporate Social Responsibility Practices and Its Implementation after the Legal Mandate: A Study of Selected Companies in India with Special Emphasis on the Mining Sector. *Global Challenges to CSR and Sustainable Development: Root Causes and Evidence from Case Studies*, pp.105-138.

Giama, E., & Papadopoulos, A. M. (2018). Carbon footprint analysis as a tool for energy and environmental management in small and medium-sized enterprises. *International Journal of Sustainable Energy, 37*(1), 21–29. DOI: 10.1080/14786451.2016.1263198

Gidage, M., Bhide, S., & Bilan, Y. (2024). Greenwashing in the Indian corporate landscape: An empirical assessment of ESG disclosures of NIFTY 50 companies. *Environment, Development and Sustainability*, •••, 1–25. DOI: 10.1007/s10668-024-05191-3

Gláserová, J. (2013). Differences in financial statements of business entities in the Czech Republic. *Acta Universitatis Agriculturae et Silviculturae Mendelianae Brunensis*, *61*(2), 335–343. DOI: 10.11118/actaun201361020335

Glaum, M., Lin, B., & Street, D. L. (2013). The Economic Consequences of IFRS Adoption: A Review of the Literature. *Accounting in Europe*, *10*(1), 1–38.

Glaum, M., Schmidt, P., Street, D. L., & Vogel, S. (2013). Compliance with IFRS 3 and IAS 36-required disclosures across 17 European countries: Company-and country-level determinants. *Accounting and Business Research*, *43*(3), 163–204. DOI: 10.1080/00014788.2012.711131

Gomes, A., Williams, S., & Brito, M. (2021). The role of financial reporting in cross-border trade. *Accounting Forum*, *45*(3), 285–299.

Gompers, P., Ishii, J., & Metrick, A. (2003). Corporate governance and equity prices. *The Quarterly Journal of Economics*, *118*(1), 107–156. DOI: 10.1162/00335530360535162

Gonfa, Y. H., Tessema, F. B., Tadesse, M. G., Bachheti, A., & Bachheti, R. K. (2023). Medicinally Important Plant Roots and Their Role in Nanoparticles Synthesis and Applications. In *Secondary Metabolites from Medicinal Plants: Nanoparticles Synthesis and their Applications*. CRC Press., DOI: 10.1201/9781003213727-11

González, J. A. (2021). Enhancing compliance through digital technologies in financial reporting. *Journal of Accounting and Technology*, *5*(2), 88–102. DOI: 10.1016/j.acctech.2020.12.001

Gopal, S., Gupta, P., & Minocha, A. (2023). Advancements in Fin-Tech and Security Challenges of Banking Industry. *4th International Conference on Intelligent Engineering and Management, ICIEM 2023*. DOI: 10.1109/ICIEM59379.2023.10165876

Gordon, L. A., Loeb, M. P., & Zhu, W. (2012). The impact of IFRS adoption on foreign direct investment. *Journal of Accounting and Public Policy*, *31*(4), 374–398. DOI: 10.1016/j.jaccpubpol.2012.06.001

Government of India. (2008). *National action plan on climate change*. Prime Minister's Council on Climate Change.

Goyal, S., Kaur, A., Sharma, V., & Batra, N. (2024). IMHS: An IoT-Based Machine Learning Healthcare System. *2024 2nd International Conference on Disruptive Technologies, ICDT 2024*, 916 – 919. DOI: 10.1109/ICDT61202.2024.10489127

Goyal, P., Kukreja, T., Agarwal, A., & Khanna, N. (2015). Narrowing awareness gap by using e-learning tools for counselling university entrants. *Conference Proceeding - 2015 International Conference on Advances in Computer Engineering and Applications, ICACEA 2015*, 847 – 851. DOI: 10.1109/ICACEA.2015.7164822

Gramling, A. A., Maletta, M. J., Schneider, A., & Church, B. K. (2004). The role of the internal audit function in corporate governance: A synthesis of the extant internal auditing literature and directions for future research. *Journal of Accounting Literature*, *23*, 194.

Grassmann, M., Fuhrmann, S., & Guenther, T. W. (2021). Assurance quality, disclosed connectivity of the capitals and information asymmetry–An interaction analysis for the case of integrated reporting. *Meditari Accountancy Research*, *30*(3), 852–892. DOI: 10.1108/MEDAR-11-2020-1087

Gray, R. (2000). Current developments and trends in social and environmental auditing, reporting and attestation: A review and comment. *International Journal of Auditing*, *4*(3), 247–268. DOI: 10.1111/1099-1123.00316

Grover, D., Sharma, S., Kaur, P., Mittal, A., & Sharma, P. K. (2024). Societal Elements that Impact the Performance of Women Entrepreneurs in Tier-II Cities: A Study of Rohilkhand Region of Uttar Pradesh. *2024 IEEE Zooming Innovation in Consumer Technologies Conference. ZINC, 2024*, 114–117. DOI: 10.1109/ZINC61849.2024.10579316

Gujarathi, M. R., & Yezegel, A. (2014). Spectacular Airlines, Inc.: Implications of the transition to IFRS in the context of cross- border acquisitions. *Issues in Accounting Education*, *29*(1), 247–257. DOI: 10.2308/iace-50583

Gul, F. A., Fung, S. Y. K., & Jaggi, B. (2009). Earnings quality: Some evidence on the role of auditor tenure and auditors' industry expertise. *Journal of Accounting and Economics*, *47*(3), 265–287. DOI: 10.1016/j.jacceco.2009.03.001

Gul, F. A., Jaggi, B. L., & Krishnan, G. V. (2007). Auditor independence: Evidence on the joint effects of auditor tenure and non-audit fees. *Auditing*, *26*(2), 117–142. DOI: 10.2308/aud.2007.26.2.117

Gul, F. A., Ma, S. M., & Lai, K. (2017). Busy auditors, partner-client tenure, and audit quality: Evidence from an emerging market. *Journal of International Accounting Research*, *16*(1), 83–105. DOI: 10.2308/jiar-51706

Gul, F. A., Tsui, J., & Dhaliwal, D. S. (2006). Non-audit services, auditor quality and the value relevance of earnings. *Accounting and Finance*, *46*(5), 797–817. DOI: 10.1111/j.1467-629X.2006.00189.x

Gul, F. A., Zhou, G. S., & Zhu, X. K. (2013). Investor protection, firm informational problems, Big N auditors, and cost of debt around the world. *Auditing*, *32*(3), 1–30. DOI: 10.2308/ajpt-50462

Gunningham, N., & Prest, J. (1993). Environmental audit as a regulatory strategy: Prospects and reform. *The Sydney Law Review*, *15*, 492.

Guo, J., & Cheng, H. (2024). Acquirers' carbon risk, environmental regulation, and cross-border mergers and acquisitions: Evidence from China. *Environment, Development and Sustainability*, *26*(6), 15861–15904. DOI: 10.1007/s10668-023-03276-z

Gupta, C., Jindal, P., & Malhotra, R. K. (2022). A Study of Increasing Adoption Trends of Digital Technologies - An Evidence from Indian Banking. In D. N. & C. A. (Eds.), *AIP Conference Proceedings* (Vol. 2481). American Institute of Physics Inc. DOI: 10.1063/5.0104572

Gupta, S., Kumar, V., & Patil, P. (2022). A Study on Recycling of Waste Solid Garbage in a City. In D. N. & C. A. (Eds.), *AIP Conference Proceedings* (Vol. 2481). American Institute of Physics Inc. DOI: 10.1063/5.0104563

Gupta, A., Dixit, A. K., Kumar, K. S., Lavanya, C., Chakravarthi, M. K., & Gangodkar, D. (2022). Analyzing Robotics and Computer Integrated Manufacturing of Key Areas Using Cloud Computing. *Proceedings of 5th International Conference on Contemporary Computing and Informatics, IC3I 2022*, 194 – 199. DOI: 10.1109/IC3I56241.2022.10072581

Gupta, M., Arora, K., & Taneja, S. (2023). Bibliometric analysis on employee engagement and human resource management. In *Enhancing Customer Engagement Through Location-Based Marketing*. IGI Global., DOI: 10.4018/978-1-6684-8177-6.ch013

Gupta, P., Gopal, S., Sharma, M., Joshi, S., Sahani, C., & Ahalawat, K. (2023). Agriculture Informatics and Communication: Paradigm of E-Governance and Drone Technology for Crop Monitoring. *9th International Conference on Smart Computing and Communications: Intelligent Technologies and Applications, ICSCC 2023*, 113 – 118. DOI: 10.1109/ICSCC59169.2023.10335058

Gurendrawati, E., Musyaffi, A. M., Wolor, C. W., Khairunnisa, H., Wibowo, S. N., Fuzianah, E., & Faturachman, M. (2024). An empirical study on the barriers to digital financial reporting adoption among non-adopting SMEs in Indonesia. *Journal of System and Management Sciences*, *14*(3), 96–114. DOI: 10.33168/JSMS.2024.0306

Gururani, P., Bhatnagar, P., Bisht, B., Jaiswal, K. K., Kumar, V., Kumar, S., Vlaskin, M. S., Grigorenko, A. V., & Rindin, K. G. (2022). Recent advances and viability in sustainable thermochemical conversion of sludge to bio-fuel production. *Fuel*, *316*, 123351. Advance online publication. DOI: 10.1016/j.fuel.2022.123351

Gusain, I., Sharma, S., Debarma, S., Kumar Sharma, A., Mishra, N., & Prakashrao Dahale, P. (2023). Study of concrete mix by adding Dolomite in conventional concrete as partial replacement with cement. *Materials Today: Proceedings*, *73*, 163–166. DOI: 10.1016/j.matpr.2022.09.583

Gusti, G. P., & da, H. (2023). The important role of e-commerce in forming community financial literacy. *Business* [BOSOC]. *Organizações & Sociedade*, *1*(1), 26–29. DOI: 10.26480/bosoc.01.2023.26.29

Habib, A., Bhuiyan, M. B. U., Huang, H. J., & Miah, M. S. (2019). Determinants of audit report lag: A meta-analysis. *International Journal of Auditing*, *23*(1), 20–44. DOI: 10.1111/ijau.12136

Hail, L., & Leuz, C. (2006). International differences in the cost of equity capital: Do legal institutions and securities regulation matter? *Journal of Accounting Research*, *44*(3), 485–531. DOI: 10.1111/j.1475-679X.2006.00209.x

Hail, L., Leuz, C., & Wysocki, P. (2010). Global accounting convergence and the potential adoption of IFRS in the United States. *Accounting Horizons*, *24*(3), 355–394. DOI: 10.2308/acch.2010.24.3.355

Hail, L., Leuz, C., & Wysocki, P. D. (2020). Globalization and accounting standards: A review of the literature. *Journal of Accounting and Economics*, *63*(1), 69–84.

Hajoary, P. K., Balachandra, P., & Garza-Reyes, J. A. (2023). Industry 4.0 maturity and readiness assessment: An empirical validation using Confirmatory Composite Analysis. *Production Planning and Control*. Advance online publication. DOI: 10.1080/09537287.2023.2210545

Han, G. (2020). Institutional Conditions of Economic Globalization: Effects of Antitrust and Merger Laws on the Global Integration of the Acquisition Market1. *Sociological Forum*, *35*(4), 1250–1271. DOI: 10.1111/socf.12646

Hardies, K., Breesch, D., & Branson, J. (2016). Do (fe) male auditors impair audit quality? Evidence from going-concern opinions. *European Accounting Review, 25*(1), 7–34. DOI: 10.1080/09638180.2014.921445

Harindahyani, S., & Agustia, D. (2023). The assurance providers' role in improving the independent assurance statement quality on sustainability reporting. *Accounting Research Journal, 36*(1), 37–54. DOI: 10.1108/ARJ-01-2021-0024

Hassan, E. A., Rankin, M., & Lu, W. (2014). The development of accounting and reporting in Iraq and the IFRS decision: An institutional perspective. *The International Journal of Accounting, 49*(3), 371–390. DOI: 10.1016/j.intacc.2014.07.001

Hassan, M. (2008). The development of accounting regulations in Egypt. *Managerial Auditing Journal, 23*(5), 467–484. DOI: 10.1108/02686900810875299

Hassan, M., & Giouvris, E. (2021). Bank mergers: The cyclical behaviour of regulation, risk and returns. *Journal of Financial Economic Policy, 13*(2), 256–284. DOI: 10.1108/JFEP-03-2020-0043

Healy, P. M., & Palepu, K. G. (2001). Information asymmetry, corporate disclosure, and the capital markets: A review of the empirical disclosure literature. *Journal of Accounting and Economics, 31*(1-3), 405–440. DOI: 10.1016/S0165-4101(01)00018-0

Hedberg, C. J., & Von Malmborg, F. (2003). The global reporting initiative and corporate sustainability reporting in Swedish companies. *Corporate Social Responsibility and Environmental Management, 10*(3), 153–164. DOI: 10.1002/csr.38

Heinemann, A. (2012). Government control of cross-border M&A: Legitimate regulation or protectionism. *Journal of International Economic Law, 15*(3), 843–870. DOI: 10.1093/jiel/jgs030

Heras-Saizarbitoria, I., Dogui, K., & Boiral, O. (2013). Shedding light on ISO 14001 certification audits. *Journal of Cleaner Production, 51*, 88–98. DOI: 10.1016/j.jclepro.2013.01.040

Hillary, R. (1998). Environmental auditing: Concepts, methods and developments. *International Journal of Auditing, 2*(1), 71–85. DOI: 10.1002/(SICI)1099-1123(199803)2:1<71::AID-IJA23>3.3.CO;2-X

Hoekman, B. M., & Kostecki, M. M. (2009). *The Political Economy of the World Trading System*. Oxford University Press. DOI: 10.1093/oso/9780199553761.001.0001

Hoekman, B., & Mavroidis, P. C. (2020). To TTIP or not to TTIP: On the future of transatlantic economic relations. *Journal of Economic Policy Reform, 23*(1), 1–21. DOI: 10.1080/17487870.2018.1425880

Holzmann, O. J. (2000). M&A accounting: FASB calls for ban on pooling. *Journal of Corporate Accounting & Finance, 11*(2), 41–50. DOI: 10.1002/(SICI)1097-0053(200001/02)11:2<41::AID-JCAF9>3.0.CO;2-G

Hong, H., Karolyi, G. A., & Scheinkman, J. A. (2019). Climate finance. *Review of Financial Studies, 33*(3), 1011–1023. DOI: 10.1093/rfs/hhz146

Hossain, M. Z., & Hammami, M. (2020). Challenges in global trade compliance and the role of IFRS in emerging markets. *International Journal of Accounting and Finance, 29*(3), 144–160.

Hsu, J., & Cao, T. L. (2021). The Antecedents of Likelihood to Completion of Cross-Border M&As: An Empirical Analysis of ASEAN Countries. *Emerging Markets Finance & Trade, 57*(10), 2888–2906. DOI: 10.1080/1540496X.2019.1668766

Hughes, L. (2022). Blockchain in cross-border transactions: Enhancing transparency and reducing fraud. *Journal of Digital Finance, 6*(2), 90–105.

Humphrey, C., Moizer, P., & Turley, S. (2006). Independence and competence? A critical questioning of auditing. *Independent Accounts*, 149-167.

Humphrey, C., Kausar, A., Loft, A., & Woods, M. (2011). Regulating audit beyond the crisis: A critical discussion of the EU Green Paper. *European Accounting Review, 20*(3), 431–457. DOI: 10.1080/09638180.2011.597201

Husson-Traore, A.-C. (2020). 12 - Sustainable Finance for Citizens. In *Making the Financial System Sustainable*. Cambridge University Press., DOI: 10.1017/9781108908269.015

Hýblová, E. (2019). The current problems of harmonization of accounting for small and medium-sized enterprises. *Ekonomska Istrazivanja, 32*(1), 604–621. DOI: 10.1080/1331677X.2018.1561317

IASB. (2020). *IFRS Foundation Annual Report*. International Accounting Standards Board.

Iatridis, G. (2010). International Financial Reporting Standards and the quality of financial statement information. *International Review of Financial Analysis, 19*(3), 193–204. DOI: 10.1016/j.irfa.2010.02.004

IFAC. (2020). *The role of IFRS in promoting transparency and enhancing compliance in international trade*. International Federation of Accountants.

IFRS Foundation. (2018). *Use of IFRS Standards around the world*. https://www.ifrs.org/content/dam/ifrs/around-the-world/adoption/use-of-ifrs-around-the-world-overview-sept-2018.pdf

IFRS Foundation. (2023). *IFRS Sustainability Disclosure Standards: Progress report*. IFRS Foundation.

IFRS Foundation. (n.d.). *Website*. Retrieved from https://www.ifrs.org

Indu, R., Dimri, S. C., & Kumar, B. (2023). Identification of Location for Police Headquarters to Deal with Crime Against Women in India Using Clustering Based on K-Means Algorithm. *International Journal of Computing and Digital Systems*, *14*(1), 965–974. DOI: 10.12785/ijcds/140175

Ingale, N. V., Saravana Kumar, G., Panduro-Ramirez, J., Raj, M., Vaseem Akram, S., & Rawat, R. (2023). Role of IOT in managing education management tools: A technical review. *2023 3rd International Conference on Advance Computing and Innovative Technologies in Engineering, ICACITE 2023*, 2056–2061. DOI: 10.1109/ICACITE57410.2023.10182953

International Accounting Standards Board. (2023). IFRS standards and global adoption. Retrieved from https://www.ifrs.org

International Federation of Accountants (IFAC). (n.d.). *Website*. Retrieved from https://www.ifac.org

Irvine, H. (2008). The global institutionalization of financial reporting: The case of the United Arab Emirates. *Accounting Forum*, *32*(2), 125–142. DOI: 10.1016/j.accfor.2007.12.003

Irwansyah, Hakim, W. and Yunus, A. (2017). Environmental audit as instrument for environmental protectioan and management. *The Business & Management Review*, *9*(2), 228–232.

Irwin, K., Gilstrap, C., McDowell, W., Drnevich, P., & Gorbett, A. (2022). How knowledge and uncertainty affect strategic international business investment decisions: Implications for cross-border mergers and acquisitions. *Journal of Business Research*, *139*, 831–842. DOI: 10.1016/j.jbusres.2021.10.001

Išoraitė, M., & Miniotienė, N. (2018). Electronic commerce: Theory and practice. *Integrated Journal of Business and Economics*, *2*(2), 194–200. DOI: 10.33019/ijbe.v2i2.78

Ittonen, K., Vähämaa, E., & Vähämaa, S. (2013). Female auditors and accruals quality. *Accounting Horizons*, *27*(2), 205–228. DOI: 10.2308/acch-50400

Jabor, L., & Hamdan, A. (2023). Digitalization in accounting and financial reporting quality: Literature review. In El Khoury, R., & Nasrallah, N. (Eds.), *Emerging trends and innovation in business and finance* (pp. 821–838). Springer., DOI: 10.1007/978-981-99-6101-6_59

Jain, P., Gupta, V. K., Tiwari, H., Shukla, A., Pandey, P., & Gupta, A. (2023). Human-Computer Interaction: A Systematic Review. In M. H.K. & S. S. (Eds.), *Proceedings - 2023 International Conference on Advanced Computing and Communication Technologies, ICACCTech 2023* (pp. 31 – 36). Institute of Electrical and Electronics Engineers Inc. DOI: 10.1109/ICACCTech61146.2023.00015

Jayadeva, S. M., Prasad Krishnam, N., Raja Mannar, B., Prakash Dabral, A., Buddhi, D., & Garg, N. (2023). An Investigation of IOT-Based Consumer Analytics to Assist Consumer Engagement Strategies in Evolving Markets. *2023 3rd International Conference on Advance Computing and Innovative Technologies in Engineering, ICACITE 2023*, 487 – 491. DOI: 10.1109/ICACITE57410.2023.10183310

Jayeoba, O. O., Ajibade, A. T., Olayinka, I. M., Ogundajo, G. O., & Kwarbai, J. D. (2016). Accounting standards and foreign direct investment inflows in selected African countries (1980–2015). *International Journal of Advanced Academic Research: Social & Management Sciences*, *2*(10), 17–25.

Jena, S., & Gairola, A. (2022). Numerical Method to Generate and Evaluate Environmental Wind Over Hills: Comparison of Pedestrian Winds Over Hills and Plains. *CFD Letters*, *14*(10), 56–67. DOI: 10.37934/cfdl.14.10.5667

Jensen, M. C., & Meckling, W. H. (1976). Theory of the firm: Managerial behavior, agency costs, and ownership structure. *Journal of Financial Economics*, *3*(4), 305–360. DOI: 10.1016/0304-405X(76)90026-X

Jha, B., Giri, P., Jha, D., & Badhera, U. (2022). Unlocking IoT: AI-enabled green fintech innovations. In *AI-Enabled Agile Internet of Things for Sustainable FinTech Ecosystems*. IGI Global., DOI: 10.4018/978-1-6684-4176-3.ch001

Jindal, G., Tiwari, V., Mahomad, R., Gehlot, A., Jindal, M., & Bordoloi, D. (2023). Predictive Design for Quality Assessment Employing Cloud Computing And Machine Learning. *2023 3rd International Conference on Advance Computing and Innovative Technologies in Engineering, ICACITE 2023*, 461 – 465. DOI: 10.1109/ICACITE57410.2023.10182915

Jindal, M., Bajal, E., Singh, P., Diwakar, M., Arya, C., & Sharma, K. (2022). Online education in Covid-19: Limitations and improvements. *2021 IEEE 8th Uttar Pradesh Section International Conference on Electrical, Electronics and Computer Engineering, UPCON 2021*. DOI: 10.1109/UPCON52273.2021.9667605

Jin, K., & Liu, J. (2020). How IFRS impacts foreign direct investment decisions: Evidence from emerging markets. *Global Finance Journal, 48*, 100–112.

Johnstone, L. (2022). The means to substantive performance improvements–environmental management control systems in ISO 14001–certified SMEs. *Sustainability Accounting. Management and Policy Journal, 13*(5), 1082–1108.

Joshi, S., Balakrishnan, S., Rawat, P., Deshpande, D., Chakravarthi, M. K., & Verma, D. (2022). A Framework of Internet of Things (Iot) for the Manufacturing and Image Classification System. In D. R.K., S. A.Kr., K. G., & B. S. (Eds.), *Proceedings of the 2022 11th International Conference on System Modeling and Advancement in Research Trends, SMART 2022* (pp. 371 – 375). Institute of Electrical and Electronics Engineers Inc. DOI: 10.1109/SMART55829.2022.10046756

Joshi, S., Kulkarni, N., & Athavale, R. (2013). Business informatics a key driver for successful strategic planning. *Proceedings - International Conference on Intelligent Systems, Modelling and Simulation, ISMS*, 305 – 309. DOI: 10.1109/ISMS.2013.111

Joshi, K., Patil, S., Gupta, S., & Khanna, R. (2022). Role of Pranayma in emotional maturity for improving health. *Journal of Medical Pharmaceutical and Allied Sciences, 11*(2), 4569–4573. DOI: 10.55522/jmpas.V11I2.2033

Joshi, S., Bisht, B., Kumar, V., Singh, N., Jameel Pasha, S. B., Singh, N., & Kumar, S. (2024). Artificial intelligence assisted food science and nutrition perspective for smart nutrition research and healthcare. *Systems Microbiology and Biomanufacturing, 4*(1), 86–101. DOI: 10.1007/s43393-023-00200-4

Joshi, S., Gangola, S., Bhandari, G., Bhandari, N. S., Nainwal, D., Rani, A., Malik, S., & Slama, P. (2023). Rhizospheric bacteria: The key to sustainable heavy metal detoxification strategies. *Frontiers in Microbiology, 14*, 1229828. Advance online publication. DOI: 10.3389/fmicb.2023.1229828 PMID: 37555069

Joshitta, S. M., Sunil, M. P., Bodhankar, A., Sreedevi, C., & Khanna, R. (2023, May). The Integration of Machine Learning Technique with the Existing System to Predict the Flight Prices. In 2023 3rd International Conference on Advance Computing and Innovative Technologies in Engineering (ICACITE) (pp. 398-402). IEEE.

Josphineleela, R., Gupta, R., Misra, N., Malik, M., Somasundaram, K., & Gangodkar, D. (2023). Blockchain Based Multi-Layer Security Network Authentication System for Uncertain Attack in the Wireless Communication System. *2023 3rd International Conference on Advance Computing and Innovative Technologies in Engineering, ICACITE 2023*, 877 – 881. DOI: 10.1109/ICACITE57410.2023.10182747

Josphineleela, R., Kaliappan, S., Natrayan, L., & Bhatt, U. M. (2023). Intelligent Virtual Laboratory Development and Implementation using the RASA Framework. *Proceedings - 7th International Conference on Computing Methodologies and Communication, ICCMC 2023*, 1172–1176. DOI: 10.1109/ICCMC56507.2023.10083701

Josphineleela, R., Siva Reddy, K. V., Reddy, M. V. S. S., & Rawat, R. S. (2023). Design and Development of a Smart Sprinkler Device for IoT-Integrated Plants Irrigation. *Proceedings of the 2023 2nd International Conference on Electronics and Renewable Systems, ICEARS 2023*, 498 – 501. DOI: 10.1109/ICEARS56392.2023.10084960

Judge, W., Li, S., & Pinsker, R. (2010). National adoption of international accounting standards: An institutional perspective. *Corporate Governance*, *18*(3), 161–174. DOI: 10.1111/j.1467-8683.2010.00798.x

Kalantzis, F., & Revoltella, D. (2019). Do energy audits help SMEs to realize energy-efficiency opportunities? *Energy Economics*, *83*, 229–239. DOI: 10.1016/j.eneco.2019.07.005

Kaliappan, S., Natrayan, L., & Garg, N. (2023). Checking and Supervisory System for Calculation of Industrial Constraints using Embedded System. *Proceedings of the 4th International Conference on Smart Electronics and Communication, ICOSEC 2023*, 87 – 90. DOI: 10.1109/ICOSEC58147.2023.10275952

Kamra, J., Mani, A. P., & Tripathi, V. M. (2023). Decarbonization Trajectory in Cement Industry. In S. P., N. S., R. J.J.P.C., R. J.J.P.C., R. J.J.P.C., L.-I. G.-A. D., P. T., C. L., & P. L. (Eds.), *2023 8th International Conference on Smart and Sustainable Technologies, SpliTech 2023*. Institute of Electrical and Electronics Engineers Inc. DOI: 10.23919/SpliTech58164.2023.10193682

Kannan, P. R., Periasamy, K., Pravin, P., & Vinod Kumaar, J. R. (2022). An experimental investigation of wire breakage and performance optimisation of WEDM process on machining of recycled aluminium alloy metal matrix composite. *Materials Science Poland*, *40*(3), 12–26. DOI: 10.2478/msp-2022-0030

Kanojia, P., Malhotra, R. K., & Uniyal, A. K. (2022). Impact of Organizational Commitment Components on the Teachers of Higher Education in Uttarakhand: An Emperical Analysis. *Proceedings - 2022 International Conference on Recent Trends in Microelectronics, Automation, Computing and Communications Systems, ICMACC 2022*, 360–364. DOI: 10.1109/ICMACC54824.2022.10093606

Kanojia, P., Malhotra, R. K., & Uniyal, A. K. (2022b). Organizational Commitment and the Academic Staff in HEI's in North West India. *Proceedings - 2022 International Conference on Recent Trends in Microelectronics, Automation, Computing and Communications Systems, ICMACC 2022*, 365–370. DOI: 10.1109/ICMACC54824.2022.10093347

Kashiwazaki, R., Sato, S., & Takeda, F. (2019). Does IFRS Adoption Accelerate M&A? The Consequences of Different Goodwill Accounting in Japan. *International Advances in Economic Research*, *25*(4), 399–415. DOI: 10.1007/s11294-019-09757-0

Kaur, J., Khanna, R., Kumar, R., & Sunil, G. (2024). Role of Blockchain Technologies in Goods and Services Tax. *Proceedings - 2024 3rd International Conference on Sentiment Analysis and Deep Learning, ICSADL 2024*, 607–612. DOI: 10.1109/ICSADL61749.2024.00104

Kaur, A., Kumar, P., Taneja, S., & Ozen, E. (2023). Fintech emergence – an opportunity or threat to banking. *International Journal of Electronic Finance*, *13*(1), 1–19. DOI: 10.1504/IJEF.2024.135163

Kaushal, D., Kumar, S., Raj, R., & Negi, A. (2022). Understanding the effect of entrepreneurial orientation, innovation capability and differentiation strategy on firm performance: A study on small and medium enterprises. *International Journal of Business and Globalisation*, *30*(1), 57–80. DOI: 10.1504/IJBG.2022.122280

Keith, R. (1992). Accounting numbers as 'inscription': Action at a distance and the development of accounting. *Accounting, Organizations and Society*, *17*(7), 685–708. DOI: 10.1016/0361-3682(92)90019-O

Kerrouche, N., & Belouadah, F. (2025). Digital transformation and the quality of financial reports: Evidence from Saudi listed companies. *International Journal of Data and Network Science*, *9*(1), 243–252. DOI: 10.5267/j.ijdns.2024.7.012

Khalaf, A. Z., & Hamad, S. B. (2023). An exploratory and analytical study of a sample of control and audit professionals' opinions on green audit techniques and methods. *Revenue Journal: Management and Entrepreneurship*, *1*(1), 11–17. DOI: 10.61650/rjme.v1i1.173

Khandelwal, C., Kumar, S., Tripathi, V., & Madhavan, V. (2023). Joint impact of corporate governance and risk disclosures on firm value: Evidence from emerging markets. *Research in International Business and Finance*, *66*, 102022. Advance online publication. DOI: 10.1016/j.ribaf.2023.102022

Khanna, R., Jindal, P., & Noja, G. G. (2023). Blockchain technologies, a catalyst for insurance sector. In *The Application of Emerging Technology and Blockchain in the Insurance Industry*. DOI: 10.1201/9781032630946-19

Kinney, W. R.Jr, Palmrose, Z. V., & Scholz, S. (2004). Auditor independence, non-audit services, and restatements: Was the US government right? *Journal of Accounting Research, 42*(3), 561–588. DOI: 10.1111/j.1475-679X.2004.t01-1-00141.x

Knechel, W. R., Krishnan, G. V., Pevzner, M., Shefchik, L. B., & Velury, U. K. (2013). Audit quality: Insights from the academic literature. *Auditing, 32*(Supplement 1), 385–421. DOI: 10.2308/ajpt-50350

Knechel, W. R., Sharma, D. S., & Sharma, V. D. (2012). Non-audit services and knowledge spillovers: Evidence from New Zealand. *Journal of Business Finance & Accounting, 39*(1-2), 60–81. DOI: 10.1111/j.1468-5957.2011.02268.x

Koh, K., Rajgopal, S., & Srinivasan, S. (2013). Non-audit services and financial reporting quality: Evidence from 1978 to 1980. *Review of Accounting Studies, 18*(1), 1–33. DOI: 10.1007/s11142-012-9187-6

Kohli, P., Sharma, S., & Matta, P. (2022). Secured Privacy Preserving Techniques Analysis of 6G Driven Vehicular Communication Network in Industry 5.0 Internet-of-Everything (IoE) Applications. *2022 International Conference on Smart Generation Computing, Communication and Networking, SMART GENCON 2022*. DOI: 10.1109/SMARTGENCON56628.2022.10084289

Kollruss, T. (2021). The interaction between combating tax avoidance and group accounting. *British Tax Review, 5*, 579 – 597. https://www.scopus.com/inward/record.uri?eid=2-s2.0-85120707622&partnerID=40&md5=86aa2b2e2cc8ae16362a8acd65b3eb03

Kolsi, M. C., Muqattash, R., & Al-Hiyari, A. (2022). How do external auditor attributes impact corporate social responsibility disclosures: Empirical evidence from ADX-listed companies. *Social Responsibility Journal, 18*(2), 293–315.

Komkowski, T., Antony, J., Garza-Reyes, J. A., Tortorella, G. L., & Pongboonchai-Empl, T. (2023a). A systematic review of the integration of Industry 4.0 with quality-related operational excellence methodologies. *The Quality Management Journal, 30*(1), 3–15. DOI: 10.1080/10686967.2022.2144783

Komkowski, T., Antony, J., Garza-Reyes, J. A., Tortorella, G. L., & Pongboonchai-Empl, T. (2023b). Integrating Lean Management with Industry 4.0: An explorative Dynamic Capabilities theory perspective. *Production Planning and Control*. Advance online publication. DOI: 10.1080/09537287.2023.2294297

Kosadi, F., Ginting, W., & Alamsyah, M. I. (2021). Online sales and payment in SMEs financial reporting preparation. *Jurnal Reviu Akuntansi dan Keuangan, 11*(1), 204-223. https://doi.org/DOI: 10.22219/jrak.v11i1.15164

Kosadi, F., Ginting, W., & Merliana, V. (2021). Digital receipts of online transactions in the reconciliation process and the preparation of financial reports. *Journal of Indonesian Economy and Business*, *36*(1), 31–50. DOI: 10.22146/jieb.59884

Kour, M., Taneja, S., Özen, E., Sood, K., & Grima, S. (2025). *Financial Landscape Transformation Technological Disruptions*.

Kowsalya, K., Rani, R. P. J., Bhiyana, M., Saini, M., & Patil, P. P. (2023, May). Blockchain-Internet of things-Machine Learning: Development of Traceable System for Multi Purposes. In 2023 3rd International Conference on Advance Computing and Innovative Technologies in Engineering (ICACITE) (pp. 1112-1115). IEEE.

KPMG. (2020). *IFRS and global trade regulations*. Retrieved from www.kpmg.com

KPMG. (2021). *IFRS and global trade regulations: Best practices for multinational enterprises*. KPMG Insights.

KPMG. (2021). The future of financial reporting in a digital world. KPMG Report.

Krahnen, J., Rocholl, J., & Thum, M. (2023). A Primer on Green Finance: From Wishful Thinking to Marginal Impact. *Review of Economics*, *74*(1), 1–19. DOI: 10.1515/roe-2023-0019

Krinichansky, K. V., & Rubtsov, B. B. (2022). Financial Sector Regulation on the Agenda of Economic Policy Reforms [Регулирование финансового сектора в повестке реформ экономической политики]. *Finance: Theory and Practice*, *26*(5), 6–21. DOI: 10.26794/2587-5671-2022-26-5-6-21

Krueger, P., Sautner, Z., Tang, D. Y., & Zhong, R. (2022). The effects of mandatory ESG disclosure around the world. European Corporate Governance Institute–Finance Working Paper, 754.

Krueger, P., Sautner, Z., & Starks, L. T. (2020). The importance of climate risks for institutional investors. *Review of Financial Studies*, *33*(3), 1067–1111. DOI: 10.1093/rfs/hhz137

Kukreti, M., Sehajpal, S., Tiwari, R., & Sood, K. (2025). *Driving Global Health and Sustainable Development Goals With Smart Technology* (Mohit, K., Sabina, S., Rajesh, T., & Kiran, S., Eds.; 1st ed.). IGI Global Scientific Publishing., DOI: 10.4018/979-8-3373-0240-9

Kumar, A. (2021). Introduction: Sustainable Development Goals, New urban agenda, and climate change. In *Sustainable Development Goals and Indian Cities* (pp. 1-41). Routledge India.

Kumar, A. S., & Desi, A. B. (2023). Collaborative logistics, tools of machine and supply chain services in the world wide industry 4.0 framework. In *Artificial Intelligence, Blockchain, Computing and Security: Volume 2* (Vol. 2). CRC Press. DOI: 10.1201/9781032684994-15

Kumar, K., Chaudhary, S., Anandaram, H., Kumar, R., Gupta, A., & Joshi, K. (2023). Industry 4.0 and Health Care System with special reference to Mental Health. *2023 1st International Conference on Intelligent Computing and Research Trends, ICRT 2023*. DOI: 10.1109/ICRT57042.2023.10146640

Kumar, M. A., Valli Mayil, V., Jeyalakshmi, T. R., Ghanshala, A., & Gupta, A. (2023). Wireless Body Area Network (WBAN) Centric Healthcare System for Continuous Monitoring. *2023 9th International Conference on Advanced Computing and Communication Systems, ICACCS 2023*, 214 – 219. DOI: 10.1109/ICACCS57279.2023.10112922

Kumar, P., Reepu, & Kaur, R. (2024). Economic and Urban Dynamics: Investigating Socioeconomic Status and Urban Density as Moderators of Mobile Wallet Adoption in Smart Cities. *Lecture Notes in Networks and Systems, 948 LNNS*, 409–417. DOI: 10.1007/978-981-97-1329-5_33

Kumar, P., Taneja, S., & Ozen, E. (2024). Exploring the influence of green bonds on sustainable development through low-carbon financing mobilization. *International Journal of Law and Management*. DOI: 10.1108/IJLMA-01-2024-0030

Kumar, R., Lande, A., Kumar, D., Malhotra, R. K., & Sharma, A. (2023). Technology Bridging -in Entrepreneurs and Consumers in Product Development. *ISED 2023 - International Conference on Intelligent Systems and Embedded Design*. DOI: 10.1109/ISED59382.2023.10444599

Kumar, R., Malhotra, R. K., Pandey, S., Gehlot, A., Gautam, I., & Chamola, S. (2023). Role of Artificial Intelligence in Input Tax Credit Reconciliation. *Proceedings - 2023 3rd International Conference on Pervasive Computing and Social Networking, ICPCSN 2023*, 497–501. DOI: 10.1109/ICPCSN58827.2023.00086

Kumar, V., & Korovin, G. (2023). A Comparision of Digital Transformation of Industry in the Russian Federation with the European Union. In K. V., K. G.L., A. V., & K. E. (Eds.), *Lecture Notes in Information Systems and Organisation: Vol. 61 LNISO* (pp. 45 – 57). Springer Science and Business Media Deutschland GmbH. DOI: 10.1007/978-3-031-30351-7_5

Kumar, V., Sharma, N. K., Mittal, A., & Verma, P. (2023). The Role of IoT and IIoT in Supplier and Customer Continuous Improvement Interface. *EAI/Springer Innovations in Communication and Computing*, 161 – 174. DOI: 10.1007/978-3-031-19711-6_7

Kumari, J., Singh, P., Mishra, A. K., Singh Meena, B. P., Singh, A., & Ojha, M. (2024). Challenges Hindering Women's Involvement in the Hospitality Industry as Entrepreneurs in the Era of Digital Economy. In *Revolutionizing the AI-Digital Landscape: A Guide to Sustainable Emerging Technologies for Marketing Professionals*. Taylor and Francis., DOI: 10.4324/9781032688305-9

Kumar, K. S., Yadav, D., Joshi, S. K., Chakravarthi, M. K., Jain, A. K., & Tripathi, V. (2022). Blockchain Technology with Applications to Distributed Control and Cooperative Robotics. *Proceedings of 5th International Conference on Contemporary Computing and Informatics, IC3I 2022*, 206 – 211. DOI: 10.1109/IC3I56241.2022.10073275

Kumar, K., Singh, V., Mishra, G., Ravindra Babu, B., Tripathi, N., & Kumar, P. (2022). Power-Efficient Secured Hardware Design of AES Algorithm on High Performance FPGA. *Proceedings of 5th International Conference on Contemporary Computing and Informatics, IC3I 2022*, 1634 – 1637. DOI: 10.1109/IC3I56241.2022.10073148

Kumar, N. M., Islam, S., Podder, A. K., Selim, A., Bajaj, M., & Kamel, S. (2023). Lifecycle-based feasibility indicators for floating solar photovoltaic plants along with implementable energy enhancement strategies and framework-driven assessment approaches leading to advancements in the simulation tool. *Frontiers in Energy Research*, *11*, 1075384. Advance online publication. DOI: 10.3389/fenrg.2023.1075384

Kumar, P., Bhatnagar, M., & Taneja, S. (2023). Investigation of the time pattern of Bit Green Crypto: An Arma modeling approach to unrave volatility. In *Algorithmic Approaches to Financial Technology: Forecasting, Trading, and Optimization*. IGI Global., DOI: 10.4018/979-8-3693-1746-4.ch001

Kumar, P., Taneja, S., Bhatnagar, M., & Kaur, A. K. (2024). Navigating the digital paradigm shift: Designing CBDCs for a transformative financial landscape. In *Exploring Central Bank Digital Currencies: Concepts, Frameworks, Models, and Challenges*. IGI Global., DOI: 10.4018/979-8-3693-1882-9.ch006

Kumar, P., Verma, P., Bhatnagar, M., Taneja, S., Seychel, S., Todorović, I., & Grim, S. (2023). The Financial Performance and Solvency Status of the Indian Public Sector Banks: A CAMELS Rating and Z Index Approach. *International Journal of Sustainable Development and Planning*, *18*(2), 367–376. DOI: 10.18280/ijsdp.180204

Kumar, R., Goel, R., Singh, T., Mohanty, S. M., Gupta, D., Alkhayyat, A., & Khanna, R. (2024). Sustainable Finance Factors in Indian Economy: Analysis on Policy of Climate Change and Energy Sector. *Fluctuation and Noise Letters*, *23*(2), 2440004. Advance online publication. DOI: 10.1142/S0219477524400042

Kumar, R., Kathuria, S., Malholtra, R. K., Kumar, A., Gehlot, A., & Joshi, K. (2023). Role of Cloud Computing in Goods and Services Tax(GST) and Future Application. *2nd International Conference on Sustainable Computing and Data Communication Systems, ICSCDS 2023 - Proceedings*, 1443–1447. DOI: 10.1109/ICSCDS56580.2023.10104597

Kumar, R., & Khanna, R. (2023a). Role of Artificial Intelligence in Digital Currency and Future Applications. *Proceedings of the 2023 2nd International Conference on Augmented Intelligence and Sustainable Systems, ICAISS 2023*, 42–46. DOI: 10.1109/ICAISS58487.2023.10250480

Kumar, R., & Khanna, R. (2023b). RPA (Robotic Process Automation) in Finance & Accounting and Future Scope. *Proceedings of the 2023 2nd International Conference on Augmented Intelligence and Sustainable Systems, ICAISS 2023*, 1640–1645. DOI: 10.1109/ICAISS58487.2023.10250496

Kumar, R., Khannna Malholtra, R., & Grover, C. A. N. (2023). Review on Artificial Intelligence Role in Implementation of Goods and Services Tax(GST) and Future Scope. *2023 International Conference on Artificial Intelligence and Smart Communication, AISC 2023*, 348–351. DOI: 10.1109/AISC56616.2023.10085030

Kumar, R., Malholtra, R. K., Singh, R., Kathuria, S., Balyan, R., & Pal, P. (2023). Artificial Intelligence Role in Electronic Invoice Under Goods and Services Tax. *2023 International Conference on Computational Intelligence, Communication Technology and Networking, CICTN 2023*, 140–143. DOI: 10.1109/CICTN57981.2023.10140870

Kumar, R., Malhotra, R. K., & Grover, N. (2023). Data Mining in Credit Scoring and Future Application. *International Conference on Innovative Data Communication Technologies and Application, ICIDCA 2023 - Proceedings*, 1096–1100. DOI: 10.1109/ICIDCA56705.2023.10100032

Kumar, R., Sexena, A., & Gehlot, A. (2023). Artificial Intelligence in Smart Education and Futuristic Challenges. *2023 International Conference on Disruptive Technologies, ICDT 2023*, 432 – 435. DOI: 10.1109/ICDT57929.2023.10151129

Kumar, R., Singh, T., Mohanty, S. N., Goel, R., Gupta, D., Alharbi, M., & Khanna, R. (2023). Study on online payments and e-commerce with SOR model. *International Journal of Retail & Distribution Management*. Advance online publication. DOI: 10.1108/IJRDM-03-2023-0137

Kumar, S. (2022). State of Play of Drives for Implementing Sustainable Procurement in India. In *Understanding Sustainable Public Procurement: Reflections from India and the World* (pp. 221–298). Springer International Publishing. DOI: 10.1007/978-3-031-08258-0_5

La Porta, R., Lopez-de-Silanes, F., Shleifer, A., & Vishny, R. W. (1998). Law and finance. *Journal of Political Economy, 106*(6), 1113–1155. DOI: 10.1086/250042

Lade, J., Mohammed, K. A., Singh, D., Prasad Verma, R., Math, P., Saraswat, M., & Raj Gupta, L. (2023). A critical review of fabrication routes and their effects on mechanical properties of AMMCs. *Materials Today: Proceedings*. Advance online publication. DOI: 10.1016/j.matpr.2023.03.041

Lang, M. H., & Möller, M. (2020). The impact of IFRS adoption on transparency and cross-border investments. *Journal of International Financial Markets, 39*(4), 315–334.

Lasmin, R. (2012). The unwanted effects of international financial reporting standards (IFRS) adoption on international trade and investments in developing countries. *Journal of Economics and Economic Education Research, 13*(1), 1–14.

Lenormand, G., & Touchais, L. (2009). Les IFRS améliorent-elles la qualité de l'information financière? Approche par la value relevance. *Comptabilité-Contrôle-Audit, 15*(2), 145–164. DOI: 10.3917/cca.152.0145

Leuz, C. (2020). Cross-border investment and IFRS adoption: A review of evidence from global markets. *Journal of Accounting Research, 58*(2), 463–504.

Leuz, C., & Wysocki, P. D. (2016). The economics of disclosure and financial reporting regulation: Evidence and suggestions for future research. *Journal of Accounting Research, 54*(2), 525–622. DOI: 10.1111/1475-679X.12115

Leventis, S., Weetman, P., & Caramanis, C. (2005). Determinants of audit report lag: Some evidence from the Athens Stock Exchange. *International Journal of Auditing, 9*(1), 45–58. DOI: 10.1111/j.1099-1123.2005.00101.x

Levine, R., Lin, C., & Shen, B. (2020). Cross-border acquisitions: Do labor regulations affect acquirer returns? *Journal of International Business Studies, 51*(2), 194–217. DOI: 10.1057/s41267-019-00281-1

Lightbody, M. (2000, June). Environmental auditing: the audit theory gap. In *Accounting Forum* (Vol. 24, No. 2, pp. 151-169). Taylor & Francis. ()DOI: 10.1111/1467-6303.00033

Li, H., He, R., & Fu, Q. (2023). Does corporate social responsibility affect the performance of cross-border M&A of emerging market multinationals? *Finance Research Letters*, *58*, 104320. Advance online publication. DOI: 10.1016/j.frl.2023.104320

Lin, D., Barth, J., Jahera, J., & Yost, K. (2013). Cross-border bank mergers and acquisitions: What factors pull and push banks together? *Review of Pacific Basin Financial Markets and Policies*, *16*(4), 1350022. Advance online publication. DOI: 10.1142/S0219091513500227

Lisauskas, A., Kveselis, V., Dzenajavičienė, E. F., Masaitis, S., & Perednis, E. (2022). Analysis of energy audits results and impacts: Case of small and medium enterprises in Lithuania. *Energy Efficiency*, *15*(7), 48. DOI: 10.1007/s12053-022-10052-x

Lisic, L. L., Myers, L. A., Pawlewicz, R., & Seidel, T. A. (2019). Do accounting firm consulting revenues affect audit quality? Evidence from the pre-and post-SOX eras. *Contemporary Accounting Research*, *36*(2), 1028–1054. DOI: 10.1111/1911-3846.12424

Liu, K., Wu, S., & Guo, N. (2021). Governmental governance of host countries and cross-border merger and acquisition performance: Evidence from listed enterprises in China. *PLoS ONE*, *16*(8 August). DOI: 10.1371/journal.pone.0256494

Liu, C., Chen, W., & Li, Z. (2019). IFRS adoption and its impact on financial transparency and cross-border investment flows. *Accounting and Finance*, *59*(2), 481–505.

Liu, J., & Liu, C. (2007). Value relevance of accounting information in different stock market segments: The case of Chinese A-, B-, and H-shares. *Journal of International Accounting Research*, *6*(2), 55–81. DOI: 10.2308/jiar.2007.6.2.55

Liu, Q., & You, Y. (2023). FinTech and Green Credit Development—Evidence from China. *Sustainability (Basel)*, *15*(7), 5903. Advance online publication. DOI: 10.3390/su15075903

Liu, X. (2017). An integrated macro-financial risk-based approach to the stressed capital requirement. *Review of Financial Economics*, *34*(1), 86–98. DOI: 10.1016/j.rfe.2017.06.002

Ljubisavljević, S., Ljubisavljević, L. and Jovanović, D., 2017. Environmental audit for environmental improvement and protection. Economic themes, 55(4), pp.521-538.

López, J. F., & Sánchez, R. (2020). The effect of harmonized accounting standards on international investment flows. *Journal of International Finance*, *33*(4), 180–193.

Lu, M., Simnett, R., & Zhou, S. (2023). Using the same provider for financial statement audit and assurance of extended external reports: Choices and consequences. *Auditing*, *42*(1), 125–154. DOI: 10.2308/AJPT-19-080

Maaze, M. R., Garg, N., Das, S. K., & Shrivastava, S. (2024). Industrial and C&D waste as precursor material in geopolymers: A state-of-the-art review. *Innovative Infrastructure Solutions*, *9*(6), 229. Advance online publication. DOI: 10.1007/s41062-024-01546-x

Mahapatra, S. K., Schoenherr, T., & Jayaram, J. (2021). An assessment of factors contributing to firms' carbon footprint reduction efforts. *International Journal of Production Economics*, *235*, 108073. DOI: 10.1016/j.ijpe.2021.108073

Mahwar, R. S., Verma, N. K., Chakrabarti, S. P., & Biswas, D. K. (1997). Environmental auditing programme in India. *The Science of the Total Environment*, *204*(1), 11–26. DOI: 10.1016/S0048-9697(97)00161-7 PMID: 9299766

Malhotra, R. K., Gupta, C., & Jindal, P. (2022). Blockchain and Smart Contracts for Insurance Industry. In *Blockchain Technology in Corporate Governance*. Transforming Business and Industries., DOI: 10.1002/9781119865247.ch11

Malhotra, R. K., Ojha, M. K., & Gupta, S. (2021). A study of assessment of knowledge, perception and attitude of using tele health services among college going students of Uttarakhand. *Journal of Medical Pharmaceutical and Allied Sciences*, *10*, 113–116. DOI: 10.22270/jmpas.VIC2I1.2020

Malik, P., Singh, A. K., Nautiyal, R., & Rawat, S. (2022). Mapping AICTE cybersecurity curriculum onto CyBOK: A case study. In *Machine Learning for Cyber Security*. De Gruyter., DOI: 10.1515/9783110766745-007

Maltby, J. (1995). Environmental audit: Theory and practices. *Managerial Auditing Journal*, *10*(8), 15–26. DOI: 10.1108/02686909510147372

Mandalapu, S. R., Sivamuni, K., Chitra Devi, D., Aswal, U. S., Sherly, S. I., & Balaji, N. A. (2023). An Architecture-based Self-Typing Service for Cloud Native Applications. *Proceedings of the 4th International Conference on Smart Electronics and Communication, ICOSEC 2023*, 562 – 566. DOI: 10.1109/ICOSEC58147.2023.10276313

Marek, P. (2024). Legal, Accounting, and Tax Implications of Mergers around the EU Countries: Pitching Research. In P. D. (Ed.), *Springer Proceedings in Business and Economics* (pp. 193 – 200). Springer Nature. DOI: 10.1007/978-3-031-62998-3_13

Marimon, F., & Casadesús, M. (2017). Reasons to adopt ISO 50001 energy management system. *Sustainability (Basel)*, *9*(10), 1740. DOI: 10.3390/su9101740

Marquez-Ramos, L. (2008). The effect of IFRS adoption on trade and foreign direct investments. *International Trade and Finance Association Conference Papers*. bepress, (19).

Marriott, N., & Marriott, P. (2000). Professional accountants and the development of a management accounting service for the small firm: Barriers and possibilities. *Management Accounting Research*, *11*(4), 475–492. DOI: 10.1006/mare.2000.0142

Martínez-Bravo, M., & Martínez-del-Río, J. (2020). Urban pollution and emission reduction. *Sustainable cities and communities*, pp.905-915.

Martynova, M., & Renneboog, L. (2008). Spillover of corporate governance standards in cross-border mergers and acquisitions. *Journal of Corporate Finance*, *14*(3), 200–223. DOI: 10.1016/j.jcorpfin.2008.03.004

Mary Joshitta, S., & Sunil, M. P. Badriasulaimanalfurhood, Bodhankar, A., Ch.Sreedevi, & Khanna, R. (2023). The Integration of Machine Learning Technique with the Existing System to Predict the Flight Prices. *2023 3rd International Conference on Advance Computing and Innovative Technologies in Engineering, ICACITE 2023*, 398–402. DOI: 10.1109/ICACITE57410.2023.10182539

Maso, L. D., Lobo, G. J., Mazzi, F., & Paugam, L. (2020). Implications of the joint provision of CSR assurance and financial audit for auditors' assessment of going-concern risk. *Contemporary Accounting Research*, *37*(2), 1248–1289. DOI: 10.1111/1911-3846.12560

Mathieson, D. J., Richards, A., & Sharma, S. (1998). Financial crises in emerging markets. *Finance & Development*, *35*(4), 28–31. https://www.scopus.com/inward/record.uri?eid=2-s2.0-0032405736&partnerID=40&md5=d04e34b5c717bbb2330d7f7ed82f4c74

Maurya, S. K., Ghosal, A., & Manna, A. (2022). Experimental investigations during fabrication and electrical discharge machining of hybrid Al/(SiC+ZrO2+NiTi) MMC. *International Journal of Machining and Machinability of Materials*, *24*(3–4), 215–230. DOI: 10.1504/IJMMM.2022.125195

Medhi, M. K., Ambust, S., Kumar, R., & Das, A. J. (2023). Characterization and Purification of Biosurfactants. In *Advancements in Biosurfactants Research*. Springer International Publishing., DOI: 10.1007/978-3-031-21682-4_4

Mehershilpa, G., Prasad, D., Sai Kiran, C., Shaikh, A., Jayashree, K., & Socrates, S. (2023). EDM machining of Ti6Al4V alloy using colloidal biosilica. *Materials Today: Proceedings*. Advance online publication. DOI: 10.1016/j.matpr.2023.02.443

Ministry of Economy and Finance (Morocco). (n.d.). *Website*. Retrieved from https://www.finances.gov.ma/Fr/Pages/index.aspx

Mir, M., & Rahaman, A. S. (2005). The adoption of International Accounting Standards in Bangladesh: An exploration of rationale and process. *Accounting, Auditing & Accountability Journal, 18*(6), 816–841. DOI: 10.1108/09513570510627720

Mishra, D., Kandpal, V., Agarwal, N., & Srivastava, B. (2024). Financial Inclusion and Its Ripple Effects on Socio-Economic Development: A Comprehensive Review. *Journal of Risk and Financial Management, 17*(3), 105. Advance online publication. DOI: 10.3390/jrfm17030105

Mishra, P., Aggarwal, P., Vidyarthi, A., Singh, P., Khan, B., Alhelou, H. H., & Siano, P. (2021). VMShield: Memory Introspection-Based Malware Detection to Secure Cloud-Based Services against Stealthy Attacks. *IEEE Transactions on Industrial Informatics, 17*(10), 6754–6764. DOI: 10.1109/TII.2020.3048791

Mishra, P., & Sant, T. G. (2024). Examine the level of environmental, social and governance disclosure in sustainability report–a study of the Indian banking sector. *International Journal of Innovation Science, 16*(2), 420–442. DOI: 10.1108/IJIS-08-2022-0136

Mitra, D., Mondal, R., Khoshru, B., Senapati, A., Radha, T. K., Mahakur, B., Uniyal, N., Myo, E. M., Boutaj, H., Sierra, B. E. G. U. E. R. R. A., Panneerselvam, P., Ganeshamurthy, A. N., Elković, S. A. N. Đ. J., Vasić, T., Rani, A., Dutta, S., & Mohapatra, P. K. D. A. S.MITRA. (2022). Actinobacteria-enhanced plant growth, nutrient acquisition, and crop protection: Advances in soil, plant, and microbial multifactorial interactions. *Pedosphere, 32*(1), 149–170. DOI: 10.1016/S1002-0160(21)60042-5

Mittal, A., Pandey, H., Arsh, M., Soni, M., Goyal, H. R., & Sharma, S. (2024). Advancements and Applications of Artificial Intelligence in Various Sectors: From Internet of Vehicles to 6G and Healthcare. *Proceedings - 2024 4th International Conference on Pervasive Computing and Social Networking, ICPCSN 2024*, 107 – 112. DOI: 10.1109/ICPCSN62568.2024.00026

Mladenovic, M., Dukic, T., & Popovic, G. (2023). Analysis of financial reporting platforms based on the PIPRECIA-S method. *Journal of Process Management and New Technologies, 11*(3-4), 95–104. DOI: 10.5937/jpmnt11-48186

Mohanty, S., Alfurhood, B. S., Bakhare, R., Poongavanam, S., & Khanna, R. (2023, January). The role and impact of artificial intelligence on retail business and its developments. In *2023 International Conference on Artificial Intelligence and Smart Communication (AISC)* (pp. 1098-1101). IEEE.

Monastyrenko, E. (2017). Eco-efficiency outcomes of mergers and acquisitions in the European electricity industry. *Energy Policy*, *107*, 258–277. DOI: 10.1016/j.enpol.2017.04.030

Monteiro, R., & Silva, S. (2022). The impact of securities regulation in the European Union on M&A: Does it compensate to go beyond borders? *Journal of Financial Regulation and Compliance*, *30*(3), 282–311. DOI: 10.1108/JFRC-08-2021-0066

Morais, A. I., & Curto, J. D. (2008). Accounting quality and the adoption of IASB standards: Portuguese evidence. *Revista Contabilidade & Finanças*, *19*(48), 103–111. DOI: 10.1590/S1519-70772008000300009

Moravcsik, A. (2020). Regulatory harmonization and investment flows: The role of international trade laws. *World Politics Review*, *62*(5), 505–523.

Müller, A., Lapsley, I., & Chua, W. F. (2020). The IFRS and the Challenges of International Financial Reporting. *Accounting and Business Research*, *50*(5), 490–513.

Musaha, A., Adjeib, E., & Ahmed, I. A. (2020). The effect of IFRS adoption on foreign direct investment in Africa. *Journal of Applied Accounting and Taxation*, *5*(2), 117–126. DOI: 10.30871/jaat.v5i2.1481

Nagila, A., Saravanakumar, P., Pranavan, S., Goutam, R., Dobhal, D. C., & Singh, G. (2023). An Innovative Approach of CNN-BiGRU Based Post-Earthquake Damage Detection of Reinforced Concrete for Frame Buildings. *International Conference on Self Sustainable Artificial Intelligence Systems, ICSSAS 2023 - Proceedings*, 56 – 61. DOI: 10.1109/ICSSAS57918.2023.10331894

Neha, M., S., Alfurhood, B. S., Bakhare, R., Poongavanam, S., & Khanna, R. (2023). The Role and Impact of Artificial Intelligence on Retail Business and its Developments. *2023 International Conference on Artificial Intelligence and Smart Communication, AISC 2023*, 1098–1101. DOI: 10.1109/AISC56616.2023.10085624

Nikolaidis, P., Ismail, M., Shuib, L., Khan, S., & Dhiman, G. (2022). Predicting Student Attrition in Higher Education through the Determinants of Learning Progress: A Structural Equation Modelling Approach. *Sustainability (Basel)*, *14*(20), 13584. Advance online publication. DOI: 10.3390/su142013584

Ningsih, D. F., Junaid, A., & Mursalim, M. (2020). Environmental audit analysis to support Sustainability Development. *Point of View Research Accounting and Auditing*, *1*(3), 101–109. DOI: 10.47090/povraa.v1i3.48

Nnadi, M., & Soobaroyen, T. (2015). International financial reporting standards and foreign direct investment: The case of Africa. *Advances in Accounting*, *31*(2), 228–238. DOI: 10.1016/j.adiac.2015.09.007

Nobes, C., & Parker, R. (2016). *Comparative International Accounting* (13th ed.). Pearson Education.

Nobes, C., & Parker, R. (2016). *Comparative international accounting*. Pearson Education.

OECD. (2021). *International trade regulations and their impact on financial reporting*. OECD Trade and Investment Report, 2021.

Okoshi, H. (2024). Attractive target for tax avoidance: Trade liberalization and entry mode. *International Tax and Public Finance*. Advance online publication. DOI: 10.1007/s10797-024-09830-3

Okpo, D. S. A., & Eshiet, U. E. (2023). Digital accounting practices and quality of financial reports. *GPH-International Journal of Business Management*, *6*(6), 21–35. DOI: 10.5281/zenodo.8103873

Oktaviani, N. F., Yusnita, R. T., Yuniar, E. S., Listanti, Y. F., Tujjahra, D. R., & Pamungkas, M. D. (2023). Analysis of the use of digital payment and financial report applications in SMSE. *Journal of International Conference Proceedings*, *6*(6), 286–294. DOI: 10.32535/jicp.v6i6.2720

Oliveira, P., Roth, A. V., & Heitor, M. V. (2001). Mergers and acquisitions: A tool for knowledge/technology transfer. *Proceedings of the Hawaii International Conference on System Sciences*, 222. DOI: 10.1109/HICSS.2001.927143

Olson, E. G. (2010). Challenges and opportunities from greenhouse gas emissions reporting and independent auditing. *Managerial Auditing Journal*, *25*(9), 934–942. DOI: 10.1108/02686901011080071

Onyema, E. M., Almuzaini, K. K., Onu, F. U., Verma, D., Gregory, U. S., Puttaramaiah, M., & Afriyie, R. K. (2022). Prospects and Challenges of Using Machine Learning for Academic Forecasting. *Computational Intelligence and Neuroscience*, *2022*, 1–7. Advance online publication. DOI: 10.1155/2022/5624475 PMID: 35909823

Organisation for Economic Co-operation and Development. (2022). *Trade and Investment Report*. OECD Publishing.

Owusu-Ansah, S., & Leventis, S. (2006). Timeliness of corporate annual financial reporting in Greece. *European Accounting Review*, *15*(2), 273–287. DOI: 10.1080/09638180500252078

Pai, H. A., Almuzaini, K. K., Ali, L., Javeed, A., Pant, B., Pareek, P. K., & Akwafo, R. (2022). Delay-Driven Opportunistic Routing with Multichannel Cooperative Neighbor Discovery for Industry 4.0 Wireless Networks Based on Power and Load Awareness. *Wireless Communications and Mobile Computing*, *2022*, 1–12. Advance online publication. DOI: 10.1155/2022/5256133

Palakshappa, N., & Dodds, S. (2020). Mobilising SDG 12: Co-creating sustainability through brands. *Marketing Intelligence & Planning*, *39*(2), 265–283. DOI: 10.1108/MIP-08-2018-0360

Pande, S. D., Bhatt, A., Chamoli, S., Saini, D. K. J. B., Kute, U. T., & Ahammad, S. H. (2023). Design of Atmel PLC and its Application as Automation of Coal Handling Plant. *2023 International Conference on Sustainable Emerging Innovations in Engineering and Technology, ICSEIET 2023*, 178 – 183. DOI: 10.1109/ICSEIET58677.2023.10303627

Pandey, N. K., Kashyap, S., Sharma, A., & Diwakar, M. (2023). Contribution of Cloud-Based Services in Post-Pandemic Technology Sustainability and Challenges: A Future Direction. In *Evolving Networking Technologies: Developments and Future Directions*. wiley. DOI: 10.1002/9781119836667.ch4

Pandey, R. P., Bansal, S., Awasthi, P., Dixit, V., Singh, R., & Yadava, V. (2023). Attitude and Myths Related to Stalking among Early and Middle Age Adults. *Psychology Hub, 40*(3), 85 – 94. DOI: 10.13133/2724-2943/17960

Pandya, D. J., Kumar, Y., Singh, D. P., Vairavel, D. K., Deepak, A., Rao, A. K., & Rana, A. (2023). Automatic Power Factor Compensation for Industrial Use to Minimize Penalty. *Proceedings of International Conference on Contemporary Computing and Informatics, IC3I 2023*, 2499 – 2504. DOI: 10.1109/IC3I59117.2023.10398095

Pant, R., Gupta, A., Pant, G., Chaubey, K. K., Kumar, G., & Patrick, N. (2022). Second-generation biofuels: Facts and future. In *Relationship between Microbes and the Environment for Sustainable Ecosystem Services: Microbial Tools for Sustainable Ecosystem Services: Volume 3* (Vol. 3). Elsevier. DOI: 10.1016/B978-0-323-89936-9.00011-4

Pant, A., Joshi, R. C., Sharma, S., & Pant, K. (2024). Air Quality and Public Health Risk Assessment: A Case of an Industrial Area in Haridwar City, Uttarakhand (India). *Indian Journal of Public Health*, *68*(2), 222–226. DOI: 10.4103/ijph.ijph_279_23 PMID: 38953809

Parker, R. (2021). Navigating IFRS and global trade: The challenges for multinational enterprises. *Accounting Horizons*, *35*(2), 169–184.

Park, H., & Kim, J. D. (2020). Transition towards green banking: Role of financial regulators and financial institutions. *Asian Journal of Sustainability and Social Responsibility*, *5*(1), 1–25. DOI: 10.1186/s41180-020-00034-3

Paterson, J. S., & Valencia, A. (2011). The effects of recurring and nonrecurring tax, audit-related, and other non-audit services on auditor independence. *Contemporary Accounting Research*, *28*(5), 1510–1536. DOI: 10.1111/j.1911-3846.2010.01060.x

Pattanshetti, M. K., Jasola, S., Rajput, A., & Pant, V. (2021). Proposed eLearning framework using open corpus web resources. *Proceedings of the 2021 1st International Conference on Advances in Electrical, Computing, Communications and Sustainable Technologies, ICAECT 2021*. DOI: 10.1109/ICAECT49130.2021.9392591

Peng, S., & van der Laan Smith, J. (2010). Chinese GAAP and IFRS: An analysis of the convergence process. *Journal of International Accounting, Auditing & Taxation*, *19*(1), 16–34. DOI: 10.1016/j.intaccaudtax.2009.12.002

Pereira, F., & Góis, M. (2020). Integrating IFRS with global trade regulations: A framework for compliance and transparency. *International Journal of Accounting and Finance*, *12*(3), 87–102.

Piecyk, M. (2010). Carbon auditing of companies, supply chains and products. 2010) Green Logistics: Improving the environmental sustainability of logistics, Kogan Page, pp.49-67.

Poniachek, H. A. (2022). Mergers and Acquisitions: Principles and Practices. In *Encyclopedia of Finance, Third Edition*. Springer International Publishing. DOI: 10.1007/978-3-030-91231-4_105

Porter, M. E., & Kramer, M. R. (2011). Creating shared value. *Harvard Business Review*, *89*(1/2), 62–77.

Poswal, P., Chauhan, A., Aarya, D. D., Boadh, R., Rajoria, Y. K., & Gaiola, S. U. (2022). Optimal strategy for remanufacturing system of sustainable products with trade credit under uncertain scenario. *Materials Today: Proceedings*, *69*, 165–173. DOI: 10.1016/j.matpr.2022.08.303

Praveenchandar, J., Vetrithangam, D., Kaliappan, S., Karthick, M., Pegada, N. K., Patil, P. P., Rao, S. G., & Umar, S. (2022). IoT-Based Harmful Toxic Gases Monitoring and Fault Detection on the Sensor Dataset Using Deep Learning Techniques. *Scientific Programming*, *2022*, 1–11. Advance online publication. DOI: 10.1155/2022/7516328

Pricope, C. F. (2017). The implications of IFRS adoption on foreign direct investment in poor countries. *The Audit Financiar Journal, 15*(146).

Prikshat, V., Kumar, S., & Nankervis, A. (2019). Work-readiness integrated competence model: Conceptualisation and scale development. *Education + Training*, *61*(5), 568–589. DOI: 10.1108/ET-05-2018-0114

Prikshat, V., Kumar, S., & Raje, P. (2017). Antecedents, consequences and strategic responses to graduate work-readiness: Challenges in India. In *Transitions from Education to Work: Workforce Ready Challenges in the Asia Pacific*. Taylor and Francis., DOI: 10.4324/9781315533971-8

Probowulan, D., & Ardianto, A. (2024). Internet financial reporting disclosure index of e-commerce businesses on social media. *International Studies of Accounting and Finance, 31*(2), Article e1550. https://doi.org/DOI: 10.1002/isaf.1550

PWC. (2019). *IFRS and beyond: Supporting the journey to financial transparency*. PricewaterhouseCoopers.

PWC. (2021). *Navigating the intersection of financial reporting and trade regulations*. PWC Publications.

PwC. (2023). *Global survey of IFRS adoption*. PricewaterhouseCoopers.

PwC. (2023). *Global sustainable finance survey: Bridging the capability gap*. PricewaterhouseCoopers.

Raghavendra, C., Rampilla, M., Thanikella, V. R., & Gupta, I. (2022). Impact of Carbon Tax and Environmental Regulation on Inbound Cross-Border Mergers and Acquisitions Volume: An Evidence from India. *International Journal of Financial Studies*, *10*(4), 106. Advance online publication. DOI: 10.3390/ijfs10040106

Raihan, A., Begum, R. A., Said, M. N. M., & Pereira, J. J. (2022). Relationship between economic growth, renewable energy use, technological innovation, and carbon emission toward achieving Malaysia's Paris agreement. *Environment Systems & Decisions*, *42*(4), 586–607. DOI: 10.1007/s10669-022-09848-0

Rajapakse, R. M. D. A. P., Azam, S. F., & Khatibi, A. (2022). The role of environmental incentives in greening the small and medium-sized enterprises: A developing economy perspective. *Management of Environmental Quality*, *33*(5), 1167–1186. DOI: 10.1108/MEQ-10-2021-0239

Rajawat, A. S., Singh, S., Gangil, B., Ranakoti, L., Sharma, S., Asyraf, M. R. M., & Razman, M. R. (2022). Effect of Marble Dust on the Mechanical, Morphological, and Wear Performance of Basalt Fibre-Reinforced Epoxy Composites for Structural Applications. *Polymers*, *14*(7), 1325. Advance online publication. DOI: 10.3390/polym14071325 PMID: 35406199

Rajbalaji, S., Raman, R., Pant, B., Rathour, N., Rajagopa, B. R., & Prasad, C. R. (2023). Design of deep learning models for the identifications of harmful attack activities in IIOT. *2023 International Conference on Artificial Intelligence and Smart Communication, AISC 2023*, 609 – 613. DOI: 10.1109/AISC56616.2023.10085088

Rajeswari, M., Kumar, N., Raman, P., Patjoshi, P. K., Singh, V., & Pundir, S. (2022). Optimal Analysis for Enterprise Financial Management Based on Artificial Intelligence and Parallel Computing Method. *Proceedings of 5th International Conference on Contemporary Computing and Informatics, IC3I 2022*, 2081 – 2086. DOI: 10.1109/IC3I56241.2022.10072851

Rajora, R., Gupta, H., Malhotra, S., Devliyal, S., & Sunil, G. (2024). Advancing Renal Health: Unleashing the Power of CNNs in Multi-Class Classification for Precise Kidney Condition Diagnosis. *2024 IEEE 9th International Conference for Convergence in Technology, I2CT 2024*. DOI: 10.1109/I2CT61223.2024.10544018

Rama, A., & Rodriguez, M. (2018). The influence of IFRS on cross-border investment decisions: A comprehensive analysis. *International Business Research*, *44*(6), 113–124.

Raman, R., Kumar, R., Ghai, S., Gehlot, A., Raju, A. M., & Barve, A. (2023). A New Method of Optical Spectrum Analysis for Advanced Wireless Communications. *2023 3rd International Conference on Advance Computing and Innovative Technologies in Engineering, ICACITE 2023*, 1719 – 1723. DOI: 10.1109/ICACITE57410.2023.10182414

Ramanan, M., Singh, L., Kumar, A. S., Suresh, A., Sampathkumar, A., Jain, V., & Bacanin, N. (2022). Secure blockchain enabled Cyber- Physical health systems using ensemble convolution neural network classification. *Computers & Electrical Engineering*, *101*, 108058. Advance online publication. DOI: 10.1016/j.compeleceng.2022.108058

Ramanna, K., & Sletten, E. (2014). Network effects in countries' adoption of IFRS. *The Accounting Review*, *89*(4), 1517–1543. DOI: 10.2308/accr-50717

Raman, R., Buddhi, D., Lakhera, G., Gupta, Z., Joshi, A., & Saini, D. (2023). An investigation on the role of artificial intelligence in scalable visual data analytics. *2023 International Conference on Artificial Intelligence and Smart Communication, AISC 2023*, 666 – 670. DOI: 10.1109/AISC56616.2023.10085495

Ramesh, B. N. (2023). Cross border mergers and acquisitions: A comparative study between India and the USA. In *Cross Border Mergers and Acquisitions: A Comparative Study between India and the USA*. Taylor and Francis., DOI: 10.4324/9781003396987

Ram, M., Negi, G., Goyal, N., & Kumar, A. (2022). Analysis of a Stochastic Model with Rework System. *Journal of Reliability and Statistical Studies*, *15*(2), 553–582. DOI: 10.13052/jrss0974-8024.1527

Ram, M., & Xing, L. (2023). Reliability Modeling in Industry 4.0. In *Reliability Modeling in Industry 4.0*. Elsevier., DOI: 10.1016/C2021-0-01679-5

Ramos, V. C., & Pereira Coelho, D. (2023). Defending victims of cross-border fraud in the EU – A Portuguese view, including the use of preventive "freezing" of bank accounts under anti-money laundering legislation. *New Journal of European Criminal Law*, *14*(3), 397–420. DOI: 10.1177/20322844231173913

Rana, M. S., Cavaliere, L. P. L., Mishra, A. B., Padhye, P., Singh, R. R., & Khanna, R. (2022). Internet of Things (IOT) Based Assessment for Effective Monitoring Data Against Malicious Attacks on Financial Collectors. *2022 2nd International Conference on Advance Computing and Innovative Technologies in Engineering, ICACITE 2022*, 177–181. DOI: 10.1109/ICACITE53722.2022.9823612

Rana, M. S., Dixit, A. K., Rajan, M. S., Malhotra, S., Radhika, S., & Pant, B. (2022). An Empirical Investigation in Applying Reliable Industry 4.0 Based Machine Learning (ML) Approaches in Analysing and Monitoring Smart Meters using Multivariate Analysis of Variance (Manova). *2022 2nd International Conference on Advance Computing and Innovative Technologies in Engineering, ICACITE 2022*, 603 – 607. DOI: 10.1109/ICACITE53722.2022.9823597

Rana, D. S., Dimri, S. C., Malik, P., & Dhondiyal, S. A. (2022). Impact of Computational Thinking in Engineering and K12 Education. *4th International Conference on Inventive Research in Computing Applications, ICIRCA 2022 - Proceedings*, 697 – 701. DOI: 10.1109/ICIRCA54612.2022.9985593

Rani, S. (2023). Initiatives on climate change mitigation. In *Climate, Land-Use Change and Hydrology of the Beas River Basin, Western Himalayas* (pp. 177–202). Springer International Publishing. DOI: 10.1007/978-3-031-29525-6_6

Rathore, R., & Goudar, R. H. (2015). SPARQL-based personalised E-Learning system designed using ontology (SPELSO): An architecture. *International Journal of Knowledge and Learning*, *10*(4), 384–416. DOI: 10.1504/IJKL.2015.077554

Ratzinger-Sakel, N. V. (2013). Auditor fees and auditor independence—Evidence from going concern reporting decisions in Germany. *Auditing*, *32*(4), 129–168. DOI: 10.2308/ajpt-50532

Ravindra, K., Bhardwaj, S., Ram, C., Goyal, A., Singh, V., Venkataraman, C., Bhan, S. C., Sokhi, R. S., & Mor, S. (2024). Temperature projections and heatwave attribution scenarios over India: A systematic review. *Heliyon, 10*(4), e26431. DOI: 10.1016/j.heliyon.2024.e26431 PMID: 38434018

Rawat, R. S., Singh, V., & Dumka, A. (2022). Complaint Management in Ethiopian Vocational and Technical Education Institutions: A Framework and Implementation of a Decision Support System. *2022 International Conference on 4th Industrial Revolution Based Technology and Practices, ICFIRTP 2022*, 73 – 79. DOI: 10.1109/ICFIRTP56122.2022.10063207

Rawat, R., Sharma, S., & Goyal, H. R. (2023). Intelligent Digital Financial Inclusion System Architectures for Industry 5.0 Enabled Digital Society. *Winter Summit on Smart Computing and Networks. WiSSCoN, 2023*, 1–5. Advance online publication. DOI: 10.1109/WiSSCoN56857.2023.10133858

Reddy, K. S., Xie, E., & Huang, Y. (2016). Cross-border acquisitions by state-owned and private enterprises: A perspective from emerging economies. *Journal of Policy Modeling, 38*(6), 1147–1170. DOI: 10.1016/j.jpolmod.2016.10.002

Reepu, R., Taneja, S., Ozen, E., & Singh, A. (2023). A globetrotter to the future of marketing: Metaverse. In *Cultural Marketing and Metaverse for Consumer Engagement*. IGI Global., DOI: 10.4018/978-1-6684-8312-1.ch001

Regulation (EU) No 537/2014 of the European Parliament and of the Council of 16 April 2014 on specific requirements regarding statutory audit of public-interest entities and repealing Commission Decision 2005/909/EC (Text with EEA relevance). (n.d.). https://eur-lex.europa.eu/legal-content/EN/TXT/PDF/?uri=CELEX:32014R0537

Rendtorff, J. D. (2023). Responsible Business and Integrated Stakeholder Reporting: Towards a Stakeholder Model for Integrated Reporting of ESG and SDG. *Ethical Economy, 64*, 49–59. DOI: 10.1007/978-3-031-26959-2_6

Renewables, A. (n.d.). Policy on Business Responsibility and Sustainability Reporting (BRSR). [online] Available at: https://www.adanigreenenergy.com/-/media/Project/GreenEnergy/Corporate-Governance/Policy/BRSR-Policy.pdf (Accessed: 23 July 2024).

Report on the Observance of Standards and Codes, Accounting & Auditing (ROSC-AA). (2002). *Kingdom of Morocco*. Retrieved from file:///C:/Users/user/Downloads/Report_on_the_observance_of_standards_an.pdf

Rika, N. (2009). What motivates environmental auditing? A public sector perspective. *Pacific Accounting Review, 21*(3), 304–318. DOI: 10.1108/01140580911012520

Röben, V. (2006). The regulation of financial services in the European Union. In *The Regulation of International Financial Markets*. Cambridge University Press., DOI: 10.1017/CBO9780511494505.007

Rodgers, W., & Housel, T. J. (2004). The effects of environmental risk information on auditors' decisions about prospective financial statements. *European Accounting Review, 13*(3), 523–540. DOI: 10.1080/0963818042000237160

Rossi, S., & Volpin, P. F. (2004). Cross-country determinants of mergers and acquisitions. *Journal of Financial Economics, 74*(2), 277–304. DOI: 10.1016/j.jfineco.2003.10.001

Rubeena, R. and Maseeh, M. (2023). "Innovative Data Collection Methods For Research In The Digital Era", *Vidya - A Journal Of Gujarat University*, Gujarat University, Vol. 2 No. 2, pp. 125–129.

Ruhnke, K., & Schmidt, M. (2014). The audit expectation gap: Existence, causes, and the impact of changes. *Accounting and Business Research, 44*(5), 572–601. DOI: 10.1080/00014788.2014.929519

Ruiz-Barbadillo, E., Gómez-Aguilar, N., De Fuentes-Barberá, C., & García-Benau, M. A. (2004). Audit quality and the going-concern decision-making process: Spanish evidence. *European Accounting Review, 13*(4), 597–620. DOI: 10.1080/0963818042000216820

Ruiz-Barbadillo, E., & Martínez-Ferrero, J. (2020). Empirical analysis of the effect of the joint provision of audit and sustainability assurance services on assurance quality. *Journal of Cleaner Production, 266*, 121943. DOI: 10.1016/j.jclepro.2020.121943

Ruiz-Barbadillo, E., & Martínez-Ferrero, J. (2022). The choice of incumbent financial auditors to provide sustainability assurance and audit services from a legitimacy perspective. *Sustainability Accounting. Management and Policy Journal, 13*(2), 459–493.

Sabu, C. (2021). Global Warming and Climate Change: Constitutional Standing and Legal Framework in India. *Indian JL & Legal Rsch., 2*, 1.

Sahithya, B., Guru Prasad, M. S., Sahithi, B., Madhu Krishna, K., Devarlla, A. C., & Yashavanth, T. R. (2024). Empowering Healthcare with AI: Advancements in Medical Image Analysis, Electronic Health Records Analysis, and AI-Driven Chatbots. *2024 3rd International Conference for Innovation in Technology, INOCON 2024*. DOI: 10.1109/INOCON60754.2024.10511753

Sahoo, I., & Chakrabarti, A. (2022). The Impact Of Protective Takeover Regulation On Acquiring Firms: Evidence From The New Bid Regime In Canada. In T. S. (Ed.), *Academy of Management Annual Meeting Proceedings* (Vol. 2022, Issue 1). Academy of Management. DOI: 10.5465/AMBPP.2022.306

Sahu, S. R., & Rawat, K. S. (2023). Analysis of Land subsidencein coastal and urban areas by using various techniques– Literature Review. *The Indonesian Journal of Geography*, *55*(3), 488–495. DOI: 10.22146/ijg.83675

Said, S. M. S., & Ali, S. I. M. (2023). The role of digital accounting in improving the quality of financial reporting information and its impact on the accuracy of financial analysts' predictions: A field study. *World Research of Business Administration Journal*, *3*(3), 175–201. DOI: 10.56830/WRBA11202304

Salama, R., Al-Turjman, F., Bordoloi, D., & Yadav, S. P. (2023). Wireless Sensor Networks and Green Networking for 6G communication- An Overview. *2023 International Conference on Computational Intelligence, Communication Technology and Networking, CICTN 2023*, 830 – 834. DOI: 10.1109/CICTN57981.2023.10141262

Salehi, M., Lari Dasht Bayaz, M., Mohammadi, S., Adibian, M. S., & Fahimifard, S. H. (2020). Auditors' response to the readability of financial statement notes. *Asian Review of Accounting*, *28*(3), 463–480. DOI: 10.1108/ARA-03-2019-0066

Sathyapriya, G., Natarajan, U., Sureshkumar, B., Navaneethakrishnan, G., Palanisamy, R., Bajaj, M., Sharma, N. K., & Kitmo, . (2022). Quality and Tool Stability Improvement in Turning Operation Using Plastic Compliant Damper. *Journal of Nanomaterials*, *2022*(1), 8654603. Advance online publication. DOI: 10.1155/2022/8654603

Sathyaseelan, K., Vyas, T., Madala, R., Chamundeeswari, V., Rai Goyal, H., & Jayaraman, R. (2023). Blockchain Enabled Intelligent Surveillance System Model with AI and IoT. *Proceedings of 8th IEEE International Conference on Science, Technology, Engineering and Mathematics, ICONSTEM 2023*. DOI: 10.1109/ICONSTEM56934.2023.10142303

Sati, P., Sharma, E., Soni, R., Dhyani, P., Solanki, A. C., Solanki, M. K., Rai, S., & Malviya, M. K. (2022). Bacterial endophytes as bioinoculant: microbial functions and applications toward sustainable farming. In *Microbial Endophytes and Plant Growth: Beneficial Interactions and Applications*. Elsevier., DOI: 10.1016/B978-0-323-90620-3.00008-8

Sauvant, K. P. (2016). The next step in governance: The need for global micro-regulatory frameworks in the context of expanding international production. *Research in Global Strategic Management*, *17*, 401–440. DOI: 10.1108/S1064-485720160000017013

Schiebel, A. (2006). Empirical value relevance of German GAAP and IFRS. *Journal of Economic and Financial Sciences, 1*(2), 141–170. DOI: 10.4102/jef.v1i2.365

Schmidt, A., & Vogl, S. (2018). The evolution of global trade and its impact on cross-border investments. *Journal of Global Trade, 22*(3), 150–165.

Searcy, C., Morali, O., Karapetrovic, S., Wichuk, K., McCartney, D., McLeod, S., & Fraser, D. (2012). Challenges in implementing a functional ISO 14001 environmental management system. *International Journal of Quality & Reliability Management, 29*(7), 779–796. DOI: 10.1108/02656711211258526

Seetharaman, A., Sun, Y., & Wang, W. (2011). Tax-related financial statement restatements and auditor-provided tax services. *Journal of Accounting, Auditing & Finance, 26*(4), 677–698. DOI: 10.1177/0148558X11409146

Sehajpal, S., & Kaur, N. (2025). Neuroscience, Nursing, and Financial Innovation : A Synergistic Approach to Optimized Patient Care and Economic Well-Being. In Sanjay, T., Bhupinderpal Pal, S. C., Amar, J., Ercan, O., & Pawan, K. (Eds.), *Neuromarketing's Role in Sustainable Finance* (pp. 133–146). IGI Global Scientific Publishing., DOI: 10.4018/979-8-3693-9117-4.ch008

Semwal, P., Painuli, S., Shabaaz Begum, J. P., Jamloki, A., Rauf, A., Olatunde, A., Mominur Rahman, M., Mukerjee, N., Khalil, A. A., Aljohani, A. S. M., Al Abdulmonem, W., & Simal-Gandara, J. (2024). Corrigendum to "Exploring the nutritional and health benefits of pulses from the Indian Himalayan region: A glimpse into the region's rich agricultural heritage" [Food Chem. 422 (2023) 136259] (Food Chemistry (2023) 422, (S0308814623008774), (. *Food Chemistry, 445*. https://doi .org/DOI: 10.1016/j.fo

Shah, J. K., Sharma, R., Misra, A., Sharma, M., Joshi, S., Kaushal, D., & Bafila, S. (2023). Industry 4.0 Enabled Smart Manufacturing: Unleashing the Power of Artificial Intelligence and Blockchain. *2023 1st DMIHER International Conference on Artificial Intelligence in Education and Industry 4.0, IDICAIEI 2023*. DOI: 10.1109/IDICAIEI58380.2023.10406671

Sharma, S., Gupta, A., & Tyagi, R. (2023). Artificial Intelligence Enabled Sustainable Education System Using Vedic Scripture and Cyber Security. *2023 2nd International Conference on Advances in Computational Intelligence and Communication, ICACIC 2023*. DOI: 10.1109/ICACIC59454.2023.10435133

Sharma, S., Gupta, A., & Tyagi, R. (2023). Sustainable Natural Resources Utilization Decision System for Better Society Using Vedic Scripture, Cloud Computing, and IoT. In B. R.C., S. K.M., & D. M. (Eds.), *Proceedings of IEEE 2023 5th International Conference on Advances in Electronics, Computers and Communications, ICAECC 2023*. Institute of Electrical and Electronics Engineers Inc. DOI: 10.1109/ICAECC59324.2023.10560335

Sharma, S., Mishra, R. R., Joshi, V., & Kour, K. (2020). Analysis and Interpretation of Global Air Quality. *2020 11th International Conference on Computing, Communication and Networking Technologies, ICCCNT 2020*. DOI: 10.1109/ICCCNT49239.2020.9225532

Sharma, S., Singh, V., & Sarkar, D. (2023). Machine Vision Enabled Fall Detection System for Specially Abled People in Limited Visibility Environment. *2023 3rd Asian Conference on Innovation in Technology, ASIANCON 2023*. DOI: 10.1109/ASIANCON58793.2023.10270769

Sharma, E., Rana, S., Sharma, I., Sati, P., & Dhyani, P. (2023). Organic polymers for CO2 capture and conversion. In *CO2-Philic Polymers, Nanocomposites and Solvents: Capture, Conversion and Industrial Products*. Elsevier., DOI: 10.1016/B978-0-323-85777-2.00002-0

Sharma, M., Kumar, A., Luthra, S., Joshi, S., & Upadhyay, A. (2022). The impact of environmental dynamism on low-carbon practices and digital supply chain networks to enhance sustainable performance: An empirical analysis. *Business Strategy and the Environment*, *31*(4), 1776–1788. DOI: 10.1002/bse.2983

Sharma, M., Luthra, S., Joshi, S., & Kumar, A. (2022). Analysing the impact of sustainable human resource management practices and industry 4.0 technologies adoption on employability skills. *International Journal of Manpower*, *43*(2), 463–485. DOI: 10.1108/IJM-02-2021-0085

Sharma, P., Mahajan, R., & Sharma, Y. (2018). Investigation of the energy audit practice in India. [IJRAR]. *International Journal of Research and Analytical Reviews*, *5*(3), 767–772.

Sharma, P., Malhotra, R. K., Ojha, M. K., & Gupta, S. (2022). Impact of meditation on mental & physical health and thereby on academic performance of students: A study of higher educational institutions of Uttarakhand. *Journal of Medical Pharmaceutical and Allied Sciences*, *11*(2), 4641–4644. DOI: 10.55522/jmpas.V11I2.2309

Sharma, P., Taneja, S., Kumar, P., Özen, E., & Singh, A. (2024). Application of the UTAUT model toward individual acceptance: Emerging trends in artificial intelligence-based banking services. *International Journal of Electronic Finance, 13*(3), 352–366. DOI: 10.1504/IJEF.2024.139584

Sharma, S., & Bhadula, S. (2023). Secure Federated Learning for Intelligent Industry 4.0 IoT Enabled Self Skin Care Application System. *Proceedings of the 2nd International Conference on Applied Artificial Intelligence and Computing, ICAAIC 2023*, 1164 – 1170. DOI: 10.1109/ICAAIC56838.2023.10141028

Sharma, S., Kadayat, Y., & Tyagi, R. (2023). Sustainable Global Democratic e-Governance System Using Vedic Scripture, Artificial Intelligence, Cloud Computing and Augmented Reality. *Proceedings of the International Conference on Circuit Power and Computing Technologies, ICCPCT 2023*, 113 – 118. DOI: 10.1109/ICCPCT58313.2023.10245405

Sharma, S., Singh Rawal, R., Pandey, D., & Pandey, N. (2021). Microbial World for Sustainable Development. In *Microbial Technology for Sustainable Environment.* Springer Nature., DOI: 10.1007/978-981-16-3840-4_1

Sharma, V., & Jain, S. (2020). Managers Training Programs Effectiveness Evaluation by using different Machine Learning Approaches. *Proceedings of the 4th International Conference on Electronics, Communication and Aerospace Technology, ICECA 2020*, 1453 – 1457. DOI: 10.1109/ICECA49313.2020.9297556

Shekhar, H. S., & Chadda, V. M. (2024). Disclosure regime for climate change: Proposal and prospects for India Inc. *Indiana Law Review, 8*(1), 42–65. DOI: 10.1080/24730580.2024.2323845

Shrivastava, A., Usha, R., Kukreti, R., Sharma, G., Srivastava, A. P., & Khan, A. K. (2023). Women Safety Precaution. *2023 1st International Conference on Circuits, Power, and Intelligent Systems, CCPIS 2023*. DOI: 10.1109/CCPIS59145.2023.10291594

Sierra García, L., Bollas-Araya, H. M., & García Benau, M. A. (2022). Sustainable development goals and assurance of non-financial information reporting in Spain. *Sustainability Accounting. Management and Policy Journal, 13*(4), 878–898.

Simnett, R., Vanstraelen, A., & Chua, W. F. (2009). Assurance on sustainability reports: An international comparison. *The Accounting Review, 84*(3), 937–967. DOI: 10.2308/accr.2009.84.3.937

Singh, A., & Srivastava, A. (2024). Innovation needed to improve road construction and road infrastructure in the future in India. In G. A. & V. R.J. (Eds.), *IOP Conference Series: Earth and Environmental Science* (Vol. 1326, Issue 1). Institute of Physics. DOI: 10.1088/1755-1315/1326/1/012097

Singh, K. D., & Singh, P. (2023). A Novel Cloud-based Framework to Predict the Employability of Students. In K. R., K. R., G. M., G. M., S. R., & S. R. (Eds.), *2023 International Conference on Advancement in Computation and Computer Technologies, InCACCT 2023* (pp. 528 – 532). Institute of Electrical and Electronics Engineers Inc. DOI: 10.1109/InCACCT57535.2023.10141760

Singh, K. D., Deep Singh, P., Bansal, A., Kaur, G., Khullar, V., & Tripathi, V. (2023). Exploratory Data Analysis and Customer Churn Prediction for the Telecommunication Industry. *ACCESS 2023 - 2023 3rd International Conference on Advances in Computing, Communication, Embedded and Secure Systems*, 197 – 201. DOI: 10.1109/ACCESS57397.2023.10199700

Singh, K. D., Singh, P., Chhabra, R., Kaur, G., Bansal, A., & Tripathi, V. (2023). Cyber-Physical Systems for Smart City Applications: A Comparative Study. In K. R., K. R., G. M., G. M., S. R., & S. R. (Eds.), *2023 International Conference on Advancement in Computation and Computer Technologies, InCACCT 2023* (pp. 871 – 876). Institute of Electrical and Electronics Engineers Inc. DOI: 10.1109/InCACCT57535.2023.10141719

Singh, K. D., Singh, P., Tripathi, V., & Khullar, V. (2022). A Novel and Secure Framework to Detect Unauthorized Access to an Optical Fog-Cloud Computing Network. In R. H.S., B. R., G. P.K., & S. V.K. (Eds.), *PDGC 2022 - 2022 7th International Conference on Parallel, Distributed and Grid Computing* (pp. 618 – 622). Institute of Electrical and Electronics Engineers Inc. DOI: 10.1109/PDGC56933.2022.10053223

Singh, P., & Singh, K. D. (2023). Fog-Centric Intelligent Surveillance System: A Novel Approach for Effective and Efficient Surveillance. In K. R., K. R., G. M., G. M., S. R., & S. R. (Eds.), *2023 International Conference on Advancement in Computation and Computer Technologies, InCACCT 2023* (pp. 762 – 766). Institute of Electrical and Electronics Engineers Inc. DOI: 10.1109/InCACCT57535.2023.10141802

Singh, S., Singh, R. B., Singh, S., & Singh, R. B. (2021). Indian Climate Policy, Programs, and Initiatives. *Simulating Climate Change and Livelihood Security: A Western Himalayan Experience, India*, pp.273-299.

Singh, A. B., Meena, H. K., Khandelwal, C., & Dangayach, G. S. (2023). Sustainability Assessment of Higher Education Institutions: A Systematic Literature Review †. *Engineering Proceedings*, *37*(1), 23. Advance online publication. DOI: 10.3390/ECP2023-14728

Singh, A. R., Vishnuram, P., Alagarsamy, S., Bajaj, M., Blazek, V., Damaj, I., Rathore, R. S., Al-Wesabi, F. N., & Othman, K. M. (2024). Electric vehicle charging technologies, infrastructure expansion, grid integration strategies, and their role in promoting sustainable e-mobility. *Alexandria Engineering Journal*, *105*, 300–330. DOI: 10.1016/j.aej.2024.06.093

Singh, A., Kumar, P., & Taneja, S. (2024). Artificial Intelligence and Machine Learning-Powered Smart Finance. In Taneja, P. K. S., & Singh, A. (Eds.), *IGI Global*. IGI Global., DOI: 10.4018/979-8-3693-3264-1

Singh, K. D., Singh, P., Kaur, G., Khullar, V., Chhabra, R., & Tripathi, V. (2023). Education 4.0: Exploring the Potential of Disruptive Technologies in Transforming Learning. *Proceedings of International Conference on Computational Intelligence and Sustainable Engineering Solution, CISES 2023*, 586 – 591. DOI: 10.1109/CISES58720.2023.10183547

Singh, K. U., Chaudhary, V., Sharma, P. K., Kumar, P., Varshney, N., & Singh, T. (2024). Integrating GPS and GSM Technologies for Enhanced Women's Safety: A Fingerprint-Activated Device Approach. *2024 International Conference on Automation and Computation, AUTOCOM 2024*, 657 – 662. DOI: 10.1109/AUTOCOM60220.2024.10486120

Singh, N. K., Singh, Y., Rahim, E. A., Senthil Siva Subramanian, T., & Sharma, A. (2023). Electric discharge machining of hybrid composite with bio-dielectrics for sustainable developments. *Australian Journal of Mechanical Engineering*. Advance online publication. DOI: 10.1080/14484846.2023.2249577

Singh, N. K., Singh, Y., Singh, Y., Rahim, E. A., Sharma, A., Singla, A., & Ranjit, P. S. (2023). The Effectiveness of Balanites aegyptiaca Oil Nanofluid Augmented with Nanoparticles as Cutting Fluids during the Turning Process. In *Biowaste and Biomass in Biofuel Applications*. CRC Press., DOI: 10.1201/9781003265597-7

Singh, P., & Singh, D. P. (2024). Role of Disruptive Technologies in the Smart Healthcare Sector of Society 5.0. In *Artificial Intelligence and Society 5.0* (pp. 143–153). Chapman and Hall/CRC.

Singh, S. K., Chauhan, A., & Sarkar, B. (2023). Sustainable biodiesel supply chain model based on waste animal fat with subsidy and advertisement. *Journal of Cleaner Production*, *382*, 134806. Advance online publication. DOI: 10.1016/j.jclepro.2022.134806

Singh, S., Singh, A., Mohan, A., Batola, M., & Kumar, N. (2024). Health Expenditures And Health Outcomes In Central Europe And The Baltic Region. *Baltic Region*, *16*(2), 126–143. DOI: 10.5922/2079-8555-2024-2-7

Sinkovics, N., Sinkovics, R. R., & Archie-Acheampong, J. (2021). Small-and medium-sized enterprises and sustainable development: In the shadows of large lead firms in global value chains. *Journal of International Business Policy*, *4*(1), 80–101. DOI: 10.1057/s42214-020-00089-z

Sirakaya-Turk, E., & Uysal, M. S. (2017). "Survey research: sampling and questionnaire design.", cabi, pp. 122–146.

Širić, I., Eid, E. M., Taher, M. A., El-Morsy, M. H. E., Osman, H. E. M., Kumar, P., Adelodun, B., Abou Fayssal, S., Mioč, B., Andabaka, Ž., Goala, M., Kumari, S., Bachheti, A., Choi, K. S., & Kumar, V. (2022). Combined Use of Spent Mushroom Substrate Biochar and PGPR Improves Growth, Yield, and Biochemical Response of Cauliflower (Brassica oleracea var. botrytis): A Preliminary Study on Greenhouse Cultivation. *Horticulturae*, *8*(9), 830. Advance online publication. DOI: 10.3390/horticulturae8090830

Smith, J., & Moore, D. (2018). Enhancing compliance and transparency through regulatory frameworks. *Journal of Financial Regulation*, *4*(1), 32–48.

Song, B., He, J., Yan, W., Hu, Q., & Zhang, T. (2017). Key technologies for knowledge-based cross-border e-commerce risk assessment - Accurate commodity classification and efficient knowledge acquisition. In C. C.-H., T. A.C., P. M., S. J., W. N., & W. N. (Eds.), *Advances in Transdisciplinary Engineering* (Vol. 5, pp. 146 – 153). IOS Press BV. DOI: 10.3233/978-1-61499-779-5-146

Sonnad, S., Awasthy, M., Rane, K., Banerjee, M., Buddhi, D., & Pant, B. (2022). Blockchain-Based Secure Mengers Authentication for Industrial IoT. In D. R.K., S. A.Kr., K. G., & B. S. (Eds.), *Proceedings of the 2022 11th International Conference on System Modeling and Advancement in Research Trends, SMART 2022* (pp. 853 – 858). Institute of Electrical and Electronics Engineers Inc. DOI: 10.1109/SMART55829.2022.10046934

Soroushyar, A. (2023). Auditor characteristics and the financial reporting quality: The moderating role of the client business strategy. *Asian Journal of Accounting Research*, *8*(1), 27–40. DOI: 10.1108/AJAR-01-2022-0020

Srivastava, B., Kandpal, V., & Jain, A. K. (2024). Financial well-being of women self-help group members: A qualitative study. *Environment, Development and Sustainability*. Advance online publication. DOI: 10.1007/s10668-024-04879-w

Stittle, J. (2004). The reformation of European corporate reporting: Towards a model of convergence or confusion? *European Business Review*, *16*(2), 139–151. DOI: 10.1108/09555340410524247

Suadiye, G. (2017). Does mandatory IFRS adoption improve financial reporting quality? Empirical evidence from an emerging economy. *European Journal of Business and Social Sciences*, *6*(5), 63–80.

Sunori, S. K., Kant, S., Agarwal, P., & Juneja, P. (2023). Development of Rainfall Prediction Models using Linear and Non-linear Regression Techniques. *2023 4th IEEE Global Conference for Advancement in Technology, GCAT 2023*. DOI: 10.1109/GCAT59970.2023.10353508

Suresh, M., Antony, J., Nair, G., & Garza-Reyes, J. A. (2023). Lean-sustainability assessment framework development: Evidence from the construction industry. *Total Quality Management & Business Excellence*, *34*(15–16), 2046–2081. DOI: 10.1080/14783363.2023.2222088

Svanström, T. (2013). Non-audit services and audit quality: Evidence from private firms. *European Accounting Review*, *22*(2), 337–366. DOI: 10.1080/09638180.2012.706398

Tamilmani, S., Mohan, T., Jeyalakshmi, S., Shukla, G. P., Gehlot, A., & Shukla, S. K. (2023). Blockchain Integrated with Industrial IOT Towards Industry 4.0. *2023 International Conference on Artificial Intelligence and Smart Communication, AISC 2023*, 575 – 581. DOI: 10.1109/AISC56616.2023.10085226

Taneja, S., Gupta, S., Singh, A., Bhatnagar, M., & Gaur, A. (2023). Green management - A new paradigm in the world of business. *Green Management - A New Paradigm in the World of Business*, 1–230. DOI: 10.52305/DLIH6622

Taneja, S., Bhatnagar, M., Kumar, P., & Grima, S. (2023). A Panel Analysis of the Effectiveness of the Asset Management in Indian Agricultural Companies. *International Journal of Sustainable Development and Planning*, *18*(3), 653–660. DOI: 10.18280/ijsdp.180301

Taneja, S., Bhatnagar, M., Kumar, P., & Rupeika-apoga, R. (2023). India ' s Total Natural Resource Rents (NRR) and GDP : An Augmented Autoregressive Distributed Lag (ARDL) Bound Test. *Journal of Risk and Financial Management*, *16*(2), 91. https://doi.org/doi.org/10.3390/jrfm16020091. DOI: 10.3390/jrfm16020091

Taneja, S., & Özen, E. (2023). To analyse the relationship between bank's green financing and environmental performance. *International Journal of Electronic Finance, 12*(2), 163–175. DOI: 10.1504/IJEF.2023.129919

Tang, D. Y., & Zhang, Y. (2020). Do shareholders benefit from green bonds? *Journal of Corporate Finance, 61*(November), 1–18. DOI: 10.1016/j.jcorpfin.2018.12.001

Task Force on Climate-related Financial Disclosures. (2023). *Status Report 2023*. Financial Stability Board.

Taylor, A. L., Levin, J., Chan, J., Lee, M., Kasitinon, D., Miller, E., & Fox, P. (2021). Improving environmental sustainability in outpatient clinics: Lessons from a waste audit. *The Journal of Climate Change and Health, 4*, 100070. DOI: 10.1016/j.joclim.2021.100070

Thakkar, J. J., & Thakkar, J. J. (2020). Applications of structural equation modelling with AMOS 21, IBM SPSS. *Structural equation modelling: application for research and practice (with AMOS and R)*, pp.35-89.

Thapa, D., Kumar, V., Naik, B., Kumar, V., Gupta, A. K., Mohanta, Y. K., Mishra, B., & Rustagi, S. (2024). Harnessing probiotic foods: Managing cancer through gut health. *Food Science and Biotechnology, 33*(9), 2141–2160. DOI: 10.1007/s10068-024-01638-5 PMID: 39130664

Thompson, D., & Wilson, M. J. (1994). Environmental auditing: Theory and applications. *Environmental Management, 18*(4), 605–615. DOI: 10.1007/BF02400863

Tian, Z.-H., & Wang, J.-J. (2007). Cross-border merger and acquisitions, government regulations and market competition. *Proceedings of 2007 International Conference on Management Science and Engineering, ICMSE'07 (14th)*, 1397 – 1403. DOI: 10.1109/ICMSE.2007.4422040

Tiwari, R., Agrawal, P., Singh, P., Bajaj, S., Verma, V., & Chauhan, A. S. (2023). Technology Enabled Integrated Fusion Teaching for Enhancing Learning Outcomes in Higher Education. *International Journal of Emerging Technologies in Learning, 18*(7), 243–249. DOI: 10.3991/ijet.v18i07.36799

Tokic, S., & Beyea, G. (2010). Changing regulations for cross-border M&As. *Journal of Corporate Accounting & Finance, 21*(2), 33–43. DOI: 10.1002/jcaf.20561

Trigo, A., Belfo, F., & Pérez Estébanez, R. (2014). Accounting information systems: The challenge of real-time reporting. *Procedia Technology, 16*, 118–127. DOI: 10.1016/j.protcy.2014.10.075

Tsepova, E. A. (2022). Prospects for the Use of Cross-Cutting Digital Technologies in the Framework of Tax and Currency Control Over Cross-Border Financial Transactions. *Smart Innovation. Systems and Technologies*, *254*, 51–64. DOI: 10.1007/978-981-16-4621-8_5

Tumwebaze, Z., Bananuka, J., Kaawaase, T. K., Bonareri, C. T., & Mutesasira, F. (2022). Audit committee effectiveness, internal audit function and sustainability reporting practices. *Asian Journal of Accounting Research*, *7*(2), 163–181. DOI: 10.1108/AJAR-03-2021-0036

Türegün, N. (2020). Accounting for e-commerce sector. *International Journal of Critical Accounting*, *11*(5), 429–438. DOI: 10.1504/IJCA.2020.111564

Tyagi, S., Krishna, K. H., Joshi, K., Ghodke, T. A., Kumar, A., & Gupta, A. (2023). Integration of PLCC modem and Wi-Fi for Campus Street Light Monitoring. In N. P., S. M., K. M., J. V., & G. K. (Eds.), *Proceedings - 4th IEEE 2023 International Conference on Computing, Communication, and Intelligent Systems, ICCCIS 2023* (pp. 1113 – 1116). Institute of Electrical and Electronics Engineers Inc. DOI: 10.1109/ICCCIS60361.2023.10425715

Tyagi, S., Mathur, K., Gupta, T., Khantwal, S., & Tripathi, V. (2023). The Effectiveness of Augmented Reality in Developing Pre-Primary Student's Cognitive Skills. *IEEE Region 10 Humanitarian Technology Conference, R10-HTC*, 997 – 1002. DOI: 10.1109/R10-HTC57504.2023.10461754

Tyagi, S., Jindal, T., Krishna, S. H., Hassen, S. M., Shukla, S. K., & Kaur, C. (2022). Comparative Analysis of Artificial Intelligence and its Powered Technologies Applications in the Finance Sector. *Proceedings of 5th International Conference on Contemporary Computing and Informatics, IC3I 2022*, 260 – 264. DOI: 10.1109/IC3I56241.2022.10073077

UNEP FI. (2022). The Climate Risk Landscape: 2022 Supplement. United Nations Environment Programme Finance Initiative.

Unhelkar, B., Joshi, S., Sharma, M., Prakash, S., Mani, A. K., & Prasad, M. (2022). Enhancing supply chain performance using RFID technology and decision support systems in the industry 4.0–A systematic literature review. *International Journal of Information Management Data Insights*, *2*(2), 100084. Advance online publication. DOI: 10.1016/j.jjimei.2022.100084

Uniyal, A. K., Kanojia, P., Khanna, R., & Dixit, A. K. (2022). Quantitative Analysis of the Impact of Demography and Job Profile on the Organizational Commitment of the Faculty Members in the HEI'S of Uttarakhand. *Communications in Computer and Information Science, 1742 CCIS*, 24–35. DOI: 10.1007/978-3-031-23647-1_3

Upreti, H., & Malhotra, R. K. (2024). Bridging The Urban-Rural Education Gap In India Through CSR (Corporate Social Responsibility) Initiatives: A Conceptual Study With Special Reference To Sustainable Development Goal 4 (Quality Education). In P. P.K. (Ed.), *E3S Web of Conferences* (Vol. 556). EDP Sciences. DOI: 10.1051/e3sconf/202455601032

Upreti, H., Uddin, Z., Pandey, A. K., & Joshi, N. (2023). Particle swarm optimization based numerical study for pressure, flow, and heat transfer over a rotating disk with temperature dependent nanofluid properties. *Numerical Heat Transfer Part A*, *83*(8), 815–844. DOI: 10.1080/10407782.2022.2156412

Van der Meulen, T. (2020). Cross-border investments and IFRS compliance: A conceptual framework. *Financial Markets and Accounting Review*, *18*(2), 95–110.

Venkatesh, J., Shukla, P. K., Ahanger, T. A., Maheshwari, M., Pant, B., Hemamalini, R. R., & Halifa, A. (2023). A Complex Brain Learning Skeleton Comprising Enriched Pattern Neural Network System for Next Era Internet of Things. *Journal of Healthcare Engineering*, *2023*(1), 2506144. Advance online publication. DOI: 10.1155/2023/2506144

Verma, A., Sharma, D., Pant, M., Khatib, M. N., Singh, M. P., Zahiruddin, Q. S., Rustagi, S., Gaidhane, S., & Gaidhane, A. M. (2024). First sighting of human H5N1 in Australia: A detailed account and public health implications. *New Microbes and New Infections*, *60–61*, 101447. Advance online publication. DOI: 10.1016/j.nmni.2024.101447 PMID: 39045288

Wahab, E. A. A., Gist, W. E., & Majid, W. Z. N. A. (2014). Characteristics of non-audit services and financial restatements in Malaysia. *Journal of Contemporary Accounting & Economics*, *10*(3), 225–247. DOI: 10.1016/j.jcae.2014.10.001

Wang, X., & Wen, H. (2022). Research on the Financing Mode of Green Bond Supporting Green Building Development. In W. Y., L. S., & S. G.Q.P. (Eds.), *ICCREM 2022: Carbon Peak and Neutrality Strategies of the Construction Industry - Proceedings of the International Conference on Construction and Real Estate Management 2022* (pp. 170 – 175). American Society of Civil Engineers (ASCE). DOI: 10.1061/9780784484562.017

Wanyonyi, A. (2020). An Insight into the Emerging Issues, Challenges and Future Prospects in Environmental Audit. Challenges and Future Prospects in Environmental Audit (June 16, 2020).

Wazid, M., Das, A. K., & Park, Y. (2021). Blockchain-Envisioned Secure Authentication Approach in AIoT: Applications, Challenges, and Future Research. *Wireless Communications and Mobile Computing*, *2021*(1), 3866006. Advance online publication. DOI: 10.1155/2021/3866006

Weitz, K. A., Thorneloe, S. A., Nishtala, S. R., Yarkosky, S., & Zannes, M. (2002). The impact of municipal solid waste management on greenhouse gas emissions in the United States. *Journal of the Air & Waste Management Association*, *52*(9), 1000–1011. DOI: 10.1080/10473289.2002.10470843 PMID: 12269661

Wen, H., & Moehrle, S. R. (2016). Accounting for goodwill: An academic literature review and analysis to inform the debate. *Research in Accounting Regulation*, *28*(1), 11–21. DOI: 10.1016/j.racreg.2016.03.002

Whelan, T., & Fink, C. (2021). The comprehensive business case for sustainability. Harvard Business Review Working Paper.

Wintergreen, J., & Delaney, T. (2007, May). ISO 14064, international standard for GHG emissions inventories and verification. In 16th annual international emissions inventory conference, Raleigh, NC.

World Bank Group. (2020). *Embedding digital finance in e-commerce platforms during the COVID-19 pandemic: Early assessment of the impact of COVID-19 on e-commerce and the provision of digital financial services for micro, small, and medium enterprises and low-income consumers*. Finance, Competitiveness & Innovation Global Practice. International Bank for Reconstruction and Development / The World Bank. https://www.worldbank.org

World Bank. (2018). *IFRS and financial reporting: Global perspectives on transparency and governance*. World Bank Group.

World Trade Organization. (2020). *Trade Policy Review: Principles and Practices*. WTO.

Wright, D. (1994). Environmental Auditing: An integral component of environmental management. Eco-Management and Auditing. *Eco-Management and Auditing*, *1*(2), 11–13. DOI: 10.1002/ema.178

Wu, M. G. (2006). An economic analysis of audit and nonaudit services: The trade-off between competition crossovers and knowledge spillovers. *Contemporary Accounting Research*, *23*(2), 527–554. DOI: 10.1506/4DA7-D9YU-P9HQ-PX82

Xia, Q. (2016). Study on the impact of electronic commerce on the development of financial accounting. *4th International Education, Economics, Social Science, Arts,Sports and Management Engineering Conference (IEESASM 2016)*, 955–957. https://doi.org/DOI: 10.2991/ieesasm-16.2016.102

Yadav, P. M., Patra, I., Mittal, V., Nagorao, C. G., Udhayanila, R., & Saranya, A. (2023). Implementation of IOT on English Language Classroom Management. *2023 3rd International Conference on Advance Computing and Innovative Technologies in Engineering, ICACITE 2023*, 1686 – 1690. DOI: 10.1109/ICACITE57410.2023.10182984

Yan, J. (2018). Do Merger Laws Deter Cross-Border Mergers and Acquisitions? *Australian Economic Papers*, *57*(3), 376–393. DOI: 10.1111/1467-8454.12118

Yarmoliuk, O., Abramov, A., Mulyk, T., Smirnova, N., & Ponomarova, N. (2024). Digital technologies in accounting and reporting: Benefits, limitations, and possible risks. *Amazonia Investiga*, *13*(74), 323–333. DOI: 10.34069/AI/2024.74.02.27

Ye, P., Carson, E., & Simnett, R. (2011). Threats to auditor independence: The impact of relationship and economic bonds. *Auditing*, *30*(1), 121–148. DOI: 10.2308/aud.2011.30.1.121

Yeruva, A. R., Vijaya Durga, C. S. L., Gokulavasan, B., Pant, K., Chaturvedi, P., & Srivastava, A. P. (2022). A Smart Healthcare Monitoring System Based on Fog Computing Architecture. *Proceedings of International Conference on Technological Advancements in Computational Sciences, ICTACS 2022*, 904 – 909. DOI: 10.1109/ICTACS56270.2022.9987881

Yessenamanova, M., Lukyanets, A., Golovina, E. and Topornin, N. (2022). Environmental Auditing: The EU Practice in the Context of Pursuing Sustainable Development Policy. *European Energy and Environmental Law Review, 31*(4).

Yousefinejad, M., Ahmad, A., Salleh, F. M., & Rahim, R. A. (2018). Causal relationship between International Financial Reporting Standard (IFRS) and foreign direct investment (FDI): A panel data analysis of ASEAN countries. *Asian Journal of Accounting and Governance*, *10*, 61–72. DOI: 10.17576/AJAG-2018-10-06

Zaheer, A., Zehra Hussain, D., Verma, A., Sah, S., Pant, M., Nazli Khatib, M., Pratap Singh, M., Syed Zahiruddin, Q., & Rustagi, S. (2024). Marburg virus: An emerging threat to global health. *Clinical Infection in Practice*, *23*, 100371. Advance online publication. DOI: 10.1016/j.clinpr.2024.100371

Zaman, R., Farooq, M. B., Khalid, F., & Mahmood, Z. (2021). Examining the extent of and determinants for sustainability assurance quality: The role of audit committees. *Business Strategy and the Environment*, *30*(7), 2887–2906. DOI: 10.1002/bse.2777

Zeghal, D., & Mhedhbi, K. (2006). An analysis of the factors affecting the adoption of International Accounting Standards by developing countries. *The International Journal of Accounting*, *41*(4), 373–386. DOI: 10.1016/j.intacc.2006.09.009

Zetzsche, D. A., Anker-Sørensen, L., Passador, M. L., & Wehrli, A. (2021). DLT-based enhancement of cross-border payment efficiency–a legal and regulatory perspective. *Law and Financial Markets Review*, *15*(1–2), 70–115. DOI: 10.1080/17521440.2022.2065809

Zhang, B., & Swanson, L. A. (2022). Discount rates and sustainability: Problems in valuation across time. *Business Ethics Quarterly*, *32*(2), 279–304.

Zhang, L., & Sun, X. (2021). Challenges in aligning trade regulations and accounting standards for cross-border investments. *Global Economy and Finance Journal*, *41*(7), 45–61.

Zhang, W. (2013). The international convergence of accounting standards: IFRS adoption in China. *Journal of International Accounting Research*, *12*(1), 1–25.

Zhang, W., He, X., & Hamori, S. (2022). Volatility spillover and investment strategies among sustainability-related financial indexes: Evidence from the DCC-GARCH-based dynamic connectedness and DCC-GARCH t-copula approach. *International Review of Financial Analysis*, *83*, 102223. Advance online publication. DOI: 10.1016/j.irfa.2022.102223

Zhang, Y., Cao, C., Gu, J., & Garg, H. (2023). The Impact of Top Management Team Characteristics on the Risk Taking of Chinese Private Construction Enterprises. *Systems*, *11*(2), 67. Advance online publication. DOI: 10.3390/systems11020067

Zhao, G., & Chen, S. (2015). Greenhouse gas emissions reduction in China by cleaner coal technology towards 2020. *Energy Strategy Reviews*, *7*, 63–70. DOI: 10.1016/j.esr.2014.08.001

Zhao, X., & Ma, J. (2018). Harmonizing international accounting standards: The role of IFRS in promoting global transparency. *The International Journal of Accounting*, *53*(3), 245–262.

Zhou, P., & Cui, L. (2023). Strategic integration of sustainability in corporate finance: Evidence from green bond issuers. *Strategic Management Journal*, *44*(2), 401–425.

Zhou, S., Simnett, R., & Green, W. J. (2016). Assuring a new market: The interplay between country-level and company-level factors on the demand for greenhouse gas (GHG) information assurance and the choice of assurance provider. *Auditing*, *35*(3), 141–168. DOI: 10.2308/ajpt-51414

Zhu, W. (2014). The evolving economic role of accounting standards: Evidence from bilateral cross-border M&A flows. *Frontiers of Business Research in China*, *8*(4), 435–479. DOI: 10.3868/s070-003-014-0020-1

Zutshi, A., & Sohal, A. S. (2004). Adoption and maintenance of environmental management systems: Critical success factors. *Management of Environmental Quality*, *15*(4), 399–419. DOI: 10.1108/14777830410540144

About the Contributors

Luan Vardari is Assistant Professor of Finance in the Faculty of Economics at University "UKSHIN HOTI" Prizren. He received his Master's degree (MA) in Finance (Balkan Countries Stock Markets) in 2012 from Trakya University and finished his Ph.D. in Business Administration at Trakya University in 2019. He teaches finance courses at graduate and undergraduate levels. His research interests include financial markets and institutions, portfolio optimizations, and international finance. Vardari is the founder and editor-in-chief of PRIZREN SOCIAL SCIENCE JOURNAL. Editor in book chapters and articles in national and international journals.

Isuf Qabrati is an accomplished Albanian economist and academic currently pursuing a Ph.D. in Economics at the South East European University (SEEU), Faculty of Business and Economics. With a Master's degree in Accounting and Auditing from the University "Ukshin Hoti" Prizren, he has showcased his expertise through a thesis on the "Financial Debt and Financial Performance of Limited Liability Companies in Kosovo." As an Assistant at the University "Ukshin Hoti" Prizren, Faculty of Economics, he imparts knowledge across various courses. Isuf's professional journey includes roles as an Accountant, Lecturer, and Trainer in diverse institutions. Holding certifications as a Certified Accountant and Accounting Technician from the Society of Certified Accountants and Auditors of Kosovo (SCAAK), Isuf has contributed to research papers in scientific journals and conferences. His dedication to academia is complemented by technical skills in time management, communication, and proficiency in Microsoft Office, SPSS, and QuickBooks. Fluent in Albanian, English, and with a foundation in German and Turkish, Isuf Qabrati is a member of SCAAK since 2018 and has received scholarships during both his bachelor and master studies.

***

Kushtrim Gashi is the Vice Dean and Assistant Professor at the Faculty of Economics, University "Ukshin Hoti" Prizren. He earned his PhD from SMC University, Switzerland, specializing in management. Dr. Gashi teaches courses such as Managerial Economics, Quality Management, Negotiation and Leadership Skills, and E-Business. He mentors Bachelor's and Master's students, guiding them through research in business and management. His professional experience includes roles as a credit analyst and managerial positions in diverse organizations. As a member of the Central Quality Assurance Committee and Faculty Council, he contributes to institutional governance. Dr. Gashi's research focuses on management, technology, and data governance, with publications in international book chapters and peer-reviewed journals. His work addresses artificial intelligence, risk management, and sustainable business practices, showcasing his dedication to advancing both academia and the business community.

A.V.Senthil Kumar is working as a Professor and Director, PG and Research Department of Computer Applications, Hindusthan College of Arts & Science, Coimbatore, Tamilnadu. To his credit he has industrial experience for five years and teaching experience of 27 years. He has also received his Doctor of Science (D.Sc in Computer Science). He has to his credit 50 Book Chapters, 225 papers in International and National Journals 64 papers in International Conferences in International and National Conferences, and edited 14 books and 2 Text books. He is as Associate Editor of IEEE Access. He is an Editor-in-Chief for many journals and Key Member for India, Machine Intelligence Research Lab (MIR Labs). He is an Editorial Board Member and Reviewer for various International Journals. He is also a Committee member for various International Conferences.

Pawan Kumar, PhD, is a prominent academic and researcher with over 20 years of expertise in business studies. A professor at Graphic Era Deemed to be University, Dehradun, India, he has supervised six PhD scholars and published over 60 research papers, including 40 in SCOPUS/ Web of Science, and 14 books, including eight indexed in Scopus. His works, featured by prominent publishers like Emerald, IGI Global, Nova Science, and Cambridge Scholars, have gained recognition. Dr. Kumar earned his PhD in Commerce from Kurukshetra University in 2007 and holds an M.Phil. and M.Com. Degrees. Specializing in finance, banking, and securities markets, he has authored books on green finance, AI, and fintech. His innovative research includes five patents and has served as a guest editor for Scopus-indexed journals. In 2022, he received the prestigious Researcher Award from Chandigarh University. Dr. Kumar's impactful work on sustainable finance, blockchain, and fintech is globally recognized. His active participation in high-impact conferences and faculty development programs reflects his commitment to advancing research, teaching, and innovation in commerce and management.

Sanjay Taneja is currently an Associate Professor in Research at Graphic Era University, Dehradun, India. His significant thrust areas are Banking Regulations, Banking and Finance (Fin Tech, Green Finance), Risks, Insurance Management, Green Economics and Management of Innovation in Insurance. He holds a double master's degree (MBA &M.Com.) in management with a specialization in Finance and Marketing. He received his PG degrees in Management (Gold Medalist) from Chaudhary Devi University, Sirsa, India in 2012. He earned his Doctor of Philosophy (Sponsored By ICSSR) in Banking and Finance entitled "An Appraisal of financial performance of Indian Banking Sector: A Comparative study of Public, Private and Foreign banks in 2016 from Chaudhary Devi University, Sirsa, India. He received his Post Doctoral Degree from faculty of Social Sciences, Department of Banking and Insurance, Usak University, Turkey entitled on "Impact of the European Green Deal on Carbon (CO2) Emission in Turkey" in 2023.

Vesel Usaj is the Head of Teaching for the Bachelor of Business Administration Program and a dedicated PhD candidate in Finance at the University of St. Clement of Ohrid. He earned his MSc in Accounting and Auditing from the University "Ukshin Hoti" Prizren in 2018, completing a thesis on diagnosing financial conditions and the impact of financial decisions at the company "Frutex." Vesel also holds a Bachelor's degree in Business Administration with a specialization in accounting, earned from the same university in 2016. Since 2019, Vesel has served as a Teaching Assistant at the University "Ukshin Hoti" Prizren, where he lectures on Financial Analysis, Financial Management, Accounting, Tax Accounting, and Microeconomics. His academic journey and teaching roles reflect a deep commitment to the fields of finance and accounting, integrating practical insights and theoretical expertise into his work. Vesel's dedication to education and research is evident in his contributions to the academic and professional growth of his students, as well as his ongoing research pursuits in finance and accounting.

Index

A

B

C

D

E

F

G

H

I

K

M

N

R

S

T

www.ingramcontent.com/pod-product-compliance
Lightning Source LLC
LaVergne TN
LVHW080609300926
849162LV00005B/1098
* 9 7 9 8 3 3 7 3 0 8 8 7 6 *